W9-BDB-530

 booksonline

Read this book online today:

With SAP PRESS BooksOnline we offer you online access to knowledge from the leading SAP experts. Whether you use it as a beneficial supplement or as an alternative to the printed book, with SAP PRESS BooksOnline you can:

- Access your book anywhere, at any time. All you need is an Internet connection.
- Perform full text searches on your book and on the entire SAP PRESS library.
- Build your own personalized SAP library.

The SAP PRESS customer advantage:

Register this book today at *www.sap-press.com* and obtain exclusive free trial access to its online version. If you like it (and we think you will), you can choose to purchase permanent, unrestricted access to the online edition at a very special price!

Here's how to get started:

1. Visit *www.sap-press.com*.
2. Click on the link for SAP PRESS BooksOnline and login (or create an account).
3. Enter your free trial license key, shown below in the corner of the page.
4. Try out your online book with full, unrestricted access for a limited time!

Your personal free trial **license key** for this online book is:

pd7n-by9r-8tif-sq2x

SAP® Solution Manager

Galileo Press is named after the Italian physicist, mathematician and philosopher Galileo Galilei (1564—1642). He is known as one of the founders of modern science and an advocate of our contemporary, heliocentric worldview. His words *Eppur si muove* (And yet it moves) have become legendary. The Galileo Press logo depicts Jupiter orbited by the four Galilean moons, which were discovered by Galileo in 1610.

Editor Florian Zimniak
English Edition Editor Laura Korslund
Translation DSC Translation
Copyeditor Julie McNamee
Cover Design Silke Braun, Graham Geary
Photo Credit iStockphoto.com/Yury Kuzmin
Layout Design Vera Brauner
Production Graham Geary, Kelly O'Callaghan
Typesetting SatzPro, Krefeld (Germany)
Printed and bound in the United States of America, on paper from sustainable sources

ISBN 978-1-59229-388-9

© 2012 by Galileo Press Inc., Boston (MA)
3rd edition 2012, 1st reprint 2012
3rd German edition published 2011 by Galileo Press, Bonn, Germany

Library of Congress Cataloging-in-Publication Data
Schäfer, Marc O.
SAP solution manager / Marc O. Schäfer and Matthias Melich. -- 1st ed.
p. cm.
Includes index.
ISBN-13: 978-1-59229-388-9
ISBN-10: 1-59229-388-3
1. SAP solution manager. 2. SAP ERP. 3. Management information systems--Computer programs. 4. Business--Data processing--Computer programs. 5. Integrated software. I. Melich, Matthias. II. Title.
T58.6.S3155 2012
658.4'038011--dc23
2011037735

Contents at a Glance

Dear Reader,

To be bold, we think that this third edition of our comprehensive book on SAP Solution Manager is something special! However, you may be thinking "It's just a book about a piece of software, so what?" To answer your question, this comprehensive book explains the software that provides functionality, scaling from solution design to the technical system monitoring, user support, and extending to the landscape transformation in a thorough and easy-to-follow process.

You'll find that this completely redesigned edition will provide you with the valuable information you need to plan, design, implement, and manage your SAP Solution Manager project. Combined with real-world scenarios and the accumulated knowledge and experience of nearly 40 experts from SAP, I'm confident that you'll find a trustworthy and essential companion on your journey with the newest release of SAP Solution Manager.

However, make sure to also share your thoughts on this book. Your comments and suggestions are the most useful tools to help us improve our books for you, the reader. Visit our website at *www.sap-press.com* to leave a review, or send me an email directly.

Thank you for purchasing a book from SAP PRESS!

Laura Korslund
Editor, SAP PRESS

Galileo Press
Boston, MA

laura.korslund@galileo-press.com
www.sap-press.com

Contents

Foreword from the Chief Operating Officer of SAP AG

After the success of the first two editions of the *SAP Solution Manager* book, I am pleased to present this third, completely reworked edition of the book.

SAP is constantly providing its customers and partners with new ways of driving innovations and adapting quickly and flexibly to the market, while at the same time reducing the *total cost of ownership* (TCO) and minimizing risks. Constantly enhancing the SAP product portfolio not only boosts SAP's strategic relevance, but it increases the company's level of ecosystem responsibility as well. SAP is committed to providing its customers and partners with end-to-end, comprehensive support and maintenance for their software-based business processes and services, both today and in the future.

To achieve this, it is my aim as Chief Operating Officer to develop and optimize best practices, processes, methods, services, and tools, and make them available for use. As such, we have been consistent in promoting the right measures in all areas related to service and support so that we can meet the needs of our customers and partners in the ecosystem more effectively.

With the new version of SAP Solution Manager and the interaction with the underlying support agreements, in particular *SAP MaxAttention*, *SAP Enterprise Support* and *Product Support for Large Enterprises* (PSLE), SAP is providing you with a cross-solution option. All the technology and application components that you need to operate your business processes, whether from SAP or other manufacturers, partner solutions, or customer specific expansions (*custom code*), are included here. SAP Solution Manager is the backbone for our customers and partners to ensure that SAP-based customer solutions and services operate as efficiently as possible.

SAP Solution Manager features specific services, methods, and tools that are aligned with our commitment to providing end-to-end support for business processes and offering open integration in the ecosystem.

Here, industry standards such as the Application Management processes described in the *IT Infrastructure Library* (ITIL) are becoming increasingly more important all the time.

The main focus of these offerings was on scalability, with a particular emphasis placed on services. Only by "productizing" our offers and standard consulting services can we adequately support customers and partners in all different sizes of companies—from small, to mid-size, to large enterprises. This applies in particular to strategic innovations such as *in memory*, *cloud computing*, and *mobility*, which strengthen SAP's vision of enabling a combination of *on demand*, *on device*, and *on premise* for your company.

In the current version of SAP Solution Manager, the range of services in particular was enhanced with regard to standardization, user-friendliness, and openness in the ecosystem. This input has enabled SAP Solution Manager to provide end-to-end, comprehensive support and maintenance for the software-based business processes and services of our customers and partners today and in the future.

With this in mind, I would like to sincerely thank the authors for their commitment to writing a book filled with collective experiences for the benefit of our customers and partners. I also hope that you, dear readers, can learn and take advantage of the great deal of valuable information about SAP Solution Manager in this book, as well as benefit from the specific practical examples by applying them to your own projects. The close working relationship with customers and user groups is an invaluable asset, and I would like to take this opportunity to give special thanks to the authors of the customer experience reports. In addition to their daily work, they have invested time in this book to report on their experience with the new version of SAP Solution Manager during the ramp-up. Thank you for the trust you have shown in us, and for your commitment!

Gerhard Oswald
Member of the board and Chief Operating Officer of SAP AG

Foreword by Andreas Oczko
Deputy Chairman of DSAG Board Area:
Operations/Service & Support

"In the next edition, we will be astounded once again by all of the newness around us." In the turbulent days of 2008, this prediction was part of the foreword I wrote for the book on SAP Solution Manager 7.0 Enterprise Edition. I, for my part, am astounded indeed.

With SAP Solution Manager 7.1, we are now 0.1 steps further and hold in our hands a milestone in the tool's history. In essence, however, SAP Solution Manager is evolving more and more from a tool into a holistic process for running SAP solutions. The new version, having been shaped by the ideas and technical skill of SAP's developers and IT architects, is also one of the main results of the joint Get-Well Initiative involving SAP and the German-speaking SAP User Group (DSAG) e.V.

Kicked off in late 2009, this initiative aims to align SAP Solution Manager more closely to customers' needs and significantly increase the utility it provides. Customers' real-world experiences have found their way into release 7.1 through workshops and development requests; detailed analysis of the tool's new features and DSAG's prompt feedback to SAP were also important parts of the development cycle. Meanwhile, DSAG worked with SAP on organizing events about specific topics in Germany and Austria. In attending these events, more than 640 people also registered their great interest in SAP Solution Manager—version 7.1 in particular. This series of events will continue next year and pass through Switzerland, as well.

That's not all, however. DSAG was also in charge of designing the licensing for SAP Solution Manager. As a result, customers with SAP Standard Support contracts can now rely on extensive protection of their investments, clear future perspectives, and the ability to set up their SAP operations according to their specific needs.

This book, which presents a summary of functions, process expertise, and customer reports that factor in the updates included in release 7.1 of the tool, rounds out our activities related to the latest version of SAP Solution Manager. I am proud to note that most of the customer reports were written by experts from the ranks of the nearly 800 companies registered to the DSAG Special Interest Group CCC/Service & Support or one of its work groups.

SAP, meanwhile, has been confidently dispelling any doubts about version 7.1 of SAP Solution Manager. The time has come to see what it can do! We will know if the tool has fulfilled the expectations soon—at the latest in the fourth edition of this book. If you would prefer not to wait that long, I can only recommend becoming an active member of DSAG and the aforementioned Special Interest Group. In it, you will have constant access to the latest unvarnished information, tips and tricks, and a functioning network of users—not to mention the chance to be a contributing part of the group.

I hope you enjoy reading the book and applying what you learn from it. If you think it might be too early to look into SAP Solution Manager 7.1, think again. You and your company can benefit thanks in part to the work of the Get-Well Initiative, which has chosen a motto befitting its aims: "Listen—Understand—Analyze—Implement."

Andreas Oczko
Deputy Chairman, German-speaking SAP User Group (DSAG) e.V.
Board Area: Operations/Service & Support

Introduction

Since the second edition of this book was published, there have been many changes in the area of SAP Solution Manager. On the publication date of this book, a new version of SAP Solution Manager is available: SAP Solution Manager 7.1. The first two editions of this book were received by readers with great excitement. We are especially pleased with this interest and with being able to present the innovations of the past two years in the general context of SAP Solution Manager throughout the following pages. This also includes an explanation of integrated partner solutions and application concepts for non-SAP components of your solutions. You will become familiar with new concepts such as the *Monitoring and Alerting Infrastructure* or the *Test Automation Framework*, as well as trusted content and content that has been adapted to meet new requirements.

What is SAP Solution Manager? and *Where can I use SAP Solution Manager?* are among the questions that excite many minds and trouble a few. We intend to answer these questions on a conceptual and strategic level, as well as a practical and application-specific level.

Therefore, we have spoken with experts at SAP and with customers and partners who gave us their personal insight, for which we owe our sincere thanks. The intense, constructive teamwork with these people to produce this book, especially with regard to development requests and concept revisions, enabled us to turn SAP Solution Manager into a standardized platform for application management and operation, and it is this platform that we would like to present to you in this book. In the future, we hope to be able to continue and build on this close working relationship.

The book comprises two sections, each of which addresses a specific topic and focuses on a specific reader base, as described here: **Layout of the book**

- A short section (**Chapters 1** to **3**) deals with the concepts and the entire spectrum of *SAP Solution Manager* from a general standpoint, explains the basic functions and fundamental content, and discusses SAP Solution Manager in the context of *Information*

Technology Infrastructure Library (ITIL) application management. Chapter 1 is dedicated to the aspect of openness toward non-SAP software and the usage rights of SAP Solution Manager. This section gives CIOs and management an overview of the capabilities and strategies employed by SAP Solution Manager and provides an outlook on future development as part of an *executive summary*.

▶ The second section (**Chapters 4 to 15**) picks up on the structure of SAP Solution Manager introduced in the first section and goes into detail on the SAP Solution Manager functions relevant to the corresponding processes. This most comprehensive single topic area is written for project teams that require more specific information about the functionality of individual scenarios. These chapters already contain customer experience reports from the ramp-up phase of SAP Solution Manager for the corresponding processes. The **Appendix** contains information about all of the authors who contributed to this book.

Overview The following is an overview of the topics addressed in each chapter.

Chapter 1 provides a brief overview of SAP Solution Manager and explains its role as an integration platform for the support options provided by SAP. We take a detailed look at the usage rights within the support options and provide an overview of how you can use SAP Solution Manager end-to-end, even for products from other manufacturers.

Chapter 2 clarifies the strategic significance of SAP Solution Manager as a platform for *Application Lifecycle Management* (ALM). Here you will learn how to use SAP Solution Manager for continuous improvements and for fundamental changes to your business processes within the release management, such as upgrades.

After the explanations of Application Lifecycle Management, **Chapter 3** shows how SAP Solution Manager provides you with long-term support during the operating phase, through automation, for example.

After these predominantly strategic and comprehensive chapters, **Chapter 4** takes up the structure of ITIL Application Management introduced in Chapter 1 and describes the *Solution Documentation* process that helps you create transparency in your business processes and the system landscapes underlying them.

The objective of **Chapter 5** is to explain the *Solution Implementation* process in more detail. Among the topics included are the SAP Solution Manager content supplied in the *Business Process Repository* (BPR), project management with SAP Solution Manager, and functions such as the *Business Blueprint* and *Roadmaps*. It also explains the configuration of the solution, knowledge transfer in the project, and reporting functions.

Chapter 6 explains how you can use SAP Solution Manager during the rollout of templates with the *Template Management* process within your company to reduce the total cost of implementation (TCI).

Testing within the entire lifecycle is a potential cost driver. **Chapter 7** presents the *Test Management* process, which provides you with optimal support for all of the tasks that arise during testing. The *Business Process Change Analyzer* concept employed in SAP Solution Manager is just one of the topics that we discuss in detail in this chapter.

To help you take your projects or maintenance activities smoothly and cost-efficiently into the operating phase, SAP Solution Manager contains the *Change Control Management* process, which provides comprehensive functions such as Quality Gate Management, the Change and Transport System (CTS), or Change Request Management. **Chapter 8** covers this process and the underlying functions in detail.

In ensuring the smooth operation of a solution, the *Application Incident Management* process is of primary significance. **Chapter 9** explains the functions and innovations of the Service Desk in SAP Solution Manager. Because partners also play a vital role in the SAP ecosystem, the chapter also discusses the integration of partners in SAP support processes, which not only increases quality but also adds value.

A central innovation of the new SAP Solution Manager is the new *Monitoring and Alerting Infrastructure* in the *Technical Operations* process. This and other functions, such as *End User Experience Monitoring* or *Data Volume Management*, are described in detail in **Chapter 10**.

Chapter 11 deals with the *Business Process Operations* process. Here the central functions *Business Process Monitoring, Job Scheduling Manage-*

ment, *Data Consistency Management*, and *Interface Monitoring* are explained in detail.

Because solutions are continually being improved and have to be adapted to changing requirements, *Maintenance Management* is an important task in the lifecycle of solutions. **Chapter 12** describes the process and functions of SAP Solution Manager that help you structure the maintenance of your solution as efficiently and effectively as possible.

Chapter 13 shows you how to use SAP Solution Manager to leverage SAP knowledge and experience in the *Upgrade Management* process.

Mergers and acquisitions present many companies with major challenges. With *SAP Landscape Transformation*, SAP provides you with an add-on for SAP Solution Manager that supports you in the tasks involved in business and IT transformations. In **Chapter 14**, you will find detailed information on this process.

Customer developments are necessary if the SAP standard software has to be expanded for specific customers to map their individual requirements. However, these developments also represent a major cost driver. The *Custom Code Management* process helps you clearly to identify which expansions are really necessary and which can be substituted for standard solutions, thus decreasing the overall operating costs. **Chapter 15** shows how you can use the process to increase the quality and the added value of your solution.

The **Appendix** contains information about all of the authors who contributed to this book.

This book is designed so that you can read it cover to cover or refer to specific chapters as needed. We hope that this book will give you a comprehensive, consistent grasp of SAP Solution Manager and enable you to recognize the benefits it can provide, as well as appreciate the new application scenarios that are possible when used at your company. We are confident that you will profit from our suggestions and be inspired to learn more. If you have any questions, comments, or criticism, please feel free to contact us by sending an email to the addresses given in Appendix A.

Acknowledgments

The making of such a comprehensive book is the product of end-to-end collaboration at many levels over the course of the project. Many people have assisted us, the authors, by providing the information necessary to present the concepts, strategy, and content of SAP Solution Manager in book form.

We especially would like to thank:

- Gerhard Oswald, Chief Operating Officer and member of the SAP AG executive board
- Dr. Uwe Hommel, Executive Vice President, SAP Active Global Support
- Helmut Fieres, Vice President, Service and Support Infrastructure
- Marc Thier, Senior Vice President, Solution Management for Application Lifecycle Management

We would also like to thank:

- Andreas Oczko for the invaluable collaboration and close support on behalf of the German-Speaking SAP User Group (DSAG)
- Eric Wannemacher, Günther Theiss, Andreas Krückendorf, Christiane Hahn, Mathias Uhlmann, Manja Müller, Andreas Diebold, Vital Anderhub, Gordon McDorman, Rüdiger Stöcker, Axel Spenneberg, Jonathan Bletscher, Claudia Kalwell, Gregory Freeman, Melanie Freeman, Thomas Zaelke, Michael Erhardt, Stefan Berndt, Christoph Nake, and Marc Arnold Bach for their active support
- Manon Fischer for her enduring commitment to proofreading and correcting the manuscript, and for supporting the project as a whole
- Our families, partners, and children for their patience and understanding

SAP Solution Manager facilitates efficient application management and collaboration with SAP. In this chapter, you'll find an overview of the crucial functional areas of SAP Solution Manager 7.1 and its underlying concepts.

1 Concept of SAP Solution Manager 7.1

SAP Solution Manager 7.1 is *the* central solution for *Application Lifecycle Management* (ALM) and the operation of software solutions. It supports heterogeneous system environments, and its functions cover all key areas, from implementation and go-live to operation and ongoing improvement of solutions. SAP Solution Manager 7.1 combines tools, content, and direct access to SAP to increase the reliability and stability of solutions and lower the *total cost of operations* (TCO). SAP Solution Manager is also the linchpin for cooperation in the SAP ecosystem; that is, cooperation between project teams, SAP partners, consultants, and SAP Active Global Support (SAP AGS), because it simplifies communication among all stakeholders of a solution.

To ensure this, SAP Solution Manager covers the entire lifecycle of a solution. To explain the lifecycle, this book uses the application management lifecycle described in version 3 of the IT Infrastructure Library (ITIL) as a generally recognized model. Application management is a comprehensive support approach in the application environment that spans the entire lifecycle of IT solutions, from planning and operation to continuous improvement of a solution.

Lifecycle

The lifecycle has six phases (see Figure 1.1):

Phases

▶ **Requirements**
Collect requirements for new applications or for the distribution of existing applications.

▶ **Design**
Convert requirements into detailed specifications.

▶ **Build & Test**
Configure the application and create an organizational model in accordance with the specifications.

▶ **Deploy**
Transfer changes and the organizational model into the existing live IT landscape.

▶ **Operate**
Provide IT services required for ongoing operations.

▶ **Optimize**
Analyze service-level fulfillment and perform any activities required to improve results.

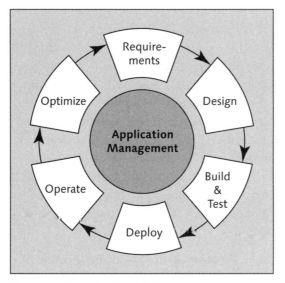

Figure 1.1 Lifecycle of IT Solutions

1.1 Effective Implementation of Changes— Projects in SAP Solution Manager

A *project* in SAP Solution Manager describes the grouping and organization of business, technical, and organizational tasks during the implementation of SAP software in an enterprise. In an implementation project, the project team performs tasks that are structured according to a common project plan and roadmap. In SAP Solution Manager, projects follow the ASAP methodology, starting with project preparation and completing the project in the go-live phase.

From the lifecycle perspective, a project covers the application management phases from requirements gathering through the Build & Test phase. All information that you collect over the course of the project is applied in the solution at the end of the Deploy phase. This includes the transfer of knowledge to the end user by means of e-learning or the implementation of the support organization.

Using SAP Solution Manager for projects has many advantages, including the following:

Benefits of SAP Solution Manager project administration

▶ Structured, systematic procedure throughout the project.

▶ Strict adherence to a process-centric approach, which is separate from individual applications and components and provides a more comprehensive view of process flows in heterogeneous system landscapes.

▶ Centralized metadata repository for solutions, including documentation, test cases, and configuration information.

▶ No information loss between project phases. Once created, content is reused throughout the software lifecycle, preventing integration gaps.

From the perspective of the lifecycle, an SAP Solution Manager project covers phases from the Requirements phase to the preparation of the go-live (Deploy phase). The scope of a project varies and can range from large-scale projects, such as upgrade projects, to smaller changes implemented during a maintenance cycle.

1.2 Efficient Operation—Solutions in SAP Solution Manager

After you have successfully completed a project, the challenges during operations are preserving the knowledge gained during the project and keeping it constantly up to date. The solution concept of SAP Solution Manager helps you do this. During import for production use, all of the information accumulated in your project is transferred into a solution. An SAP Solution Manager solution contains all of the information about systems, software components, and business processes (scenarios) needed in the operation and continuous optimization of your IT solution. This ensures that all information remains accessible and can be consolidated when a project is over.

Information about systems, software components, and business processes

A solution naturally spans a longer period of time than a project. However, the operational phase is also the phase of the lifecycle in which you create value from your investments in projects. Therefore, the integrity of your solution is the key to successful operation.

A differentiation is made between two dimensions in which the solution serves as an information source for operation: Horizontally, each software component that is required for the execution of the business processes of the customer in accordance with the solution documentation can be administered with the SAP Solution Manager processes. Vertically, every layer of the solution can also use these processes, including databases and IT assets, for example.

Solutions in SAP Solution Manager offer the following advantages:

- **All assignments are in the SAP Solution Manager project**
  - Scenario and business process structures are transferred to the solution.
  - Configuration object assignments are readily available.
  - Test cases in the structure can be used to test changes that have been made.
  - E-learning materials from projects in the solution can be reused.
  - The solution has the same system landscape as the project, so you can reuse the structure when you upgrade.
- **Solution components, such as servers, systems, business processes, and scenarios, are provided in a standard presentation.**
  - The display of graphics and diagrams is clear.
  - You can export graphics to Microsoft Office or HTML.

From the perspective of the application management lifecycle, the solution in SAP Solution Manager covers the phases from handover into operation (the Deploy phase) to operation (the Operate phase) to optimization (the Optimize phase).

1.3   Processes in SAP Solution Manager

To cover the entire lifecycle, SAP Solution Manager offers 12 processes. These processes bundle functions in SAP Solution Manager that support you in the respective focus areas on a long-term basis. As previously mentioned, this book is structured according to these processes (Chapter 4 to 15); only a brief overview is to be given here:

► **Solution Documentation**
The Solution Documentation includes the documentation of the technical landscape as well as the business process documentation. It forms the basis for all other functions of SAP Solution Manager. It describes a customer's SAP and non-SAP technical components, core business processes, and interfaces. The documentation also includes custom code and modification documentation, as well as links to supporting technical objects, such as transactions and programs.

► **Solution Implementation**
Solution Implementation involves the identification, adaptation, and implementation of new and enhanced future-oriented business and technical scenarios. It's designed to decouple technical installation from business innovation and uses SAP Solution Manager to implement innovation within the system landscape.

► **Template Management**
Using this process, customers with SAP installations that include multiple locations can also efficiently administer their business processes over long distances. Template Management is part of a global rollout approach and includes template definitions, template implementation, and template optimization.

► **Test Management**
Here you define the integration testing requirements and test scope based on a change impact analysis. You can also develop automatic and manual test cases, manage the testers, and report on the test progress and test results.

► **Change Control Management**
This process offers workflow-based management of changes to use to improve a business or technological aspect. Integrated functions for project management, quality management, and synchronized provisioning support you in the optimal management of risks associated with the implementation of the solution and in ensuring technical and functional stability.

► **Technical Operations**
This process includes all capabilities for monitoring, alerting,

analyzing, and administering SAP solutions, and allows customers to reduce total cost of ownership (TCO) by using predefined content and centralized tools for all aspects of SAP Solution Manager operations. It provides end-to-end reporting functionality either out of the box or as individually created by customers.

▶ **Business Process Operations**
This process covers the most important application-related aspects of operation. It's necessary to take these aspects into account to ensure a smooth and reliable flow of the core business processes, and thus the fulfillment of the business requirements.

▶ **Application Incident Management**
This process enables centralized and common incident and problem message processing on multiple organization levels and offers a communication channel with all relevant stakeholders of an incident. The process includes business users, SAP experts at the customer site, SAP AGS, and partner support employees. It's integrated in all processes of SAP Solution Manager and in any SAP Business Suite solution, can be connected to a non-SAP help desk application, and includes follow-up activities such as knowledge research, root cause analysis, and change management.

▶ **Maintenance Management**
This process includes packages for software correction from identification and provisioning to optimization of the test scope. These packages can be optionally imported into the production environment on an automatic basis.

▶ **Upgrade Management**
This process includes the identification, adaptation, and implementation of new and enhanced business and technical scenarios, and it uses SAP Solution Manager to holistically and effectively manage the upgrade project end to end. It allows SAP customers to better understand and manage the major technical risks and challenges within an upgrade project and to make the upgrade project a non-event for the business.

▶ **Landscape Transformation Management**
This process helps you to accelerate business and IT transformations, in case of mergers or acquisitions, for example, and to plan, analyze, organize, and implement complex business requirements using standardized transformation solutions.

► **Custom Code Management**
Includes tools and methods that support you in analyzing custom code and in deciding whether individual developments can be replaced by standard software to minimize the TCO with upgrade projects, for example.

1.4   From SAP-Centered to Solution-Wide Use

SAP Solution Manager[1] was often criticized in the past for only providing really good support to SAP solutions. When customers looked for a tool for their complete solution, including the software of third-party providers connected with SAP components, or even the entire IT system, SAP Solution Manager had the reputation of being developed "only for SAP." As a result, other tools were often purchased and implemented. That is unfortunate because SAP has the objective—especially in the context of its *premium engagements*[2]—of offering all functions that enterprises need for universal management of their applications.

1.4.1   Simple Usage for the Overall Customer Solution

The question of why this opinion is so pervasive was regularly answered by naming two main aspects. First, the user environment was said to be too inconvenient. Users claimed that the user interfaces were accepted by SAP users, to be sure, but not by other user groups in the enterprise. Second, the technical support of non-SAP components was said to be insufficient; the users also claimed that only SAP components were well supported. The bottom line is that SAP Solution Manager is often not considered to be a possible solution, not even in comparative assessments before the selection of such tools. That is why the goal was set to fare better in such comparisons with the new version of SAP Solution Manager by greatly expanding the functional footprint. For you as a customer, this

Main aspects of the criticism

---

1 Depending on the support agreement, different usage rights apply for SAP Solution Manager. These are described in detail in Section 1.6. When mentioning SAP Solution Manager, this book assumes the use of SAP Solution Manager under SAP Enterprise Support.

2 When SAP Enterprise Support is mentioned in the following, this includes SAP Product Support for Large Enterprises (SAP PSLE) and SAP MaxAttention.

means that you can avoid additional investments because corresponding functions are already made available by SAP Solution Manager under SAP Enterprise Support.

A good example of this is the process for processing and resolving errors. This is especially clear and prevalent, but the example applies to all other scenarios covered by SAP Solution Manager.

New user interface

The completely revised *Service Desk* of SAP Solution Manager offers a state-of-the-art user interface that allows customers to ensure broad acceptance in the entire company beyond the previous circle of SAP users.

New monitoring infrastructure

The same applies for the new *End-to-End Monitoring and Alerting*, which offers SAP Enterprise Support customers an infrastructure with which they can monitor the availability of the systems and business processes—across different technologies and with integration with both the Service Desk and *Root Cause Analysis*. In this way, SAP Solution Manager can either be used exclusively for monitoring and alerting or for the complete problem handling and resolution process within the overall solution.

Extension of usage rights

Beyond all technical arguments, the expansion of usage rights is another good example of how SAP makes it easy for its customers to use SAP Solution Manager for the overall customer solution. SAP Enterprise Support customers can use the SAP Solution Manager as a general Service Desk tool without additional license costs, for example. This is possible because SAP has extended the usage rights for the Service Desk to all software components of third-party providers that are used in conjunction with SAP business processes. For example, if a customer uses mobile communication devices to accept orders, SAP Enterprise Resource Planning (SAP ERP) and SAP Customer Relationship Management (SAP CRM) to process them, a database provided by a third-party provider to process them, and printers to print the delivery notes, all of these are components of the SAP customer solution—and exempted from being subject to separate charges for licensing from the SAP price list. Thus, the Service Desk can be used without additional license fees within the scope of SAP Enterprise Support (see Section 1.6).

1.4.2 Openness: Integration of Partner Products

Another frequently mentioned point of criticism was that customers had already invested in management software in the past and understandably did not want to write off these investments to henceforth use SAP Solution Manager. Such misgivings are not justified because SAP Solution Manager is already well integrated with tools from third-party providers such as SAP Quality Center by HP, so that customers can use these third-party products together with SAP Solution Manager. This strategy of openness is further pursued with the new SAP Solution Manager under SAP Enterprise Support, as both of the following examples show.

The integration with the *IBM Rational test software* allows you to better test your own *IBM WebSphere* developments to supplement your SAP solution. This is better because IBM and SAP have integrated SAP Solution Manager and *IBM Rational Quality Manager* for their common customers under SAP Enterprise Support—in the newest version of both of these tools in each case.

IBM tools

Other partners with which SAP works on the ever greater openness of SAP Solution Manager include the following:

▶ Software AG with *ARIS* (previously from IDS Scheer) for business process modeling (*SAP Enterprise Modeling Applications by IDS Scheer*)

▶ Ancile (formerly RWD) with the *SAP Productivity Pack by Ancile* for training management

▶ Redwood with *SAP Central Process Scheduling by Redwood* for job scheduling management

▶ Hewlett-Packard with *SAP Quality Center by HP*, including *Quality Test Pro* for the area of test management and *SAP LoadRunner by HP* for mass performance tests

▶ IBM with *Requisite Pro* as part of the test integration, as well as *ClearQuest* and *Requisite Testing*

At the time of the printing of this book, these and other partners and their products are integrated with SAP Solution Manager.

1.4.3 Openness: SAP Solution Manager for Non-SAP Software

Along with SAP components, non-SAP software components, which are often based on the infrastructures of third-party providers such as *Microsoft .NET* or *IBM WebSphere*, can be connected to SAP Solution Manager. The following integration options are available to you:

▶ Register the required non-SAP components in the *Maintenance Optimizer* or landscape management.

▶ Integrate the non-SAP components into the *Enhanced Change and Transport System* (CTS+).

▶ Instrument the non-SAP components so that you can provide metrics for the *Root Cause Analysis*.

▶ Integrate non-SAP process steps into the *Solution Documentation*, the *Business Processes Monitoring*, and the *Business Processes Analytics*.

▶ Integrate non-SAP reporting data into the *Management Dashboards*.

Landscape Management

Landscape Management Database (LMDB)

The registration of all technical components at a central location is a basic requirement for successful management of heterogeneous SAP solutions. The *Landscape Management Database* (LMDB), an open and expandable landscape modeling environment based on the *Common Information Model* (CIM), is available with SAP Solution Manager 7.1. This makes it possible to supply SAP Solution Manager without further modeling information for all types of technical components, such as technical systems, instances, or scenarios. Detailed information about the LMDB can be found in Chapter 4, Section 4.1.2, subsection "Landscape Management Database."

You can manually expand the LMDB by entering your technical systems using what is known as the *Technical System Editor*. To facilitate this, immediately usable ("out-of-the-box") and predefined system types are available, including IBM WebSphere and Apache Tomcat, for example. There are also generic system types, such as *unspecific system* or *unspecific cluster*. Manual modeling can relate to these predefined system types. To avoid manual modeling, it is possible to use *data suppliers* supplied by SAP or customer-specific ones. Correct technical modeling is the prerequisite for root cause analysis or technical monitoring in SAP Solution Manager, for example.

Enhanced Change and Transport System (CTS+)

The enhanced Change and Transport System (CTS+) provides you with a variety of options for integrating your own transport logics into the change process. When content from the development system is to be transported into a production system, and the SAP transport mechanisms do not support this content in the standard, you can develop the required logic on the basis of CTS+ itself. SAP makes two options available: file transfer and script-based importing.

File transfer is the simplest way to integrate non-SAP applications into the transport process. CTS+ supports the transport of every file type. In the parameter settings of CTS+, you can define a dedicated export folder for manual uploading. Changes to a non-SAP object are attached to a transport order, released, exported, and imported into the follow-on systems. CTS+ supports these activities, but you need to manually execute the additional activation and configuration steps in the target system. You can use CTS+ to monitor imports and analyze errors. The queue and import histories of CTS+ give you an overview of the imports that have already been executed or that are being planned.

File transfer

Batch or shell scripts on SAP Solution Manager can be used to integrate non-SAP applications into CTS+. For Windows platforms, *Standard Batch Scripts* (*.bat* files) are used, and for UNIX, *Standard Shell Scripts* (*.sh* files) are used. The *CTS+ Deploy Web Service* calls a separate script for each transport object. Understandable *return codes* must be implemented to control and monitor the monitoring and import process. These are read in by the *CTS Script Caller* and entered into the *CTS Deployment Log*.

Script-based importing

Business Process Monitoring

The operation of business processes includes the entirety of the most important application-related activities needed to ensure a stable and problem-free process flow of the core business processes within a company. A comprehensive representation of the process can be found in Chapter 11, Section 11.1.

Monitoring of business processes offers you a variety of options for integrating non-SAP technologies throughout the monitoring process:

▶ ABAP Database Connectivity (ADBC)

▶ Web services

▶ SAP NetWeaver Business Warehouse (BW)

General functions such as integration into the Service Desk, trend reporting, or alerting and messaging mechanisms are available with these integration scenarios.

ADBC monitoring for non-SAP systems

Integration via ADBC is the simplest and most flexible way to integrate customer-specific functions into the monitoring of business processes. The only prerequisite is that a secondary database connection from SAP Solution Manager to the database of the non-SAP system exists and that the user has basic knowledge of the data model of this system.

In the setup of Business Process Monitoring, you can define the database tables and fields needed to fulfill your requirements easily and without programming effort. You can use the familiar *user exit framework* to extend the existing monitoring functions. Using ABAP, you can develop complex scenarios for non-SAP systems. Using this approach, you can better mask the complexity of the underlying data models of the non-SAP systems, thus making the work of the end users easier.

As already mentioned, the work required for the development of ADBC-based monitoring depends to a great extent on how well you know the data model of the non-SAP system. While the required effort is often less with custom-developed systems because you know the data model well, you can expect that more effort will be required for the connection of third-party systems because you need to implement the integration through trial and error or with the support of partners.

Web service-based monitoring for non-SAP systems

Although the ADBC-based solution is very powerful, it is a good idea in many cases to completely separate the data model of the non-SAP system from the implementation in SAP Solution Manager; for example, when the non-SAP system is still being developed and the data model could still change. In this case, you can access the non-

SAP system via Web services to keep the monitoring of business processes stable in SAP Solution Manager even if changes are carried out in the non-SAP system.

Both *push* and *pull* mechanisms are supported here; for example, you can use SAP Solution Manager as a server to send data from the non-SAP system, or as a client that queries the monitoring data from the third-party system. With the pull mechanism, you need to implement a web service on a third-party system for transferring the monitoring data over the interface defined by SAP. For the push method, a consumer for the SAP Web service needs to be implemented on the non-SAP system.

Third-party systems are often connected to an SAP NetWeaver Business Warehouse (BW) system to enable reporting. In this case, you can connect SAP Solution Manager with the relevant BW system and use the existing data of the *InfoObjects* for the monitoring of business processes. This is especially important if you want to monitor the aggregated throughput data, such as the number of sales orders that need to be created on a daily basis.

BW-based monitoring for non-SAP systems

Root Cause Analysis

SAP supplies a standardized and central suite of tools for root cause analysis with SAP Solution Manager. You can use these tools for all technologies of SAP and third-party providers. SAP Solution Manager supports classic ABAP components, various versions of Java and J2EE, Microsoft .NET, and Internet Information Services (IIS), as well as native components.

The objective is to offer the following tools for all supported technologies:

Tools

▶ The *Exception Analysis* allows you to centrally analyze all exceptions from connected systems, such as serious error messages in logs or dumps. From here, you can start component-specific tools.

▶ The *Workload Analysis* comprises server-related workload statistics for the connected systems.

▶ The *Change Analysis* creates transparency for all changes (technical configuration, code, content) that have been made in the connected system landscape. This is particularly useful in the event of faults that occur after changes have been made to the production landscape.

▶ The *Trace Analysis* records performance-related and functional faults in a specific user activity from the user's browser to the storage subsystem. The measurement is triggered by the user interface and automatically activates recording of the relevant traces on every component processed by the user query.

It is not SAP's objective to replace all local tools for root cause analysis, but instead to make the previously mentioned information available in SAP Solution Manager on a standardized and centralized basis. SAP Solution Manager contains instrumentation for the most common SAP and non-SAP technologies, as well for a wide range of other technologies. In the case of non-ABAP technologies, the instrumentation is carried out using *CA Wily Introscope*, which is also supplied with SAP Solution Manager. You can find more information about Root Cause Analysis in Section 1.4.

SAP Extended Diagnostics

However, you can also extend the supplied instrumentation to include additional technologies or customer-specific developments, for example. For this, SAP offers the product *SAP Extended Diagnostics*, which contains a full version of CA Wily Introscope. Using this product, you can extend the functions of Root Cause Analysis to the entire customer solution.

Technical Monitoring

With SAP Solution Manager 7.1, a new infrastructure for central technical monitoring of system landscapes was introduced that consists of the following components:

Components of technical monitoring

▶ In the *Alert Inbox*, all incoming alerts of the various monitoring applications are shown.

▶ The *System Monitoring* application allows monitoring of the current status of technical systems, as well their instances, databases, and hosts.

▶ In *End User Experience Monitoring*, recorded scripts are executed from several locations on an automated basis, and their results are evaluated to draw conclusions about the availability and performance of scenarios from the perspective of the end user.

▶ In *Connection Monitoring*, remote function call (RFC) and HTTP connections from ABAP systems are tested in regard to their availability and performance.

▶ *Process Integration Monitoring* (PI Monitoring) enables monitoring of the runtime components of all SAP NetWeaver Process Integration (PI) domains that are connected to SAP Solution Manager.

▶ In *Business Intelligence Monitoring* (BI Monitoring), both the process chains of connected BW systems and the status of the components of one or more SAP BusinessObjects systems are monitored.

End User Experience Monitoring, PI Monitoring, and BI Monitoring are known as *scenario-specific applications*, which were developed for a certain use type. For this reason, no provision is made to extend these applications. In contrast, the Alert Inbox and System Monitoring are generic functions for all types of managed objects. SAP covers the most common SAP and non-SAP technologies with content that is ready for immediate use for monitoring, alerting, and analysis. You can nevertheless extend this content if your application requires it.

For extension, the monitoring and alerting infrastructure offers fully configured templates that are based on approaches proven in practice. You can adjust these templates to your requirements and deactivate, adjust, or define your own SAP metrics (e.g., thresholds), alerts, and events. You can also make your own data providers available as RFC-based function modules or Web services to procure data via pull mechanisms or diagnostic agents for push mechanisms. You can also subscribe to CA Wily Introscope metrics so that data is supplied to SAP Solution Manager from Introscope using push methods. Whether you decide in favor of push or pull methods depends on the expected data volumes and how often the data is to be acquired.

Template-based extension

For alerts that arise, you can decide whether an incident is to be automatically created, an automatic reaction is to occur, or a connection to a third-party system is to be established. All of these activities can be configured using a *business add-on* (BAdI). For example, you can integrate an incident management application of a third-party provider or dynamically determine who will be notified in case of an alert.

1.5 Improved User-Friendliness

Special attention was paid to the user interfaces of SAP Solution Manager in the development of the new version. Two main aspects were important here: improved usability and targeted user groups.

Improved usability | Improved usability helps existing users with the effective and efficient execution of their tasks. Within enterprises, this improved usability also makes it easier for the SAP community to find acceptance for SAP Solution Manager and thus establish it as a central IT tool.

A quick glance at the examples in the following sections shows that the user interfaces of the new SAP Solution Manager target different user groups. They are designed strictly according to the requirements resulting from the various user roles. For example, SAP Solution Manager offers an interface for IT decision makers focused on *key performance indicators* (KPIs), reports, and graphical navigation to enable a fast, intuitive understanding of complex relationships.

1.5.1 Maintaining an Overview with Management Dashboards

Management dashboards in SAP Solution Manager are a new development that gives IT managers the ability to use the data available about the customer solution in SAP Solution Manager in such a manner that it is possible to have better control over the IT.

With version 7.1, SAP Solution Manager is offering a *dashboard framework* that allows you to configure dashboards that you need for your daily work. The data needed for this is made available centrally by SAP NetWeaver BW (in SAP Solution Manager or from other BW systems as well), including filtering and aggregation of the data.

Dashboards and dashboard apps | On the dashboard, the data is displayed on dashboard apps. A *dashboard app* is an Adobe Flash application that shows the status of an individual KPI on its dashboard—system availability, for example. SAP develops standard dashboard apps using *SAP BusinessObjects Dashboards* and supplies them via the *Dashboard App Store* in SAP Solution Manager (see Figure 1.2). It is important to emphasize here that you do not need additional licenses to work with the management dashboards. That's because the dashboard apps are supplied as

Flash applications and can be integrated, configured, and adjusted to your requirements on the dashboard. The apps use queries to access the SAP NetWeaver BW data in SAP Solution Manager.

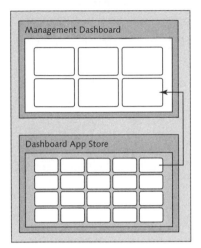

Figure 1.2 Management Dashboards and Dashboard Apps

To integrate a dashboard app into your management dashboard, simply select CONFIGURE in the upper-right corner of the dashboard. You can select the relevant app from the Dashboard App Store of SAP Solution Manager. In the configuration dialog that follows (CONFIGURATION UI), you can quickly and flexibly adjust the app to your requirements. After you have saved your configuration, the app is displayed on your dashboard. You can also display several instances of the same app on your dashboard—to compare KPIs across several time periods, for example. The management dashboard adjusts the size of the individual apps automatically when you add new apps. In configuration mode, you can add new apps to your dashboard, remove apps from the dashboard, copy existing apps, and change the layout of your dashboard by using drag and drop to move the apps into other areas of the dashboard.

Working with dashboard apps

With SP02 of SAP Solution Manager 7.1, the following dashboard apps were supplied in the standard system (see Figure 1.3):

▶ Technical Operations

  ▶ System performance

  ▶ System availability

  ▶ End User Experience Monitoring

> ▶ Business Process Operations
>
>   ▶ Monitoring of business processes
>
>   ▶ Static rating tables

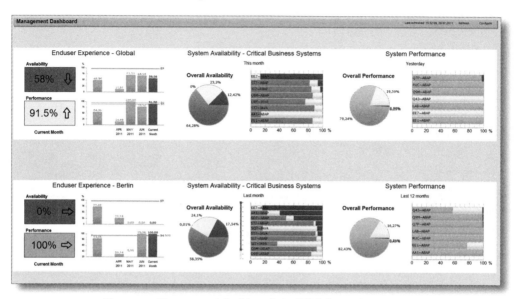

Figure 1.3 Management Dashboards in SAP Solution Manager

Other dashboard apps are planned for future functional deployments of SAP Solution Manager.

Openness

Because the management dashboard framework is open, you can also use SAP BusinessObjects Dashboards to develop your own dashboard apps in SAP Solution Manager. However, you need a licensed version of SAP BusinessObjects Dashboards for this.

Integration of non-SAP data

As already mentioned in Section 1.1.3, SAP Solution Manager is also open for non-SAP systems. If you want to include data from non-SAP systems in your dashboard, you can do this in a variety of ways.

Integration using a BAdI

You can use BAdIs to access data that is not available in SAP NetWeaver BW.

Manual entry of data

You can also use SAP BusinessObjects Dashboards to create an app on a manual basis with data calculated with Microsoft Excel. After you have registered the app in the Dashboard App Store of SAP Solution Manager, the app shows the statistical data that was entered in Excel on the dashboard. You can manually change the data in the tables and re-register the app to update your data.

Another option is to use the standard functions of SAP BusinessObjects Dashboards to access other data sources, such as Enterprise Server, for example. You can display the data dynamically on your dashboard, making the manual entry described in the previous paragraph unnecessary.

Connecting to other data sources

1.5.2 End-to-End Monitoring and Alerting

The new monitoring and alerting infrastructure (see Figure 1.4) is largely intended for Basis administrators responsible for the performance and stability of the SAP solution. The function enables fast drill-down to the technical causes of business process-related warnings.

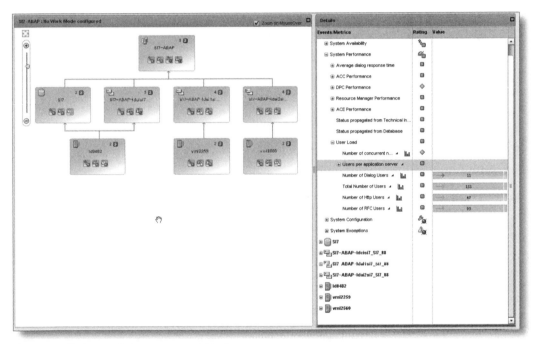

Figure 1.4 End-to-End Monitoring and Alerting

1.5.3 SAP CRM User Interface Web Client UI and Work Center Increase User-Friendliness

Along with increased technical and financial benefits of SAP Solution Manager, user-friendliness was also greatly improved, so that practiced and occasional users alike can profit from achievable productivity increases.

Because the new SAP Solution Manager is delivered with SAP CRM 7.01, the *Web client UI* for the IT service management processes (Service Desk, incident, problem, and change request management) is also available. This new user interface concept is based on the proven *Interaction Center Web client* technology, and in contrast to the previous *People-Centric UI*, it does not require the SAP NetWeaver Portal. The excellent usability of the new solution has been convincing and has led to consistently positive responses. This is of particular interest when user groups beyond the enterprise's existing SAP community are to be reached. The appearance is maintained in the style of familiar web applications (see Figure 1.5). The navigation is clear and intuitive. Higher productivity is provided by groupware integration, the option to print directly from the browser, and a search function that can be extended on a flexible basis. In addition, the SAP GUI can continue to be used, but only by administrators and developers and for Customizing tasks.

Objectives of the web client concept

The original objectives of the web client concept were the following:

▸ To provide a framework that was as comprehensive as possible to make the creation of applications easier

▸ To make available a standardized interface to the various business objects that is independent of the user interface

▸ To enable applications from various components that are also reusable

▸ To offer a standardized structure of the user interface and user guidance

The user interfaces should be able to be changed by system administrators without requiring programming effort, should be able to be easily adjusted to the customer style specifications, and should also be based on the newest standards of Internet technology. These objectives were not just fulfilled, but additional important add-ons were also developed: The web client offers a platform for the development or extension of applications. On the one hand, it makes available functions that allow simple applications to be created in the shortest possible time with the support of configuration tools. On the other hand, the various components of the web client applications can be used as interchangeable components. Instead of standard components with a broad functional scope, self-programmed elements can be integrated. The interface also permits the use of *HTML*, *JavaScript*, and *Cascading Style Sheets* (CSS).

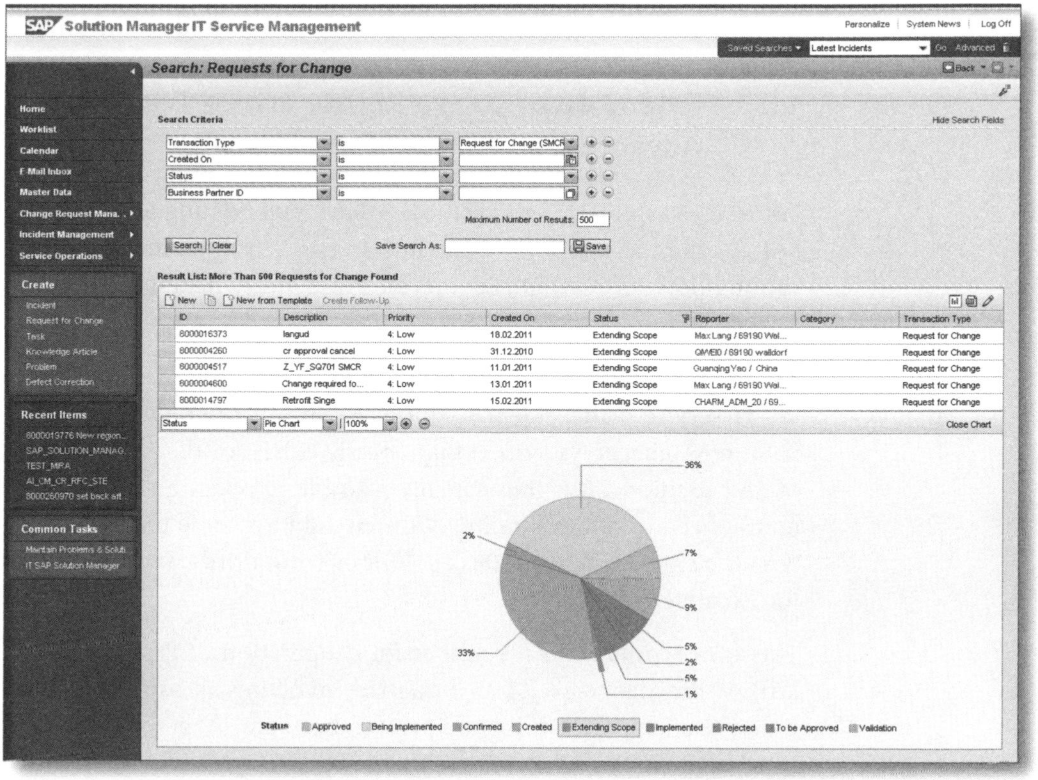

Figure 1.5 The SAP CRM User Interface Web Client UI

In this way, the web client UI framework makes it possible to optimally create applications that have a standardized appearance and that can be used and programmed in a standardized manner. It also leaves the option open to insert your own programs at locations where this uniformity would not be advantageous or where the standard components of the web client do not make sufficient functions available. These properties make the web client interesting for projects in which customers place special emphasis on precise implementation of their requirements, and SAP Solution Manager 7.1 is thus made even more attractive due to its high level of flexibility.

The Service Desk is a central tool for the handling and resolution of problems, as well as for common processing of problem resolutions with SAP and the SAP Partner Support Network. The new SAP Solu-

Service Desk

tion Manager offers a web-based Service Desk user interface for IT employees that can be easily tailored to the individual requirements of the respective area of responsibility.

1.6 Extension of Usage Rights Brings Cost Advantages

For many customers, however, the greatly extended usage rights for SAP Solution Manager are more important than the functional innovations because real money can be saved here, depending on the applicable support agreement.

For example, the Service Desk should be able to be scaled up into a full IT service management solution. All of this can be done by SAP Solution Manager—a system that already exists for the management of SAP solutions. It is thus actually possible to operate the scenarios mentioned at the beginning without additional license costs as would be due for Service Desk solutions from third-party providers, for example.

This idea results from the successful cooperation of customers and SAP within the scope of an initiative involving all aspects of SAP Enterprise Support. During the project, both parties determined that the definition of SAP Solution Manager usage rights was too narrow and that this was keeping customers from using SAP Solution Manager. This led to a complete overhaul of the usage rights for SAP Solution Manager under SAP Enterprise Support. For example, now every SAP Enterprise Support customer can use the Service Desk not just for SAP components (as is the case with SAP Standard Support customers) but for the overall solution as well. This difference may not seem dramatic at first, but it can actually have enormous effects. That's because the scope of application was extended beyond SAP products to all components of the customer solution that are needed for the full processing of business processes in accordance with the solution documentation.

"Additionally supported assets" In the language of the agreement, reference is made here to "additionally supported assets." A real-life example provides information about what concrete effects this inconspicuous formulation can have. As previously mentioned, the usage rights apply not just to the Service Desk mentioned in the example but also to all other functions and processes of SAP Solution Manager under SAP Enterprise Support.

Suppose that one morning the employee responsible for printers in the enterprise comes into the printer room in which the shipping documents are printed from the SAP system and finds a serious problem with one of the printers. Under the aspect of license and usage rights, there is now the interesting question of whether he can record a malfunction report in SAP Solution Manager without incurring additional costs. Within the scope of SAP Enterprise Support, the simple answer is *Yes*! Support employees can also process the report without having to buy an engine from the SAP price list, for example, because the printers are part of the customer solution and fall under the category of "additionally supported assets." The other items included in this category can be found in Figure 1.6. They show that it is not just printers but also PCs, the entire middleware, databases, IT management software, and non-SAP applications for the customer solution in the sense of the SAP Enterprise Support agreement that is binding for the extended usage rights. The only condition is that these software and IT components are operated in conjunction with the SAP system that is, they are used for the execution of an SAP business process that is documented in SAP Solution Manager.

Example: Printing

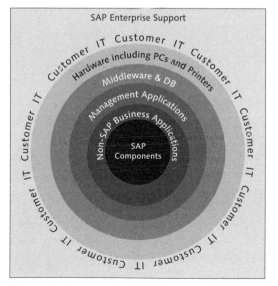

Figure 1.6 Components of the Customer Solution under SAP Enterprise Support

Example: A business process across several systems

Another example shows the resulting implications. Figure 1.7 shows a typical end-to-end process with SAP software. New orders are accepted by sales employees using mobile devices. This data is transmitted to an SAP CRM or SAP ERP system and saved to a database of a third-party provider, and then invoices and shipping documents are ultimately printed.

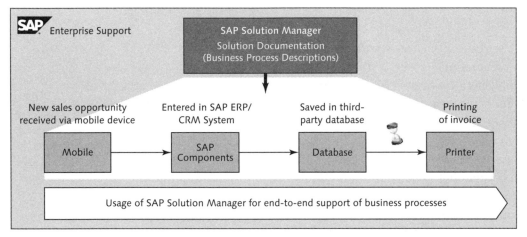

Figure 1.7 Scope of Applicability of Usage Rights in SAP Enterprise Support

The entire business process is actually covered within the scope of the applicable definition of the term *customer solution* in SAP Enterprise Support. That means you can use the SAP Solution Manager Service Desk for incident and problem management at no cost.

SAP Standard Support

In SAP Standard Support, the situation is completely different, as shown by Figure 1.8. SAP Standard Support customers are permitted to use SAP Solution Manager exclusively for SAP software components.

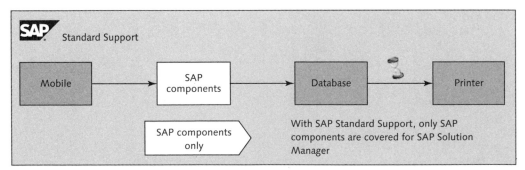

Figure 1.8 Scope of Applicability of Usage Rights in SAP Standard Support

Let's return to the topic of SAP Enterprise Support and how far the corresponding solution definition can really extend. Suppose that the employee responsible for printers who was mentioned in the first example finds another problem with one of the other printers that is not used for SAP documents and is completely independent from the solution in the sense defined previously. The employee can also enter a malfunction report for this printer in SAP Solution Manager. But why do that if the applicable solution definition states that a connection to SAP must exist? This may initially appear to be illogical.

However, it was the objective of SAP to make work with SAP Solution Manager as simple as possible. An objective consideration of the matter resulted in the conclusion that it would be nearly impossible to reliably determine whether each individual printer, each individual mobile device, or each hardware item is used exclusively for non-SAP applications. That is why the *one-for-all principle* came to be used here. Staying with the example with the printers, this principle means that as soon as one of these printers is used for the SAP solution, all of these printers are part of the solution in the sense of the SAP Enterprise Support definition. This means that for the overwhelming majority of SAP customers, the solution definition in SAP Enterprise Support covers practically everything that is operating in your IT department. In turn, this means that the Service Desk, for example, can be used in its entirety at no additional cost.

A one-for-all principle

A question that goes even further in this direction is whether the solution definition also applies to SAP CRM installations protected by SAP Enterprise Support. The technical background of this question is that the SAP Solution Manager uses the IT service management components from the SAP CRM system. However, the solution definition applies only to SAP Solution Manager. If you want to use a standalone SAP CRM system for incident and problem management, you need to purchase the corresponding licenses for the SAP CRM engine in accordance with the SAP price list. That's why we recommend that you implement incident and problem management for IT with the new SAP Solution Manager because it already has the newest SAP CRM technology on board. If you use SAP Solution Manager, you not only avoid having to install a separate SAP CRM system, but you also don't have to manually connect this system to SAP Solution Manager. Under SAP Enterprise Support, you can instead

Independent incident and problem management

use integrated Application Lifecycle Management (ALM) and IT service management with incident and problem management without additional licenses. This is a convincing offering that is unique in the entire IT industry and that also contributes to savings in the TCO through the lower number of systems.

From an SAP perspective, this offering should be very attractive first and foremost for customers in the following situations:

▶ If you operate a third-party provider's greatly modified IT management tool that is to be superseded soon. Why not also take SAP Solution Manager into account when making a decision? It is a tool that is needed anyway and results in no additional costs under SAP Enterprise Support.

▶ If you intend to invest in IT service management and follow the current developments in the market. SAP Solution Manager under SAP Enterprise Support allows you to pursue IT service management on a completely risk-free basis because incident and problem management are already included, for example. And further savings result from the fact that no additional systems need to purchased and operated.

▶ If you are satisfied with your current IT tools but have to pay high maintenance fees for them. In this case, SAP Solution Manager and SAP Enterprise Support should be considered, but the changeover costs also need to be taken into account.

After this holistic overview of the new SAP Solution Manager, its processes, and the central aspects of the platform, in the following two chapters, we will go into the specifics of how its functions can be used strategically and profitably for the introduction of new functions and processes, as well as for efficient and effective operations in your company.

SAP Solution Manager supports the centralized control of all types of changes that become necessary during the lifecycle of solutions. To coordinate these changes, SAP offers Application Lifecycle Management. This chapter explains how you use this approach to accelerate innovations and reduce total cost of ownership.

2   Application Lifecycle Management (ALM)

SAP Solution Manager is SAP's central application management solution. It greatly simplifies the implementation, operation, monitoring, and support of SAP solutions in the enterprise. The functions SAP Solution Manager brings together cover the phases of the overall lifecycle of SAP solutions. This integration allows customers to achieve greater added value from their SAP solution. SAP Solution Manager 7.1 allows SAP customers to determine their current SAP usage, quickly analyze potential, and more easily profit from SAP innovations, as is explained in the following examples featuring various phases of Application Lifecycle Management (ALM) and the corresponding processes.

2.1   Phases and Topic Blocks

The term *application management* comes from the IT Infrastructure   ITIL
Library (ITIL) environment. ITIL is the de facto standard when it comes to service management and includes documentation on planning, providing, and supporting IT services. ITIL comprises several basic elements, including *service delivery*, *service support*, *infrastructure management*, and *application management*.

Application management (see Figure 2.1) includes a comprehensive support approach in the application environment. It involves the entire lifecycle of IT solutions. Here, the lifecycle is subdivided into six phases in accordance with ITIL:

▶ **Requirements**
Collection of requirements for new applications or for adapting existing applications.

▶ **Design**
Conversion of requirements into detailed specifications.

▶ **Build & Test**
Application configuration and creation of an operating model in accordance with the specifications.

▶ **Deploy**
Transfer of any changes and the operating model into the existing, live IT landscape.

▶ **Operate**
Provision of IT services required for business operations.

▶ **Optimize**
Analysis of service level fulfillment and possible start of activities to improve results.

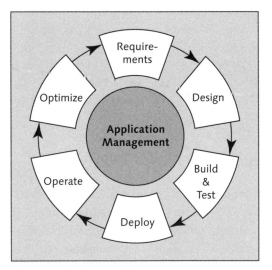

Figure 2.1 Application Management

In ALM, a holistic approach is needed to accelerate innovations while simultaneously reducing risks and TCO. Effective operation and management of an SAP solution requires current knowledge about this solution. This section provides you with an overview of the scope and processes of ALM, and it explains what help SAP Solution Manager offers you in the implementation of the activities occurring in the individual phases.

SAP differentiates between two types of changes depending on the time that is needed to execute and use the change. The bigger category is *major releases*, which have a duration of three to six months and have changes that influence the core business processes over the long term. There are also *minor releases*, which have a duration of a month or less and are primarily used to make error corrections available, as well as to meet lesser requirements.

Major and minor releases

Figure 2.2 shows the major topic blocks of significance for ALM for managing your solution:

▶ Portfolio and Project Management

▶ Solution Documentation and Implementation

▶ Change, Test, and Release Management

▶ Incident, Problem, and Request Management

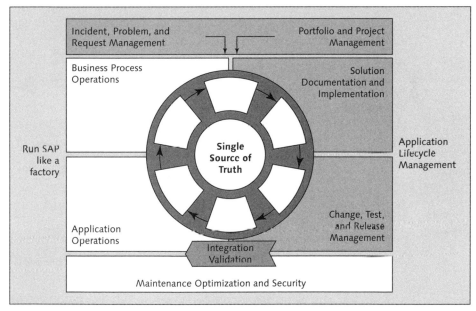

Figure 2.2 Managing the Solution with Application Lifecycle Management

The first three topic blocks are primarily for the major release, and incident, problem, and request management are more relevant for the minor release.

Portfolio and project management

Portfolio and project management allows you to manage requirements from the business areas from the initial idea to the conception and project management; that is, all relevant information is available to all parties involved from the very beginning. The project management software *SAP cProjects* is used here to collect all changes that are to be carried out in a certain time period so that their execution can be planned. Resource planning, as well as integration into back-end systems (such as CATS), is available to document the effort for individual changes. SAP cProjects can also be used to plan changes that have gone through the approval workflow. The resulting project plan is integrated into the corresponding project in SAP Solution Manager. This enables comprehensive control of projects because all project phases are centrally managed in SAP Solution Manager.

Implementation of the solution

During the *implementation of the solution*, you can control the software production process in SAP Solution Manager. SAP Solution Manager functions as an information container for the relevant projects. A project in SAP Solution Manager describes how the business, technical, and organizational processes are set up and structured, and how they can be changed. Within the scope of a project, all changes that need to be implemented in a certain time period can be planned and monitored.

In ALM, a project covers the ITIL phases from Requirements and Design to Build & Test and Deploy. All information that accrues during the project is transferred to the solution at the end of the Deploy phase, including the knowledge transfer to end users using e-learning management, implementation of a support organization, and so on.

Advantages of project management with SAP Solution Manager 7.1

Using SAP Solution Manager for projects provides the following advantages:

▸ A structured, systematic approach for the project

▸ A strictly process-oriented approach that is not bound to individual applications or components and that allows a comprehensive view of process flows in heterogeneous system landscapes

▸ A central metadata repository for the respective solutions with documentation, test cases, and configuration information

▸ Fewer information losses between individual project phases because after the content is created, it is used over the entire solution lifecycle, which helps avoid integration gaps

All changes during the implementation of the solution can be monitored and controlled through *Quality Gate Management*. This function integrates all persons involved in the release into the change process and offers defined milestones and handover processes in case of significant phase transitions of the project—from the Build to Test phases, for example.

Change, test, and release management

This includes effective and efficient *test management*. SAP Solution Manager offers functions for test automation that allow you to ensure that all required test cases are available and that they support automated regression tests, as well as improved maintenance of test scripts. You can also define your test scope on a risk basis.

The underlying transport management system (TMS) brings transparency in regard to risks and risk minimization, as well as protection from over-shooters and dependencies for SAP and non-SAP software changes in your business processes.

In many system landscapes, several projects run in parallel, and often in different development systems as well. It is possible that there is a new development in a project development system, while errors must be simultaneously corrected in a maintenance system for the production environment. The development teams must not hinder each other in their activities—such as by blocking access. In such a scenario, it's important that the teams proceed in a planned manner and coordinate on a regular basis. When various work streams have run in parallel, you cannot just propagate the resulting changes into the follow-on systems using a transport request. This would mean that current software states would be overwritten and that inconsistencies could arise. To prevent this, SAP Solution Manager offers controlled imports into the respective target system in a procedure called *retrofit*.

Retrofit

During the entire project, the knowledge accumulated here is continuously expanded and recorded in the solution documentation in a visible and understandable manner. After going live, all information from the project is transferred to the solution in SAP Solution Manager. The advantage of this approach is that the collected knowledge from the project is made available to the teams who operate the live solution without media discontinuities.

Single source of
truth

SAP calls this knowledge the *single source of truth*—a structured, comprehensive, standardized, and, above all, reliable collection of information about all ongoing projects and the status of the productive SAP solution. In turn, the solution is the basis for informed, fact-based decisions and measures during the entire lifecycle of the solution.

Incident, problem,
and request
management

As previously mentioned, in addition to major releases, there are also releases that have a much shorter term. These minor releases are used to correct errors and to make smaller changes. Minor releases are triggered by requirements in the operational phase of the solution and usually need to be implemented in a month or a shorter period of time. The requirements are documented as *service requests* or, in the case of disruptive events, as *problems* in the *IT service management* of SAP Solution Manager.

For the requirements and problems that require corrective action, *requests for change* are created. These are checked and approved or rejected by the quality manager according to the standards of the IT Infrastructure Library (ITIL V3). The actual change is controlled by *Change Request Management*. In this way, you can implement changes that need to be quickly carried out and still document them well. These changes are needed if an error endangers the production system environment, for example. For this application case, SAP Solution Manager offers a dedicated change type called an *urgent change*.

2.2 Implementation of Changes Using Releases (Major Release)

Highly integrated solution landscapes require a well-controlled, quality-oriented change management process to make solution operations highly available on a reliable basis. In regard to the lifecycle of SAP solutions, it is apparent that most changes and enhancements are motivated by changes in the application layer. Customer-specific developments and Customizing activities are managed in projects of a major release and transported to the production systems from development systems via test systems. These change types require a formal quality management process (see Figure 2.3) that covers the Requirements to Deploy phases of ALM down to the final transport to the production landscape.

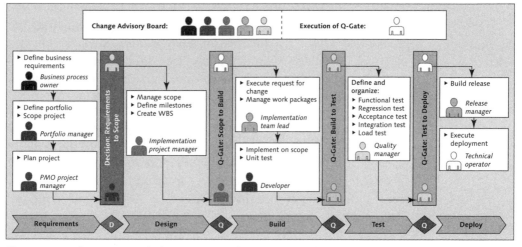

Figure 2.3 Implementation of Changes Using Releases (Major Release)

2.2.1 Requirements Phase

During the Requirements phase, attention is focused primarily on the scenarios with the corresponding business processes and the extent to which these are important to the project. In the SAP Solution Manager environment, *Business Function Prediction for SAP ERP* (*www.service.sap.com/erp-ehp*, see Figure 2.4) can be used. This simplifies the identification of SAP innovations because it recommends the business functions relevant for your solution that are provided with the SAP enhancement packages.

Business function prediction

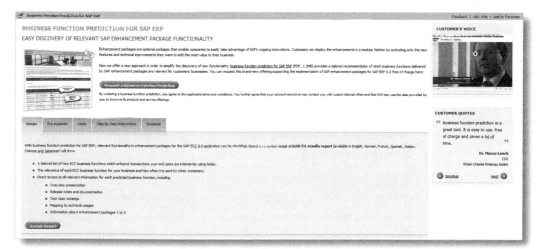

Figure 2.4 Business Function Prediction for SAP ERP

Solution
documentation
assistant
However, in many projects, it's necessary to first analyze which transactions and processes are being used at the moment to define the project scope. For this reason, SAP Solution Manager offers a function that allows automatic analysis of the systems and business processes called the *Solution Documentation Assistant* (see Chapter 4, Section 4.2).

To quickly and appropriately react to bottlenecks, it is important to establish clearly identifiable project management procedures and a cleanly defined project scope. Not until you do this is it possible to protect investments, assign resources according to the specifications, set priorities, and ensure that all project participants are communicating well with each other.

Release process
The release process begins with the persons responsible for the business process or key users that have extension requirements for the existing solution. These requirements are documented via *service requests* or via *incidents* that arise repeatedly and are logged in the IT service management of SAP Solution Manager. For requirements and problems that require corrective measures, *requests for change* are created. These are evaluated by the quality manager and the Change Advisory Board according to ITIL V3 standards.

Approved change requests are used by the portfolio manager to define the scope of the release with SAP cProjects. The portfolio manager is also responsible for budget decisions and the entire investment strategy. In addition, SAP Solution Manager makes the functions of SAP Portfolio and Project Management available to you. These functions support you in the portfolio planning for your solution.

The project manager plans the project within the scope of the time- and budget-relevant limitations and ensures that the project develops in the direction of the expected benefits as defined in the business case. During a *quality gate*, the scope of the project is approved by all stakeholders.

Quality Gate Management
A quality gate (Q-Gate) is a special milestone of projects managed with SAP Solution Manager. It controls the import of project data in downstream systems; data can be propagated when the Q-Gate has the status SUCCESSFULLY COMPLETED; that is, it ran through successfully. All activities of the Quality Gate Management process, as well

as the synchronized transport management, are controlled in SAP Solution Manager. In the process, SAP Solution Manager uses extended transport management (CTS+) to support not just ABAP but also Java, .NET, C, and C++. Details regarding these functions are explained in Chapter 8, Section 8.4.

To provide further support to the process, Quality Gate Management offers an overview of all projects in the customer solution. This view is shown in the *Quality Gate Calendar* of SAP Solution Manager (see Figure 2.5) and makes it possible to get a quick overview of what progress the projects are making and the status of the Q-Gates. You can find detailed information about Quality Gate Management in Chapter 8, Section 8.1.

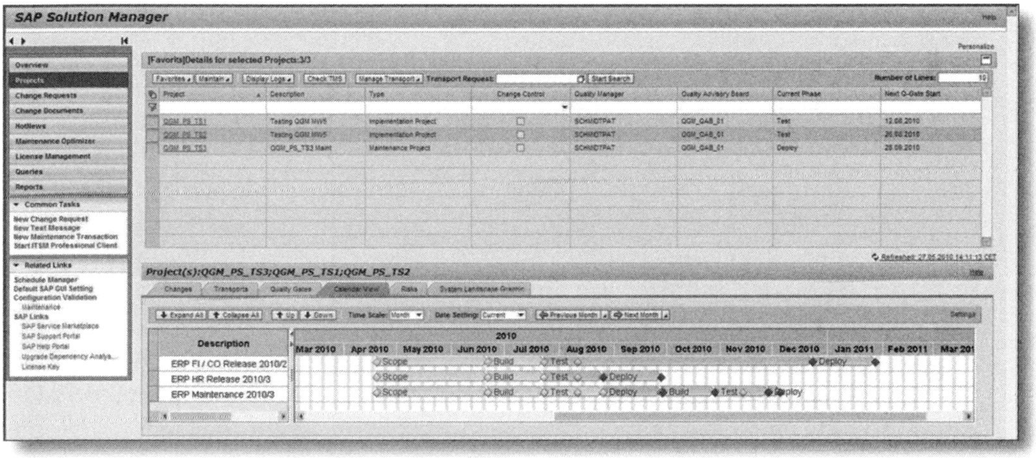

Figure 2.5 Quality Gate Calendar in SAP Solution Manager

2.2.2 Design Phase

In the Design phase, an implementation project manager oversees the project and heads up the introduction of new products, services, or projects for an organization. He defines the milestones of the project and creates the *work breakdown structure* (WBS).

The role of SAP Solution Manager in this phase includes offering *roadmaps*, proven procedures for project management that can be used to clearly structure project management activities, with tools such as *Project Administration* used in the process (see also Chapter 5, Section 5.3.1).

Roadmaps

Business Blueprint SAP Solution Manager also supports the drafting of a well-defined, comprehensive conception design—the *Business Blueprint* (see Figure 2.6). This describes how a company intends to map its business processes with SAP and non-SAP systems and includes the following steps:

1. Revise the original project goals and requirements.

2. Finalize the overall project plan.

3. Implement organization and change management.

4. Define functional standards and document customer-specific developments.

5. Define requirements for the authorization concept, security guidelines, and end-user training.

6. Plan the system environment for production operation.

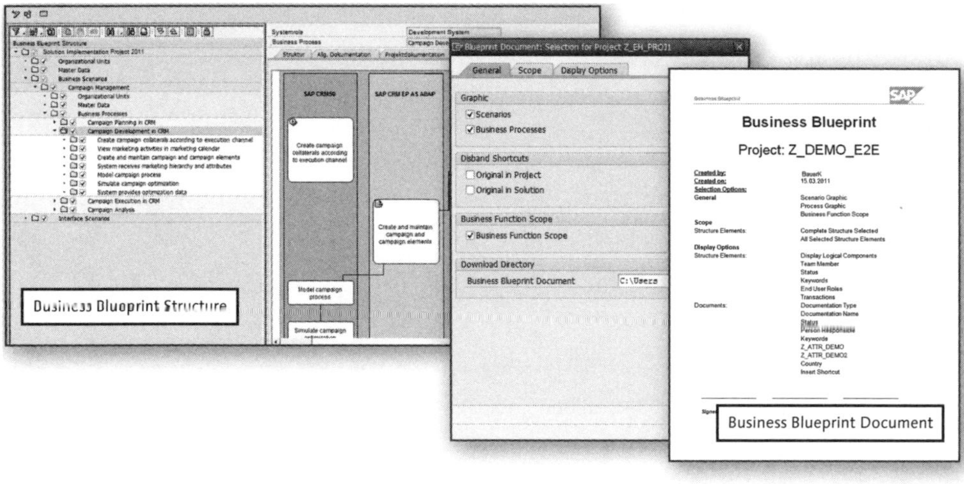

Figure 2.6 Business Blueprint in SAP Solution Manager

The project structure created in this way maps the businesses processes to technical objects. SAP Solution Manager is used as a repository for the entire project documentation, technical specifications, technical objects, and test cases. This documentation is uploaded into the specific project structure. An approval process for the documentation is implemented in SAP Solution Manager. SAP Solution Manager thus supports you in configuring the system according to your own processes and in documenting the configuration settings on a centralized basis. For more information, see Chapter 5, Section 5.4.

The decision of whether planned changes can go into the Build phase is assigned to the people involved in the Q-Gate *scope to build*. During the Q-Gate meeting, all aspects are examined and discussed, including the reasons for certain changes, priorities, associated risks, affected core business processes, budget availability, and so on. The decision is documented and signed by the involved decision makers.

Q-Gate scope to build

2.2.3 Build Phase

During the Build phase, changes are implemented. It can involve a solution extension with customer-specific developments, Customizing changes, interface changes, or the integration of a third-party application. Developers carry out *unit tests*, and the quality assurance department prepares function and user acceptance tests. A change impact analysis should be carried out to check whether core business processes are affected by the changes. It is also recommended that the solution operation be prepared through the *Solution Documentation*, for example.

For implementation of the business functions defined during the Requirements phase, you use the Build phase to set up a system landscape in which the scenarios and business processes run. The structure created in the Business Blueprint is used to help with the configuration of the solution for the business processes and with the control of the test activities. The implementation includes the following steps:

1. Continuously monitor project targets, especially costs, deadlines, and resources.

2. Actively implement organization and change management.

3. Develop training documents and user documentation.

4. Create user roles, and implement the authorization and security concept.

5. Develop the specification for customer-specific developments.

Business functions can be activated directly from SAP Solution Manager (see Figure 2.7).

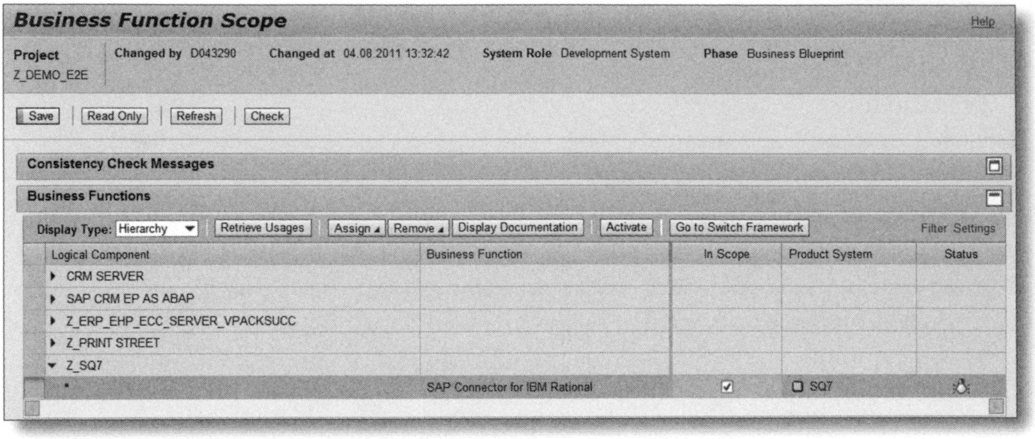

Figure 2.7 Activation of Business Functions

Q-Gate Build to Test

The implementation team lead ensures the implementation of the products as defined by the project manager, that is, with the appropriate level of quality, within the time frame, and at costs that are acceptable to the Change Advisory Board. During the Q-Gate *build to test*, all stakeholders decide whether new developments and other system changes have reached the point that they can be transported from the development environment into the test environment, thus beginning the Test phase. The decisions and justifications are documented and signed off by the involved parties of the Q-Gate. You can't import into the downstream system until the Q-Gate has been successfully completed because the transport lock is not opened until this point. The quality manager defines and organizes the test management for the release, including function, regression, acceptance, integration, and load tests.

2.2.4   Test Phase

For today's software solutions, several development environments are used, and a wide variety of file types and transport objects are created. Many business processes also require the availability of several systems; for example, the business process *trade promotion management* requires SAP NetWeaver Portal, SAP CRM, and SAP ERP. Transports thus need to be synchronized to enable problem-free testing. During the Test phase, all of the following relevant tests are carried out:

- Regression tests
- Integration tests
- Scenario tests
- User acceptance tests
- Performance tests

When an SAP solution is implemented (for example, SAP CRM as an extension of an existing SAP ERP implementation), a certain number of business processes are adjusted, reconfigured, and documented in the Business Blueprint. The scope of the test is derived from the list of adjusted business processes.

The actual Test Management process is subdivided into the following steps:

Test management process

1. Create the test plan.
2. Generate test packages.
3. Assign test packages to the testers.
4. Carry out tests, and log results.
5. Evaluate results.

It's possible to generate test plans and test packages based on the SAP Solution Manager project structure (see Figure 2.8). Test packages can include manual and automatic test cases. The eCATT framework for automatic tests is used as a tool for automating the test process and for generating test data for user acceptance tests. With SAP Solution Manager, test packages can be assigned to the various testers, and the test progress can be tracked. During the execution of the test, the cooperation between users and developers can be supported with internal news, test logs, and analyses of the test status. At the end of a test cycle, the test results can be evaluated.

After a planned change has been approved, an initial risk assessment should first be made. It should take into account what effects the planned changes have on the core business processes. Other detailed risk assessments then follow, both after the implementation of the change in the development system and when the tests are conducted in the test system. In this way, the scope of the test can be concentrated on the changes for which a risk for the core business processes cannot be excluded. This greatly reduces the test scope and thus enables targeted use of the test resources.

Risk assessment

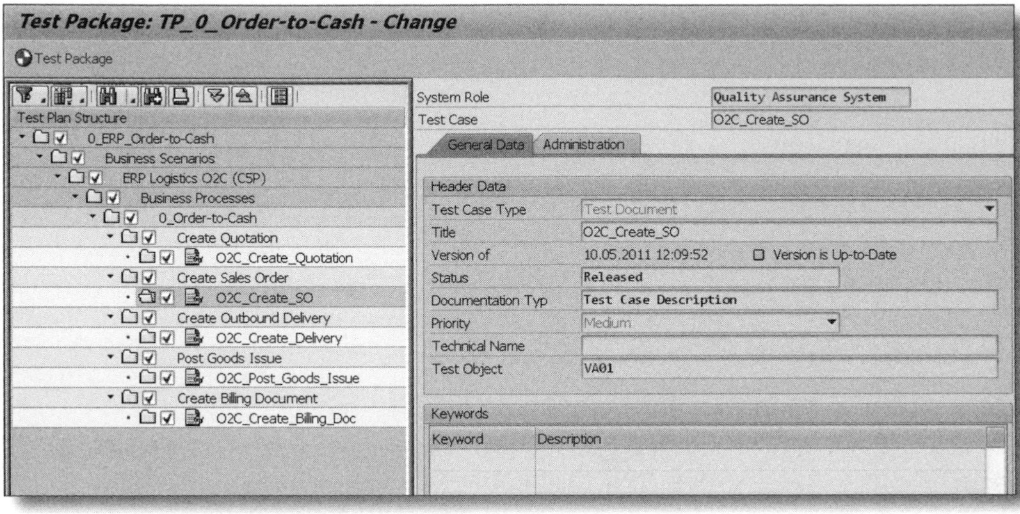

Figure 2.8 Creation of the Test Packages

To support this approach, SAP Solution Manager offers the *Business Process Change Analyzer* (BPCA; see Figure 2.9), a tool for general analysis of what effects the changes have on the business processes (*Change Impact Analysis*). You can change the TEST COVERAGE (%) so that the percentage of modified objects is displayed, which is covered by the test scope displayed below. You can also specify the available TOTAL TEST EFFORT (capacity) to see which test coverage is possible with the selected test effort. Because BPCA is a crucial component of the end-to-end quality management process within the scope of SAP Enterprise Support, it is only available to SAP Enterprise Support customers. To also study customer-specific business processes, the BPCA functional scope was expanded. The BPCA begins with the new option PLANNED BUSINESS FUNCTION ACTIVATION, which allows the user to select one or more business functions that were not yet activated. The number available for selection depends on the installed enhancement packages.

After the test scope has been optimized using BPCA, the actual testing can begin. Testers or automatic test tools document problems and errors in the incident management process. Complex problems are judged and evaluated using root cause analysis. Problems that need to be fixed require additional activities in the development system with subsequent transports into the test system landscape.

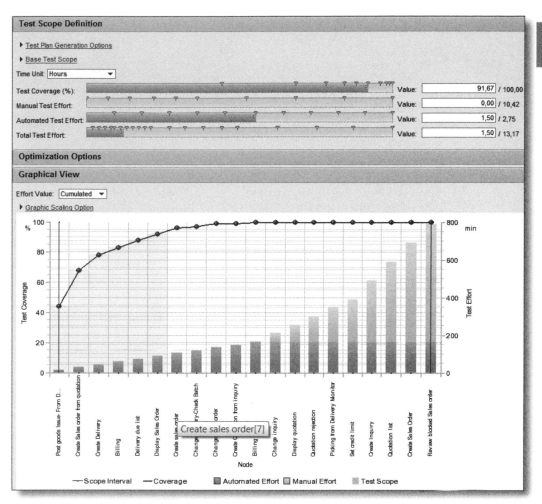

Figure 2.9 Optimization of the Test Scope with the BPCA

Test coordinators monitor the progress of the test activities, the number of open messages with high priority, and the repetition of the tests after the problem has been rectified. Test criteria need to be created to ensure the following at a minimum:

▶ User acceptance tests verify that the business side agrees with the planned changes.

▶ Integration tests ensure that processes distributed over several instances run correctly.

▸ Regression tests validate that all core business processes can be executed with correct system behavior and produce the correct results.

▸ Performance tests show that the changed solution shows acceptable response time behavior.

Final activities of this phase include updating the user documentation and other pre-go-live activities.

Integration validation

After the functional quality assurance, SAP recommends that the core business processes be checked in single-user mode to find problems before the load tests, such as problems in regard to performance, data consistency, or technical compliance. It also allows you to avoid effects on production operation. An *E2E Trace Analysis* can be used to anticipate problems that occur in a multi-user environment. Problems with data consistency can also be avoided by analyzing the transfer behavior (on the SQL level) with an E2E trace. This also helps avoid technical exceptions that are not visible in the user interface but nonetheless can have significant effects on production operation.

A detailed check of the program flow using an E2E Trace Analysis even allows load tests to be reduced or avoided. The continuity of the business processes can also be improved after changes. The simulation of parallel executions in load tests means a great amount of work in script management and the provision of test data. Every reduction of this effort has a major influence on the TCO. If load tests are nevertheless needed, they can be monitored and statistically evaluated with *E2E Workload Analysis* and *E2E Exception Analysis*. And instead of having to individually log on to each system, the tests can be executed centrally and from a single access point, SAP Solution Manager. This procedure to analyze performance, data consistency, and technical compliance systematically after the functional integration test is called *integration validation*. SAP supplements classic quality management with best practices and a validation of the solutions integrated across various technologies and components.

Q-Gate test to deploy

After the Test phase is complete, the last Q-Gate *test to deploy* (see Figure 2.10) must be passed to enable the production start of the release. The release manager is then responsible for ensuring that the implementation of the changes in the IT infrastructure is carried out in an effective, safe, and verifiable manner. Only at that point can the technical operator import the changes into the production environment.

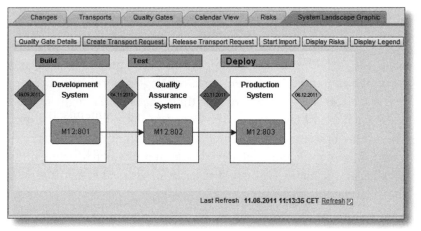

Figure 2.10 Quality Gate Test to Deploy

2.2.5 Deploy Phase

After the Q-Gate test to deploy has been successfully completed, the transport lock can be lifted, and the last synchronized transport can be carried out. The project ends when the changed solution is handed over to the solution operation.

The objective in the Deploy phase is to complete the transition from the development and quality assurance environment into production operation. It is important to establish support structures for the end users that are available over the long term, not just in the critical phase after the go-live. The Service Desk integrated in SAP Solution Manager is very well suited for this.

A prerequisite for the go-live is that the cutover plans are implemented, which includes, for example, the transfer of the datasets verified in the implementation phase from the legacy system to the current production system. Tested configuration settings as well as modifications and customer-specific developments are also transferred to the production system.

The Go-Live and Support phase is when the users gain initial practical experiences with the solution. In this phase, the monitoring of the system transactions also takes place, along with optimization of the general system performance. SAP Solution Manager offers a wide range of resources and tools that help operate the solution. For instance, the implemented processes can be monitored across all systems.

Test management

As is the case during the Build & Test phase, test management in SAP Solution Manager is also extremely helpful in the Deploy phase as well. The same resources and tools are also used here to execute and document a number of system tests relating to performance, load, and interfaces, for example. At this time, the learning maps created in SAP Solution Manager are distributed to the relevant end users. The users can use these to become familiar with new functions relevant for their work and to give feedback on individual learning units or all learning maps. The feedback can be evaluated and used to improve training materials.

SAP EarlyWatch

Particularly when a system has not been in operation for very long, it is recommend that *SAP EarlyWatch* be executed, which analyzes the system proactively. The goal is to recognize potential problems at an early point in time, to avoid bottlenecks, and to regularly and automatically monitor system performance by activating *SAP EarlyWatch Alert* in SAP Solution Manager. There is also the *SAP EarlyWatch Check*, a service that proactively analyzes the operating system, the database, and the SAP system with the goal of optimizing performance and providing additional recommendations and suggestions for further action.

2.3 Implementation of Requirements through Maintenance (Minor Release)

In contrast to the major releases described in the previous section, the minor release offers the option to carry out changes quickly and flexibly but in a manner that is traceable. If a user in a business department sees potential for improvement for a certain transaction, he can create an incident message directly from the relevant transaction. Alternatively, a business process owner can request a small change. The incident appears in the worklist of the Service Desk employee, who processes the incident and generates a request for change if required. The request is approved and classified as an urgent change (see Figure 2.11).

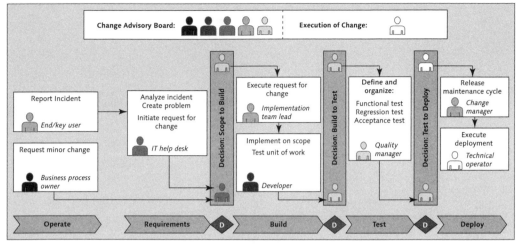

Figure 2.11 Delivery of Requirements through Maintenance

Because urgent changes need to be made in the minor release, the decisions that are made during the *Change Request Management* process are sufficient. This saves time without neglecting a seamless documentation of the change.

Then the developers take care of design and programming, including adjustment and customizing of the solution. They also carry out the unit tests of their developments.

As soon as the developers have completed the corrections, testers can test them. Change Request Management ensures the transport of the changes into the test system. SAP Solution Manager supports a dual control principle here to ensure that the developers and testers are different people. It is possible to transport the changes into the production environment only after the changes have been successfully tested.

The release manager is responsible for ensuring that the implementation of the changes in the IT infrastructure is carried out in an effective, safe, and verifiable manner. The technical operator can then import the changes into the production environment. After successful transport into production, the requirement is implemented, and the request for change can be concluded.

In the operational phase of a solution, you reap actual bene-fits from the software introduced during the implementation phase. For this reason, SAP pays particular attention to this important phase. In this chapter, you will learn more about how SAP Solution Manager uses automation to support you when operating the solution.

3 Effective and Efficient Operation

SAP's approach to equally effective and efficient application management and solution operation can be summed up with the motto "Run SAP like a factory." In the process, SAP Solution Manager creates a central *Operations Control Center* that provides all of the important status and runtime information on the most important business processes, their critical interfaces, and the underlying software components. This chapter provides an overview of the operating phase; you will find detailed presentations of the underlying processes and functions in Chapters 10 and 11.

SAP Solution Manager collects and analyzes alert information from all SAP and non-SAP backend components. The user of the Operations Control Center is actively informed if critical alerts occur and can immediately start the necessary error analysis in SAP Solution Manager. SAP provides adapters and interfaces to enable the integration of any existing Java and .NET applications, in addition to the automatically integrated SAP systems.

Alerts

Specifically, you can use this approach to carry out the following tasks:

- Ensure that the most important business processes run correctly and perform well, without any communication breaks or data losses.
- Monitor the components of the complete business processes to ensure that they are and remain available, both for daily transaction-based work and batch processing overnight.

▶ Handle business process exceptions that are practically unavoidable in solutions with a high data volume and a high level of complexity.

▶ Quickly find the cause of a problem and restore services if interfaces or components fail.

▶ Integrate all of the solution components in an Operations Control Center to provide all of the support required to achieve the business goals around the clock, also known as *24 x 7 Mission Critical Support* (MCS).

3.1 Operations Control Center

In the Operations Control Center that provides MCS, the technology support staff, IT experts, and all external support providers all work together, connected by videoconferencing, if necessary.

Alert Inbox   The Operations Control Center employees mainly work with the central Alert Inbox of SAP Solution Manager, which displays technical and functional alerts for all components on a single screen. Filters can be set to display only technical alerts, for example.

The threshold values for performance alerts are set so that alerts occur before critical situations arise. This leaves more time to correct errors before end users on the business side are affected. For other types of alerts, there are clear instructions on whether an immediate reaction is necessary or whether it is acceptable to act at a later time.

Troubleshooting   There are additional tools and methods for troubleshooting: The *Root Cause Analysis* tools help identify components with errors that are causing performance problems. An SAP *Exception Management Cockpit* helps when analyzing technical and business process exceptions. When the problematic component has been found, locally executed *expert analysis transactions* provide additional options for performing more in-depth analysis. Figure 3.1 shows the overview monitors for technical staff. The monitors can be tailored to meet the requirements of specific users.

All of these tools for SAP operations are seamlessly integrated with each other. This is particularly important for the Service Desk, whether it is the recommended Service Desk in SAP Solution Manager or a third-party product that is part of the Incident Management process, and also for all of the tools that are used for Change Management, Monitoring, and Job Scheduling Management.

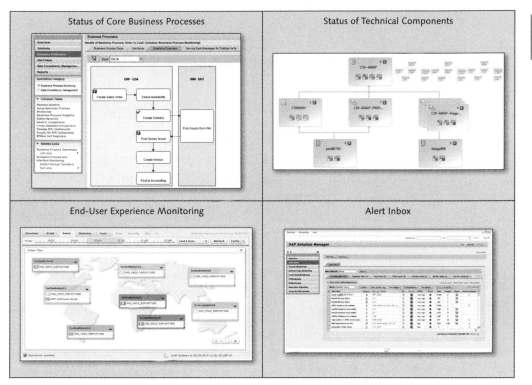

Figure 3.1 Overview Monitors for Technical Staff

The concept of the Operations Control Center ("Run SAP like a factory") is powerful enough for just a few staff members to operate complex solutions. Their activities are as follows:

Tasks for IT staff

▸ The main tasks involve working with the central Alert Inbox in SAP Solution Manager. The Alert Inbox is permanently displayed on the main screen and is updated automatically.

▸ Critical processes and the system performance can be continuously monitored proactively. At all times, you can access an overview display on the main screen as a starting point for monitoring tasks.

▸ The Technical Administration covers all of the periodic tasks, such as cleaning up the operating system, monitoring transportation or the backup environment, and meeting basic service requirements (e.g., restarting a process or system, manually moving data between servers, or generating technical reports).

77

Most of the time is spent processing the alerts that go into the central Alert Inbox. If no urgent alerts appear, the other displays are checked regularly, and the MCS staff works on their scheduled tasks.

3.2 Proactive Monitoring and Working with the Alert Inbox

The status of a solution is recorded for four core areas:

▸ **Status of core business processes**
This monitor displays the core business processes. Color-coded signals show whether there have been serious exceptions or whether a process has been completely stopped, for example, in processes in the day-end closing. In these cases, an immediate reaction is required.

▸ **Status of technical components**
A graphic representation of the solution landscape visualizes all of the components involved. The color code of the respective component shows whether it is working correctly or whether errors have occurred.

▸ **End User Experience Monitoring**
This monitors the response times that the users are experiencing on the business side, including the transmission times through the network.

▸ **Alert Inbox**
This is the main work area for the MCS staff of the Operation Control Center, which contains the technical and functional alerts. All of the alerts received must be processed as soon as they appear. For particularly critical alerts, messages can also be sent by SMS, pager, or email.

You have the option of displaying these monitors around the clock on large screens in your command center. They are updated automatically, and all of the important support activities begin there.

The Alert Inbox complements the overview monitors (see Figure 3.2). The layout can be adapted to meet the employees' personal requirements. When a lot of alerts are received, they can be grouped to provide a better overview. The Alert Inbox is checked at regular intervals and at the latest when a red signal appears on one of the other monitors.

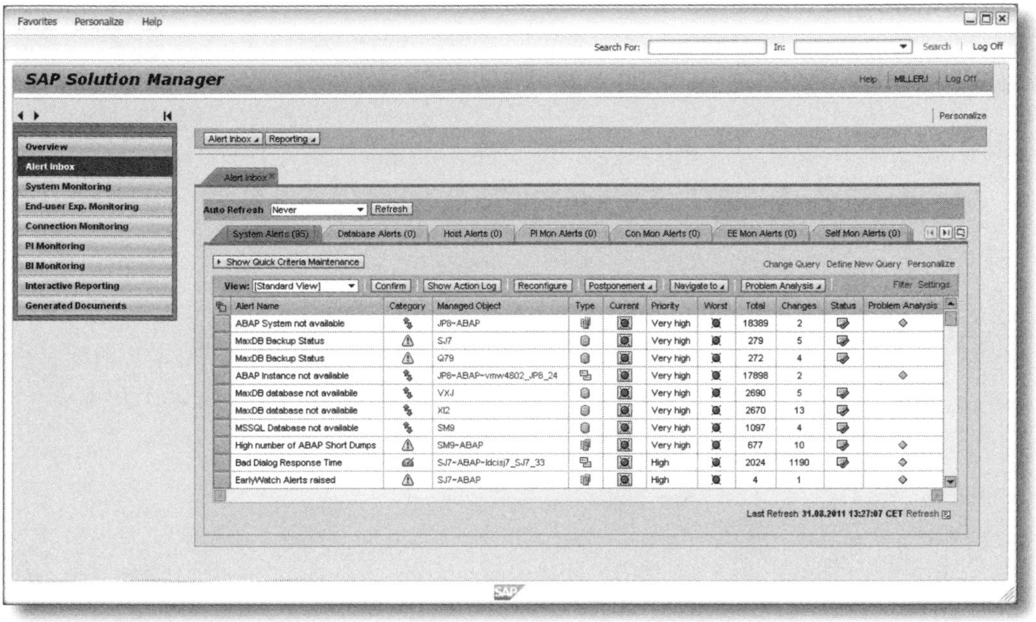

Figure 3.2 Alert Inbox

When you open an alert and enter yourself as the processor, you see a detailed description, recommended instructions for what to do, escalation instructions and contacts, and other context information such as details of the performance history for the relevant system. You can start a keyword search to obtain additional information. However, the alert engine of SAP Solution Manager already contains micro-monitoring information on the alert context to supplement the alert information. This includes tips as to what could be causing the problem or at least where to begin looking. The system already starts any automatic reaction or self-healing method that is available. In many cases, a *guided procedure* is offered in addition to the manual check. This is an analysis wizard that provides additional documentation and leads you through the process step by step. The corresponding backend transactions are also called without you having to intervene manually.

Alert details

If the problem cannot be removed, one mouse-click changes the alert to an *incident* and forwards it to the Service Desk for processing on the next level of the technical or functional support. Depending on

Escalation

79

how critical the incident is, the next-level support is informed automatically. A support expert, who has additional powerful tools for finding the cause and resolving the incident, takes over the processing.

If the cause of the alert has been found and removed, the alert is also closed. It is then no longer displayed in the Alert Inbox, but it can be selected from the history tables if necessary. Therefore, during normal processing, it is important to keep the Alert Inbox free for critical alerts.

Dashboards   In addition to the monitors, a number of dashboards can be requested (see Figure 3.3). These dashboards show the history of the most important key performance indicators (KPIs) for technical processes and business processes. The dashboards have both drill-down and forecast functions. This helps you with the following tasks:

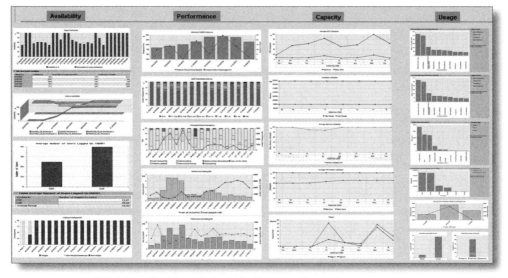

Figure 3.3 Dashboards for IT Performance Reporting

▶ Checking the current system behavior (Is is better or worse than on the day before? If there a negative trend when the month-end closing is being performed?).

▶ Checking what has changed between yesterday and today (as in: "Yesterday everything was fine").

▶ Estimating the risk of breaching service level agreements (SLAs), from which the priority of an incident can be derived.

The other overview monitors can also be checked.

The *status monitor for business processes* provides a graphic overview of all of the process steps in individual business processes:

Status monitor for business processes

▶ For processes running in dialog mode, the monitor displays whether there are critical exceptions, such as system crashes with memory extracts. Errors on interfaces between components are also displayed.

▶ For processes running in background mode (e.g., day-end closings), the monitor displays application errors in red in the reports. Additionally, certain steps are displayed in red if the processing speed falls below a specific value or comes to a complete stop.

▶ Every yellow entry in this monitor should be investigated. Clicking once with the mouse takes you to other related alerts in the inbox or, if everything is okay, to other performance and log data.

The *status monitor for technical components* displays the technical status of systems or whole system groups. For example, a component turns red if it is not available technically, if there are performance problems, or if other technical exceptions occur. A double-click on the relevant component takes you to the corresponding alerts in the Alert Inbox or displays the historical values of the performance key figures, including their related threshold values. If a productive component is not available, the effects on the business must be checked immediately, and it must be established whether there is a redundant second component to which you could switch without any problems. Once the switch has been performed, an incident must be entered for the primary component so that it can be made available again.

Status monitor for technical components

The *status monitor for business users*, which uses the End User Experience Monitoring to represent the end users' perceived response time, should also be checked regularly. Based on an artificial load generated by so-called robots, this monitor displays the same response times that end users would also experience at their workplaces on the business side. With a click on a red box, you can display a detailed performance history and open additional drill-down options.

Status monitor for business users

3.3   Technical Administration

Clean-up tasks are part of the day-to-day work. These activities are predefined by the technical support manager, or they are received in the form of service requests from other support teams. In general, the planning and execution of these clean-up tasks are managed with the IT Calendar in SAP Solution Manager (see Figure 3.4), which centrally displays the planned status of a system (e.g., business and break times, maintenance scheduling, etc.).

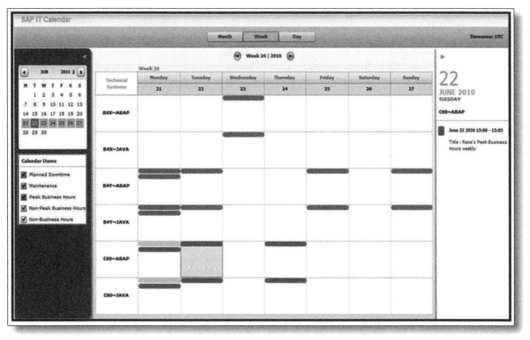

Figure 3.4 The IT Calendar in SAP Solution Manager

Based on the IT Calendar, the technical administration tasks can be started. For removing leftovers from the last scheduled maintenance weekend from the system, for example, you receive a list of all related tasks that shows the completed and outstanding subtasks. In general, database maintenance is also usually performed, as well as following up on transport errors.

3.4 Business Process Operations for the Example of "Monitoring the Day-End Closing"

The following example shows how exceptions during the processing of the day-end closing are processed in collaboration with a function support expert. The day-end closing runs are background jobs that are scheduled with the central *Job Scheduling Management* and often do not require any interaction with users. Some of these jobs use the *Parallel Processing Framework* to process large data volumes in parallel. The day-end closing is a time-critical process because it must be finished before the next day's business begins. Critical technical and application-specific exceptions in the day-end closing must be removed immediately; otherwise, the processing can be delayed, and the regular business operations can be severely restricted.

As one of the most commonly used and, for some industries, most important processes, the day-end closing processing is presented in an aggregated form in the process overview monitor. When you click on individual process steps, you receive performance data such as the number of objects to be processed (*due objects*), the throughput, and the estimated duration. This information is automatically compiled by *Business Process Monitoring* and should be compared to data from the past (e.g., from yesterday or from last month) to find out whether the performance has changed. This trend analysis can also be represented in dashboards, together with the applicable SLAs.

Process overview monitor

The most important thing is to ensure that the job chain runs for the day-end closing. To do so, you select the alerts marked in red in the Alert Inbox.

From the alert, you go directly to the detailed list of the process steps (see Figure 3.5). The step list in SAP Solution Manager displays all of the steps that have already been processed with a color code—red or green. If there is a complete process standstill, for example, because a technical job was terminated and cannot be started again, an incident must be created with the priority *very high*, which is then passed to the support team on the next level for further processing. Support experts that are on call, both for the technical and functional levels, can then act immediately.

List of process steps

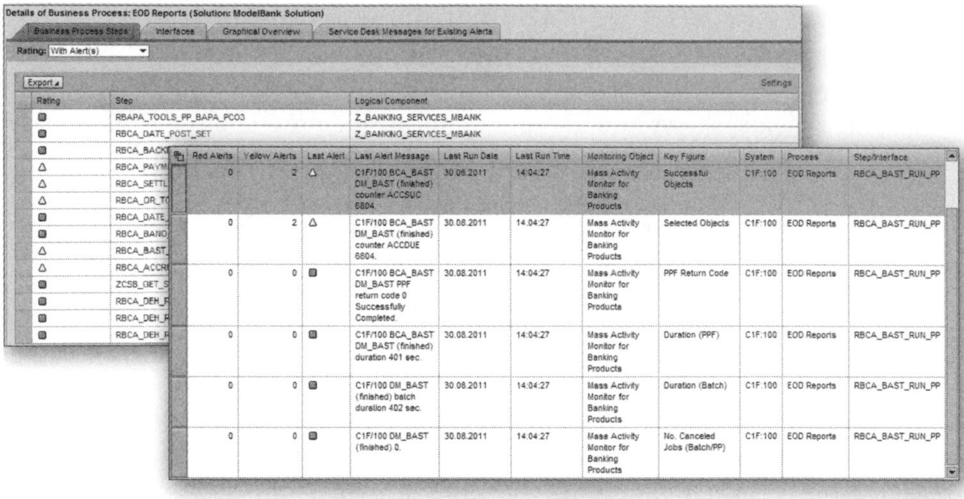

Figure 3.5 List of Process Steps and Key Figures in the "Business Process Operations" Work Center

However, the job chain often keeps running. In this case, you should analyze the status of the jobs. With one click, you can switch from the central alert list in SAP Solution Manager into the local job management transaction of the respective SAP system. Here you can check both the technical and application return codes for the jobs. It is certainly possible for a job to run without any technical errors while the return code on the application level indicates individual or even multiple application errors.

For jobs in which errors occur, the central job documentation is opened, which is part of the operation management manual. There you will find a detailed description of what to do in the case of an error. Sometimes a simple restart is sufficient, and you can execute this directly. However, in other cases, it may be necessary to record an incident and forward this to a specific processing queue for further processing.

Central job scheduling

Because of the heterogeneous character of typical SAP landscapes, it's very probable that central job scheduling is performed using tools such as *SAP Central Process Scheduling by Redwood* (SAP CPS by Redwood). SAP CPS by Redwood can react to both technical and application return codes. If the business procedure allows this, the scheduling tool automatically restarts the job instance in which the error occurred to enable the completion of the processing. In this case, the checking must be started in SAP CPS by Redwood, and it must be ensured that the process that was restarted automatically was completed successfully.

If an application error is still there, a message should be recorded for further processing by the support team for the business area. The support experts there start their analysis in the *Business Process Operations* work center. From there they are taken directly to the corresponding local transaction of the respective backend system to analyze the relevant jobs. All job activities are listed there together with context information in a clear list.

Post Processing Office

From this user interface, the support expert for the business area can navigate directly to other detailed analysis transactions. Jobs with the status "P" must be processed further in the Post Processing Office (PPO). These entries are business-critical and are therefore also highlighted in SAP Solution Manager. From SAP Solution Manager, the support expert can jump directly to the PPO (see Figure 3.6).

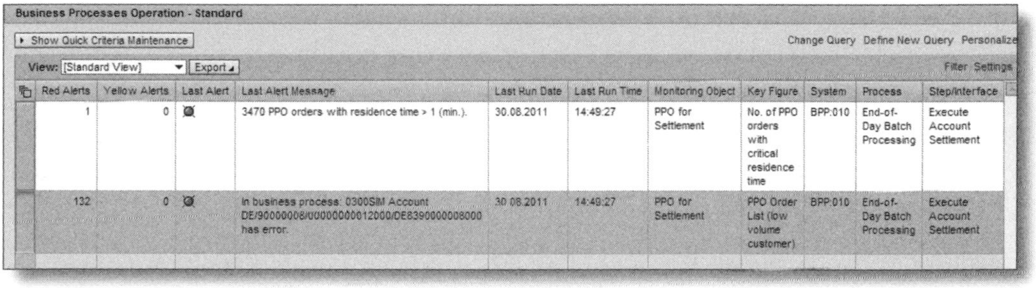
Business Processes Operation - Standard
Show Quick Criteria Maintenance
Change Query Define New Query Personalize
View: [Standard View] Export
Filter Settings
Red Alerts | Yellow Alerts | Last Alert | Last Alert Message | Last Run Date | Last Run Time | Monitoring Object | Key Figure | System | Process | Step/Interface
1 | 0 | | 3470 PPO orders with residence time > 1 (min.). | 30.08.2011 | 14:49:27 | PPO for Settlement | No. of PPO orders with critical residence time | BPP:010 | End-of-Day Batch Processing | Execute Account Settlement
132 | 0 | | In business process: 0300SIM Account DE/90000008/00000000012000/DE8390000008000 has error. | 30.08.2011 | 14:49:27 | PPO for Settlement | PPO Order List (low volume customer) | BPP:010 | End-of-Day Batch Processing | Execute Account Settlement

Figure 3.6 Post Processing Office Alerts in SAP Solution Manager

The PPO contains the business objects that require further processing. All object data required for the error handling is displayed here in the correct sequence for further processing. If a process is not executed correctly, the PPO also displays the corresponding metadata and the related log entries to make the error-correction process more convenient. If the cause of an error has been removed, the execution of the job or the individual object should be started again. Either this occurs automatically, or a service request informs you to restart the job manually. Afterwards, the support expert for the business area closes the incident.

3.5 Business Process Operations for the Example of "Automatic Business Exception Management"

The following example shows how the Operations Control Center staff and the support experts for the business area work together in handling exceptions in business processes in the online day-to-day business, whereby multiple dialog transactions are processed in parallel.

During the daily dialog operation periods, you must ensure that the general system performance is sufficient by periodically checking the overview monitors. If, for example, ABAP dumps occur when you are monitoring the Alert Inbox, you can simply look for solution proposals in the database for guided procedures. However, alerts often occur that indicate exceptions (business exceptions) due to communication problems between components. Such exceptions require special knowledge of the application to perform an analysis. Therefore, the alert and the context information are converted into a message, which is then given a high priority and forwarded to the support team of the corresponding business area on the second level for further processing.

Exception Management Cockpit

The support expert opens the *Exception Management Cockpit* (EMC) in SAP Solution Manager. The EMC centrally gathers the entire process flow and all of the log information that is automatically created during the regular business procedure. For certain business process errors, it also provides tracing information. Based on this error information, SAP Solution Manager makes a preliminary selection of specific guided procedures from the database.

In the cockpit, the support expert sees the complete flow of the business procedure and the error environment. This is necessary to get a clear picture of what has happened in the component affected, and why. If applicable, the support expert must also confirm whether the instance of the business process was completed or not. It can be difficult to answer this question when there are multiple interfaces between the components. Incomplete process instances can cause data inconsistencies, which can in turn have serious financial consequences if they remain undiscovered. To avoid having to check the business process instances manually, log information is gathered continually when web services are called. SAP Solution Manager collects this information in a process journal, which you can view in the *Business Process Completeness Check*. Here the entire process flow is represented, including error, database, commit, and rollback information.

The support expert starts a guided procedure either to resolve the error or to clean up the system. This guided procedure calls the required business functions and the saved business variables to complete the process in the backend and correct the data inconsistencies.

If the process cannot be executed again, the service expert must perform clean-up activities in all of the components that have already been updated. Whether this can be offered as a guided procedure or not depends on the business process itself and on the status of the process instance. If the clean-up cannot be provided as a guided procedure, the consistency of the data must be restored manually. The trace information stored in the EMC helps you find out what exactly has to be corrected.

3.6 Technical Operations for the Example of "Analysis of Complex Technical Problems"

The next example describes how the Operations Control Center staff and the technical support experts work together to solve complex technical problems. The business user overview monitor can be checked at all times.

If, for example, online transactions on the SAP NetWeaver portal are running slowly, and the threshold values for the response times are exceeded, the overview monitor changes to red. Corresponding alerts on the response times also appear in the central Alert Inbox. Ideally, the threshold values are selected so that this occurs before the end users start complaining.

In the monitor for the business users, you can check that the infrastructure is working correctly and that no critical alert has been triggered, for example. You can see how the performance has been recently by opening the dashboards.

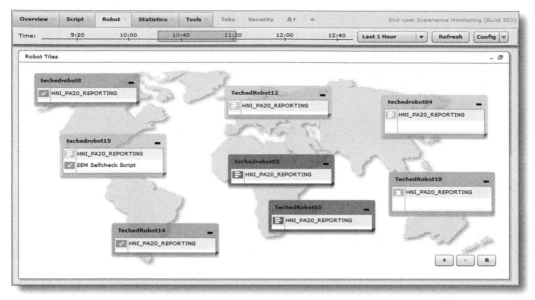

Figure 3.7 End User Experience Monitoring

The alert details also provide additional information on what has to be done. In the first step, you should check whether the relevant system and all its instances are even available. If the entire production system is not available anymore, the alert should be converted into an incident with a very high priority and forwarded to the second level of the technical SAP support. The escalation is triggered automatically, for example, with notifications by means of distribution lists or telephone conferences.

Workload Analysis If the component is still working but has poor response behavior, you try to find out whether the problem with the response time persists or resolves itself. You can then start a *Workload Analysis* in SAP Solution Manager that depicts the current performance of systems. If an SLA for the response time is at risk, an incident must be created. Sometimes you'll find that the response time in the SAP system is good, even though the end users have to deal with poor performance. In such a case, the message can be passed on directly to the network team for processing.

Trace Analysis The technical support expert also sees all of the context information in the message. Many components can be involved. Therefore, the most important question is which component is not working correctly. In some cases, the answer can already be derived from the

Workload Analysis. If not, the support expert can call up the *Trace Analysis* (see Figure 3.8). It shows all of the SAP components involved, and how much time every one of these components requires for the processing. The analysis can also be activated in the overview monitor for the users on the business side. The next automatic calling of the robots is then executed in trace mode.

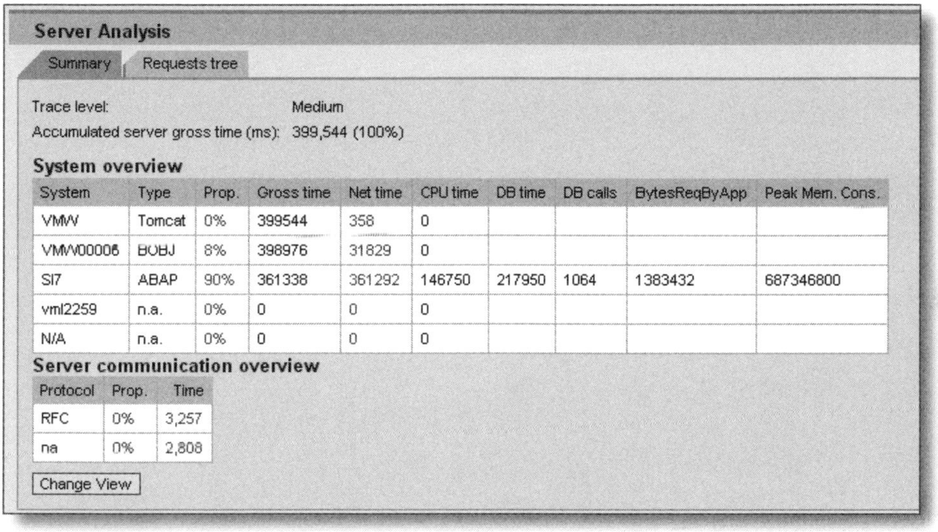

Server Analysis

| | Summary | Requests tree |

Trace level: Medium
Accumulated server gross time (ms): 399,544 (100%)

System overview

System	Type	Prop.	Gross time	Net time	CPU time	DB time	DB calls	BytesReqByApp	Peak Mem. Cons.
VMW	Tomcat	0%	399544	358	0				
VMW00006	BOBJ	8%	398976	31829	0				
SI7	ABAP	90%	361338	361292	146750	217950	1064	1383432	687346800
vml2259	n.a.	0%	0	0	0				
N/A	n.a.	0%	0	0	0				

Server communication overview

Protocol	Prop.	Time
RFC	0%	3,257
na	0%	2,808

Change View

Figure 3.8 Identifying Bottlenecks Using the End-to-End Trace

The Trace Analysis can help locate performance bottlenecks in processes that are run over multiple components. In Figure 3.8, System SI7 is the weak point.

A second scenario in SAP Solution Manager, the *Change Analysis*, tells the support expert whether changes have been made recently to the component that is not working correctly. Technical support then often starts CA Wily Introscope to perform a detailed trace analysis for an individual component. Based on this analysis, the reason why the component is running slowly can be found. Afterwards, you can remove the cause by means of a change request.

Change Analysis

Solution documentation in SAP Solution Manager forms the basis for many other elements of Application Lifecycle Management. This chapter explains how SAP Solution Manager supports you in documenting your system landscape and your business processes.

4   Solution Documentation in SAP Solution Manager

Efficient planning, reporting, and operation of your SAP solutions require clear and reliable documentation for these solutions. The documentation of your system landscape and your business processes in SAP Solution Manager is the basis for the additional usage of the comprehensive Application Lifecycle Management (ALM) functions provided by SAP Solution Manager. The documented business processes are used in many ALM phases; for example, in the Implementation phase by the template management (see Chapter 6), in the test environment by the Test Workbench and the Business Process Change Analyzer (BPCA; see Chapter 7), or in the monitoring environment by the Business Process Monitoring (see Chapter 11). Therefore, up-to-date documentation of your core business processes is a basic prerequisite for realizing the full potential of SAP Solution Manager.

SAP distinguishes between two types of interconnected solution documentation:

- Documentation for the technical system landscape
- Business process documentation

You'll find a detailed description of the documentation for the technical system landscape in Section 4.1, so there is no need for an additional presentation here.

There are two different ways of obtaining documentation for your business processes: the *initial documentation* within a template or implementation project or the *re-documentation* of existing business processes.

Initial documentation

When template or implementation projects are being used in SAP Solution Manager, comprehensive documentation is created when the business process structure to be implemented is being set up, and technical objects, configuration elements, test cases, and other documents are added to this structure in the course of the project. The most important elements are used again as solution documentation during operations after the productive start.

Re-documentation

If you only start setting up solution documentation during operations after the productive start, it's possible to perform a re-documentation of your business processes. The *Solution Documentation Assistant*, including the *Reverse Business Process Documentation Content* in SAP Solution Manager, provides support in setting up this re-documentation. The supporting functions are described in detail in the following sections.

The most important functions for the solution documentation in SAP Solution Manager are listed here:

▶ SAP Solution Manager System Landscape
▶ Business Blueprint (Transaction SOLAR01)
▶ Solution Configuration (Transaction SOLAR02)
▶ Solution Documentation Assistant

The goal of solution documentation in SAP Solution Manager is to have central documentation for IT-supported business processes and technical information about SAP and non-SAP solutions in order to have transparency and efficient collaboration.

Core elements of the solution documentation

The solution documentation is made up of the following core elements:

▶ Documentation of your IT-supported core business processes
▶ Documentation of the technical objects belonging to these, such as transactions, programs, customer-defined objects, background jobs, and interfaces
▶ Documentation about the corresponding systems and software components (SAP and non-SAP)

The documentation of your IT-supported business processes in SAP Solution Manager is performed in a three-level hierarchy consisting of the following hierarchy levels: business scenario, business process, and business process step. This hierarchy enables a standardized and uniform view of your processes and ensures its reusability in all phases of Application Lifecycle Management.

4.1 Technical Landscape Documentation

Landscape data describes the way in which company software is installed. On one hand, this data is available to applications that require information about systems in the landscape and the software installed on it, and on the other, it forms the basis for the management of these systems in SAP Solution Manager. Figure 4.1 shows an example of the cycle for the landscape data and a simplification of how this data flows through the systems, and how it is managed in SAP Solution Manager.

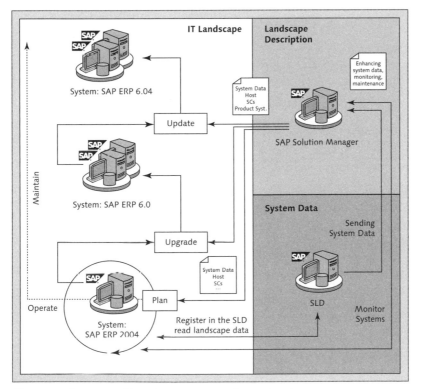

Figure 4.1 Overview of Data Flow Usage in a System Landscape

Data supplier   Systems that have a *data supplier* report their system data to a *System Landscape Directory* (SLD). These are SAP systems in particular that are based on SAP NetWeaver AS ABAP or AS Java, such as SAP Solution Manager itself, TREX systems, and others. Additionally, there are generic data suppliers with which third-party systems can also send their data to the SLD. Data transfer by means of data suppliers should be used wherever possible because it delivers up-to-date system data automatically and regularly.

Some systems, depending on their application, use data from the SLD themselves (the specific users of landscape data are shown in Figure 4.2). The SLD sends the collected data to SAP Solution Manager.

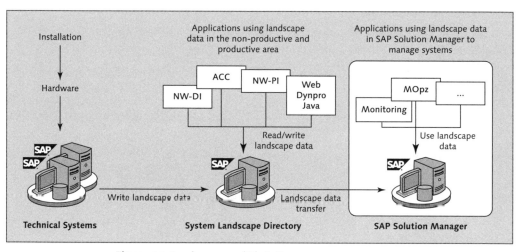

Figure 4.2 Landscapes and Their Users

Therefore, while the SLD collects data and provides SAP Solution Manager with business applications, SAP Solution Manager uses the data to monitor systems and add to their scope of functions by means of updates and upgrades.

Changes made through the installation of updates and upgrades are recorded automatically by means of the regular registration of the technical systems to the SLD, thus keeping the landscape description up to date.

The components and applications that provide landscape descriptions and use the recorded data are represented in Figure 4.2.

The technical systems created through the installation of SAP company software register themselves in the SLD. The SLD collects the data for the system landscape. Manual creation is only necessary in a few cases. The data collected with the first registration is used directly by other applications, such as the *Adaptive Computing Controller* (ACC). These applications in turn write their own data to the SLD or create new data based on the data that already exists in the SLD. The SLD sends this data to SAP Solution Manager, which also has its own applications that require landscape data.

As administrator of a landscape, it is your task to keep your landscape description up to date. This should be ensured, above all, by setting up the connections to the SLD for new systems, and only maintaining data manually when it cannot be entered automatically. You thus spare time and work while also improving the quality of your landscape data.

4.1.1 Landscape Data, Tools for Administration, and Processes to Use

Let's take a detailed look at the data collected in the IT landscape and how it is used in the systems for landscape administration. This data consists of the following:

▸ Products

▸ Technical systems

▸ Product systems

▸ Landscape patterns

To understand the difference between the landscape description and system data, you require an explanation of the terms *technical system* and *product system*. While the technical system comes about through the installation of SAP software on the hardware, the product system is a description of functional dependencies between technical systems. Figure 4.3 provides a simplified illustration of modules of products and technical systems.

Automated SLD registration

Technical system and product system

95

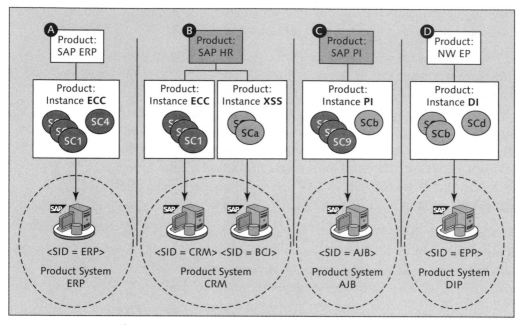

Figure 4.3 Product, Product Instance, Technical System, and Product System

Software components *Products* are developed in the form of software components (SC). Depending on how they are used, various dependencies exist between these software components. The components that have to be installed together on a technical system are combined into product instances. Therefore, the installation of product instances on the hardware leads to a technical system, which is given a *system ID* (SID). Information on the product instances of a technical system is necessary for calculating updates and upgrades using the Maintenance Optimizer, and it must be manually entered or completed for systems that do not report this information automatically to the SLD. The new EHP version of SAP Solution Manager is an example of the automatic reporting of the product version with the product instances.

As can be seen in Figure 4.3, different types of product instance distribution to the hardware are possible:

▸ **A and D**: All product instances are of the same type, so for A, they must all be used on the SAP NetWeaver Application Server (AS) ABAP, and for D, all on the SAP NetWeaver AS Java. Additionally, they are all installed on a technical system—A for an ABAP-based product, and D for a Java-based product. Note that the real products have more product instances than are shown in the figure.

- ▶ **B**: The product has product instances divided between ABAP and Java that are installed on separate technical systems.

- ▶ **C**: The product has both ABAP and Java elements in the product instances. These automatically result in an obligatory dual-stack system.

You can also see from the example that many software components appear in multiple product instances.

As previously mentioned, technical systems result from the installation of SAP software on the hardware. A technical system can also be installed, for example, on separate host systems for databases, servers, and message servers. That is, the hardware does not have to correspond to a physical computer. The technical system reports the installed software components to the SLD on the dates named. This information is required in particular by SAP Solution Manager to calculate the objects required for updating a system because technical systems are the goal of the maintenance and update processes. Additionally, aside from the software components, the information on the product instances and product version(s) of a technical system must be maintained. You have to do this yourself in SAP Solution Manager. For more recent releases, the product information is filled in during the installation and forwarded automatically to the SLD.

Technical systems

An example of a technical system is an SAP ERP system or an SAP NetWeaver Portal. The latter can be operated alone but is often used together with other applications.

As shown in Figure 4.3, however, in many cases multiple technical systems have to be considered in combination to map a business process of a product. To create this combination, you have to maintain product system definitions.

A *product system* consists of one or more *technical systems* that are required to operate a *product* or part of a product. Often, though not always, this will affect more than one technical system. For example, to operate an HR application with *Employee Self-Services (ESS)*, you will install the ABAP-based backend system separately from the portal system. However, during maintenance, you have to view the two technical systems as one unit because there can be dependencies on

Product systems

the level of the compatible versions of the two systems. For this reason, you combine the two technical systems into one *product system*. This information is not sent automatically by the system. The allocation is a manual activity that you perform in SAP Solution Manager. With this allocation, you define your landscape pattern and thus define the maintenance strategy for your systems.

Landscape pattern Landscape patterns describe the various options for you to assign technical systems to your product systems. Interestingly, they allow you to assign a technical system to multiple product systems. You can, for example, also assign an SAP NetWeaver Portal on which the product instances of the ESS are installed, along with the product system of your HR application, to a product system for SAP CRM, for example, which also uses functions of the SAP NetWeaver Portal.

In principle, there are two forms of landscape pattern: *hub* and *sidecar*:

Hub
▶ A technical system functions as a hub when it has been assigned to multiple product systems. When a product system is updated, only urgently required changes are made to the hub system to avoid forcing all the other systems that also use the hub system to update. If the information on the landscape pattern is not maintained, a system is treated as a hub.

Sidecar
▶ A technical system that is only used in one product system is always updated with the other system. This means that the AS Java-based part is updated together with the AS ABAP-based part.

In principle, you can use a technical system both in a hub and also in a separate product system. The assignment to a separate product system allows this system to be handled separately; the example in Figure 4.4 shows a specific upgrade of only the portal system.

In Figure 4.4, both the ABAP-based HR and SAP CRM systems use an SAP NetWeaver Portal system. Through this usage in multiple product systems, the SAP NetWeaver Portal becomes a hub system. What is this information used for? In the example shown, when the HR system is updated to a new release, the new version can often work with the existing version of the SAP NetWeaver Portal system. Due to the possible dependencies between various systems, the maintenance for product systems is calculated, and not only for calculated systems. In this case, the *Maintenance Optimizer* does not include the

SAP NetWeaver system EPP in the upgrade because it is possible that this would force the SAP CRM system to upgrade as well. This keeps the effects of the system upgrade to a minimum. If the SAP NetWeaver Portal system were only used in the HR product system as a sidecar, it would always be maintained together with the ABAP system. On the other hand, the definition of a portal product system allows the isolated upgrade of the SAP NetWeaver Portal system to benefit, for example, from the improved performance of a new version of SAP NetWeaver. However, a prerequisite for this type of upgrade is compatibility with both applications, HR and SAP CRM.

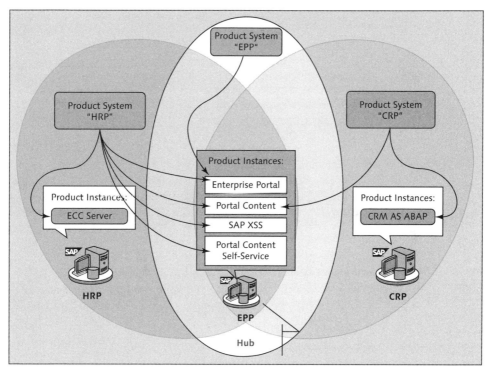

Figure 4.4 Landscape Pattern—an SAP NetWeaver Portal as a Hub System for CRM and HR

4.1.2 Handling Landscape Data

Technical systems, product systems, and landscape patterns are the basic elements of the landscape description. Other concepts, such as logical components, use this data. This section describes the steps and tools required to collect, manage, and update this data for the landscape description.

Process overview

As described in the introduction, the SLD and SAP Solution Manager are the most important systems in the landscape data maintenance. The sequence for the collection, management, and updating of the data is based on the steps for the installation, the registration on SLD, and the data forwarding to SAP Solution Manager:

Data collection

Figure 4.5 provides an overview of the processes for collecting landscape data. Deviations from the steps shown here will be discussed in later sections. Details relating to the SLD are only touched on here. You will find more information in the SAP Developer Network (SDN) under *http://sdn.sap.com/irj/sdn/nw-sld* and in a book[1] on this topic.

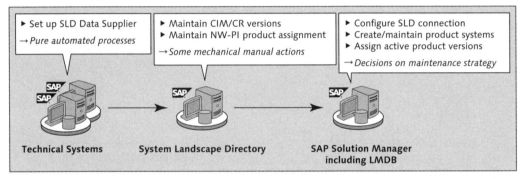

Figure 4.5 Overview—System Data, Steps, and Tools for Maintenance

Technical systems should always report to SLD by means of a *data supplier* whenever one is available. The advantage of this is that regular reporting—for example, changed software statuses due to system maintenance—ensures that your data is automatically updated when changes are made. There are examples of systems with a data supplier at the start of this chapter.

The data of the technical systems forms the basis of the data in the SLD. To also process the data from new systems, all you have to do is update the *software catalog* in the SLD (supplied as component repository content) and the underlying model, so that every SLD system of any release can process data from all technical systems—as long as they are

---

1 Hengevoss, Wolf; Linke, Andreas: *SAP NetWeaver System Landscape Directory. Grundlagen und Praxis. Bonn: SAP PRESS 2009. (This book is currently only available in German.)*

known in the latest software catalog. They are either directly consumed by the applications named at the start or are used for the development of application data. Examples of this are business systems in the SAP NetWeaver Process Integration (PI), or destinations for Web Dynpro Java that define sources and destinations for messages. The updating of the software catalog and the required model is a mechanical activity that, in principle, does not require a decision. In SAP Solution Manager, you make decisions about the maintenance and expansion of your systems.

The software catalog describes which software versions are available. It is developed in the *Products and Production Management System* (PPMS) and is supplied by SAP by means of a central SLD (the *Master Component Repository*) together with the required *Common Information Model* (CIM), in which the landscape data in SLD is described, through the SAP Service Marketplace (step ❶ in Figure 4.6). You must import this data into your SLD systems ❷ and update it in SAP Solution Manager ❷*. Here, the software catalog data enables you to interpret data from the technical systems that register on the SLD ❸. You use automated processes to transfer this data into SAP Solution Manager ❹. You create the landscape description on the basis of the system data. Some manual steps are required here when defining the product systems (and thus also when defining the landscape pattern) and when assigning installed product instances. In older installations, the installed product version must also be assigned. During the installation of newer product versions that are based on SAP NetWeaver 7.0 EHP 2 or higher versions—for example, SAP Solution Manager 7.1—this step is performed automatically. The landscape description is the basis for the processes of the ALM, such as the monitoring and maintenance of the systems ❺. Changes to the technical system that you made by, for example, importing an SAP EHP are automatically reported to the SLD during the next run of the self-registration, and the landscape data is updated accordingly.

Software catalog

The SLD primarily collects the data that technical systems send through their *data suppliers*. For AS ABAP-based systems and AS Java-based systems, these are directly available, whereas for third-party systems, a generic data supplier (sldreg) can be used. System data is used directly; however, it is mainly business systems that are used as the destinations of the middleware-supported system communication by means of the SAP NetWeaver Process Integration (PI).

Collecting landscape data in the SLD

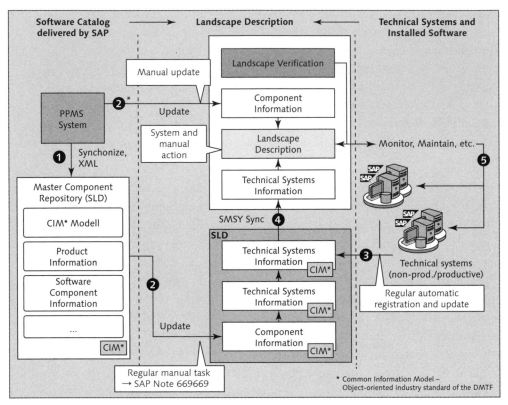

Figure 4.6 Maintaining System Landscape Data

To display the information that the technical systems send correctly, the SLD contains the software catalog in which information is supplied about the software supplied by SAP. You can add to the software catalog as you wish by creating your own products and software components—mainly for the SAP NetWeaver use types Process Integration (PI) and Development Infrastructure (DI). For the use with DI, the name reservation in the SLD is also available to ensure unique naming for development objects. In Figure 4.7, you can see how the data named is represented on the start page of an SLD system.

Along with the use of the data from business processes, the SLD also forwards the data to SAP Solution Manager. Although a local SLD only receives the data of the technical systems in release 7.0 of SAP Solution Manager, with the new SAP Solution Manager, much more comprehensive data is transferred, namely the entire content of the SLD. This also includes, for example, the *business systems* required for the PI Monitoring. Thus, the SLD is the most important source for landscape data for SAP Solution Manager. Its use is absolutely essential for efficient landscape administration. You will find more information on the SLD in the SDN under *http://sdn.sap.com/irj/sdn/ nw-sld*.

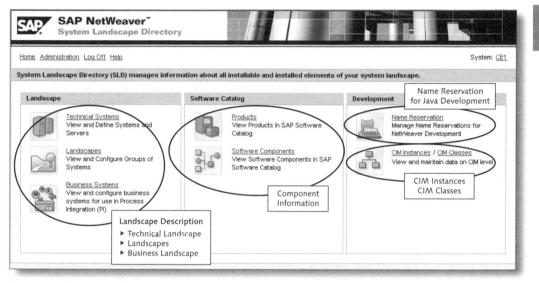

Figure 4.7 Data on the Start Page of the System Landscape Directory

The new SAP Solution Manager uses practically the entire range of landscape data from the SLD. In the standard case, this data is no longer collected in a local SLD running on the system of SAP Solution Manager, but in the newly developed *Landscape Management Database* (LMDB). In an automated process, the LMDB takes over all of the data, or the changes to the data, from one or more SLD systems in the landscape and immediately forwards the changes to the client applications. From the management point of view, this enables a more complete record of information and a clear savings with regard to manual work and the wait time for visualizing changes to the landscape data. In earlier releases of SAP Solution Manager, data was taken over from the SLD in a landscape fetch, which usually ran during the day, so that updated data only became visible after the job was complete. The main tools for managing the landscape data are the SLD, the LMDB, the system landscape (Transaction SMSY), and the Landscape Verification Tool, introduced with SAP Solution Manager 7.0.

Management of landscape data in LMDB, SMSY, and the Landscape Verification Tool

The connections between the technical systems and the tools in the new SAP Solution Manger are shown in Figure 4.8.

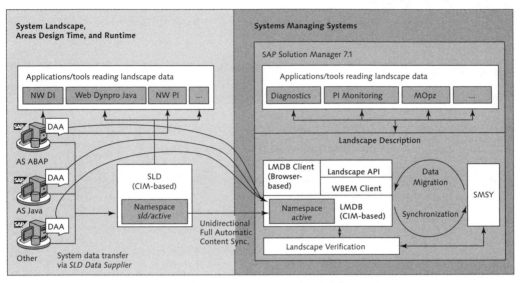

Figure 4.8 Landscape Data in SLD and SAP Solution Manager

As already mentioned, you set up the registration in the SLD for the technical systems. All of the data is transferred from one (or multiple) SLD(s) into the LMDB by means of a one-sided, complete, and automatic synchronization only in the direction from the SLD to the LMDB. From here, the data is synchronized in the tables of the system landscape (Transaction SMSY). Data from (usually older) systems that only exists in the system landscape but not in the SLD can be migrated to the LMDB. You make all changes to technical systems, including their initial creation, in the LMDB. In addition to the data from the SLD, the LMDB receives data from *diagnostics agents* (DAA, Figure 4.8) installed on the technical systems, which supply data to the database and the host. To use the data further configuration steps are necessary. Choose the CONFIGURE SYSTEM button to access the configuration (see Figure 4.11).

You still perform the product and product system assignment in the system landscape maintenance (Transaction SMSY). The Landscape Verification Tool, which is now also part of SAP Solution Manager, can continue being used to verify the data of the system landscape. You can also maintain the product system definition here.

The landscape data is thus available to the applications in SAP Solution Manager. Some of these read LMDB data directly, such as the *Diagnostics Framework*, while others still read the tables of the system landscape. As a user, you are automatically taken from the interfaces to the correct application. If you want to make changes to technical systems, the LMDB opens automatically. From here, you can, for example, open product systems for maintenance in the *Landscape Verification Tool* or the system landscape; the Landscape Verification Tool is connected to both the LMDB and the system landscape.

Landscape Management Database (LMDB)

The LMDB is supplied as part of the new SAP Solution Manager. As Figure 4.8 shows, the LMDB—like the SLD—implements the CIM, a model that's based on open standards for managing the landscape data, thus taking a significant step toward the standardization of the landscape data maintenance. The connection to the SLD has already been described briefly. However, the LMDB cannot be used without an SLD, as illustrated by Figure 4.9.

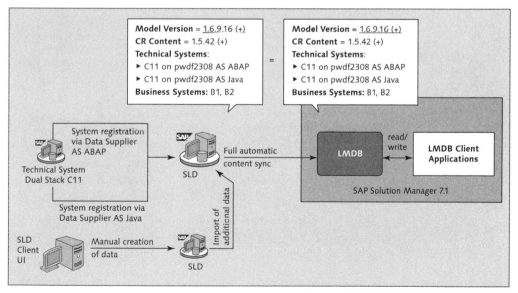

Figure 4.9 Data Flow in the Complete, Automated Synchronization from SLD to LMDB

We recommend using an SLD system that is operating in the production environment to collect the data from technical systems, and providing an SLD system in the development landscape for PI and Web Dynpro developments. When a complete, automated synchronization from the SLD to the LMDB is set up, the CIM, CR content, and all other data are taken over from the SLD in the production environment.

Configuration of the LMDB

You'll find the configuration of the LMDB in the SAP Solution Manager Configuration (Transaction SOLMAN_SETUP), in the step SYSTEM PREPARATION (see Figure 4.10).

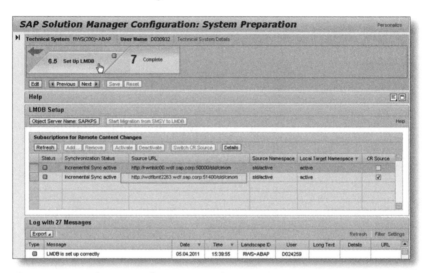

Figure 4.10 Configuration of the LMDB in the Procedure SOLMAN_SETUP with Source SLDs Highlighted

In the SAP Solution Manager Configuration screen, you set up the LMDB by entering one or more SLD systems as the source for the data. Exactly one SLD must be the source for the CR content, that is, for the software catalog. When the connection to an SLD system is activated, the data transfer begins (*Full-Sync phase*). When all of the data has been transferred, the phase begins in which changes are now taken over from the SLD only individually and directly (*Incremental-Sync phase*).

Conflicts

Because you can change the data for technical systems in both the SLD and the LMDB, a conflict can arise if data for a technical system in SLD and LMDB was changed in parallel and then resent by the SLD. Such conflicts are resolved automatically by means of a rank that you assign to an SLD or to the LMDB in a synchronization connection: The higher-ranking system wins in this case. We recommend assigning the highest rank to the LMDB. This prevents changes that were made in the LMDB from being overwritten by changes from the SLD. However, there are a number of important points that you should consider here:

▶ Only make manual changes when it is absolutely necessary.

▶ Change or delete data in the place where it was created, that is, automatically reported data in the SLD, and data manually created in the LMDB there.

You also call the LMDB itself under the SAP Solution Manager Configuration (Transaction SOLMAN_SETUP). Under the menu item MANAGED SYSTEMS CONFIGURATIONS, you will find the list of the TECHNICAL SYSTEMS known in SAP Solution Manager, as well as the TECHNICAL SCENARIOS (groupings of technical systems that are to be monitored together, for example), and DATABASES (see Figure 4.11).

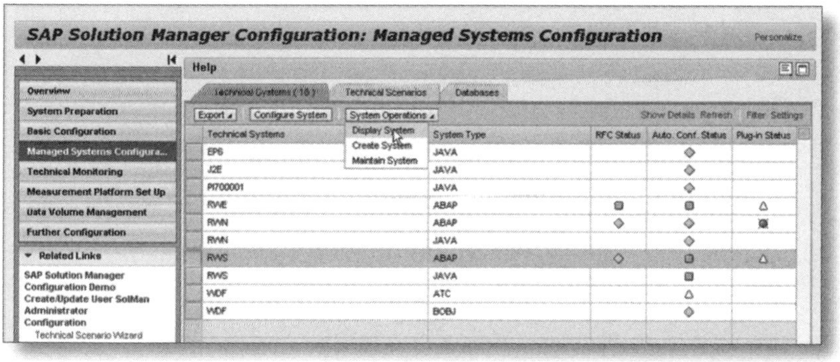

Figure 4.11 Technical Systems, Scenarios, and Databases in SAP Solution Manager

The LMDB manages the data received from the SLD and the diagnostics agents. The *Technical System Editor* (see Figure 4.12) of the LMDB allows you to display, create, and change your data.

Creating, displaying, and changing data in the LMDB

The editor shows the data for the selected technical system, as it is supplied by the SLD and added by the diagnostics agent, if this is installed on the system. Figure 4.12 also illustrates that the use of a technical system in the product system is also shown. The following data is sent by the SLD: SID, extended SID, database host, release, installation number, license key, software components, and free text entries, as well as the product version, if the installation tool wrote this to the system. In addition, the use of the technical system in technical scenarios and product systems is displayed. In the new SAP

Solution Manager, you'll find a centrally located, clearly improved, and expanded view of the systems in the landscape.

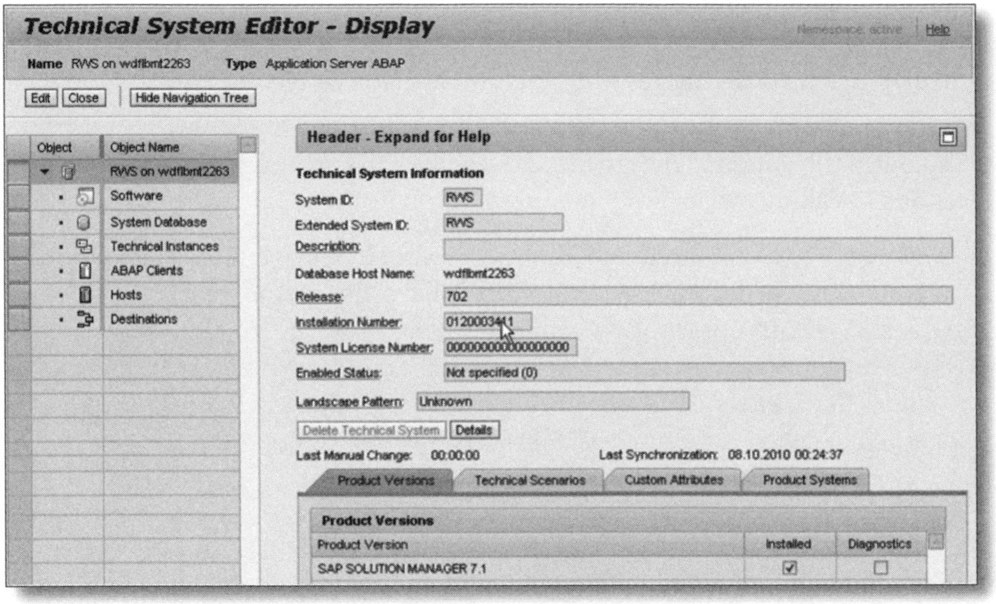

Figure 4.12 Editor for the Data of Technical Systems in the LMDB in Display Mode

For the systems for which a data supplier is not (or not yet) available, the LMDB provides an enhanced function for manually creating these system types.

With a defined sequence of steps (*guided procedure*), the LMDB supports you in creating your technical systems (see Figure 4.13). In addition to adding a database—in step 2—a list of the database hosts already known is also provided for selection. This helps you avoid making incorrect manual entries by offering validated entries for selection.

Manual creation   SAP BusinessObjects systems are good examples of manual creation. Data suppliers are not available in all cases here. However, the system data is still required to view an SAP BusinessObjects system together with an AS ABAP-based system and to monitor all of the systems involved in this scenario in a shared monitoring process. This is also a type of technical scenario that you can create with the help of LMDB by means of a guided procedure. The option to call this function using the TECHNICAL SCENARIOS tab page was shown earlier in Figure 4.11.

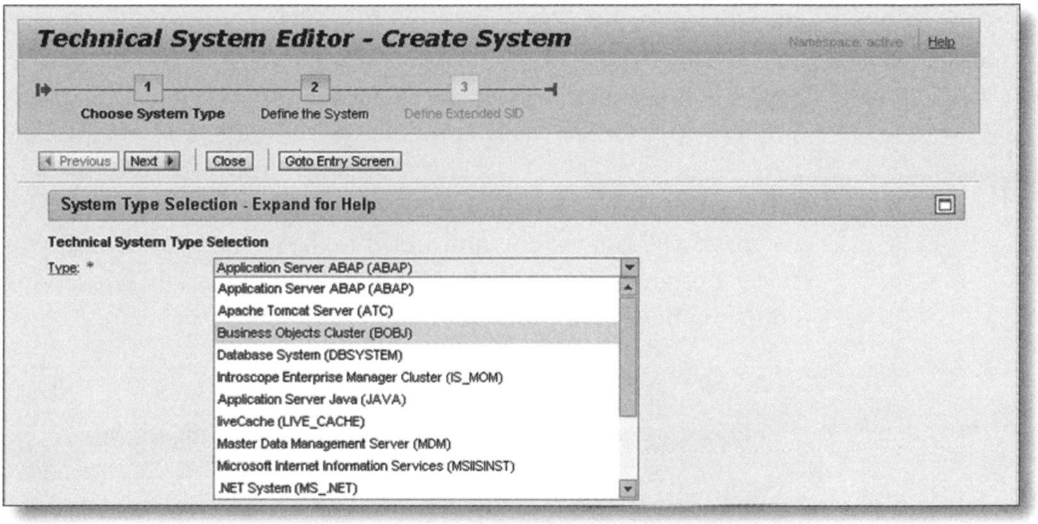

Figure 4.13 Guided Procedure for Creating a Technical System—Selecting the System Type

As previously mentioned, the LMDB supports you in managing landscape data through improved synchronization with the SLD and standardization in the data model. The combination of the starting points for maintaining the various system data is an additional improvement. The data that is not maintained in the LMDB, in particular the definition of the product systems, can be selected centrally from the LMDB.

On the PRODUCT SYSTEMS tab page of a technical system, the use of this technical system in one or more product systems is displayed. Because this assignment cannot be changed in the LMDB in the current version, you have the option to go to the system landscape or to the Landscape Verification Tool (see Figure 4.14).

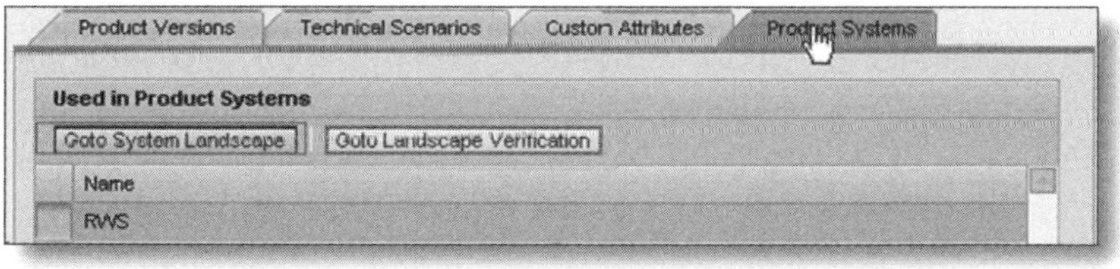

Figure 4.14 Maintenance of Product Systems—Goto System Landscape and the Landscape Verification Tool in the LMDB

System Landscape in SAP Solution Manager

Transaction SMSY In the maintenance of the system landscape (Transaction SMSY; see Figure 4.15), you can display the data for technical systems and product systems. You can change product systems here, but you can neither create nor change technical systems. You are automatically taken to the LMDB for editing. An exception is data that is read by means of RFC connections and added to the technical system. If you select a product system in the LMDB, it is automatically opened for editing in the system landscape.

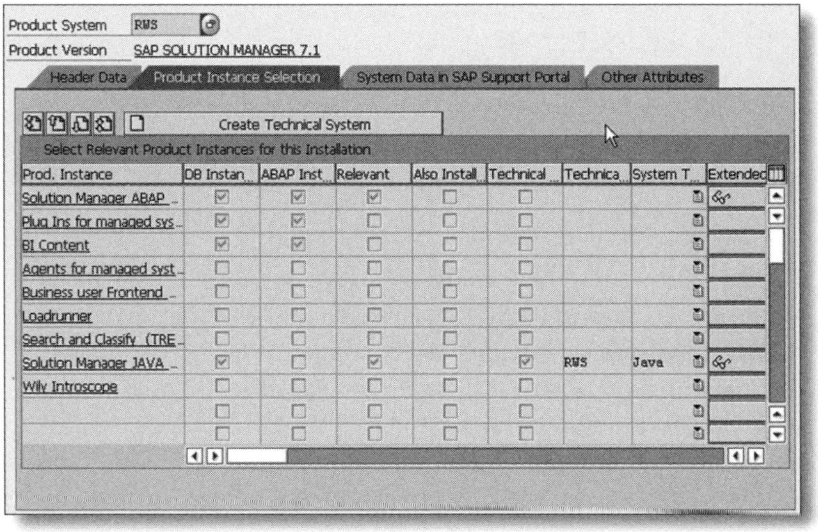

Figure 4.15 A Product System with Product Instances in Transaction SMSY

As previously noted, you can add product instances to the product system in the system landscape, manage the data from the SAP Service Marketplace, delete transport buffer data where necessary, and maintain landscape patterns (under the OTHER ATTRIBUTES tab).

The Maintenance Optimizer, which is responsible for calculating the download stacks, reads landscape data from the system landscape. Therefore, the quality of this data is decisive for the success and the duration of the maintenance process, so it makes a lot of sense to invest in the quality of this data. The *Landscape Verification Tool* supports you here.

Landscape Verification Tool

In October 2010, the optional add-on Landscape Verification 1.0 for SAP Solution Manager was released for use with SAP Solution Manager 7.0 (from SP 18). With the new SAP Solution Manager, the Landscape Verification Tool is integrated.

As shown in Figure 4.16, the Landscape Verification Tool reads data from the tables of the system landscape and helps verify the data. For this purpose, extended checks on existing information are implemented in the Landscape Verification Tool and the SAP Service Marketplace that support you in analyzing your landscape data, especially on the level of the product systems. When you select the LANDSCAPE VERIFICATION TOOL function for the product system, an overview opens with the errors and warnings found in your landscape. You can see the selected system in the detail view.

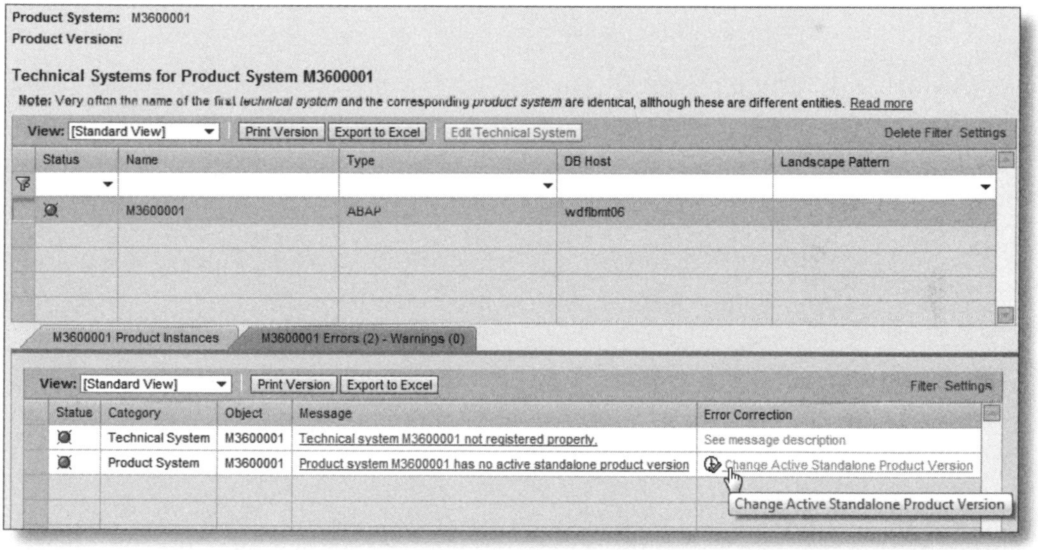

Figure 4.16 A Product System in the Landscape Verification Tool

All of the errors found for a product system or technical system are displayed. In the example shown, a guided procedure is also provided for the assignment of the product version in which the Landscape Verification Tool offers you for manual selection only those product versions that correspond to the installed software component versions.

We recommend using the Landscape Verification Tool, in particular before installing an update (e.g., an EHP) or an upgrade, to find and remove errors in the landscape description because the quality of the calculation of the download stack in the Maintenance Optimizer depends directly on the quality of the landscape description.

4.1.3 Topology of the Tools for Managing Landscape Data

With the System Landscape Directory (SLD), the landscape management database (LMDB), and SAP Solution Manager (with system management and the Landscape Verification Tool), you are now familiar with all of the applications for managing landscape data. An important task in the design of IT landscapes is to distribute the landscape data so that all applications receive the required landscape data quickly, correctly, and with as little manual work as possible; in other words, you need to find a suitable *topology* for the applications named.

Links between SLDs and client applications

The topology shown in Figure 4.17 has proven itself suitable for most customers who also operate applications such as SAP NetWeaver PI.

For setting up SLD systems and SAP Solution Manager, this means the following:

► All technical systems register on a central SLD

► The central SLD forwards the data to all other SLD systems (the non-production SLDs can also be further divided into development and quality assurance systems, for example).

► SLD-relevant objects that are created during development are distributed by means of export/import processes from the development to the quality assurance systems, and then into the (central) SLD for the production systems (e.g., with the expanded transporting of the SAP NetWeaver AS ABAP).

► Optionally, a hot backup SLD system can be set up (independent SLD installations are required that are connected by means of a bidirectional, complete, automatic synchronization, as well as a virtual IP address).

► The data is forwarded to the LMDB in SAP Solution Manager by means of unidirectional, complete, automatic synchronization.

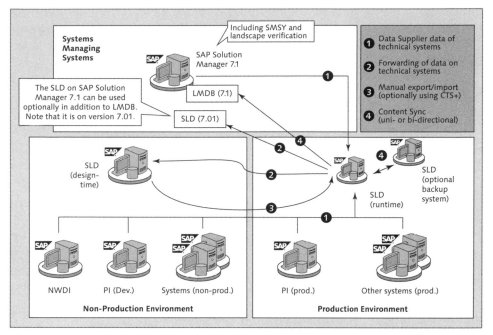

Figure 4.17 Topology of Applications for the Landscape Management

4.2   Solution Documentation Assistant

The Solution Documentation Assistant enables you to automatically evaluate business processes in SAP Solution Manager. It helps you prepare implementation or upgrade projects, evaluate new functions, and analyze customer-specific developments. You can, for instance, determine which business processes are being used actively in production systems and view this information graphically. This has benefits for standardization and thus supports the optimization of your business processes.

Above all, existing customers already operating a live solution can benefit from the capability to create solution documentation for their existing solution quickly and efficiently with the Solution Documentation Assistant. Its scope, however, is not limited to the initial creation of solution documentation; you can also use it to continuously verify and update your solution documentation. In this sense, the Solution Documentation Assistant makes a lasting contribution to the reduction of your operating costs as well as the transparency of the solution.

Identifying
core business
processes

Identification of core business processes, a process supported by the Solution Documentation Assistant, is divided into the following process steps:

- ▶ Document the system landscape.
- ▶ Automatically assign the analysis results to a process structure.
- ▶ Create the Business Blueprint.

Central access

This SAP Solution Manager function cuts the time you need to achieve the goal of making solution documentation for all your core business processes available centrally in SAP Solution Manager, serving as a single source of truth and supporting you in other scenarios of SAP Solution Manager that are based on this information. For example, this solution documentation can help you in setting up Business Process Monitoring (see Chapter 11, Section 11.1) or using the Business Process Change Analyzer (see Chapter 7, Section 7.1).

4.2.1 Documentation of the System Landscape

Entry points

You have three possible entry points for inputting the components of the landscape of the managed systems that you want to document:

- ▶ Transfer existing system documentation from previous implementation or upgrade projects
- ▶ Transfer documentation from existing solutions in SAP Solution Manager
- ▶ Previously undocumented solution and system landscapes that are already up and running

If the managed systems in your system landscape are already connected to SAP Solution Manager, no further activity is required here. If the systems have not yet been connected, enter them in Transaction SMSY (Solution Manager System Landscape; see Section 4.1.3).

4.2.2 Automatically Assigning the Results of the Analysis to a Business Process Structure

Sources

You can use the Solution Documentation Assistant to automatically analyze your business processes and draw on different sources to reuse existing process documentation:

- Documentation from existing implementation and upgrade projects in SAP Solution Manager
- Documentation for SAP partner products
- Documentation from existing solutions in SAP Solution Manager
- Documentation for SAP standard processes in the Business Process Repository, which is integrated into SAP Solution Manager

Check any existing documentation from existing projects or solutions. If no documentation yet exists, create a project in SAP Solution Manager (see Chapter 5, Section 5.3.2) to create the documentation automatically with the Solution Documentation Assistant.

The existing structures and data from projects and solutions are copied to the analysis projects. You can also base the analysis projects on imported data from a different SAP Solution Manager system.

The analyses show the results based on structures. In addition, all data used is comprehensively analyzed. This means that the result of an analysis may reveal objects that are not assigned to the structure but are still used in production. This approach ensures that all objects used in production are available in the solution documentation.

Structure-based mapping

The analysis results are presented in such a way that they can be used for considering higher-level business aspects as well as taking a more detailed look at the analyzed technical objects, such as transactions or reports. The Solution Documentation Assistant distinguishes here between objects that result from real production data or, for example, data created for test purposes. The analysis findings can be transferred from the Solution Documentation Assistant to the underlying SAP Solution Manager project at the touch of a button. The project can be updated in this way.

When analyzing live solutions, you can verify the correctness and consistency of existing documentation at reasonable intervals. Because the solution acts as the source in this case, you are not required to create an SAP Solution Manager project before you start the analysis. If the analysis reveals that the existing solution documentation needs to be updated, you can create a new project from within the analysis and copy the analysis results to it. This poses no threat to the production solution, which can be updated at a defined time by transferring project data to the solution under controlled circumstances.

Updating and consistency check

You also have access to the analysis results in the form of an extensive HTML report, as well as in various graphic representations.

Work center You can call up all of the tasks relevant to working with the Solution Documentation Assistant from the *Solution Documentation Assistant* work center. The work center (see Figure 4.18) presents several views to enable you to manage analysis projects, process analyses and their results, and process check steps in the rule database.

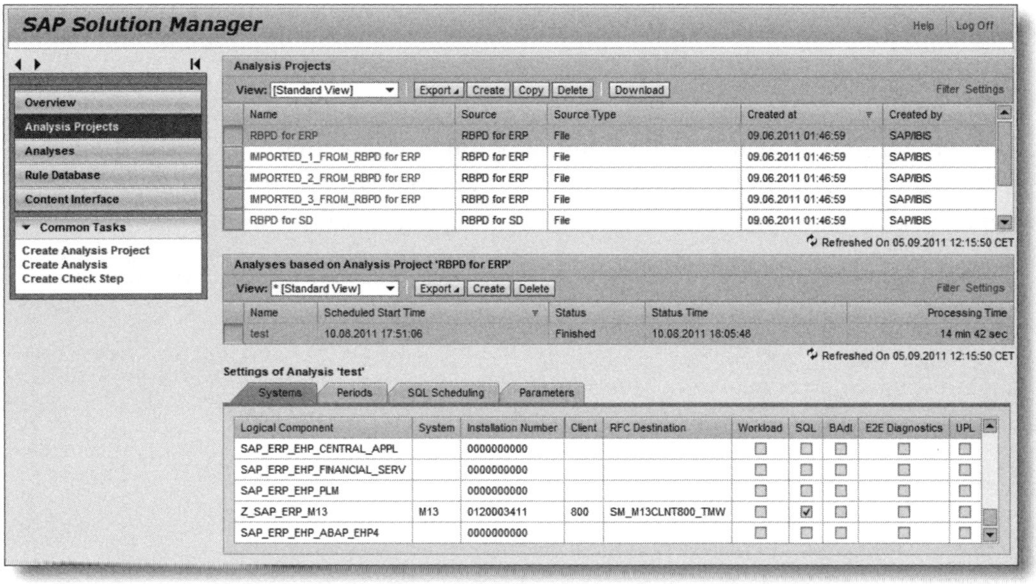

Figure 4.18 "Solution Documentation Assistant" Work Center

Views The following views are provided:

▶ An OVERVIEW that gives you fast access to your current projects and analyses

▶ ANALYSIS PROJECTS to provide a detailed view of all analysis projects and the analyses created for a given project. You can also open an individual analysis project to display and edit the view of the analysis structure and check rules of the analysis project.

▶ ANALYSES for a detailed view of all analyses. You can search for particular analyses and open a view showing the results of a given analysis.

▶ A RULE DATABASE to allow you to see all of the check steps that exist; you can create, edit, or delete check steps.

► The CONTENT INTERFACE enables you to export or import analysis projects or check rules as files. For instance, you can use this function to import and make use of analysis projects provided by SAP partners.

The work center supports you with guided procedures when you are creating analysis projects and analyses, and it allows you to create check steps:

Guided procedures

► CREATE ANALYSIS PROJECT
You create a new analysis project on the basis of an SAP Solution Manager project, a solution, or an imported analysis project. You can also call up the guided procedure from the view for analysis projects.

► CREATE ANALYSIS
You create an analysis on the basis of an existing analysis project and plan the time it is to be performed. You can also start the guided procedure from the view for existing analyses.

The *Solution Documentation Assistant* work center offers you a view showing the structure and details of an individual analysis project. You can use the view to display and edit the check rules that are assigned to the nodes in the analysis structure, for example.

Analysis project

In the analysis, check rules enable nodes in the analysis structure to be rated. Check rules denote check sets and check steps belonging to a structure node, for example, a business process.

The *Solution Documentation Assistant* work center displays the check rules of an analysis project in the CHECK RULES area of the detailed view of the analysis project. Check rules are automatically copied from the source (project, solution, or imported data) when the analysis project is being created. You can edit and extend check rules to increase the quality of the analysis.

Check rules

The check rules are split into two levels:

► Check sets
► Check steps

In the analysis, check sets enable nodes in the analysis structure to be rated. This rating is based on the results of check steps that have been assigned to the check sets. You can assign as many check steps as you

Check sets

like to each check set, and as many check sets to every structure node.

Check step   A check step is an object to be analyzed, such as a transaction, a report, or an SQL statement. The check step is the smallest unit in the check rules. The following types of check step exist:

- ▶ **Transaction**
  Checks whether a specific transaction is used.

- ▶ **Report**
  Checks whether a specific report is used.

- ▶ **SQL statement**
  Enables you to create in detail your own check rules, for example, for checking whether specific tables, table fields, or table entries occur.

- ▶ **BAdI**
  Enables you to check whether specific business add-ins (BAdIs) are used.

The following elements use the data from the End-to-End Diagnostics as the basis for the usage check:

- ▶ Web Dynpro application/Web Dynpro component
- ▶ Java web service
- ▶ Servlet
- ▶ iView

You also have the option of using SAP kernel logs as the data source: *Usage procedure logging* enables you to check whether individual methods, classes, function modules, or reports are used with SAP kernel logs as the data source.

A threshold value is assigned to check steps and is taken as a rating criterion for analysis purposes. For example, you can define that the CREATE DOCUMENT check step can only be rated as productive if it has been executed more than 100 times a month.

Rule database   The rule database provides an overview of all of the available check steps, including those that have not been assigned to analysis projects. You can use the rule database to search for check steps and display detailed information for them. You can also edit the check steps and create new ones.

The view of an individual analysis project shows the analysis structure, for instance, how it is based on the underlying SAP Solution Manager project, and the check rules that are assigned to the nodes in the analysis structure.

Analysis structure

The work center depicts the structure of an analysis project as a tree in the ANALYSIS STRUCTURE area (see Figure 4.19). Some of the nodes in the structure are abstract. Their purpose is to organize the items listed below them, namely concrete business scenarios or processes and their individual steps. Examples of such nodes include the following:

Analysis structure

▸ Organizational units

▸ Master data

▸ Business scenarios

▸ Business processes

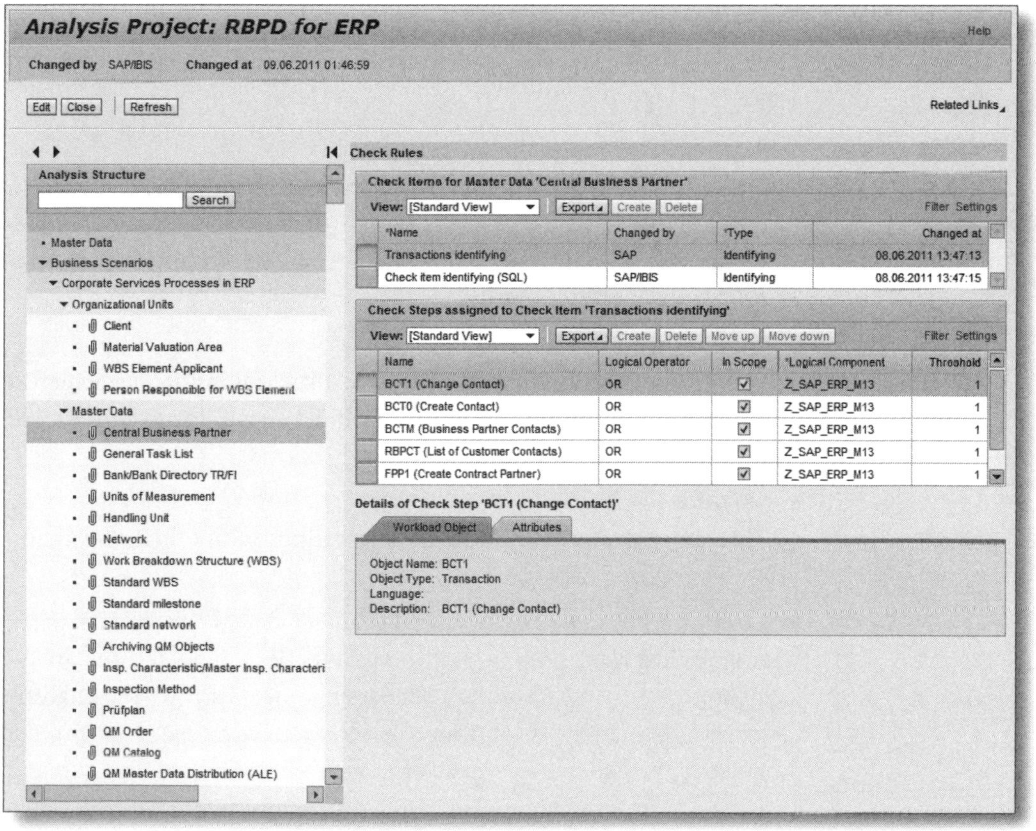

Figure 4.19 View of an Analysis Project in the Solution Documentation Assistant

The other nodes represent concrete business scenarios, business processes, and process steps. Their names stem from the underlying SAP Solution Manager projects, solutions, or imported analysis projects. This type of node might, for instance, represent the process for creating a purchase order.

These nodes are assigned check sets and check steps that enable the nodes to be rated during the analysis. The attachment symbol displayed in the structure indicates the nodes that have been assigned check sets already (see Figure 4.19).

The hierarchy of the analysis structure is also taken into account when the results of the analysis are determined. This means that a business scenario groups together the rating results of all of the business processes that belong to it, and a business process groups together the results of all of the process steps that belong to it.

Analysis results The Solution Documentation Assistant gives you a detailed view of the results of an analysis. The analysis results are arranged according to the following aspects and presented on the corresponding tab pages (see Figure 4.20):

▶ ANALYSIS RESULTS
This tab page represents the results of the analysis with regard to the structure and visualizes the use of individual structure elements. The GRAPHICS tab page also provides a graphic representation of the analysis results.

▶ OBJECT USAGE
This is a summary of the analysis results looking in particular at the success of the analysis and the object usage, for example, SAP or customer-specific transactions and reports..

▶ SETTINGS
This tab page summarizes all of the settings with which the analysis was carried out.

▶ CHAIN
A graphical representation of the connections between the analysis source (e.g., SAP Solution Manager project or file), the analysis project, the analysis, and any resulting new projects or project updates, provides a clearer overview.

▶ REPORT
This tab page provides various evaluation options for the results,

including the representation of the entire analysis results in an HTML report.

▸ LOG

The automatically filled log lists all of the actions carried out and makes it easier to reproduce the analysis at a later time.

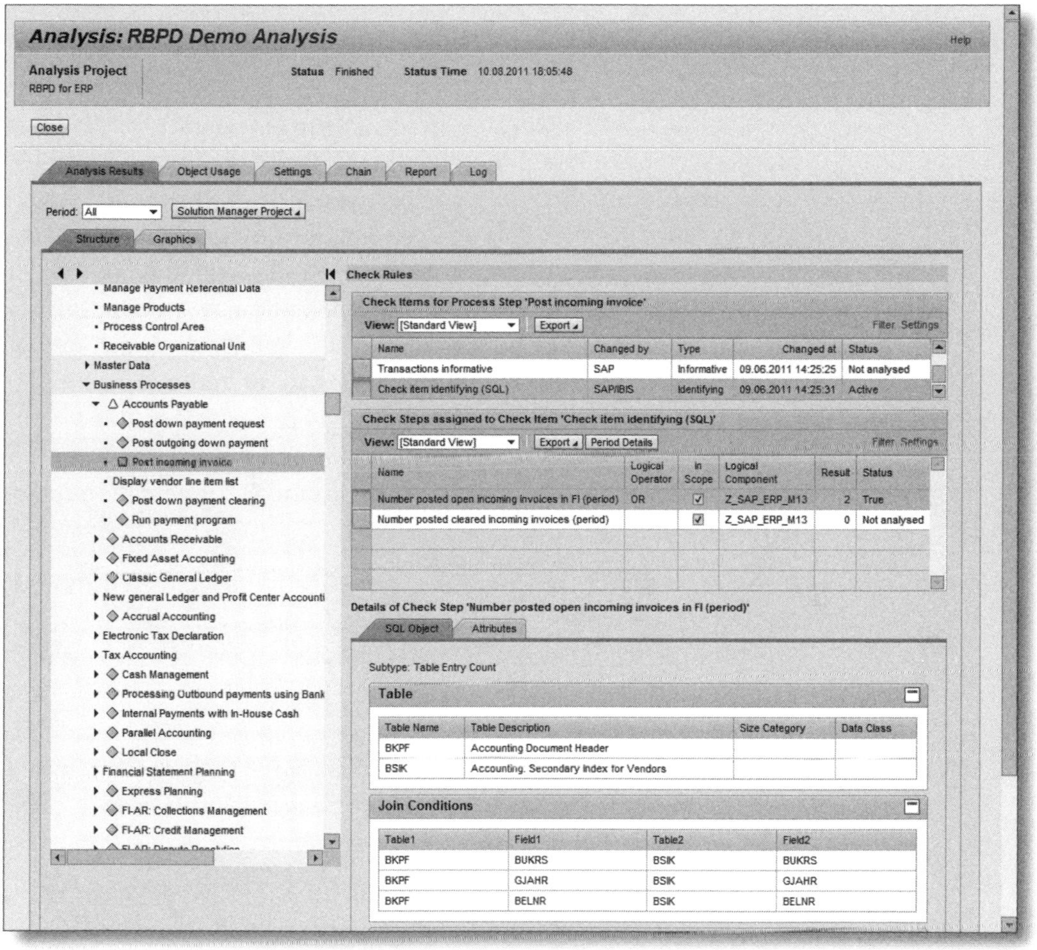

Figure 4.20 Overview of the Analysis Results

4.2.3 Updating Analysis Results in a Project or Transferring Results to a Solution

After you have successfully completed an analysis project, you can update the data in your SAP Solution Manager project at the touch of a button. You are free to edit the resulting Business Blueprint if necessary (see Chapter 5, Section 5.4). You transfer the project to your solution documentation using the standardized procedures for implementing solutions.

4.3   Reverse Business Process Documentation

Many of your SAP systems have been operating in production for years—but often no one remembers which business processes are used in which way in which variants on which systems. To solve this problem, and to obtain—quickly and with as little effort as possible—documentation of your core business processes based on the actual use of these processes, SAP has developed content for *Reverse Business Process Documentation* (RBPD content) that will help you when setting up initial business process documentation, with support from the many years' experience of IBIS Prof. Thome AG in the area of process identification. The content consists of more than 14,000 check rules linked to standard business processes that enable you to document your business processes faster and holistically based on usage and intensity of usage with the Solution Documentation Assistant.

Based on the business processes predefined and delivered by SAP (BPR), the managed systems are checked. Along with the use of the SAP transactions, master and transaction data, Customizing settings, and the control of functional procedures in the business, processes are also rated. If processes are used according to the SAP standard, they are flagged and can be copied into an initial project. Objects and variants developed by the customer are detected and are added manually in a second step.

Use and application of the RBPD content
The RBPD content was developed precisely for SAP Solution Manager 7.1 and is available for customers with SAP Enterprise Support. When loading the content to the Solution Documentation Assistant, you have the option of making a preselection and only uploading specific excerpts from the RBPD content for an analysis.

After the content is uploaded, the Solution Documentation Assistant automatically creates an analysis project with the corresponding business scenarios and stores the check rules in the rule database.

The RBPD content is supplied as a business process structure with attached check rules. The business process structure is mainly based on the predelivered structures of the BPR, while the check rules were assigned to the processes and process steps to enable quick analysis.

After the RBPD content is uploaded, the Solution Documentation Assistant automatically creates an analysis project containing the standardized business process structure and the check rules. Based on this analysis project, you can now perform the analysis of your system.

The analysis result you receive is the use frequency of your business processes and business process steps, and that of the technical objects connected to them.

The results of the analysis can then be transferred to an SAP Solution Manager project, where you can modify or expand your business process documentation accordingly.

What benefits can you derive from an RBPD analysis?

▶ **Better positioning of IT with respect to the business departments**
RBPD analysis results provide transparency in the use of the SAP systems and the IT implementation of project specifications.

▶ **Identification of optimization potential for IT investments**
With information about the actual use of the business processes, IT investments can be implemented meaningfully and with greater focus.

▶ **Find out and improve the standardization level for business processes**
RBPD analysis results show how close to the SAP standard the actual use of your system is. This can be used to optimize the process. Additionally, processes that are close to the standard can lower costs by reducing the maintenance required.

▶ **Identification of customer-defined developments**
If the analysis reveals the use of customer-defined developments, these can be managed using Custom Code Management in SAP Solution Manager or be changed back to the standard (see Chapter 15).

▶ **Up-to-date, clearly structured, and verified solution documentation**
RBPD helps you quickly set up up-to-date documentation of your business processes as the basis for ALM with SAP Solution Manager. This creates the basis for many additional saving opportunities and efficiency improvements through reusing the solution documentation in other areas of the ALM.

4.4 Initial Setup of a Business Blueprint Structure with the Excel Upload Interface

To speed up the initial setup of a Business Blueprint structure, for example, by importing existing business process documentation from other tools (such as ARIS), a new interface in Microsoft Excel format was developed for the initial upload of business process structures.

Creating a template
To use the interface, you must have created a new project in SAP Solution Manager (see Chapter 5, Section 5.3.2). To now set up a business process structure using the Excel interface, in the first step you can go to the Project Administration (Transaction SOLAR_PROJECT_ADMIN) and use the menu entry EDIT • BUSINESS BLUE-PRINT • FILL • CREATE TEMPLATE FILE to have SAP Solution Manager create an Excel template. This template contains information about how exactly you can include your documentation in this template, so that you can then upload it directly to SAP Solution Manager.

The interface is based on an incremental working method with which you can fill the Business Blueprint step by step. In a first step, the interface provides the Excel template for the initial filling of the business process structure. After this operation is complete and your business process structure is included in the Business Blueprint, you can use the same procedure—create an Excel template, fill this template, and upload the file to SAP Solution Manager—to gradually fill the individual tab pages (TRANSACTIONS, PROJECT DOCUMENTATION, TEST CASES, etc.).

The Excel interface is created for the quick initial filling of the Business Blueprint with process content (e.g., from other tools such as ARIS), whereby only basic checks are performed on the correct upload format. Therefore, it can only be used once for each project (and there once for each tab page). Further maintenance of the uploaded content is then performed in a controlled environment with more comprehensive consistency checks in the Business Blueprint of SAP Solution Manager.

If you want to use the interface again to upload additional process structure content for an existing project, you must perform the upload to a new SAP Solution Manager project. You can then merge the newly uploaded content with the structures of existing projects using the function COMPARE AND ADJUST, which uses appropriate checking mechanisms to ensure the consistency of your existing project structures.

Compare and Adjust function

4.5 Documentation of the Solution

IT landscapes are regularly maintained throughout their lifecycle and adapted to new business requirements if necessary. The planning and reporting for the respective initiatives are therefore irreplaceable instruments for operating the solution successfully. Detailed documentation of the existing solution is the basis for efficient planning and reporting. You must completely and accurately describe the individual components in your solution landscape as well as the business processes running on it. This documentation is referred to frequently during the implementation project and later when operating the solution.

A good approach to modeling your solution is to first concentrate on a few core business processes. These are the processes that are particularly important for the economic success of your company. Disruptions to these processes have a negative effect on the success of your business.

Core business processes

To create the documentation, you should first concentrate on the system that performs the most important process steps. This system is also described as a *critical system* for a business process because the failure of the system greatly impairs the process. Because the later operation of the solution essentially focuses on the critical systems, particular care is required to describe these systems and the corresponding process steps. Next, you integrate the description of the

Critical system

other systems involved, the process steps run on them, and the interfaces used, until all interfaces that transfer critical data for the business process have been documented.

The documentation of the business processes initially includes the individual process steps. It should be described in a standardized format. As well as the actual process, you also document more detailed information, such as the roles involved or possible dependencies. Table 4.1 contains a template for documenting business process steps. In addition to describing the individual process steps, the documentation also presents information about the whole process, such as the purpose of the process or relevant key performance indicators (KPIs).

Process Step	\<Name of the Process Step>
Description	\<Short description of the business process step (target state)>
Who performs the step?	\<Responsible role or function for performing the step>
When is the step performed?	\<Fixed date or triggering event>
What information or documents are required?	\<Documents with information required to perform the step (paper or system documents)>
Which tool is used?	\<System function used (dialog, batch, or program) or other required media>
What is the result of the activity?	\<Generated/changed data and documents (if relevant: Who is the recipient?)>
Comments	\<Reference to further information; related business processes; critical factors>
Specifications for master data	\<Which master data is required, and how is it replicated?>
Specifications for reporting	\<Information required for reporting>
Specifications for system configuration	\<Required Customizing settings or system configuration (including customer development requirement)>
Person(s) involved/date	\<Name of project team members who created the documentation>

Table 4.1 Template for Documenting Business Process Steps

The business process documentation is generally created as part of an implementation, maintenance, or upgrade project. To do this, use Transactions SOLAR01 (Business Blueprint) and SOLAR02 (Configuration) in SAP Solution Manager in particular; both are available from the *Implementation/Upgrade* work center. You will find more detailed information about documenting your solution with these transactions in Chapter 5, Sections 5.4 and 5.5. You can obtain more support for documenting your existing solution from the Solution Documentation Assistant (see Section 4.2).

The system documentation contains technical information about the system; for example, the product and release, the server and database on which it is installed, the software components it contains and their Support Package level, the clients that are configured, and how you can connect to them (see Figure 4.21). Information about the corresponding system landscape (development, quality assurance, and production systems) and the respective transport routes of software logistics is also relevant here.

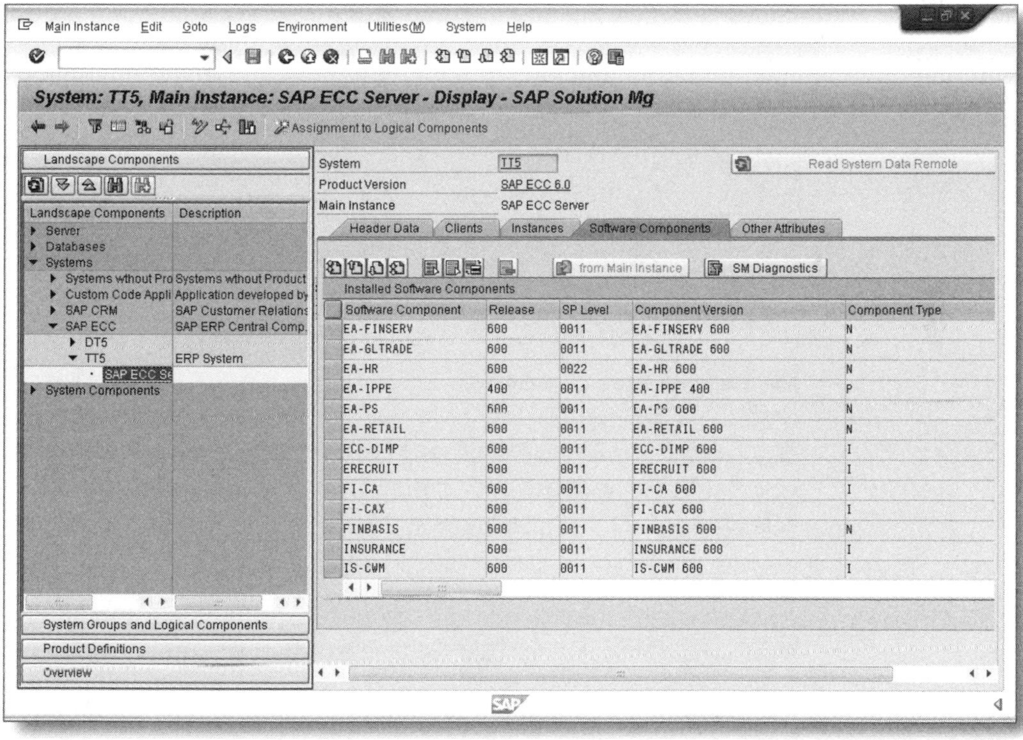

System documentation

Figure 4.21 Displaying System Documentation

The documentation of the systems in the solution landscape is generally created automatically for SAP applications and applications that are registered in the SLD by connecting the systems to SAP Solution

Manager. It is also possible to manually enter the data for non-SAP applications in the SAP Solution Manager system landscape (Transaction SMSY). This transaction can be reached through the *SAP Solution Manager Administration* work center.

Views of a solution The information in the solution documentation is required by many people to complete their tasks. However, different data are required depending on the person's role. SAP Solution Manager therefore provides different views of your solution (see Figure 4.22).

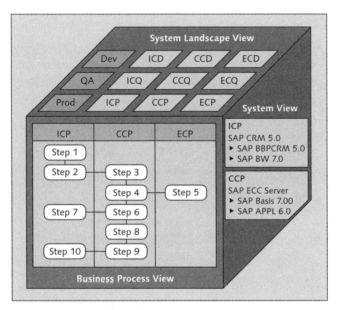

Figure 4.22 Views of a Solution

Business process view The *business process view* shows the core business processes. The process steps contained are each assigned to logical components (products or product versions). You use this view in projects, in particular to store the project documentation in a structured way.

System view The *system view* focuses more on technical aspects. It contains all systems/logical components that are operated by a certain organization. This view makes it possible to view the system, its product versions, and software components in greater detail. A connection to the business process view and the system view is created by assigning business process steps to systems.

System landscape view The *system landscape view* arranges all logical components to be operated and monitored into system landscapes. This view defines the relationships between production and non-production systems (e.g., development, quality assurance) in a system landscape and, in particular, the transport rules relevant for monitoring changes. For this reason, this view is particularly relevant for software logistics tasks.

The topic of traceability is becoming increasingly important not only due to legal regulations such as the Sarbanes-Oxley Act (SOX) or the requirements of the Food and Drug Administration (FDA) but also in the light of general IT governance. In close collaboration with customers, SAP has introduced new functions for traceability management in SAP Solution Manager.

Traceability

Traceability management extends the SAP Solution Manager options in the *document management* and *project structure editing* areas.

The digital signature plays an important role in document management in a regulated environment. You can use a digital signature to sign electronic documents digitally. When you process digital data, a digital signature has the same function as a written signature on printed documents. Digital signatures uniquely identify the signer of a digital document.

Document management

Digital signatures can be used in a wide range of scenarios, enabling you to do the following:

► Confirm that a document has been read or approved (e.g., approval of final document versions for Business Blueprint documents).

► Protect the integrity of data (e.g., signatures on tester notes or other documents for auditing purposes).

SAP Solution Manager offers functions that make it possible to trace changes:

► When digitally signed documents are displayed and printed, the signature is always displayed or printed automatically. To ensure the security and integrity of your data, this function cannot be suppressed.

► The history of documents shows all of the information about the changes made to documents, including the digital signature processes.

► Reporting enables you to create reports for documents.

Editing the project structure

To facilitate working with project structures in a regulated environment, SAP Solution Manager provides corresponding functions:

► As an example, you can lock structure nodes that you have finished editing in the project structure, for example, in the Business Blueprint (Transaction SOLAR01). This is especially important if the steering committee of the project has approved a structure. By locking these structure nodes, you can prevent project members from making changes to parts of the project structure at a later date. To ensure the security and integrity of the data, you can use the digital signature to identify the user who has locked the nodes.

► Locking a structure still allows the tabs of the structure, for example, DOCUMENTATION, to be changed.

► If you have finished editing tab data in the project, you can lock the areas of the tab and therefore prevent other project members from making changes. Depending on the structure nodes, you can lock and unlock entries on the following tabs (tabs can also be locked with a digital signature):

  ► GEN. DOCUMENTATION

  ► PROJECT DOCUMENTATION

  ► ADMINISTRATION

  ► TRANSACTIONS

  ► END USER ROLES

  ► CONFIGURATION

  ► TEST CASES

  ► DEVELOPMENT

  ► TRAINING MATERIALS

Free attributes   To facilitate transparent documentation of your projects and to provide information exactly where it is needed, you can assign customer-specific attributes to the project at different levels. You can define these attributes for structure nodes in the project structure or assign attributes to certain objects.

Depending on the object, the following tabs are available for assigning attributes:

▶ GENERAL
General information about the object and assignment of keywords.

▶ CONNECTIONS
Assignment of documents.

▶ OTHER ATTRIBUTES
Customer-specific attributes and their assignment.

▶ HISTORY
Editing history.

After editing the attributes, you can lock them so that it is no longer possible for other project members to make changes.

The attribute values of an object are assigned to the combination of object and logical component. If you use the same object with the same logical component again in the project, the system automatically adopts the assigned attribute values so that you have centralized access to integrated system documentation.

4.6   SAP Solution Manager at Sanofi-Aventis Deutschland GmbH

The software met our expectations and was unusually easy to use. We have been able to further improve the quality of our system data, which is particularly important for maintenance and update processes, as well as the processes based on these. The integration of the individual tools in the environment of the system landscape management is effected even better than before in the new release of SAP Solution Manager, and it is particularly important for correct system data maintenance in the long term.

Ralf Punga, Sanofi

As one of the leading health companies worldwide, Sanofi researches, develops, and sells therapeutic solutions tailored to the patient's needs. The seven continually growing areas that are the strengths of Sanofi and that determine its product portfolio are diabetes, vaccines, innovative medication, rare diseases, consumer health, new markets, and animal health.

Sanofi-Aventis Deutschland GmbH

As a company in the pharmaceutical industry, quality and quality control are of great importance to us. Therefore, it is always of immediate interest to us to be offered opportunities for further improvement and automation in these areas and to evaluate these opportunities.

Project overview

With our ramp-up participation in the add-on *Landscape Verification 1.0 for SAP Solution Manager* in the fall of 2010, we were able to introduce a new tool with which, in combination with the System Landscape Directory (SLD) and the system landscape (Transaction SMSY) of SAP Solution Manager, we anticipated another step toward automating work steps that had previously been carried out manually for the correct maintenance of the product versions. Another object was to identify and correct potential errors or any incomplete system data descriptions.

Motivation

The main motivation for our early involvement and our participation in the ramp-up was to further increase the quality of our system data description, also with the objective of supporting our maintenance processes. In addition, we expected a reduction in the work required for our system data description.

The software met our expectations and was unusually easy to use.

We have been able to further improve the quality of our system data, which is particularly important for maintenance and update processes, as well as the processes based on these.

The integration of the individual tools in the environment of the system landscape management is effected even better than before in the new release of SAP Solution Manager, and it is particularly important for correct system data maintenance in the long term.

Project report

Our system landscape is largely made up of SAP applications, SAP BusinessObjects applications, and non-SAP applications, and is therefore very heterogeneous. On the one hand, this is dictated by the size and global orientation of our group, and on the other, by numerous large fusions in the group's history.

Starting situation and goals

Maintaining our system landscape in the Sanofi SAP Solution Manager constantly requires a lot of work and involves comprehensive manual maintenance tasks. However, as manual maintenance always comes with a certain risk of error, our interest in automating these processes was significant. Along with reducing the risk of error, the system data quality has always been a particular focus of our interest. Another goal was to reduce the maintenance workload.

The manual maintenance of system data in the central SAP Solution Manager had become more work-intensive and complex for us over time. Changes to the system data maintenance introduced by SAP, such as the handling of active or installed product versions, add-ons, and product instances from EHP systems that were dependent on the SAP Solution Manager stack used, made the correct manual system data maintenance very difficult and error-prone.

Manual system data maintenance

For this reason, we wanted to achieve automation for these process steps. By introducing and using a central SLD and making the corresponding adjustments in the SAP satellite systems worldwide, we got the SAP systems to report their system data automatically to the central SLD. With this central SLD as the data source, a corresponding system data entry is automatically created in the system landscape of the central SAP Solution Manager. Thus, a large part of the system data description for SAP Solution Manager is automated and free from potential errors due to manual data maintenance. However, this has not been the case for the product versions up to this point. These still had to be maintained manually.

Routes to automation

The Landscape Verification Tool closes this gap. It checks the product versions and generates the necessary correction proposals. The version of the Landscape Verification Tool available since December 2010 provides an assistant function to help the user make corrections, thus further improving the convenience of automatic data maintenance. After the required adjustments are completed, the synchronization of the system landscape can be performed.

Landscape verification

The Landscape Verification Tool was supplied as an add-on and thus enabled us to perform a comparatively fast software implementation. A stack update and related work-intensive test runs were therefore not required. At only 2MB, the add-on was relatively small. The minimum requirement was SAP Solution Manager 7.0 EHP1 SPS 18, and Sanofi already had SPS 20.

Implementation

After the implementation, we initially omitted an SAP Note search for the software component of the Landscape Verification Tool (ST-LV100).

Analysis of the
system landscape
data

The software description initially required the loading of the system data from the system landscape to a separate SMSY area. This was achieved in 20 to 30 minutes on the development system. The result we received was a list of systems that were classified as incomplete or containing errors. The classification of the missing system data descriptions and the errors was very precise. A check of these results revealed many unexpected warnings, and also a number of errors that we had to adjust immediately. However, some of the change proposals made by the tool were evaluated as definitely incorrect. As a consequence, we implemented various SAP Notes for the software component and repeated the loading procedure.

The second check on the proposed adjustments showed that the change proposals detected as incorrect in the first run were now detected correctly.

After the adjustment has been made in Transaction SMSY, in a final step, the changes have to be copied to the system landscape.

The Landscape Verification Tool is thus an ideal addition to the existing process. For the important product version assignment, the Landscape Verification Tool closes a gap in the SLD and allows the customer to make the required adjustments that are identified. In larger system landscapes, in which multiple SLDs are used, it is decisive to set up a coordinated SLD hierarchy. To achieve good results on a long-term basis, the SLD requires that the underlying CIM and the content repository (CR) be updated at specific intervals.

Another important point that is often overlooked is the regular maintenance of the Product and Production Management System Catalog (PPMS) in the system landscape of SAP Solution Manager.

Landscape
management
database

Along with its greater range of functions when compared to the system landscape, the landscape management database (LMDB) used in SAP Solution Manager 7.1 comprises a complete integration with regard to collaboration in the system data management for the managed systems connected to SAP Solution Manager, the SLD, and the SAP Service Marketplace (SMP). Additional convenience is also provided by the integration or connection of the Landscape Verification Tool in the LMDB. Thus the former add-on is copied into the SAP Solution Manager standard system and made available to all customers. This integration of the individual tools is of major significance for long-term correct system data management.

In the course of the introduction of the Landscape Verification Tool, we also realized that every installed software component in the system landscape of SAP Solution Manager should have a product version written to it (e.g., VIRSA, SAP GRC, products from third parties).

Conclusion

Finally, we conclude that the software was easy to use and provided us with very good support in the maintenance of our system landscapes. Using it improved our system data quality very significantly, and we would unreservedly recommend using it, even to experienced SAP Solution Manager experts.

The Author

Ralf Punga studied Computer Science at Darmstadt University from 1983 to 1987. In 1987, he joined Hoechst AG in IT Pharma Controlling, where he was responsible for the introduction of a new global reporting system. In the course of a number of major fusions, he switched responsibilities to the areas of *Financial Reporting/Management IS*, and later *Global Finance Integration IS*. Since 2006, he has been at the SAP Customer Competence Center Network Management (CCC) and is responsible for SAP Solution Manager in the Sanofi Group.

When implementing software solutions, you first define your requirements, initiate a project, and execute this using your selected procedure model. SAP supports you with methods, content, and tools.

5   Implementing Solutions

The following sections present tools and functions in SAP Solution Manager that support you when implementing solutions. The *Solution Implementation* process in Application Lifecycle Management (ALM) includes the *Requirements, Design, Build & Test*, and *Deploy* project phases. Before a project begins, you collect and evaluate all functional and non-functional requirements during *the Requirements* phase. In the *Design* phase, you define the scope of your project in the Business Blueprint based on the results of the *Requirements* phase. It documents how your applications or business processes are planned and in which application or IT environment they are to be mapped. The goal of the *Build & Test* phase is to implement the business processes defined in the Business Blueprint according to the defined requirements. For this, you configure the planned business processes, add your company-specific requirements to them, and test them. In the *Deploy* phase, you pass the application on for live operation. Your communication channels are critical for the implementation of solutions because they enable the smooth transfer of information to end users before the solutions go live. When the application has been passed on for live operation and the go-live has been completed, the newly introduced or changed business processes can be used in the daily operations.

5.1 Accelerated and Process-Oriented Implementation by Means of SAP Standard Content

Challenges

Innovation versus stability is the pair of opposites that companies find themselves confronted with when implementing solutions. Fast and efficient introduction of new business processes with minimal risk for live operations is the challenge posed for companies seeking to maintain and increase their competitiveness. Optimizing value chains has become a major objective, demanding a greater emphasis on individual business processes. IT must be able to support changes in your company flexibly and quickly. This also means performing a business process-oriented software implementation quickly and efficiently. The SAP standard content supports you here, in particular in the *Requirements, Design*, and *Build & Test* project phases.

Optimizing value chains

The *Business Process Repository* (BPR) supplied in SAP Solution Manager, also known as the SAP standard content, provides you with a good starting point for introducing SAP solutions. Predefined process models help you during the definition and company-specific modeling of business procedures; configuration information supports you in implementing them on the system side. In just a few steps, you can add the special features in process flows specific to your company, as well as the required software configuration connected to this, and integrate them into the overall model.

5.1.1 Structure

Business Process Repository (BPR)

The BPR is a structured directory of business processes. All the scenarios and processes are available centrally and are grouped together based on business and content factors.

The meta model of these supplied business processes is made up of three levels (see Figure 5.1):

▶ **Business scenario**
The *business scenario* is an element of the SAP reference structure. A scenario represents a comprehensive business process as a

sequence of various individual processes that are connected with each other in terms of chronology and logic. To graphically represent a scenario, the design model of the event-driven process chain is used.

▶ **Business process**

A *business process* is a chronological–logical sequence of processes and functions that caters for an external or internal target group in providing a defined service.

▶ **Process step**

The *process step* is the smallest self-contained unit in a business scenario. The process step is an action item within the framework of a business task (action item within the framework of a process). A process step is run in precisely one SAP application component.

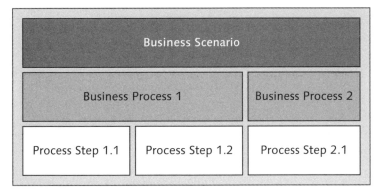

Figure 5.1 Meta Model for Business Processes

The overall structure of the BPR (see Figure 5.2) is divided into the *Organizational* and *Solutions/Applications* areas. The *Organizational* area is made up of all the available processes. To make it clearer and easier to use, this section is arranged on the basis of the areas in a generic value chain (such as sales, marketing, and purchasing). The *Solutions/Applications* area contains the cross-scenario basic settings and all the scenarios and processes, arranged based on solutions — including the industries.

Figure 5.2 Structure of the Business Process Repository

5.1.2 Contents

On every level of business processes (business scenario, business process, and process step), you will find information that supports you when carrying out your *Design* and *Build & Test* phases.

Textual and graphical descriptions

The description of the business significance of the business scenario and the business process is comprised of the technical requirements as well as a textual and graphical illustration. The text description contains the business context of the business process. The graphic description represents the business process in the form of a flow diagram and also maps the corresponding underlying software solutions. Figure 5.3 shows what is known as the component view. The component view is automatically derived from the structural description of the business process. Process steps in the business process structure that are defined by you are also automatically integrated into the component view and represented accordingly.

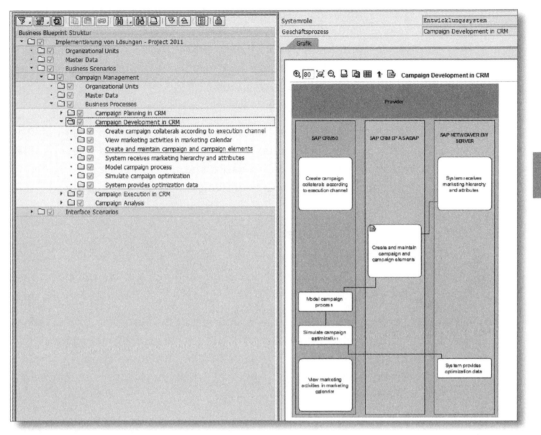

Figure 5.3 Component View

The process level contains the actual content for the implementation. This content can be found in Transactions SOLAR01 and SOLAR02, on the TRANSACTIONS and CONFIGURATION tab pages for the business process selected. From here, SAP Solution Manager grants you direct access to the customizing of the relevant development and Customizing system. There, you can quickly make the necessary entries in the specified sequence. Additional documentation on Customizing gives you a better understanding of the business context of the system settings you need to make, thereby enabling you to tailor the customer-specific requirements flexibly and optimally. Where necessary and practical, comparable content also exists on the business scenario and individual process step levels.

Basic settings   Basic settings are system settings that have to be made for all business processes. As they apply to all scenarios, they can be found at the level of the component(s) on which the respective business process is based. Basic settings also include Customizing settings, transactions, and further explanations.

Portal roles   Scenarios and processes can be grouped to form *portal roles*. A role therefore comprises scenarios and processes for a user group. The BPR contains configuration information for standard roles. As roles often comprise multiple scenarios and processes, they are stored in the context of the relevant component (like the basic settings).

5.1.3   Product Dependency

The BPR is constantly evolving, partly in a process of continuous improvement, but also to reflect developments in the associated software products.

Versioning   To take into account the release dependency of the SAP standard content, different content versions are created, and these are shown in accordance with the selected software constellation (i.e., which products go with which release) when the business scenarios are selected.

5.1.4   Outlook

Value chains and their business processes continue to change in a dynamic economic environment. As software solutions are always evolving, the BPR adapts to any changes. The content and the modeling are optimized and expanded at regular intervals, and they are updated by means of the ST-ICO software component of SAP Solution Manager.

You will find the current status in the online version of the BPR (*https://implementationcontent.sap.com/bpr*). Here you can view the business scenarios and business processes available along with the relevant descriptions and graphics.

5.2   ASAP Implementation Method

The *ASAP implementation method* is the proven, reusable, and successful SAP method for implementing SAP solutions in all industries and customer environments. The ASAP implementation method is divided into phases and is a result-oriented method that streamlines implementation projects, minimizes risks, and reduces the overall implementation costs. ASAP provides a consistent approach for project management, organizational change management, solution management, and for other disciplines applied when implementing SAP solutions. The method supports project teams with templates, tools, questionnaires, and checklists, such as guidelines and accelerators. With ASAP, companies can utilize the benefits of the accelerated functions and tools already integrated into the SAP solutions.

5.2.1   Scope and Usage

The ASAP implementation method is provided in the form of a road-map that reflects years of experience with SAP projects. The ASAP Implementation Roadmap comprises the following:

Scope of the roadmap

▶ Provides processes and proven business procedures for the implementation of SAP applications and solutions.

▶ Provides a framework for project management that complies with the *Project Management Institute Project Management Body Of Knowledge* (PMI PMBOK) industry standard.

▶ Covers all the project activities required for the implementation of SAP solutions and applications, whereby a significant emphasis is on guiding the project team through the lifecycle of project management, value management, business process management, and ALM in the course of the project.

▶ Provides clear recommendations for projects that intend to provide one or more services at a global level. Global sourcing enables major savings to be made in all types of projects.

▶ Deals with technical aspects of the implementation process, such as planning and designing the infrastructure, setting up the system landscape, and installing and configuring the software.

The benefits of ASAP include the following:

► Faster implementations with a fast and focused method.

► More reliable projects thanks to proven tools, accelerators, and business procedures.

► Less risk due to the use of a formal quality management process.

► Lower costs due to use of accelerating techniques and the more efficient use of project resources.

► Effective project management based on the standards of the PMI.

5.2.2 Roadmap Phases

The ASAP Implementation Roadmap is divided into six phases:

► **Phase 1: Project Preparation**
In this phase, the project team initiates, plans, and prepares your SAP project. You define the main characteristics of your project plan, agree on project standards, draw up a schedule, and assemble the project team. This is also the point at which you implement the business case in the implementation scope and plan the technical requirements and the infrastructure.

► **Phase 2: Business Blueprint**
In this phase, the project team works out how the enterprise wants to conduct its business operations with the SAP application. In the process, the project team uses proven business procedures from SAP to achieve an optimal relationship between using Best Practices and using its own procedures for the specific business processes of the enterprise. The result is a Business Blueprint, a compilation of process requirements on the basis of business scenarios describing how the system should work. The document also exposes gaps for which you have to develop expansions. This phase is completed when all the people involved have approved the Business Blueprint.

► **Phase 3: Realization**
In this phase, the requirements worked out in the Business Blueprint phase are implemented in the development system, and the functions are tested in the quality assurance system. In larger projects, you can break down the implementation process into a series of cycles to give you more control over how the business

processes are configured, developed, and tested. Integration tests are performed after the configuration phase to ensure that the system is ready to go live. In this phase, the project team also puts together solution-related documentation and prepares training materials, so that user training can begin.

▶ **Phase 4: Preparations for Going Live**
In this phase, the team finalizes plans for the cutover activities, the data transfer, and the production operation. The user training courses are completed. The team performs non-functional tests, including the performance and system load tests. Any critical open items should be addressed during this phase. When this phase is complete, the solution is ready to go live. A support organization has been set up to provide solution support.

▶ **Phase 5: Support for Going Live**
In this phase, the team provides support for the solution. This is during the period that directly follows the cutover into the production system. Unforeseen aspects such as additional production support, extraordinary monitoring processes, and special technical support are planned and implemented in this phase. At the end of the additional support phase, sustainable production support processes that are planned in the go-live preparation and executed as part of the go-live support become the central support to ensure continuous improvement of the production solution. In this project phase, the project is formally completed.

▶ **Phase 6: Operation**
In this phase, IT departments are provided with structured support when setting up efficient ALM processes and standards, with which the solution's readiness for operation can be ensured. *Readiness for operation* means the ability to keep IT solutions in a functioning state. In the process, the system availability and the required performance level are ensured, among other things, and this guarantees that the business processes flow smoothly. The central operating platform is SAP Solution Manager, together with the solution documented in the project documentation.

5.2.3 Structure of the ASAP Method

The ASAP method is structured according to project activities (deliverables). On the highest level are the *roadmap phases* (level 1), which comprise *project work streams* (level 2). These, in turn, are grouped into *project activities (deliverables)* (level 3).

To completely reflect the terminology and the principle of the breakdown of the project structure plan of the PMI, the terms *deliverable* and *subdeliverable* are used in ASAP. Subdeliverables are occasionally used to break down larger and more complex deliverables. Project managers can thus plan and control the work more efficiently over the entire project lifecycle.

Deliverables   The ASAP Roadmap provides access to *accelerator documents and tools* throughout the structure. With the accelerators and their templates, patterns, and other aids that can be used by the project team, your project deliverables can be performed more quickly.

The advantages of this new, streamlined project planning structure are obvious: Project managers can better manage deliverables and therefore better monitor the current status of the project.

5.2.4   Business Add-Ons for the ASAP Method

The *business add-ons for the ASAP method* add modular implementation content to the ASAP Roadmap. Business add-ons contain tried and tested content for the implementation of various industry solutions and solution packages, as well as content for other areas, such as the method of agile software development, business process management, service-oriented architecture, and EA governance and strategy frameworks. You can find more information on business add-ons for the ASAP method on the SAP Service Marketplace under *http://service.sap.com/asap-business-add-ons*.

5.2.5   Working with the Run SAP and ASAP Implementation Roadmaps

The roadmap structure is made up of *phases*, *work streams* or *project activities (deliverables)*. You can see these on the left side of the screen (see Figure 5.4). On the top-right, you see the *topic node description texts* that describe the *inputs, the outputs*, and the *activities* and *tasks* that are required to complete the project deliverables.

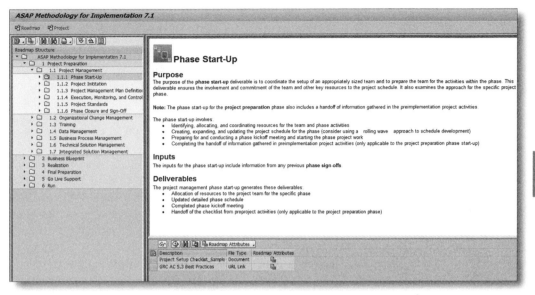

Figure 5.4 Structure of the ASAP Roadmap

At the bottom-right, you can see the *accelerators* available for the selected roadmap nodes. These include examples, templates, white papers, guidelines, and links to the SAP Help Portal and to further information on the SAP Service Marketplace, namely additional material that will help you complete your implementation project more quickly.

Auxiliary material

The roadmap itself comprises accelerators that explain how SAP Solution Manager can be used optimally to enable the project teams to achieve their implementation goals in every project phase.

Material for the implementation with Run SAP

The Run SAP roadmap provides the following accelerators for implementing end-to-end operating standards:

▶ **Documentation of the standard**
Each standard contains Best Practice descriptions of specific tasks, explanations of the tools used in SAP Solution Manager, and training and services available from SAP, which support you when implementing the standard.

▶ **Implementation methods for the standard**
These documents describe the steps required to define, implement, and deploy end-to-end operating processes, and to adapt them to new scenarios.

▶ **Documentation of industry-specific aspects of operation**
Best Practice documents for specific industries, such as retail, util-
ities, or banking, can be selected by using an attribute filter (see
the section on *Attributes*). These documents relate to industry-specific aspects of IT operations; for example, mass data processing or
period-end closing.

**Material for the
implementation
with ASAP**

SAP Solution Manager supports the project team in all the phases of
the ASAP Implementation Roadmap. Project teams are expressly
advised to use the following SAP Solution Manager guidelines:

▶ **"SAP Solution Manager Usage Guidelines" deliverable in the
project preparation phase**
Detailed guidelines for the project team that describe how SAP
Solution Manager is set up and used in the course of an implementation project. It explains how SAP Solution Manager is used, from
the project preparation, blueprint creation, configuration, development, and testing, to the transfer of the solution documentation
into the Solution Directory for daily operation.

▶ **"SAP Solution Manager and Business Process Management"
deliverable in the Business Blueprint phase**
This deliverable provides the project team with clear guidelines
for using SAP Solution Manager in the Business Blueprint phase. It
comprises a number of helpful accelerators that support the
project team when setting up SAP Solution Manager to get optimal results when creating the blueprint. It also contains up-to-date
templates for the solution documentation that are recommended
for all implementation projects.

Attributes

In addition to accelerators, every structure node has the following
attributes, making it easier for project teams to find the correct information:

▶ **Subject areas**
Deliverables are assigned to one or more subject areas, which represent the different fields of knowledge and experience in the
implementation project. Examples are business process management, organization change management, project management and
training.

▶ **Variants**

A variant shows which area of the structure is relevant for a specific solution. Selecting a variant allows you to generate a solution-specific view of the roadmap, showing only the content that applies to the solution that your team is implementing. You choose the variant when you create a project in SAP Solution Manager and define the solution scope (see Section 5.2.1). Since ASAP Implementation Roadmap version 7.0, variants are used to provide business add-ons for the ASAP method, which add solution-specific or cross-solution content to the central ASAP method.

▶ **Roles**

The ROLE attribute shows which roles are involved in the execution of tasks, activities, or outputs. The role description represents expert knowledge for various project team roles, such as business consultant or project manager. This information can be used to create a roles and responsibilities matrix for the project or for a part of the project.

You can combine these attributes to define your own filters that display the information you want to find, such as which business process requirements an application consultant has to fulfill for the implementation of an SAP for Retail application.

5.3 Project Administration as the Cornerstone of Project Preparation

Project Administration as the cornerstone of project preparation is the starting point of the *Design* phase. When you define this general project data at an early stage, you provide a solid basis for implementing your software successfully and running your project efficiently. All the information and steps required for this, which are generally valid for all projects, regardless of the objectives, scope, and priorities, are provided for you by means of the ASAP Roadmap.

Defining basic conditions

With the Project Administration (Transaction SOLAR_PROJECT_ ADMIN or PLANNING view in the *Implementation/Upgrade* work center), SAP Solution Manager offers support for managing project standards and project team members, rough time planning, and project-related structuring of the system landscape.

5.3.1 Project Administration

All projects and project types

Project Administration gives you an overview of all the projects in SAP Solution Manager. Here, you create new projects and administer all existing projects. When implementing SAP solutions, you work with an implementation project. You can easily apply the knowledge gathered here to other project types because the functions in SAP Solution Manager are essentially identical for all project types. Other project types include the following:

▸ *Template projects* for creating global templates as a starting point for global rollouts or SAP partner solutions

▸ *Upgrade projects* for upgrading a solution

▸ *Maintenance projects* for continuous solution maintenance and managing requests for change

5.3.2 Creating an Implementation Project

Documentation of the general data

The implementation project is used to implement solutions. When creating an implementation project, you first assign a project ID abbreviation and a meaningful project title. If the planned project is based on an existing solution, you can select this when creating the project, thus achieving the desired transparency. The general data is entered on the GENERAL DATA tab page. Here, you store information on the areas of responsibility of the project manager, the project status, the basic project data (e.g., start of project, end of project), and the project language. The project language is valid for the entire project duration and is relevant for the documentation of business scenarios[1] and business processes.[2] After the project is saved, it is no longer possible to change the project language. In the project description, you can outline your project roughly and, for example, store your project setup checklist, which is provided in the ASAP Roadmap. This includes, for example, information on the project planning, organization, change tracking, monitoring, and quality assurance.

---

1 The term *business scenario* is used in SAP Solution Manager, also referred to here as *scenario*. The equivalent term *business scenario* is also used in the documentation of these scenarios.

2 The term *business process* is used in SAP Solution Manager, also referred to here as simply *process*.

5.3.3 Defining the Project Scope and the Procedure

The project scope—that is, the definition of the changes or improvements to be introduced in your company in the course of the project—is based on an as-is analysis and customer-specific requirements.

For assessing and representing the business benefits of innovation, SAP tools such as the *Business Function Prediction Service for SAP ERP* (*www.service.sap.com/erp-ehp*) or the *SAP Solution Composer* (*www.service.sap.com/bmet*) provide you with an initial approach. You prepare and specify the project scope in the Business Blueprint. For more information, see Section 5.4.

Assessing and defining local innovations

In the Project Administration, you define the project-specific methodology, and, if applicable, select template projects that are to provide the basis for the implementation.

The roadmap supports you when carrying out a project. Templates and information on the project preparation for an implementation project are available to you directly in the ASAP Roadmap. The corresponding templates are used as accelerators for your project. You can save time by copying these templates as standards or adjusting them to meet your requirements. You will find the corresponding templates and information in the roadmap structure. You use the *roadmap selection* to select the current version of the ASAP Roadmap for your implementation project. You can now use the selected roadmap for your specific project, which means that you can enter statuses and notes in the project phases, assign employees to individual work steps, create messages and project documentation, and add keywords. The existing filter functions enable every project employee to restrict the roadmap structure according to their requirements. For more information on working with roadmaps, see Section 5.2. If your implementation project is based on globally defined template projects or on predefined implementation packages (solution packages), you can select these in the Project Administration as a basis for the implementation. Selecting and using global templates, and implementing them worldwide, is dealt with in the template management process (Chapter 6), so we will not be looking at it in detail here.

Methodology and templates as basis and accelerator

5.3.4 Managing Project Team Members

Creating project team members

You use the resource assignment in the Project Administration to centrally manage the task distribution in your implementation project. Before project team members can be assigned to a project, you require a system user. If no system user has been created for your planned team members yet, you can perform this task directly using the PROJECT TEAM MEMBERS tab page. The link to the USER ADMINISTRATION (Transaction SU01) makes your maintenance work easier. You can quickly create new system users from the project or select existing system users and add them to the project. You thus identify them as project team members. In the ROLE DESCRIPTION column, you define the tasks for which the project team member is responsible. The project team members are assigned the authorizations they require to complete their tasks in the project. SAP Solution Manager provides predefined authorization roles for defined target groups, which you can adjust to meet your requirements at any time. You will find up-to-date information on system roles and authorizations in the security guide of SAP Solution Manager on the SAP Service Marketplace under *www.service.sap.com/instguides*.

Project authorizations

The assignment of project team members in the implementation project is used again in the roadmap, the Business Blueprint, and the configuration. All project team members have change authorization for the whole project. However, you can use the *Project Administration* to restrict access in the Business Blueprint and configuration areas to the project team members assigned to the business processes. This control is based on the RESTRICT CHANGING NODES IN THE PROJECT TO ASSIGNED TEAM MEMBERS indicator in the Project Administration.

Changing the project team

The assignment of team members to the project structure leads to a better overview for the individual employees in the project work. The project team members can use the filter function to restrict the project structure so that only the parts assigned to a certain team member are displayed. You can also reduce the administration work you have to do when organizational changes are made during the project. In the central administration for project team members, you can replace or remove team members centrally. A history of all changes is recorded, guaranteeing complete traceability.

If your implementation project is used by external resources, you often have central contact persons in the partner company. You can also maintain these project team members here.

Storing partner companies

5.3.5 Defining the System Landscape

In the central maintenance of the system landscape of SAP Solution Manager (see Figure 5.5), your system administrator defines the relevant physical systems, creates the communication with the systems using suitable RFC connections, and groups the systems into logical components. A logical component combines various physical systems with the same SAP product release according to their role in the system group (e.g., development system, quality assurance system, production system).

Fast project start with logical components

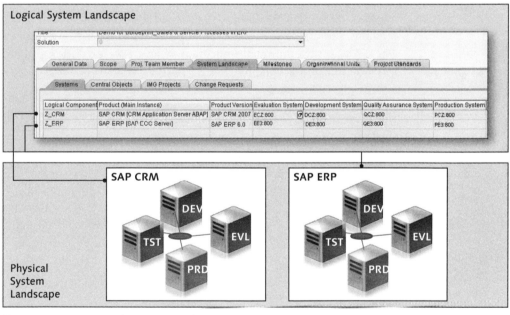

Figure 5.5 Maintaining the System Landscape

In the Project Administration, you select the logical components affected by the implementation.

If no physical systems exist yet at the start of the project, it's sufficient if you only define the logical components and add the systems at a later time. This enables you to document the process model in the Business Blueprint without any physical systems existing, even though the system landscape is not yet complete at the start of the project. It's only important that the development system is set up at the time of the configuration and the system landscape maintenance is known. Here, the configuration settings in the development system are controlled by SAP Solution Manager using the RFC connections. The separation of logical components and physical systems also enables you to manage the systems centrally and make changes in all the projects affected without any extra work. For more information on maintaining the system landscape, see Chapter 4, Section 4.1.

5.3.6 Defining the Project-Specific Milestones

Milestones are an important part of the project controlling and also play a role in other phases of the ALMs in SAP Solution Manager (for information on Quality Gate Management and change control management, see Chapter 8). SAP supplies a series of defined milestones that represent the minimal basic data of an implementation project and are indicated as quality gates (Q-Gates).

Milestones and quality gates

In a Q-Gate, you decide whether a project can proceed to the next phase. In Quality Gate Management, for example, you can control whether transports can be imported into systems or not. In the Project Administration, you can assign document templates to a Q-Gate as standards for the Q-Gate documents. If you have selected a roadmap for implementing your project, it can contain milestones that go beyond the predefined basic data. You can also take over these milestones and flag them as Q-Gates if required. You can also manually add milestones, thus modifying your project individually.

5.3.7 Storing Organizational Units

To ensure transparency between your implementation project and organizational units that are affected by your project, it helps to store the organizational units in the Project Administration. You have the option of distinguishing central organizational units using relevant information data such as number of employees, location, function in company, or time zone.

5.3.8 Defining Project Standards

As the project manager, you define your project standards centrally in the Project Administration. The objective is for your project team members to work consistently during the implementation project according to the standards you defined. This makes standardized communication within the project easier (e.g., for project progress and assessments) and reduces unnecessary searching for document templates. Project standards in the Project Administration comprise standard status values, keywords, and documentation types:

▶ **Central status values**
Central status values help you with the administration of your implementation project, in the Business Blueprint and the configuration.

▶ **Keywords**
Keywords support you to filter the project scope by team, subproject, or scenario in subsequent project phases, for example.

▶ **Structure and object attributes**
Structure and object attributes support you in all types of filter and reporting functions over the entire lifecycle. In contrast to keywords, these attributes are passed on through all phases of the implementation, thus enabling you to use them even after the go-live.

▶ **Standardized documentation types**
Standardized documentation types (see Figure 5.6) are used for documentation in the Business Blueprint and the configuration.

Standard documents, keywords, and status

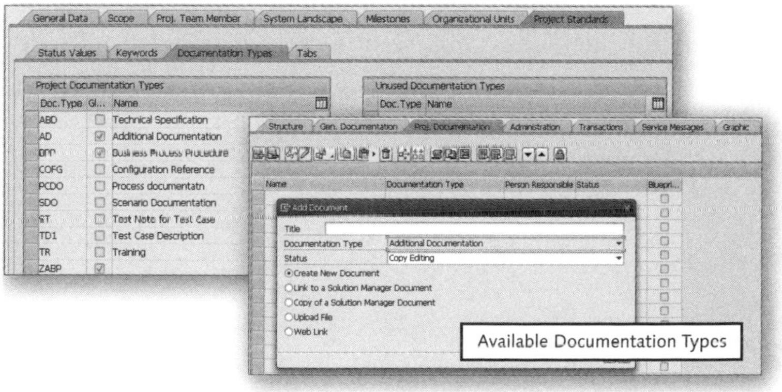

Figure 5.6 Defined and Available Documentation Types

With the documentation types, you have the option of storing document templates. These are then called up when a document is created, and they guarantee you standardized documentation in your project. Status values give you an effective means of monitoring how work is progressing in different project phases. SAP supplies default values for documentation types and status values. You can also change these standards to meet your requirements or define your own standards. For the documentation of an implementation project, we recommend creating the following documentation types, which you can then use as a standard:

Recommended documentation types

▶ Business process description

▶ Functional specification

▶ Configuration description

▶ Authorization concept

▶ Technical specification

▶ Test case description

▶ Template for user training

Which documentation types you actually use will vary greatly from project to project. As such, the document types listed here are intended only as a recommendation. We do not recommend that you include documentation types for the project control; for example, meeting minutes, status reports, and organizational diagrams.

Status values for project versus status values for documentation types

Documentation types are stored using the *project template*. Status values can also be assigned to the documentation types. However, these values differ from the status values that define the progress of the project. Status profiles for documentation types are also used for digital signatures in documents, which is particularly helpful to customers working in validated environments. Suitable status profiles for documents include the following:

▶ Z_NEW

▶ Z_PROCESS

▶ Z_APPROVAL

▶ Z_RELEASED

You define status profiles for document types in Customizing using the Implementation Guide (IMG) for SAP Solution Manager.

5.4 Business Blueprint—Conceptual Design for Your Solution

The objective of the Business Blueprint is to define the project scope; that is, to document the conceptual design of the solution being implemented and the resultant requirements. The design drawn up describes how your enterprise wants to map its business processes using SAP and non-SAP systems.

SAP Solution Manager supports you in creating this conceptual design with Transaction SOLAR1 (Business Blueprint) and the PLAN-NING view of the *Implementation/Upgrade* work center.

5.4.1 Structure of the Business Blueprint

Implementation projects can have very different starting points. Some projects have only a broadly defined scope and use the *BPR* (see Section 5.1) as a starting point for the implementation project. Other projects may be based on the results of the analysis of the Solution Documentation Assistant (see Chapter 4, Section 4.2) or on process models or documentation outside SAP Solution Manager. Irrespective of the starting point, the goal is always to find the optimal way of integrating or setting up existing processes as part of a harmonized overall concept. The team usually holds a series of workshops to gradually break down the requirements from solution level to business process level. The ASAP Roadmap provides you with templates and information for setting up the documentation of the Business Blueprint.

Integrating existing processes

In the Business Blueprint transaction (SOLAR01), you depict your conceptual design as a process-oriented structure (process structure) with, similarly to the meta model of the BPR, three levels: business scenarios, business processes, and process steps (see Figure 5.7). Organizational units, master data, and interfaces complete your conceptual design. These elements are also referred to as *structure items*.

Concept of the process structure

If you're using additional levels, we recommend working with virtual levels by using naming conventions for prefixes (short names or numbers). Your project work will be easier if you use no more than five levels. The process-centric view you draw up for the Business Blueprint is the basis for all subsequent project stages of your implementation project, and it can also be used for business process monitoring in daily operation (see Chapter 11, Section 11.1). The required work that you put in here pays off in later project phases. It is not generally advisable to structure your model based on functional units, such as organizations, business departments, persons responsible, or SAP components. You can deal with these aspects by assigning keywords or structure and object attributes. A reduced display in the structure level, views required for user groups, for example, can be created using filter functions in the Business Blueprint and the configuration.

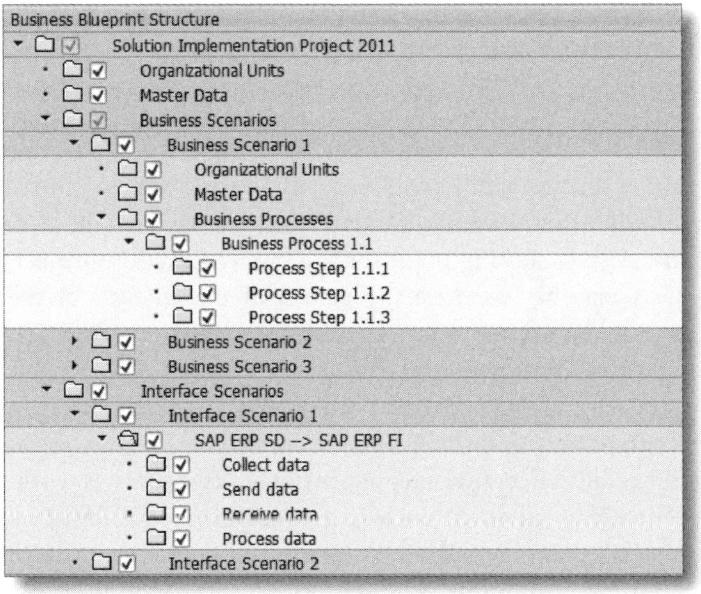

Figure 5.7 Concept of the Business Blueprint Structure

Lifecycle of business processes

Before setting up your Business Blueprint, you should consider that business processes, like systems, are also subject to a lifecycle (see Figure 5.8). Optimizing and adjusting operative business processes requires, among other things, changes in organizational areas, system adjustments, and therefore the necessity of updating your documentation. If you set up your Business Blueprint on the basis of process structures already documented—such as BPR content or templates—the match function gives you a quick overview of whether and how this process has changed. If the adjustments made to the process also affect your implementation project, use the match function to copy them to your project, thus reducing the documentation work you have to do and ensuring that the new process flow is also in your Business Blueprint.

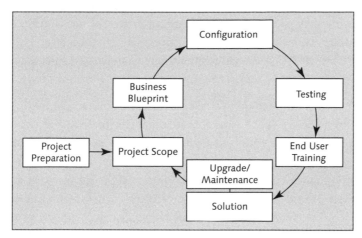

Figure 5.8 Lifecycle of Projects and Business Processes

The structure of the Business Blueprint can be based on various sources:

► Using predefined business processes from the BPR

► Reusing business processes from operative solutions

► Reusing business processes from other projects

► Setting up customer-specific business processes without a reference

In the BPR, SAP supplies predefined content for SAP applications and solutions (see Section 5.1). This includes the business processes supported by the application, business descriptions, assignments to business functions in the application, assignments to SAP functions in the form of transactions, Web Dynpro applications, URLs, and so on, as well as assignments to the configuration. The assignments to business functions support you in the technical implementation of innovations using enhancement packages. Building on this content in your project reduces the effort you spend on implementing and adjustments. On the STRUCTURE tab page, if you use the input help to select the elements that correspond to your implementation scope from the BPR, you are shown the SAP product combinations that you require as a minimum to operate the corresponding scenario. If you have already defined a system landscape in your Project Administration that maps this

Structure setup based on the BPR

scenario, the corresponding version is dark, and otherwise has a gray background. You can also select the versions with a gray background. If necessary, the system advises you about whether you need additional system components to run the corresponding processes and automatically matches the project system landscape. When SAP reference elements are selected, all the existing assignments are copied into your project. SAP reference elements are available in different languages.

Customer-specific adjustments

Because customers almost always need to make some adjustments, you can adjust the reference elements (project documentation, process graphics, etc.) and add your own content. In addition to the options just described, you can insert new process steps into the processes without losing the information about the origin of the process. Keeping the relationship to the original SAP reference elements is important for the lifecycle model of processes because it equips you for quick changes and future upgrades, enabling you to use the match function to identify and copy relevant new features and changes.

Reusing processes from operative solutions

Not all customers who use SAP Solution Manager start by implementing new solutions. Customers who deploy Business Process Monitoring for an operational solution must have already defined business processes, which they can reuse in an implementation project. They need only assign the operational solution to the project. This enables you to copy business processes to your project from the customer solution using input help. The reference relationship is also kept during the copying process, and you can update your Business Blueprint using the match function.

Reusing processes from other projects

Business processes already defined can also be used in other projects to map the process structure, reducing the time and effort required to describe the processes. In particular, you can map your customer-specific processes as a reference in a template project. You can thus also use other projects as a data source for setting up the process structure, and also use the match function.

Setting up customer-specific processes without a reference

You can also set up a partial or complete process structure without using reference elements. However, in this case, you will not be able to compare your processes against SAP reference processes at a later stage, for example, as part of an upgrade project. You also have to make all assignments yourself, such as transactions and IMG assignments for the configuration. Therefore, always investigate the possibility of referring to SAP reference elements at least at the process level, even if you change these later for your specific project. However, you always have access to comparison functions for viewing changes to SAP reference elements that are relevant to a particular project and copying them if necessary. You can delete redundant reference elements that you have copied from the BPR, provided you have made a conscious decision that they are definitely not needed. If you cannot confirm this, or if certain processes might be implemented in a subsequent phase, we recommend that you use the scoping function to hide processes from the project scope that will be implemented later on.

However, if you still decide to set up the process structure without reference elements, along with manually setting up the structure of your processes, you can create the partially automated transfer of analysis results from the Solution Documentation Assistant or external process documentation, for example. Selecting and handling the automatic setting up of the process structure is described in the *Solution Documentation* process (see Chapter 4, Section 4.5).

You assign general, cross-scenario master data (such as material masters, business partners, countries, measurement units) directly to the implementation project (MASTER DATA structure node) above the scenarios. You must define scenario-specific master data below the respective scenarios. The same applies to ORGANIZATIONAL UNITS.

Master data and organizational units

If a structure item appears more than once in the project structure, it is advisable to define a master structure item, such as a dominant process, as a template for other processes. If you change the master process, you can transfer changes easily to the copied processes (ADJUST TO ORIGINAL on the STRUCTURE tab page).

Multiple use of structure items

You document interfaces on the INTERFACE SCENARIOS structure node and map these on the interface scenario, interface, and interface attributes levels. To not lose your overview, you can define naming conventions for the interfaces. Here you can use, for example, your different interface technologies or your system landscape as a guideline. You store the documentation on the PROJECT DOCUMENTATION tab page. You maintain technical information for the interface, such as program names, as attribute values on the STRUCTURE tab page. In the graphic, you can assign these interfaces to business processes to complete your conceptual design.

Storing interfaces

5.4.2 Documenting the Conceptual Design

In the Business Blueprint, you describe the business objects (master data and organization) as well as the business process structure. By assigning software functions to business processes (as transactions, for instance), you define how the business processes run in the system on a daily basis. If you use predefined implementation content from the BPR, the scenario and business process descriptions are also supplied on the GEN. DOCUMENTATION tab page. You cannot change this documentation during implementation projects. Therefore, if you need to create project-specific documentation, you use the PROJ. DOCUMENTATION tab page. From the TRANSACTIONS tab page, you can call transactions, URLs, and programs to navigate to the relevant applications. This means that you can start conducting initial tests on these functions when creating the Business Blueprint, after you have already connected systems at this time. The BUSINESS FUNCTIONS tab page shows you the business functions that are relevant for the corresponding business process. Here, you can navigate to the documentation of the individual business functions and copy relevant business functions into the scope of your Business Blueprint.

Requirements in the conceptual design

In its documentation, the Business Blueprint contains information for the current situation, the requirements and implementation options, and the process flow—also displayed graphically. A functional vulnerability analysis can supply input for requirements regarding enhancements and customer developments (including interface definition, program developments, and data transfer). Furthermore, you can record requirements for end user training here, and for setting up authorizations and end user roles. Specifying the requirements therefore gives you a firm and comprehensive basis for implementing your solution.

When documenting the conceptual design, you can draw on SAP- or customer-specific documentation types and templates that you defined in the Project Administration (Transaction SOLAR_ PROJECT_ADMIN; see Section 5.3) and thereby ensure that the documentation process observes project standards. Project team members can refer to precompleted sample documents for a clear and consistent illustration of how to fill out the documents. It is also possible to attribute the documents and thus structure them more easily.

When you create project documentation in SAP Solution Manager, you can use the documents in various ways. Documentation is stored in the Knowledge Warehouse (KW), which is integrated into SAP Solution Manager. The following information refers to processes but also applies to other structure items in the project structure. You can do the following:

Storing and handling documents

▸ Use the templates defined in the Project Administration to create new documents.

▸ Create references to existing documents, that is, link to a particular document at a different place in the structure. You use this option if, for example, a process is used in multiple scenarios, and the process documentation is applicable to all the scenarios.

▸ Copy an existing document. This option is recommended if processes or scenarios are similar but not identical. You can use documentation for a similar process as a basis for tailoring the documentation from other processes. You need fewer resources to create documents, but the number of documents to be managed in SAP KW increases.

▸ Upload documents and therefore integrate existing documents from a central repository.

▸ Connect documents using links that were created in a different (external) repository, such as an intranet or file server, and for which migration is not economically feasible. This option has performance-related advantages too for all types of materials that require substantial memory space, such as web-based tutorials. Although such materials are stored locally, you can still incorporate and access them centrally via SAP Solution Manager.

▸ Check documents in and out. You can check documents out to edit offline. Checked-out documents are automatically locked against editing in SAP Solution Manager until they are checked in again.

▸ Use documentation from SAP or a template in your project documentation. Documents from SAP and templates are displayed on the GEN. DOCUMENTATION tab page; they must not be changed during implementation projects. You can refer to these documents from the project documentation. We recommend this option if you do not want to change the documents but still want to include them in the Business Blueprint document. Alternatively, you can copy documents, which is recommended if you want to tailor standard documentation.

User-specific
settings

User settings allow you to show and hide individual tab pages and to control the editing and displaying of documentation.

Process flow as
graphic

Besides documenting the business processes, you can also use graphics to display the actual process flow, and you can assign interfaces to the process flow. A graphic lets you store information that cannot otherwise be depicted in the process structure due to the structure's linear nature. The graphic on the tab page of the same name enables you to navigate between the structure levels and allows you to view how your conceptual design is made up. This includes business processes, logical components, and any products from third parties on which the processes run. One advantage of SAP Solution Manager is that it automatically proposes basic scenario and process graphics based on the process structure, which you can process further if necessary. For detailed modeling, you can embed graphics created in external modeling tools into your project as a separate documentation type, such as a process graphic.

5.4.3 Defining Persons Responsible

Organizationally, it is important to allocate persons responsible for the individual structure items in the process structure. Particularly in the case of cross-functional processes, clearly defined responsibilities are critical for efficient communication during the project, both when processes are mapped and when they are changed subsequently. You maintain information concerning team member responsibilities and other administrative data such as keywords on the ADMINISTRATION tab page.

Defining persons
responsible

You can also assign responsible project team members for the project documents; they need not be identical to the persons responsible for the processes or scenarios. On the PROJ. DOCUMENTATION tab page, the persons responsible for the documents set the current editing status, and thus create a basis for analysis. You can use the HISTORY tab page to trace the changes to the documents with the person responsible for it.

5.4.4 Completing the Business Blueprint

You can create an interim or final version of your Business Blueprint at any time as a Business Blueprint document and adjust the layout according to your requirements in the IMG (see Figure 5.9). You indicate any documents that you want to be included as BLUEPRINT-RELEVANT on the corresponding tab pages. You can select additional content when creating the Business Blueprint document. The document includes information relating to the following:

▸ Business areas

▸ Requirements regarding master data, organizational units, scenarios, and processes that are to be created

▸ Components required

▸ Scenario and process graphics

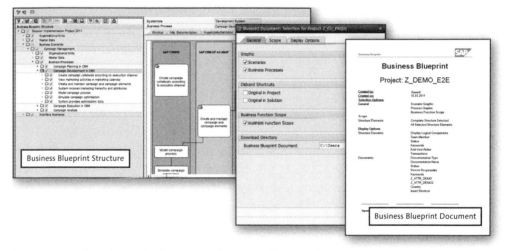

Figure 5.9 Business Blueprint Structure and Business Blueprint Document

One of the many options for generating documents is creating document parts. By selecting a suitable documentation type (such as *management summary*), you can merge (interim) status reports maintained by the document owners to form a complete management document. If necessary, you can also include the project description and other project planning documents in the Business Blueprint document by assigning them to the project documentation accordingly.

Creating document parts

The Business Blueprint phase ends with the *Blueprint sign-off*. The Business Blueprint is frozen at a particular point and signed off by process owners and IT managers from the individual areas. You freeze the Business Blueprint by setting a lock in the Project Administration. This specifically prevents changes being made to the

Blueprint sign-off

process structure, blueprint-relevant documents, or administrative data (SCOPE tab page, Transaction SOLAR_PROJECT_ADMIN; see Section 5.3). Subsequent changes must be requested explicitly and systematically using a Change Request Management procedure (see Chapter 8, Section 8.2).

5.5 Solution Configuration

The configuration of the solution is the starting point of the *Build* phase of your implementation project. The objective is to perform the configuration of your business processes based on the specification of the conceptual design. For this, the structure of the Business Blueprint is copied and implemented here. The results of this are the basis for customer enhancements and the subsequent testing.

In SAP Solution Manager, the Configuration transaction (Transaction SOLAR02) and the create view of the *Implementation/Upgrade* work center provide all the functions required for this. All the relevant information, such as the documentation, is found in the process structure. RFC connections link you to all the systems defined in the SAP Solution Manager system landscape, so that you can make settings directly in the respective systems.

5.5.1 Prerequisites for Configuration

Setting up and connecting the physical systems

To perform the configuration directly in the systems, the systems must be available and technically up to date. The Maintenance Optimizer (described in detail in the *Maintenance Management* process; see Chapter 12) helps you with installing and updating your system landscape. After the technical installation, the systems are connected to the Project Administration with the corresponding system roles. The configuration requires setting up and connecting development systems, and subsequent tests require connecting quality assurance systems. Additional preparations also required for performing the configuration are described in the following section.

Activating the business function

When implementing business functions, you have to activate them previously in the development system. All the business functions flagged with IN SCOPE in your Business Blueprint are considered for activation in the system landscape. To identify technical inconsistencies, you have the option of running *consistency checks* directly and, if necessary, making adjustments accordingly. The status displayed informs you which business functions in your system landscape are already activated and which still require activation. The actual activation is performed in the *Switch Framework* of the selected physical system in SAP Solution Manager.

Another prerequisite for the configuration is the creation of an IMG project. To perform the configuration, in the Project Administration (IMG PROJECTS tab page) of SAP Solution Manager, you create the corresponding IMG project used to make the basic and project-related configuration settings and group them into transport requests.

Creating a project-related IMG project

5.5.2 Basic Principles of the Configuration

In the Configuration transaction (Transaction SOLAR02), you configure your solution. Note that with the exception of documentation, all configuration settings are shipped with the respective application, not with SAP Solution Manager. What SAP Solution Manager does is provide an infrastructure for centrally accessing the system settings in the administered systems.

The configuration of your system landscape is based on the following configuration scenarios:

► Cross-scenario configuration

► Scenario- and process-specific configuration

The objective of the cross-scenario configuration is to make basic and global settings and cross-scenario settings in the systems relevant to your implementation project. Basic and global settings are required settings for performing the configuration of your conceptual design.

Cross-scenario configuration

Cross-scenario settings are relevant for multiple business processes and are often maintained in the same way. To set up the cross-scenario configuration structure, you select the STRUCTURE tab page on the CONFIGURATION node and create your configuration structure. You then have the option to access the content of the BPR or set up or create cross-scenario structures based on projects already documented. The configuration structure is not subject to any fixed level structure and can therefore be set up to any depth. To have a better overview, we recommend limiting yourself to three to five levels and defining the naming convention in advance.

If you use the SAP content in the BPR, you can access sources during the configuration, such as setting up communication connections between systems and scenario-related settings, which are valid for multiple scenarios or processes. If you are implementing only selected scenarios from a solution, the system proposes the configuration structures relevant to your selection, which you can amend if necessary. By selecting specific countries and industries, you can reduce the scope of the system's proposal. The settings listed on the CONFIGURATION tab page not only include individual IMG activities or groups of activities but also configuration documents for topics such as non-ABAP components, which supplement the IMG documentation. Preconfigured *Business Configuration Sets* (BC Sets) are available for certain solutions. You can activate them in the target system and adapt them as required.

Scenario- and process-specific configuration

The business scenario- and business process-specific configuration is derived from the structure of your conceptual design in the Business Blueprint transaction. Only in the Configuration transaction are you able to make configuration settings. There is no plan to expand the structure levels for the scenario- and process-specific configuration. Here it is also the case that if you use the content of the BPR, during the configuration, you can access information stored on the CONFIGURATION tab page.

Phased configuration

With complex or lengthy implementation projects, it can be helpful to break down the configuration process into a number of phases:

▶ **Baseline configuration**
The baseline configuration has a previously defined and agreed upon configuration level that contains high-priority requirements that need to be implemented quickly. The baseline generally covers the implementation of organizational units and core processes (main scope).

▶ **Final configuration**
The baseline configuration is finalized in a series of cycles. This is an iterative process in which you finish planning, configuring, documenting, and testing your process configurations. This includes working on customer developments and master data.

You can use keywords on the ADMINISTRATION tab page to classify the relevant master data, organizational units, and business processes by baseline and cycle for the final configuration.

There are essentially two methods for documenting configuration settings:

▶ **Documentation in IMG project**
You document your settings directly in the IMG project for the development system and can therefore analyze the IMG project at any time. The advantage here is that you save the documentation once, centrally, in the IMG project. All processes or process steps that are customized in this IMG activity therefore refer automatically to one and the same configuration document.

▶ **Documentation in SAP Solution Manager**
Alternatively, you can document your settings on the CONFIGURATION tab page for the structure item in question and assign the documentation to processes or process steps that are customized in the same IMG activity. You can view a where-used list at any time showing you where in the process structure a particular document is assigned. Furthermore, the system logs all changes made to the documentation; different versions let you see successive document changes.

You can also combine the two methods. This enables you to generate a URL in the attributes of every document in SAP Solution Manager, which you simply copy and paste into the corresponding configuration document and call from there. In technical terms, the URL points to a *Logical Information Object* (LOIO), which means that when the document is accessed, the system links to the most recent version in the form of *Physical Information Objects* (PHIOs). As such, the link in the IMG documentation always refers to the current document content. If you compile your documentation in SAP Solution Manager, the processes and process steps make suitable levels for storing configuration settings that need documenting.

No matter which method you opt for, as in the Business Blueprint phase, it is important to assign responsibilities and (document) status values, from the process level right down to the level of IMG activities. Particularly in the case of cross-process IMG settings, this makes coordination and communication easier.

Configuration guide — You can create an interim or final version of your configuration at any time as a configuration guide and adjust the layout according to your requirements. To do so, you select either the entire structure or specific parts of it. In contrast to the Business Blueprint document, when you generate a configuration guide, the system considers only documents from the CONFIGURATION tab page.

Training materials — Throughout the configuration phase, we recommend that you describe procedures so that you can compile end user documentation. Using the template for *Business Process Procedures* (BPPs) in SAP Solution Manager, you can draft step-by-step instructions for working with selected transactions. The description explains how to use the given transaction in context, which prerequisites apply, and how to complete individual activities, which are supplemented ideally by some sample data. After you have filled out this form, you can include it in the process structure at the process step level, on the TRAINING MATERIALS tab page. This gives you a building block for creating training materials specifically for end users. For more information, see Section 5.7.

5.5.3 Implementing Customer Developments

You may need customer developments before you can configure your processes completely. You usually define the functional scope for enhancements to reports, interfaces, forms, user exits, migration programs, and new developments in the Business Blueprint phase at the same time as the functional documentation. You can supplement the functional documentation with realization specifications, which state how enhancements are to be implemented in technical terms. You store these specifications, along with links to objects that are to be enhanced or created specifically for your company in the development system, on the DEVELOPMENTS tab page. The object types you can use include programs, transactions, Internet services, BSP applications and extensions, function groups and modules, and includes. This assignment lets you call the relevant object directly in the development system. For a better overview of the development progress, it is helpful to store responsibilities and a status for each object.

Setting up separate development structures — Complex development requirements may call for a separate development structure. In this case, you would enter development-related documents and objects in this structure. You can also link the documents to structure items that the customer development affects, such as processes. This enables you to create different views on the same content.

Additionally, this is the project phase in which you also implement the authorization and security concept and create end user roles. When you define roles for end users, you can assign organizational units or items on the END USER ROLES tab page. The project analysis (Transaction SOLAR_EVAL) lets you run CROSS-TAB ANALYSES, which indicate which process steps are assigned to which transactions and end user roles and, consequently, provide input for the functional scope of the roles. For more information on processing and documenting user-defined developments, see Chapter 15; for reporting, see Section 5.8.

5.5.4 Working with Service Messages

Queries and obstacles that arise over the course of the project should be recorded and addressed as soon as possible. Here, SAP Solution Manager enables the project team members to use service messages (incidents, requests for change, and issues) to address existing problems, changes in the scope, and questions relating to the implementation. The function enables you to access the questions from team members directly from the project context and view the corresponding requests.

During your implementation project, it is possible for changes to be made to your defined and agreed-on implementation scope, and these must be considered. The requests and approvals for these changes are processed in the Change Request Management in SAP Solution Manager. By means of an approval workflow, requests for change go through a clearly regulated process and provide seamless documentation. To trace the technical effects, schedule changes, and any resource bottlenecks due to these requests for change in your implementation project, you assign the changes to the business process on the SERVICE MESSAGES tab page. For more information on Change Request Management and possible application scenarios, see Chapter 8, Section 8.3.

Traceability of changes to the scope

You record messages using the Service Desk. You can use the Service Desk for a range of tasks, from recording and classifying all types of

Traceability of issues and messages

171

errors and monitoring how they are processed (where appropriate, with escalation to other departments or specialists) to resolving the problem, either by Service Desk staff or, if the problem message is forwarded, by experts from SAP Active Global Support (SAP AGS).

In implementation projects, you can use the message function without having to configure the Service Desk completely. You set up the minimum functions by making basic settings for the Service Desk in Customizing for SAP Solution Manager; most of the settings are made automatically.

Assigning a message to a project

If messages have not been assigned, they must be assigned centrally (e.g., by the project management) to a particular topic. They are assigned to the appropriate project or subproject automatically on the basis of the project context in which they are created. Even when used in this way, the Service Desk outperforms external tools, such as Microsoft Excel, when it comes to managing open error messages.

In an implementation project, the end users are project team members working during the Business Blueprint, configuration, and later testing phases. The messages created here can cover a broad range of subjects, from open items and business requirements to actual error messages. You need to ensure that messages and their solutions are described in sufficient detail for third parties to understand. Although it is possible to forward messages directly to SAP, you rarely need to do so with project-related messages.

Besides being able to enter messages in the project context based on the process structure (SERVICE MESSAGES tab page), employees can submit messages directly from the environment in which the problem arises, for instance, when configuring the development system. To report on messages, you can use general analyses for problem messages in the Service Desk and a project-specific analysis of the problem messages using the evaluation transaction (Transaction SOLAR_EVAL). Chapter 9 provides more information about the Service Desk and how it can be used.

5.6 Test Management

Before transferring your solution configuration to your production system landscape and thus making it available for your operative business processes, you must first check that all changes have been made correctly and do not have a negative impact on other business processes. SAP Solution Manager provides extensive test functions for this purpose. The topic of test management is treated as a separate process in the ALM and is therefore described separately in Chapter 7.

5.7 E-Learning Management—Efficient Knowledge Transfer During Projects

E-Learning Management in SAP Solution Manager enables you to transfer knowledge in your projects effectively, efficiently, and promptly. The purpose of E-Learning Management is to create user training courses on new and changed processes and make them available to end users as *e-learning materials*. The advantages are that you can manage learning materials, reuse them at any time, adapt them where necessary, and thus improve efficiency in the user training. E-learning also reduces travel and training location expenses, as users can complete training activities independently at the workplace, which in turn reduces absence from work. It presents another attractive way to transfer knowledge and supplement project-related classroom training. When you adapt your IT solution to meet changing requirements, you have to notify users who work with the solution daily about changes, for example, to the interface.

In SAP Solution Manager, the Configuration (Transaction SOLAR02) and Learning Map (Transaction SOLAR_LEARNING_MAP) transactions and the CREATE view of the *Implementation/Upgrade* work center provide you with the central infrastructure for creating, organizing, and distributing learning content and learning units.

5.7.1 Creating Learning Materials

Figure 5.10 shows an overview of E-Learning Management. In the first step, you create e-learning materials, for example, in the form of presentations, documentation, or application simulations. You can use the existing business process structure to organize and categorize individual learning objects in SAP Solution Manager. If you have saved end-user roles in your project, you can use them to distribute the learning materials to specific end users. This is because every user has different training requirements. A project manager, for example, would prefer an overview, whereas a technology consultant or specialist department user would like to understand functions in detail.

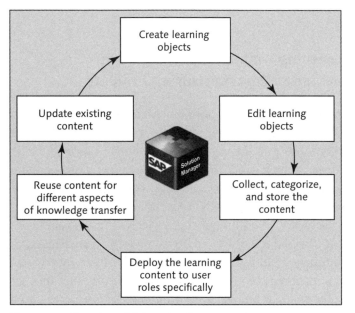

Figure 5.10 Overview of E-Learning Management

5.7.2 SAP Productivity Pak by ANCILE Adapter for SAP Solution Manager

With *SAP Productivity Pak by ANCILE Adapter for SAP Solution Manager*, SAP Solution Manager provides an interface to the software product *SAP Productivity Pak by ANCILE*.[3] The product supports you when developing documentation in various output formats (HTML, PDF, Flash, Microsoft Word) with an integrated workflow, and thus the exchange of knowledge and the collaboration between authors, editors, and users. The re-recording function allows you to create new versions and replace original screenshots with new language versions.

The adapter enables you to store documents created with the SAP Productivity Pak by ANCILE centrally in SAP Solution Manager and

---

3   Registered trademarks: RWD uPerform by Ancile Solutions, Inc.

later edit and manage them. Additionally, you can create, edit, and delete new documents in SAP Solution Manager. Thus all the functions of both products are available to you in full.

The following section provides you with application examples of how to created learning materials with the SAP Productivity Pak by ANCILE.

Project documentation is one case where the adapter is used: For example, it enables a project team to create documentation for the project configuration directly from SAP Solution Manager using SAP Productivity Pak by ANCILE. The created documents are integrated in SAP Solution Manager on the appropriate tab pages (e.g. CONFIGURATION, PROJECT DOCUMENTATION, or TRAINING MATERIALS).

Documentation of the project configuration

The adapter can also be used to create application simulations, for example, as training material or for training purposes. The adapter enables you to go directly to the relevant transaction from SAP Solution Manager for recording with the SAP Productivity Pak by ANCILE. When recording is complete (and any postprocessing in SAP Productivity Pak by RWD), end users can access the simulation in SAP Solution Manager on the relevant tab pages (such as TRAINING MATERIALS) or using the functions of SAP Productivity Pak by ANCILE.

Creating application simulations

The adapter also allows you to add the documentation for test cases created with SAP Productivity Pak by ANCILE. The integration enables you to directly record, create, and store these documents on the TEST CASES tab page in SAP Solution Manager.

Documentation of test cases

5.7.3 Organizing and Distributing Training Content

Edited training content is collected, categorized, and stored in SAP Solution Manager. To integrate e-learning content in your project and distribute it to your end users by mail using the Learning Map function of SAP Solution Manager, it must be integrated into the Configuration transaction (Transaction SOLAR02) on the TRAINING MATERIALS tab page for the respective business process or business process step. For organization purposes, you can define status values and attributes for the learning units. For attributes, you can store values that are useful for distribution and training later on. Examples include the description of the learning object or the duration

Organizing training content

required to complete the training. On the END USER tab page, you can also define the end users for which the process step is relevant. You can copy predefined roles from the HR organization and technical profiles, or you can define separate roles.

Creating a
Learning Map

When you have stored learning content in the project, you can use the Learning Map builder transaction (Transaction SOLAR_LEARNING_MAP; see Figure 5.11) to generate a Learning Map and send it to the relevant end users.

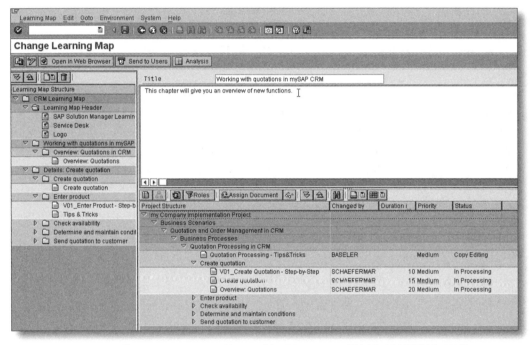

Figure 5.11 Learning Map Builder (Transaction SOLAR_LEARNING_MAP)

SAP Solution Manager takes the project structure and uses it to generate a proposed chapter structure. You can then enter a title for the Learning Map, a company logo, and, for example, the URL of your company's web page at the header level.

Integrating service
messages

Another important function integrates the Service Desk into the Learning Map, which makes it possible to create and send a support message directly. The message window already contains certain information, and end users can add their own text if they have questions or problems regarding the Learning Map. In this way, technical problems can be reported directly to the relevant support organization without any integration gaps. Detailed information on the Service Desk is not included here, but you will find it in Chapter 9.

You can change the chapter structure of the Learning Map, remove proposed chapters, and add new ones. To assign learning objects to the chapters, you can use drag and drop to move learning objects from the project structure into the relevant chapters. You can also add more detailed information to the chapters and display the current status directly as a preview of the Learning Map in the web browser (see Figure 5.12).

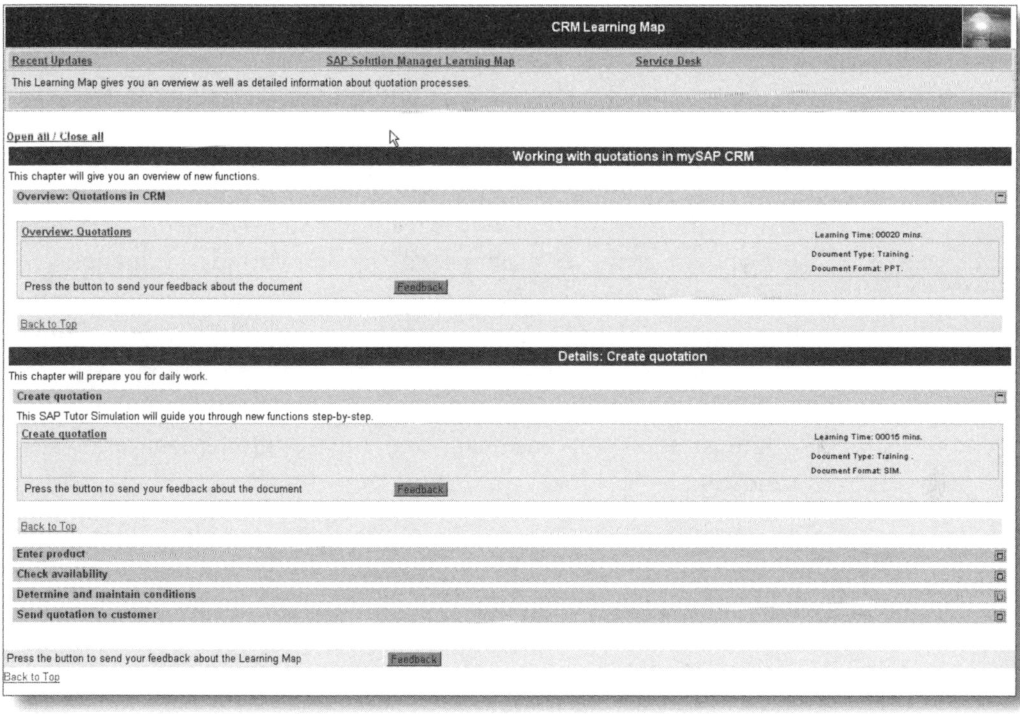

Changing the chapter structure

Figure 5.12 Completed Learning Map in a Web Browser

For users to be able to complete the training independently at their workplace, you can inform them by email about the availability of the Learning Map. This email contains a text and the URL for the corresponding Learning Map. You can insert this text in your email, adapt it to meet your requirements, and send it to the users assigned to the selected end user role. This approach ensures that information is communicated efficiently to a specific audience.

However, this is not the end of the e-learning lifecycle. The Learning Map is subject to continual improvement. The feedback function in E-Learning Management helps you in this process. Users who use the Learning Map to complete the training can directly submit anonymous evaluations and comments about the content of this Learning Map. Such information is an important element that enables those responsible to respond to requirements. E-learning can be conducted at any time, directly at the workplace, with the help of SAP Solution Manager as a document server. You can view the feedback information in reporting and, depending on the result, make adjustments and/or improvements. For more detailed information on reporting, see Chapter 10.

5.8 Reporting for Your Implementation Project

SAP Solution Manager therefore features extensive reporting options for you to create evaluations efficiently. Various evaluations for phase-dependent and phase-independent data are possible. Phase-dependent evaluations are available; for example, for the Business Blueprint, the configuration, the testing, and the Learning Map. You will find phase-independent evaluations, for example, in the Project Administration, the roadmap, and the Solution Manager System Landscape.

In SAP Solution Manager, the EVALUATION function (Transaction SOLAR_EVAL) and the EVALUATIONS view of the *Implementation/Upgrade* work center provide the functions for the project reporting.

5.8.1 Reporting Roadmap

You can use the evaluation function of the Roadmap to evaluate accelerators, statuses, service messages, and project documents of the roadmaps that are assigned to a project.

5.8.2 Reporting—Business Blueprint

The evaluation functions for your Business Blueprint let you analyze information stored in your project, such as business scenarios, business processes, status values, project deadlines, and transactions. The more detailed the information stored by your project team when creating the Business Blueprint, the more wide-ranging are your evaluation options. You can analyze data for a single project or for several projects, depending on the scope of your project or the purpose of your analysis.

For the Business Blueprint, evaluations are available to you for the ADMINISTRATION and ASSIGNMENTS areas (see Figure 5.13). Evaluations of the ADMINISTRATION provide you with a quick overview of administrative data. In ASSIGNMENTS, you can show the assignments for the project structure (business scenario, business process, business process step). Additionally, other cross-phase evaluations in the Business Blueprint can be of interest to you, such as the evaluations for the system landscape or the project data history. For all evaluations, you can store selection variants that are available to all users and that can be executed directly to respond to FAQs without any errors.

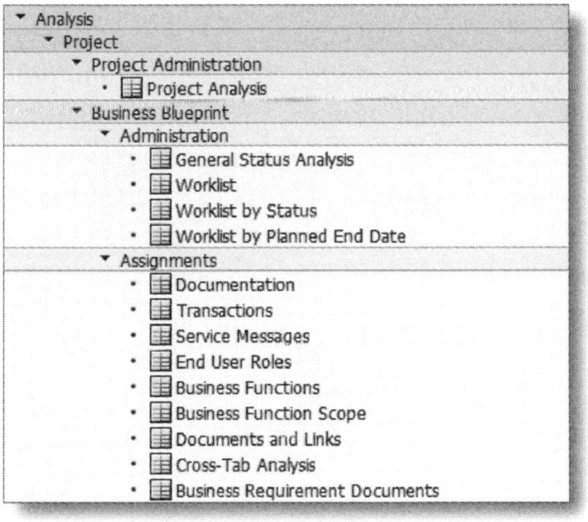

Evaluation areas

Figure 5.13 Evaluation Options of the Business Blueprint

Administration

The reports listed under ADMINISTRATION help you to analyze administrative data. Besides the general status evaluation, you can evaluate the worklists of one or more members of the project team and focus specifically on, for example, the status or planned end date.

You can use predefined reports or execute individual ones, which you can define as standard reports, if necessary.

179

Examples of data you might analyze in your project are listed here:

▶ **Incomplete elements**

The report analyzes all elements of the project structure for which the planned project end falls within the period specified in PLANNED END and which are not 100% complete.

▶ **All completed elements**

The report analyzes all activities for which the actual project end (from the actual status information) falls within the analysis period you specified.

▶ **Individual reports**

You can run individual reports in addition to those just mentioned. To compare individual values in the analysis result to each other, you can calculate column totals.

Project Structure Assignments

All scenario and process structures must contain blueprint-specific assignments for the individual structure items. The scenario and process structure itself only provides an item-specific view of existing assignments. Assignment reporting provides a higher-level view. You can make various settings to create user-specific report variants for specific queries. You can also define the variants as standard project variants so that all team members can use them.

You can analyze the following assignments in the Business Blueprint phase:

▶ Documentation

▶ Transaction

▶ Service messages

▶ End user roles

▶ Business functions

▶ Business function scope

▶ Documents and links

▶ Cross-tab page evaluations

▶ Business requirement documents

You can display report results in two ways: as a tree structure or as a table. The tree structure gives you a quick overview and, having the same structure as the project, is instantly familiar.

The table, on the other hand, is attractive because it offers numerous technical functions that are vital for detailed reporting. Such functions include the following:

▸ Sorting project results

▸ Restricting the results display using a filter

▸ Totaling

▸ Defining and displaying layouts

▸ Downloading evaluation results

▸ Exporting evaluation results using Microsoft Excel

Comparing reports

All the reports for analyzing assignments in SAP Solution Manager have the same structure. This makes it easier for you to work with various reports simultaneously. It can be particularly useful to compare two reports, for instance.

5.8.3 Reporting—Configuration

As with the reports for the Business Blueprint, in the configuration, you have the option of analyzing the information you stored in the implementation project. The more detailed the information stored by your project team when creating the configuration, the more wide-ranging are your evaluation options. Depending on the project scope or purpose of your evaluation, you can also evaluate the data for one or more projects and differentiate between ADMINISTRATION and ASSIGNMENTS (see Figure 5.14).

The reports listed under ADMINISTRATION behave the same in the configuration as in the BUSINESS BLUEPRINT section. The only difference is the data itself.

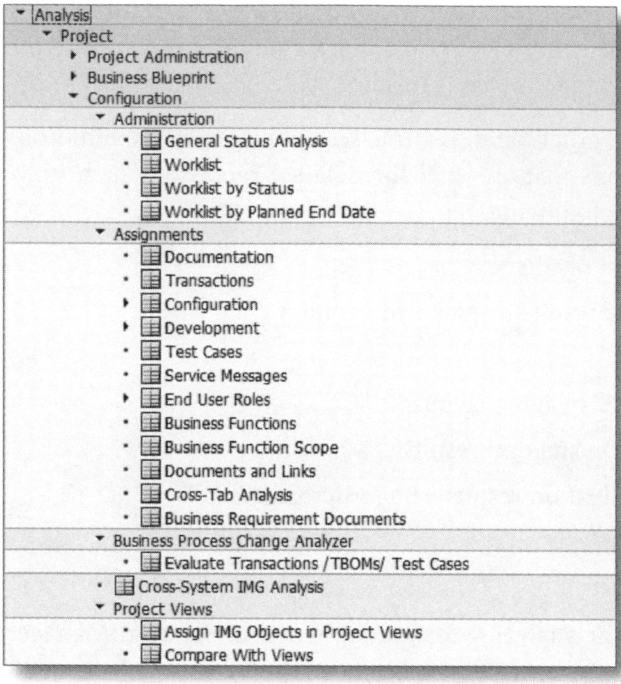

Figure 5.14 Reporting Options for the Configuration

Assignments to the project structure

In addition to the assignments from the Business Blueprint evaluation, the configuration contains the following information, which is stored as assignments:

- Configuration
- Development
- Test cases
- Learning materials

The report results (see Figure 5.15) show the configuration elements assigned to the different structure items. Here you can also access configuration documents, which fully explain the procedure and configuration steps used in the configuration. You will also find IMG objects and transactions that you can use to make the settings described.

Additionally, you are also provided with cross-system IMG evaluations, evaluations for different project views, and evaluations for the Business Process Change Analyzer (BPCA).

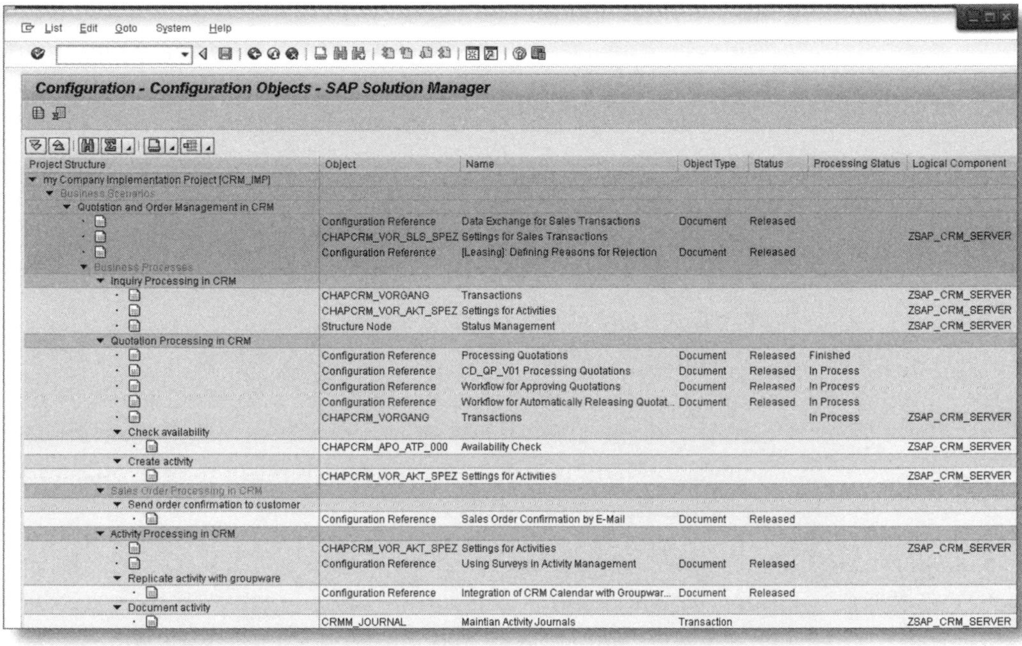

Figure 5.15 Result — Evaluations for the Configuration

The evaluation for the *cross-system IMG evaluations* is based on the information that you can store for every step in the IMG project. We refer to IMG activities for simplification purposes, but you can also store and analyze status information for structure nodes in the project IMG.

You can analyze data for a single project or for several projects, depending on the scope of your project or the purpose of your analysis.

Cross-system IMG evaluations

Examples of data you might analyze in your project are given here:

▶ **Planned activities without actual data**
The system analyzes all activities whose planned project start falls within the period you specified for PLANNED START and for which no actual status information yet exists.

▶ **Activities not yet completed**
The system analyzes all activities for which the planned project end falls within the period you specified for PLANNED END, and which are not yet 100% complete.

▶ **All activities started**
The system analyzes all activities for which the actual project start (from the actual status information data) falls within the period you specified for PROJECT START, and for which the actual project end is still open.

▶ **All completed activities**
The report analyzes all activities for which the actual project end (from the actual status information) falls within the analysis period you specified.

▶ **Individual analyses**
You can perform individual analyses, as well as the analysis scenarios just described, and define them as standard analyses. To compare individual values in the analysis result to each other, you can calculate column totals.

Business Process Change Analyzer

BPCA allows you to perform a completeness check. This check is to ensure that the requirements for the BPCA are met. This means that, depending on your selection criteria, you are provided with a result informing you for which business processes and technical objects documentation has been maintained completely or incompletely. Incomplete documentation must be completed to meet the requirements for the BPCA. Using the BPCA, you create information for preparing tests, which is used in test management. For more information about BPCA, see Chapter 7, Section 7.1.

5.8.4 Reporting—Training Materials

When a project is transferred to production operation, one of the most important success factors is that end users know how to use new or changed processes in their daily activities. To monitor this transfer of knowledge, SAP Solution Manager provides special reporting functions.

With SAP Solution Manager, you generate Learning Maps from the existing project structure for the respective task areas of end users, for example, to show the buyers in your company how to use new functions. A Learning Map is the structured table of contents of a computer-supported, self-learning training course, which presents information about the learning units and links to the learning material in HTML format.

End users can evaluate Learning Maps using an HTML-based feedback option. All the feedback from end users of the Learning Map is saved anonymously. You can display the results of these evaluations in Learning Maps Management (Transaction SOLAR_LEARNING_MAP). When doing so, you can analyze four different criteria: **Feedback**

▶ Number of times the Learning Map was called

▶ Individual evaluations

▶ Average evaluation

▶ Feedback on individual learning units and the overall Learning Map

The analysis (see Figure 5.16) provides information about the usage rate and quality of Learning Maps. It also lets you display the feedback as text.

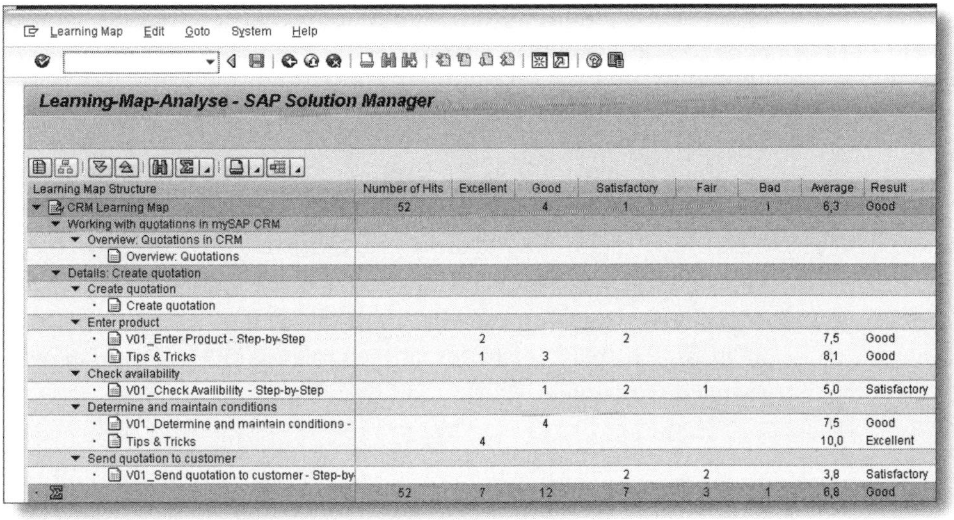

Learning-Map-Analyse - SAP Solution Manager

Learning Map Structure	Number of Hits	Excellent	Good	Satisfactory	Fair	Bad	Average	Result
▼ CRM Learning Map	52		4	1		1	6,3	Good
▼ Working with quotations in mySAP CRM								
▼ Overview: Quotations in CRM								
· Overview: Quotations								
▼ Details: Create quotation								
▼ Create quotation								
· Create quotation								
▼ Enter product								
· V01_Enter Product - Step-by-Step		2		2			7,5	Good
· Tips & Tricks		1	3				8,1	Good
▼ Check availability								
· V01_Check Availibility - Step-by-Step			1	2	1		5,0	Satisfactory
▼ Determine and maintain conditions								
· V01_Determine and maintain conditions -			4				7,5	Good
· Tips & Tricks		4					10,0	Excellent
▼ Send quotation to customer								
· V01_Send quotation to customer - Step-by				2	2		3,8	Satisfactory
· Σ	52	7	12	7	3	1	6,8	Good

Figure 5.16 Result—Evaluations of Learning Materials

5.8.5 Reporting—Test

Reports for different test functions are described in Chapter 7, Section 7.4.5, of the *Test Management* for the process, rather than here.

5.8.6 Reporting—System Landscape

You can use the system landscape report in the planning, Business Blueprint, configuration, and test phases. It determines which components are assigned to individual process steps and in which systems they are executed. You can therefore get an overview of the systems and processes at any time.

5.8.7 Reporting—History

SAP Solution Manager logs a large number of changes so that they can be traced. For projects, the main purpose is to record changes to the business scenarios, the business process structure, and the assigned elements. Another important aspect is the history management for document. To enable changes to be displayed by topic, SAP Solution Manager offers two cross-phase reports:

▸ **History of elements assigned to the structure (tab pages)**
This report enables you to trace all the assignments made during a particular period. It shows you what was changed when, where, how, and by whom (e.g., it would indicate that a transaction was added to or deleted from a process).

▸ **History of documents**
Contrary to transactions and configuration elements, documents are independent objects in SAP Solution Manager (transactions and configuration elements are links to objects in managed systems). SAP Solution Manager therefore logs changes to these objects as well, which you can analyze using a separate report for documents. Here you can also trace all changes made to a document and display its history. It enables you to see what was changed when, where, how, and by whom.

5.9 SAP Solution Manager at the HARTMANN GROUP

The seamless integration of SAP Solution Manager functions has made it possible not only to establish a link to the affected business processes in requests for change (and vice versa), but also to automatically generate risk-based test plans using the Business Process Change Analyzer and integrate them in the change procedure—ALM in its purest form.

Dr. Björn Gelhausen, SNP AG

The introduction of SAP Solution Manager with all of its modules and functions is best done in several steps. It typically begins with the functions of the monitoring and operations area. This is generally followed by the Service Desk and Change Request Management. The central component—the implementation part—is usually implemented at a later stage with a focus on the use of Test Management and then connected to Change Request Management to constitute the Application Lifecycle Management (ALM) solution. SAP Solution Manager thereby becomes the central point of access to the *current documentation* of a company with regard to business and IT processes.

Project goals

Looking at the HARTMANN GROUP, one of the leading European providers of medical and hygiene products, we will show how the global group successfully implemented the documentation of business processes and introduced the practice worldwide. To achieve the objective of continuous access to the company's current process and technical documentation, the project placed special focus on ensuring that all modules of SAP Solution Manager work together with a high degree of integration.

HARTMANN GROUP

SNP AG has assisted the HARTMANN GROUP in the implementation of SAP Solution Manager and all its functions since 2005.

SNP AG, Heidelberg

Based in Heidelberg, SNP AG is a leading provider of software and software-related services for the transformation of IT systems such as in the course of company restructurings or technical upgrades. SNP AG was founded in Heidelberg in 1994 and has roughly 190 employees at five locations in Germany, Austria, Switzerland, the United States, and South Africa.

After evaluating other products, the globally active HARTMANN GROUP identified SAP Solution Manager as the central solution on the way to establishing a *single point of truth* through the documentation of business processes and their changes. In this regard, the various components of SAP Solution Manager were implemented in succession and integrated with each other. The initial setup of the business-related and technical documentation of the utilized processes was done as part of an SAP release changeover.

Strategy

With the primary goal of optimizing test management, a year prior to the actual release changeover the company began to implement

Introduction of the solution documentation

the *Solution Documentation*, building on the Service Desk and Change Request Management functions already in place. To get the process started, business processes were analyzed in a series of workshops, and the previous testing procedure was examined and evaluated to identify optimization potential.

In workshops with the responsible module managers, initial ideas about how to structure business processes in SAP Solution Manager were developed. In the subsequent proof of concept phase—together with a release changeover for a small SAP landscape—participants began to gather common experiences with the modular structure of process mapping, the use of customer-specific attributes, the possibilities for mapping interfaces with other systems, mapping SAP interfaces with SAP NetWeaver Business Warehouse systems (SAP NetWeaver BW), the possibility of documenting jobs and authorizations, as well as the general use of documents in SAP Solution Manager. The proof of concept phase also saw the development of the first templates for the required document types (e.g., business process description, customizing process description, customizing object value description, and development description). From the outset, particular attention was paid to ensuring that the structure enables not only a unified view of all business processes in the group but also clear display options for the individual companies.

The initial setup of the process structure was done through an implementation project because this enabled an uncomplicated and simple structuring of processes. The mapping of numerous (country-specific) variants of processes in an implementation project also enables a view of the processes using a unified template. Using appropriate filter criteria, this enables the identification of both differences and similarities across country borders. If these processes run in a client, this procedure is recommended because the options for unifying processes become evident at a glance.

Processes were structured on a modular basis. This can lead to increased work later when setting up integration tests but simplifies the setup of subprocesses together with the respective module manager. A total of 39 scenarios, 240 processes, and nearly 1,000 process steps were mapped. Care was taken to ensure that process steps actually represented business-related steps and not just transaction-oriented steps. After completely defining the process structure, the plan calls for the transfer of the Business Blueprint to a solution in order to use the functions of Business Process Monitoring.

A side effect of the release changeover was cleansing the custom code in the ERP system. To this purpose, the *Solution Documentation Assistant* was used to analyze the used translations and business processes. Based on the analysis results, more than 600 objects, 270 Z transactions, and 547 temporary objects were deleted. The result was reducing custom code by 18% without affecting existing processes.

Introduction of the Solution Documentation Assistant

To execute and check the dual maintenance phase during the release changeover, the *Retrofit* procedure in SAP Solution Manager was also used. This procedure enables quick comparison of changes made in the maintenance landscape with the landscape in the new release.

Retrofit

To replace an existing Lotus Notes-based solution, the first step was implementing—alongside the functions of the monitoring and operation area—the *Service Desk* and *Incident Management* for SAP and non-SAP message processing. To improve the interaction between users and support employees, the company's support portal (a customer-specific, browser-based solution) was rolled out to every workplace to handle messages of all types in a simple way and exchange additional information with support if necessary. The multilingual support portal also enables the user to track the processing status and use numerous services, such as requests for new authorizations.

Implementing the Service Desk

After the worldwide rollout of the *Service Desk* in all branches of the HARTMANN GROUP, *Change Request Management* was also implemented. In a series of rollout and optimization phases, custom-tailored procedures for requests for change were developed that covered the special requirements in the areas of change contents, change classification, time management, process automation, and, above all, increased security with greater flexibility. Transports, for example, are only transferred to production systems when they have been explicitly released following successful integration tests. Thanks to another test during import into production that checks whether the change belonging to the transport has really been released, the imports can now be performed in a time-controlled automated process. This is of particular importance for globally active groups with small time windows for maintenance

Implementing Change Request Management

activities on central systems. Further enhancements enabled greater user-friendliness and thereby acceptance of the solution.

To support the worldwide rollout of the *Service Desk* and *Change Request Management*, a *management information system* was developed on the basis of the central SAP NetWeaver BW. The decision makers and users can thereby access overview graphics and, if required, details, via the group-wide intranet. In addition to information about the availability of the systems, there are also overviews of current Service Desk messages and requests for changes by type, system, and region. To ensure that this information can also be displayed in a current form, the extractors in SAP Solution Manager were enhanced to enable the transfer of additional, customer-specific data to the BW. The clear and current display of IT key figures (e.g., still available person-days for projects) has made a major contribution to improving support processes and optimizing the central IT environment in terms of capabilities, availability, and internal coordination.

Test management

Building on the display of the processes in the implementation part of SAP Solution Manager, a total of 43,000 transaction steps (including country-specific repetitions) were identified as test-relevant for the individual test phases of the release changeover and tested by up to 300 testers (122 test plans with 750 test packages). The required test scope was coordinated in advance with the auditing company and was reduced step by step in subsequent test phases with the help of risk assessments (phase 2: 34,000 transaction steps; phase 3: 5,700 transaction steps). The integration of the Service Desk with test management was used to track errors worldwide.

Application Lifecycle Management

After completing the release changeover and thus also the documentation of the central business processes, the implementation area and test management were fully integrated with Change Request Management through an enhancement. This made it possible not only to establish a link to the affected business processes in requests for changes (and vice versa) but also to automatically generate risk-based test plans using the *Business Process Change Analyzer* and integrate them in the change procedure—ALM in its purest form.

Conclusion and recommendations

From these descriptions of the implementation steps for SAP Solution Manager at a globally active group, we can draw the following conclusions:

▸ Schedule enough time for the introduction of the individual SAP Solution Manager modules. A step-by-step approach is definitely preferable to a big-bang approach.

▸ The comprehensive and integrated use of SAP Solution Manager processes should be the objective. This requires optimized and partially automated support processes.

▸ The introduction of process documentation is best done as part of a larger project such as a release changeover or transformation project.

▸ The introduction of test management is not strictly an IT project, but is largely borne by the departments. A key-user concept can be very helpful here.

▸ The introduction of SAP Solution Manager represents a major change in a company and must be accompanied by organizational measures. The consistent optimization of processes in terms of user-friendliness and automation promotes the acceptance and penetration of SAP Solution Manager in the company.

The Authors

Dr. Björn Gelhausen is the head of the Training and Quality Management department at SNP AG. Since 1999, he has directed numerous SAP Solution Manager implementation projects as a consultant and project manager. His special area of expertise is the efficient linking of solution documentation, test management, and Change Request Management.

Johannes Hurst is the Head of Consulting at SNP AG. He has more than 20 years' experience in consulting, and he and his team have been working with SAP Solution Manager since 2002. His special focus is on Change Request Management and integration with non-SAP products. Since 2007, he has been the spokesperson of the DSAG SAP Solution Manager work stream.

You can use templates to design a company-wide business process library and reuse process-related content both locally and globally for efficient and faster implementation.

6 Template Management

Business processes that are experienced identically or in a similar way throughout a company have a strong potential for standardization. It therefore makes sense to harmonize and standardize procedures for implementing and tailoring such processes, so that the company need only design them once and can provide or reuse them in various solutions.

Identical business processes company-wide

The growing importance of business processes that are standardized group-wide can be put down to various factors: The increasing internationalization and globalization coupled with a simultaneous expansion of company operations is one reason. This tendency goes hand in hand with the dynamics of technological and economic change, which creates the need to adapt existing business models to new situations at ever-shorter intervals. At the same time, group-wide process harmonization and standardization should improve the organization's efficiency and decrease overall operating costs. This then leads to the need for a standard, company-wide business process model for certain lines of business. This is where SAP Solution Manager comes in.

6.1 Application Areas for Templates

SAP Solution Manager makes it possible for you to create designed scenarios and processes as templates. These templates are stored in a central process library and can be used for local implementation projects and group rollouts. This chapter gives you an overview of the process library application areas and global rollout of the templates you create.

Templates

6.1.1 The Company-Wide Process Library

When it comes to building up a company-wide process library such as the Business Process Repository (BPR), which contains business processes provided by SAP, templates offer many advantages.

Templates enable centralized definition and harmonization of company-specific processes that are applicable throughout the company or that are intended to be so in the future. The structure of the solution documentation forms the basis of this harmonization. The documentation can be formulated on three levels: from the business scenario, through the processes, and down to the level of the individual process steps.

In addition to the associated process documentation, this structure can be enriched successively with implementation-related content—from configuration settings, own developments, through to test cases and training material for end users.

The design of this process library can be organized specifically for your needs. One option is to create templates on the basis of entire business scenarios that recur, and another option is to group individual, component-related process steps that are reused in many processes.

6.1.2 Global Rollout

In addition to local implementation projects, you can reuse the business scenarios included in the templates straightaway in rollout projects without intensive preparatory work. The result is that you require fewer resources and less time for the go-live project because business processes only need tailoring and testing in line with local requirements.

When identifying and comparing changes to templates and getting feedback about template-relevant changes during implementation, the adjustment work can be reduced by using a comparison tool. This tool automatically highlights changes and new features in a template and provides comparison functions that ensure the integrity of the template through to the live solution. The global rollout process is explained in the following. Figure 6.1 shows an overview of the group rollout.

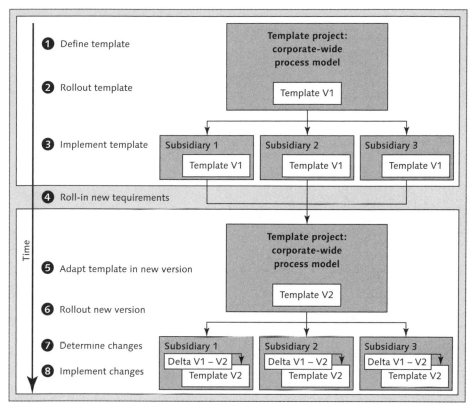

Figure 6.1 Global Rollout: Overview

A cross-functional team (subsequently referred to as template team) is enlisted to create a global template ❶. Based on the processes tested in the implementation project, the team creates a template project and defines the template, taking into account business- and organization-related issues. The template includes business processes and other content such as process documentation, cross-functional configuration structures, preconfiguration, and test documents—all the materials that bring about faster implementations in rollout projects.

Defining a template

The template completed in the first rollout phase is made available to selected local sites, for instance, in Europe ❷. Strictly speaking, this process is also a rollout. The application scenario dictates how this process is approached. If the template and implementation projects are in the same SAP Solution Manager system, you don't need to transport the template. In other cases, you need to transport the template to the relevant rollout target system of SAP Solution Manager.

Rolling out the template

You also have to copy any content that was created locally in the reference systems, such as the preconfiguration, to target systems.

Implementing the template

Next, the rollout team responsible implements the template ❸. The procedure is similar to a standard implementation project, as described in Chapter 5. To implement the template, the team creates a rollout project of type *implementation*. In this case, however, the source for the implementation is the template that has been rolled out, not the BPR. The template's *global attributes*, in turn, can dictate the scope of the changes that can be made to a global template when actually implementing it.

Rolling in new requirements

After piloting the template at the first location, the template team checks the change requests defined by the rollouts and gradually transfers them to a new template version ❹. If applicable, the team copies existing implementations and changes that are relevant to the template from successfully completed rollout projects.

Adapting the template and rolling it out again

In the course of this, a scenario is adjusted; for example, so that it can be planned, carried out, and evaluated more cost-efficiently ❺. Part of the adjustment step entails considering local processes in terms of local requirements and making them known in the template project, if company policy is to store all processes centrally, both global and local. An alternative would be to define the local processes in the rollout projects. In the second rollout phase, new versions of the templates are rolled out at locations two and three ❻.

Identifying and implementing changes

The rollout team integrates new scenarios by selecting and implementing templates again. In the case of existing scenarios, it uses a comparison tool that compares the old and new template versions and lists any changes that have been made to processes and the assigned objects. This enables the rollout team to identify changes as quickly as possible and to include and implement them in the rollout projects (❼ and ❽).

6.2 Template Management in Detail

This section provides information about which steps you need to take from planning and designing your templates, through to implementation. Additionally, it contains valuable tips and tricks on working with templates.

6.2.1 Template Management in the Context of Application Lifecycle Management

To establish long-term template management in your company, it's important to create a consistent design in advance for templates, projects, and solutions, as well as for the way they interact.

SAP Solution Manager provides various project types and design options that make it possible to create an individual lifecycle model that is oriented toward both your development planning and your release and change management.

These are the application areas and special features of the most important project types and the solution:

Project types

- **Template project**
  The template project is used to create and design templates and their content, as well as to specify how the template content can be changed during later rollouts, if they are used for global rollout projects.

- **Implementation project**
  The implementation project is used to implement template content. In the context of release management, implementation projects are used to provide a *major release* of template content. After the project ends or the go-live starts, the content provided is transferred to a live solution.

- **Solution**
  The solution represents the business processes that are currently used productively.

- **Maintenance project**
  Maintenance projects make it possible to carry out tasks on the solution that have a more limited scope than an implementation project. To integrate with change management, a maintenance project can be allocated to a solution and changes can be carried out using a check-out/check-in mechanism. In the context of release management, a maintenance project results in a *minor release*.

- **Upgrade project**
  The upgrade project is used to upgrade or reconfigure the technical systems on which the business processes are based.

Project and solution design

The project and solution design should be oriented toward the special features and possible uses of the various project types in Figure 6.2. This enables full support of the lifecycle, from designing the templates through to live operation, including maintenance and upgrade cycles.

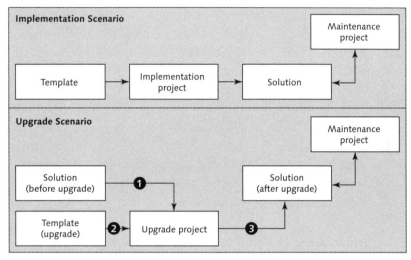

Figure 6.2 Project and Solution Design

Predecessor/ successor relationship

The transition of the template from implementation in a project, or from the project to productive use in the solution, is a critical stage. During this transition, the predecessor/successor relationship between the project and template (or between solution and project) that's relevant to the lifecycle is created. This is the only way that technical support can be provided when rolling changes in or out using the comparison tool.[1]

As can be seen in the project and solution design sketched in Figure 6.2, the implementation is carried out in one or more templates with implementation projects, which are transferred to a live solution when the implementation is complete (major release).

Minor enhancements or adjustments to the solution (minor release) are either carried out by means of a maintenance project using the check-out/check-in mechanism, or by means of multiple parallel maintenance projects without check-out (not shown).

---

1 For recommendations about safeguarding the predecessor/successor relationship between stages, see SAP Note 603336.

Changes to the templates can either be transferred to a new implementation project or, via the *Compare and Adjust* function, into an ongoing implementation project (if the scope of changes is larger) or maintenance project (if the scope of changes is smaller), where it can be implemented and prepared for productive use.

Compare and Adjust function

If there is a system upgrade pending, it is advisable to copy the entire solution to an upgrade project ❶ to implement and test an adjusted template from the current solution ❷ without risking live operation. After the implementation of the upgrade is complete, the final status of the upgrade project is transferred to the solution, thereby replacing the old solution ❸.

6.2.2 Methodical Support from the Global ASAP Template Roadmap

The *Global ASAP Template Roadmap* contains methodical guidelines for organizing projects aimed at compiling and delivering (rolling out) global templates. It's designed for complex implementation and harmonization projects, which generally span multiple solutions or applications, various locations, and, in some cases, various countries. Project managers, support managers, solution and technical consultants, as well as partners will find the roadmap useful.

SAP recommends this roadmap because it provides valuable information for all phases, from *Global Program Setup* and *Global Blueprint and Global Realization* to *Global Maintenance and Support*, and from planning a project of this kind to designing a roll-in procedure. It centrally addresses all the basic strategic issues relating to template management, such as program management, creation and delivery of templates, system landscape aspects, Customer Center of Expertise (CCoE) organization, support infrastructures, and procedures for global and local change requests. The *Global ASAP Rollout Roadmap* provides guidance for individual rollout projects. You can also tailor the roadmap's content to your organization's requirements and reuse it to define and implement templates (see Chapter 5, Section 5.2.5).

Phases

Building on expertise validated in practice in other projects, the roadmap helps you to achieve better results, coordinate a cross-functional team effectively, and simultaneously minimize the costs, risks, and time involved in implementing software across various sites.

6.2.3 Creating Templates

You create a template project in the *Implementation/Upgrade* work center or directly in the Project Administration transaction (Transaction SOLAR_PROJECT_ADMIN) by selecting the type TEMPLATE PROJECT. You define the actual template in the TEMPLATES tab page (see Figure 6.3). Here, you create the TEMPLATE SHELL in the customer namespace to gather the corresponding processes and implementation-relevant assignments. You can customize templates on the basis of organizational, regional, component-related, or business criteria. Other potential criteria include the release dependency and the rollout phase. We recommend that you define separate templates for general organizational units, master data, or scenarios that are used in multiple rollouts. As a naming convention, you could include company codes, countries, and components in the template ID.

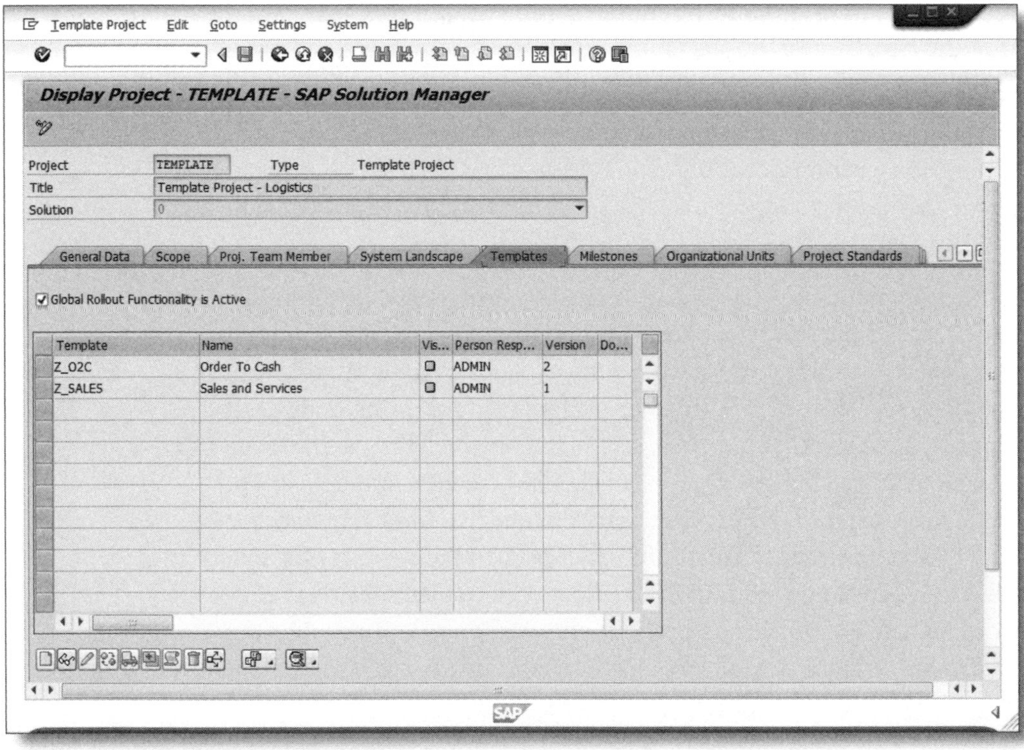

Figure 6.3 Template Definition in a Template Project

You can create one or more templates for each project. If you want to roll out the template in a different SAP Solution Manager system, you must specify a transportable package when you define the template. We recommend that you enter this on the TRANSPORT REQUESTS tab page straightaway, so that the system offers the package you assign as the standard package for all subsequent templates that you create.

The *visibility* of a template is important for later implementation. You can specify whether a template is still being edited and consequently not yet available (PRIVATE) or has been released for usage (PUBLIC). This is important as a means of preventing an unfinished template or new template version being used for an implementation, particularly when the template and implementation projects are in the same SAP Solution Manager system.

VISIBILITY

In addition, you can set the GLOBAL ROLLOUT FUNCTIONALITY IS ACTIVE indicator to specify to what extent rollout projects can effect changes in delivered templates that are being implemented. The range of *global attributes* spans from GLOBAL, which does not permit changes to standard company-wide processes, across various other levels, down to LOCAL, which lends rollouts the most flexibility.

Global attributes

You define your individual project standards, which can take different forms, depending on whether you want to bundle only global processes or all the processes used across the company centrally in one template. The general project data is similar to the data for implementation projects. The system landscape defines which systems should be used as a reference for creating and extracting the preconfiguration, test cases, and similar objects.

Project standards

6.2.4 Business Blueprint Definition and Configuration Structure

After you have created the template(s), you create the reference process structure (Business Blueprint) with all the assignments relevant to the implementation—similar to an implementation project—in the Business Blueprint (SOLAR01) and Configuration (SOLAR02) transactions.

Reference process structure

To make the processes available for use in a template, you assign individual scenarios to the templates with which the corresponding processes are to be delivered. For business scenarios and configuration structures, you use input help on the STRUCTURE tab page to assign the required templates in the TEMPLATES column. The GLOBAL ROLLOUT FUNCTIONALITY IS ACTIVE indicator selected in the Project Administration transaction, along with the global attributes, lets you define the scope of changes that can be made in rollout projects. Initially, these settings apply only to the scenario, but you can transfer them to the lower-level processes and process steps by choosing PASS ON GLOBAL ATTRIBUTE.

6.2.5 Releasing and Implementing Templates

Releasing the template

When you have finished working on the template, you release it for usage in the Project Administration transaction (see Chapter 5, Section 5.3). You must always set the visibility to PUBLIC by choosing CHANGE VISIBILITY. If you are transporting the template to a different SAP Solution Manager system, you need to use the TEMPLATE COLLECTOR with the DELIVER function to include it in a transport request. You are guided step by step through all the necessary activities until you have collected the template content (process structure with implementation-relevant assignments) in a transport request, which you can transport directly to an SAP Solution Manager target system or to the consolidation system via a standard transport route. Note that the objects created in the managed reference systems, such as separate reports or preconfigurations, have to be transported separately; the template contains only the references to these objects.

The procedure is different for template documentation created locally in SAP Solution Manager on the GEN. DOCUMENTATION, CONFIGURATION, DEVELOPMENT, and TEST CASES tab pages. This documentation is entered directly in the template collector and does not have to be transported separately. During the course of the rollout, you also need to ensure consistency between the template system landscape and the rollout system landscape, which means that the components listed in the template actually have to be physically available. For example, if you extend a template to include the implementation of an SAP NetWeaver Business Warehouse (BW), you must ensure that a BW system has been added to the managed system landscape before you implement the template in the rollout. Otherwise, you will not be able to use certain content relevant for the implementation.

You can now use the released templates for implementation in implementation projects. In the Project Administration transaction, the rollout team calls up the rollout project and selects the relevant templates on the SCOPE tab page. When the project is saved, the process structure is decoupled from the template and referenced, and the system creates copies and notes their origin (template). This reference relationship enables the rollout team to run comparisons against more recent template versions and copy changes at any time. It also allows them to roll in local, template-relevant changes to the template during implementation. Alternatively, the template documentation is not copied when a rollout project is created; it is only flagged for copying. The result is that the shipped documents are not copied until they are transferred to the project documentation area in the rollout project and actually changed.

Generating implementation projects

The global attribute, which controls the scope of the changes, comes into play during the rollout project. Globally defined scenarios, processes, and process steps offer few options for changing the process structure or implementation-relevant assignments. You can tailor local scenarios and processes to a specific rollout by using the BPR or by adding or deleting assigned objects such as local programs, Customizing settings, or test cases. Between these two extremes, there is also the option of permitting enhancements but prohibiting deletions.

Because the functions that SAP Solution Manager provides for rollouts are based on those provided for implementation projects, you should also refer to the information in Chapter 5, Sections 5.3 onward.

6.2.6 Tips and Tricks for Working with Templates

In addition to the methodical instructions in the Global ASAP Template Roadmap, certain aspects need to be noted when using template and rollout projects in SAP Solution Manager itself.

Restrictions and Recommendations

Make sure to read FAQ Note 603336, which contains the latest restrictions and recommendations for creating and using templates.

Working with Authorizations

When you carry out template and rollout projects in a centralized SAP Solution Manager system, it's particularly important to assign authorizations at the project level to protect the template and rollout teams' work against unauthorized access. You can do this by adapting authorization object S_PROJECT, PROJECT MANAGEMENT: PROJECT AUTHORIZATION, and assigning the relevant project ID. We also recommend using different document contexts for SAP Solution Manager templates and rollout projects to provide additional protection against unwanted or unauthorized changes.

Restricting changes

Additionally, the RESTRICT CHANGES TO NODES IN PROJECT TO ASSIGNED TEAM MEMBERS indicator in the Project Administration transaction enables you to specify that only users assigned to particular business scenarios or processes may edit those parts of the process structure. This can be useful if global and country-specific templates are being created as part of one template project but are edited by different template teams.

Project Documentation

To enable members of the template team to create documentation, we recommend that you configure the Knowledge Warehouse (KW) authorization object S_IWB to give members authorization for the folder group belonging to the project ID. If maintenance is required, you may also need to assign authorizations for editing (creating, changing, deleting) template documentation, general documentation, configuration documentation, and test case and development documentation (folder group SOLAR00), as well as the document templates (folder group TEMPLATES). The rollout team, alternatively, usually needs display authorization only for document templates and general documentation delivered with the template. The same applies to project documentation as for template projects.

Delete structure elements

In individual cases, you may need to change or delete global structure items. Only selected super users, such as project managers, should be authorized to do so. To delete structure elements from a template, you need authorization for authorization object PROJECT MANAGEMENT: AUTHORIZATION FOR GENERAL PROJECT FUNCTIONS (S_PROJ_GEN) with the value "GLOB" in the PROJ_FUNC field.

Working with Different Template Versions

You cannot display template versions that were created explicitly in the Project Administration transaction at a later date. However, if you want to reproduce the different versions and processing statuses and therefore display the versions, copy the relevant master project, and indicate the versions in the project name and ID. If you still intend to deliver a template's predecessor version, you need to freeze the appropriate template state in a transport request, which you should create using the template collector in the Project Administration transaction.

If the template and rollout projects are in the same SAP Solution Manager system, you need to consider the following points. The template documentation is referenced on a 1:1 basis in the rollout project. If documentation is changed in the template project, it becomes visible immediately in the rollout project, even if it cannot be changed there. Consequently, the documentation ceases to correlate with the business processes currently implemented. We therefore recommend that you change documents in the template project using copies by first copying the documents with a new name to indicate the version and then making your changes. This also applies for other objects that contain version-dependent content, such as test cases or Business Configuration Sets (BC Sets). Make sure that the template is not public while it is being processed. Otherwise, the matching process could accidentally copy inconsistent intermediary stages from the rollout projects.

Working with Multilevel Templates

You can use multilevel templates in SAP Solution Manager. This means that you can use a given template, Template A, to enhance Template A and use Template A as the final basis for the rollout. It's an approach that lets you create country-specific variants from an international master template, for example. It also allows you to copy processes from the BPR to a template project to be modified and rolled out in the template.

Transporting Templates and Template Projects

Always deliver templates from the original projects only (the template projects in which they were created), not from copied projects. This is a basic condition for the comparison to function correctly; when you compare templates, the tool determines only the sources of the direct predecessor.

6.3 Template Management and Lifecycle

Adjusting the templates

Over time, you normally need to make changes to both the template and within the implementation projects or solutions. This is triggered by different situations; for example, new requirements can be included in the template or enhancements made to the solution by means of a maintenance project that could, under certain circumstances, also be relevant to the template. A pending release upgrade could also kick off the next update cycle. The template team makes any necessary changes to the template content in the original template. For major changes, it uses the version counter on the TEMPLATES tab page in the Project Administration transaction and creates a backup copy. When the new version is complete, it needs to be distributed again to the local implementation projects and solutions, as well as to the target organizations for the rollouts.

6.3.1 Comparing and Adjusting Changes

Comparison tool

This is where the comparison tool (Transaction SA_PROJECT_UPGRADE) comes in. It enables the implementation teams to quickly identify changes made to a specific template and copy them to the relevant implementation or rollout projects (rollout), and to return template-relevant changes to the template (roll-in).

This comparison and adjustment functions for successors that have adopted a process structure element and, in the opposite direction, it can carry out a comparison and adjustment with the source. Figure 6.4 shows the most common routes for the comparison and adjustment. For the sake of clarity, the various different project types are grouped together under the umbrella term *project*.

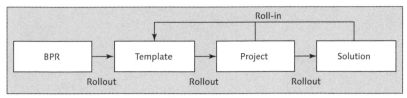

Figure 6.4 Roll-In and Rollout of Changes

In the comparison, a project or solution is taken as the basis. The process and configuration structures implemented in the project or solution, together with their allocations, are compared to the associated comparison nodes of a predecessor or successor. This means that the comparison report automatically identifies the origin or destination of each structure element, which it was either copied from or to (e.g., from the template to the implementation project). Other possible sources include structure items from the BPR and structure items that were copied and possibly changed during the project. The implemented scope can have one single source or a combination of sources. You can always access details about the origin of structure items on the STRUCTURE tab page (ORIGIN column).

Note that there is only one production version of a template per SAP Solution Manager system. This is the version last set to public or transported to a system. The system automatically uses this version as the source for comparison without you having to select it explicitly. Figure 6.5 shows the initial screen of Transaction SA_PROJECT_UPGRADE.

Besides the process structure, the comparison tool also compares the following assignments that you made in the Business Blueprint (SOLAR01) and configuration (SOLAR02) transactions:

- General documentation
- Transactions
- Configuration
- Development
- Test cases
- Training materials
- End-user roles
- Business functions

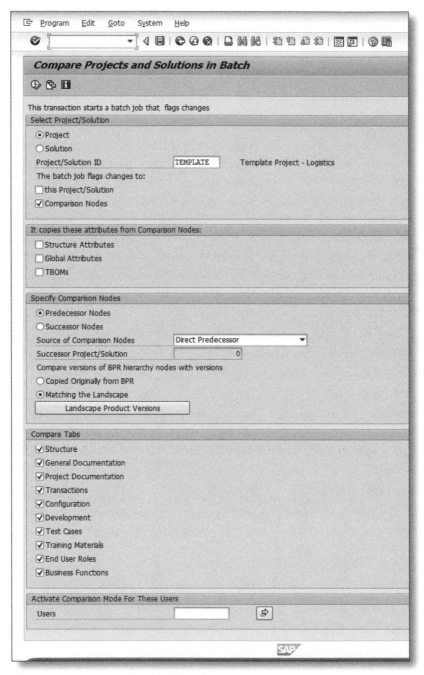

Figure 6.5 Transaction SA_PROJECT_UPGRADE Entry Screen

Note that the system compares only assignments. You cannot com-pare changes to the objects themselves. You can bypass these restrictions as follows:

Pure assignment comparison

Constraint	... and how to tackle it
Changes to implementation-relevant assignments not displayed for BC Sets, CATT/eCATT scripts, general documentation (with a few exceptions)	In the template project, create a new BC Set, CATT/eCATT script, or document by copying the existing objects, for instance. Assign this to the relevant structure item, and remove the old assignment.
New scenarios not displayed	In the rollout project, copy new scenarios on the SCOPE tab page in the Project Administration transaction.

As you can see, the comparison tool is not only designed to identify differences between projects or solutions and their underlying templates, but it can also be used earlier in the process. If you base your template on BPR structure items, you can track down release-related changes and align your template or projects with current processes if necessary. Furthermore, when you copy objects (such as a dominant process) within a project, you can use the comparison tool to update the copies with changes made to the master process.

When the comparison report has run, the comparison results are displayed in the Business Blueprint and Configuration transactions by the Change symbol, in Adjustment mode. (You must have selected the ADJUSTMENT MODE indicator by using the menu path SETTINGS • USER-SPECIFIC, ADJUSTMENT MODE indicator). The log for background job SPROJECT_PROJECT_UPGRADE contains statistics for the changes detected by the tool. Changes are listed in the process structure as well as on the tab page where the change was found. You can easily identify and copy the detected changes by accessing each next change via menu item FIND • NEXT COMPARISON DIFFERENCE.

Comparison results

For reasons of transparency, changes are only flagged for transfer and not copied to the existing project immediately.

You can now run a detailed comparison. The ADJUST TO ORIGINAL function shows you details for the following:

Detailed comparison

- ▶ Changes (new features/deletions in original) detected by the comparison tool (New Version of Original)
- ▶ Changes that were made in the project after the template was copied (Current Version from tab)

Switching comparison nodes

During a detailed comparison, you can also select a different predecessor or successor of the current structure element for comparison using the Switch Comparison Node function. This way you can detect changes that have occurred from one version of the BPR to the next, for example, or see whether a change to a template has not simply reached the subsequent rollout project but has also been transferred to the solution.

6.3.2   Copying Template Changes (Rollout)

To copy template changes, you can configure the comparison tool so that only changes to the implemented templates are considered. To do this, choose the implementation project in the comparison tool, and select the identifier for changes to the comparison nodes.

If you select a predecessor comparison with the source as the comparison node, the comparison only considers template changes in the current project scope. After the background job has been executed, the template changes that were detected can be copied to the Business Blueprint and the configuration.

If you look at the Compare and Adjust dialog box in Figure 6.6, the area on the left shows you that a process step has been delivered with the new template version. First, the rollout team can copy changes resulting from the template to the rollout project and then implement them step-by-step. To confirm the scope of the changes adopted and close the comparison for the tab page in question, you choose Complete (not shown in the figure). This means that you have verified all the tabs indicated as changed for a given structure item. In subsequent comparison runs, the system displays only new changes made to the original, not ones that you have already accepted or ignored. Changes already made locally in the rollout project are never affected when you transfer current template content.

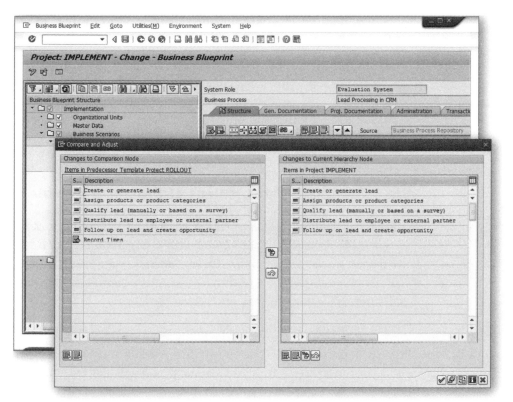

Figure 6.6 Detailed Comparison

6.3.3 Feeding Local Changes Back into the Template (Roll-In)

To feed local changes back, change request mechanisms are used to set up a process that takes into account local requirements the next time a template is changed. You also need to check which changes already made locally need to be rolled back into the central template to aid standardization.

The purpose is to define the scope of the roll-in process in detail, that is, which elements from the process structure are to be transferred with which implementation-relevant assignments; for example, documentation, transactions, configuration, customer developments, and test cases. Other purely local objects, such as local documents, which are of no additional use to the template or other locations, and

Scope of the roll-in

BC Sets with purely local customizing values are not usually relevant for the roll-in process.

From a technical perspective, the roll-in procedure and configuration for the comparison tool is the same as for the rollout. However, the comparison is only configured on the basis of the template project, and a successor comparison of the appropriate type (such as implementation) is specified as the comparison node.

6.4   Template Management at Procter & Gamble

From our point of view, the greatest strength of SAP Solution Manager is the possibility of storing technical information across all systems in a single solution, which can be connected to business processes. This continuous coverage of the ALM processes guarantees that our libraries are kept up to date, now and in the long term.

Gerd Siemering, Procter & Gamble

Procter & Gamble

Procter & Gamble (P&G) is one of the world's biggest consumer goods manufacturers, with brands such as Ariel, Lenor, Duracell, Oral-B, Wick, Pampers, Pantene, Head & Shoulders, Gillette, and Braun. The issue of sustainability is very important to us. This is deeply rooted in our corporate culture and applies not just to the environmental sustainability of our products but also to socially and economically responsible behavior. These are key to the long-term success of our company. On September 29, 2010, in the context of its continuing sustainability strategy, the corporation announced a long-term ecological sustainability vision and corresponding objectives for 2020 that provide measurable advances toward making that vision a reality.

IT at P&G belongs to the Global Business Services organization (GBS). As part of IT Develop and Operate (ITDO), our application management horizontal team is responsible for the IT processes for developing, implementing, and delivering all solutions.

Motivation

For years, SAP Solution Manager has been, for us, a strategic platform that not only offers functions for our IT processes, but which represents a single source of truth in the form of centralized libraries for the Application Lifecycle Management (ALM) for all SAP solutions. Our focus is not so much on process-oriented storage; instead, we concentrate on storage directed at technical components. From our point of view, the greatest strength of SAP Solution Manager is the possibility of continuously storing technical information across all systems in a single solution, which can be connected to usage data for business processes. This continuous coverage of the ALM processes guarantees that our libraries are kept up to date, now and in the long term. We believe that ALM library systems that do not include this sustainability are doomed to failure.

Despite the fact that it did not cover all our requirements to start with, it made sense for us to position SAP Solution Manager as the ALM platform in our company. When we discussed matters with SAP, it became clear that this was the right decision, and missing functions could be implemented by means of co-innovation projects with SAP's development and product management (see Chapter 15, Section 15.5).

The documentation of the solutions is the starting point and the result of each application management lifecycle, so it should also form the basis of the SAP Solution Manager processes' *single source of truth* approach. Since 2008, we have been successfully using the functions available in the SAP Solution Manager's project administration environment to document our projects. This approach enables us to monitor our projects and create transparency about the status of each project. The solution was successively expanded after successful pilot stages and has been used very effectively for projects that are probably among the largest SAP implementation projects in the world.

Global rollout scenario

SAP Solution Manager offers two options for using templates that have been created previously. On the one hand, templates can be used to build up a company-specific library. On the other hand, they can form the basis for group rollout in implementation projects. From the start, we have used the group rollout scenario for our projects. This allows us to implement templates both locally and regionally, as well as manage the necessary changes and expansions of the global template. This task is delegated to projects, which are responsible for changes to the template documentation throughout the project, during implementation of the template. This way, the templates are continuously improved by means of tried-and-tested procedures.

We maintain our centralized design documents in SAP Solution Manager's template environment. These design documents describe the entire global solution, not simply the most recent changes. We differentiate here between functional and technical design and use our own document types. In an environment in which information is constantly being removed from storage and in which implementation partners and developer teams change frequently, this type of centralized documentation library is essential.

Lifecycle design

In our system, the distribution of templates (rollout) is designed as a lifecycle design solution. Dedicated document types in the project environment are assigned in mirror-image to the two central document types for design management from the template environment. These dedicated document types are used to specify and document changes to the solution on each design level (first the functional, then the technical) (see Figure 6.7). This results in a clear understanding of which documents in the template environment need to be adjusted by the project after the specified changes are implemented. These adjustments are made for the solution that reflects the new overall design (roll-in). The documents from the template are therefore the start and end points of the design process when it comes to changes, and they are an additional end product when it comes to new solutions. The design of changes is documented in the SAP Solution Manager by means of implementation projects and is also managed using the same library hierarchy as in the template environment. In the template roll-out scenario, the higher-level complete documents, the *functional solution document* and the *technical solution document* from the template, are made available as reference documentation on a separate tab in the implementation project. The additional functional requirements and the functional design are documented in the *gap sheet*. The technical design, on the other hand, is mapped in the document type *technical specification*. These two document types are always assigned to the same nodes as the reference documentation, but they are attached on a separate tab for production documentation. Additionally, links are used to provide a standard function that allows you to refer directly to the specific reference template documents from document attributes maintenance.

We create these technical and functional design documents in accordance with the specifications of Capability Maturity Model Integration (CMMI) because the external partners who carry out the implementation projects at P&G are generally certified to CMMI Level 5. Unlike ITIL, CMMI provides a reference model for software engineering (CMMI-DEV) and software purchasing (CMMI-ACQ), as well as for the degree of maturity and quality management of these processes. Due to the fact that we cooperate with different external partners, our contact persons often change during the Blueprint, Design, and Build phases. This makes it vital, especially in our major projects, that the documentation is of a high quality and that standardized document templates are used. Using different document types in SAP Solution Manager makes management considerably easier.

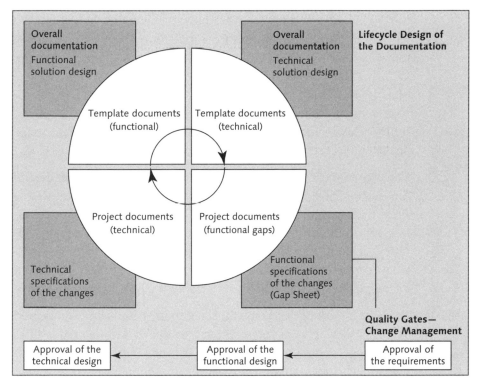

Figure 6.7 Lifecycle Design of the Documentation

At present, we also use template management to manage change management approvals that have an effect on transport management. The transport orders are created locally in the managed systems. The technical name of the SAP Solution Manager document is referenced as an *attribute*. SAP Solution Manager then checks whether the document has the correct status for a transport release, meaning that the change gate criteria for the change are fulfilled

Change management

because both the functional and technical design documents have been approved (refer to Figure 6.7).

Together with SAP, we are working on a solution that will allow us in the future to map the workflow and the transport connection via change management. The aim is to employ an integrated solution to guarantee that the right documents are used in the hierarchy nodes of the implementation projects and to connect the lifecycle design created in accordance with our documentation standards to the actual standard change management tool in SAP Solution Manager.

Technical objects

In addition to the documentation, technical objects in the configuration can be assigned to template nodes (Transaction SOLAR02). We have used this function at P&G for a long time. The focus of our customer developments is mainly on transactions, programs, and tables. With the introduction of the new application *Custom Code Lifecycle Management*, which SAP developed as a co-innovation with P&G, management of these objects will be expanded and simplified in the future. This includes ownership of the objects, cross-system usage analyses, lifecycle attributes, criticality, and so on.

We will connect the management of our custom developments in Transaction SOLAR02 with this new central library. Connecting these two central libraries of the SAP Solution Manager offers countless opportunities for aligning information and interesting opportunities for the change management process. The aim is to make it possible to plan and measure an organizational reduction of custom developments (see also Chapter 15, Section 15.5).

Project monitoring

Using a reporting add-on (Excel output) based on Transaction SOLAR_EVAL, it is possible to finely manage all documentation tasks and change management workflows in our template projects. This lends transparency to project advances in the Blueprint, Design, and Build phases of very complex implementation projects that integrate hundreds of resources. This makes it possible to identify tasks that last too long and the people responsible for them. All types of development are represented by documents and scheduled using milestones. This makes it possible to carry out and document rollout customizing projects that are based purely on cookbooks. In the long term, we are planning to discuss with SAP the option of mapping this type of monitoring information in the SAP Solution Manager's BW.

The measurement results of quality objectives are also evident for each project. To comply with the defined documentation standards, the content of the relevant project documents is also subjected to quality inspections. This type of information will later be included in a Quality Gate Management system for the projects.

Integration with test management is not yet covered by an automated interface as we currently have difficulties with addressing specific test cases from the library for the template processes defined in the scope for our projects. This involves tens of thousands of test cases. We have not yet been able to map the transfer of the projects to the SAP Solution Manager's Solution Directory and therefore to the support for the operating stage. However, we are planning to implement this with the improved opportunities of the Compare and Adjust function in the new Release 7.1 of SAP Solution Manager (see Section 6.3.1).

Testing and operation

The template management process integrated in SAP Solution Manager to provide support for the group rollout enables us to standardize software quality management in our projects and always keep our template documentation up to date. This means that the template management methods play an important role in standardizing our processes. Additionally, introducing the library for managing custom developments makes reducing customer code a measurable goal. For our largest projects, we already use the template rollout application provided in SAP Solution Manager. In the future, we are planning to establish this as the global standard for all SAP implementation projects.

Conclusion

The Author

Gerd Siemering is an Application Manager for SAP Solution Manager and other Application Lifecycle Management tools at Procter & Gamble. He has a total of 13 years of experience with SAP, as an in-house consultant in industrial enterprises and an application manager, also for mega solutions (such as SAP SD/MM at Wella). He has been working with SAP Solution Manager for 7 years. He currently works in the Application Management Horizontal Team at P&G, where he shares responsibility for global IT processes in the development, implementation, and delivery stages.

Before transferring your solution configuration to your pro-
duction system landscape and thus making it available for
your operative business processes, you must first check that
all changes have been made correctly and do not have a
negative impact on other business processes. This chapter
provides an overview of the extensive test functions in SAP
Solution Manager

7   Test Management

These days, typical customer solutions look like this: Customers use SAP software to map their business processes end to end, whereby they adjust the SAP standard software to their individual requirements during the initial implementation. Many SAP customers supplement their SAP solution with partner and third-party products that they integrate with the SAP solution. In selected areas, additional developments are made to map missing functions that are required for the individual customer situation and that are not included in the SAP standard software. This heterogeneous SAP-centric solution is customer-specific and therefore needs to be tested extensively before being used in production. Among others, the following test types are used:

Motivation for testing SAP-centric solutions

- ▶ Functional tests of individual business process steps
- ▶ Functional tests of end-to-end business processes
- ▶ Interface and integration tests
- ▶ End user tests
- ▶ Performance and load tests

Even after the go-live, numerous software changes require test activities:

- Maintenance activities, including the activation of SAP support packages (SPs)
- Functional enhancements made by activating SAP enhancement packages (EHPs)
- Upgrades to higher releases of SAP solutions
- Customer-specific enhancements made through configuration or software developments
- Changes and enhancements to interfaces
- Integration of additional partner or third-party applications into the overall solution

7.1 Procedure from Test Planning to Test Execution

Determining the test scope Different ways of determining the test scope must be used depending on the type of change made to the software (see Figure 7.1). If you are implementing a new SAP solution or want to model additional business processes, we recommend that you supplement the business process hierarchy in the solution document in SAP Solution Manager. That way, the delta test scope can be determined automatically.

In contrast, if you want to make changes to technical SAP objects, you should execute a *Change Impact Analysis* to discover what impact these changes have on important business processes and to develop a suitable test plan on that basis.

Test planning During test planning, you either create the required test cases in manual tests, in which process descriptions and expected results are described, or through automatic tests using SAP or partner tools that automate the manual test process. You can assign these tests to the corresponding business processes and then select them for a test cycle.

For a concrete test cycle, start by determining the test scope, then derive suitable test cases and summarize everything in a test plan. The test plan is usually divided into smaller test packages that are assigned to participating testers and thus make it easier to coordinate the test tasks for your test manager.

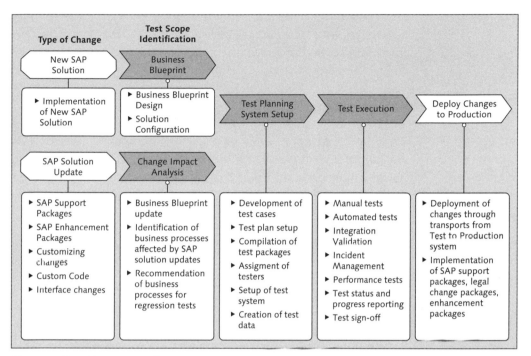

Figure 7.1 Test Management Process

All software changes must be transferred to the test systems for testing the changed functions and updated configuration of your business processes. In addition, you have to provide suitable test data in the test systems to execute all business processes to be tested with realistic variants.

Test system structure

At the start of the test cycle, all involved persons are informed, and the testers start to execute the manual and automatic tests. In addition to the functional tests, it might be necessary to test changed interfaces. Users who know the business processes well participate in user tests. When functions are changed, these users usually also take care of the formal acceptance (user test). Performance and load tests take place after the functional tests. If you detect errors during testing, you can record these directly in problem messages and let experts analyze them. After the errors have been corrected in the development system, the corrections are transported back into the test system where you can then retest. Reporting enables your test coordinators to gain an overview of the current state of activities, test packages still to be processed, and the status of open problem messages.

Executing tests

Activating software
changes

After you have completed your tests, corrections, and the final release, you can transport all software changes to your production environment and implement the SPs or EHPs.

7.2   Options for Test Tools

A number of integrated tools are available for organizing and executing the various test types. In addition to SAP tools, non-SAP tools are also integrated into SAP Solution Manager (see Figure 7.2). With the new SAP Solution Manager, you have more options for executing your functional tests, which we explain in the following sections.

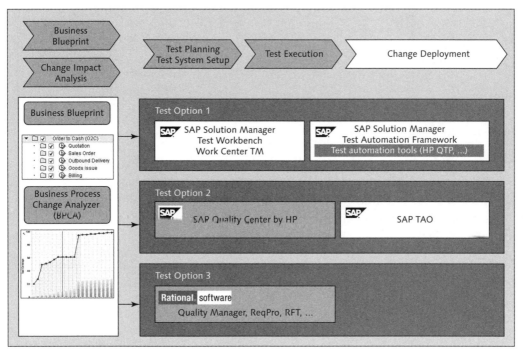

Figure 7.2 Test Options for Organizing and Executing Functional Tests

7.2.1   Test Option 1

You define and document your business processes in the *Test Workbench* (TWB) of the *Business Blueprint* integrated into SAP Solution Manager. The Test Workbench helps you organize and execute your tests. The *Business Process Change Analyzer* (BPCA) is used for the risk-based derivation of the test scope and can directly generate a test plan for TWB integration. With the new SAP Solution Manager, the new *Test Automation Framework* enables you to easily integrate eCATT as well as powerful partner tools for test automation (e.g., HP QuickTest Professional). During the test phases, you can use the SAP Solution Manager Service Desk to manage your problem messages. This is integrated into the TWB. Extensive reporting in SAP Solution Manager and an integrated SAP NetWeaver Business Warehouse (SAP NetWeaver BW) complement the functions for test coordinators. Test option 1 therefore makes it possible to completely cover all business processes based on SAP, partner, and non-SAP applications.

7.2.2 Test Option 2

You use the *Business Blueprint* to define and document business processes. An interface transmits your business process hierarchy as well as links to process requirements to the *Requirements* module of the SAP Quality Center by HP. You can use the BPCA to determine the business processes that are affected by software changes. The SAP Quality Center helps you organize your tests and plan and execute your test cycles. The SAP Quality Center module—HP QuickTest Professional—supports automatic tests. The supplementary SAP Test Acceleration and Optimization product lets you create automatic tests in a quick and convenient fashion. During your test phase, you manage problems using *defect management*, which is integrated into the SAP Quality Center module. The SAP Quality Center is rounded off with extensive reporting and the option to create dashboards for management. You can transmit all test results and open problem messages to SAP Solution Manager using the aforementioned interface. The integration makes it possible for your support staff and SAP to work on solving the problems, transfer corrections back to the SAP Quality Center, and then request retesting. In SAP Solution Manager, the project manager can call up reports that display the test results in connection with the status of the implementation.

SAP Quality Center by HP

7.2.3 Test Option 3

With the new SAP Solution Manager, we have a third test option. Like the other two test options, it uses both the Business Blueprint and the BPCA of SAP Solution Manager. A new standard interface integrates the *Requirements* module by IBM Rational (ReqPro) and *SAP Quality Manager*, the test management module by IBM Rational.

IBM Rational

The test organization, the setup of manual and automatic tests, and the management of problem messages are handled using various IBM Rational modules. You can use the same standard interface to return your test results and open problem messages to SAP Solution Manager.

7.2.4 Supplementary Products

As an option, we recommend considering the SAP Test Data Migration Server (TDMS) for setting up test data in lean test systems. SAP recommends using SAP LoadRunner by HP for performance and load tests.

7.3 Business Process Change Analyzer

Changes to SAP solutions

You often have to make changes to your SAP applications after they have gone live. Changes are often due to maintenance work or functional enhancements of business processes that were required by departments or changes caused by SPs and EHPs. Changes bear a risk with regard to the availability and performance of your mission-critical business processes. Before you implement the changes, you have to test your applications. However, there is often not enough time to really test everything. You thus need to have an option to test only those business processes and scenarios that are affected by the change. Such an analysis is often a time-consuming and error-prone process in which several SAP transactions are checked, and data is exported into a standalone reporting tool such as Microsoft Excel.

Change Impact Analysis

With SAP Solution Manager 7.0 EHP1, a new option was introduced for analyzing the effects of changes in the scope of the general test management process. SAP therefore introduced the Business Process Change Analyzer (BPCA) we mentioned earlier, which enables you to analyze the effects of a technical change to determine which business processes are affected. Based on customer feedback, the BPCA was enhanced significantly in SAP Solution Manager 7.1.

7.3.1 Use Case 1: Customizing Changes

Most business processes that are executed in SAP applications are adjustable. The Customizing options provided by SAP—such as the IMG—enable you to adjust your applications to your business requirements. Most of the customizing is made during the initial implementation of the application, but you can also change the customizing afterwards, for example, due to business changes.

The BPCA enables you to exactly identify the effects of customizing changes on existing business processes. For changes to Customizing, the tables in the backend are usually changed. Many backend tables are generic; that is, they are used for numerous business processes so that an analysis that is based only on table names is not precise. BPCA in SAP Solution Manager 7.1 provides analyses that go beyond table names and now also supports, where possible, analyses that are based on table names and the corresponding keys. With such an analysis of table names and the corresponding keys, the BPCA can identify exactly which business processes are affected by customizing changes.

Analysis of tables

The effects of customizing changes are analyzed as follows (see Figure 7.3):

Procedure

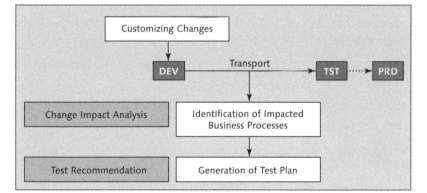

Figure 7.3 Analysis of Customizing Changes

1. The user (application consultant, developer, or business process expert) uses a standard Customizing application (e.g., the IMG) to make changes in a test system.

2. The user executes module tests for this Customizing change and creates a transport request for it. A test manager executes a BPCA analysis of the change (in the transport request).

3. The test manager checks the results of the Change Impact Analysis and creates a test plan for the affected business processes.

7.3.2 Use Case 2: Changing Custom Code

Code changes or developments occur during the initial implementation of a SAP application as well as in the context of ongoing maintenance work. Many customers create or change custom code in the form of modified function modules, transactions, user exits, UI objects, and so on, to adjust SAP applications to their business requirements. Just like customizing changes, code changes are made during the initial implementation of the application or due to business changes, code changes and enhancements, or as part of ongoing maintenance work.

The BPCA can identify exactly what impact the changes to custom code have on existing business processes. The Change Impact Analysis for changes to custom code is comparable to the analysis for customizing changes (see Figure 7.4).

1. The user (developer) uses a standard development environment (e.g., ABAP Workbench) to make the changes in a development system. In the development environment, the user performs module tests for the custom code development and creates a transport request for it.

2. A test manager executes BPCA of the change (in the transport request).

3. The test manager checks the results of the Change Impact Analysis and creates a test plan for the affected business processes

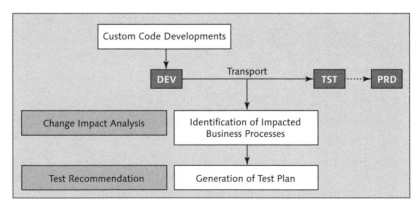

Figure 7.4 Analysis of Changes to Customer Code

Test managers can use the Change Impact Analysis to determine the regression test scope for software changes. The test scope includes potential side effects of the changes, which developers or function consultants might not detect. This avoids potential risks in the production environment, which might be caused by these changes.

7.3.3 Use Case 3: Enhancement Package—Business Function Analysis

With EHPs, you profit from constant innovation in various SAP applications. As an SAP customer, you can implement these enhancements in a modular fashion by activating new functions and technical improvements only to the extent appropriate for your business requirements.

These new enhancements are bundled as business functions in EHPs and controlled using a switch framework with which you can selectively activate new functions when desired and to the extent desired.

Business functions

These functions are new and many of them cannot be "turned off" after they have been activated. Therefore, the change and test managers in the IT department have to identify the impact of activating new enhancements.

The BPCA offers innovative new functions that you can use to analyze the effects of business function changes before you activate them. A test manager can thus see the impact of activating new business functions required by the company.

The effects of planned business function changes are analyzed as follows (see Figure 7.5):

Process flow

1. The business user changes the business functions available in an SAP EHP and decides that the new functions are useful to the company and triggers a request for change to activate the new business functions.

2. A test manager responds to this application for activation of a business function by executing the corresponding business function before activating a BPCA analysis.

3. A test manager checks the results of the Change Impact Analysis and designs a temporary view of potential impacts of the activation of new functions. These results can later be reused to create a regression test plan for the affected business processes if the new business function is activated.

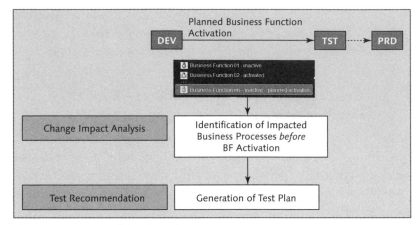

Figure 7.5 Analysis of the Planned Business Function Activation

This function is useful for test managers because applications for activating new business functions are often submitted when a new SAP EHP has been implemented. In many cases, potential training requirements are also recognized with the business processes affected by these new enhancements.

7.3.4 Use Case 4: Optimization of the Test Scope for SAP Support Packages or SAP Enhancement Packages

SAP customers regularly have to update their systems with the latest SPs or EHPs from SAP to minimize risks for their production environments, reduce their support costs, and profit from the latest SAP innovations. To make large implementations, you must perform extensive regression tests of your critical business processes. Handling these projects is a huge challenge for the IT teams, especially in an environment with limited resources.

Effectively planning regression tests

They look for ways to effectively plan regression tests for major changes such as SPs or EHPs. The BPCA has a function for detecting the impact of these major changes on existing productive business scenarios, but the results of such an analysis often show that the regression test scope is too large. In SAP Solution Manager 7.1, the BPCA offers a new function with which you can use various criteria to determine and optimize the test scope for your regression tests for SPs and other major change events (see Figure 7.6).

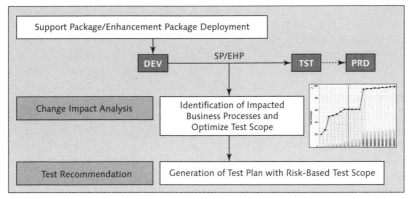

Figure 7.6 Analysis of Extensive Changes Such as SAP Support Packages

The BPCA can compare objects that have been changed in an SP to objects that are used in various business scenarios to analyze the impact of a technical change. With such a comparison, the BPCA can determine which scenarios—if they were tested first—would cover the greatest portion of objects changed in an support package. With this approach, the BPCA can recommend an optimized test scope so that all objects modified in a change event are only tested once, and the test scope is reduced to a minimum.

Test scope optimization

The following section uses an example to illustrate this concept. First, the test manager executes a preliminary Change Impact Analysis for SAP ECC 6.0 SP04. It bases this on a sample Business Blueprint for sales order processing. The initial BPCA results are displayed in Figure 7.7.

Change Impact Analysis

The last column shows the number of affected objects for each business process step. The step CREATE SALES ORDER FROM QUOTATION has 57 objects that were changed in the support package and the QUOTATION LIST process step has five. The five objects in the QUOTATION LIST process step could be a subset of the 57 objects in the CREATE SALES ORDER FROM QUOTATION process step. That is, if the CREATE SALES ORDER FROM QUOTATION step is tested, it may no longer be necessary to test the QUOTATION LIST step because the affected objects have already been tested.

Business Process	Business Process Step	Referred Object	Test case available?	Num - All
Pre- Sales Processing	Create Inquiry	VA11	☑	43
Pre- Sales Processing	Change inquiry	VA12	☑	45
Pre- Sales Processing	Create Quotation from inquiry	VA21	☑	36
Pre- Sales Processing	Display quotation	VA23	☑	30
Pre- Sales Processing	Create Sales order from quotation	VA01	☑	57
Pre- Sales Processing	Quotation list	VA25	☑	5
Pre- Sales Processing	Quotation rejection	VA22	☑	44
Sales Order Processing for Prospect	Create Sales Order	VA01	☑	53
Sales Order Processing for Prospect	Change Sales order	VA02	☑	53
Sales Order Processing for Prospect	Delivery due list	VL10C	☑	66
Sales Order Processing for Prospect	Display Sales Order	VA03	☑	34
Sales Order Processing for Prospect	Picking from Delivery Monitor	VL06O	☑	43
Sales Order Processing for Prospect	Change Delivery-Check Batch	VL02N	☑	22
Sales Order Processing for Prospect	Post goods Issue- From Delivery Monitor	VL06O	☑	68
Sales Order Processing for Prospect	Billing	VF01	☑	17
Credit Management	Set credit limit	FD32	☑	29
Credit Management	Create sales order	VA01	☑	43
Credit Management	Review blocked Sales order	VKM1	☑	1
Credit Management	Create Delivery	VL01N	☑	31
Credit Management	Billing	VF01	☑	2

Figure 7.7 Initial Results of the Change Impact Analysis for the SAP Support Package

Optimizing the test scope

The next step is to show how the BPCA can optimize the test scope in this example. In the new optimization interface, users can use various optimization procedures to reduce the test scope as much as possible. Figure 7.8 shows the aforementioned interface for optimizing the test scope for the preceding example.

The interface shows that the user can change the test coverage percentage (currently 100%) so that it shows the percentage of modified objects covered by the test scope displayed below. The user can also specify the available overall test effort (capacity) to see which test coverage is possible with the selected test effort.

As you can see in Figure 7.9, the user needs a total of 3.67 hours to get 100% test coverage. If such an optimization was not possible, the overall test scope would be 14.08 hours. The BPCA has determined that it is not necessary to test the QUOTATION LIST to cover 100% of test objects if CREATE SALES ORDER FROM QUOTATION is tested. This example uses a simple process structure with about 25 process steps. For real customer scenarios, the savings can be much greater.

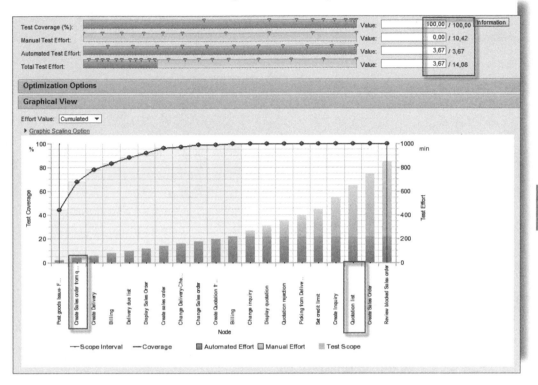

Figure 7.8 Optimized Test Scope

You want to make sure that your high priority business processes are protected by such optimization procedures for tests. That is why users can use certain parameters to determine a basic test scope in BPCA. The business processes included in such a basic test scope are not subject to the optimization criteria and are always included in the test scope. Figure 7.9 shows the interface for test scope optimization. Here, a basic test scope is defined so that the *billing* process steps are included, and optimization is not applied to these processes (this is represented by a black line in Figure 7.9).

Protecting
mission-critical
processes

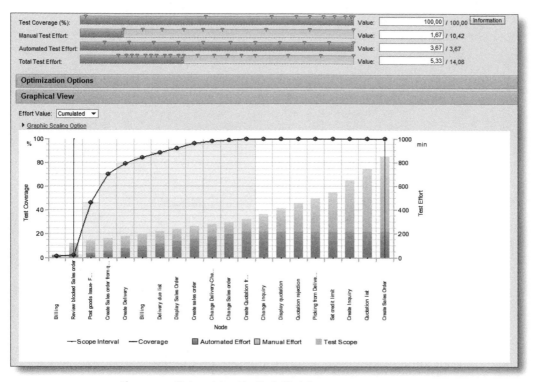

Figure 7.9 Determining the Basic Test Scope

7.3.5 Preparations

Prerequisites Before you can use the BPCA, two main prerequisites must be met.

- In SAP Solution Manager, precise information about the Business Blueprint and the SAP system must be available. The Business Blueprint should describe in detail how users on the customer side use the SAP applications.

- There should be a technical bill of material (TBOM); that is, a list of all technical SAP objects that are used or accessed when a business transaction is executed, for each process step in the Business Blueprint. The following section describes these two important steps in more detail.

Preparatory Step 1a: Connectivity of Managed Systems

RFC connections To make sure the BPCA can technically analyze software changes, the corresponding managed systems (SAP application systems) must be connected to SAP Solution Manager via RFC connections. This is the only way the tool can access change-related information for analysis and activate traces in the managed system if TBOMs have to be created.

Preparatory Step 1b: Documentation of Business Processes

The results of the BPCA Impact Analysis show which business processes are affected by the Change Planned Software changes. For this analysis, the BPCA needs a well-documented Business Blueprint in SAP Solution Manager. The process hierarchy and the corresponding executable units (SAP transaction codes, SAP CRM application URLs, etc.) must be documented for the BPCA to work properly. Chapter 4, Section 4.2, explains the best practice procedure for documenting such a process hierarchy and alternative ways for creating such documentation.

Preparatory Step 2: Technical Bill of Materials (TBOM)

To ensure the BPCA can technically analyze software changes, a TBOM must be created and maintained for each business process step (depicted in Figure 7.10). TBOMs represent a collection of names of technical SAP objects that were used or accessed when a business process step was executed. To ensure that the BPCA can compile such a list of object names, the customer must execute the business process in the SAP system, and the BPCA must have a trace function that is used to collect all the names of SAP objects in the background. This trace is then compiled in a TBOM and saved in the corresponding process step in SAP Solution Manager.

Creation using trace

Here, this concept is explained using an example in which a customer uses an SAP ERP system that includes a CREATE SALES ORDER business process in which the business users create sales orders in the SAP system. For this process step, the business users could use standard SAP Transaction VA01. To ensure that BPCA can identify the effects on the CREATE SALES ORDER process step, a TBOM must be created for Transaction VA01. To do so, the customer must first document the information on the process step and the corresponding transaction code in a *project* or a *solution* in SAP Solution Manager. As soon as the documentation has been created, the user can execute Transaction VA01 in SAP Solution Manager to create the TBOM. If the transaction is executed in the SAP ERP system, a trace is activated. If the user then actually executes the transaction by entering the right data and performing various actions on the screen, this trace collects all objects used during execution. As soon as the execution is completed, a TBOM is compiled and stored under the documented transaction code (in our example, Transaction VA01) in the SAP Solution Manager system.

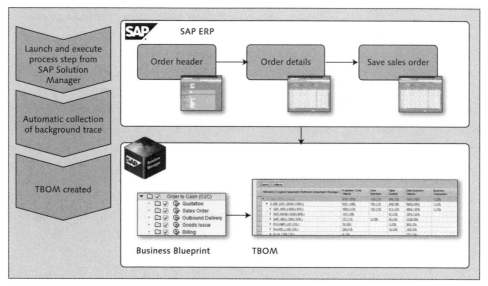

Figure 7.10 Technical Bill of Materials (TBOM)

In the example shown in Figure 7.11, the TBOM for Transaction VA01 contains 8,315 objects in total. Different object types were collected: 6,253 program or code objects, 132 user interfaces, 469 table contents, and so on. These figures differ for different customer situations and execution variants of the same transaction code.

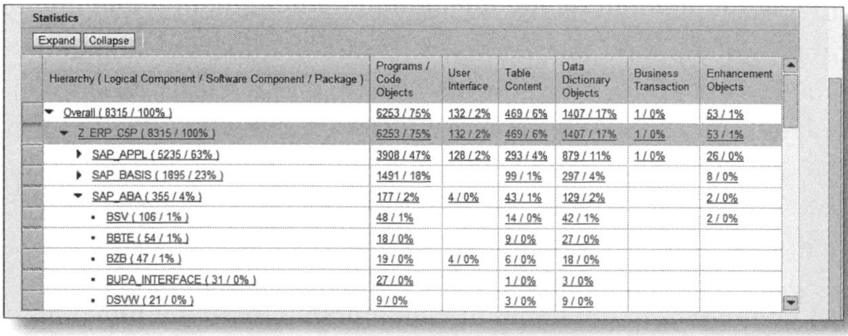

Hierarchy (Logical Component / Software Component / Package)	Programs / Code Objects	User Interface	Table Content	Data Dictionary Objects	Business Transaction	Enhancement Objects
▾ Overall (8315 / 100%)	6253 / 75%	132 / 2%	469 / 6%	1407 / 17%	1 / 0%	53 / 1%
▾ Z_ERP_CSP (8315 / 100%)	6253 / 75%	132 / 2%	469 / 6%	1407 / 17%	1 / 0%	53 / 1%
▸ SAP_APPL (5235 / 63%)	3908 / 47%	128 / 2%	293 / 4%	879 / 11%	1 / 0%	26 / 0%
▸ SAP_BASIS (1895 / 23%)	1491 / 18%	99 / 1%	297 / 4%			8 / 0%
▾ SAP_ABA (355 / 4%)	177 / 2%	4 / 0%	43 / 1%	129 / 2%		2 / 0%
• BSV (106 / 1%)	48 / 1%		14 / 0%	42 / 1%		2 / 0%
• BBTE (54 / 1%)	18 / 0%		9 / 0%	27 / 0%		
• BZB (47 / 1%)	19 / 0%	4 / 0%	6 / 0%	18 / 0%		
• BUPA_INTERFACE (31 / 0%)	27 / 0%		1 / 0%	3 / 0%		
• DSVW (21 / 0%)	9 / 0%		3 / 0%	9 / 0%		

Figure 7.11 Sample Content of a TBOM for Transaction VA01—Create Sales Order Process

TBOMs can be created for all ABAP-based SAP applications; for example, transaction codes, Web Dynpro ABAP applications, applications based on the SAP Web client, business server pages (BSPs), and so on. Manually creating a TBOM can be both time consuming and hard to organize for many IT teams. In SAP Solution Manager 7.1, there are numerous new options for creating these TBOMs, which replace manual creation.

All ABAP applications

Reusing Automatic Test Scripts

To create a TBOM, the business process must be executed in exactly the same way a business user would execute it. Customers who have invested in test automation try to ensure that the same business processes are automated using an automation tool so that regression tests can be executed. Because these automatic scripts also execute business process steps, the same automatic scripts/test cases can be used to automatically create the TBOM (see Figure 7.12).

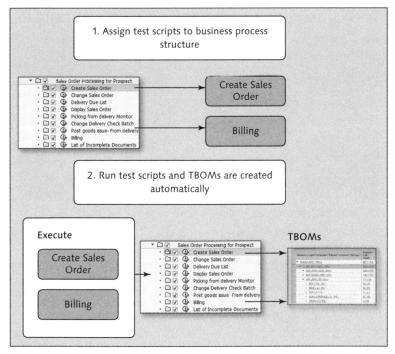

Figure 7.12 Reusing Automatic Test Scripts for Creating a TBOM

For customers who use SAP Solution Manager for test management, Release 7.1 provides a new Test Automation Framework that can be

Test option 1

used to reuse automatic scripts to create TBOMs. For more information, see Section 7.4.

Test option 2

For customers who use the HP Quality Center and SAP Test Acceleration and Optimization, SAP TAO 2.0 SP04 assists with the creation and maintenance of automatic scripts. For more information, see Section 7.5.

Assistance from Business Users

If you have to create TBOMs manually, you need some help from a person who knows the business processes well. Even though this knowledge can be useful to quality teams with regard to executing a change influence analysis with BPCA, many IT teams do not have this knowledge. The teams depend on business process experts or departments when they have to create TBOMs.

These business users generally know little about SAP Solution Manager and do not have the technical skills to understand the projects and solutions in SAP Solution Manager. In addition, tracking an activity in which business users have to execute processes in a complex SAP landscape with many business scenarios can be a challenge for quality teams.

"TBOM tasks" function

To assist business users with the execution of the processes and support the creation of TBOMs, BPCA has the new *TBOM Tasks* function in SAP Solution Manager 7.1. Quality assurance (QA) teams can use this function to create tasks for business process steps that do not have a TBOM (e.g., in the form of a to-do list) and assign these tasks to specialist teams. Business users can then be informed of the tasks via email and receive an easy access link to their personal worklists. In their worklists, business users see a list of business transactions that have been assigned to them. Business users execute the transactions in sequence and work their way through the worklist.

While a business user is executing the transactions, BPCA activates the trace in the relevant systems in the background, compiles a TBOM, and assigns it to the corresponding process step in SAP Solution Manager. The business user is completely unaffected by this complex process. The quality team can now create the TBOMs with the specialist team.

Reusing a Manual Test Cycle

Another option to create a TBOM is to reuse a pending test cycle. In a normal regression cycle for a comprehensive change, all critical business scenarios are tested. In such a test cycle, individual testers are assigned test packages with corresponding test case information so that they can execute the tests. Because the execution of the process steps in such a test cycle corresponds to the steps for creating a TBOM, you can reuse the test cycle for creating TBOMs. If a tester executes a business transaction directly from the worklist in the TWB of SAP Solution Manager, he can activate TBOM traces so that a TBOM is created in the background while the business transaction is executed.

You can use the already scheduled, planned test effort to create TBOMs. However, this is only possible if you use the TWB to manage your manual tests (similar to test option 1 in Section 7.4).

7.3.6 Customer Benefits

The technical Change Impact Analysis in the BPCA lets you manage changes to SAP software more efficiently. The use cases in Sections 7.3.1 to 7.3.4 show how valuable it is to execute a Change Impact Analysis for each software change in the SAP environment. The benefits include the following:

▶ Reduction of business risks due to potential side effects of software changes and determination of a risk-based test scope for all SAP software changes

▶ Reduction of tests costs thanks to the precise determination of the test scope for all SAP modifications

▶ Reduction of maintenance costs for automatic test scripts by identifying negative effects of software changes on these scripts

▶ Implementation of support packages with information about their potential impact

7.4   Test Option 1

Test option 1 represents the use of the original SAP Solution Manager functionality. That is, SAP Solution Manager provides all tools and functions for test management. Test option 1 supports the entire test process and enables you to cover all your business processes.

7.4.1 Overview of Test Functions and Tools for Test Option 1

Most of the functions and tools for testing offered by option 1 are provided by SAP Solution Manager and SAP Test Data Migration Server (SAP TDMS). As of SAP Solution Manager 7.1, you have the additional option to use the new Test Automation Framework to integrate test automation tools from partners and third-party providers. You can thus complement SAP's own test automation functions in a sensible manner (see Figure 7.13).

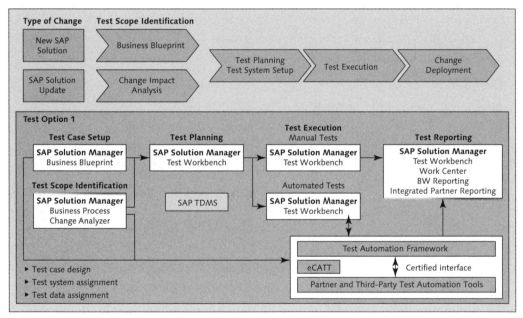

Figure 7.13 Test Functions and Tools of Test Option 1

Business Blueprint   The Business Blueprint function enables you to design, document, and hierarchically catalog your business processes (see Chapter 5, Section 5.4). The next step is to configure or adapt the business processes in the assigned SAP application systems (see Chapter 5, Section 5.5).

Your user departments can store their *business requirements* from a test management viewpoint. At a later point in time, the manual and automatic test cases are also assigned to the business processes using the Business Blueprint. This provides a holistic view of the business processes—all technical and business aspects are entered centrally using the Business Blueprint and then centrally adjusted if changes are made later on.

By taking this centralized approach to modeling, managing, and documenting business processes using the Business Blueprint, you significantly improve efficiency compared to a decentralized approach, which often leads to documentation becoming quickly outdated.

When you make changes to an existing SAP solution, this raises the question of whether important applications or critical processes are affected. It does not matter if SAP source code is adjusted due to EHPs or customer enhancements, or if the configuration or interfaces have been changed. The question of which areas of the solution are affected by the change must always be addressed. SAP Solution Manager provides the Business Process Change Analyzer function for this purpose (BPCA; see also Section 7.3).

Business Process Change Analyzer (BPCA)

SAP TDMS accelerates the process of automatically building test systems and other, nonproduction SAP systems. It draws on the configuration, master, and transaction data from a source system such as your production system and uses it to build the target system. In addition to creating an initial test system, you can also add data to an existing system or replace it.

SAP Test Data Migration Server (SAP TDMS)

The system setup using SAP TDMS is quite different from a simple system copy because the data volume in the test system is kept significantly smaller, and sensitive data is avoided or made anonymous. For instance, you can restrict the transaction data that is transferred to one or more periods or organizational units. For sensitive data, for example, from SAP ERP Human Capital Management (SAP ERP IICM), you can apply preconfigured data anonymization methods.

After the initial build is complete, SAP TDMS also supports specific items of data to be updated. To this end, documents from the source system can be selected and copied to the target system together with all preceding documents.

After the test coverage based on the planned changes is known, you can create the test cases and test plans. Following that, you create and assign test packages to each tester. In option 1, you use the TWB

Test Workbench

for this purpose. The TWB also supports the execution of manual and automatic tests, the entry of malfunction or problem messages, and test status management and status reporting.

7.4.2 "Test Management" Work Center

The *Test Management* work center enables web-based access to all functions and tools available in SAP Solution Manager for planning, executing, and analyzing functional tests. For each role (e.g., test organizer, test engineer, or tester), the relevant functions of test management are thus available through a central access point (see Figure 7.14).

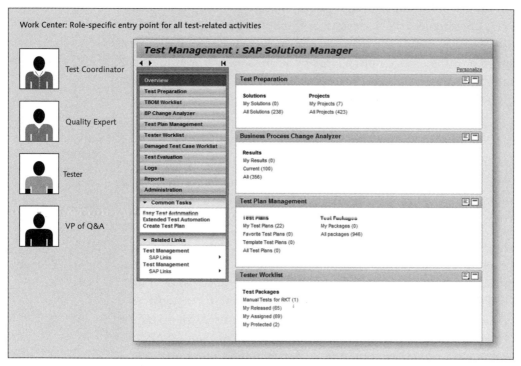

Figure 7.14 Work Center "Test Management" as the Central Access Point

Structure of the work center

The structure of the *Test Management* work center basically follows the individual phases of the test process:

▶ **Overview**
The OVERVIEW view provides a general summary of all important *Test Management* work center content and also makes it possible to directly access the queries in the individual views. A personal-

ization function also enables you to adapt the contents displayed in the OVERVIEW according to your requirements.

▶ **Test preparation**

This view includes a list of your projects and gives you quick access to the Business Blueprint function and the configuration of your business processes.

▶ **TBOM worklist**

In this area, you—the business process expert—find recording tasks that have been requested by quality experts. After you have completed a recording task, the respective quality expert is automatically informed of the completion of the recording by email.

▶ **BP Change Analyzer**

In this view, you can execute Change Impact Analyses and generate appropriate test plans based on the analysis results.

▶ **Test plan management**

In TEST PLAN MANAGEMENT, you can access all functions for managing your test plans and packages in the test coordinator role. You can, for example, do the following:

▷ Create, edit, copy, transport, and delete test plans for your project.

▷ Edit test plan attributes, such as planning data for test times and budgets.

▷ Create test packages and assign them to testers.

▷ Arrange test cases within a test package in a test sequence.

▷ Execute mass changes of test plan and test package attributes (e.g., priority, responsible employee, planning data).

▶ **Tester worklist**

The TESTER WORKLIST view is the central work environment for executing manual and automated test cases. This view gives you an overview of all test packages that are assigned to you for testing. In addition, it provides information about the current test status and shows you at a glance whether there are open messages for a certain test package.

With the new SAP Solution Manager, the TESTER WORKLIST also provides the option to schedule the execution of automated test cases and report damaged test cases (for more information, see Section 7.4.4).

▶ **Worklist for damaged test cases**
As the test engineer you find an overview of messages for damaged test cases that are assigned to you here. This view thus supports the repair process for damaged test cases (for more information, see Section 7.4.4).

▶ **Test evaluation**
This view provides a list of your test plans as well as an aggregated status overview of the test cases contained therein. In addition, this gives you access to additional functions for the detailed evaluation of your test plans and the corresponding test cases. In addition to various evaluation options of the TWB, this also includes SAP NetWeaver BW-based reports, which are suited in particular to evaluating extensive test plans.

▶ **Administration**
In the ADMINISTRATION view, you can make the basic settings for various test functions. Among other things, this view is designed for registering third-party or partner tools, test automation, and activating SAP NetWeaver BW-based reports.

7.4.3   Manual Testing

Planning manual tests

You can use the following functions to plan manual tests with the TWB:

▶ **Business requirements**
When designing and documenting business processes, you can save requirements that are relevant for creating test cases.

▶ **Manual test cases**
You have the option of creating test documents that contain instructions to help manual testers perform tests. You can enter test case descriptions directly as text or create them in a word processing program and upload them to the test case. Because the number of test cases usually grows as time progresses, you are able to assign a range of attributes, for example, priority and keywords, to make the cases easier to catalog and locate. You can also, in turn, link each test case to the previously mentioned business requirements, which means it is possible to check whether all requirements have been covered in test cases.

▶ **Cataloging test cases**
We recommend that you assign all test cases directly to the business processes by configuring the business processes in SAP Solution Manager at any time after the modeling stage is complete.

▶ **Test plan**
All relevant test cases are grouped together in one or more test plans for an actual test cycle. The following procedures are available for test plan creation:

  ▶ Manual selection of suitable test cases based on the business process hierarchy

  ▶ Filtering of test cases by business process attributes (e.g., status, keywords, customer attributes)

  ▶ Filtering of test cases by test case attributes (e.g., test case type, priority, test object)

  ▶ Automatic selection of test cases based on the events of a BPCA analysis

▶ **Test packages**
Test persons are assigned test cases via test packages. Similar to the process of creating test plans, you can create the packages manually from the test cases found in the test plan or generate them by selecting test case attributes. You can assign one or more testers to each test package.

▶ **Test sequences**
To run tests on complex process chains, you often require different testers with different process knowledge. To this end, test packages enable test sequences to be established. For each sequence, you can define which test cases are to be executed in which order and by which testers.

▶ **Release procedures and digital signatures**
To ensure statutory requirements are met and enable a formal release procedure, the TWB allows you to use a release status schema. In this schema, you can define that test plans and test packages may only be used after they have been released explicitly. After test activities have been completed, you can lock the test plan and test packages. To comply with stringent legal standards, all status activities can be documented by the respective users with digital signatures.

Start Test Activities

Email notification
To ensure that test activities can start smoothly, manual testers are informed about the availability of the test packages assigned to them through automatic email notification. The corresponding links in the email notification give testers direct access to their test packages.

The email notification function is particularly useful when testing process chains because these tend to involve different testers, and their test activities are interdependent. For test cases for which you have defined a test sequence, only the first tester is notified at first. It's only when the first tester has successfully completed the test and set the corresponding test status that the next tester in the test sequence receives an email notification.

Manual test execution
To enable test persons to access the test case descriptions in a way that is as easy and intuitive as possible and give them access to the business transactions to be tested, SAP Solution Manager offers not only a user-friendly tester worklist in the *Test Management* work center, but also a completely new environment for executing manual test cases.

As already mentioned, the tester worklist contains a list of all test cases that are assigned to you in your role as tester through one or more test packages. From here, you get to a new display for manual test cases where all data and functions that you need to execute the tests are made available (see Figure 7.15).

This includes the title and author of the respective test case as well as information about the test object and the priority of the test.

In addition, this display includes the test case description, which provides testers with all the information required for executing the manual test.

A pushbutton enables you to directly call the respective transaction or application in the assigned test system so you do not need to know any other details about the test environment.

Following the manual test execution, you assign a test case status, which basically forms the basis for the test evaluation of the test coordinator. You can also enter the time you took for executing the test.

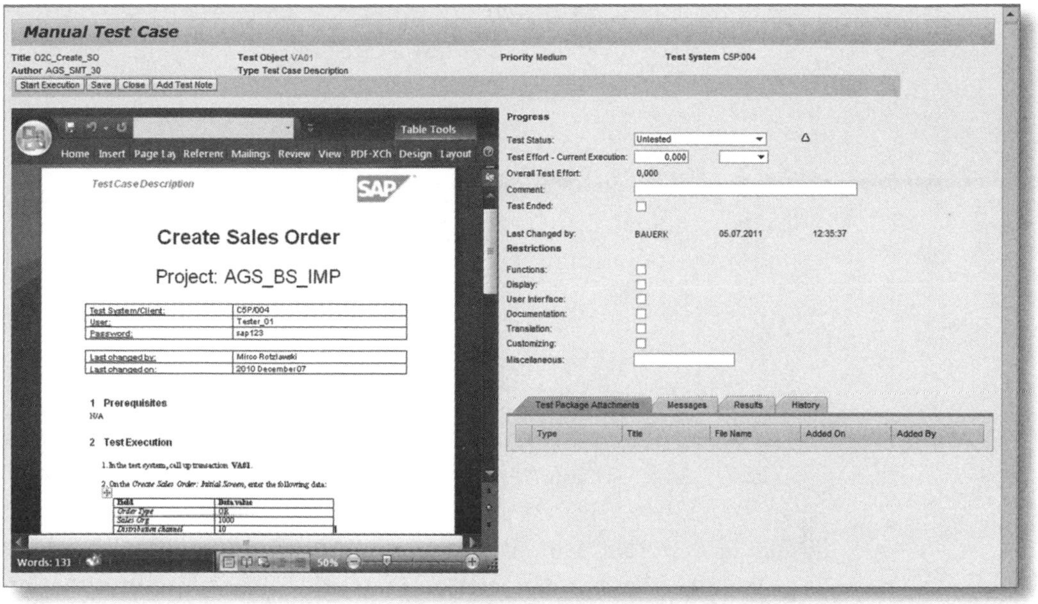

Figure 7.15 Display for Manual Test Cases

To document the test results, you can also create an optional test memo. Here you can use the test case description as the template and supplement it with test results, comments, screenshots, and so on. This offers a convenient way to document all the results of the test execution and create the basis for executing audits.

Test documentation

Error messages

If problems or errors occur while tests are being executed, you can enter them directly in the integrated incident management application in SAP Solution Manager—the *Service Desk* (see Chapter 9). The function for creating error messages is also available in the display for manual test cases. To make incident handling as efficient as possible, SAP Solution Manager thus offers the option to create messages directly during test execution.

When you create a test-specific error message, the message is connected to the respective test case. Certain information, such as the test system and the corresponding application component, is derived directly from the respective test case and copied into the Service Desk message. This ensures that all relevant information is available to all parties involved at any time. This simplifies the handling of

Creating an error message

error messages and speeds up problem solving. After the error has been corrected, you as the tester are automatically informed by email.

7.4.4 Test Automation

To create automatic test cases, you can use the SAP tool eCatt and the new Test Automation Framework (as of SAP Solution Manager 7.1) in test option 1.

eCATT (Extended Computer Aided Test Tool)

eCATT test script · The eCATT SAP tool is suited to the automatic testing of SAP GUI and Web Dynpro user interfaces. For automatic testing of other SAP user interfaces (e.g., SAP Web Client) and non-SAP applications, you should therefore use partner tools. You can easily integrate these tools using the Test Automation Framework (for more information on the Test Automation Framework, see the next section). To record an eCATT test script, you as the user merely have to execute the transaction to be automated. eCATT records the used SAP objects and user activities and compiles them in a test script.

To enable the dynamic use and transfer of test data between process steps, you can add parameters to the test script in a follow-on step.

You start eCATT tests from the test package just like manual tests. After the test has been executed, the application sets the test status itself. For each test execution, a detailed log, which documents the test process and the results, is also created automatically.

In addition, eCATT test scripts enable test results to be checked extensively. For example, after a test has been executed, you can check the accuracy of data posted in the respective SAP tables using eCATT check functions.

Test Automation Framework

As already mentioned, the new SAP Solution Manager provides the Test Automation Framework, which provides you with an easy way to integrate certified test automation tools from partners and third-party providers[1] with SAP Solution Manager to enable you to easily test non-SAP GUI or Web Dynpro-based user interfaces. The Test

Automation Framework is thus an efficient supplement to the eCATT SAP tool and is well suited to create automatic tests for complex business processes.

The features of the Test Automation Framework basically cover the following four areas:

Features of the Test Automation Framework

1. Creation of test configurations using external test tools and assignment of test configurations to the business process hierarchy in the Business Blueprint

2. Scheduling the execution of automated test cases

3. Integration of status and progress reporting between SAP Solution Manager and the third-party provider tool used

4. Workflow for accelerated repair of damaged test cases

The following sections explain these areas in more detail.

Creation of Test Configurations Using External Test Tools

Thanks to the seamless integration between SAP Solution Manager and external test automation tools, the Test Automation Framework provides you with an easy way to create test configurations. The starting point for creating a test configuration is the business process hierarchy so that you can specify directly to which business process or process step the test configuration is to be assigned (see Figure 7.16).

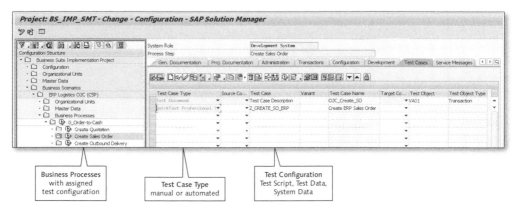

Figure 7.16 Definition of a Test Configuration and Assignment to the Business Blueprint

---

1 The following products are currently certified: HP QuickTest Professional, Worksoft Certify, and IBM Rational Functional Tester.

Parts   A test configuration in the Test Automation Framework consists of the following three parts:

▶ **Test script**
The test script contains a recorded transaction. To create test scripts, you can use an external test automation tool of your choice.

After you have used the external tool to create a test script, you can add parameters to the test script in SAP Solution Manager. This offers the option to use test data dynamically and transfer it from one process step to the next.

▶ **Test data container**
Test data containers enable you to store test data separately from the test scripts, which improves reusability and maintainability. This in turn can significantly reduce test costs. In SAP Solution Manager, you establish a connection between the test data from a test data container and the parameters of the external test script. It is only during test execution that the test data is transferred to the test script. This enables you to centrally and flexibly plan test data for complex business processes (such as order processing). Hence, you can vary the test data used for test execution without having to change the test script.

▶ **System data container**
A system data container is designed for determining the system in which an automatic test is supposed to be executed. The fact that system data and test scripts are separated means that you can change the systems to be tested without having to change the test script.

Scheduling the Execution of Automated Test Cases
With SAP Solution Manager 7.1, the tester worklist of the *Test Management* work center provides a new function that you can use to schedule the execution of test packages that contain automated test cases.

Lights-out tests   The unsupervised execution of automated test cases is also referred to as *lights-out tests*.

For scheduling, you can specify a start date and time so that the test execution of the respective job is automatically started at the desired time. The execution can take place both on a local PC or on a remote computer. During execution, SAP Solution Manager transfers the test data and system landscape information to the automated test cases.

After the automated tests have been executed, the results are transferred to the status analysis of the TWB. Optionally, the test engineer or test coordinator can also receive an automatic email notification, which provides a summary of the execution status (see Figure 7.17).

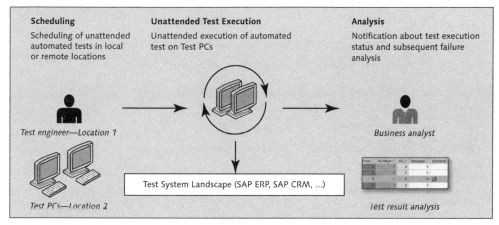

Figure 7.17 Scheduling and Execution of Automated Tests

Integrated Status and Progress Reporting for Automated Test Cases

As already mentioned, after the execution of the automated test cases, the test automation tool transfers the test results to SAP Solution Manager. There, the test results are immediately available for extensive reporting in all the analysis tools of the TWB.

For more information on reporting for your test activities, see Section 7.4.5.

Repair Process for Damaged Test Cases

Changes to an SAP solution often damage the automated test cases, which causes the test case execution to fail.

To get damaged test cases to run again as soon as possible, SAP Solution Manager offers functions that facilitate the reporting, analyzing, and repairing of damaged test cases.

As the tester, you can easily create a message for a damaged test case in the tester worklist to trigger appropriate repair measures. The message is transferred directly to the responsible test engineer so that he can first test the respective test case and then repair it.

Workflow for accelerated repair of damaged test cases

As the test engineer, the *Test Management* work center provides you with a *worklist for damaged test cases*, which gives you an overview of damaged test cases that you have to repair.

From here, you can access a central repair environment, which displays the most important information about the test case and the test environment. In addition, the repair environment provides direct access to different functions for determining the cause of the error and repairing the test case. You can, for example, do the following:

▸ Display the log of the last execution of the test case.

▸ Re-execute the test case to be repaired.

▸ Execute a Change Impact Analysis using the BPCA to check whether changes in the system to be tested have caused the test case to fail.

▸ Edit and repair the respective test script.

▸ Flag a repaired test case as completed to inform the person who created the message of the repair and request retesting.

Figure 7.18 shows the entire workflow from reporting a damaged test case, to analysis and repair activities by the test engineers, to the confirmation of the repaired test case by the person who reported it.

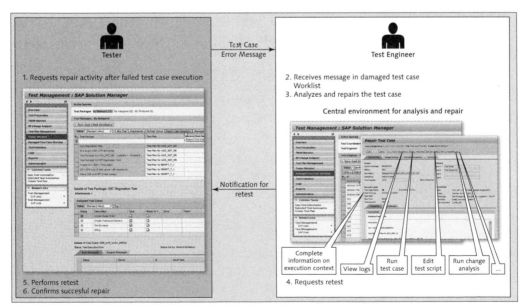

Figure 7.18 Workflow for Repairing Damaged Test Cases

7.4.5 Test Reporting

The TWB provides numerous reports for analyzing your test activities. As the test coordinator, you thus have the option to monitor the test progress and analyze the number and priority of errors that have occurred, even if tests are distributed globally.

Thanks to the integration with SAP NetWeaver Business Warehouse (BW), you can also use the reporting tools of the TWB as well as BW-based reports for analyzing your tests. These also enable you to graphically display the results of your reports. You can use the BW system in SAP Solution Manager so no additional costs are incurred.

BW reports

TWB reporting offers the following functions and options:

Test Reporting using the Test Workbench

▶ **Checking the test case coverage**
In the TWB, you can use a reporting function with which you can check whether all business processes in your project have been assigned test cases and current TBOMs. This enables you to efficiently identify gaps in your test scope and helps you meet the prerequisites for using the BPCA.

▶ **Determination of inconsistent test plans**
Changes to the Business Blueprint structure and/or test case description are often made after the test plans for the respective project have already been generated. The consequence of this is that test cases no longer reflect the current status of your project.

To avoid such inconsistencies in your test plans and to increase flexibility in the test process, an appropriate report is available as of SAP Solution Manager 7.1. This report enables you to determine test plans affected by possible changes to the business process structure or changed test documents. You can then easily generate the determined test plans so that the latest status of your processes and test case descriptions is taken into account.

▶ **Status reporting**
SAP Solution Manager provides different functions for efficient status reporting.

You can use the Status Info System of the TWB to get a flexible and efficient overview of all current and completed test activities and monitor the progress of one or more test plans. The information is available in aggregated form and at the detail level.

Status Info System

Status analysis

In addition, the *status analysis* provides a detailed overview of all the data for a selected test plan, for example, test status, test result documentation, messages and test memos, and so on.

▶ **Message overview**
You can use the TWB message overview to get an overview of all messages that testers have created in the context of a certain test plan. In addition to general information such as message status, priority, reported by, and processed by, you also find information about the corresponding test case and test plan. In addition, the message overview provides direct access to the individual messages so that you can display and edit these in Service Desk.

BW-based test reporting

In the TEST EVALUATION area of the *Test Management* work center, you have access to the following BW reports:

▶ **Status report**
You can use this report to display a status overview for selected test plans at a certain time. In addition, you also get an overview of existing messages and their priorities here.

All data is displayed graphically as well as in table form.

▶ **Progress report**
The progress report shows how the test case status information has developed over a certain period of time. Hence, the progress report provides project managers and test coordinators with a good way to detect possible delays or resource bottlenecks.

▶ **Message report**
This report provides an overview of all messages that were entered within a certain test plan. You receive information about the number, respective priority, and processing status of the messages at a certain time.

A table overview provides a list of all messages in which you have the option to access the individual messages directly to find out more details.

▶ **Test effort report**
The test effort provides an overview of the test budget and lets you check whether the expected test effort has been observed or exceeded.

Figure 7.19 shows an example of a test effort report where the development of status values is displayed in combination with the progress of test efforts.

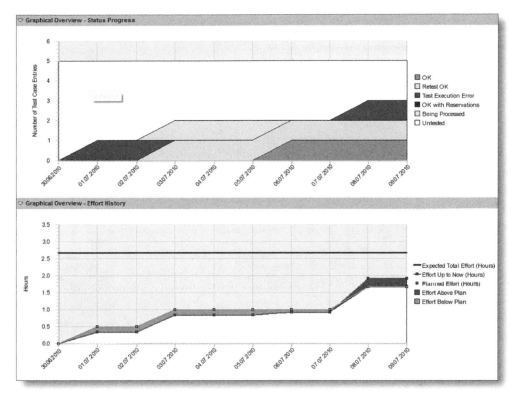

Figure 7.19 BW-Based Test Effort Report

In each BW report, you have flexible filter and analysis options that allow you to combine several characteristics and thus achieve a higher granularity for your data.

In addition, you can supplement the aforementioned BW-based reports with customer reports and dashboards.

7.5 Test Option 2—Testing with the SAP Quality Center by HP

Many customers already use the product SAP Quality Center by HP to organize and execute tests. All tools described in test option 2 are available for a fee and sold by SAP.

7.5.1 Overview of Test Functions and Tools for Test Option 2

The tools and functions in test option 2 are provided by SAP Solution Manager, *SAP Quality Center by HP (SAP Quality Center)*, *SAP Test Data Migration Server (SAP TDMS)*, as well as *SAP Test Acceleration and Optimization (SAP TAO)*.

SAP Quality Center
In test option 2 (see Figure 7.20), the SAP Quality Center plays an important role in the administration of manual and automatic tests. It is made up of a range of modules that boast highly sophisticated user guidance. It also combines the following test management processes: requirements management, test planning, defect management, and test reporting. In addition, you can use a test modeling environment in which you can create test cases for test components.

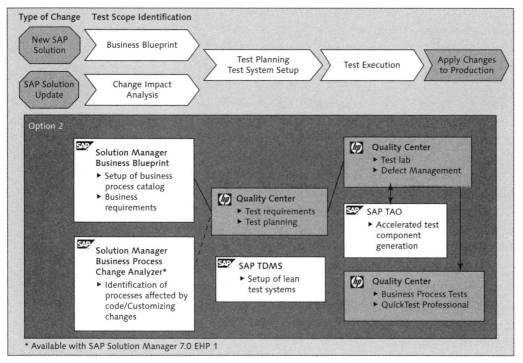

Figure 7.20 Test Option 2

The test components are located in the *Business Process Testing (BPT)* module of the SAP Quality Center.

The *HP QuickTest Professional* module is part of the SAP Quality Center and is used to automate functional and regression tests. It supports both keyword and scripting interfaces and uses Visual Basic scripting languages for editing the objects of the applications to be tested.

The SAP Solution Manager adapter for SAP Quality Center transfers the information between SAP Solution Manager and the SAP Quality Center. Thanks to this integration, functional experts of the project team can check the status of the business process test in SAP Solution Manager while the quality team continues working in the SAP Quality Center.

The adapter transfers the information as follows:

▶ **Transfer from SAP Solution Manager to SAP Quality Center (outbound)**
The adapter transfers the Business Blueprint structure and all related documents, including specifications, business requirements, links, and test objects such as transactions, IMG activities, and own programs. The quality managers use this information to effectively plan and structure their test projects.

▶ **Transfer from the SAP Quality Center to SAP Solution Manager (inbound)**
The test results can be sent to SAP Solution Manager. This enables your project managers to get an overview of all projects. Defects that the SAP Quality Center has found can be transferred to SAP Solution Manager for further processing and solution determination (see Figure 7.21).

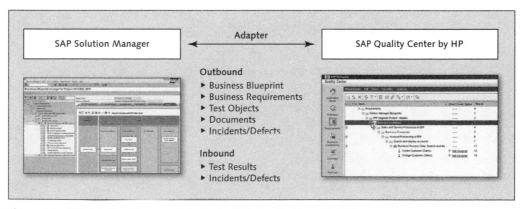

Figure 7.21 SAP Solution Manager Adapter for SAP Quality Center by HP

255

SAP TAO   The *SAP Test Acceleration and Optimization (SAP TAO)* application helps you automate your business process tests with automatically generated test case drafts and test components. SAP TAO is completely integrated into SAP Solution Manager and helps you identify test cases and test components that are affected by software changes in your system landscape. SAP TAO generates modular test cases that are easier to manage if there is a change.

SAP TAO helps you convert your test procedure from manually testing to testing on the basis of generated test components. This reduces your costs and minimizes the risk of testing SAP solutions incompletely. Additional benefits are the reduction of administrative effort for automatic tests, risk minimization thanks to improved test coverage, and increased capacities for managing changes. The tool is permanently integrated into BPCA and enables you to report test cases and test components affected by changes.

Thanks to the modular approach for generating test cases, SAP TAO enables you to automate your tests quicker and significantly facilitates the maintenance of your test cases. Another advantage compared to manual testing is that the test scripts generated with SAP TAO require fewer resources for execution (see Figure 7.22).

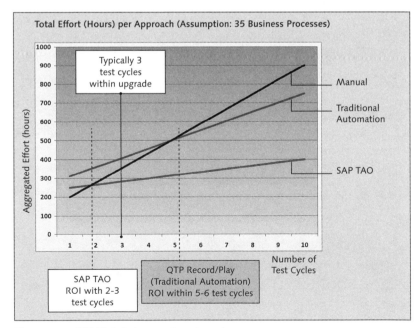

Figure 7.22 SAP TAO Return on Investment

7.5.2 Transfer to the Business Blueprint

To ensure that you can transfer the SAP Solution Manager Business Blueprint to the SAP Quality Center, you should first connect the projects of the two applications. This helps you exchange information between the projects.

You can assign several SAP Solution Manager projects to one SAP Quality Center project (1:*n* assignment). For each SAP Solution Manager project, a new node is created in the SAP Solution Manager project Blueprint folder in the *Requirements* module of the SAP Quality Center.

Project assignment

While you link the two projects, you can schedule and configure periodic updates of your test requirements in the SAP Quality Center as well as updates for your test results in SAP Solution Manager (see Figure 7.23). Whenever you add new test requirements using the TRANSFER TO SAP QC BY HP tab, structures already transferred to the SAP Quality Center are updated automatically. In addition, your test results can be automatically updated with SAP Solution Manager, and you no longer have to execute this activity manually.

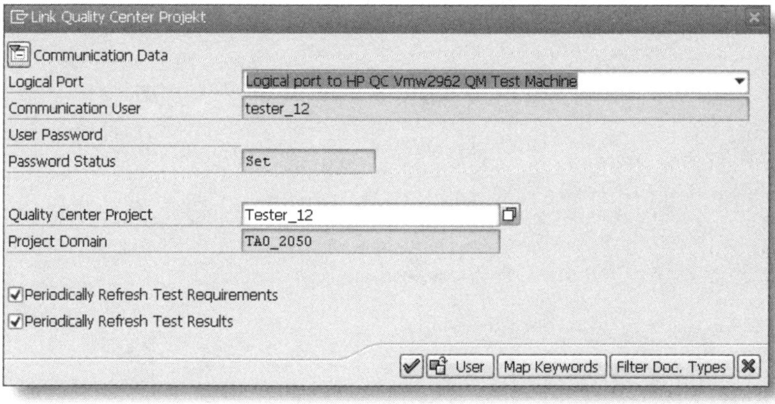

Figure 7.23 Establishing a Connection to an SAP Quality Center Project

After the connection between the projects has been established, you can edit the Business Blueprint of the project using the Configuration transaction (Transaction SOLAR02). Both your business requirements and your test objects have to be assigned to the TRANSFER TO SAP QC BY HP tab. Following that, all Business Blueprint structures as well as entries on the TRANSFER TO SAP QC BY HP tab can be transferred to the SAP Quality Center for testing.

You can transfer the document with the business requirements to the SAP Quality Center and select it in the Business Blueprint via the GENERAL DOCUMENTATION, PROJECT DOCUMENTATION, or TRAINING MATERIAL tabs. You can select test objects using the TRANSACTIONS, DEVELOPMENT, or CONFIGURATION tab pages.

Note that you can only select for transfer Business Blueprint structures or test objects that you have assigned using the TRANSFER TO SAP QC BY HP tab. This ensures that only node structures with entries for testing are contained in the SAP Quality Center.

7.5.3 Creating Test Plans

You can call the Business Blueprint transferred to the SAP Quality Center in the Requirements module of the SAP Quality Center. Table 7.1 provides an overview of the assignment of the data from the Business Blueprint of SAP Solution Manager to the Requirements module of the SAP Quality Center.

SAP Solution Manager (Business Blueprint)		SAP Quality Center (Requirements)
ADMINISTRATION tab		DETAILS (see Requirement Details Transferred to SAP Solution Manager)
GENERAL DOCUMENTATION tab		Appendix*
PROJECT DOCUMENTATION tab		Appendix*
TRANSFER TO SAP QC BY HP tab	Business requirements	Business Requirements (the document is transferred as an attachment)
	Test object	Test requirement*
(*) The documents are transferred to SAP Solution Manager as links.		

Table 7.1 Assignment of Data from the Business Blueprint in the "Requirements" Module

Attributes SM OBJECT CODE and SM LOGICAL COMPONENT provide information about executable and logical components of your test objects (see Figure 7.24). The tester in the SAP Quality Center thus knows which transaction is to be tested in which system.

To generate the test plans for the transferred requirements, choose CONVERT TO TESTS in the context menu of the SAP Quality Center. In addition, you can delete your manual test cases by converting the requirements on the lowest level (see Figure 7.25).

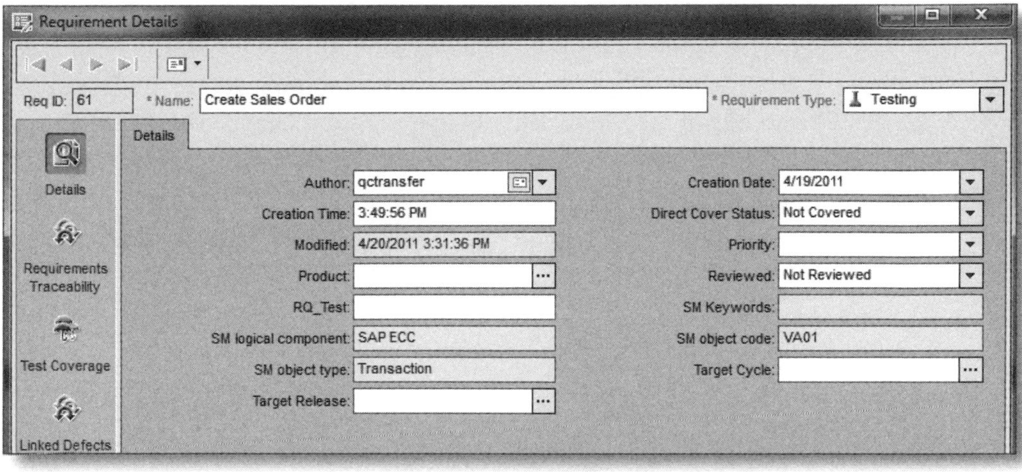

Figure 7.24 Requirement Details Transferred to SAP Solution Manager

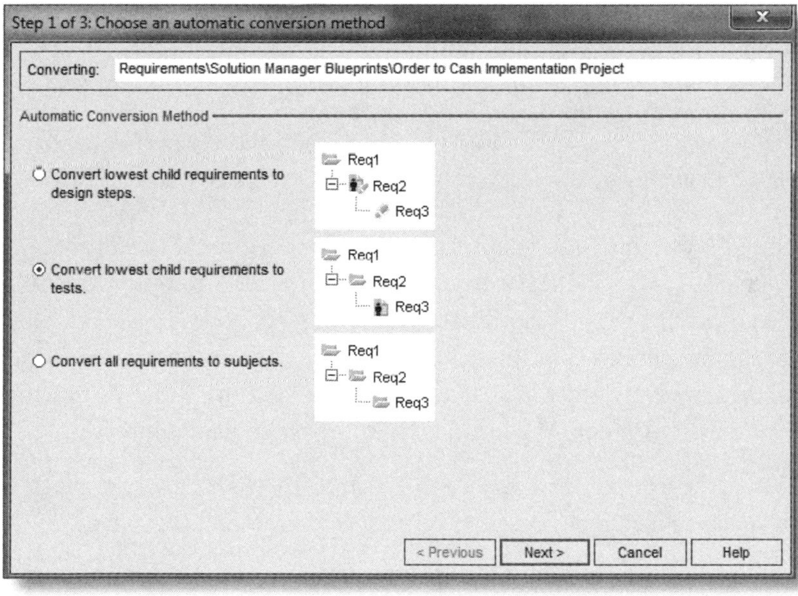

Figure 7.25 Converting Requirements of the Lowest Level into Test Cases In SAP Quality Center by HP

7.5.4 Generating Test Cases Using SAP Test Acceleration and Optimization

As a test engineer or business user, you can use SAP TAO to generate automatic test cases with a modular structure. To create test components, the test designer uses the *Process Flow Analyzer* function (PFA;

Process Flow Analyzer (PFA)

see Figure 7.26) to go through the business process flow of the desired transaction. The business process flow is recorded using the PFA. The result of the PFA can then be uploaded to the Test Plan module of the SAP Quality Center. You can change the test cases you have uploaded at any time to adjust them to your test requirements.

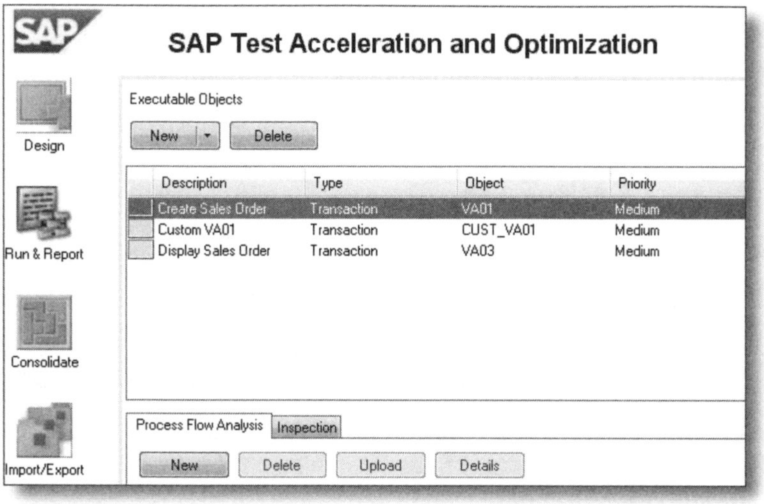

Figure 7.26 Process Flow Analyzer in SAP Test Acceleration and Optimization

Check points   The PFA function also enables you to enter additional *check points* in your test cases. The test designer can use the PFA function to enter check points while recording the business process flow and then determine certain conditions for these. The check points are inserted as components into the test cases generated using SAP TAO in the SAP Quality Center. The test fails as soon as the validation fails.

When the check point has been created, the value of the selected property is automatically fetched and set as the default value.

The test cases uploaded to the SAP Quality Center are components of the SAP TAO library or screen components. They are sorted, and the relevant input fields have parameters. SAP TAO provides many library components that you can use to fine-tune your test cases.

7.5.5 Executing Test Cases Using SAP Test Acceleration and Optimization and the SAP Quality Center

There are different ways of executing the test cases based on SAP TAO, for example:

▶ You can use the SAP TAO module RUN & REPORT to generate TBOMs for your Business Blueprint objects in SAP Solution Manager (see Figure 7.27). Before you generate TBOMs, all test cases should be connected to the Business Blueprint objects from SAP Solution Manager.

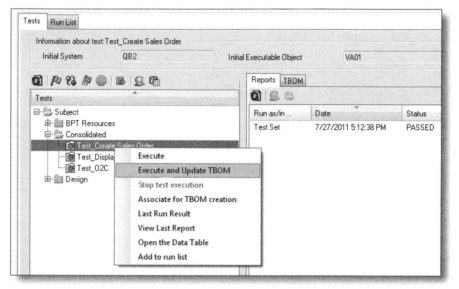

Figure 7.27 Test Execution with SAP TAO for Generating TBOMs

▶ You can use the TEST PLAN module of the SAP Quality Center to eliminate errors.

▶ You can use the TEST LAB module of the SAP Quality Center to execute functional tests (see Figure 7.28).

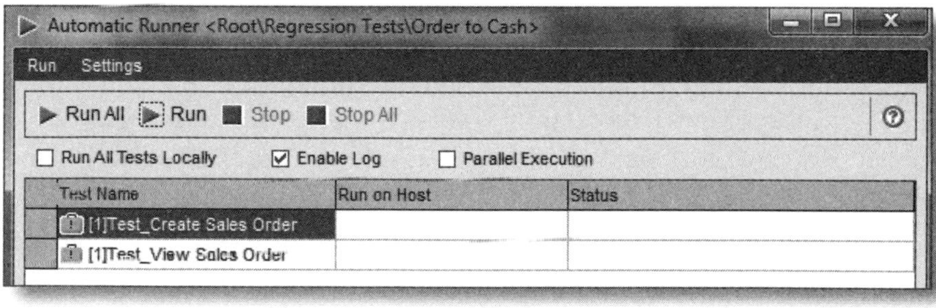

Figure 7.28 Test Execution Using the SAP Quality Center

We recommend consolidating the components of the test cases based on SAP TAO into one component. This accelerates the execu-   Consolidating tion of test cases. You can use the Consolidate function in the SAP TAO client to do so. Test cases that you select for consolidation are added to the Consolidation List. Additional test cases depending on your test cases are automatically included in the Consolidation List (see Figure 7.29).

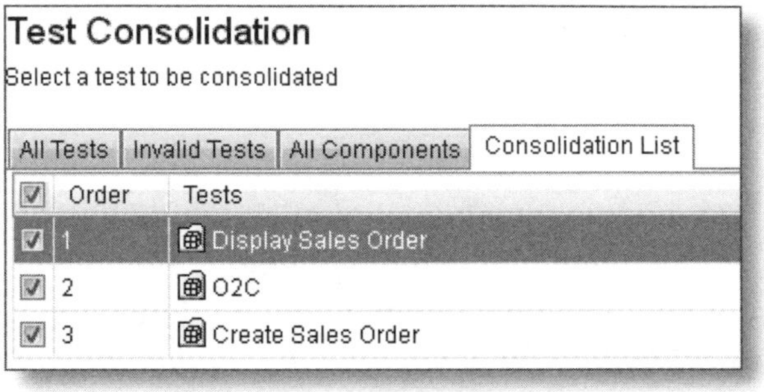

Test Consolidation
Select a test to be consolidated

	Order	Tests
☑	1	Display Sales Order
☑	2	O2C
☑	3	Create Sales Order

Tabs: All Tests | Invalid Tests | All Components | Consolidation List

Figure 7.29 Consolidation List in the SAP TAO Client

The Invalid Tests tab in the Consolidation module recommends test cases to you for consolidation. Cases are recommended if they have changes caused by SAP TAO functions; PFA, import/export, and so on. You have the option to flag tests that have been changed in the SAP Quality Center as invalid and use them for consolidation.

Test reports   After the test cases have been executed using SAP TAO or the SAP Quality Center, you can display two types of test reports:

► **SAP TAO test report**
You can call the SAP TAO test report for each test case using the Run & Report module. The test case reports are generated during test execution in SAP TAO or the SAP Quality Center. You can adjust the report view as required and save the changes you have made.

The log shown in Figure 7.30 contains important information, for example, the system in which a test is executed, input values, the output document, execution time of the tests, and so on.

► **SAP Quality Center test report**
The SAP Quality Center also saves detailed test execution logs that you can call using the Test Lab module in the SAP Quality Center.

Reports | TBOM | 7/27/2011 5:12:38 PM

Advanced

Step Details | Step Result | None ▼ | HTML Report | Close

Execution Time	Step Result	Step Description
7/27/2011 5:12:38 PM		
7/27/2011 5:12:38 ...	DONE	DataTable: C:\saptaort\DATA\DT_Create Sales Order.xls Import was successfull. RowCount = 1
7/27/2011 5:12:38 ...	INFO	System: QB2 Client: 800 User: TESTER_12 Language: EN
7/27/2011 5:12:38 ...	DONE	---- Declared Libraries ---- CBASE_Foundation_DT.vbs CBASE_Foundation_Reports.vbs CBASE_Foundatio...
7/27/2011 5:12:38 ...	INFO	TAO Report is at: ...\Logs\TestSet_Create Sales Order\2011-07-27_17-12-38_Test_Create Sales Order
7/27/2011 5:12:47 PM		
7/27/2011 5:12:47 ...	PASSED	Current Transaction is: VA01
7/27/2011 5:12:47 ...	INFO	Create Sales Order: Initial Screen
7/27/2011 5:12:48 PM		
7/27/2011 5:12:48 ...	INFO	Distribution Channel - (Text = 10)
7/27/2011 5:12:48 ...	INFO	Target: Division
7/27/2011 5:12:48 ...	INFO	Control: Enter - Key Pressed: 0
7/27/2011 5:12:48 ...	INFO	Sales Doc. Type - (Text = OR)
7/27/2011 5:12:48 ...	INFO	Sales Organization - (Text = 1000)
7/27/2011 5:12:48 ...	INFO	Division - (Text = 00)

Figure 7.30 SAP TAO Test Report

7.5.6 Exchanging Error Messages Between the SAP Quality Center by HP and SAP Solution Manager

Errors discovered during test execution in the SAP Quality Center by HP can be forwarded to SAP Solution Manager for solution determination or to SAP to submit a change request (see Figure 7.31).

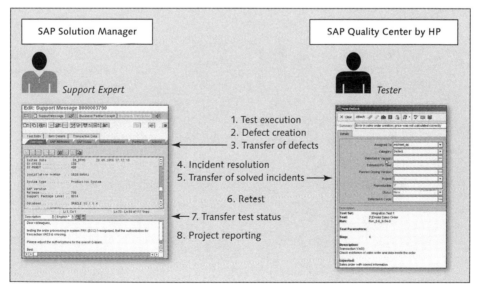

Figure 7.31 Exchange of Error Messages between the SAP Quality Center and SAP Solution Manager

You can display the errors transferred to SAP Solution Manager in the SAP Web Client, if you have been assigned the user role SOL-MANPRO. After editing the error message, it is sent back to the SAP Quality Center to inform the tester that the solution needs to be checked.

7.5.7 Reporting in SAP Solution Manager and the SAP Quality Center by HP

Test report

The *Test Management* work center in SAP Solution Manager gives you central access to your test results in the form of a test report. You can execute this report using the SAP Solution Manager project (see Figure 7.32).

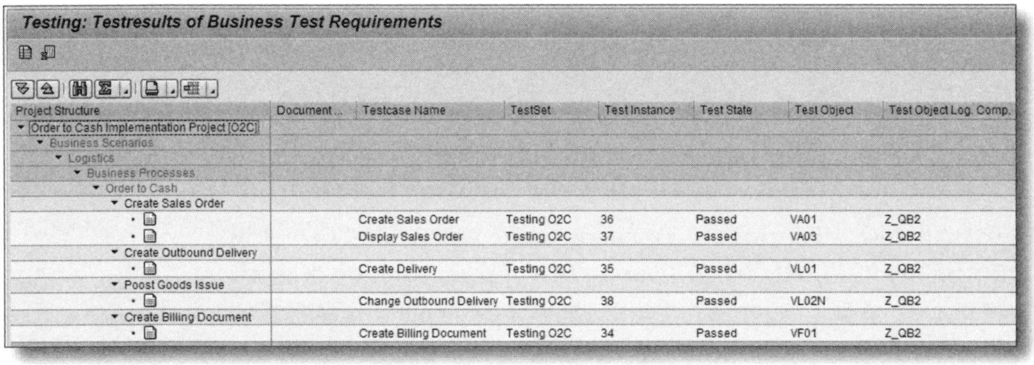

Testing: Testresults of Business Test Requirements

Project Structure	Document...	Testcase Name	TestSet	Test Instance	Test State	Test Object	Test Object Log. Comp.
▼ [Order to Cash Implementation Project [O2C]]							
▼ Business Scenarios							
▼ Logistics							
▼ Business Processes							
▼ Order to Cash							
▼ Create Sales Order							
▪ 🗎		Create Sales Order	Testing O2C	36	Passed	VA01	Z_QB2
▪ 🗎		Display Sales Order	Testing O2C	37	Passed	VA03	Z_QB2
▼ Create Outbound Delivery							
▪ 🗎		Create Delivery	Testing O2C	35	Passed	VL01	Z_QB2
▼ Poost Goods Issue							
▪ 🗎		Change Outbound Delivery	Testing O2C	38	Passed	VL02N	Z_QB2
▼ Create Billing Document							
▪ 🗎		Create Billing Document	Testing O2C	34	Passed	VF01	Z_QB2

Figure 7.32 SAP Solution Manager Test Report

The SAP Quality Center offers you many different reports and graphs for different target groups, from manual testers to senior management.

You can call the reports in the Dashboard, Requirements, Test Plan, Test Lab, or Defects modules in the SAP Quality Center.

The Dashboards module lets you display analysis reports using different graphs next to each other (see Figure 7.33).

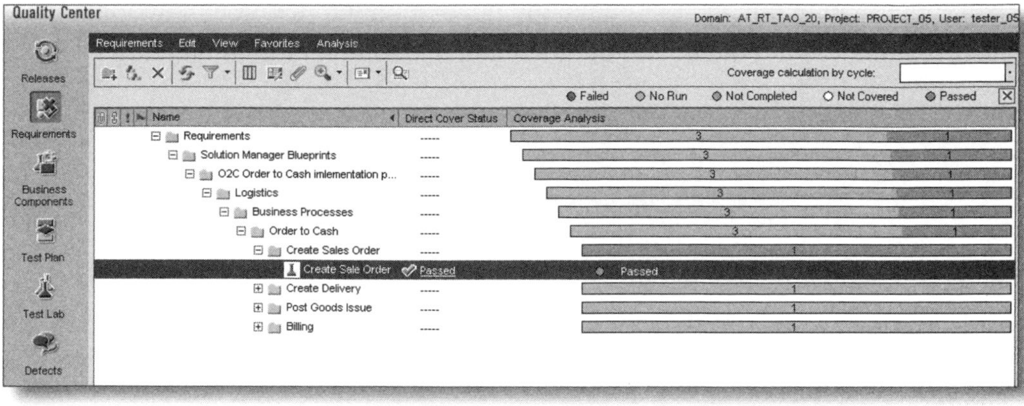

Figure 7.33 Test Report in the SAP Quality Center

7.5.8 Maintenance of Test Cases Using SAP Test Acceleration and Optimization

Test cases created in SAP TAO are easier to repair thanks to their modular structure. This means that if a test case is damaged, you only have to repair the affected components rather than the whole test case. You can identify affected test cases manually or automatically using SAP Solution Manager.

The *Change Analyzer* function included in SAP TAO helps you find damaged test cases and repair components affected by software changes. SAP TAO is based on the BPCA that is integrated into SAP Solution Manager. You can find the BPCA results using the ID of your solution or your project in SAP TAO. Proceed as follows to repair a test case based on SAP TAO:

1. After introducing software changes in your system landscape it is possible that many test cases are damaged. The test engineer can find damaged cases either manually or automatically using the Change Analyzer in SAP TAO. In case of a manual search, he would discuss the changes with the person responsible and execute the test cases to see where they fail (see Figure 7.34).

2. The affected test components are identified manually or automatically using the Change Analyzer in SAP TAO (see Figure 7.35). It is often not necessary to repair these test components because they already include all user interface fields unless new fields have been added. New fields are typically used in modified views.

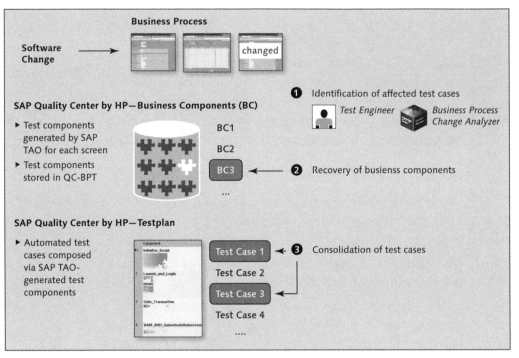

Figure 7.34 Identifying Damaged Test Cases and Components

Figure 7.35 Affected Test Components

3. The damaged test cases are repaired using appropriate new parameter values and data for new mandatory fields in the test case. However, this means that the test cases and test files have to be changed, and the individual test cases have to be consolidated. This is the only way to repair all higher level test cases automatically.

7.6   Test Option 3—Integration Using IBM Rational Tools

Many customers use the tools by IBM Rational for managing their IT requirements and for quality management. Some customers also want to implement SAP Solution Manager because this solution provides the BPCA, support for operating technical and business processes, and extensive governance functions. Combining the functions for application management in SAP Solution Manager with the IBM Rational software means that there is comprehensive support for quality management, which can be used to increase efficiency and lower costs. In addition, business and IT requirements are consolidated.

You can integrate SAP Solution Manager 7.1 with IBM Rational tools to get an end-to-end quality management solution.

7.6.1   An Automated, Integrated, and Standardized Approach

Manually managing test tasks can be time consuming and expensive. To be on schedule and within the budget, your quality teams might have to delay the release of new technologies or skip important tests. Quality managers need more transparency and better collaboration in dynamic environments. To use resources more effectively, you also have to reconcile your test effort with your business requirements.

SAP and IBM have developed a tool that combines the Application Lifecycle Management (ALM) functions in SAP Solution Manager with the governance and quality management support of the IBM Rational software (see Figure 7.36). This integration of software functions lets you automate, integrate, and standardize your entire test management process. You can use SAP and IBM Best Practices and standards to manage SAP and third-party software testing. A single, consolidated view increases transparency and makes it easier to make informed release decisions.

SAP Solution Manager and IBM Rational

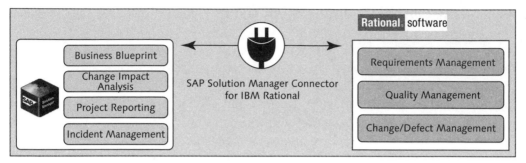

Figure 7.36 Integration of SAP Solution Manager with IBM Rational Software

7.6.2 Creating Business Blueprints and Requirements Management

This powerful support is available via the start menu of your quality management program. The Business Blueprint function in SAP Solution Manager lets you set up your business process hierarchy and identify your business requirements.

SAP Solution Manager provides a centralized, easily accessible repository for information about your business processes and systems, as long as they are related to your software. Business process contents from the repository can be extended to maintain contents for systems, interfaces, software providers, transaction codes, training materials, and process documentation.

Transferring the Business Blueprint
You can transfer the Business Blueprint into the IBM software for requirements management and thus increase transparency and establish a connection with the quality management process. You profit from a powerful environment for requirements editing as well as governance support for managing your business goals, rules, dependencies, and priorities.

7.6.3 Change Impact Analysis

You can use the BPCA in SAP Solution Manager to detect how installing or adjusting SPs or EHPs would affect mission-critical business processes in your current software. For more information, see Section 7.3.

7.6.4 Test Planning

As soon as you have identified your requirements and how these affect your business processes, you can use IBM Rational to plan and set up your quality management project. This web-based software promotes effective collaboration of all parties involved by doing the following:

▶ Defining business goals

▶ Specifying starting and completion criteria for the quality management project

▶ Defining the roles and responsibilities of project teams and their members

▶ Leading the teams through the tasks, handovers, checks, approvals, and acceptances

The quality management method improves the productivity of individual employees and entire teams by combining processes and workflows and thus improving the integrity of the updated business processes.

IBM Rational provides live documentation and reports of your quality goals at the business level. This software also provides a central repository for the most important project parts, for example, business requirements, available resources, and the applications that you manage.

Live documentation and reports

The Service Desk in SAP Solution Manager assists you with the processing of messages and supplements IBM Rational during the test and implementation phase. This can be useful if incidents that are managed in IBM Rational have to be sent to SAP Support for better integration in the change process and if you send a message to SAP for resolving an incident. As a key user (restricted functionality) or processor, you can check messages when you look for solutions, communicate with the people involved in the solution process, or use SAP Support to test the collaboration.

7.6.5 Testing

During testing, IBM Rational supports labor management, error tracking and management, and Change Request Management.

Best Practice templates
The software includes Best Practice templates for managing enhancement requests, project activities, change requests, and known errors during the implementation of SAP or third-party software. Electronic signatures and revision functions help you enhance and adjust SAP processes so that the statutory requirements are met and data are recorded internally.

Workflows
With IBM Rational, you can create flexible, adjustable, and automatic workflows. This means that you then have repeatable, implementable, and predictable processes with which you can complete projects quicker. IBM Rational enables all parties involved to cooperate in a secure, role-based, and cross-project manner. This applies to global teams as well as internal teams. The software offers version management of the highest standard, supports parallel developments, and provides functions for creating and releasing your new software.

The automatic test functions of IBM Rational include natural language tests and screenshots of SAP applications, which make it easier for users to read and edit test scripts. Wizards help new users create automatic test scripts quickly. They also assist with editing these test scripts by providing scripts, texts or dynpros for more text flexibility.

Scripts
With scripts that are easily adapted to changes in your IT landscape, IBM Rational reduces the effort required for editing tests to a minimum. If offers a consistent, integrated environment for function or performance tests with a strong script language, integration with standard development tools for professional testers, and support for team-based parallel developments.

The load and stress test functions speed up the creation of tests, simplify test execution, and quickly detect performance problems as well as their causes. An engine for automatic data correlation enables you to significantly reduce your test development effort.

7.6.6 Customer Benefits

With SAP Solution Manager and IBM Rational, you can minimize errors and other risks and also improve your operating results because your test program is standardized, and cooperation is improved between the parties involved on the business side and the IT team. You can make better decisions about your test priorities by detecting and managing risks more effectively. The end-to-end traceability of test results back to the original business requirements guarantees that these requirements are met and implemented without affecting other areas of the software.

With the assistance of SAP Solution Manager and IBM Rational, managers in your company get better insights into the business environment in which changes are made. Managers can also run reports more easily. Real-time dashboards enable proactive risk management. Adaptable reports make it easier to constantly improve the processes.

7.7 SAP Solution Manager at Colgate-Palmolive

An average time savings of over 90% was achieved when the test processes were run in an automated mode rather than executing the processes manually.

Warren Kaufman, Colgate-Palmolive

Colgate-Palmolive—headquartered in New York—is continuously innovating, as evidenced by our position as a market-leading provider of oral care, personal care, home care, and pet nutrition. We sell our products in over 200 countries and territories around the world, under internationally recognized brand names such as Colgate, Palmolive, Mennen, Softsoap, Irish Spring, Protex, Sorriso, Kolynos, Elmex, Tom's of Maine, Ajax, Axion, Fabuloso, Soupline and Suavitel, as well as Hill's Science Diet, and Hill's Prescription Diet.

Colgate-Palmolive

We have achieved our long history of success by consistently identifying opportunities for growth. Our company's technology platform is very complex, and we use SAP software to manage 99% of our business processes, including all our supply-chain processes, demand chain, finance, customer relationship management, technology, and business warehousing. Although Colgate-Palmolive has a complex IT environment, the systems are built to simplify business processes. As part of our continuous innovation, we are always looking for opportunities to enhance our project lifecycles, thereby increasing performance and reliability while lowering the total cost of ownership (TCO). To reduce TCO, Colgate-Palmolive was an early

Project overview

adopter of SAP Solution Manager. Our first project on SAP Solution Manager was to use Change Request Management to standardize our transport management processes and change control activities across the entire company. Since 2005, application development and support teams have leveraged SAP Solution Manager for our Application Lifecycle Management functionality. This has included using the roadmap for project management, outlining the business processes via the Business Blueprint functionality (Transaction SOLAR01), as well as documenting the configuration and transports in the SOLAR02 configuration transaction. Most importantly, Colgate-Palmolive has maximized the functionality of the Test Workbench to manage all testing activities across all IT divisions, although manually.

In regards to Application Lifecycle Management, Colgate-Palmolive considers testing to be one of the greatest opportunities for return on investment (ROI). Automating repeatable testing processes with easy-to-use tools would make the development process more efficient, and improve performance and reliability. The amount of time and resources required to test the increasingly complex environment and processes are growing, not just for IT, but for business users as well. Even a small increase in efficiency in this area would drive ROI for the company and reduce TCO.

Project report To validate this premise, Colgate-Palmolive conducted an extensive ROI study to determine the cost savings and benefits of automating its testing activities. The study identified the amount of time spent on testing activities, ranging from new functionality bundles, to technical and enhancement packages, to all the testing being conducted in support of break fixes. The research showed that if we could optimize the automation of testing in SAP Solution Manager, we would achieve a high ROI through cost avoidance and better use of our most important resource—our staff.

End-to-end integrated automated testing Recognizing an opportunity, Colgate-Palmolive turned to SAP to establish an end-to-end integrated, automated testing approach through SAP Solution Manager that will allow us to leverage our current investment in SAP Solution Manager, while taking advantage of third-party automation engines.

Colgate-Palmolive worked closely with SAP development to define an end-to-end test-automation framework which is featured in the standard SAP Solution Manager 7.1 release. This functionality will allow us—and any other customers—to integrate SAP Solution Manager directly into any certified third-party vendor product.

The design of the Test Automation Framework is defined by four areas:

Test Automation Framework

▶ **Test Case Design**

  ▸ Test case design: Seamless integration of third-party testing tools into SAP Solution Manager blueprinting and configuration transactions via Test Workbench.

  ▸ Test data and system landscape: Test data planning and system landscape information integrated for test execution is managed in SAP Solution Manager and passed to the third-party testing engine.

▶ **Test Case Execution**

  ▸ Unattended test case execution: Scheduling of automated tests for unattended execution at local or remote sites (lights out).

  ▸ Exception reporting: Exception-based reporting for test engineers, testers, and managers for reviewing test results and logs in SAP Solution Manager.

  ▸ Business process Change Analyzer (BPCA): Leverage Change Impact Analysis to define risk-based test scope.

▶ **Test Case Repair**

  ▸ Change Impact Analysis: Integrated Change Impact Analysis with workflow to identify and initiate accelerated repair activities on potentially damaged automation scripts.

▶ **Test Case Reporting**

  ▸ SAP NetWeaver Business Warehouse (BW): Extended BW reporting to analyze test results and trends

  ▸ Status reporting/results: Transactional reporting to analyze test coverage, status, and results, including logs and screen captures which are captured by the third-party engines.

To validate the design provided by SAP, Colgate-Palmolive conducted a series of proofs of concept (POC). The first POC tested the different testing engines available from third-party vendors on as many of the SAP Graphical User Interfaces (SAP GUI) currently employed in its environment. The team focused on using just the third-party testing engines on the most complex business processes

Series of proofs of concept

within the demand chain, supply chain, and technology categories. This included SAP GUIs on SAP CRM, Web Dynpro, Java, .NET, BW, and even Microsoft Excel (MS Excel). In addition to the SAP GUI validation, the POC also confirmed that the third-party engine met Colgate-Palmolive's minimum requirements, ranging from vendor assessment and product offerings to Gartner's magic quadrant rankings. Each requirement was weighted to provide an overall objective score for each vendor and product offering.

Once the vendor was selected, we focused on the integration of the third-party engine with SAP Solution Manager, while also validating the SAP Solution Manager 7.1 release. In preparation of the second POC, the entire Test Automation Framework within SAP Solution Manager was configured and unit tested by a joint team consisting of Colgate-Palmolive analysts and SAP development.

After the functionality was confirmed, business blueprints were defined in support of the POC. Selected manual test scripts from across demand chain, finance and supply chain categories were automated via the third-party testing engine and integrated into the documented business blueprint. The second POC was then conducted, testing the wide range of functionality within the Test Automation Framework of SAP Solution Manager 7.1, as well as the integration of the third-party testing engine within the framework.

In summary, the POC validated:

▶ Running tests directly from the business blueprint for both automated and manual execution

▶ Scheduling tests for lights out execution

▶ Using Business Process Change Analyzer (BPCA) to determine test scope for risk-based test planning and execution

▶ Using automated test repair workflows to fix damaged tests

▶ Passing information about systems, as well as test data, between SAP Solution Manager and third-party software, using System Data Container (SDC) and Test Data Container (TDC)

▶ Creating Technical Bill of Materials (TBOM) via third-party tools, as well as directly in SAP Solution Manager, in support of BPCA activities

▸ Test results from the third-party testing engine in SAP Solution Manager, including screen captures/prints, error logs, and test management reporting

▸ Executing BW reporting of all test execution

▸ Transactional reporting to analyze test coverage, status, and results

Table 7.2 shows some of the end-to-end business processes which were automated and integrated. An average time savings of over 90% was achieved when the test processes were run in an automated mode, rather than executing the processes manually. In fact, most of our analysts felt the administrative savings from the automated self-documentation of the results and logs outweighed the potential setup cost of automation. Extrapolating these savings over a larger set of core business processes, as well as multiplying the savings by the number of times a process is tested, yields a compelling ROI.

POC results

Function	Processes	Transactions	Steps	Manual Test Time	Third-Party's Automated Test Time	Savings
Change Request Management	Creation of Service Message	ZNOTIFCREATE	32	20 min	90 sec	92.5%
Change Request Management	Display Service Message	ZMONITOR	15	20 min	45 sec	96.25%
Demand	SO Create, Change, Credit Release, Delivery, Invoice	VA01, VA02, VKM3, VL01N, VF01	202	30 min	4.5 min	85%
FICO	Product Costing	OKKS, CK11N, CK24, CK13N, KP27, GR55, KKS5	116	25 min	3.5 min	86%
Supply	Purchase Order, Goods Receipt	ME21N, MIGO	72	30 min	2.5 min	91.6%

Table 7.2 Examples of Prototype Results

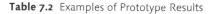

The way ahead Over the next several months, our company will be working on a testing strategy to realize the following benefits:

- Expansion of test coverage by automating all critical processes
- A centralized data strategy that outlines the critical variants and drives a set of critical conditions and validates complex table structures
- A global strategy for defining automated test scripts as part of standard release of application functionality bundles that can be leveraged by the implementation teams across all divisions
- Shorten the development cycle, by reducing time for system testing
- Reduce the need for business resources for testing, especially technical upgrades
- Retain knowledge of processes within automated-script and data sources
- Improve end-to-end traceability and reporting
- Test standardization across the entire organization
- Analyze change impact at an object level to determine test scope (risk-based approach)
- Leverage the change analysis during EHP testing to better scope and understand impact
- Support best place to work initiatives by automating repetitive testing tasks
- Improve resource management by freeing up resources from testing activities

Our next step will be to implement SAP Solution Manager 7.1, and automate our critical processes, with the goal of automating all our disaster recovery and monthly maintenance activities. We will then expand our automation to include all regression testing of our new application bundles and releases. We will also be looking at building automated TBOMs using the third-party vendor in order to leverage the BPCA functionality in support of its planned EHP and SP upgrades.

This is a very good opportunity for us to automate our testing across a wide range of areas that we believe will expedite delivery of new functionality to our user community, while, at the same time, improving our performance and reliability.

In keeping with the company's commitment to ongoing innovation, we continually evaluate our solution landscape to find opportunities to become more efficient and effective. In this case, SAP Solution Manager's tight integration with third-party testing automation software provides an end-to-end testing framework that leverages our initial investment in SAP Solution Manager, while expanding the functionality into areas that were initially not available with previous releases of SAP Solution Manager.

The Author

Warren Kaufman is Director of the Governance IT organization at Colgate-Palmolive. The key responsibility of the Governance organization is to ensure the effective and efficient use of IT resources in order for Colgate to achieve its corporate goals. To that end, Warren's primary focus for the past several years has been to standardize the Application Lifecycle Management processes by maximizing Colgate's investment in SAP tools. Warren and his team have implemented global processes and applications consisting of portfolio management and resource planning, project management frameworks and methodologies, project turnover procedures, change management, and business process monitoring. Most recently, Warren and his team have been working on the implementation of an end-to-end test automation framework as well as implementing a centralized governance, risk, and compliance process and tools.

You can use the key figures and data collected from the live solution to reduce expenditures or boost performance. The important thing is that you can retrace any changes made in the solution. This chapter explains the change control management process. It also explains in detail how Change Request Management, Quality Gate Management, retrofit, and the supporting services work.

8   Change Control Management

The change control management process ensures that changes are planned and made in a consistent manner. The important thing is that all changes are traceable in the solution and the risk they pose in relation to stability and security can be checked at any time.

SAP Solution Manager supports you with a range of functions. ITIL-certified *Change Request Management* enables the highest integration into your change management process. *Quality Gate Management* also provides an additional quality inspection for projects and ensures changes are transported correctly to the production systems. In the upgrade environment, global rollouts or functional enhancements, risks, and efforts arise in the synchronization of developments. You use the *Retrofit* function to completely synchronize dual landscapes with minimal manual effort. To keep an overview of all the changes in the landscape, the *change analysis* provides information about the current status and history of changes. It records changes to the configuration of a system from the operating system, database, application server parameters, transport requests, to notes and support packages (SPs). You can use *configuration validation* to compare configuration settings and thus ensure, for example, the homogeneity of the configuration within the solution landscape. Based on SAP Support experience, the guided self-service *Transport Execution Analysis* provides a best practice recommendation from SAP that is adjusted to your transport environment. You can use this to derive a corresponding action plan for you that can contain organizational-, process-, or plant-specific aspects.

SAP Solution
Manager functions

8.1 Quality Gate Management

For end-to-end solution landscapes, Quality Gate Management ensures that the areas of design and development as well as the implementation of a new service are efficiently and effectively embedded in projects. The aim is to establish an integrated and consistent quality process in the company and to integrate all departments involved.

Quality Gate Management supports *release management* for customer implementation and maintenance projects. A distinction is frequently made between two types of *releases*:

Collaboration with release management

▶ **Major release**
A *major release* is marked by a three- to six-month term. Customers develop two to four releases over a year. Such a release includes all types of changes, including those that significantly impact core business processes. Hence, a major release requires a complete regression test.

▶ **Minor release**
A *minor release* is marked by a significantly shorter runtime of one to four weeks. The objective of such a release is to bundle error corrections and minor functional enhancements and make them available. Here, test coverage can be limited to core business processes and the enhancements provided.

The procedure has the following advantages:

▶ It reduces the frequency of changes in the production system.

▶ Changes happen at clearly defined points in time.

▶ End users are happier thanks to timely communication and training.

▶ A suitable test method is available for each change.

▶ Daily changes are reduced to emergency corrections.

▶ Reduced risk of inconsistencies due to missing transports or transports imported in the wrong order.

▶ Reduced workload for transport management thanks to bundling.

Figure 8.1 provides an overview of release management (minor and major release) and transport management; that is, import into the following systems.

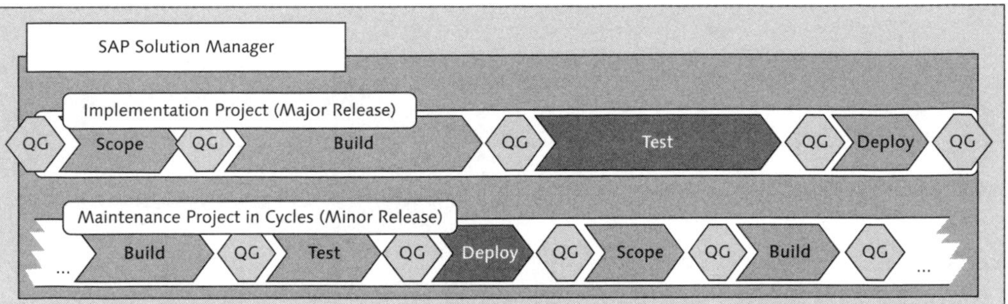

Figure 8.1 Release and Deployment Management

	Major Release	Minor Release
Transport Cycle every...	3-6 months	1-4 weeks
Change Categories	All types of changes including invasive changes	Bug fixes and small enhancements (and re-import of emergency changes)
Priorities	Normal	Normal
Test Focus	Complete test scope	Core processes and new features
Examples	New (major Functions, Support/ Enhancement Packages, Upgrades	Non-critical configuration, meduim- or low-priority incidents

8.1.1   "Change Management" Work Center

The *Change Management* work center in SAP Solution Manager represents the central access point for creating and administering projects for Quality Gate Management. The display enables the user to obtain a quick overview of the different software development projects and their statuses. Quality Gate Management supports both implementation and maintenance projects.

In the overview, you see which tasks have to be performed or in which projects you are involved, and which role you are assigned. You can directly process the tasks to be completed by you. The automatic update ensures that you always work with the latest dataset. You can use favorites to summarize several projects and display them user specifically. The projects view enables you to visualize a range of information. Various tabs are available in the projects view (Figure 8.2).

Views

281

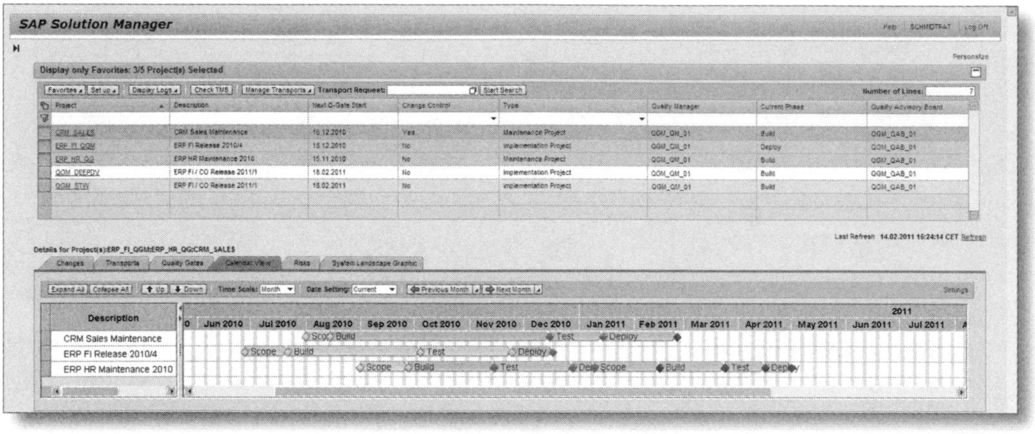

Figure 8.2 Project Overview in the Quality Gate Calendar

You can use the CALENDAR VIEW tab to use the quality gate (Q-Gate) calendar to display all currently created or active projects as well as their active phase. In addition, the overview visualizes both the *Q-Gates* and the *milestones*. With the multiple selection of projects, the calendar view makes it possible to visualize the project terms and their current statuses. This view makes it possible to detect possible time conflicts at an early stage and to initiate corresponding actions.

Procedure   To use a project in Quality Gate Management, certain requirements must be met. You have to create a Solution Manager project (Transaction SOLAR_PROJECT_ADMIN) and then record the system landscape in Transaction SMSY (see Chapter 5, Section 5.3.1). This can be a maintenance or an implementation project. Only then can you see the project in the selection box. After you have selected the desired project, you can use the menu option SET UP • QUALITY GATE MANAGEMENT to make outstanding configurations. After clicking the menu item, a wizard opens. In the first step, you can specify the start times of the individual phases. The standard contains the following four phases with corresponding Q-Gates:

▸ Scope

▸ Build

▸ Test

▸ Deploy

A *quality gate (Q-Gate)* is a special milestone in a project. Q-Gates come between the phases in the project that are especially dependent on the results of the preceding phase or in which special attention must be paid to technical dependencies. A Q-Gate involves checking the results of the preceding phase. You can upload the necessary result types and requirements placed on these phases in the form of checklists for a Q-Gate. The check is performed by those responsible for the project and experts on the particular phases during a session. Depending on the outcome, the project may continue as planned or be canceled or delayed. If you use Quality Gate Management, it's not possible to import transports in follow-on systems without a Q-Gate having been processed successfully. This *import lock* enables a high level of control over your projects and the transport system. It is only after a successful Q-Gate check that the import lock on the following system is lifted.

Quality gate

Figure 8.3 shows an example of the Quality Gate Management process flow.

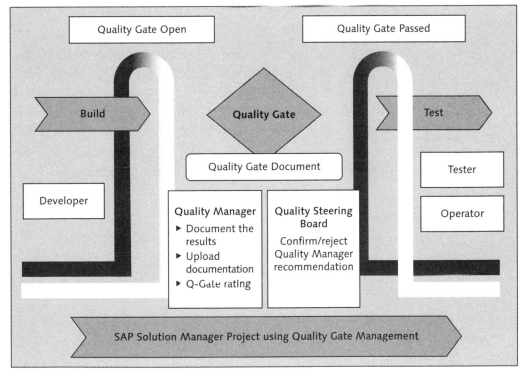

Figure 8.3 Quality Gate Management Process Flow

Milestones
In addition to the existing Q-Gates, you can create *milestones* that represent a particular point in time in your project. A milestone is an event with special significance. In project management, these events are usually interim goals or stopovers in a project. These goals are connected to the completion of an important project result. To emphasize the importance of a milestone, you can also add a Q-Gate to it.

Quality manager and quality advisory board
In the second step, you define the quality manager and the quality advisory board. This establishes a principle of dual control in the project and the process (segregation of duties). The import lock for the system assigned to the Q-Gate is only lifted if both persons or groups confirm that the Q-Gate has been passed successfully. It is then possible to import into the system. You can import transports with different developments into the system by using transport management.

In the third step, the logical component that you previously created in system landscape maintenance (Transaction SMSY) is displayed with the systems defined therein and verified against the transport route configuration.

In another step, you then assign the individual Q-Gate to the phases and system roles. This flexible assignment of Q-Gates makes it possible, for example, to not set a Q-Gate between the development system and the quality assurance (QA) system. This enables iterative testing while protecting the production system.

After the configuration is finished, the wizard displays the project landscape with the individual phases, systems, and Q-Gates (see see Figure 8.4).

Q-Gate calendar
After you have saved the configuration, the different milestones and Q-Gates appear in a Q-Gate calendar. With different filter options, you can user-specifically adjust the view on projects. Click the processed Q-Gate to see the results and requirements that are fixed in the form of checklists and documents (see Figure 8.5).

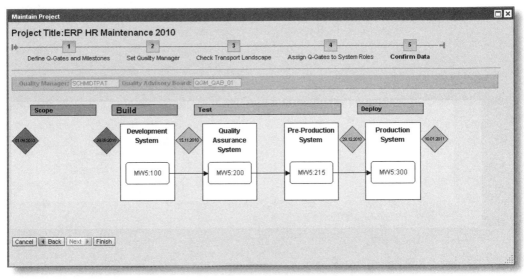

Figure 8.4 Project Landscape after Configuration

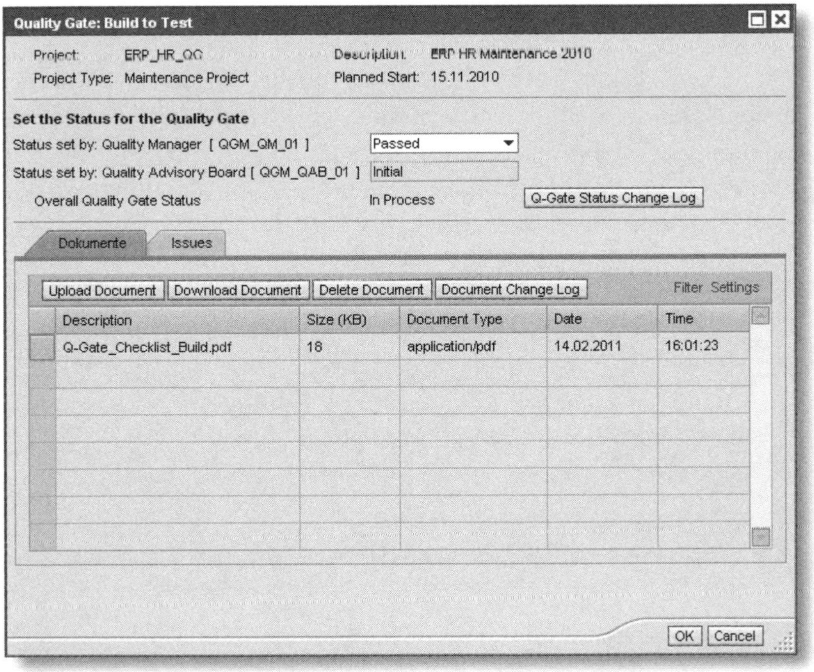

Figure 8.5 Q-Gate Documentation

The quality manager is responsible for the transition between the individual project phases (Scope, Build, Test, and Deploy). The check is performed by those responsible for the project and experts on the particular phases during a session. You also have a variety of information and views at your disposal for your software development projects. You can always keep an overview using the tabs in the work center (see Figure 8.6).

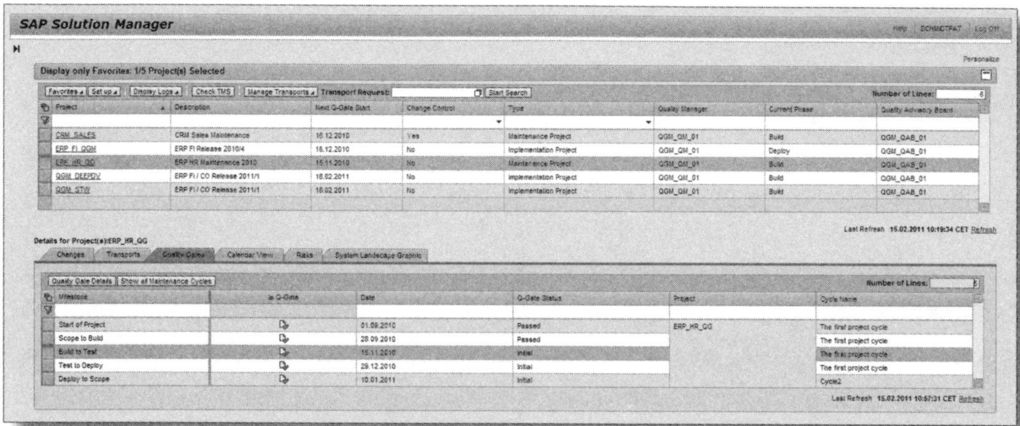

Figure 8.6 Q-Gate Information

By clicking the respective project, the quality manager can access general and detailed information on various tabs. This includes, for example, defined project phases, number of changes and transport requests belonging to the project, and information about the persons responsible for the project (see Figure 8.7).

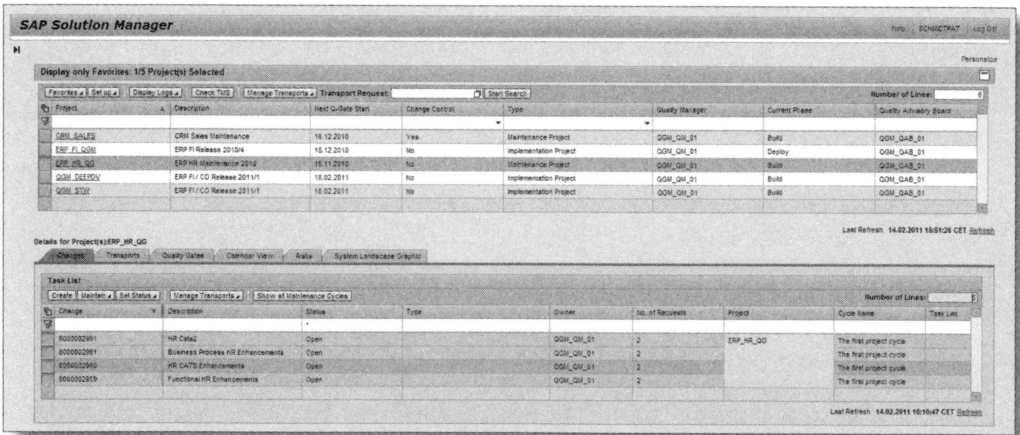

Figure 8.7 Project with Changes and Their Respective Transports

Log   An action or application log logs all activities with a timestamp and user to ensure auditing acceptability.

8.1.2 Central Transport Management with Quality Gate Management

In today's heterogeneous, distributed customer solutions, it's necessary to ensure that a new service can be implemented efficiently and effectively where end-to-end solution landscapes are concerned. While the main focus used to be on the dependencies of objects in a system landscape, it is now on the dependencies of objects in a solution landscape. This means systems that are completely independent in a technical sense are becoming more and more functionally dependent on each other. The aim must be to establish central transport management for the entire solution landscape.

With Quality Gate Management, SAP Solution Manager provides the administration interface for central transport management (see Figure 8.8) in the *Change Management* work center.

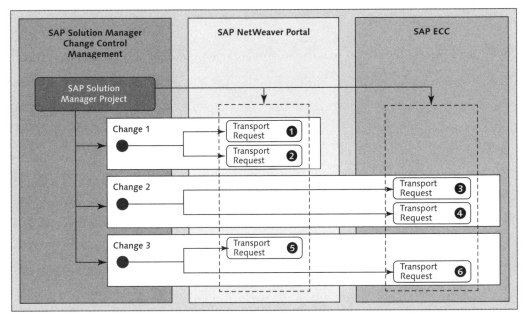

Figure 8.8 Central Transport Management

By clicking the SYSTEM LANDSCAPE GRAPHIC tab after selecting the project, the person responsible for the transport can see the defined solution landscape graphically and in detail (see Figure 8.9). The solution landscape mirrors the customer-specific transport configuration and its transport routes. A wizard enables you to set up the solution landscape for a project quickly, easily, and based on SAP

Transport configuration and risks

Solution Manager projects (see Section 8.1.1). The visualization shows the phase of the project that is currently active and the Q-Gates that have been passed and those that are still pending. In addition, possible transport risks are highlighted in color in the system graphic.

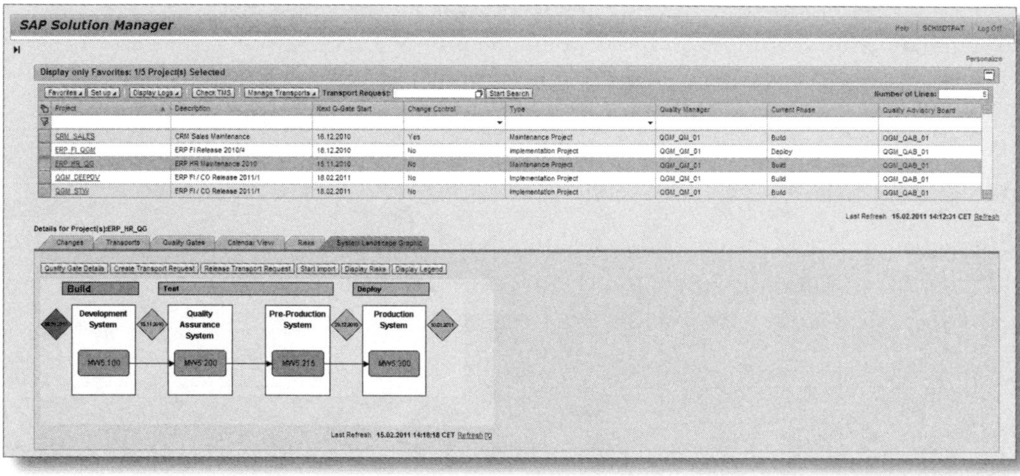

Figure 8.9 System Landscape Graphic

The transport risks of the corresponding system are also made available in table form on the RISKS tab (see Figure 8.10). The system automatically collects the risks. This way, the quality manager can assess before each phase or phase completion, which transports have been released or are still awaiting release. He can also see whether all transports were imported correctly into the system. Based on this information, he can decide which measures are required.

Examples of risks include the following:

▶ Transport error (return code 8)

▶ Missing transport requests in the systems

▶ Transports that are logically interdependent and have not been imported completely

▶ Open transport requests that are awaiting release in the development system

This way, the quality manager can effectively counteract critical situations with the corresponding activities and assess the risk of the project.

Figure 8.10 Transport Risks in Solution Landscapes

Based on the selection of a project, the CHANGES tab displays the project-specific changes as well as the number of transport requests contained therein. Any number of changes can be created for a project. You can create the individual changes for the respective project on the CHANGES tab. After creating a change, you can assign any number of transport requests (WORKBENCH REQUEST/CUSTOMIZING REQUEST) to it. You can create transport requests using the MANAGE TRANSPORTS pushbutton on the CHANGES tab. Alternatively, you can use the CREATE button on the TRANSPORTS tab. The changes form a reference unit for the transport requests that are assigned to them. Change and Transport System (CTS) projects form the basis for this.

Changes to the project

You can also create the changes and transport requests for a project discussed in Section 8.1.1 using Change Request Management. You can then display them in Quality Gate Management (see Figure 8.11; see Section 8.2.9).

This concept makes it possible to logically group related transport requests and those that are dependent on each other specific to the system or solution. Depending on the current phase, you can import entire projects or individual changes in one or more transport requests into downstream systems. In the Test phase, the administrator can, after consulting with the quality manager and other experts, assign transport requests to other projects and their changes. In the

Grouping transport requests logically

Test phase of the software development project, the quality manager can consolidate the project before the last phase of the project is activated. In the Deploy phase, the entire project with all its transport requests can be imported using the tried and tested SAP approach (SAP Best Practices). This ensures that all transport requests in a project are imported into the production systems completely and in the right order at a defined time. If a project import (IMPORT ALL) cannot be executed, the import of individual changes is also available for the Deploy phase. With this functionality, you can synchronously change business processes in ABAP and non-ABAP across solution landscapes.

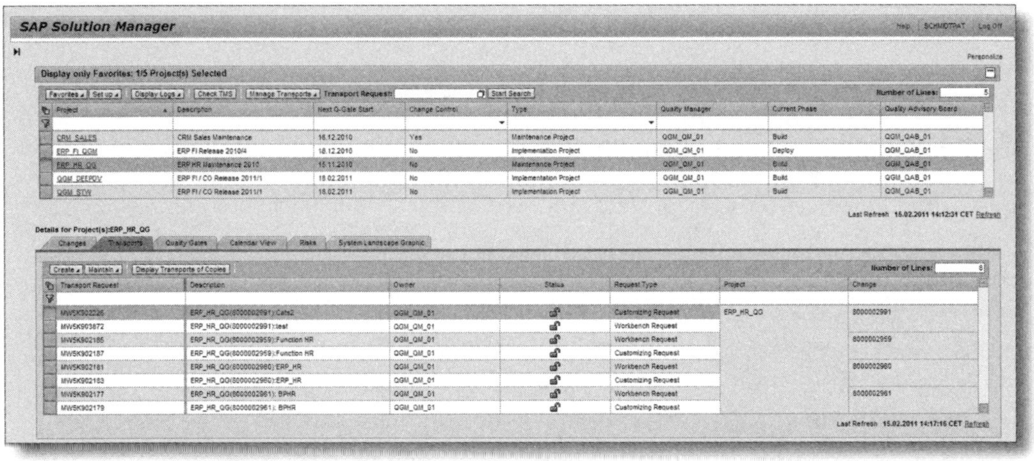

Figure 8.11 Overview of Transport Requests Assigned to a Project

8.1.3   SAP Best Practices in the Transport Area

To support you with your changes as best as possible, Quality Gate Management was developed under consideration of the SAP Best Practices in the transport area. These are based on experience from numerous customer projects:

▶ **Transport of copies**
This function makes it possible to block an original transport request and the objects contained therein in the development system until the developed functionality has been successfully tested in the QA system. It is only then that the final release of the original transport request takes place. Hence, the developer uses the transport of copies as long as possible.

This procedure has two main advantages. On the one hand, it reduces the number of transport requests that are imported into the production system. Because the original transport only contains the final version of the changed object and not the previously developed versions, this reduces the number of object versions in the production system as well as the import time for the transport requests.

The second advantage is that the transport of copies significantly reduces the overshooting risk because the developed objects remain locked in the development system as long as possible. You can thus prevent version conflicts.

Overshooting

▶ **Cross-system object lock**
You can use the cross-system object lock to operate several implementation or maintenance projects in the same system landscape. If a developer changes an object in a project, this object can no longer be changed by any other developers. This applies to this and other projects in the same system landscape if the developer uses the cross-system object lock. Depending on the settings of this lock, changes can be made after the final release of the transport request at the earliest. This prevents version conflicts at an early stage. This function is available for ABAP Workbench objects as well as Customizing settings.

▶ **Urgent corrections**
An urgent correction makes it possible to implement a correction in the production system as quickly as possible by using a preliminary transport. Thanks to the assignment to a project, the transport order and the consistency of the production system are retained.

For more details on SAP Best Practices in the transport area, see Section 8.3.

8.2 Change Request Management

The ability to trace changes is one of the most important factors for guaranteeing quality and transparency in a software solution while ensuring that IT standards are met. This applies in particular to changes to actual software components and changes to the configuration. This section illustrates how SAP Solution Manager helps you implement changes to software components or the configuration with clearly regulated process flows and seamless documentation. It thus enables you to manage your changes and transports centrally.

Changes in a company tend to originate from a user department. The reasons for these changes are either that innovation is needed to ensure growth or the company is evolving in a constantly changing market environment. Other reasons for changes are disruptions or technical problems occurring in daily operation, which can only be resolved by making a change to the system or replacing an IT component.

Requests for change

In Change Request Management, all of these requests end up in requests for change. Change Request Management offers functions for managing, executing, and documenting all these changes, requirements, and requests for change. It not only provides status tracing but also improves integration between user departments and IT in this process. The application supports changes from the initial request until final deployment in the system. The prerequisite for this is a close integration between SAP Solution Manager and the managed systems as well as a close integration between Change Request Management and the SAP transport system. This integration starts at the business and change process level and extends to the technical level of transports and development objects.

Major and minor releases

SAP distinguishes between different types of changes. Based on the time that is required for making and implementing the changes, these are divided into different types of releases. As discussed earlier in this chapter, the larger category is major releases, which have a term of three to six months and have changes that influence the core business processes over the long term. The minor releases have a much shorter term and are primarily used to make error corrections available, as well as to meet lesser requirements.

Implementation or maintenance project

Within the IT organization, these changes or releases are either implemented directly in an implementation project or through a maintenance project, which enables ongoing changes to the system. The projects are always split into phases to support project management and release control. For a detailed depiction of the phases used in Change Request Management, see Section 8.2.3.

Change Request Management can also be used in combination with the Quality Gate Management of SAP Solution Manager to check the different phases and sections of an implementation project. This integration enables you to ensure that quality criteria and project standards are observed before a phase of a project can be completed. For more information about the integration of Change Request Management and Quality Gate Management, see Section 8.2.9 at the end of this chapter.

As already mentioned, both applications are closely integrated into the SAP transport infrastructure, which makes it possible to trace changes from the request in the user department to the implementation in IT. Here, Change Request Management centrally manages the transports, and manual activities are reduced to a minimum.

8.2.1 Change Request Management in Detail

Change Request Management is a flexible tool that helps you check developments and changes to your entire system landscape centrally in SAP Solution Manager. Change Request Management offers a range of functions for this purpose.

The concept on which the processes are based consists of two types of documents: the request for change and the change transaction.

The request for change is the initial document in which the requirement or change to be made is documented and described for the first time. It also documents the approval or approval procedure of the request.

Request for change

As soon as you have approved a request for change, one or more change transactions are generated as follow-on documents with direct reference to the original request. Change transactions distinguish between different types of changes. This depends on whether a change is a change to a system or an IT component and the urgency of the change. In the change transaction, you can document and execute all activities that are necessary for making this change.

Change transaction

You can see at any time where an actual change originated, who approved it, who implemented it, and who imported it into the production system. One of the main benefits of this transparency is that all this information is available at a central point, SAP Solution Manager, where you can access it at any time.

Example scenario A brief example (see Figure 8.12) of a typical change process with Change Request Management illustrates this approach: A processor in the business department discovers a change requirement in a transaction that he uses. The user can enter a Service Desk message directly from the transaction in question, describing the context and requesting a change. The message appears in the worklist of a Service Desk employee, who processes the message and generates a change request, if appropriate (see Section 8.2.4). Next, the system forwards the change request to the central person in the scenario, the change manager. The change manager is responsible for assessing, categorizing, and approving or rejecting the request. If he approves the request, a change transaction is generated, which forms the functional basis in subsequent stages for developers, testers, and IT administrators. The Change Manager comes back into play after the processes described next have been completed and concludes the request for change.

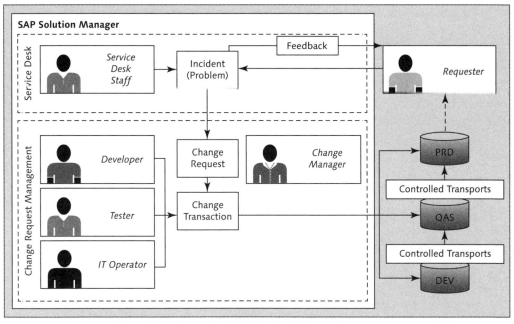

Figure 8.12 Overview of the Standard Change Request Management Process

The Change transaction appears in the worklist of a developer, who implements the change and releases it for testing. At this point, it is transferred to a tester. The change cannot be transported into the production system until it has been tested successfully.

You can use the Change Request Management functions to manage releases and projects in a number of ways. Within a given project, you can plan any changes that are to be implemented over a certain period and monitor their implementation. You can also document and resolve changes efficiently that are not part of a project plan but call for swift attention (*urgent changes*), for instance, if an error occurs that could jeopardize a production environment.

Release management using Change Request Management

Another option for managing releases using Change Request Management is the integration with *SAP cProjects*, the SAP project planning tool. Your organization can record and plan all the changes that need to be implemented in a project in a cProjects project plan. You can plan resources and also establish a connection to the backend, for example, to the *Cross-Application Time Sheet* (CATS) component for recording tasks. Requests for change that have undergone the approval procedure can be scheduled here. The project plan is integrated in the project in SAP Solution Manager, which passes through several phases in what is known as a *project cycle*. The phases are controlled centrally from SAP Solution Manager and set forth basic conditions that cannot be sidestepped.

Project plan

In this regard, SAP Solution Manager closes a gap that exists in many change management solutions: When databases or lists, for example, are used to depict change management processes and log requests for change and approvals, manual intervention becomes absolutely necessary when a transport request needs to be created or imported. The transport request number has to be copied to the database by hand, which is a potential source of errors. A typo or mistake when copying invalidates the entire process. With Change Request Management, transport requests are generated centrally from SAP Solution Manager. A reference to the corresponding request for change is created automatically (with the ID and description copied to the transport request's name), enabling a clear relationship to be identified at any time. The Change Request Management scenario lets you track all transports relating to a specific project, enabling you to check where they were created and in which systems they have been

Integration of Change Request Management with the transport system

imported. From SAP Solution Manager, you can navigate to the transport logs and import queue, as well as to the SAP Solution Manager maintenance project, the project plan, and the connected systems. Each change transaction provides an overview of all transports and transport tasks created for it. From there, you can monitor the status of transports at any time and also branch directly into the log file.

You can also record changes in Change Request Management that do not require a transport connection. As with all other changes, you produce a request for change that goes through all the approval steps. You document the required steps in the request for change itself. SAP Solution Manager therefore advances SAP's vision of application management and IT governance by providing enterprises with indispensable functions for implementing and running solutions transparently. This forms the basis for many statutory requirements: It supplies answers to the question of who did what when, and who checked and approved the measures.

For an organization to run a system landscape smoothly in the face of constantly changing requirements, it must take into account the following aspects:

▶ Request for changes, whether resulting from error messages or from idea management processes, must be classified and approved centrally.

▶ When a request has been approved, reliable procedures must be followed to apply the change, transport it to follow-on systems (QA and production), and conduct tests. These procedures should be complemented by meticulous documentation containing all change-related information and data on all persons involved in the process.

▶ The status of a request for change must be traceable at all times.

Integrated teams

Equally important is the integration of people within the organization, whereby SAP Solution Manager's focus on processes is instrumental in enabling communication between business departments and IT administrators. Everyone involved in implementing a change can always access all the relevant information, such as requirements, specifications, documentation, test cases, test results, and status analyses, which are organized using the business process hierarchy in SAP Solution Manager and stored centrally.

This offering from SAP is designed in line with the processes in the IT Infrastructure Library (ITIL). ITIL defines the objective of change management as ensuring that changes are made economically and promptly with minimum risk. Change Request Management includes the following processes: change request management, project management, and change logistics.

Conformity and IT standards

In addition, Change Request Management enables your company to use these processes in a very easy way by offering predefined processes. It also helps you meet audit requirements—for example, for SOX (Sarbanes Oxley Act)—by forcing all users to make the changes centrally using the defined change management processes using SAP Solution Manager.

A major advantage of Change Request Management is, as already mentioned, that standard processes and functions are supplied and can be used quickly.

Ready to run out of the box

SAP Solution Manager is supplied with preconfigured workflows for the request for change and change execution (change transactions). These workflows are based on SAP's experience with change management and transport management influenced by numerous customer projects. The following change types are predefined:

▶ **Normal change**
Normal changes refer to requests for regular system maintenance activities, such as requests for SPs or SAP Notes to be imported.

▶ **Error correction**
An error correction reports errors that are discovered during testing to the development team. The developer can then also correct the error at a later date using this document, even though it is not possible to create a new normal change during the Test phase.

▶ **Urgent change**
An urgent change enables you to react quickly and flexibly if a malfunction threatens to disrupt the operation of your solution. This enables you to import changes from urgent changes into production systems before importing the normal change in the Go-Live phase of the maintenance cycle.

▶ **Administrative change**
An administration change concerns changes that do not require transporting, such as changes to number ranges.

▶ **General change**
A general change concerns changes that do not require a transport connection and that are not related to an SAP or IT system, for example, changes to IT components such as printers or mobile devices.

Roles and authorization profiles

To make it possible to get started with Change Request Management quickly and smoothly, SAP also provides a range of predefined roles and authorization profiles. These roles and processes can initially be used to create a feasibility report using Change Request Management. Later on, they can serve as the basis for adjusting Change Request Management to the individual requirements or change management processes of your company.

8.2.2 Architecture

To understand the architecture of Change Request Management in SAP Solution Manager, you need to know how the individual entities interact.

Solution Manager project

The basis of Change Request Management is the Solution Manager project (see Section 8.1.1). A project contains the following information:

▶ **Logical components**
A logical component contains all systems that supply a production system (e.g., a production client). The assigned systems are usually connected to each other through transport routes.

▶ **IMG project**
From project administration in SAP Solution Manager (Transaction SOLAR_PROJECT_ADMIN), you create an IMG project in managed systems to group settings made in the SAP Implementation Guide (IMG) for a Solution Manager project in one system.

▶ **CTS project**
A container in a logical system (system/client combination) that bundles transport requests that belong to one IMG project.

Change Request Management supports the implementation, upgrade, template, and maintenance project types.

Depending on the type of change transaction the change manager assigns in the request for change before approval, two types of Change Request Management cycles are possible: project cycle and maintenance cycle. Designed to meet different requirements, the cycles differ in scope and are therefore explained in Section 8.2.3.

The *task list* in Change Request Management provides system admin-   Task list
istrators with an overview of implemented and scheduled actions. It summarizes all the systems and necessary tasks and displays them in the correct sequence. Any tasks that you execute by performing actions on the corrections or project cycle user interfaces in SAP Solution Manager (such as system logon, create transport request, or import transport request) are defined in the task list. For more information on the task list, see Section 8.3.1, subsection "Central Transport Management."

8.2.3 Project Cycle and Maintenance Cycle

We have already mentioned implementation and maintenance projects several times. This section explains the concepts and differences between the two project types in more detail.

To support implementation, upgrade, and template projects in the   Project cycle
Change Request Management scenario, SAP Solution Manager offers the *project cycle*.

The project cycle (depicted in Figure 8.13) is a preconfigured service process (transaction type SMDV) that allows you to control the following activities over the course of a project:

► Requests for change and the resulting changes in systems used in your project

► Transport requests required to transport changes to follow-on systems

► Complete change logistics, that is, when certain transports can be imported into follow-on systems

Structured as a series of phases, the project cycle provides a functional supplement to the project plan. A single project cycle has the following phases:

- ▶ Development without Release
- ▶ Development with Release
- ▶ Test
- ▶ Preparation for Go-Live
- ▶ Go-Live

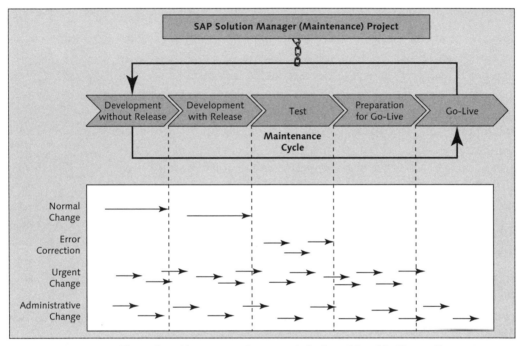

Figure 8.13 Maintenance Project with Cycle and Possible Change Transactions

You close the project cycle after going live. The maintenance cycle is a special type of project cycle in which it is possible to run through the phases several times (as explained later in this section).

In the Development without Release phase, a transport request can be created but not released. This phase can thus be defined also as the initial specification phase or planning phase. We do not recommend using this phase with normal changes (transaction type SMMJ) because it is not possible to generate test transports during this phase. Transport requests cannot be released until the Development with Release phase. It is initiated by a central body (Change Advisory Board or a change manager) and permits transports to be released and imported into the test environment for unit tests. After project changes have been imported into the test environment, the Test phase can be opened so that integration testing can begin. New requests for change can no longer be created for this project; only bugs that are discovered during testing are fixed. The preparation for the Go-Live phase enables users with appropriate authorization to make other necessary changes before the changes are imported into the production environment in the Go-Live phase. However, you cannot import any changes that do not have the status TESTED SUCCESSFULLY.

Consistent with the lifecycle model, you use an implementation project in SAP Solution Manager to implement a solution. You conclude the implementation project successfully and the solution goes live. During this process, you copy the project data into a solution (see Section 8.1.1). To keep the solution current, you assign it a maintenance project with a maintenance cycle.

Differences between maintenance cycles and project cycles

A maintenance cycle is a project cycle that has been adapted to meet the special requirements of maintenance projects. A maintenance project does have a defined start time. However, in contrast to a development project, it is a continuous, ongoing process. The individual phases of the maintenance cycle will continue to run.

The maintenance cycle has the same phases as the project cycle but with certain additional features. First, the maintenance cycle has an extra correction type (urgent changes), which gives you the flexibility to make urgent corrections at short notice (see Section 8.2.5). Second, if you work with maintenance cycles, we advise adopting a different approach that meets the requirements posed by maintaining a solution.

Phase model of a maintenance cycle

We recommend that you assign a maintenance project to a solution, lasting for the same amount of time as you intend to run the solution. Within the maintenance project, any necessary corrections are effected in a series of maintenance cycles. The change manager defines the duration of a maintenance cycle, for example, one month. During this period, the project runs through all the phases in the cycle, from In Development without Release to Go-Live. At the end of the Go-Live phase, you do not close the cycle. It is checked for open and incomplete business transactions and transport requests. Documents that have not been closed are then carried over when a new maintenance cycle is created.

From a technical point of view, it is possible not to close the maintenance cycle but to reset its phase to In Development without Release and to run through the same cycle again. However, closing and recreating the maintenance cycle facilitates and guarantees clearer and more traceable reporting, which is why we recommend it.

Example   The following example shows the benefits of this approach. You have defined the scope of your maintenance cycle by assessing and approving submitted requests for change. Ten normal changes have been approved for the current maintenance cycle (e.g., October). During the development phase, you find that one of the normal changes, change number nine, cannot be realized in the time allotted to the phase.

As project manager, you have two options for dealing with the delay. You can increase the amount of time available for this correction so that it can be realized in the current maintenance cycle. Or, if the change is not critical and has no dependencies with the other changes, you can decide to complete it in the next maintenance cycle—November. In this case, the status of the change remains IN DEVELOPMENT. The other nine changes go through the Test and Go-Live phases and are imported into the production systems. Now you close the October cycle, and the open change is ready to be carried over into the new cycle. When the November cycle is created, the change is automatically carried over to this cycle and processed together with the new changes in this cycle.

In this regard, this approach differs from that of the project cycle. If normal changes with a status other than TESTED SUCCESSFULLY still exist when you move from the Development with Release phase of the maintenance cycle to the Test phase, the system only issues a warning message. These corrections are excluded from integration tests and cannot be released.

During maintenance, errors that demand a swift resolution can be reported at any time, for example, if production systems are likely to be jeopardized. A normal change does not allow you to respond to such problems quickly enough because it is dependent on the maintenance cycle phase. If the maintenance cycle is in the Test phase, you cannot enter new changes for this cycle. That is why Change Request Management offers the urgent change, which is explained in more detail in Section 8.2.5.

8.2.4 Request for Change

You can assign any number of requests for change to a project or maintenance cycle. Like a Service Desk message, a *request for change*, (transaction type SMCR; see Figure 8.14) is a preconfigured service process, which contains all of the following data relevant to the change:

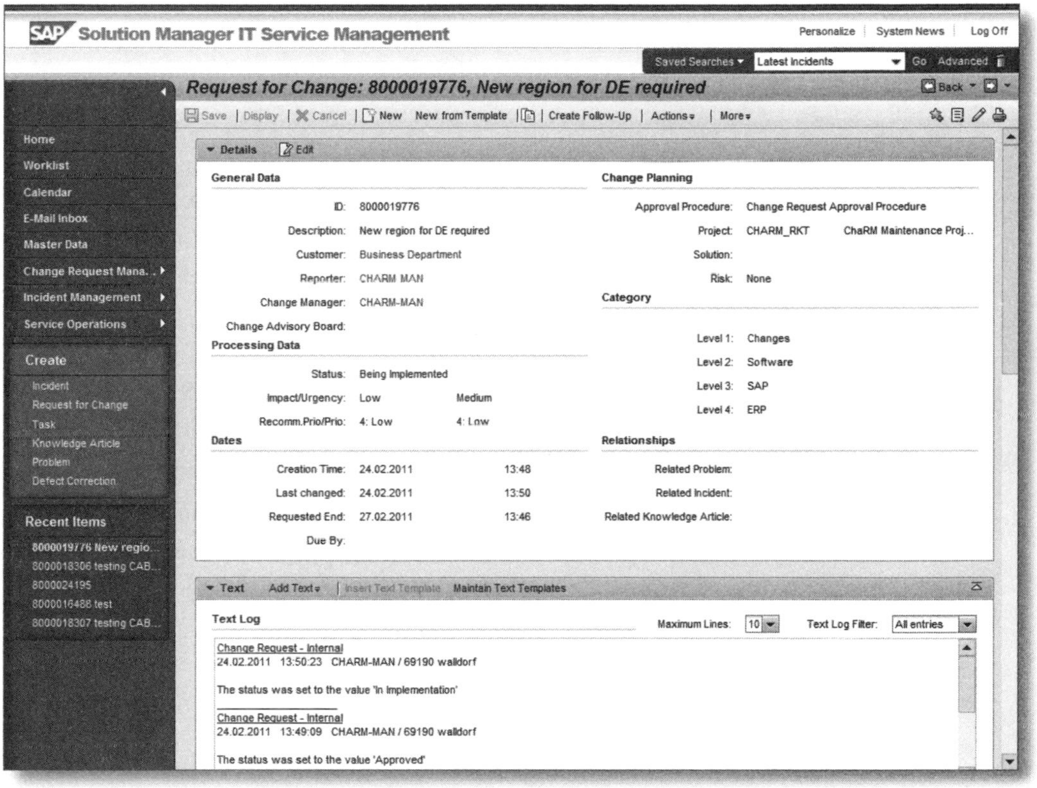

Figure 8.14 The Request for Change in the New Web Client Interface

▶ Persons involved (ordering party, requester, change manager, Change Advisory Board)

▶ System affected by the change (installed base/component)

▶ Corresponding Solution Manager project

▶ Priority

▶ Effect

▶ Urgency

▶ Risk

> ▶ Scope of the change

> ▶ Texts that safeguard communication (e.g., description of change, reason for change, implications for business partners, implications for systems, etc.)

Change Request Management therefore covers the complete lifecycle, from gathering requirements to implementing, testing, running, and continuously improving a solution. It is integrated in SAP Solution Manager's extensive range of functions, which include incident management, E-Learning Management, and upgrade support.

Scope of the change

In the assignment block SCOPE OF THE CHANGE REQUEST (see Figure 8.15), you can define which type of change you are dealing with and in which system/component this change is supposed to be made.

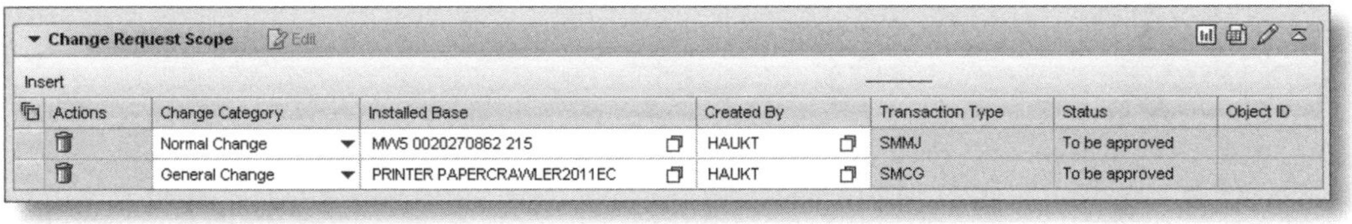

Figure 8.15 Scope of the Change Request Assignment Block

Types of change

Depending on which change category you choose, the system creates other follow-on activities when the change is released for development. A project cycle supports four types of change, enabling the change manager to classify requests for change:

> ▶ Normal change

> ▶ Error correction

> ▶ Administrative change

> ▶ General change

In contrast to the previous version of Change Request Management, you can now combine different types of changes within a request for change. For each new change transaction, the change manager can create a new entry in the table of the assignment block SCOPE OF THE CHANGE REQUEST. In general, you can combine any types of changes. The available systems or components also have a relation to the Solution Manager project that has been assigned to the document in the DETAILS assignment block. You can only select components that are part of the system landscape of this project. General changes are an exception to this. Because this change type is to be viewed independently of an SAP or IT system, there is no dependency on components that can be selected.

You can assign an approval transaction to the request for change. This transaction must then be processed before the request receives the status APPROVED.

Approval transactions

An approval transaction is an approval process that consists of a defined sequence of approval steps (see Figure 8.16). For each approval transaction, you can define in Customizing which approval steps must be completed. In doing so, you can choose which steps can run in parallel and which steps are interdependent.

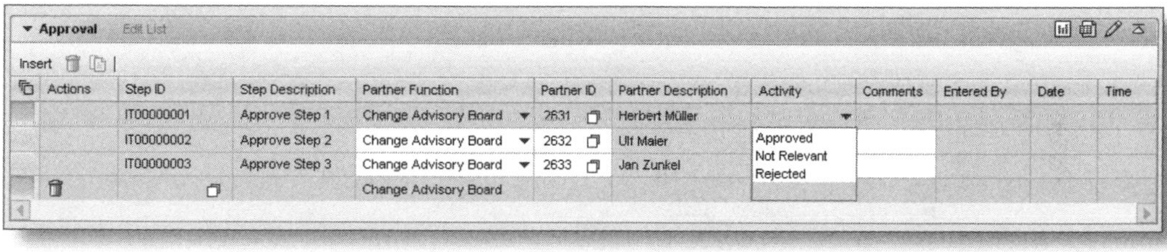

Actions	Step ID	Step Description	Partner Function		Partner ID		Partner Description	Activity		Comments	Entered By	Date	Time
	IT00000001	Approve Step 1	Change Advisory Board	▼	2631	🗇	Herbert Müller		▼				
	IT00000002	Approve Step 2	Change Advisory Board	▼	2632	🗇	Ulf Maier	Approved					
	IT00000003	Approve Step 3	Change Advisory Board	▼	2633	🗇	Jan Zunkel	Not Relevant					
			Change Advisory Board					Rejected					

Figure 8.16 Approval Assignment Block

For each approval step, you can define which business partner role is responsible for executing it. If you later select the approval transaction in the request for change, you have to assign a concrete business partner to each step. Each business partner can be informed through a workflow item or email from the SAP Business Workflow, if he needs to make a decision.

Assigning business partners

To execute the approval, you can choose from three options: APPROVED, REJECTED, and NOT RELEVANT. In addition, the approver can enter a comment for each approval step when executing this step. All this information is also recorded in the change log and can be called up at any time.

You can define any number of approval transactions in Customizing. You can assign these to a request in line with the change type. In addition, you can also use a set of rules to define your own rules. These rules can, for example, assign a certain approval transaction on the basis of field values (e.g., if the urgency and priority of the change are very high, a different approval transaction is to be used than for a normal change).

In the standard system, SAP provides a simple approval transaction that consists of just one approval step for the change manager. You can adjust and enhance this as required.

Change request process

The change request process starts with the creation of the request by the requester. This requester is either a Service Desk employee or, in the case of a new requirement, a member of the business department. It describes the required change and provides all other necessary information, for example, specifications or screenshots. Following that, the change manager accepts the document and changes its status from CREATED to REVIEW. In this review step, the change manager completes the request for change with other relevant information and answers, among others, the following questions:

- Which system and which change type are required (definition of the change scope)?
- Which SAP Solution Manager project is supposed to be used?
- Which solution and business process are affected?
- Which approval transaction is supposed to be used?
- How high is the risk for this change?
- Which effect and urgency has the change, and which priority should it be given?

Figure 8.17 outlines the change request process.

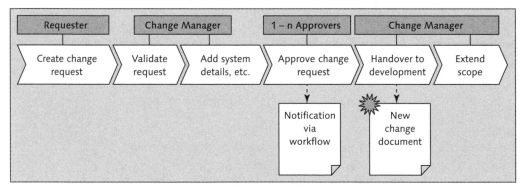

Figure 8.17 Overview of the Process for a Change Request

Approval procedure

After all these questions have been answered and the information has been gathered and entered in the request, the change manager submits the request for approval. The assigned approval transaction now starts. In addition, the change manager has the option to reject the request for change if it cannot be implemented or if a similar request already exists.

If all approval steps have been processed successfully and the result of the approval transaction is positive, the status of the request is set to APPROVED. The change manager can now release the request for development or implementation. With this release, the change transactions defined in the change scope are created, and the status of the request is changed to CURRENT IMPLEMENTATION.

After all assigned change transactions have reached their final status, the status of the request automatically changes to IMPLEMENTED. As the last step, the change manager can now check the request and implementation once more before setting the status to CONFIRMED after consulting the requester.

Another new feature in the change request process using the new SAP Solution Manager is the option to extend the scope of the change during implementation. You can use the EXTEND SCOPE action to extend the defined scope of the request for change and add additional change transactions. This means you keep an overview of all connected changes, even if they are added subsequently.

Scope extension

8.2.5 Change Types in Change Request Management in Detail

In Change Request Management, you distinguish between a range of change types as discussed briefly in the preceding section. This section covers the individual change types in more detail and describes the use case, process, and particularities of the different change types in more detail.

Normal Change

A normal change (transaction type SMMJ) represents the corrections or changes made in a project and has the following status profile:

Status profile

▶ Created

▶ In Development

▶ To Be Tested

▶ Successfully Tested

▶ Imported into Production

▶ Withdrawn

The workflow for a normal change is explained in detail next.

Process description A user detects missing functions in a system. The user can report the fault directly from the relevant transaction by sending a Service Desk message to SAP Solution Manager. The Service Desk message contains all of the relevant system data and describes the request.

The Service Desk employee processing the message finds that the request requires a request for change. This employee then chooses the CREATE FOLLOW-UP ACTIVITY action to create a request for change in incident management.

The request for change appears in the change manager's worklist. The change manager classifies the request, specifies how it is to be handled (normal correction), and finally approves or rejects it. The priority of the request for change is an important factor here. For details on the process for the change request, see Section 8.2.4.

If the request for change is approved as a normal change, SAP Solution Manager automatically generates a change transaction of the normal change type as soon as the request is released for development. The request for change and the change transaction are linked by the document flow, and the assignment is always visible.

The change transaction is the functional basis for developers, testers, and system administrators. First, the developer is notified that a new change needs processing. The developer works on the correction and selects the appropriate action to set the status to IN DEVELOPMENT.

The developer creates a transport request in the development system, logs on to the development system directly, and when the correction is ready, releases the transport tasks in the development system (Transaction SE09). When development is completed, the developer generates a test transport by means of an action in the change transaction, which is then imported into the test system. The developer then tests the new development. If this test is successful, the developer sets the status to TO BE TESTED. This has the effect that, if not already arranged by the developer, the system generates a transport of copies, which can be imported into the test system. On the basis of a scheduled job (in the managed system), the newly developed function is imported into a test system during one of the regular imports of the project buffer. It undergoes another function test there first. The tester can access all of the necessary functions in one place, for example, system logon, and the complete change history for the change transaction. The Change Request Management scenario supports the principle of dual control, enabling you to specify that the developer and tester must not be the same person.

If this test was successful, the tester uses an action to change the status of the change to Tested Successfully. The request from the development system is now exported to the test system. All of the activities described can be executed directly from the change transaction using actions.

The normal change ends with this step. From now on, it only contains descriptive status values but is handed over to the project cycle from a technical perspective and pursued further by it.

The following prerequisites must be met before changes can be imported into production systems:

Importing changes

▶ The system administrator cannot import a change into the production system unless the corresponding project cycle is in the Go-Live phase.

▶ The status cannot be set to Imported into Production unless all normal changes for the project have been imported successfully into the production systems. You can set this status for all imported normal corrections at the end of a project cycle by scheduling job CRM_SOCM_SERVICE_REPORT.

Normal changes whose status is still In Development trigger a warning in the corresponding project cycle if the status is set during the Test phase.

Urgent Change

Urgent changes (transaction type SMHF) have their own task list. They can be transported regardless of the phase of the assigned maintenance cycle. This enables you to import changes from urgent changes into production systems before importing the normal change in the Go-Live phase of the maintenance cycle. Urgent changes can only be created in connection with a maintenance project and are not available for implementation projects.

Transport control The IMPORT_SUBSET transport method is used in this case. That is, transport requests generated from an urgent correction are written to the transport buffer and imported into the follow-on systems. They remain in the buffer after the import. With regular imports based on the task list for the maintenance cycle, the entire transport buffer for the project is consolidated and imported using the Import_Project_All method. That is to say, the urgent changes are imported a second time to ensure data consistency.

Status profile Urgent changes have the following status profile:

- Created
- In Development
- To Be Tested
- Successfully Tested
- Release for Production
- Imported into Production
- Confirmed
- Completed
- Withdrawn

In the standard release, SAP Solution Manager automatically imports transport requests relating to an urgent change into the test system when you set the status to To Be Tested. This setting is intended to accelerate the process further, but you can change it in Customizing if necessary.

Administration Change

An *administration change* (transaction type SMAD) lets you keep a complete change history for changes that do not require transporting, such as changes to number ranges or user data. It provides access to the task list as well as to activities such as system logon. It has the following status profile:

Status profile
- Created
- In Process
- Completed
- Confirmed
- Withdrawn

General Change

A *general change* (transaction type SMCG) is designed for mapping changes to objects not relevant in the system, which do not require any transports and can be independent of Solution Manager projects. These can be, for example, changes to a mobile device or printer.

For this purpose, the general change offers an abstract status profile, which you can adapt to your requirements at any time:

▸ Created

Status profile

▸ In Process

▸ To Be Tested

▸ Change Documentation

▸ Change Report

▸ Failed

▸ Restore Original

▸ Confirmed

▸ Canceled

▸ Withdrawn

The processing of a general change, like the other changes, starts when the person who makes the change sets the corresponding status. After successful testing, the change might have to be documented and evaluated again. If this evaluation is successful, the change can be confirmed. However, it can also be necessary to reverse the change if implementing it as-is would result in a deterioration of the situation.

Error Correction

You can only create *error corrections* (transaction type SMTM) during the Test phase of the project or maintenance cycle. Because a test message is used for integration testing, which applies to the entire project (all changes), it does not refer to one single change or request for change. You use test messages to report errors found during testing to the development team so that the relevant developer can fix the problem by creating a transport request. Because the project scope has been approved on the basis of the requests for change, an

Only in Test phase

error correction does not require any approval steps. It has the following status profile:

▸ Created

▸ In Correction

▸ For Retesting

▸ Confirmed

▸ Withdrawn

Error corrections are vital because you cannot create new normal changes in the Test phase. Doing so would distort the project's defined and approved scope.

A tester creates an error correction and describes the symptoms. A developer processes the message, creates one or more transport requests, and fixes the bug in the development system. To submit the change for retesting, the developer sets the status to FOR RESTESTING. After the re-import of the transport buffer into the test system, the tester checks the functions and confirms successful testing by setting the status to CONFIRMED. During the project import in the Go-Live phase, all changes and error corrections are imported into the production system together.

8.2.6 Change Management Using Change Request Management

All Change Request Management functions that have been described so far are very flexible and can be adapted to individual company requirements. This starts with the implementation of different technologies and system landscapes and ends with the design and modeling of complex workflows and individual processes.

Change Request Management is as flexible as your business and supports many different system landscapes. In addition to a three-system system landscape, you can also manage significantly more complex landscapes with Change Request Management.

In addition to the different sequential types of system landscapes, Change Request Management is also able to manage other types of landscapes. For example, it can manage dual landscapes, that is, supplying parallel test systems or synchronizing parallel development and maintenance landscapes (see Section 8.3.2). You can also integrate independent sandbox systems into the process and supply them adequately with transports. Change Request Management supports all landscapes that can be mapped using SAP's transport management system (TMS).

Change Request Management can not only be used to manage changes to SAP landscapes, but also integration with the enhanced Change and Transport System (CTS+) enables you to manage non-ABAP and even non-SAP technologies such as Java, C++, or Microsoft .NET with Change Request Management change transactions.

Openness

Within a change transaction, you can display the complete system landscape or the transport path, including the system roles generated by Change Request Management at any time.

The system landscape in the change transaction

The SYSTEM LANDSCAPE assignment block shows an overview table of the individual systems that have been assigned to the current project using logical components. In the ACTIONS column, you can log on to the system directly to make a change there or test a changed function. Hence, the assignment block in the standard release only shows the currently relevant system. This is determined using the current status of the change transaction. For example, if the change transaction is in the status IN DEVELOPMENT, the relevant system is the development system.

As already defined, each type of change transaction follows its own predefined workflow, which makes it easy to use these functions immediately.

Flexible workflows

However, many companies already have an established change management process and do not want to change this just because they are introducing a new application. Hence, all Change Request Management processes are very flexible and can be adjusted to your individual requirements.

This starts with the definition of the approval transactions and finishes with the definition and modeling of the different process steps in detail. You can also copy existing change transactions to edit existing actions and their conditions, or you can define completely new actions and conditions.

Multilevel categorization

Multilevel categorization enables you to categories every document in Change Request Management and SAP IT service management in detail. The standard provides four category levels for this. These levels are set up in a tree structure and are interdependent.

For more information on this function, see Chapter 9, Section 9.1.7, subsection "Multilevel Categorization."

Transport management in Change Request Management

The integration of Change Request Management and the transport system becomes apparent in particular in the TRANSPORT MANAGEMENT assignment block of a change transaction (see Figure 8.18). The assignment block is assigned to the following transaction types: normal change, urgent change, and error correction.

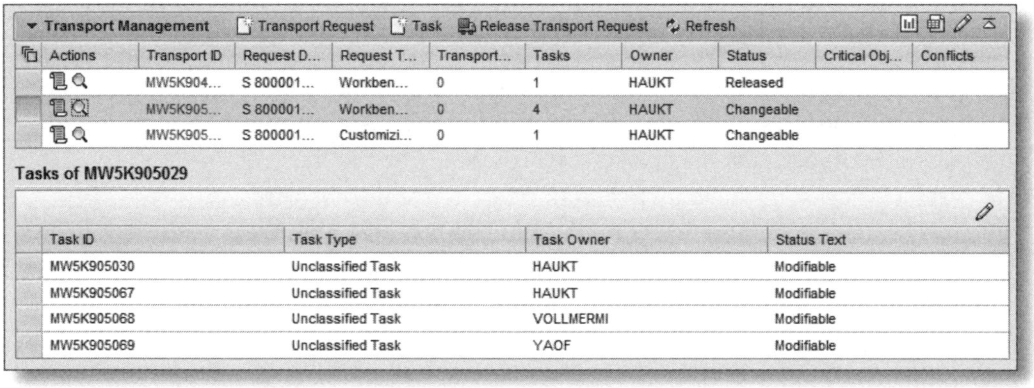

▼ Transport Management		🗋 Transport Request	🗋 Task	🗐 Release Transport Request	↻ Refresh					
🗇 Actions	Transport ID	Request D...	Request T...	Transport...	Tasks	Owner	Status	Critical Obj...	Conflicts
📋🔍	MW5K904...	S 800001...	Workben...	0	1	HAUKT	Released		
📋🔍	MW5K905...	S 800001...	Workben...	0	4	HAUKT	Changeable		
📋🔍	MW5K905...	S 800001...	Customizi...	0	1	HAUKT	Changeable		

Tasks of MW5K905029

Task ID	Task Type	Task Owner	Status Text
MW5K905030	Unclassified Task	HAUKT	Modifiable
MW5K905067	Unclassified Task	HAUKT	Modifiable
MW5K905068	Unclassified Task	VOLLMERMI	Modifiable
MW5K905069	Unclassified Task	YAOF	Modifiable

Figure 8.18 Transport Management Assignment Block

In addition to an overview of all relevant transport requests and transport tasks of a request for change, the assignment block provides a central point of access for all transport-relevant actions and functions.

You can use buttons to create new transport requests or transport tasks, release requests, and approve critical objects. A table lists all transports and additional detailed information, including the owner of the transport, type of request, status, and number of transport tasks. Just one click suffices to access the transport logs or bill of materials (BOM) of the transport request.

If copies of a transport have already been created, this is also displayed. A dialog box shows you how often a copy transport has been generated and what the current copy transport is. In addition, other columns of the table show whether the transport contains critical objects or whether conflicts with other transports have been detected.

8.2.7 Central Change Control

One of the objectives of Change Request Management is to provide a control mechanism for ensuring a safe and smooth software deployment process. To achieve this, Change Request Management uses a range of functions that can help you keep your changes consistent and minimize the number of malfunctions and problems during process execution in various situations.

The most important thing in change management is to maintain an overview of which changes are installed in the production environment and which transports may be transported from the development system to the production system via the test system. Of course, the integrity of the individual systems must not be put at risk at any time.

Built-in transport Best Practices

Change Request Management has built-in transport Best Practices from SAP, which facilitate working with changes and help you avoid errors. An example if this is the use of transport copies.

For more information on this, see also Section 8.3, which deals specifically with the subject of transport management.

Day-to-day activities will make it necessary to combine normal and urgent changes in the same system landscape, even if regular maintenance is still in process. If an object is changed that is also affected by the new development, this can lead to problems if you do not import the transports in the right order. Change Request Management has a built-in safety function for ensuring the safe processing of normal and urgent changes and importing them in the right order.

Consistent transports

For transport control, Change Request Management uses transport method `IMPORT_PROJECT_ALL`. The advantage of this is that you can work on specific projects and import the transport requests into the follow-on systems at the end of the cycle phases, harmonized, consolidated, and in the sequence in which they were released. This approach minimizes the risk of *overshooters* in the transport system. At the end of the project, you can import all of the changes into the production systems and close the project. During the project import, this means that all urgent changes are taken into account and once again imported in the right order to make sure there are no inconsistencies.

Cross-system object lock

Imagine different implementation and maintenance projects that take place in your system landscape at the same time. Some of these projects even work in the same system landscape. If a developer changes an object, which is subsequently changed by another developer, all of the changes that the first developer made are lost. This problem can be prevented by using the *cross-system object lock*.

The cross-system object lock ensures that when an object is changed in a managed system, a lock entry is created for this object in the central SAP Solution Manager system. Depending on the configuration of the object lock, this entry then prevents any other change to the same object being made in any other transport request. The cross-system object lock can not only protect ABAP but also Customizing objects. Using it minimizes the risk of a downgrade due to different go-live times of changes from projects running in parallel. For details, see Section 8.3.1.

Critical objects

For *sensitive* or *critical objects*, that is, objects that directly affect the core business, you can activate a check that is executed before a transport request is exported. Transport requests that contain critical objects must be approved separately.

You can activate the check at the system-specific or client-specific level. If a transport request is exported, the system calculates the target client and the target system. If the check for critical objects has been activated for the respective target client or target system, the system checks whether the request contains critical objects or subobjects. If that is the case, the export is not executed.

To execute the transport nonetheless, a responsible person has to approve the object and release it for export. This is a very easy way to get additional protection for your applications.

Project Phase Management

The built-in phase control in Change Request Management ensures that only the right and approved transport actions can be executed. If you are managing and checking the phases of the maintenance and implementation projects, you can, for example, ensure that the status of your test system remains constant during the Test phase. This also means that no new changes can be imported, which could then enter the production system without being tested (see Figure 8.19).

Figure 8.19 The Maintenance Cycle in the New Web Client Interface

Phase control is integrated with different change types to ensure that only the correct change transactions are used in certain phases, such as error corrections in the Test phase. This enables you to centrally check all your maintenance and implementation projects in SAP Solution Manager.

Here is a brief example to explain the project cycle concept: The project manager creates a project in SAP Solution Manager (implementation, upgrade, or template project) and generates IMG and CTS projects, as well as a project cycle for the project. The system administrator activates the project cycle in the document (transaction type SMMN) using the corresponding action. You can now begin creating,

Working with project cycles

classifying, and approving requests for change. You therefore already specify the project scope in this phase.

After changes are approved, SAP Solution Manager assigns the resulting change transactions to the project cycle. If you have several projects open at the same time, there will be more than one project cycle. In this case, you already assign a project to the request for change in advance and thus specify which cycle is used.

In Development without Release phase

The change manager sets the project cycle status to In Development without Release. With this status, developers can work on changes in the system. They can create transport requests and tasks but cannot release or export them. This phase can thus be defined also as the initial specification phase or planning phase. We do not recommend using this phase with normal changes (transaction type SMMJ) because it is not possible to generate test transports during this phase.

In Development with Release phase

When the change manager changes the project cycle status from IN DEVELOPMENT WITHOUT RELEASE to IN DEVELOPMENT WITH RELEASE, developers can generate transports of copies of the changes they have made, which are imported into the test system for test purposes. Ideally, scheduled jobs perform this job, but the system administrator can also perform it manually in the task list.

In many cases, development systems do not contain the master or transaction data that would enable developers to test their changes. Such data is often only available in test systems. This is why you have the option of scheduling unit tests in this phase of the project cycle, that is, before integration testing. This gives developers time to test their corrections after they have been imported to the test systems and to set their status to TO BE TESTED. This is followed by another transport of copies into the test system. The tester then sees the change to be tested in the worklist in the work center or SAP Web Client and can perform the test. If the test was successful, the tester sets the status of the correction to TESTED SUCCESSFULLY, triggering the correction to be exported from the development system in the background.

Test phase

After moving to the Test phase, transport requests of all changes that do not yet have the status TO BE TESTED can no longer be exported. Users are warned of this when they switch phases in the document (transaction type SMMN), as recommended by SAP. This freezes the code from the beginning of the TEST phase. Urgent changes are not affected by this behavior and can still be used.

During the Test phase, testers can check that corrections are acceptable in terms of functionality and business relevance. If they discover a mistake, they can document it in an error correction document (transaction type SMTM) and notify the relevant developer. After receiving this error correction, the developer can create a new transport request in the development system and fix the bug. The Test phase is complete when all changes and error corrections have the status TESTED SUCCESSFULLY. Changes that do not have this status cannot be excluded from testing. That is, they must either be tested successfully or be withdrawn.

If you need to make other changes after the Test phase is complete, you can create, release, and move transport requests and tasks during the emergency correction phase. However, you can only do so using the task list for the project cycle and with the appropriate authorizations. Urgent changes are not affected by this and can still be used.

Preparation for Go-Live phase (emergency correction)

In the Go-Live phase, the entire transport buffer for the CTS project is imported into the production systems in the order of the releases. Transport requests cannot be created or released during this phase. It is not possible to use urgent changes either. Following the import to the production system environment, no open transport requests remain, and the transport buffer is empty. You can now close the project cycle by setting the status to CONFIRMED. The project is then considered to be complete.

Go-Live phase

The project phase should be moved on only using the appropriate action in the document (transaction type SMMN). In a three-system landscape, for example, you will find all transport requests for urgent changes with the TO BE TESTED status in the import buffer of the production system. If the phase cannot be switched using the document but only using the task list, the user is not warned of this. Urgent corrections are therefore imported untested. When the phase is switched using the SMMN document, tests are performed so that the user is warned and can react accordingly.

8.2.8 Transparency of Change Processes

Change Request Management is not just a tool for checking and managing your changes. It also enables you to get detailed information about the status of the overall change management process at any time. The following sections provide a short overview of the different monitoring and reporting functions.

Monitoring Functions

The new Change Request Management interface offers numerous options for processing and for monitoring the status of the individual requests for change and change transaction. All of these enable you to get an overview of the overall status of change management.

In the ADMINISTRATION OF CHANGE REQUESTS area in the SAP IT service management user role, you can use a range of preconfigured search screens to search for change transactions. The search screens are divided into the CHANGE REQUEST, CHANGE TRANSACTION, and PROJECT CYCLE areas (see Figure 8.20).

Saved search Each page offers a range of search criteria that can be combined in any way. This gives you the option to create individual search queries. Every user can therefore generate a personalized worklist because each combination can be saved as a *saved search*.

You can select the saved searches centrally in the top part of the user interface and call them at any time, irrespective of the current position in the application.

The results of the search are neatly displayed in a table, whereby you can sort and filter each table column any way you like. Every user can use the personalization functions to determine which table columns are relevant, in which order they should be displayed, and which information should be hidden.

In addition to the display in table form, the search result can also be displayed graphically, as an interactive pie or bar chart. A click on a certain segment causes the system to filter the search results automatically. For further processing, the search results can also be exported into a table-processing program.

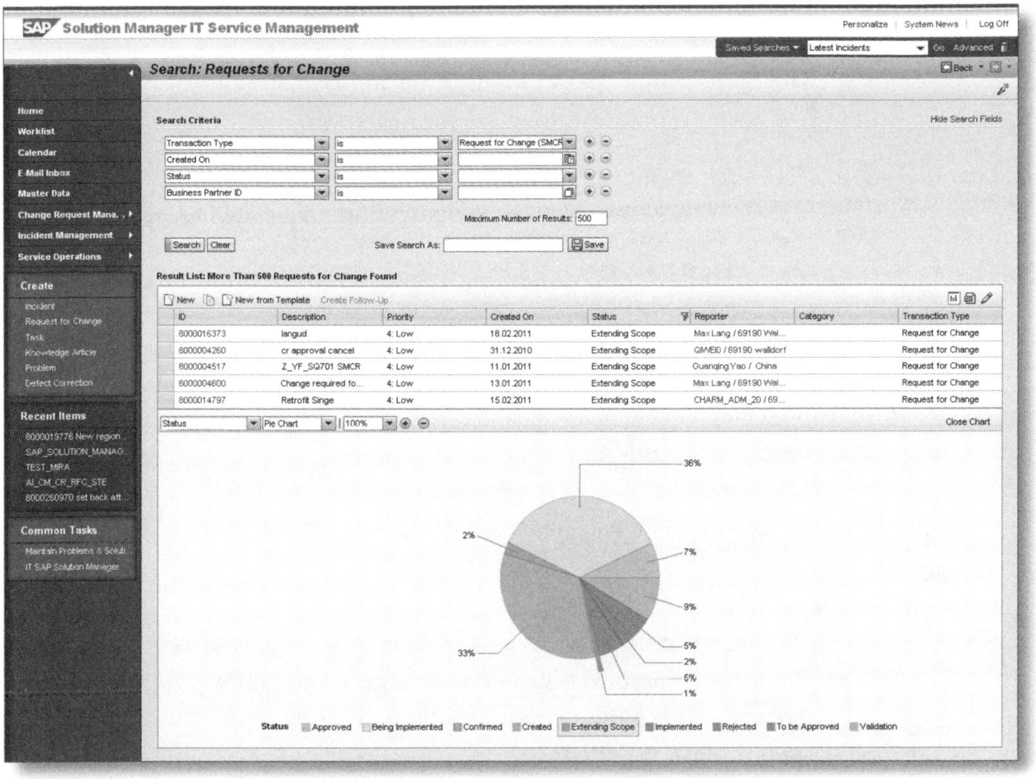

Figure 8.20 Search for New Change Requests in the New Web Client Interface

You can use the Change Request Management reporting functions without much set-up effort. They are thus also available out-of-the-box. All query options and results lists are already predefined and ready to use. In addition, a range of filter and setting options are available.

Change Request Management reporting

Change Request Management events, such as changing a DDIC (Data Dictionary) object in a development system or implementing an SAP Note, are always executed in the context of Solution Manager projects or solutions. The events that are executed when processing a change transaction are distributed across the system landscape. They require authorizations and a clear assignment of tasks.

The reporting function of Change Request Management analyzes these transactions and the corresponding events. It then consolidates them and displays them in an overview. You do not need to provide a separate SAP NetWeaver Business Warehouse (BW) because you can use the BW system integrated into SAP Solution Manager. A reporting service running in the background automatically collects the data from SAP Solution Manager as well as from the managed systems.

Recorded entities The reporting transaction (Transaction /N/TMWFLOW/REPORT-INGN) enables the display and selection using the following entities:

▶ Change transactions and requests for change

▶ SAP Solution Manager solutions and projects

▶ Change Request Management task lists

▶ Systems

▶ Support packages

▶ SAP Notes

▶ Transport requests

▶ Transport objects

Users can decide freely which data they need and can also specify additional filter criteria. The result appears in an overview that offers many additional functions and branches (e.g., into the change transaction, task list, etc.).

As with the monitoring functions, you can export all this data into a table-processing program for further processing.

Tracking changes In addition to reporting, Change Request Management also offers tracking functions (Transaction /TMWFLOW/TRMO). A special overview contains a range of information and allows an in-depth analysis.

For example, you can track the following information:

▶ The source system in which a certain transport request was generated

▶ The target system into which a certain transport request was transported

▶ The number of transport requests exported from the target system

▶ The number of transport requests that have been created but have not been released yet

▶ The number of transport requests that have generated an import error

▸ Whether changes have been imported into the target system in the right order or whether there are inconsistencies between the source and target system with regard to the exporting and importing of changes

Another function of Change Request Management tracking is to compare two systems to find out whether all transport requests have been exported and imported correctly, or whether there are differences. You can first display all objects per system on a split screen. For example, if you want to find out what differences exist, you can click to activate a filter that displays the result in an easy-to-read form.

Comparing systems

8.2.9 Integration of Change Request Management with Other Application Lifecycle Management Functions

Change Request Management is not only integrated with the transport system. It is also integrated with many other processes and applications of SAP Solution Manger (see Figure 8.21) and can be used together with these. This section provides an overview of the different integration aspects of Change Request Management, which now exist in addition to the integration into the technical infrastructure.

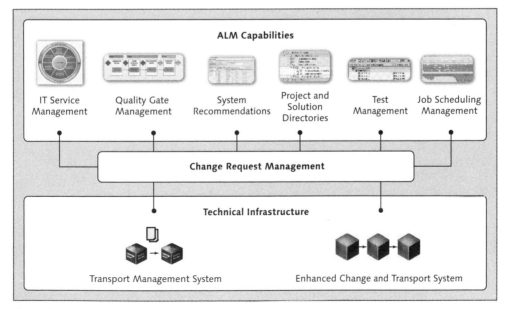

Figure 8.21 Overview of the Integrations of Change Request Management

Integration with
Quality Gate
Management

By using the same basic technologies, it is possible to operate Quality Gate Management and Change Request Management in integrated form and in the same landscape for several different project types in parallel.

For example, you can use Change Request Management for a maintenance project and Quality Gate Management for an implementation project. A maintenance project is typically based on individual changes that must be approved and documented. An implementation or release project, in contrast, covers a defined scope that is first approved and then implemented. Consequently, implementing SAP Best Practices for transport protects both projects from inconsistencies and overshooters (see Section 8.1.3).

You can also integrate the two tools. You can easily activate this integration by defining Q-Gates in a Solution Manager project defined for Change Request Management. Hence, users can operate Quality Gate Management integrated with Change Request Management.

In this scenario, Change Request Management controls the entire change process. This process includes the creation, approval, and documentation of all changes as well the creation, release, and import of all transport requests belonging to the project. Quality Gate Management controls the phases and visualizes the contents of the Change Request Management project. Quality Gate Management thus displays the Q-Gate calendar, the change transactions, transport requests, and the risks of the Change Request Management project. In this role, it acts as a type of *change management dashboard* that enables the project management team to provide useful information to detect and eliminate potential risks at an early stage. For more information on the functions of Quality Gate Management, see Section 8.1.

Integration with
IT service
management

As already mentioned, Change Request Management is strongly based on the specifications of the IT Infrastructure Library (ITIL). Hence, the other IT service management areas of SAP Solution Manager are integrated: If you have an incident or problem in your Service Desk, you can directly create a request for change as a follow-on document. Important information such as texts and the assigned component are automatically transferred to the request for change, and a relationship is established between the two documents. Hence, you can trace the request for change back to its origin at any time.

You can configure Change Request Management so that when a request for change is completed, that is, as soon as the change has been made successfully and confirmed, the corresponding incident or problem is closed automatically.

All of the changes you make with Change Request Management are always based on a Solution Manager project. You can also use the information in these projects in Change Request Management and assign it to change transactions. This enables you to classify and categorize your change transactions and requests for change.

Integration with documentation

In the SOLUTION and PROJECT assignment blocks, you can assign information such as business process scenarios, business processes, or business process steps. Change Request Management reporting supports this assignment. In reporting, you therefore also have the option to display only change transactions that are related to a certain business process.

You can reference the underlying documents of the project or solution, such as test case descriptions or specifications in the DOCUMENTS assignment block.

If you assign a solution to a change transaction, and this solution is connected to maintenance object used, you can also use the *Check-In/ Check-Out* function. As soon as you have activated this function, it is no longer possible to edit the content and structure of the solution directly. Instead, you can check out parts of the solution that have to be changed into the maintenance project by using the change transaction. There, you can update the documents and processes in line with the corresponding software or configuration change that is made simultaneously using the change transaction. Following that, you can check the structure back in as soon as the change is complete.

Check-in/check-out function

As a result, you not only get a change configuration at the technical level but also changed or updated documentation of your business process. This is particularly important if you want to use other functions of SAP Solution Manager that require correct solution documentation (e.g., Business Process Monitoring).

Test management is a subject that is closely related to changes and change management. In SAP Solution Manager, there are numerous functions and applications for checking and administering test transac-

Integration with test management

tions and test processes in the customer landscape. These functions are also integrated with Change Request Management. For requests for change or change transactions, you therefore establish a relationship between these and entities from test management (see Chapter 7).

The TEST MANAGEMENT assignment block enables you to assign test plans or test packages from SAP Solution Manager to a Change Request Management document. This enables a change manager or test coordinator, for example, to assign in advance a change to a test plan that contains test cases that are supposed to be used for testing the planned change.

In another step, you can also configure Change Request Management by implementing your own condition so that the process control is dependent on the successful execution of the assigned test packages or test plans. This makes it possible to implement a change that, for example, enables the status to be changed from TO BE TESTED to TESTED SUCCESSFULLY only if the assigned test cases have been tested positively. This adds further stability to your software and minimizes the risk of errors in the production system.

Integration with maintenance management

Maintaining an SAP landscape is also closely related to change management. The *System Recommendations* function is a part of the maintenance management process. Here, the system suggests SAP Notes for implementation in your system landscape (e.g., SAP Notes relevant for security or performance, etc.).

If you decide to implement such an SAP Note, or your company uses the Change Request Management process and you want to trigger an implementation via a change request, you can create a request for change directly from the System Recommendations application. This already contains all of the required information about the SAP Note to be implemented.

For more information on the System Recommendations function, see Chapter 12.

Integration with job scheduling management

JOB SCHEDULING MANAGEMENT deals with the numerous background applications and batch processing programs that are scheduled in an SAP system. If the system landscape gets more complex and the number of these jobs increases massively, it is difficult to keep track. *Job scheduling management* enables you to centrally manage the scheduling and execution of such applications.

Thanks to the integration with Change Request Management, you can also map the scheduling of such a background application using a change management process. Change Request Management provides a special assignment block for this purpose.

For more information on job scheduling management, see Chapter 11.

8.3 Transport Management

In integrated system landscapes, it is important to manage all changes in a central system. This is the only way to synchronously execute changes that affect more than one production system, such as simultaneous changes in the SAP NetWeaver Portal and in the SAP ERP backend system. SAP Solution Manager also provides central transport functions for the entire system landscape, such as the synchronization of development systems or the cross-system object lock.

8.3.1 SAP Change and Transport System (CTS)

SAP Change and Transport System (CTS) is the central tool for managing changes made to Customizing and repository data in the IMG and the ABAP Workbench. CTS automatically collects all changes and records them in transport requests. Logically related and interdependent changes can be recorded in the same transport request. Members of a team can use one common transport request. In the documentation for the transport request, the recorded changes can be described in greater detail. This makes it possible to trace which user changed what data and for which purpose.

Central tool

You release the transport request after work in the IMG or ABAP Workbench has been completed or an interim status has been reached. The transport request is now used to copy the changes from the clients where they were implemented to other clients or systems automatically. This automatic transfer is referred to as a *transport*. CTS therefore provides the opportunity to make changes in a separate development environment, test them in a test environment, and adopt them in production operations after they have been tested suc-

Transport

cessfully. This ensures that production operations are not out at risk at any time by incorrect settings or programming errors.

SAP NetWeaver 7.0 SPS 12 has enhanced the existing CTS and now also provides the option to manage and transport non-ABAP components. This enhancement was motivated by the request to provide central transport management for SAP environments and thereby utilize an established standard for non-ABAP components. On the other hand, you can reuse existing strategies and expertise as-is. This therefore protects your investment and keeps operating costs stable. This enhancement makes the transport functions of the *transport organizer* and the transport management system (TMS) available for non-ABAP objects also. This means that you can transport, for example, the following SAP NetWeaver usage type objects in CTS:

▶ Objects of SAP NetWeaver usage type EP (Enterprise Portal Archive, EPA)

▶ Objects of SAP NetWeaver usage type PI (XI/PI transport files, TPZ)

▶ Objects of SAP NetWeaver usage type DI (software component archives [SCAs] and development component archives [SDA])

▶ Objects of SAP NetWeaver usage type SLD (SLD objects, ZIP)

▶ Objects of SAP NetWeaver usage type MDM (SLD objects, XML)

▶ Objects of SAP NetWeaver usage type SAP BusinessObjects

You can connect additional applications to CTS using a released interface for third-party providers. There are three different options for this:

▶ **File transfer**
The transport file is transferred from system 1 to system 2 and stored in a certain directory of the file system.

▶ **Scripting**
The transport file is transferred in the same way as in the file transfer. Following that, an operating system script is called in the target system. This script processes the file further.

▶ **Program interface (API)**
CTS transfers the transport file using a release program interface. This makes it possible to make third-party provider applications available to a *deploy controller*, who receives the transport file and

processes it further. The result is reported back to CTS. This integration was already implemented with Duet as an example. In a customer project, a deploy controller that uses the CTS program interface was developed for Microsoft SharePoint. Changes to Microsoft SharePoint can thus be distributed via CTS.

You add non-ABAP objects to transport requests using the newly developed Web Dynpro user interface of the transport organizer. This newly developed interface offers a range of information, such as transport status display or export and import logs. As a consequence, you can also manage transports to non-ABAP SAP systems with one central transport tool (see Figure 8.22).

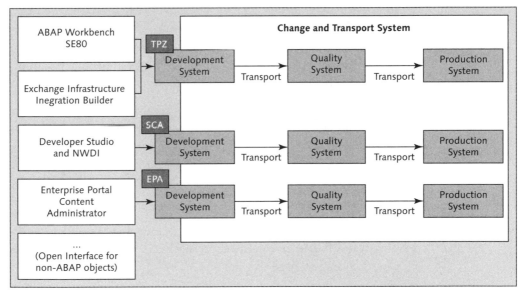

Figure 8.22 Connected Development Environments

To make your company's development process as integrated as possible, SAP-specific development environments (e.g., NWDI, Portal Content Administrator, PI Integration Builder, SLD, and SAP BusinessObjects) are connected to CTS. After being developed, the completed objects are automatically appended to the transport request provided for this. Hence, the development process and its completion receive the best possible support. In the future, SAP's aim is to connect all SAP development environments and SAP applications to CTS and integrate them.

Changes are transported between clients and systems according to traceable rules that are defined in the CTS configuration in a system landscape. For example, a rule might state that changes are first transported to the test environment before they can be copied to the production environment. All transports are also logged so that it is possible to trace when a transport request was transported in a client or a system and whether any errors occurred.

As a result, CTS comprises all tools required to support SAP change and transport management for ABAP and non-ABAP products.

CTS projects

Based on CTS, transport management offers you the chance to plan and transport your development and Customizing activities in project structures using CTS projects. Changes that are independent of each other can be split into different projects and imported separately into follow-on systems. This is recommended, for example, if various projects are to be used at different times in production operations or to form content assignments.

The assignment of a request for change to a project is displayed in the import queue so that imports to the follow-on systems can also take place for each project. It is important to ensure that projects are as independent as possible even during planning.

However, CTS also supports minor project overlaps: If you cannot keep projects completely separate, you have to define dependency relationships between the orders that belong to different projects but contain (in part) the same objects. This is necessary to maintain the correct import order.

Transports of Copies

Import time reduction

Large SAP implementation projects or long release cycles result in many transport requests that have to be imported into the production system for the go-live. This import often takes many hours. During this time, the production system is not available to users or only to a limited extent. When this happens, the same objects are often transported in different versions. However, it would suffice to import only the last successfully tested object version. This would significantly reduce the number of transports and thus the import time. That is where transports of copies come in handy.

Transports of copies are available as part of the basic functionality in every SAP system. However, you cannot use them to store changes to ABAP Workbench or Customizing settings in the respective object editor. You need ABAP Workbench or Customizing transports for that. In transports of copies, you can merely add objects that have not been changed. You can either select these objects manually or copy object lists from other transport requests. In the connection to SAP TMS, the transports of copies respond differently from ABAP Workbench or Customizing transports. During the import into the test system, these are automatically forwarded to the import buffer of the downstream test or production system. The path has thus been determined. This ensures that every change is recorded automatically and gets into all systems of the transport landscape. Transports of copies offer more flexibility: You can specify the transport target manually and thus copy the contained objects into all systems that are known to TMS. These can be, for example, systems that are not connected through transport routes. They are used for exceptions and special cases. Transports of copies also do not follow the transport routes into the downstream systems. They are only copied into a system once and then no longer exist in the import buffers.

What are transports of copies?

Change Request Management and Quality Gate Management use transports of copies to import objects in a transport request that has not been released yet into a test system. If errors are detected during testing, you can carry out further development in the originally created transport request and then import a new transport of copies into the test system. You repeat this process until the test is successful. You then release the original transport request. Only the original transport request with the successfully tested object versions is imported into the production system. All previously created transports of copies are only imported into the test system. This significantly reduces the number of transport requests that have to be imported into the production system (see Figure 8.23).

Use in SAP Solution Manager

The transport tools in SAP Solution Manage execute the following steps:

1. Create a transport of copies with the naming convention *<original transport request number>: Generated test transport.*

2. Copy objects from the original transport request into the transport of copies.

3. Release the transport of copies and add it to the import buffer of the test system.

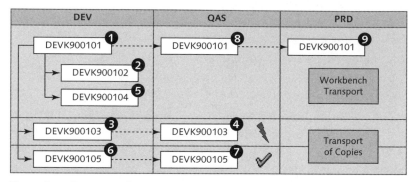

Figure 8.23 Transport of Copies in SAP Solution Manager

Normal change

If you use the normal change in Change Request Management, there is further integration: After developers have finished their work, they set the status of the normal change to To Be Tested. In the background, the system generates a transport of copies and sends it to the test system. If the test is successful, the status is set to Tested Successfully. It is only then that you release the original transport request. In contrast, if the test is not successful, the status is reset to In Development, and the developer can continue working on the same transport request.

Transports of copies are best used in a four-system landscape. The first test system acts as the unit test system for the developers and is supplied with transports of copies. The second test system is used for the final project test. Only original transport requests that have already been tested individually make it into this system. You must not use transports of copies in a two system landscape because the second system is already the production system. SAP Note 1419150 describes this case in detail.

Additional benefits

If you use transports of copies, the original transport requests only have to be released at a later time. This has two important advantages:

▶ Let's assume that different developer teams work on different projects in the same development system. You want to prevent simultaneous changes to an object in any case. Thanks to the later transport release with transports of copies, the objects remain locked for longer. This prevents the inadvertent simultaneous changing of an object by different teams of developers.

▶ The transports only have to be released when final testing of the entire project commences. If a transport request is not supposed to be imported into production with the current project but rather at a later time, for example, because the business requirement has changed, the corresponding transport request stays open in the development system. It does not have to stay longer in the test system before being imported into the production system. You thus avoid sequence problems.

Cross-System Object Lock

The cross-system object lock is a function of SAP Solution Manager that enables you to execute projects in parallel. Typical scenarios that need this extended lock mechanism are listed here:

▶ In addition to normal maintenance for production operation, new functions are being developed.

▶ Due to urgent business requirements, projects with different production start-up dates have to overlap or be executed in parallel. That means that every second or even third development project starts before the first one is completed.

It does not matter whether every project uses a separate development system or whether the projects share a development system. If projects are supposed to be imported into the same production system, you must prevent different teams from working on the same object at the same time, which would lead to inconsistencies. Hence, from the first change onward, the object must stay locked until it has been imported into the production system.

If the cross-system object lock is active, changing an object in a managed system causes a lock entry to be generated for this object in SAP Solution Manager. This prevents objects from being assigned transport requests that would generate the same lock entry. The lock entry is only deleted after the locked object is imported into the production system.

Different configuration options (see Figure 8.24) are available for covering different requirements. Depending on the configuration,

Configuration

certain conflicts only appear as warnings that can be ignored. For others, an error message appears that can only be avoided through the intervention of an administrator with the corresponding authorizations.

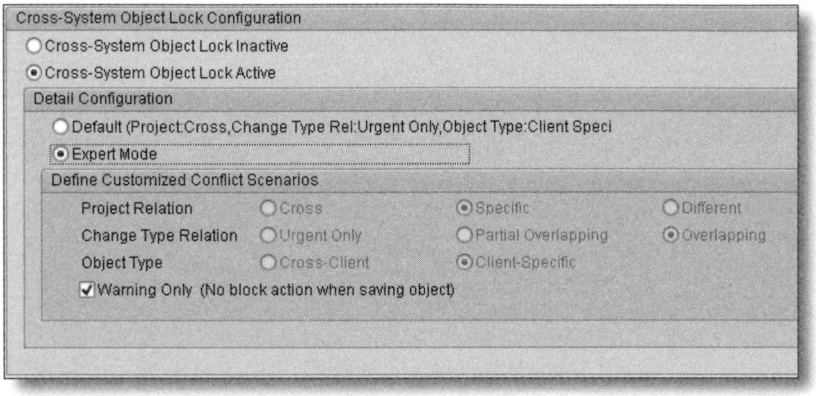

Figure 8.24 Cross-System Object Lock Options

For example, a developer makes a Customizing change to Table V_T005S. As soon as he saves the change in a transport request, a lock entry is generated in SAP Solution Manager.

If a developer wants to change the same Customizing entry, he sees the existing lock entries in SAP Solution Manager with all relevant information (see Figure 8.25). In the example, the lock is configured as just a warning. You can avoid it by clicking NEXT. If a stricter check variant had been set, the system would not have allowed the developer to save his change in a transport request. He would then have to agree on the final version with the first developer or ask a central transport manager with enhanced authorizations to delete the object lock. The transport manager can use Transaction /TMWFLOW/ LOCKMON in SAP Solution Manager to display and possibly delete existing locks (see Figure 8.26).

Prerequisites To use the cross-system object lock, you must complete the basic configuration of Change Request Management in SAP Solution Manager. You must create, release, and import transport requests centrally in the task list or in Quality Gate Management. There is no need to use workflow-based change documents.

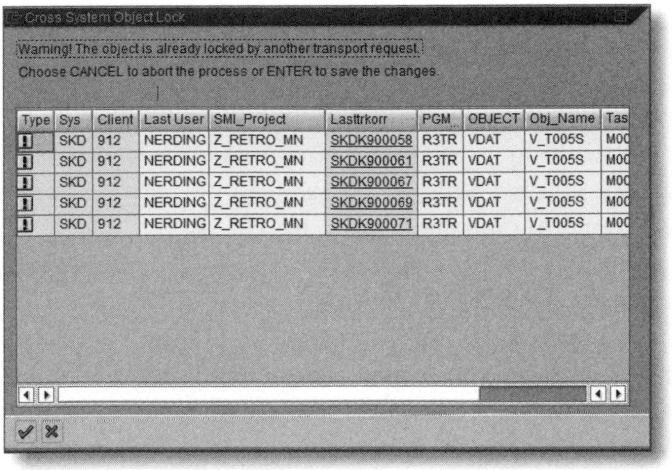

Figure 8.25 Information for the Developer

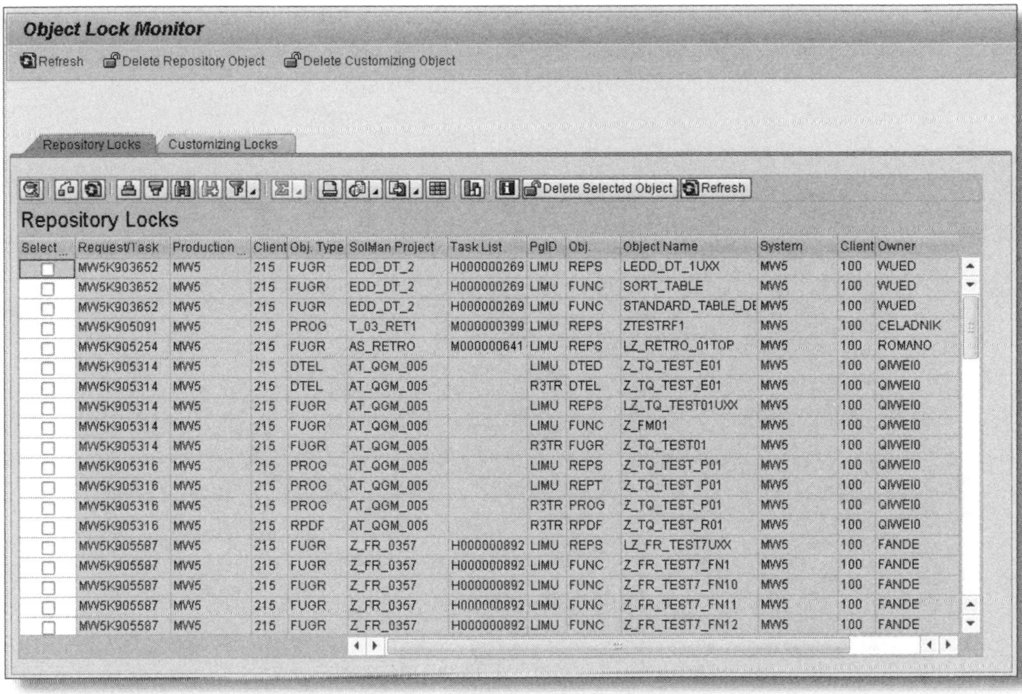

Figure 8.26 Monitor for the Cross-System Object Lock

Central Transport Management

SAP Solution Manager provides the option to centrally create and manage transports for all development systems in the landscape.

Technical task list   The central task list (Transaction SCMA; see Figure 8.27) provides system administrators with an overview of completed and scheduled actions. It summarizes all of the systems and necessary tasks and displays them in the correct sequence. Any tasks that you execute by performing actions on the change documents or project cycle user interfaces in SAP Solution Manager (system logon, create transport request, import transport request, etc.) are also stored here. You choose the implementation or maintenance project in which you want to work. For this project, you first have to activate Change Request Management using Transaction SOLAR_PROJECT_ADMIN. After you have selected the corresponding project, you can perform various administrative activities. In the task list, you can, in particular, create, release, and import transport requests as well as create transports of copies or start the *retrofit* (see Section 8.3.2). You also add additional administrative activities to the task list. These are activities that are to be performed in connection with transports, for example, locking users or stopping the interface. You can adjust the task list to your individual requirements.

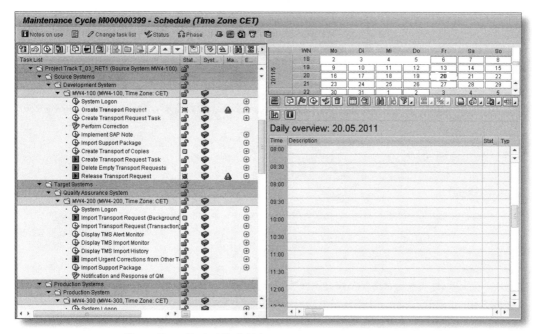

Figure 8.27 Central Task List

With Quality Gate Management, SAP Solution Manager provides another administration interface for central transport management in the *Change Management* work center (see Figure 8.28). Under PROJECTS, choose the project in which you want to work. Following that, choose the TRANSPORTS category to create or release transports. In Quality Gate Management, you can also create *changes* to group transports that logically belong together. The import always takes place for all transports of a change together. A change can also contain transports from different transport tracks. This can be, for example, an SAP NetWeaver Portal transport and a related transport for the SAP ERP backend system.

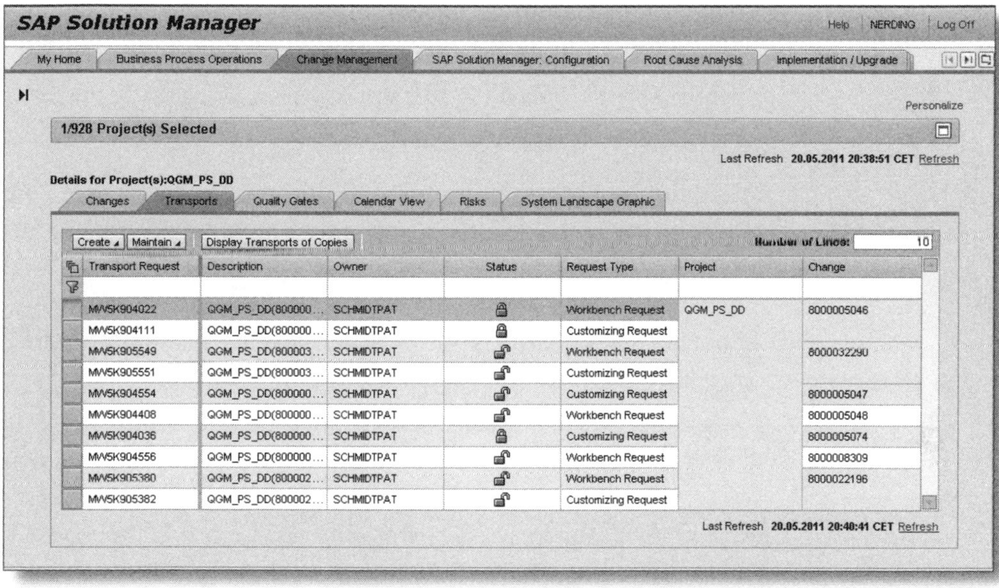

Quality Gate Management

Figure 8.28 Central Transport Management in Quality Gate Management

The RISKS tab of Quality Gate Management lists transport risks that the system collects automatically. This way, before each phase or phase completion, the quality manager can assess which transports have been released or are still awaiting release, or whether all transports have been correctly imported into the system.

Transport risks

Quality Gate Management also displays the transports and transport risks if the transports were not created in Quality Gate Management but in Change Request Management or the central task list. Instead of the change, the normal or urgent correction or the number of the task list then appears (see Sections 8.1 and 8.2).

8.3.2 Synchronizing Development Systems

Retrofit
In system landscapes where work takes place on several projects at the same time, changes are often made in several development systems at the same time. For example, you can develop new features in the project development system and correct errors for the production system landscape in a maintenance system at the same time without the developers locking each other. In this scenario, it is very important to synchronize the development systems regularly. Because work was carried out in parallel, it is not possible to make changes by simply transporting requests to another system as there is a danger here that current software levels will be overwritten, resulting in inconsistencies. To avoid this, a controlled import into the target system can be performed. This procedure is called a *retro-fit*.

Dual system landscapes
Typical customer scenarios are listed here:

▶ In addition to normal maintenance for production operation, new functions are developed in a separate development system over an extended period of time. After a development project has been imported into production, development of the next project commences. This scenario requires a permanent dual system landscape (also called *phase landscape* or *N+1 landscape*).

▶ For an individual project, for example, an upgrade, a separate development system is set up temporarily. While a development system is being prepared for the new release, the second development system remains in the same state as the production system and thus continues to be available for error corrections.

A dual system landscape (see Figure 8.29) consists of a regular landscape (e.g., three-system landscape) and an additional project landscape (e.g., a two-system landscape). All maintenance activities can be performed without conflicts with project development in the maintenance development system. This ensures that problems in production can be resolved quickly and smoothly. At the same time, project development is detached from maintenance activities and can work independently for the time being.

However, in such a dual system landscape, all changes in the maintenance system have to be manually transferred to the project development system to ensure that error corrections are still available after the project production starts. This requires significant manual effort. In addition, there is the risk that the manual duplicate maintenance is forgotten in individual cases. This leads to inconsistencies between the development systems and to significant problems in the subsequent project production startup.

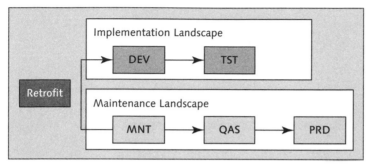

Figure 8.29 Dual System Landscape

The *Retrofit* tool in SAP Solution Manager automatically records all changes in the maintenance landscape and transfers them into the project development system. Different retrofit categories are available:

Retrofit categories

▶ **Auto-import**
If the development object has only been changed in the maintenance system but not in the development system, the object can be automatically transferred into the development system. The old version in the development system is overwritten automatically. This supports all object types that can be saved in transport requests.

▶ **Automatic reconciliation with the SAP Correction Workbench**
If a development object has been changed in both development systems at the same time, you can execute a semiautomatic synchronization using the SAP Correction Workbench that is integrated in the Retrofit tool. Just like when you import an SAP Note, this has the effect that only changed or added source code lines are transferred from the maintenance system into the development system. Both object versions are reconciled automatically.

▶ **Semiautomatic reconciliation using BC Sets**
If a Customizing setting has been changed in both development systems at the same time, you can use *Business Configuration Sets* (BC Sets) for semiautomatic reconciliation. They enable the user to

first compare the Customizing settings in both systems and then make a decision about the final version.

▶ **Manual reconciliation**

Manual reconciliation is rarely necessary—only if you cannot use any of the methods just described. In this case, you have to manually change the development object in both systems. The successful completion of the manual reconciliation must also be confirmed in the Retrofit tool.

The classification of objects takes place automatically and separately for each object in a transport request. For example, if a transport request contains 10 objects of which only 1 has to be transferred manually, the other 9 objects can still be transferred automatically.

The Retrofit tool (see Figure 8.30) provides extensive information, for example, an overview of all outstanding retrofit requests or logs for already-completed retrofit requests. If retrofit requests have to be executed in a certain order, it also displays this information.

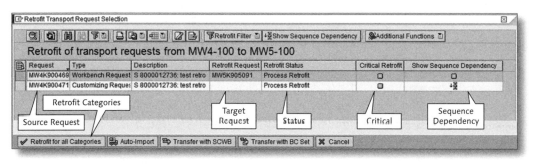

Figure 8.30 The Retrofit Interface

Prerequisites   To use Retrofit, you need to complete a basic configuration of Change Request Management in SAP Solution Manager. You also have to activate the cross-system object lock. You must create, release, and import transport requests centrally. There is no need to use workflow-based change documents.

8.3.3   SAP Transport Execution Analysis Service

SAP service for analyzing transport requests   *SAP Transport Execution Analysis Service* analyzes the transport response in a customer system and determines indicators for the quality of software changes. It collects data from the development, test, and production systems. This enables the quality manager to identify issues in the change process and take countermeasures by arranging for technical settings and process changes.

We can divide the measured indicators into the following areas:

▶ **Transport frequency**
The number of transport requests and transported objects is an important cost driver. This number should be low if no planned projects are transported into production. The import history shows whether changes are imported into production in bundled form and whether, for example, there are daily or weekly import windows. This tells you whether planned maintenance windows were observed in the past.

▶ **Emergency changes**
Transports that are transported from development into production particularly quickly and transports that are created directly in the production system appear as emergency changes. These transports have often not been tested sufficiently.

▶ **Incorrect changes**
Transports with import errors, sequence violations, and objects that have been changed particularly frequently appear as incorrect changes.

▶ **Transport backlog**
Open transports in the development system that are older than six months are flagged as development backlog. Transports that are in the import buffer of the production system for more than six months appear as production backlog. If these obsolete transports are imported, this frequently causes problems because the system environment has changed in the meantime.

▶ **Number of modifications and customer objects**
Modified SAP objects and customer objects in the system are also measured. This enables you to derive how strongly the system has been modified and how much effort a future upgrade would require.

▶ **Software maintenance**
In the SOFTWARE MAINTENANCE area, the installed SPs, SAP Notes, and activated business functions are measured, and the system checks whether these settings match in the development, test, and production systems.

Guided self-service All SAP Enterprise Support customers have access to the SAP Transport Execution Analysis Service as a guided self-service in the work center for *SAP Engagement and Service Delivery* (see Figure 8.31). Choose SERVICES • CREATE • GUIDED SELF SERVICE • TRANSPORT EXECUTION ANALYSIS. Enter the required data in the following dialogs. After you have made these entries, you can generate a report with suitable recommendations for your system.

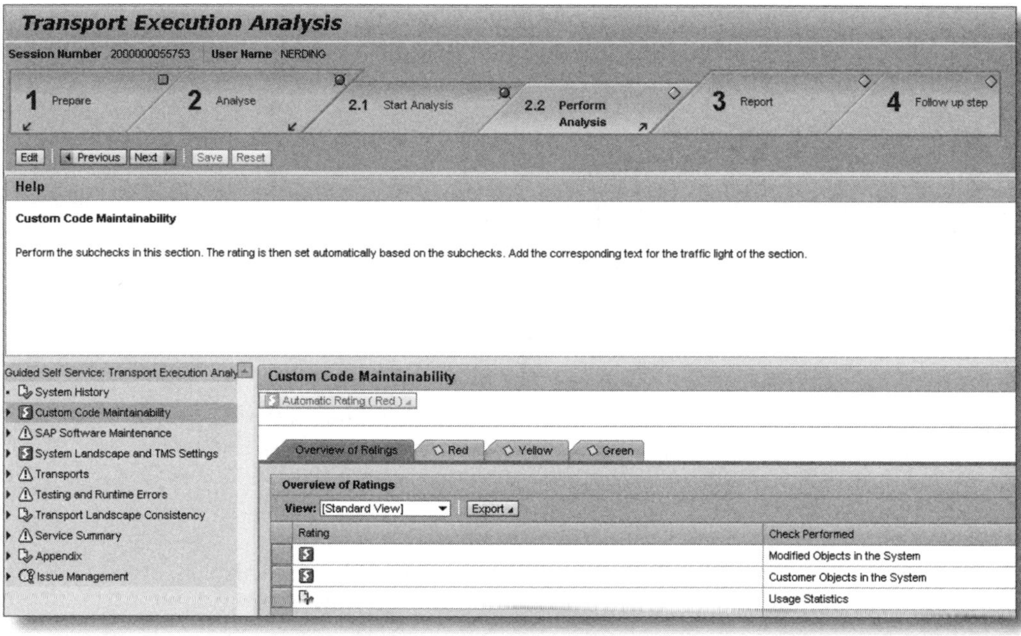

Figure 8.31 Guided Self-Service for Transport Execution Analysis

8.4 Change Diagnosis

The functions and elements of the SAP Solution Manager change diagnosis include the end-to-end change analysis, change reporting, configuration validation, and configuration and change database (as the central repository for configuration elements).

Why execute a change diagnosis? The change diagnosis function is available after you have set up SAP Solution Manager for a managed system. The change diagnosis determines and records general technical changes in a managed system. Changes are traced independently of the change management process (see Change Request Management in Section 8.2 or Quality Gate

Management in Section 8.1). This is a central function of SAP Solution Manager.

8.4.1 Tracing Changes

Changes are traced and saved in the configuration and change database (see Figure 8.32). The configuration data of the managed system is saved in *configuration repositories*. The configuration repositories are an integral part of the database and contain all configuration details. The Extractor Framework collects the configuration data daily and uploads it from the managed systems into the configuration and change database.

Figure with tabs: Status / Exception; General / Technical Systems / Cross Selection; buttons: Trigger Store Check, Trigger Change Analysis update, Trigger Administration Tasks, Recalculate Statistics.

CCDB Infrastructure

Mode	Read and write operations allowed	
Store Check	Successful	31.03.2011 01:00:47
Change Analysis update	Successful	31.03.2011 17:15:28
Administration tasks	Failed	31.03.2011 02:00:33

Statistics

Date of analysis 31.03.2011 01:19:08

| Store status of technical systems | 6 | △ 0 | 118 | ○ 13 |
| Status of overall collected stores | 5.033 | △ 13.482 | 294 | ○ 10.277 |

Max. Stores per Technical system 4.097

Number of Stores per Type and Size

Amount of elements	Property Store	Ini Store	Table Store	Text Store	Xml Store	Event Store
0 - 99	20.059	17	1.115	1.335	2.034	19
100 - 499	399	0	181	104	2.804	4
500 - 999	11	0	48	1	206	3
1000 - 4999	68	0	69	0	572	7
>= 5000	0	0	6	0	9	11

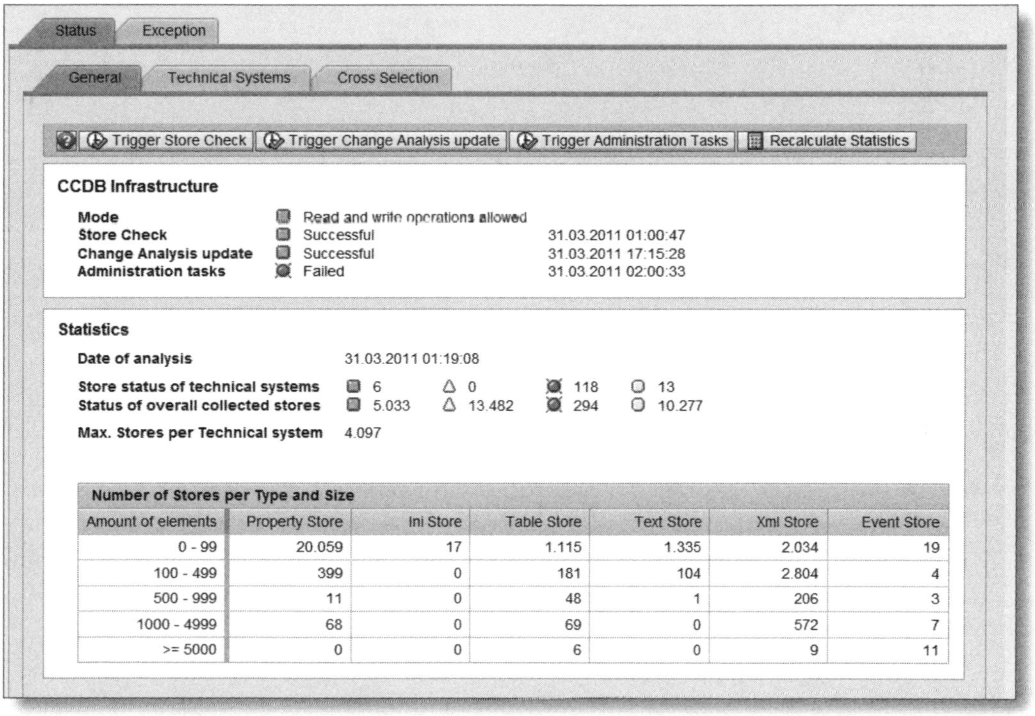

Figure 8.32 Example of the Administration of the Configuration and Change Database

8.4.2 Change Reporting

Change reports are based on the data of the configuration and change database in the configuration repositories in SAP Solution Manager. In addition, all determined changes are aggregated in SAP

NetWeaver in the change analysis InfoProvider to make change statistics available.

You can access change reports (see Figure 8.33) through the *Root Cause Analysis* work center in the system analysis or via the change detail display in the context of the change analysis.

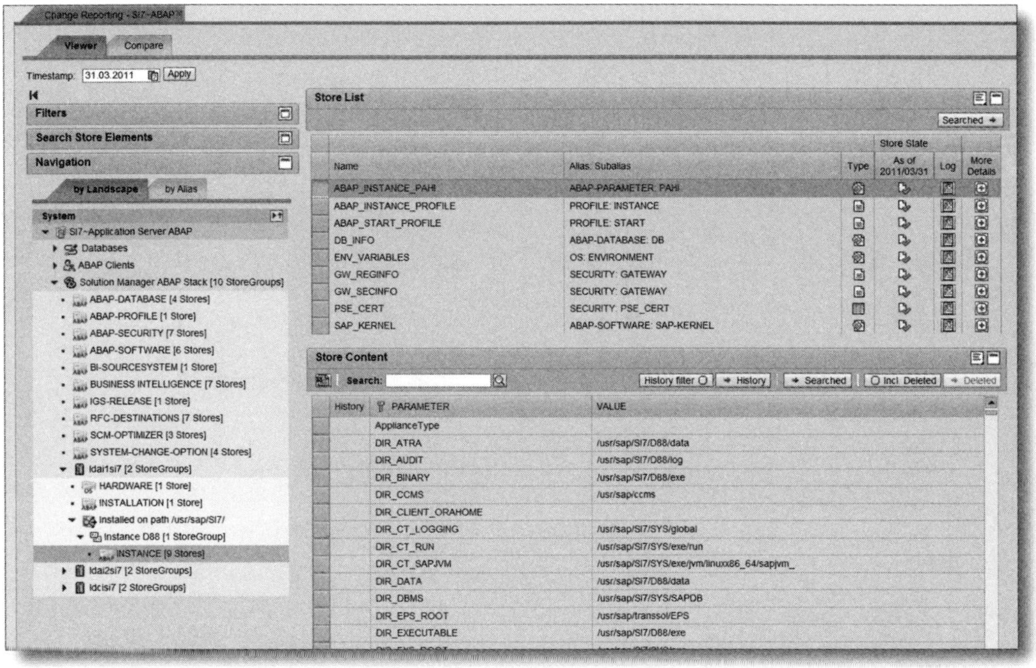

Figure 8.33 Example of a Change Report

Change reports provide information about changes in a system landscape. This enables you to query, for example, actual and historical values of configuration parameters, transport requests, or software maintenance activities of monitored systems. All software changes remain transparent and traceable. This improves the quality and availability of the software landscape. You can monitor changes end to end in the entire software application lifecycle.

8.4.3 End-to-End Change Analysis

A change analysis is a subprocess of an end-to-end change analysis in the context of root cause analysis. The change analysis accesses the change reporting data viewer to display detailed configuration data retrieved from the configuration repositories of the configuration and change database as well as the change statistics in SAP NetWeaver BW (see Figure 8.34).

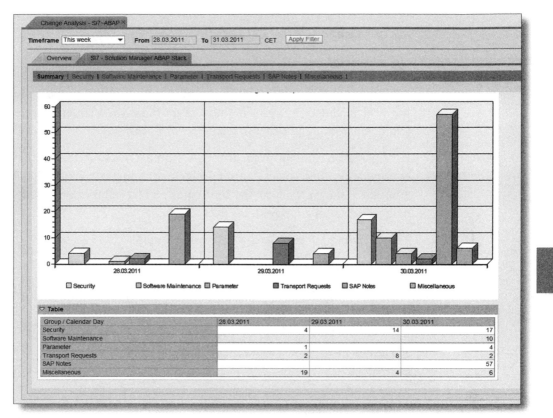

Figure 8.34 Example of an End-to-End Change Analysis

The change analysis provides an overview of changes that have been made in a managed system. It shows the number of changes per system, the change category, and the date. The change analysis determines the changed configuration elements in a system (database, ABAP, and Java parameters, transport requests, SPs, etc.).

Scope of the analysis

A change analysis traces the changes in your solution landscape. For example, it is possible that your development system responds differently than your production system or that the J2EE instances in your production system respond differently. Of course, you want to find out why that is the case. The system regularly generates snapshots of the configuration settings and saves these in the configuration and change database. The change analysis function accesses this information to determine the changes. It shows the total number of

345

changes, and, using the data viewer, it also displays the details and history of a change.

8.4.4 Configuration Validation

The configuration validation checks whether the systems of your system landscape are configured consistently and according to the requirements. You can check the current configuration of a system in the system landscape with a defined target status (or a target system) and compare it to an existing system.

Concept of configuration validation

Configuration validation analyzes the homogeneity of the system configuration. It accesses centrally saved configuration data of SAP Solution Manager to check the configuration of a number of systems using a subset of configuration data.

The following aspects are checked, for example:

- Do all systems have a certain database version?
- Has the template configuration (SAP or DB parameters) been applied to all systems?
- Are there systems with kernels that are older than six months?
- Have security policies and security standard been observed?
- Have the transports arrived in the system?

Target systems

In the configuration validation, you can access a reference system as the baseline for the comparison with other systems. For example, you can use the data of a managed system as the reference system to compare the configuration data of a system with the configuration data of another available system. You can also create a target system for which you edit the configuration data of an existing system to get a validation baseline independent of the current system settings.

Compliant/ non-compliant elements

You can create a compliance rule for each configuration item in the target system. If the rule applies to the corresponding configuration item, the configuration item receives the status COMPLIANT in the report. Otherwise, the configuration item receives the status NON COMPLIANT.

Using operators

In SAP Solution Manager 7.1, you can use rules in an even more transparent way by using operators. Operators determine the rule set for the validation of configuration items. Operators are available for all configuration items (property, table, text, and XML).

You use the configuration validation reports for configuration items to get an overview of the settings of the configuration item in your system landscape without having to execute a validation (see Figure 8.35).

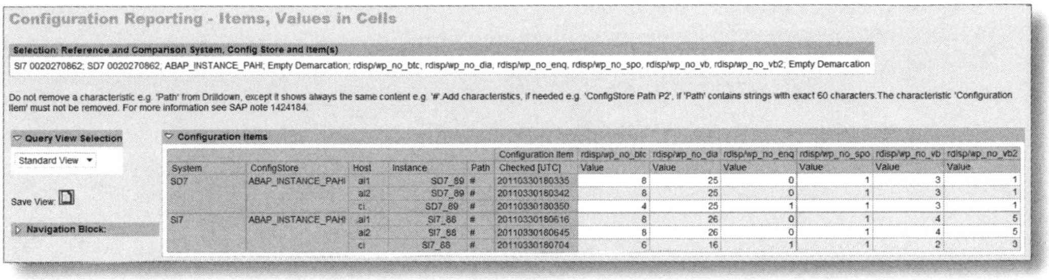

Reports

Figure 8.35 Report Shows ABAP Instance Parameters that Determine the Number of Processes

In a configuration validation, the check is based on the configuration items that are collected for a managed system (see Figure 8.36).

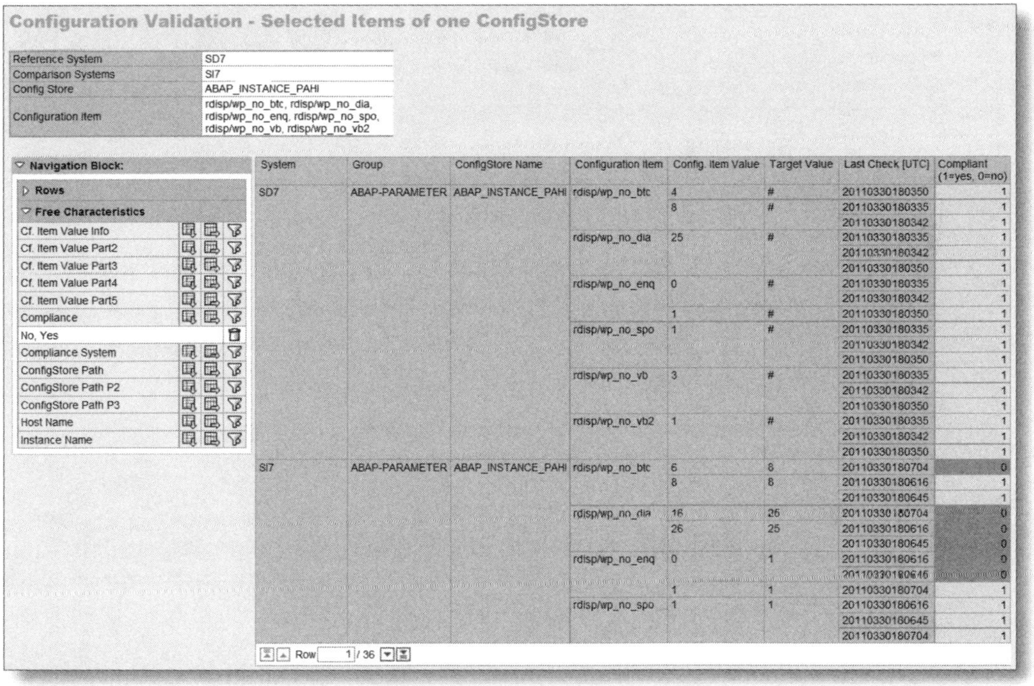

Using a real system as the baseline

Figure 8.36 Sample Report Shows Whether ABAP Instance Parameters that Determine the Number of Processes Are Compatible with the Reference System Used

Using the target system as the baseline

For configuration reports, you can specify a target system as the reference for validation (see Figure 8.37).

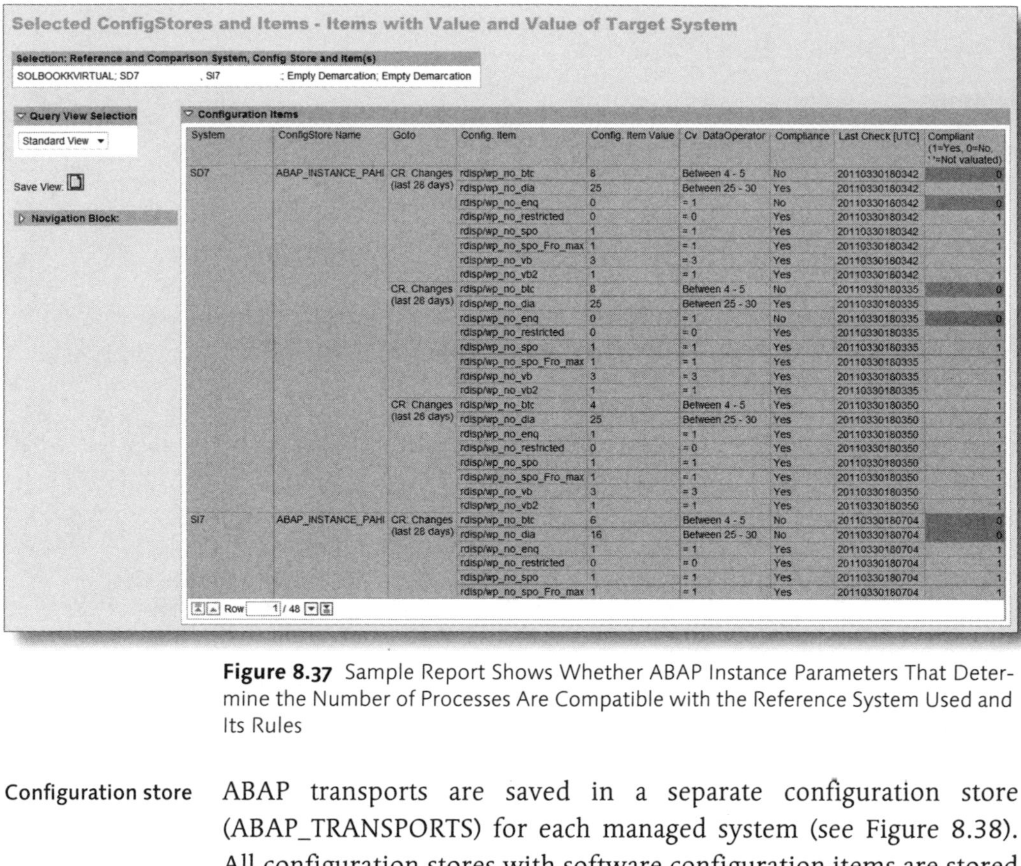

Figure 8.37 Sample Report Shows Whether ABAP Instance Parameters That Determine the Number of Processes Are Compatible with the Reference System Used and Its Rules

Configuration store

ABAP transports are saved in a separate configuration store (ABAP_TRANSPORTS) for each managed system (see Figure 8.38). All configuration stores with software configuration items are stored in configuration store group ABAP-SOFTWARE.

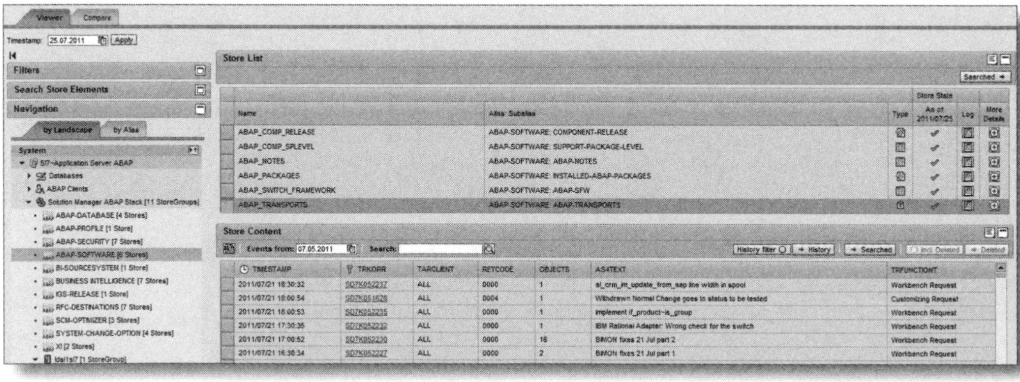

Figure 8.38 Change Report with Configuration Store ABAP_TRANSPORTS

Configuration validation uses the report directory to provide various transport reports, for example:

Transport reports

▶ **Backlog in the production system**
This report determines transports that have been released in the development system (DEV) but have not been imported into the production system (PROD) yet. A target system is generated and filled with transport requests that have been created in the development system (DEV) and have a TRSTATUS other than "D."

▶ **Backlog in the development system**
This report determines transports that have been created in the development system (DEV) but have not been released yet.

▶ **Failed transports**
This report determines failed transports (RETCOD > 4).

▶ **Local transports**
This report determines the transports that were created in the current system.

In Figure 8.39, the reports in the SECURITY, SOFTWARE, and TRANSPORTS group have predefined rules for retrieving a specific report instantly. They can thus be used immediately unlike the customer-defined group, for example, where a target system has to be defined first.

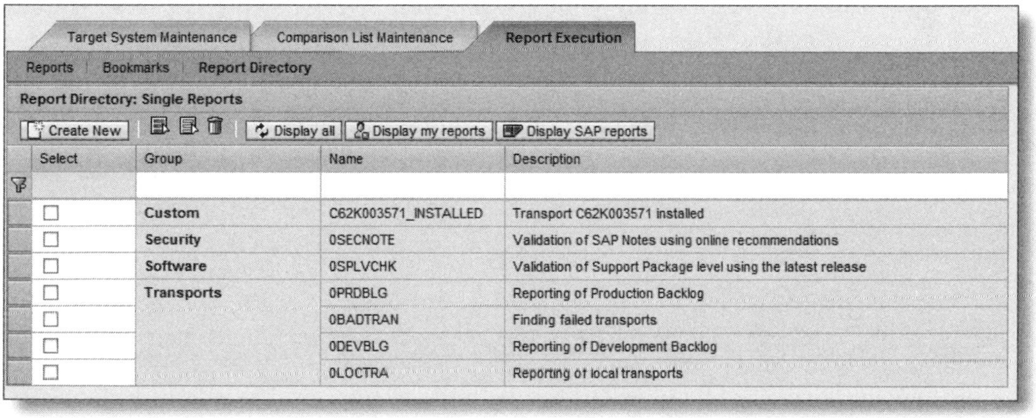

Select	Group	Name	Description
☐	Custom	C62K003571_INSTALLED	Transport C62K003571 installed
☐	Security	0SECNOTE	Validation of SAP Notes using online recommendations
☐	Software	0SPLVCHK	Validation of Support Package level using the latest release
☐	Transports	0PRDBLG	Reporting of Production Backlog
☐		0BADTRAN	Finding failed transports
☐		0DEVBLG	Reporting of Development Backlog
☐		0LOCTRA	Reporting of local transports

Figure 8.39 Report Directory, Display SAP Reports Function

8.5 SAP Solution Manager at Ferrero Deutschland MSC GmbH & Co. KG

We think it is great that only relevant information is stored directly in the change document. The new, web-based UI and the display in assignment blocks have improved the clarity so much that we are planning to use SAP Solution Manager as the central information tool for future audits.

Martin Flegenheimer, Ferrero Deutschland MSC GmbH & Co. KG

Ferrero is an international confectionery company founded in Italy in 1946 and is still family-owned to this day. Ferrero has 18 production plants worldwide. In 1956, the German company was founded with sites in Stadtallendorf (production) and Frankfurt/Main (administration).

Initial situation

In 2004, we converted all existing IT systems that had not been converted already to SAP systems. Our IT has been using SAP Solution Manager since 2006. In particular, we use incident management, Change Request Management, and the Test Workbench. The initial skepticism has since given way to high levels of acceptance in our company. Our developers and IT managers use SAP Solution Manager extensively.

In addition to request, approval, development, and testing, our change processes also include the complete documentation. This documentation is stored in our central solution on the level of the corresponding business scenario, process, or process step.

We were happy to accept SAP's offer to first test the new SAP Solution Manager release in a customer validation before participating in the ramp-up.

Project overview

Since Ferrero Deutschland GmbH has been using SAP Solution Manager Change Request Management and document management for all SAP systems from the start of 2010, our biggest priority in the customer validation project was to test the previously used functions of these modules to ensure that our processes would continue to run in case of an upgrade.

For us, it was important to get a feel for whether it has become easier to use and whether the transparency of the requests for change had improved, for example, thanks to a clearer display of the actions. Our developers had requested these things in the past. We create about 500 requests for change a month, and most of them are implemented as urgent corrections. Most change documents are linked to the implemented solution in which all business scenarios, business processes, and process steps of our company are modeled. We also tested new functions in this area.

From the new version of SAP Solution Manager, we expected, in particular, improvements in the areas of usability, requests for change for several systems, and transparency of IT processes and reporting. In addition, we expected support with the introduction and upgrades of SAP products, for example, preliminary checks on whether all prerequisites are met, improved documentation options, and assistance with system and application tests.

Overall, we had six weeks for the project. Initial issues with the installation of the pilot version of the new SAP Solution Manager and the subsequent system configuration were resolved quickly. This was possible, in particular, thanks to the on-site support provided by SAP product specialists. Overall, SAP provided excellent support. Messages were processed quickly and without delay. The specialists also contacted us directly to analyze the reported problems in our systems.

Project report

Unfortunately, there was limited time for testing due to the short project period. In general, our tests were thus limited to existing processes and a selection of new functions. To make sure we could test as realistically as possible, we set up a test system from a copy of our production system. This enabled us to test whether existing documents could be processed further without errors, and we could also compare the new version to the current production system. Figure 8.40 illustrates the system landscape that we used for our project.

In Figure 8.40, you see the current test environment at Ferrero that was used for the customer validation. Two ABAP and two Java test systems were available. Hence, we could also test changes to heterogeneous system landscapes where both ABAP and Java changes were made within one Change Request Management project.

Test environment and tests

The processes in Change Request Management are mapped according to the standards of the ITIL. We use these standards at Ferrero.

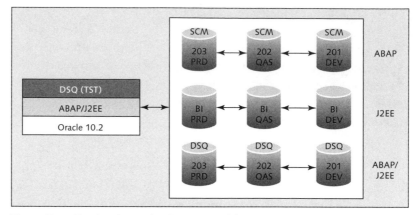

Figure 8.40 Test Landscape for Customer Validation

For example, we first record a problem in SAP Solution Manager and then generate a request for change from it, if appropriate.

We first tested our standard processes with the Change Request Management document types. After we had corrected all errors, we copied all documents into the Z namespace, as recommended by SAP. Following that, we could adapt the documents and include our own actions in the partner schema. We had no problems copying our existing profiles, for example, partner profiles, text profiles, and so on.

SAP Web Client   The most notable difference compared to previous releases of SAP Solution Manager is certainly the new SAP CRM user interface of the SAP Web Client that Change Request Management uses. Functions that could previously be called via different tabs are now mapped as separate assignment blocks. As users, we can adjust the interface according to our requirements and priorities at any time. This has the advantage that, for example, we can define the order of the displayed blocks and hide/show the fields and attributes displayed in the blocks as required. This means that a frequently voiced request from our users has been fulfilled. The requested clarity, combined with the new flexibility, makes the system easier to use and significantly improves acceptance of Change Request Management.

Improved central   The search options, which were also redesigned completely with the
search   SAP Web Client, not only provide more clarity but also offer additional benefits, for example, combining different search criteria for the search query.

Additional improvements were made to the approval procedure for requests for change. Before the actual approval, there is now a check that first clarifies whether a request is actually possible, which resources are needed, and which systems are affected. In addition, you can now also specify whether several persons from different areas are affected by the planned change and have to approve this request for change. In doing so, you can enter rules that have the effect that the intended approvers are automatically entered. Here, you can also decide individually and define your own rules. This new step makes work significantly easier for our change managers because the details of the change are already clarified at the time of the actual approval.

Enhanced approval procedure

Another important enhancement is that multiple changes are now possible. That is, we can include several target systems in one request for change. So far, a separate request for change was necessary for each system, and a corresponding amount of time was therefore required. With this enhancement, we can now ensure that our developments are transported into the defined target systems at the same time. This request was presented to our SAP Solution Manager team with increasing frequency over the past few years because the complexity of developments is constantly on the rise due to cross-system processes. Clarity has now been improved greatlybecause all the logs and documentation are now stored in one document. This enables us to quickly and easily respond to queries at a later stage.

Multiple changes

The newly designed text field for describing the change and all related activities also occupies a central place. This field has now been enlarged, and we can now quickly find information about the current status of a specific change.

Another new feature since the last release of SAP Solution Manager is that the approval procedure for requests for change now meets ITIL guidelines. Our change managers can still approve and reject requests for change. However, they can now choose the additional status NOT RELEVANT for requests for change. This status documents that an area has been informed of a request for change, but this area will not be affected by the decision of the change manager.

Approval procedure according to ITIL

The approval no longer has the effect that a change document is automatically created in the background. This only happens when the status is set to CURRENT IMPLEMENTATION. This enables our change managers to start developments and assign developers at a later point in time. This improves and supports the use and careful planning of our resources. In addition, our developers can now branch to all involved systems and not just into the system to which the current status points (which used to be the case).

Linking the changes to test plans and test packages is also an improvement for us. Both developers and departments are always prompted to use test plans to document and test their developments and adjustments. This process has been simplified significantly because we can branch directly to the Test Workbench to execute our tests.

Linking changes to a test plan

We can now create and store different templates for the different document types in Change Request Management. This facilitates routine changes, for example, in the HR area at the end of the month or the implementation of SAP Notes. However, developers who mainly implement requests for change for a certain target system at Ferrero also benefit from the creation of templates since the responsible change manager, developer, or testers are already specified. The templates can be adjusted at any time.

Templates for document types

For our developers, the information in the new TRANSPORTS assignment block is useful. With the new SAP Solution Manager release, this displays all relevant information such as the status of the transport and its transport tasks, information about transports of copies and critical objects or conflicts. Some of these used to require tedious research. Now they are all made available in one location. In addition, the assignment block offers direct branches into the transport logs for detailed analyses.

In the request for change, there are assignment blocks for storing documents to assign the request for change to a project structure and link it to a solution. Unfortunately, the function for document management has not been enhanced, and it has not been migrated to the new SAP Web Client UI either. Hence, the SAP GUI is still required as a user interface.

Change Management and document management

Because it is now possible to maintain multilevel categories for each request for change or change transaction, you can use these for reporting or as search criteria. SAP provides a sample schema with some categories. However, you can easily enhance categories or

Reporting

define customized categories and specify these individually for each document type.

We implemented reports across activities in Change Request Management in our central SAP NetWeaver BW system. An extractor transfers the data, which is then formatted according to predefined criteria.

We assume that user training will require the most effort. Because the interface and handling have changed completely, new handbooks have to be created, and courses must be prepared and held. However, we have already decided to switch to the new SAP Solution Manager for all systems as soon as possible. All production systems (ABAP and Java) are connected to SAP Solution Manager (DSP) (see Figure 8.41). We will make sure that all changes are implemented using Change Request Management. The SAP Solution Manager team has access to a development system (DSD). This is where Customizing entries are made, SAP Notes are implemented, new functions are tested, and so on. The team also has access to a test system where the development, QA, and production environments are simulated with different clients.

SAP Solution Manager is already our central IT tool. We are convinced that the new SAP Solution Manager release is even more integrated into the SAP landscapes. We will use additional functions step by step and thus expand the use of SAP Solution Manager. As examples of this, we would like to mention monitoring, release management with SAP Solution Manager, and custom code management.

Outlook

We are convinced that the new SAP Solution Manager will be very quickly accepted in the change management area. This is due in particular to the new and clearer SAP Web Client UI in Change Request Management of SAP Solution Manager, which significantly facilitates the whole change process; starting with the request and finishing with the completion of the request for change.

We also regard it as a good solution that now all relevant information is stored in the change document, for example, information about the system landscape of the change document and the corresponding transport orders. Thanks to the display in assignment blocks, the clarity has been raised to such a degree that we are now planning to employ SAP Solution Manager as the primary information tool for audits in the future.

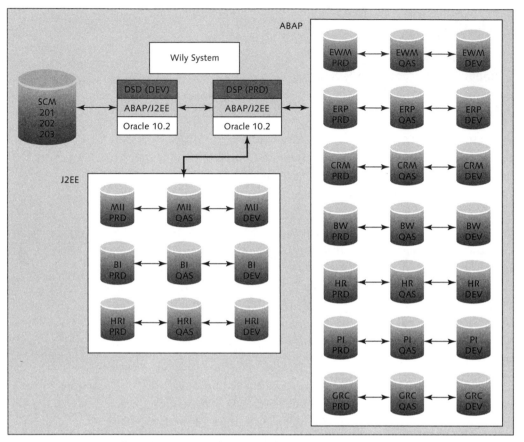

Figure 8.41 SAP Production Landscape at Ferrero

As the new SAP Web Client UI only requires a browser, a change process can be made on a BlackBerry, an iPhone, or any other mobile device that is capable of accessing a browser. This makes it possible, for example, for our change managers to approve urgent corrections from anywhere.

We are convinced that the minor problems that are yet to be solved will be solved during the ramp-up phase, and we are looking forward to using SAP Solution Manager, which will hopefully be as soon as possible.

The Author

Since 2003, Martin Flegenheimer has worked at Ferrero, where as IT Director, he is responsible for the Central and East European regions (Germany, Austria, Switzerland, Scandinavia, Poland, and other East European countries). In the Ferrero Group, he shares responsibility for the strategy and design of the entire SAP system architecture. He is also responsible for the complete lifecycles of all IT applications and for all the technologies used in the company.

SAP Solution Manager supports all of incident and problem management for a company's IT landscape and provides a high level of integration with SAP solutions. This helps you shorten the length of time needed to restore an interrupted service, significantly increasing the availability of business processes.

9 Application Incident Management

According to the definition of the IT Infrastructure Library (ITIL V3), an *incident* is any unplanned event that affects standard operation of a service and leads to an interruption or impairment of the quality of the service. This chapter explains how SAP Solution Manager can support the entire process, from entering a disruption as a message, through various processing levels and support organizations, to the fastest possible solution to the disruption.

9.1 Incident and Problem Management

Fundamental changes to the new SAP Solution Manager compared to the predecessor release can be seen in the *incident management* process or in the function of the Service Desk. Whereas SAP Solution Manager 7.0 was strongly focused on simply supporting rapid error handling in SAP systems, the integration of a comprehensive IT service management solution (ITSM) now gives you the option of supporting the entire IT area. To achieve this, the SAP Customer Relationship Management application (SAP CRM) that was already included in SAP Solution Manager was increased to the latest version of SAP CRM of SAP Business Suite Release 7.01. This makes the SAP CRM service function available in full in SAP Solution Manager. The SAP CRM service includes an ITIL-compatible IT service management (ITSM) solution. SAP Solution Manager's usage rights define the scope and functions with which the SAP CRM service solution can be used (see Section 9.3). However, these can also be extended

What's new in SAP Solution Manager 7.1?

359

on SAP Solution Manager with the corresponding SAP CRM license packages.

The integration of the SAP ITSM solution replaced the previous purely Service Desk application for processing SAP-related messages. Messages are now processed on new Web-based interfaces; the benefits of this are explained in Section 9.1.7. Furthermore, *Problem Management* introduces an additional optional document type that you can use if you want to align your IT processes to ITIL. You can now create a *problem* as a follow-on document to an *incident* to manage a more comprehensive investigation of the cause of the malfunction. If many malfunction messages are reported by different users, you can also use the problem to group together multiple incident messages in one document. Essentially, the incident and problem documents provide you with the same functions.

The following sections present the new functions included in SAP Solution Manager for supporting your ITSM processes. The various possible uses of Application Incident Management are also explained in this context; from the easy-to-use ticket system for sending messages to SAP, through to a comprehensive ITSM tool, with integration in other Application Lifecycle Management (ALM) processes and in SAP ERP solutions.

9.1.1   IT Service Management According to ITIL

ITIL describes the world's most commonly used and accepted standard for ITSM. Among other things, the content of ITIL deals with the following issues:

▶ Which services do you provide for your customers, how do you safeguard them, and what do they cost?

▶ How do customers order and query services, and which other IT components that are not controlled directly are needed to provide the services?

The answers to these questions vary from company to company because the details of the IT processes and requirements differ. However, the common thread of IT service processes is the same everywhere and can therefore be described in abstract in the ITIL books of the *Office of Government Commerce (OGC)*. These books provide a standard that many companies use as the basis for structuring their IT processes and organization.

The ITIL processes that will be examined here, together with their implementation in SAP Solution Manager, are *incident management* and *problem management*.

An incident is an unplanned interruption of an IT service or a reduction in the quality of an IT service. The aim of incident management is to restore normal service as quickly as possible to minimize the negative impact on operations. Incidents are often identified by means of events or alerts, or when the user contacts the Service Desk. Incidents are categorized for later analysis so that responsibilities can be established. Additionally, they are prioritized by urgency and business process impact. If an incident cannot be solved quickly, it can be escalated. A functional escalation forwards the incident to a technical support team with the relevant expertise; a hierarchical escalation involves the relevant management levels. After the incident has been investigated and solved, and the solution has been successfully tested, the Service Desk employee should check whether the user is satisfied with the solution before the incident is closed. An incident management tool is therefore crucial for recording and managing information about the incident.

A *problem* is the cause of one or more incidents. The cause is generally not known when the problem message is created. The problem management process is then responsible for investigating further.

The most important aims of problem management consist of preventing problems and the resultant incidents, eliminating recurring incidents, and minimizing the effects of incidents that cannot be prevented. Problem management includes diagnosing the causes of incidents, finding an adequate solution, and ensuring that the solution is implemented. Information about the problems and the corresponding workarounds and solutions are also documented in problem management. The problems are categorized in a similar way to incidents, but the aim here is solve the problems permanently. Workarounds are documented in a knowledge database, which improves the efficiency and effectiveness of incident management.

9.1.2 SAP IT Service Management (SAP ITSM)

The SAP solution for supporting the ITSM processes includes, in addition to incident and problem management, other processes that are supplied in the SAP ITSM solution (see Figure 9.1):

SAP ITSM
processes

- ▶ Service Request Management
- ▶ Change Management
- ▶ Knowledge Management
- ▶ Installed Base (IBASE) and Object Management (for Configuration Management)
- ▶ Service Level Management
- ▶ Financial Management
- ▶ IT Service Desk
- ▶ IT analytics

The processes are closely integrated, so their functions are examined more specifically in the following sections.

An independent certification authority (Pink Elephant) confirmed that the SAP ITSM tools that support these processes genuinely comply with the ITIL guidelines.

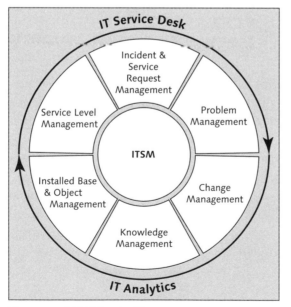

Figure 9.1 SAP IT Service Management

Like SAP CRM, SAP Solution Manager is an additional platform to operate the SAP ITSM processes on; however, it has certain cost and functional benefits for SAP Enterprise Support customers.[1] The ALM processes that were previously possible with SAP Solution Manager 7.0 were integrated into the ITSM solution. In the following section, you will see that it is precisely this integration that is the unique feature of the SAP ITSM solution in SAP Solution Manager.

9.1.3 Integration Concept

Incident and problem management is a very important process in the interaction between the components in a homogenized ALM and ITSM. It is the core process that includes other ITSM functions, such as service level agreements (SLA), knowledge management, or object management.

Incident management as a central process

ALM Integration

In the following example, you can see how closely interwoven the activities between ITSM and ALM are (see Figure 9.2).

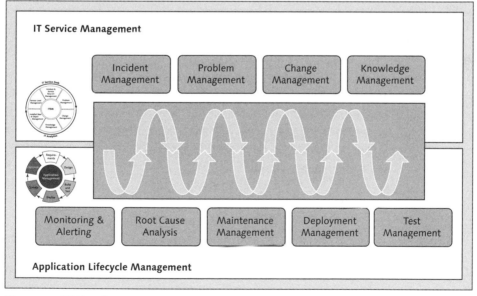

Figure 9.2 ITSM and ALM Integration

---

1 This also applies to SAP Product Support for Large Enterprises (SAP PSLE) and SAP MaxAttention; see also Section 9.3.

SAP Solution Manager monitors your company's business processes and its entire system infrastructure. Previously defined thresholds can now automatically generate an alert (event management), which automatically creates an incident. If the employees who are processing the incident in SAP Solution Manager's Service Desk do not have an immediate solution to the incident, they create a problem message as a follow-on document to the incident. Next, a detailed root cause analysis is carried out with the help of other SAP Solution Manager applications, such as *Trace, Change,* or *Exception Analyses,* and the relationships to other IT objects are considered (impact analysis).

To examine the cause of the alert in more detail, you generate a problem message from the incident. The problem management process is integrated into SAP support message processing, from where you receive an SAP Note as a solution proposal, which you can then implement with the SAP Notes Assistant (Maintenance Management). However, because this leads to a change in the live system, you start a *change request* (Change Request Management) from the problem message, which, after it is approved, is implemented by means of a correction from the development system to the production system (deployment management).

ALM and ITSM

Because the incident documents which business process is affected by the change, it is possible to identify an appropriate test case in SAP Solution Manager's Solution Documentation, to test the business process either manually or automatically (Test Management). Finally, the problem and incident messages are closed, and a knowledge article is generated documenting the solution method for the problem, in case the same alert occurs again in another system (knowledge management).

SAP Business Suite Integration

SAP CRM

Integration beyond the areas of ITSM and ALM is possible with further SAP CRM and SAP ERP functions. SAP Solution Manager is technically able to use any SAP CRM function on the basis of SAP NetWeaver. In the *SAP CRM Service* area, there are some processes that provide an ideal complement to the ITSM processes of SAP Solution Manager. The SAP *CRM middleware* can be used to synchronize data from a managed SAP ERP system. In these cases, you should contact your SAP sales representative because this could lead to you using SAP price list products that are not covered by the usage approved in SAP Solution Manager. Here are some examples of useful extensions:

▶ SAP CRM Interaction Center

▶ SAP Business Communication Management

▶ SAP CRM Service Contract Management

▶ SAP CRM Confirmation Management

▶ SAP ERP Asset Management

▶ SAP ERP Financial Management

SAP Support and Partner Integration

For SAP-specific message processing, SAP Solution Manager can be uniquely integrated into your SAP applications for notification creation. Furthermore, SAP Solution Manager allows message processing between users, an internal support organization, the SAP Active Global Support (SAP AGS), and with SAP partners. The process is described in detail in the following section.

9.1.4 Application Scenarios

With SAP Solution Manager, SAP intends to provide the best possible assistance to all SAP support customers. No one doubts the need for a support message process. However, the intensity with which individual customers use this process may vary. Added to this, there could be company-wide specifications for third-party tools or other restrictions. In this section, we present four example application scenarios of Application Incident Management, which can be combined in any way. These combinations and individual adjustment options can only be provided by a solution based on a configurable and expandable framework, such as SAP on the basis of SAP NetWeaver.

SAP Support

The process, which was already available in previous SAP Solution Manager versions, is the SAP-specific message processing. SAP Solution Manager contains a preconfigured process for processing malfunctions that can occur in day-to-day operations of SAP systems.

You can use Application Incident Management in SAP Solution Manager to operate your own SAP-specific support, for example, in the context of a Customer Center of Expertise (Customer CoE), to process malfunction messages from SAP users or key users. SAP Solution Manager provides certain functions here that significantly improve the process and ensure rapid restoration of normal business processes. This can include integrating a notification creation window in all SAP frontends, or the option of forwarding messages to the SAP global support backbone without having to worry about an integration gap.

Cooperation with SAP

Messages are created by SAP users from the SAP transaction in question, or directly via a *Self-Service* work center in SAP Solution Manager. Users can enter short and long texts and attach files. When the message is sent, it is routed to your company's Service Desk. In the background, a variety of information is attached to the message regarding the user and the system from which the malfunction was reported. This data can be used to directly forward the message to a team of specialists, for example. The user receives an email with access data for the self-service portal, where he can track the status of the message at any time and add further information subsequently, if necessary. The support colleagues can now search for a solution in dedicated information databases. To achieve this, SAP provides a link to the new *xSearch*, where you can search through SAP Notes and many other sources of SAP information. If no solution is found, and a root cause analysis is unsuccessful, you can use the forwarding function to send the message to the SAP global support backbone.

All of the data and any documented solution attempts are transferred to SAP, making the solution process more efficient. Service connections can also be controlled from the document, giving SAP Support specialists remote access to your systems. Further communication with SAP Support takes place via the same message. In individual cases, existing messages are even forwarded to SAP partners, if the customer has integrated partner products in the SAP system. In general, after a solution is found, the document is confirmed by the user in the self-service portal, which closes the message.

Configuration

The scenario is preconfigured before delivery. If you do not require any process adjustments, the Customizing can be left 1:1. However, it is normally advisable to copy the preconfigured Customizing to the customer namespace because any changes to the SAP default Customizing are overwritten during upgrades. The major task that you have to complete before using the process is maintaining the master data. This means creating the users and business partners in SAP Solution Manager; allocating these to the various organizational units (teams), if necessary; and assigning the user or processor roles via the SAP authorization concept. The standard version provides values for categories, statuses, and priorities. You can adjust these to your individual processes, as required.

The advantages of an application scenario like this are the following: Advantages

▶ A quicker and more effective solution process because there are no media discontinuities to worry about

▶ Greater transparency about the status for all the support levels involved, including for users

▶ A preconfigured incident management solution ready for use in SAP Solution Manager

▶ Standardization of incident processing in the SAP Support process

▶ The option of building up a solution database or directly accessing existing SAP infrastructure to minimize downtime caused by malfunctions.

Figure 9.3 shows the SAP Support process.

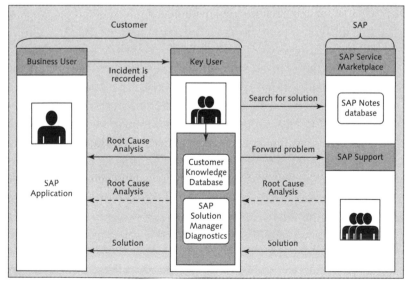

Figure 9.3 SAP Support Process

Incident and Problem Management for the Overall IT

A more comprehensive application case would be using incident and problem management in the context of an ITSM landscape in SAP Solution Manager. The focus here is on the entire IT and the services provided by an IT department for your company. The departments that use IT services are treated like IT customers, which creates the need to manage an IT department like a company that has to offer high-quality, readily available products in line with demand. The fundamental processes are defined using the ITIL framework.

IT-wide incident management

These ITIL processes are supported by relevant SAP Solution Manager functions. Finally, the interaction between these processes and the organizational approach results in the overall solution for ITSM. Next, there is a brief description of the individual SAP ITSM processes.

IT Service Desk

The IT Service Desk in SAP Solution Manager provides *call center agents* with a high-performance processing interface with integrated communication tools. This area of the SAP ITSM provides tools that help you cooperate and communicate with your customers across various channels, ensuring efficient and consistent service. It supports telephone agents and managers working in the call center.

Agents can process inbound or outbound incident or service request operations via telephone, email, fax, or Internet. They can create messages on behalf of users and increase their productivity by using alerts, scripting, and proposed solution searches. All of the relevant information about the reporting business partner is available in a clear user interface.

Incident management (including service request fulfillment)

Creating incidents and service requests includes all of the relevant information with references to configuration objects. It enables rule-based distribution to support teams and escalation management. Incidents can be categorized, thereby enabling solution proposals and autocompletion. When searching for solutions to the incident, the tool helps support employees find relevant knowledge articles in the knowledge database and provide the best solution for the end user. Confirming the solution proposal closes the incident, and optional follow-up activities, such as entering working hours, solution categorization, and so on can be triggered.

In problem management, the causes of disruptions are investigated to provide solutions that prevent the disruptive event or at least allow the event to be quickly remedied by means of documented workarounds. All of the information relating to the disruptive event is documented in the problem document.

Problem management

This includes a reference to all of the incident messages that were used as the basis for creating the problem. Problems can initially also be created without a reference to incidents if you want to use trend analyses to prevent disruptive cases. Problems can also be forwarded to SAP Support or included in change requests. Essentially, all of the functions in message processing are identical for problems and incidents because they are based on the same document type. Using problem management in SAP Solution Manager is optional. However, it offers many advantages if you want to structure your own support organization in accordance with the ITIL recommendations.

These processes can be complemented by other applications in the areas of change management, service level management, knowledge management, service asset, configuration management, and IT analytics (see Figure 9.4).

An ITSM solution should be configured in an implementation project. The duration of this type of project can last from a few days, if the SAP standard system covers most requirements, to a few weeks, if your requirements are very customer-specific. In every case, the basis is the preconfigured standard Application Incident Management system. Other functions are developed in accordance with the process requirements on this basis.

Implementation project

Why should you choose an ITSM solution in SAP Solution Manager over other providers of ITSM solutions? The most obvious benefits are the following:

Why ITSM in SAP Solution Manager?

▸ The more effective use of SAP Solution Manager provided to you as part of an SAP Support agreement makes it possible to consolidate the IT processes for ITSM and application management (transport management, root cause analysis, etc.).

▸ The expansion of SAP Solution Manager to your entire IT landscape makes it possible to consolidate all the IT-relevant processes in one centralized system (single source of truth).

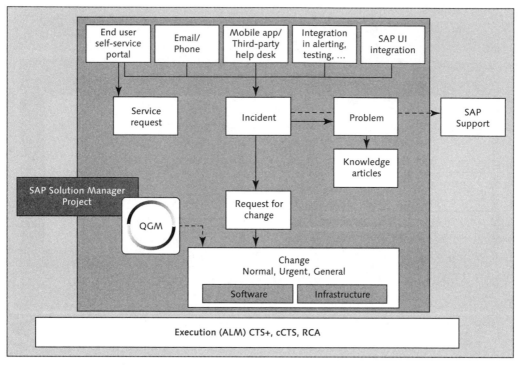

Figure 9.4 ITSM Document Overview

▶ An end-to-end IT service process safeguards ITIL compliance and effectiveness, especially by integrating the various contact channels for users (call center, email, web self-service, SAP Support, etc.).

▶ The SAP ITSM solution can be scaled to map the requirements of small businesses through to global IT processes for corporations.

▶ Thanks to the connection with the SAP ERP system, the IT processes can be integrated in the overall company control system, such as by exchanging data in the hardware purchasing process or verifying hours in personnel processes.

▶ One major benefit here is the new web interfaces in the SAP Solution Manager 7.1 that can be personalized with just a few clicks and that can also be adjusted to individual user interfaces by means of a role concept.

ALM Support from Incident Management

Integration of the Application Incident Management in many of SAP Solution Manager's ALM processes leads to some further use cases. Unlike a normal case, where a business process user reports an incident in operations or makes a service request, the process starts here when a message is triggered in other phases of application management, such as during testing or from implementation projects, or the message is triggered automatically from an event in System Monitoring.

The following areas of SAP Solution Manager include integration options with incident processes (see Figure 9.5):

ALM integration

- ▶ **Implementation**
  In the early phase of implementing solutions in the context of projects, there can be problems or unresolved issues that you want to be able to document in the project and, possibly, map using a system-supported process. It is therefore possible to enter a message in the Business Blueprint at any level of the business process structure. This is then created as an incident or, if necessary, in a customized transaction type. Then, the processing or solution process for the unresolved issue can be controlled and documented. The reference to the business process in the message and vice versa (the reference from the business process documentation to the message) are always guaranteed.

- ▶ **Test Management**
  When processing test cases, the tester has the option of setting an error status and, at the same time, posting a detailed error description in the form of a message. The message now contains the test plan, test case, and tester as a reference, as well as other details and references. This makes it possible to check and control the process for eliminating errors identified during testing.

- ▶ **Technical alerting**
  Technical alerting provides the opportunity to specify threshold values for warnings and alerts based on the monitoring of the systems managed by SAP Solution Manager. Now, automatic generation of incident messages in the event of an alert can be used to trigger an immediate solution process. The functions provided in incident management for notifying via email or text message are used here to inform the relevant agent as quickly as possible.

▶ **Business Process Monitoring**

The integration of incident management in Business Process Monitoring is based on a similar concept to technical alerting. Here, alerts or warning threshold values are stored in reference to previously defined business processes. In other words, the modeling is based on the business processes stored in the Solution Documentation The automatically generated message then contains references to the business process, which the agent processing the message can use to quickly gather detailed information about the alert.

▶ **SAP Service Delivery**

When services are provided by SAP experts, they often use *Issue Management*, which was developed specifically for this purpose, to document the current causes of the problems that are investigated by SAP as part of the service delivery. If this results in follow-up activities that have to be processed further internally, it is possible to create an incident or change message from the issue.

▶ **Job Scheduling**

The *Job Scheduling Management* component gives you an overview of and control over all of the jobs running in the background of your system landscape. End users create requests for new background processing. A job request is based on an incident message with added information about the job and job documentation.

The configuration of these applications is generally already a component of the preconfigured deliveries of each ALM process. However, Application Incident Management should always be configured using the SAP Solution Manager Configuration (Transaction SOLMAN_SETUP). This is also the crucial benefit of Application Incident Management in SAP Solution Manager. You can reuse a standardized process for incidents at any time to also support other processes without using other applications or platforms. This increases transparency because errors that occur during testing or system monitoring are often directly related to incidents that have already been reported by users. Furthermore, it is useful in early stages, such as implementation, to document the errors that occur in configuration or testing, in line with the processes because in some cases the errors will occur again during operations. If that happens, you can refer to solution proposals from the Implementation phase, and you do not have to start a new error analysis.

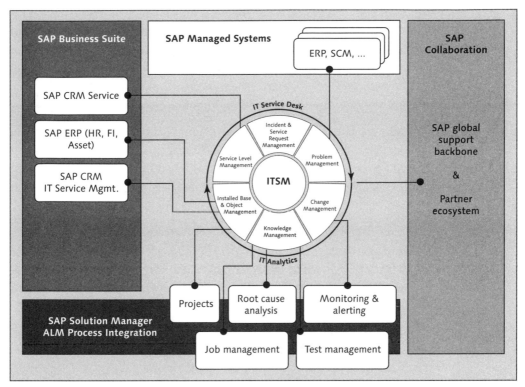

Figure 9.5 ITSM Infrastructure

Connecting Help Desk Systems from Other Manufacturers

An application example that can also be combined with the use cases mentioned previously is implementing the interface to a help desk system from another manufacturer.

Incident management in SAP Solution Manager provides an open Web service interface that can be used by customers and by other manufacturers to exchange incident messages between SAP Solution Manager and one or more ticket systems. The typical use case is that you are already using an ITSM or help desk tool and do not want to replace it. However, you still want to benefit from the advantages of the Application Incident Management, particularly due to the many integration opportunities. Here, you can make use of the bidirectional interface to create messages initially in SAP Solution Manager and then transfer the messages to another tool (help desk from another provider) for further processing. The opposite is also possible, with you creating the message first in another help desk system

Open interface

and then forwarding it to SAP Solution Manager, in accordance with certain criteria. In this case, further processing is carried out within SAP Solution Manager. The fields in the source system are synchronized, but the message can only be processed further in the target system.

It is possible to develop the interface to enable the use of multiple systems at the same time. In addition to connecting products from external manufacturers, two SAP Solution Managers can be linked using the same technology, which can also be used to connect to an SAP ITSM incident management process if it is operated on a standalone SAP CRM system.

Data is exchanged via XML. You can find the relevant Customizing settings, such as for defining mapping on the field level, together with documentation in SAP Solution Manager's IMG. Furthermore, SAP provides a more detailed technical description of the interface on the SAP Service Marketplace.

Some providers of these types of products have standardized the SAP Solution Manager linkage to their products and are certified by SAP. It is therefore advisable, before a planned implementation, to ask the manufacturer whether they offer a standard implementation of the interface to the SAP Solution Manager. You can find an overview of certified providers at *http://www.sap.com/ecosystem/customers/directories/SearchSolution.epx*.

9.1.5 The Central Incident and Problem Management Process

The following sections present three areas of an incident and problem management process that can be found, in varying form, in every customer process:

▶ **Recording**
Recording incident or service request messages via various channels to the support organization.

▶ **Processing**
The processing steps within the support organization that are intended to lead to a solution to the disruption.

▶ **Activities**

The activities and processes that can arise from the incident and problem processing.

Figure 9.6 shows an overview of the incident and problem management process.

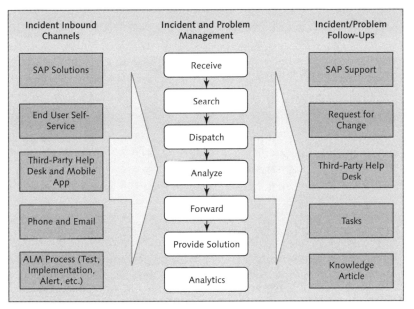

Figure 9.6 Incident and Problem Management—Process Overview

Entry Channels for Malfunction Reports

SAP Solution Manager provides you with various opportunities for entering incident or service request messages. The choice of which entry channel to use depends on the processes within your support organization. Essentially, you have to decide whether only your key users are to be allowed to create messages, as is often the case in the SAP support only process, or if you want to offer every employee in the company the option of entering tickets. Other considerations include whether the enterer can create the message online directly and forward the message directly to specialists by assigning a category. Alternatively, some customers operate a centralized Service Desk that primarily accepts messages from users by phone or email. Each variant or combination is possible.

Creating messages

SAP Solution Manager supports the following entry channels for ITSM processes:

- ► **SAP frontend**
  SAP offers direct SAP Solution Manager integration from the following SAP frontends for message creation:

  - ► SAP GUI
  - ► SAP NetWeaver Portal
  - ► SAP NetWeaver Business Client
  - ► SAP CRM Web Client

  If a user uses an SAP application within these frontends, he can enter a malfunction message directly from the current transaction. The message is then forwarded to SAP Solution Manager's incident management process. The user receives a message number immediately after saving the message; the user can use this number to track the progress of the message via the Web self-service or via the Service Desk. When the message is sent, the frontend gathers other background information about the system from which the message was sent and adds this automatically to the ticket. This provides the support agent with important information that could make it easier to find a solution.

- ► **Web self-service**
  The self-service offers the message enterer the option of creating an incident or service request and provides an overview of messages that have already been entered, plus their statuses. In addition, users can also interact with the support team regarding existing messages. In other words, users can cancel their messages if the malfunction no longer exists, they can add further information subsequently, reply to queries from support, and finally accept the solution proposal.

  Regardless of which entry channel was used to enter the message, the concept in SAP Solution Manager is that the reporter closes the message at the end of the process after receiving an acceptable solution proposal. In the default case, the user therefore receives an email after the support agent has stored a solution proposal in the ticket. The email contains a link to the self-service portal so that the user can check and accept the proposal, if appropriate.

  SAP Solution Manager 7.1 offers two web self-service portals. One is a preconfigured self-service for end users based on the work center. This is configured accordingly via the composite role SAP_SUPPDESK_CREATE_COMP provided by SAP.

The second variant is using the business role (ITSERVREQU) on the basis of the SAP CRM Web Client. SAP ITSM provides a basic role here that customers can very easily adjust to their individual requirements by making use of the flexible interface adjustments.

- **IT Service Desk**

  SAP ITSM provides a dedicated business role for assisting first-level support as a separate price list component. The interface is very efficiently designed for mass editing of messages so that the call center agent can enter the caller's information very quickly. The interface is also designed to be integrated with computer-supported telephony. Receiving emails from users who want to report an incident is also integrated into the interface because, in most cases, the Service Desk or first-level support agent should pre-qualify the situation before an email is turned into an incident or a service request.

- **SAP Solution Manager ALM processes**

  With regard to the ALM-centric usage case, messages cannot be created by users only. Particularly within ALM processes in the various stages of an application's lifecycle, it can be useful to use a structured and documented process such as incident management to solve test error or problems in projects. In these cases, the message is entered by the tester or the project member (such as the consultant or developer). By categorizing the messages accordingly, you can keep their processing separate from the processing of the operational maintenance process (classic incident management).

  You can set up system-controlled creation of messages by combining Technical Monitoring and Alerting or Business Process Monitoring with Application Incident Management. If specific threshold values are exceeded when monitoring the system infrastructure or the business processes, alerts are generated. These, in turn, can generate an incident either automatically or manually.

- **Help desk systems from other providers**

  Finally, it is also possible for a malfunction message to be created from another incident management tool or another SAP Solution Manager. For this to happen, the relevant interface must have been implemented. This makes it possible to receive messages that are to be processed further in SAP Solution Manager. The changed data can be synchronized back to the source application. This synchronization can be set using data mapping tables.

Message Processing

The message processing process consists of the following five steps that occur in almost every incident and problem management scenario:

1. **Receiving messages**

   The message processor starts in the business role SOLMANPRO. The processor can use the WORKLIST area to display all of the messages that are available for processing by the processor or his team. Alternatively, the processor can store user-defined search favorites on the start page to enable quick access to a predefined search, such as all incidents that were recorded on the same day and still have the status NEW. In general, when the enterer creates a malfunction, he stores a categorization or an SAP component that can be used for automatic distribution to processor groups or employees, by means of the corresponding rule determination. If there is no categorization, all messages can be initially forwarded to a central Service Desk.

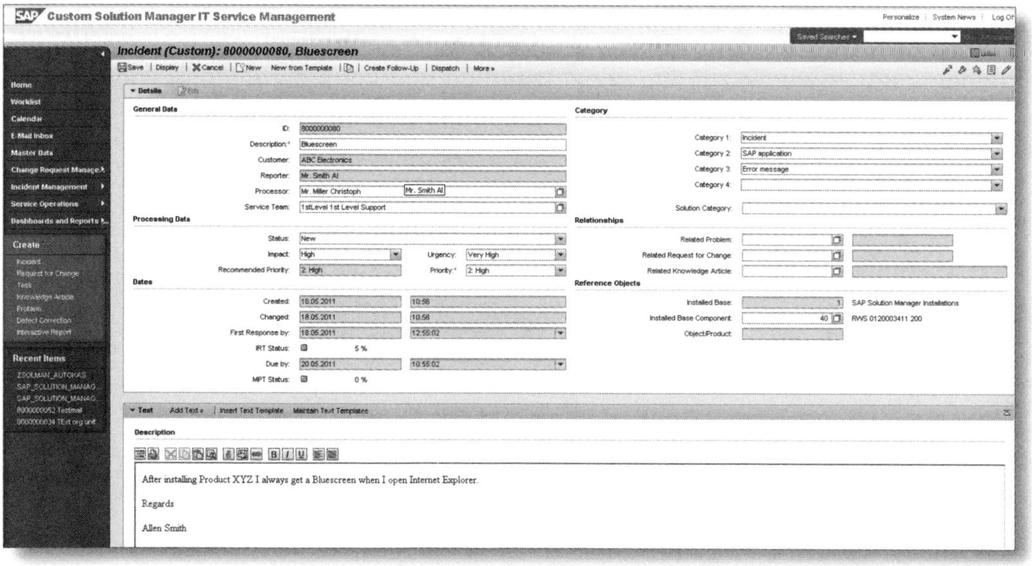

Figure 9.7 Incident Processing

2. **Searching for a solution**

After the message processor has started processing the incident, he first turns to information such as the descriptive text, attachments, system information, and other references to evaluate the urgency of the message and its effect on operations and then to correctly assess its overall priority.

▶ The enterer's initial categorization assessment can still be refined because the system already offers a few solution proposals at this stage on the basis of the categorization. The message processor can use search queries in the menu to display existing problem messages in the same category to allocate the incident directly to a problem. Further support is provided by the search, based on the same categorization, for existing knowledge articles. These articles may already contain a documented solution to the malfunction, meaning the processor can very quickly return an initial solution proposal.

Searching for a solution

3. **Forwarding the incident**

If there is no known solution available, the processor forwards the incident to an expert. The incident can be transferred to another team in various ways. You can define rules that use categories to find appropriate teams from the organization model. You can also search for other teams or processors manually and assign the message directly.

▶ ITIL also allows you to generate a problem message from your incident and have the message processed further by a problem management process. In any case, the status schema is crucial in this process because it should always be clear who in your organization is responsible for which status in the processing process.

Problem

4. **Detailed analysis**

When the incident or problem is being processed by experts, analysis tools from SAP Solution Manager can be used to localize the cause of the malfunction more closely. Performance measurements or log analyses are used to identify where exactly the root cause is located. Next, the processor analyzes additional information about the system or IT object in question and the relationships to other objects.

▶ For SAP-related incidents, there are additional sources of solutions available, such as the xSearch in the SAP Service Marketplace,

Analysis

which searches for SAP Notes, and in other SAP sources (SDN, Help Portal, etc.).

5. **Returning a solution proposal**

After a solution to the malfunction has been found, or at least a workaround has been created to restore normal operations as quickly as possible, the processor writes a description of the solution in the document and changes the status, which leads to the enterer receiving an email with the solution proposal or a link to the web self-service. The message is not closed until the enterer accepts the solution proposal. In message processing, a final categorization of the solution can also be carried out for evaluation purposes, among other reasons, making it possible to assess how the malfunction could be solved. Furthermore, the processor can record how long he took to process the message in the document.

Follow-Up Activities for Incidents and Problems

In the message processing process, it is possible to add further processes and employees to the activities. Follow-up activities can be used to generate additional documents that still retain a reference to the original message. This makes it possible to represent a document flow, and, especially when processors change, it can make the entire message process transparent and understandable.

Follow-up transactions

Of the many activities, the following are important:

▸ You can forward the incident or problem message on a specific SAP component to SAP Support to include SAP experts in the search for a solution.

▸ To rectify an error, it is often necessary to make appropriate changes to the target system. In this case, you can create a change request from the incident or problem itself. This process is described in detail in Chapter 8, Section 8.2.

▸ The document type TASK (as shown earlier in Figure 9.7) is available for further delegating tasks from an incident or problem. The processor normally creates multiple tasks and assigns them to other processors if it seems that the problem analysis will be time-consuming or complex, and multiple employees will have to become involved. After these other processors have completed their task, they report this in the document.

> ► To build up a knowledge database, it is necessary to document previously unknown problems and their solutions so that a simple search comes up with a solution in a knowledge article the next time the disruption occurs. For this reason, solution texts from incidents or problems can be copied directly to knowledge articles via a follow-up activity. These texts can be processed further in knowledge management, as required, and indexed for searches.

9.1.6 Master Data

This chapter briefly explains the few types of master data that you require in incident management. A large share of this involves master data for documenting the details of the process users.

Business Partner and Organizational Unit

Before you can create or process messages in incident management, you must save master data. *Business partners* in SAP Solution Manager guarantee effective and easy communication among all employees involved in the incident management process. All relevant information on a business partner can be accessed from one central point.

User master data

When you need to, you create individual business partners manually in SAP Solution Manager with the appropriate administration authorization in the business role SOLMANPRO, for example. In general, however, the business partners are migrated from connected SAP systems by means of background processing. The report copies all or selected users (including their email addresses) from other systems and generates all of the necessary business partner functions in the SAP Solution Manager (contact, employee, general). In addition to this, you can also generate an *SAP Solution Manager Login User* if you want and assign a template authorization role to the user. You can make the relevant settings in SAP Solution Manager's IMG.

Master data generation

Here, it does not matter in which part of a process the business partners are involved. For example, a single employee can also function as a processor and a reporter. Therefore, you can use SAP Solution Manager to assign a business partner different roles and relationships to other business partners.

In the incident management configuration shipped by SAP, some partner functions have been defined. You can adapt these by making the following Customizing settings:

- CUSTOMER
  Represents the role of the business process organization and answers the question, "Which organization does the message creator belong to?" The SOLD-TO PARTY partner function behind this is mandatory and cannot be deleted.

- REPORTED BY
  Answers the question, "Who created the message?"

- SUPPORT TEAM
  Represents the respective support team in the customer's organization.

- CURRENT PROCESSOR
  Represents the employee responsible for the message.

Organizational model

The organizational schema in SAP Solution Manager (Transaction PPOMA_CRM) should reflect the organization of the support department. You use this to define the various levels and assign employees to the various groups of experts. This is the prerequisite for activating automatic rule determination that finds a responsible group within your support organization on the basis of message characteristics (such as the category).

Developing an end-to-end support concept requires the definition and transparent mapping of internal support processes in your company.

Support levels

In the SAP support process, you can implement a four-stage concept for processing messages, for example. This architecture is structured as follows:

- **First-level support**
  First-level support forms the *single point of contact* from the end user to the customer's support organization. *Key users* are involved at this level, or designated users in the managed system who also work in SAP Solution Manager. As mentioned earlier, the following options, which can be combined with one another, are available for creating a message:

  - End users can create support messages from managed systems.

> ▶ Key users can create support messages for end users from managed systems.

> ▶ Key users can create support messages for end users directly in SAP Solution Manager.

▶ **Second-level support**
Second-level support involves employees who are familiar with the details of a customer's own applications and business processes, and assume the role of system administrator. Second-level support therefore comprises application and technology experts.

▶ **Third-level support (Customer CoE level)**
Third-level support tasks include the following:

> ▶ Searching for SAP Notes

> ▶ Managing and using a solution database in the incident management process

▶ Those responsible for third-level support typically are a function of the company's size. For smaller companies and customers that do not have a Customer CoE, this level corresponds to fourth-level support. In this case, the tasks associated with the Customer CoE level are assumed by the customer in second-level support.

▶ **Fourth-level support (SAP AGS)**
Fourth-level support represents SAP AGS. This is the final message processing level for large customers and customers with a Customer CoE. This support level also includes certified partners that are involved in processing and resolving messages through the SAP global support backbone.

This structure allows problem messages to be handled and resolved efficiently with focus on the solution throughout the entire SAP ecosystem. If required, you can use the organizational model to set up additional support levels in SAP Solution Manager.

IBASE (Installed Base) and IT Objects

To use incident management in SAP Solution Manager, you must first define the installation (IBASE). An Installed Base (IBASE) component must be created for each component system used to send messages to SAP Solution Manager. An IBASE component therefore represents a managed system in your solution.

IBASE components

383

IBASE components in SAP Solution Manager are managed in the IBASE structure SOL_MAN_DATA_REP (installation 1) in the standard and updated automatically with subsequent enhancements to the system landscape (Transaction SMSY).

IT objects

All of the IT objects in your landscape that you want to process in incident management also have to be created as objects in the IBASE. The IBASE of the IT objects can be maintained manually or synchronized with an SAP ERP system, such as asset management, via SAP CRM middleware. It is already possible, on the basis of a project, to connect configuration management tools (configuration management database, CMDB) for automatically entering the IT infrastructure. Standardization with an SAP partner product is in planning.

9.1.7 Best Practice Functions

The constraints of this publication do not allow a detailed presentation of all the functional possibilities of the ITSM. For this reason, in the following sections, we will examine a few functions in detail, while representing many others.

Knowledge Management

Knowledge articles

You can use the *knowledge article* to access saved information, such as how-to documents, user manuals, or frequently asked questions (FAQ), to more quickly process malfunctions, problems, and change requests reported by your customers, for example.

You can compile knowledge databases to make searches quicker. If you create a knowledge article in another language, the system automatically creates a knowledge database index and automatically updates the existing index to include new or changed knowledge articles. As a support manager, you can delete an index, create a new one, or update an existing index, as well as specify the date and time for compilation.

You can assign knowledge articles to other activities, such as incidents, problems, or change requests, to enable direct access to similar situations that were reported by the customer previously. To save time, you can create knowledge articles with the help of a template.

For example, a Service Desk employee receives a call from a customer who is having trouble with his monitor. The employee then creates an incident and looks for a related knowledge article. The employee finds a document about error analysis and elimination that is relevant to the incident and helps the customer solve the problem with the monitor. At the end of the call, the agent adds this knowledge article to the incident so that other employees can access it in the future.

Interaction with SAP Active Global Support

If the various support levels of the customer support organization cannot solve the problem, you send the support message along with an SAP information note (including attachments, if necessary) to SAP AGS.

Every aspect of interaction with SAP AGS was grouped together in an assignment block in SAP Solution Manager 7.1. A six-step process was defined for sending a message to SAP. This makes it easier to compile all of the necessary information for successful transfer to SAP (see Figure 9.8).

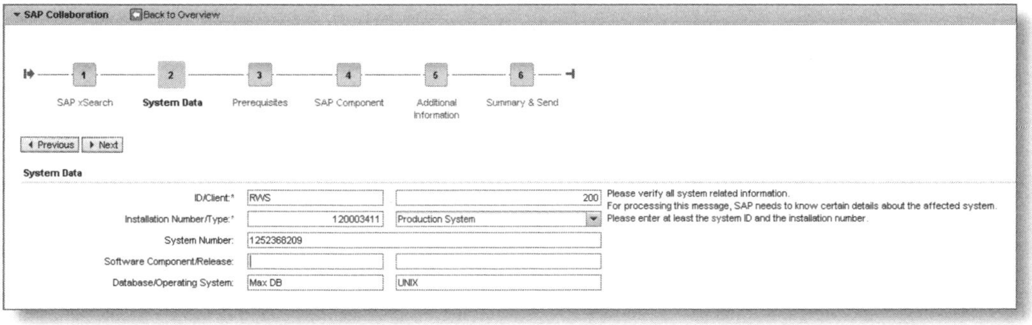

Figure 9.8 Guided SAP Message Processing

One of the unique features of incident management in SAP Solution Manager is the option of collaborating with SAP AGS to achieve shorter solution times, as targeted information allows SAP Support to better process your message. Service connections are an important part of this collaboration because they give SAP Support the opportunity to access your system from a remote location to understand the nature of the problems occurring in your environment.

Guided SAP message processing

Secure area

Access information is saved in what is known as the *secure area* for secure support. This area allows only authorized support employees to access your systems, thereby protecting your applications from unauthorized access.

As of SAP Solution Manager 7.0, the secure area is integrated into SAP Solution Manager so that the logon data for SAP AGS can be saved to the secure area directly from the support message. To do this, choose SAP COLLABORATION in the assignment block for the message in the menu MAINTAIN LOGON DATA. You can display your existing systems and add new systems on the following screen. You can include the system, client, user, and password, as well as the amount of access time assigned to the user.

SAP AGS processes the message and returns it to you along with a proposed solution or a question and an updated status. You can track the status of the message at any time in your incident in the SAP COLLABORATION assignment block. After a message has been successfully confirmed, a link appears for an online evaluation of your satisfaction with SAP Support (*positive call closure*).

If a partner's software is affected by a problem, the SAP global support backbone gives the partner access to all of the functions available to SAP AGS, for instance, root cause analysis or the ability to create notes.

Escalation Process

If you are subject to time restrictions in message processing, such as service agreements (SLA), you can use the functions for *SLA escalation*.

SLA and escalation

The prerequisite for this is that you have defined service times and SLA agreements (i.e., reaction and processing times) on the basis of priorities. Your objects (applications, IT hardware, etc.) have assigned SLAs, or you use a service contract to determine SLA times. Furthermore, you should define the statuses that are not relevant to SLA in your support, such as CUSTOMER ACTION or SENT TO SAP. This means that over the course of processing the message, you continuously receive updated, calculated times by which the message should be completed. A color bar in the document shows you what percentage of the reaction or processing time has passed at all times (see Figure 9.9). If the percentage reaches 60%, the first escalation status is automatically set.

If 90% is reached, the status is raised to escalation level 2. You can address this status with separate actions and, if necessary, send emails to the processor or team leader to point out the escalation.

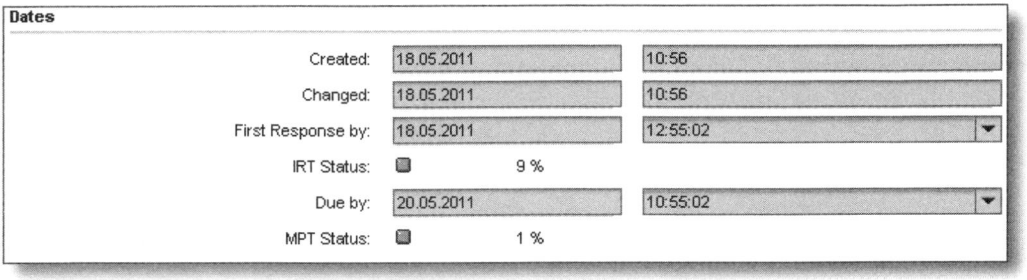

Dates		
Created:	18.05.2011	10:56
Changed:	18.05.2011	10:56
First Response by:	18.05.2011	12:55:02
IRT Status:	▣	9 %
Due by:	20.05.2011	10:55:02
MPT Status:	▣	1 %

Figure 9.9 SLA Status Display

Multi-Level Categorization

The categorization plays an important role in the incident and problem management process.

You can define various levels yourself. SAP Solution Manager provides a template schema that provides you with a starting point for defining your own categories. First, you should decide how many levels you want to use. In the standard system, the process is designed for four levels, with the person who enters the message only selecting the first two levels.

Figure 9.10 shows an example of a categorization.

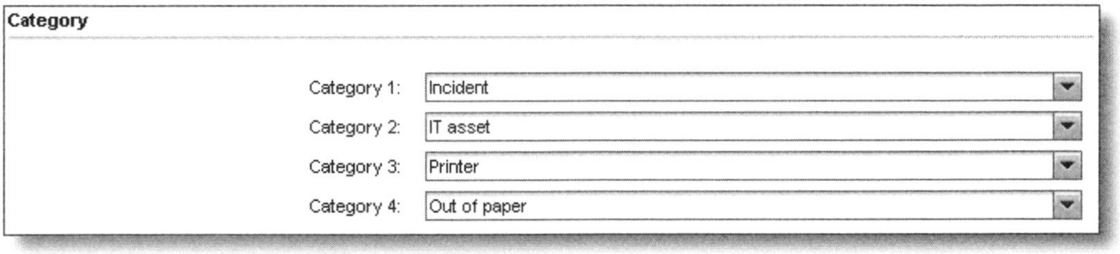

Categorization

Category	
Category 1:	Incident
Category 2:	IT asset
Category 3:	Printer
Category 4:	Out of paper

Figure 9.10 Categorization in Incident Management

▸ Level 1: Typing the document (incident, service request, test error, alarm)

▸ Level 2: Typing the IT area (SAP, IT hardware, mobile application)

▸ Level 3: Typing the error (error message, crash, missing data)

▸ Level 4: Specific error ("Cannot create data in SM7," "Error 6734")

A good categorization has fundamental benefits during later processing of the message:

- The categorization enables automatic assignment to a processor or
  a support team, reducing the workload of the first support level or
  even bypassing them completely.

- The categorization is used to propose knowledge articles with the
  same category to the processor; these can be assigned to the incident and maybe already provide a solution.

- The categorization is used to display problem messages with the
  same category (if any exist) to the incident processor. The processor could, for example, assign the incident to a problem that is
  currently dealing with the same root cause.

- The category is used as the basis for displaying a template to the
  processor; the processor can adopt the template and automatically
  generate some standard texts for the message, such as a standard
  reply for resetting a password.

- Finally, the categorization plays an important role in evaluating
  incidents to identify trends or gain a filtered view of error messages.

Web Client Interface in SAP ITSM

Integrating the SAP ITSM solution into SAP Solution Manager has led
to change interface technology. In previous releases, the Service Desk
processes could be carried out on the web interface of the *Incident
Management* work center or on the original SAP GUI transactions
(CRMD_ORDER). In SAP Solution Manager 7.1, incident messages are
only processed in the new SAP Web Client interfaces. You reach these
directly by entering a URL or via the SAP GUI with Transaction
CRM_UI. The work centers are still used in SAP Solution Manager, so
you can still access the ITSM processes via the *Incident Management*
work center.

New web UI Essentially, however, the web client interface technology has advantages over previous interface technologies:

▶ Users can personalize the interface according to their tastes, such as visible fields, colors, arrangement of the assignment blocks, or integration in Microsoft Outlook.

▶ An interface administrator can also rename fields and easily add new, individual fields.

These interfaces are controlled by means of *business roles*, several templates SAP provides according to the tasks of each role. In the ITSM scenario in SAP Solution Manager, the business role for support employees is SOLMANPRO. In addition to this, there are other roles for SAP CRM ITSM that you can use as templates. We recommend making an initial copy of the SAP standard business role that you want to use.

Business roles

The roles only define the layout and display of fields and assignment blocks. The authorizations are controlled via the SAP authorization concept, as with all SAP NetWeaver applications.

9.2 Incident Management with Help Desk Systems from Other Providers

Since Release 7.0, SAP Solution Manager has included an open interface for exchanging messages with help desk systems from other providers. Customers requested this feature because in addition to having an existing support infrastructure, they wanted to use the extended options of the Service Desk to provide support for SAP applications.

Interface to help desk systems from other providers

The purpose of the open interface is to act as a central access point for message creators and support employees. The interface, for which providers can be certified by SAP, is accessible to all customers and SAP partners and can be implemented in their tools. This means you can integrate SAP Solution Manager incident management in your existing help desk systems. Messages are exchanged in SAP Solution Manager with web services for simple, flexible, and platform-independent operation.

This combined solution offers functions that allow you to fulfill the following tasks:

> ▸ Improve the quality of information
> ▸ Increase communication options
> ▸ Simplify message processing management

You can configure message exchange in SAP Solution Manager IMG.

Architecture   The architecture of the interface is designed for SAP Solution Manager to process SAP-specific incidents and information queries, while the external help desk system handles all messages not affecting SAP applications, such as hardware queries and problems in applications from other providers.

You can forward messages from SAP ITSM to an external help desk and vice versa. Here, the system creates a corresponding message that can be uniquely identified and is assigned to the original message in another system. The message can only be processed by one of the other connected help desks. In other words, either SAP Solution Manager or the external help desk assumes the responsibility. Additional information such as message texts can be exchanged asynchronously.

A message can be exchanged several times between the SAP Solution Manager incident management and the external help desk application as the message is being processed. It is important to have the responsibilities of the respective help desk system clarified for this purpose. The following is a possible scenario:

Master/slave   The external help desk assumes the role of general first-level support, where all messages are entered. Those messages not related to an SAP-specific problem are either resolved or forwarded to second-level support in the external help desk. SAP Solution Manager assumes the role of second-level support for SAP. In the event of an SAP problem, for example, the message is forwarded to the incident management used by SAP experts at the customer service organization. Collaboration with SAP AGS is very easy at this point. As already mentioned, messages can also be returned to the external help desk. Communication is possible at any time, and central access ensures that no information is lost because every processor can read all of the information contained in the message.

This does not mean that messages cannot be sent directly from the transaction in the SAP system. This support channel is still valuable for message processing thanks to the background information it provides. When configuring the interface, you can alternatively specify automatic generation of a corresponding message in the external help desk for messages created in SAP Solution Manager. This message then appears with SENT TO SAP SOLUTION MANAGER status, and an overview of all messages can be viewed at any time from the leading help desk.

Sending a message from a transaction

The second alternative is to generate messages only when a message is explicitly sent to the external help desk (on demand). Here, it is important to know that messages processed and resolved in SAP Solution Manager will not appear in external help desk reports.

If a message is closed in the current help desk, the status of the message is automatically set to COMPLETED in the other help desk. Automatic synchronization also does not occur.

9.3   Incident Management for IT Service Providers

From the start, partners have been an essential component in collaboration between SAP and its customers. Most customers have known their IT service providers for a long time. SAP Solution Manager offers many functions, playing a crucial role in integrating the customer, SAP, and partners. In incident management, the Solution Manager offers everything that SAP, customers, and partners need. Figure 9.11 shows the interaction between customers, partners, and SAP.

Complete integration of partners in SAP support processes

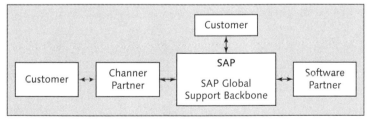

Figure 9.11 Collaboration between Customers, Partners, and SAP

Cooperation with IT service providers as channel partners has been very valuable to SAP right from the company's beginnings. Customers are supported by partners throughout the lifecycle of business processes; from selecting the right solution, through operation to continuous improvement.

All around the world, partners work together with SAP to offer customers the best possible solution for their business processes. Employees of the IT service providers go to frequent SAP training courses so that certified support employees can also offer their customers the best possible quality of service.

Right from the start, SAP Solution Manager has played an important role in cooperation with IT service providers' customers. This initial importance has increased substantially with the ongoing function enhancements. For IT service providers, SAP Solution Manager has now become a fixed anchor between the various customer systems on the one side and SAP on the other (see Figure 9.12).

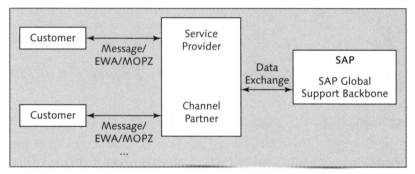

Figure 9.12 Collaboration with IT Service Providers

Many customers want support from a partner from whom they bought their SAP solution, who they have possibly known for years or who is based in the same city as them. Thanks to their partner's SAP Solution Manager, these customers can receive all the necessary services directly. A direct connection between the customer's SAP systems and the IT service provider's SAP Solution Manager has proven to be especially beneficial because some services, such as SAP EarlyWatch Alert, cannot be implemented without a direct connection.

Incident management is the core area in the relationship between the customer and partners. Whenever customers have a question, they can turn to the SAP partner company that they signed a maintenance contract with, which is generally the partner from whom the customer also bought his SAP solution.

If there is a contractual agreement between you and your partner company that maintenance of one or more of your installations is the responsibility of your partner, SAP is also informed of this, and everything is set up so that the interaction between customer, partner, and SAP works smoothly. When the maintenance contract starts, the partner has all of the necessary master data for the installation, and you are automatically given access data for the partner's SAP Solution Manager. You can then log on to your partner's SAP Solution Manager with the same S-user that you use for the SAP Service Marketplace. The option of creating messages for this installation is then normally no longer available via the message assistant in the SAP Service Marketplace. Instead, there is a link on the Marketplace to the IT service provider with whom you signed the maintenance contract for the installation.

Exchanging master data

As a customer, you might have already set up your own SAP Solution Manager and the Service Desk for your incident management. In this case, you can use the standard interface to connect to a second Service Desk. Now, the difference in your Service Desk is that you send each message TO EXTERNAL SERVICE DESK instead of to SAP.

A work center with customer-specific information is made available to each customer by a web link through the partner's SAP Solution Manager. The work center offers each customer user a range of options that provide help in various situations. If, for example, you go on vacation, you can define other users as your representatives. Of course, email and the telephone are also available, and the message can be transferred to a message document on the partner's side, either manually or using the automatic options provided by ITSM (see Figure 9.13), as described in Section 9.1.2 under "IT Service Desk."

Customer work center

If you want to send a customer message to your partner's support department, you can first use a link in the work center to the xSearch in the SAP Service Marketplace to find a possible solution to your question yourself. Links that a partner makes available to its customers in the navigation bar can be adjusted individually.

Message processing process

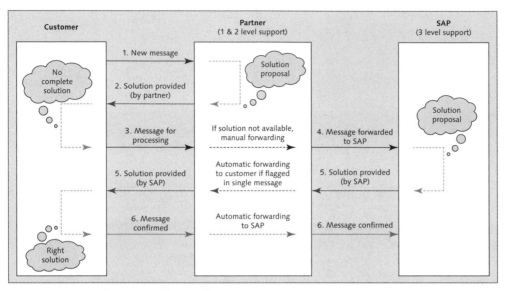

Figure 9.13 Message Process

The employee in the partner's first-level support receives the customer message in his inbox in the SAP Solution Manager Service Desk (Figure 9.14). Depending on the subject of the message (i.e., the message component) or depending on the customer number, the priority or other criteria that a partner can define, the message is forwarded from first-level support to a specialist. The specialist who is responsible in the partner's enterprise for this type of message processes the message as quickly as possible and provides an answer for the customer.

Maintaining working time — When processing a message, it can be useful for the processor to make a note of the individual working hours, according to various categories. This option is also helpful if various transactions are handled through a single message, that is, if there is also additional consulting work or services have to be performed other than simply finding a solution. These additional services can be recorded easily and evaluated later using the comprehensive options in SAP NetWeaver Business Intelligence incident management reporting, which was developed especially for IT service providers.

When you receive a solution proposal from your partner, you implement the proposal in your system, and, if it works, you mark the message as completed. This incident is then finished as far as the message processor at the IT service provider is concerned.

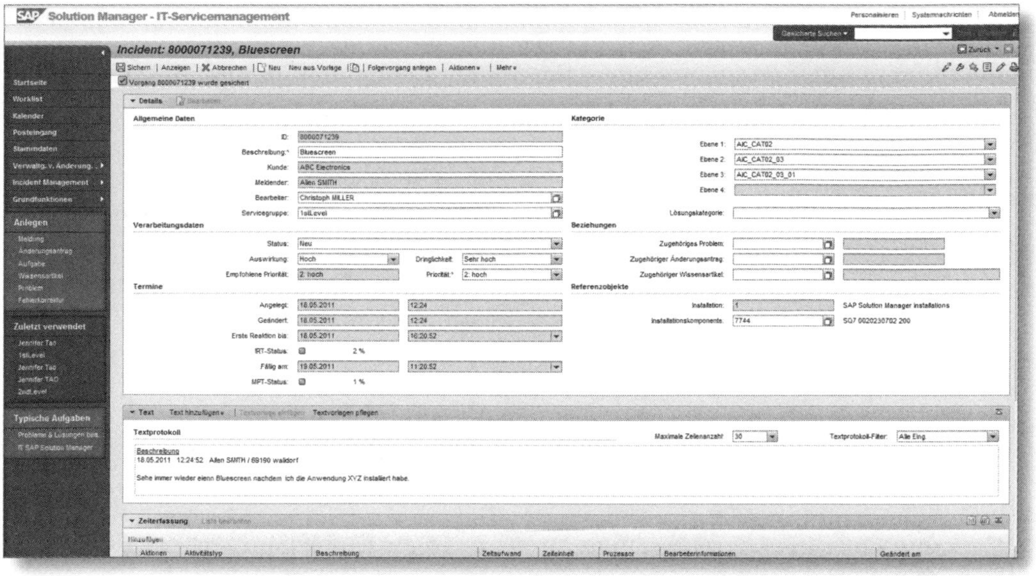

Figure 9.14 Message in the Service Desk for Partners

If a solution proposal does not immediately have the desired effect, your customer message is returned to the partner's support department with a reply in the status SENT TO SUPPORT. A support employee can now develop a more comprehensive solution proposal. The employee can, of course, also access the large range of options for finding solutions from SAP, some of which are only available to partners. Additionally, it is possible to build up a customized knowledge database in the partner's SAP Solution Manager by creating knowledge articles about every possible subject and assigning attributes to these. This is a good way of making available the knowledge gathered by the partner. It can be made available to all employees or, depending on the release status, it can be attached to a customer message like an SAP Note.

In any case, the partner can keep the customer updated each time a message's status changes thanks to automatic emails.

Sometimes, multiple customer messages from different customers or various messages from one customer are created for the same subject in the partner's Service Desk. In this case, the individual messages can be grouped together as a problem message that contains an underlying problem description and is linked to the individual messages. The individual messages are locked for processing. To make

Linking messages

the process more effective, only the problem message is processed further, not the individual customer messages. After a solution has been developed for the problem, it is passed on to the individual messages.

Forwarding to SAP If the problem involves a special topic or the possibility of a program error, the message can be forwarded to SAP AGS on behalf of the customer. There, your message is processed further, an answer is attached, and it is returned. Whether this answer appears first in the partner's worklist or is forwarded directly to you depends on the Customizing in the partner's SAP Solution Manager.

If the answer to the message solved the problem, you can confirm the message, which marks it as completed in the partner's and SAP's systems.

Automatic forwarding to SAP A critical situation can occur in a customer's operations, making it necessary to report a malfunction to your IT service provider during the weekend or at night. Because IT service providers do not generally need to provide round-the-clock support, a message like this would arrive outside the partner's business hours. If you create the message with the priority "Very high" because fundamental business processes are impaired, the message is automatically forwarded to SAP so there is no delay in processing the most urgent messages (see Figure 9.15).

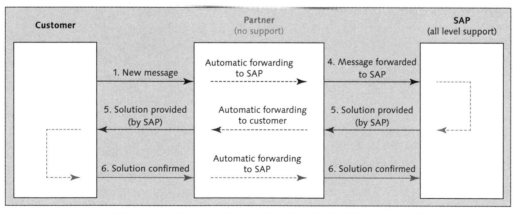

Figure 9.15 Automatic Forwarding Outside the IT Service Provider's Business Hours

The IT service provider can track the procedure once back at work during normal business hours.

Some messages on specific components can't, in general, be processed by an IT service provider and have to be processed by SAP directly. These include malfunctions when accessing the SAP Service Marketplace or SAProuter, for example. For these components, the IT service provider can also set up permanent automatic forwarding to SAP so that this type of message never even appears in the worklist of the message employee at the partner enterprise.

In many cases, processing a message makes it necessary to start an error analysis in your affected system and, possibly, make changes. To do this, your IT service provider can access a customer system from a message. Each customer has a service connection to SAP to make remote support possible. Besides this, many customers have an additional virtual private network (VPN) connection directly to their IT service provider, enabling remote support and a range of other services (see Figure 9.16).

Remote support

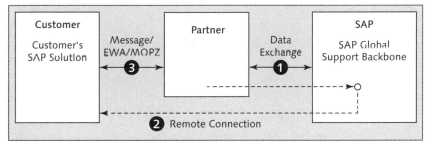

Figure 9.16 Remote Connection via SAP

You can store the logon data for the system in question in the customer message that you enter in your IT service provider's Service Desk, at any time. The information is stored in a secure area at SAP. The support employee from your IT service provider can use this logon data to connect to the SAP Service Marketplace from the message. There, the employee first selects the customer's target system and determines the type of connection. For your safety, a connection to the customer system is always logged.

There is currently a choice of two methods here: a direct system logon and—if a GUI logon is not possible or not desired—a desktop sharing connection with Netviewer. To make an SAP GUI connection possible, the access data and logon period are stored, and the partner's support employee can use these for remote support.

Connection types

For the second option of desktop sharing, SAP integrated the Netviewer solution in its system to adjust it to the specific requirements. There are safeguards to ensure that only the processor of a message can connect to a customer system.

If the support employee has agreed on Netviewer as the connection method with his customer, the support employee opens a new Netviewer session. The customer employee receives an invitation to this Netviewer session by email. If it has not yet been installed, the customer employee can install the Netviewer client via a link in the email. After the client is started, the employee enters the session ID, and the view must be approved or permission must be gained to control the customer desktop. Remote support then starts.

After the remote support session has finished, the malfunction analysis is complete, and the root cause has been rectified, the support employee terminates the remote connection and enters the concluding information in your customer message. The employee assigns the status CUSTOMER ACTION or SOLUTION PROPOSAL. If you agree with the proposal, confirm the solution proposal, and the message is marked as completed for support in your partner's system and—if the message was processed at SAP in the meantime—in SAP's system. If the customer does not confirm a solution as completed after a specific period of time (which can be defined by the IT service provider), or if the solution is sent back with an answer, a job normally automatically sets the message to the status CONFIRMED.

9.4   Incident Management for Software Partners

In various specialized areas, SAP partners offers their own products as solution extensions. Software partners come directly after SAP Support in the support chain as third-level support, or they cover all of the support levels. This depends on the product.

In general, you the customer send a message as usual to SAP via your own Service Desk, via the SAP Service Marketplace, or, in special cases, by telephone, using the contact options of the global SAP support centers. In the SAP global service backbone, a decision is then made about how to proceed with the message, regardless of the application components. The components from software partners follow the pattern XX-PART-abc for SAP software solution partners (reseller or OEM) or XX-PART-EBS-abc for partners with endorsed business solutions (EBS).

The support process is regulated in cooperation with SAP, depending on the partner type. EBS partners are responsible for all support levels. Software solution partners, on the other hand, share the support service with SAP (see Figure 9.17).

Message processing process

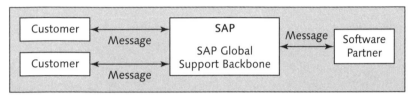

Figure 9.17 Collaboration with Software Partners

If the message component belongs to a product from an OEM partner (original equipment manufacturer), the first-level support at SAP initially searches for a possible solution and sends a proposal back to you, if possible. It is possible that the solution proposal is insufficient and does not solve the problem. In this case, you return the message to SAP with your comments.

The first-level support at SAP now decides, on the basis of specific criteria, that the malfunction should be examined further by the manufacturer itself and marks your message accordingly.

In the software partner's SAP Solution Manager, a job runs at regular intervals, checking if there are any changed messages for the software partner's support department. If new messages are ready for collection, they are copied to the partner's SAP Solution Manager for further processing.

When a message appears in your SAP Solution Manager for the first time, there is no master data for your SAP solution, unlike in an IT service provider's Service Desk. This master data (minimum system data and business partners), which has to be available in the Service Desk for processing, is automatically generated from the data in the message when a new message is created in SAP Solution Manager. If a message has already been processed in the software partner's Service Desk, the master data is compared to the available data and updated, as necessary.

A support employee or a team at the software partner's enterprise now receives a notification by email stating that there is a new message awaiting processing (if this option was set up in the Service Desk).

If there is also a multi-level support model in the partner organization, the new message is first taken up by the first-level support for preliminary clarification. It might be possible at this stage to offer a solution to the customer problem and therefore send you an answer. If the situation is not that simple, the message is forwarded to second-level support.

In second-level support, there are support engineers or employees from development who are very familiar with the partner product and have a good insight into eliminating errors and possible solutions. Their answer includes a description of the solution and, generally, a note on the solution.

Partner note — Notes are always created if a solution proposal is not just specifically suitable for one single message but solves several users' problem. If no note has yet been created for this case, the support employee can create a new partner note on the subject via the SAP infrastructure. There is an application developed specifically for software partners for this purpose, which can be accessed via the partner's SAP Solution Manager (see Figure 9.18).

A partner note is a special note with information similar to an SAP Note. The partner note contains various text sections, the note text itself in the form of a description of the solution, and the option of internal notes. Objects, additional documents, or corrections can be attached. Partner notes can be found via the SAP Notes search or via the normal SAP xSearch.

After a solution has been developed for your malfunction, a solution proposal is attached to the message, possibly together with an SAP Note or a partner note, and returned to you. To do this, the support employee assigns the message the status CUSTOMER ACTION and returns the message to SAP. On the SAP side, the message is placed in the SAP Service Marketplace inbox, or, if you also use SAP Solution Manager Service Desk for your incident management, it is made ready for collection in your Service Desk.

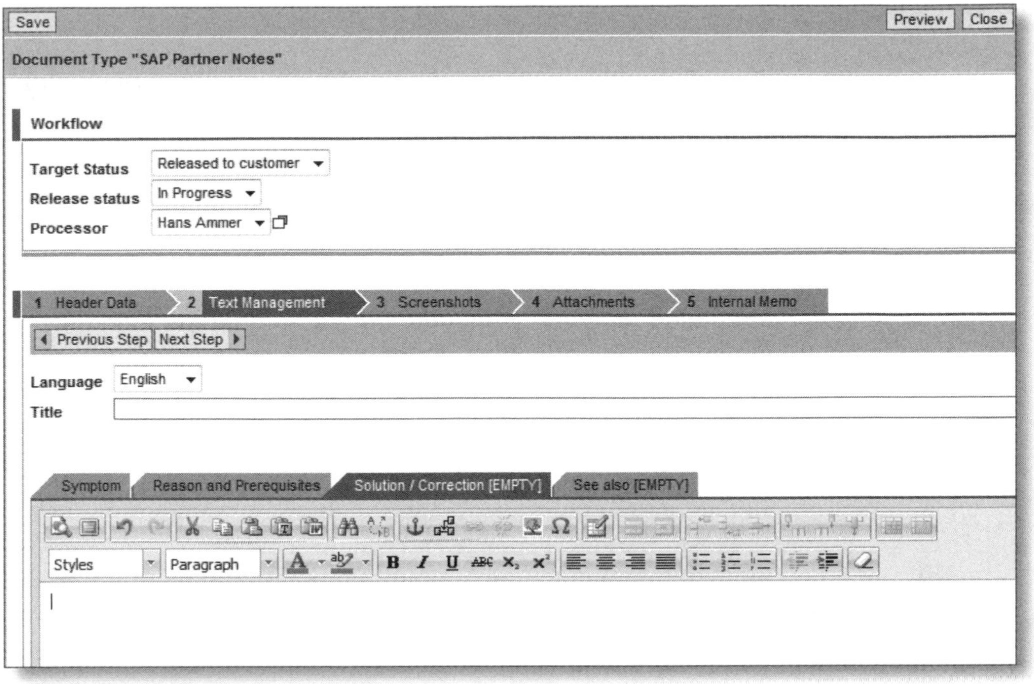

Figure 9.18 Creating a New Partner Note

If you have any questions about the solution proposed, you can send information to support at any time without having to change the status of the message. The partner employee can react accordingly and call you or send you information. If the solution proposal is successful, confirm the solution and close the message. The message confirmation is forwarded to the underlying system as a status change, and the message is then also marked as completed in the partner's Service Desk.

In certain situations, a customer message may have been created on a partner's application component, but the problem does not involve the partner application. Depending on the partner, your customer message appears, via SAP, as a new message directly in the partner's Service Desk. The software partner's employee now establishes that he cannot provide a solution because the problem is not part of the partner's subject area. To return this message to a specialist at SAP, the partner employee adds a short internal note to the message, sets it to the right component, and selects the action Send Message to SAP.

Remote support   If remote support has to be carried out in your system to process your message, the employee who is currently processing your message can establish a remote service connection to your customer system. In many cases, this is useful if the cause of a malfunction has to be analyzed in the system itself or if settings have to be changed. Depending on the customer solution, two different methods can be used for remote support. In every case, you have to agree to the access to your customer system by storing in the secure area at SAP the temporary logon data and times for an SAP GUI logon, or by agreeing to the connection for desktop sharing via Netviewer and determining the release method.

Connection is always possible via Netviewer, but an SAP GUI logon is only possible for SAP Business All-in-One. This ensures that only authorized employees at the partner company access the system after various safety measures have been fulfilled. These safety measures check that the access is legitimate before the connection is established.

After the root cause of the malfunction has been rectified and your system is back in normal operation, the final information is exchanged via the message, and you can confirm the support employee's solution proposal.

9.5   SAP Solution Manager at Ferrero Deutschland MSC GmbH & Co. KG

Incident Management of SAP Solution Manager was so well-received by users and internal IT that they also wanted to use it in the Logistics/EWM area after the go-live. At the current stage of development of ITSM, the new SAP Solution Manager makes it possible to map all errors and problems (that are related to SAP in the wider sense of the word, i.e., including connected peripheral devices, subsystems, and similar) in one system.

Klaus Wehrle, Ferrero Deutschland MSC GmbH & Co. KG

Ferrero is an international confectionery company founded in Italy in 1946 and is still family owned to this day. Ferrero has 18 production plants worldwide. In 1956, the German company was founded with sites in Stadtallendorf (production) and Frankfurt/Main (administration).

Ferrero Deutschland MSC GmbH & Co. KG

In 2004, we converted all existing IT systems that had not been converted already to SAP systems. Our IT has been using SAP Solution Manager since 2006. In particular, we use *incident management*, *Change Request Management*, and the *Test Workbench*. The initial skepticism has since given way to high levels of acceptance in our company. Our developers and IT managers use SAP Solution Manager extensively.

Initial situation

In the context of the implementation project for introducing *SAP Extended Warehouse Management* (EWM, ramp-up 2007, production startup in 2008), we extensively used the *implementation/upgrade* functions of SAP Solution Manager in project management at Ferrero for the first time.

Project description

In doing so, we mapped all scenarios and processes down to the process step level and documented them completely. Of course, it made sense to use this documentation as the basis for the necessary tests in subsequent project phases (function, integration, and regression testing).

We used the *Test Workbench* (TWB) of SAP Solution Manager for that. Until the go-live in May 2008, we executed a total of 23 test plans with more than 100 test packages and more than 3,000 test steps. With such extensive test plans, we had to ask ourselves how we would organize the errors that were bound to be detected. Because this was a ramp-up project, we assumed that we would also have to communicate extensively with SAP with regard to the errors. Project management was also very interested in being able to check the current test progress and corresponding errors at any time.

After internally checking the alternatives (Microsoft Excel for error management, SAP OSS, internal emails, etc.) we decided to handle errors using the incident management of SAP Solution Manager.

Process Step	Executed By	Comments
Create a message	Key users	Directly in SAP Solution Manager or from test execution
Assign to processor	Support team for application area	Optional, if the key user only enters the team
Process a message	Support team	
Forward to SAP	Support team	Optional
Correct the problem	Support team	Then *Solution Proposal* status
Test the solution	Key users	
Response to support team	Key users	If OK, close message. If not OK, back to *In Process*

Table 9.1 Ticket Processing Process

Benefits of this solution

This solution has the following benefits:

▶ The testers (mainly key users) can open a message directly from the test case.

▶ It was easy to learn how to enter errors because an SAP system was also used for this.

▶ When necessary, the internal processors (IT and SAP consultants) could forward these messages to SAP and monitor them.

▶ The current status of the messages could always be accessed at one central point.

▶ Reporting for the tests and the messages and their status was easy to integrate into overall project reporting.

Integration of the Service Desk with the Corporate Service Desk

In the context of the tests for this project, more than 200 messages were processed in this way.

SAP Solution Manager incident management was so well-received by users (key users) and internal IT (ticket processors) that they also wanted to use it in the Logistics/EWM area after the go-live.

Challenges

There was a potential conflict here because Ferrero was using a group-wide ticket system (Corporate Service Desk, CSD) for managing all messages, including those that are not SAP related. The internal service organization uses this system, which also serves as the central basis for management reporting in relation to the services. Hence, it was not possible to use an independent parallel system for managing SAP messages.

This situation was resolved by linking SAP Solution Manager to the existing system. To do so, the standard application programming interface (API) of SAP Solution Manager was configured and activated.

With some adjustments on the side of the group-wide Service Desk (CSD), this solution could go live after a few weeks. Nothing was programmed or modified in SAP Solution Manager. All it took was some additional configuration settings in the action profile to trigger the desired processes for the desired status and times.

The interface has been set up for bidirectional communication so that SAP-related messages are also transferred from the central Service Desk to SAP Solution Manager for further processing there. This is of particular benefit if forwarding to SAP is necessary.

Next we provide a short description of the functions offered by this link: The transfer of messages from the central system to SAP Solution Manager takes place according to specific rules, for example, the message affects an SAP system and is created in the German folder in CSD.

Function scope of the central Service Desk

▶ **Transfer of a message (processing in SAP Solution Manager)**
A message can automatically be transferred from CSD to the Service Desk of SAP Solution Manager. In this case, further processing takes place in SAP Solution Manager.

Rules for ticket transfer

▶ **Transfer of a message (processing in CSD)**
A message can be automatically transferred from the Service Desk to SAP Solution Manager for information purposes. In this case, further processing takes place in the central Service Desk.

▶ **Transferring additional information**
If additional information becomes known during the processing of a support enquiry, this information can be forwarded directly to the SAP Solution Manager Service Desk.

▶ **Message processing transfer**
For each support enquiry, there is a *leading system*. This property

can be transferred. However, this is only possible from the leading system. To transfer the *Active System* status, it then suffices to change the active system in the central service desk and save the support enquiry.

▶ **Closing a message**
If a support enquiry is closed in the central Service Desk, this status is automatically transferred to the Service Desk of SAP Solution Manager. As a result, the support enquiry is also closed. The support enquiry in the SAP Solution Manager Service Desk is set to *Closed* and the solution is documented as *Information*.

Service Desk of SAP Solution Manager

The function scope of the SAP Solution Manager Service Desk is identical to that of the central Service Desk.

In the SAP system, no configuration other than the interface configuration was necessary for operation. In addition, however, the actions for creating and regularly updating the message contents in CSD were automated:

▶ If the message is created as new and without errors in SAP Solution Manager, it is transferred directly to CSD when it is saved.

▶ If an error-free message does not have the status *New* or *Closed*, that is, when it is being processed, the additional contents of the message are transferred for updating in CSD when the message is saved in SAP Solution Manager.

All other functions except for the closing of messages are controlled using the menu. The respective actions are always executed when the support message is saved.

Transfer and processing of messages using the central Service Desk

To transfer the processing of a support message created in SAP Solution Manager to CSD, you choose the action SENDING TO EXTERNAL SERVICE DESK. In Service Desk, a new message is created with the transferred data. The active system for this support message is then CSD.

▶ **Transferring a message or updating content (processing in SAP Solution Manager)**
As described previously, the messages from SAP Solution Manager are automatically transferred to CSD, and all changes are updated as soon the message has at least the status *In Process*. Each subsequent saving (irrespective of the status) in SAP Solution Manager has the effect that the contents are also updated in CSD.

If the message does not exist there yet, a new message is created. The active system for this support message is then SAP Solution Manager.

This action can also be called manually, but this is not necessary because the transfer has been automated. To do so, you can select the action UPDATE IN EXT. SERVICE DESK.

▶ **Transferring additional information**
Additional information is transferred with the text type *Description*. When you save the message, these additions are also transferred automatically to the CSD, and the message there is updated.

▶ **Message processing transfer**
If a support message is *In Internal Processing* in the Service Desk of SAP Solution Manager, processing can be transferred to CSD. This happens with the action SEND TO EXTERNAL SERVICE DESK and the subsequent saving of the support enquiry.

▶ **Closing a support message (in SAP Solution Manager)**
A support message is closed by changing the status to *Closed*. When the message is then saved, an action starts automatically, and the status of the support enquiry in CSD is also set to *Closed*.

Hence, the requirements of the central Service Desk are met; all messages are transferred there and constantly updated. The key users and the IT group of the EWM application could therefore still open and process their messages (now also in production) in SAP Solution Manager.

This approach has turned out to be very useful in a subsequent EWM upgrade to release 7.0 as well.

After the solution in the incident management area was introduced to our internal IT, other SAP areas (SAP NetWeaver BW, SAP ERP, and SAP CRM) announced that they would also like to test this form of message processing and use it in production, if appropriate.

Extension of usage areas

In the BW team, there was the particularity that support is organized in a decentralized manner, and various additional functions were thus required.

All incoming messages of the area are assigned to processors by a central position (*dispatcher*). The processors are then notified of the assignment of new messages through an email function. That is, the support team does not always have to be logged on to SAP Solution Manager to find out about new tasks. However, these requirements could be easily met by adjusting the status profile and enhancing the action profile.

Today, SAP Solution Manager manages the messages of almost all SAP areas, and the link to CSD means that all of the group's reporting requirements are met.

In 2010, the Change Request Management functions provided by SAP Solution Manager were progressively introduced to all SAP system landscapes. These days, these functions are, in most cases, used to generate follow-on documents of the change request type and thus form the basis of the integrated change process.

In the context of our ramp-up participation for SAP Solution Manager 7.1, we have already gained some experience with incident management in the new release.

The function was transferred to the new *IT service management (ITSM)* and now runs on the SAP CRM user interface of the web client UI. With this new interface, the integration of incident management into existing Web applications can be extended further. We are thus planning to integrate the creation of messages in our company portal. Depending on the role of the user, different input screens that are adapted to the tasks are displayed in the SAP CRM Web Client UI. Compared to an IT employee, a key user in the department, for example, sees a simplified input screen that is reduced to the minimum.

In particular, the standard document types have changed (e.g., SMIN instead of SLFN). The customer adjustments made to the copied document type SLFN → ZLFN had to be checked and implemented using the new document type SMIN → ZMIN. This basically meant customizing various profiles (also copied into the Z namespace) to meet the requirements for additional statuses, actions, and so on.

This could also mean customer adjustments that are now part of the standard. For example, with the link to the external Service Desk, messages are now synchronized automatically. Before this, a separate automatic action was required for this.

There was no problem applying the link to the central Service Desk. In the new 7.1 system, only standard customizing was necessary. After that was done, communication was restored.

The *Incident Management* work center enables access to old and new documents. Depending on the case, work continues in the GUI or SAP CRM Web Client UI. This is useful in particular in the transition phase after the upgrade. Due to the change of document type, active messages of both document types exist in the system for a certain period. This is due to the fact that messages of the old type that have not been closed yet are not converted to the new document type but are processed in the same way as before (in the work center and GUI) until they are closed. After they are closed, a complete switch to SAP CRM Web Client UI processing is possible. To keep this period as brief as possible, we tried to process old messages as completely as possible in preparation for the upgrade.

The processing of messages has also changed. Central action control no longer exists. Instead, processing now takes place in the respective subject area assignment blocks. For example, there is a separate assignment block for communication with SAP. This now includes the corresponding actions for message processing.

At the current stage of development of ITSM, the new SAP Solution Manager now makes it possible to map all errors and problems (that are SAP related in the wider sense of the word, i.e., including connected peripheral devices, subsystems, and similar) in one system.

This means that the next step toward central service management in SAP Solution Manager can now be taken.

As the next step, we are planning to use the Service Desk for the entire SAP system landscape.

The Author

Klaus Wehrle has worked in IT at Ferrero Deutschland GmbH since 1991. In this time, he has completed a variety of tasks in the development and IT administration areas. He has been head of the SAP Solution Manager IT area for two years. There he is responsible for all SAP Solution Manager processes, for the coordination with all other IT areas, and for training SAP Solution Manager users.

9.6   SAP Solution Manager at itelligence AG

The global use of our SAP Solution Manager Service Desk has become a central component of our operating model. The use of a common tool is what really makes international coordination and cooperation possible. For example, to express it in numbers, this means that from 2009 to 2010, we were able to increase our revenues by far more than 50% in application management services (AMS) due to harmonized processes.

Armin Eckert, Global Service Manager, itelligence AG

Use of SAP Solution Manager

At itelligence AG, SAP Solution Manager is used as an integrated service and support tool in the local and global environment. It supports implementation projects (e.g., as a documentation platform) and is the central service desk tool for our SAP maintenance, hosting, and application management customers. Thus our customers worldwide can send all relevant incidents and queries directly to itelligence Support and track their progress on a standardized interface.

In addition to processing messages, we also use SAP Solution Manager to provide other services to our SAP maintenance customers. The EWA reports are provided through the central system, and our customers have the option to use the Maintenance Optimizer for the download of support packages and patches. Current maintenance certificates can also be distributed to our customer systems.

For more and more international consulting projects, the project management in SAP Solution Manager is used for documentation of business processes. This is also the case for delivery of itelligence industry solutions.

The SAP systems of our hosting and application management customers are also connected to the central SAP Solution Manager. Here, functions such as Computing Center Management System Monitoring (CCMS Monitoring), service level agreement reporting (SLA), the Maintenance Optimizer, and automatic distribution of maintenance certificates are used.

itelligence AG

As one of the leading international IT complete service providers in the SAP environment, itelligence AG is represented by more than 2,000 highly qualified employees in 20 countries and 5 regions (Asia, America, Western Europe, Germany/Austria/Switzerland, and

Eastern Europe). As a member of the SAP Business and Support Alliance, and as a Global Partner Hosting, Global Partner Services, and Global Value-Added Reseller, itelligence implements complex projects in the SAP environment for more than 4,000 customers worldwide. In 2006, itelligence received SAP Gold Partner status in Germany, in 2007 in the United States. With its comprehensive range of services—from SAP strategy consulting and SAP license sales to in-house development of SAP industry solutions to hosting and application management services (AMS), the company achieved total revenue of €272.2 million in 2010. In July 2010, itelligence was honored with the title of *Top Consultant*.

itelligence operates data centers in Germany, Malaysia, Poland, Switzerland, and the United States. As a certified SAP Global Partner Hosting, we are regularly checked by SAP AG for the safety and quality of the organization and processes. The service and support portfolio extends from SAP maintenance and hosting services to Application Management services. In the area of outsourcing and services, more than 1,000 customers are currently assisted by approximately 500 support employees in 15 international locations.

Although a few years ago, SAP Solution Manager was still primarily introduced in the context of consulting projects, integrated use increased continuously within the various departments at the international locations of itelligence AG.

Incident management represents the largest proportion of use of SAP Solution Manager. The mapping of all service processes using a central tool began in 2008 and is continuously further developed.

Service Desk

The strategic decision in favor of SAP Solution Manager as a central message processing tool within itelligence AG was already made at an early stage. The necessity of this project was given support in no small part by the decision of SAP to no longer process SAP maintenance for customers of value-added resellers using the shared SAP Support system CSS. Instead, SAP AG expanded the Service Desk function in SAP Solution Manager to include specific value-added reseller functions that allow value-added resellers to process messages using this tool.

CSS

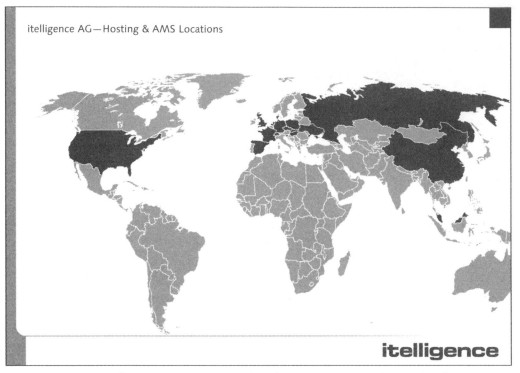

itelligence AG—Hosting & AMS Locations

itelligence

Figure 9.19 Site Hosting and Application Management Services (AMS)

Message processing   Access to the messages first needed to be designed to be more user-friendly for the customer. Here, special emphasis was given to the authorization-side separation of access to the messages for the various customers. We needed to ensure that the customers were clearly separated from each other and would only have access to their own messages.

Web service portal   Another new function was the enhanced integration into the SAP Support process. With the changeover to SAP Solution Manager, it was no longer possible for the maintenance customers of the value-added resellers to open their problem messages in SAP Service Marketplace. That's why we made a separate Web service portal available to our customers, one in which malfunction reports and other messages could be created within the scope of SAP maintenance. To continue to forward messages created in the SAP Solution Manager of itelligence AG to SAP Support, the corresponding interface needed to be enhanced. This also included automatic forwarding of messages with the priority *Very High* if these were submitted outside of the service times agreed with itelligence AG.

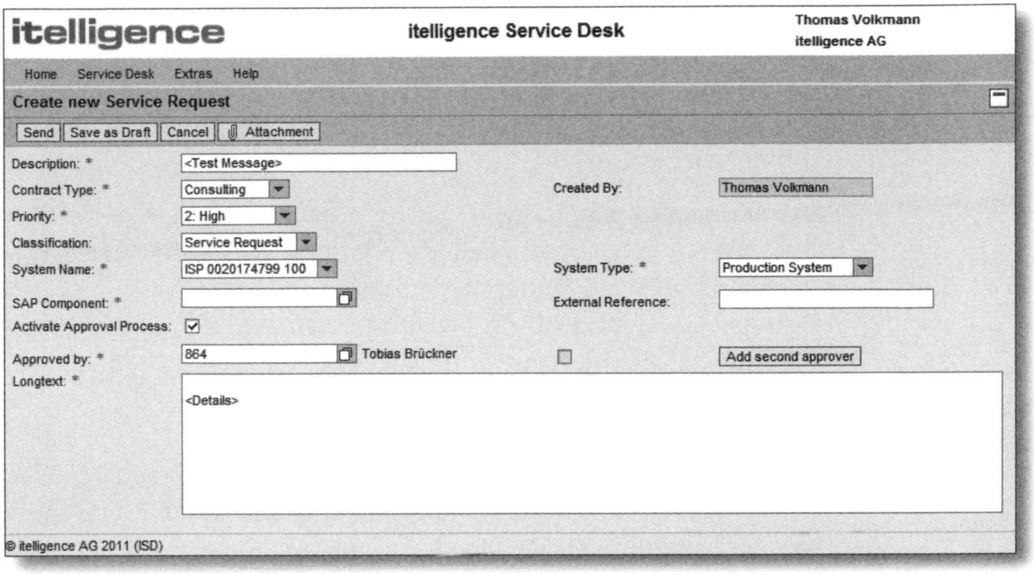

Figure 9.20 Creating a New Procedure

This somewhat difficult transition in the maintenance area from the message processing system shared with SAP Support to SAP Solution Manager began intensively in 2008 and lasted until the end of 2009. During this period, all itelligence maintenance customers were set up in a new SAP Solution Manager system. This affected the customers of all countries in which itelligence maintenance agreements exist.

This change also offered the opportunity to harmonize the various service processes that cater to our customers. In addition to maintenance, this applied and continues to apply to our consulting, hosting, and application management services, whose customers now direct their queries and problems to the respective area using this tool.

With the newly implemented web service portal, a "single point of contact" was made available to our customers, allowing them to contact itelligence Support with all questions. Within the scope of the application management services, our customers can also commission smaller developments or Customizing changes, or allow the entire end user support to be processed by the support staff of itelligence AG. The application management services are usually based on an individual agreement that regulates the scope, type of processing, and other delivery terms. For example, the service level can be agreed upon as part of this agreement. The service level can include priority-dependent reaction times or other service times (also within the framework of on-call services). A component of the ticket process is also an approval process for release of expenses by a certain customer contact.

In addition to pure incident management, a problem process and a change process were also defined in hosting, for example. The *problem* process is used for tracking and solving general problems, even if the associated incident was already resolved with a workaround that was provided. The *change* process includes an approval process subject to the principle of dual control or the inclusion of a change advisory board, as well as additional safety features, such as the *digital signature* for ensuring that only authorized persons grant approval. These processes were defined in such a way that they meet the strict requirements of the FDA (Food and Drug Administration), GxP, and ISAE 3402 (SOX compliance), as well as the standards ISO/IEC 20000-1:2005 in accordance with ITIL and the global requirements of SAP for hosting and application management services (SAP Global Hosting Partner and Global SAP-Certified Provider of Application Management Services).

Enhancements in incident management In addition to the standard functions of incident management in the Service Desk of the SAP Solution Manager for value-added resellers, a series of enhancements were made to meet the special requirements of itelligence AG:

- ▶ Integration of SLA times (initial reaction and solution times) depending on the customer, system, system location, priority, and category (incident, change request, service request), taking into account the respective service times of the responsible support organization

- ▶ Email integration that provides automatic notification via email in case of status change and escalation (the SLA times are about to be exceeded)

- ▶ Approval process for release of expenses

- ▶ Delegation provisions

- ▶ Ticket-based time recording with integration in the time sheet (CATS)

- SAP Solution Manager interface for connection to the custom Service Desk of SAP Solution Manager

- Within itelligence AG, all live customer services (SAP maintenance, hosting, Application Management services) are processed through SAP Solution Manager. For example, the SAP Maintenance and Application Management Service teams of itelligence in the countries of China, Denmark, Germany, Malaysia, the Netherlands, Poland, Switzerland, Spain, the United Kingdom, and the United States, as well as the Hosting teams in the data centers in Denmark, Germany (Bautzen and Bielefeld), Malaysia, Poland, Switzerland, and the United States, use this tool.

But that's not all—the SAP Solution Manager of itelligence is subject to ongoing further development and expansion of use. For the coming months, we have planned the following enhancements:

Further use of SAP Solution Manager

- Full-text searches for customers and support staff (in the message long text and attached documents)

- Integration of external partners in the delivery process

- Release upgrade to SAP Solution Manager 7.1 with new web client UI

As previously mentioned, the use of SAP Solution Manager at itelligence AG is not just restricted to service and support. It is recommended to customers that they use SAP Solution Manager project management for documentation of business processes and project results in implementation projects. Within the scope of the project, the range of use extends from the central document repository to the mapping of the Business Blueprint to the documentation of all individual developments and Customizing settings in the configuration. The structures created can be used for test management in SAP Solution Manager. itelligence supplies customers with guidelines for content structure, document templates, and content.

This is also the basis for an uninterrupted transition from implementation to live support through SAP maintenance, hosting, and Application Management.

SAP Solution Manager is also a central tool of the *Business Solution Platform* for internal management of itelligence industry solutions. The itelligence industry solutions are fully documented in the SAP Solution Manager of itelligence AG. Templates and Business Configuration Sets

Template management

(BC sets) are used for the delivery of the system settings of the solution itself. The structure and documentation are delivered to customers as the SAP Solution Manager project transport for the itelligence systems.

In the hosting environment in the data centers of itelligence AG, we also use SAP Solution Manager in other areas. In this way, all supported customer systems are monitored with system monitoring. The alerts generated there guarantee continuous monitoring and thus ensure high availability for these systems. The collected data, together with the EWA reports created, also goes into the reporting made available to our customers. The other services mentioned earlier (Maintenance Optimizer and maintenance certificates) are called up in the data centers using a central SAP Solution Manager.

The Author

Thomas Volkmann studied Sports Science at Bielefeld University and Economics at Bielefeld Technical College. Since 2002, he has been one of the SAP Solution Manager experts at itelligence AG in Bielefeld. Along with overseeing numerous consulting projects in the various areas of SAP Solution Manager, he shares the responsibility for supporting and developing the global SAP Solution Manager used by itelligence AG for the processes designed for customers.

Technical Operations with SAP Solution Manager consist, in part, of operating the technical infrastructure, but they mainly concern the applications that are operated on this infrastructure. This chapter gives you an overview of the tools and functions that are available for technical operations in SAP Solution Manager.

10   Technical Operations

The high demand for new information technology over the past 30 years has accelerated the ever-growing market of software solutions. Solutions now become outdated in a matter of a few years, with solution landscapes becoming more powerful and thus increasingly heterogeneous and complex all the time. Consequently, IT organizations responsible for maintaining solution landscapes have been under more constant pressure than almost any other department. Operating costs need to be kept as low as possible, while at the same time ensuring the stability of the solutions and the integration of new products.

Despite the more complex requirements, operating costs are frequently brought down by downsizing teams or delegating tasks to central service providers that oversee many systems. Transferring the knowledge necessary to perform new tasks, substituting experienced staff, and monitoring systems efficiently are becoming increasingly difficult. To counteract this, there is an increasing focus in the area of technical operations on preconfigured content based on best practices, together with as much automation of the operating processes as possible.

Essentially, SAP solutions can be divided into three areas, from a technical operations perspective: Business processes, applications, and infrastructure (see Figure 10.1).

Areas of technical operations

Technical Operations with SAP Solution Manager include, in part, operating the technical infrastructure (such as network, storage subsystems, hardware, and printers) but mainly the applications that are operated on this infrastructure. In most enterprises, the area of infrastructure operations is covered by integration partners.

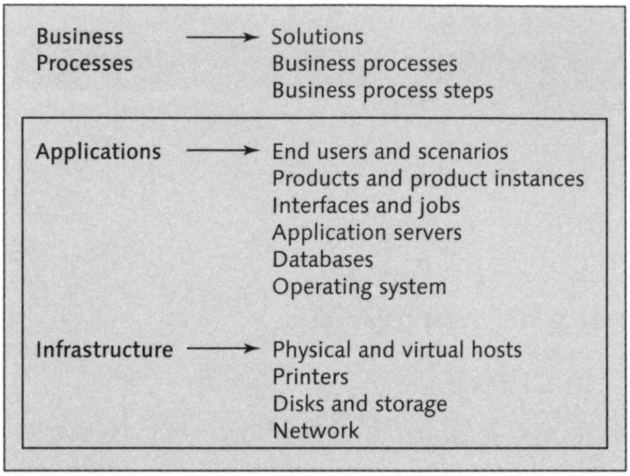

```
Business          ────────▶  Solutions
Processes                    Business processes
                             Business process steps

Applications      ────────▶  End users and scenarios
                             Products and product instances
                             Interfaces and jobs
                             Application servers
                             Databases
                             Operating system

Infrastructure    ────────▶  Physical and virtual hosts
                             Printers
                             Disks and storage
                             Network
```

Figure 10.1 Scope of Technical Operations

Application   Application operations are focused on operating systems, databases, and application servers. Different applications run on the application servers (such as SAP CRM, SAP NetWeaver Portal). Essentially, no distinction is made between SAP and non-SAP applications. Multiple applications and the connections between them (on the basis of RFC or HTTP) are grouped together in technical scenarios that can also include the end users of the applications (for End User Experience Monitoring, EEM).

Operating the actual business processes and solutions on these applications is part of the *operating business processes* process (see Chapter 11). Technical Operations with SAP Solution Manager include all of the necessary tools for a heterogeneous customer landscape.

Monitoring   If you examine the process of Technical Operations (see Figure 10.2), each customer normally starts by manually monitoring his system. To minimize the work in monitoring, threshold values are defined. If the monitored values exceed or fall below these thresholds, the administrator is automatically alerted. The challenge here is to not generate a separate alarm for each threshold infringement, as this would inundate the administrator with messages. The aim is to group together the events that occur into useful alerts. In the new SAP Solution Manager, there is a new infrastructure for Technical Monitoring and Alerting that makes it possible to monitor systems, databases, and hosts. In addition to this, special applications are provided for monitoring SAP NetWeaver Process Integration systems (SAP NetWeaver PI) and SAP NetWeaver Business Warehouse scenarios (BW), which also include SAP BusinessObjects solutions. End User Experience Monitoring (EEM) makes it possible to monitor the availability and response times of a previously defined scenario from the point of view of the end user (from various distributed locations). EEM also makes it possible to ensure that performance problems (either in the application or in the location's connection) are automatically reported before an end user notices the problem and has to create a message in the Service Desk.

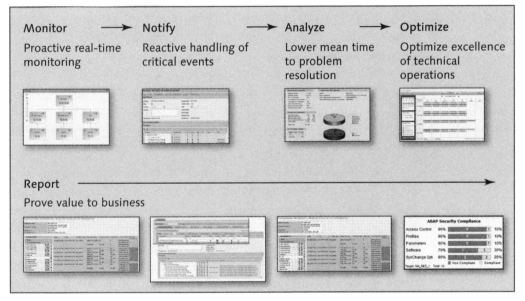

Figure 10.2 Process of Technical Operations

Furthermore, Connection Monitoring provides the opportunity of monitoring the connections between systems, and self-monitoring makes sure that the SAP Solution Manager itself, as well as all of the necessary infrastructure, is available.

When a problem is identified, you can notify the relevant contact person (or the group) by various means. These include, of course, email and SMS, and also integration into the incident management included in SAP Solution Manager (based on SAP CRM 7.0). The automatically generated message can then be used as a container to

Notification

document all changes and the entire analysis that is carried out during the course of processing the alert.

Analysis The Root Cause Analysis in Technical Operations provides a tool aimed at identifying underlying problems and including experts who can help solve the problems, if needed. It is important here to have standardized tools that always function the same, regardless of the type of technical system, thereby enabling an initial analysis without strong background knowledge of the technology or application.

If the solution to the problem requires changing the technical systems, this can be carried out and scheduled using the Technical Administration. The IT Calendar included in this clearly shows the work modes (such as maintenance window or downtime) that have already been scheduled. Additionally, you have the option of managing work modes and scheduling new work modes, as well as shutting down the systems. You can also use the integrated Notification Management to inform end users of the systems about any schedule maintenance windows and non-availability. Each user can decide how he wants to be notified. You also have access to tools for task management and planning of regular administrator tasks.

Reporting Another important aspect is reporting. In the *Technical Analysis* area (see Section 10.6), a distinction is made between two reporting methods. The technical key performance indicator (KPI) reporting is based on technical key figures that are used in operations to optimize system or create capacity plans. Tools available here include *SAP EarlyWatch Alert* or *Interactive Reporting*. If the reports delivered in the standard system are not sufficient, customers can define their own reports on the same data basis and insert these into the navigation. In the area of management reporting, on the other hand, more highly aggregated information is used. This data is prepared and made available in the form of service level reports or management dashboards. Customers can also define their own dashboard applications and integrate them in the standard system supplied.

Work center The diverse tasks within solution operations are spread out clearly across the following work centers:

- ▶ Technical Monitoring
- ▶ Technical Administration
- ▶ Root Cause Analysis

The personalized user interface, ability to work centrally, automation, and efficient transfer of knowledge give experts the time they need to concentrate on their core competencies.

This, in turn, allows small teams to monitor and manage complex system landscapes, while making the services they offer transparent to the user. SAP Solution Manager therefore makes it possible to keep IT know-how inside companies or outsource it and monitor the services provided.

10.1 Technical Monitoring

With SAP Solution Manager 7.1, a new infrastructure for central Technical Monitoring of system landscapes was introduced. These new applications are grouped together in the *Technical Monitoring* work center (see Figure 10.3).

New monitoring and alerting infrastructure

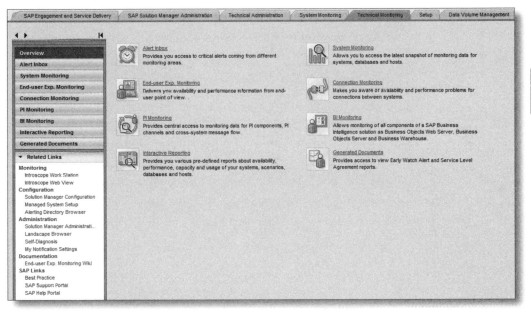

Figure 10.3 "Technical Monitoring" Work Center

The work center offers the following views (as listed in the next section in Figure 10.4):

▶ In the ALERT INBOX, all incoming alerts of the work center's various monitoring applications are displayed.

- The SYSTEM MONITORING application allows monitoring of the current status of technical systems, as well their instances, databases, and hosts.

- In END-USER EXP. MONITORING, recorded scripts are executed from several locations on an automated basis, and their results are evaluated to draw conclusions about the availability and performance of scenarios from the perspective of the end user.

- In CONNECTION MONITORING, RFC, and HTTP connections from ABAP systems are tested for their availability and performance.

- PI MONITORING enables monitoring of the runtime components of all SAP NetWeaver PI domains that are connected to SAP Solution Manager.

- In BI MONITORING, both the process chains of connected BW systems and the status of the components of one or more SAP business object systems are monitored.

- In the INTERACTIVE REPORTS area, you can centrally display the development over time of the most important metrics for your managed systems and solutions, at any time.

10.1.1   Alert Inbox

The Alert Inbox (see Figure 10.4) provides an overview of all the alerts generated from the various applications of the *Technical Monitoring* work center. This application can therefore be used to create centralized reactive alerting for all of the technical components in the landscape. Whereas the monitoring applications typically map the current state of the landscape and its components, the Alert Inbox can also be used to investigate problems that occurred in the past.

Queries The Alert Inbox enables various views of the existing alerts by means of configurable queries. The standard system includes preconfigured queries that group together the existing alerts in the Alert Inbox according to scenarios or object types, for example. There are prepared queries for database alerts or alerts that were generated for the various EEM scenarios, for example. Additionally, users can define and save their own queries. The Alert Inbox makes it possible to automatically refresh the display after a specified time. This means that the window containing the Alert Inbox can be left permanently open without the need for manual updating.

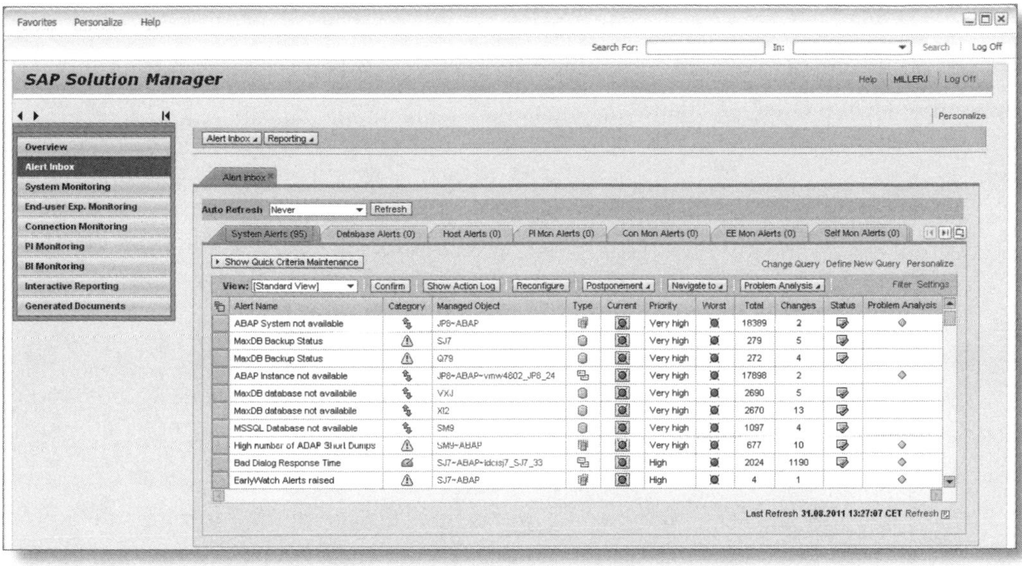

Figure 10.4 Alert Inbox

The top part of the Alert Inbox displays the current (i.e., unconfirmed) alerts. One line displays the alert and the landscape object on which the alert was generated. For each alert, the inbox displays the last reported status and the worst reported status. This makes it possible to display a problem that was already rectified, such as the non-availability of an important system. Even if the system is available at the current point in time and is therefore displayed with a green status in terms of availability, the Alert Inbox could still contain alerts for periods in which the system was not available. In this case, the system's current availability status is displayed as green, and the worst status is displayed in red. If this alert is selected, the lower part of the table displays all of the periods in which the system was not available.

The alerts displayed in the alert table can be sorted or filtered according to various criteria. The filter criteria can be saved. This way, the user can generate a filter that only displays alerts that belong to a specific category or only display alerts that currently have a red status.

Filter

423

Confirmation and
follow-up actions

All the alerts displayed in the Alert Inbox can be confirmed. Here, you have the option of confirming one or more alerts together with all their alert groups, or you can confirm individual alert groups. Follow-up actions can be generated from alerts for further processing. This type of follow-up action can consist of a Service Desk message or a notification by email or SMS. Depending on the configuration, Service Desk messages are either generated automatically or manually, that is, from an existing alert. The most important information from the alert is copied here to the Service Desk message. The number and the current processing status of a Service Desk message generated from an alert are displayed in the Alert Inbox as additional information. It is also possible to go directly from an alert in the Alert Inbox to the generated Service Desk message. If a Service Desk message that was generated from the Alert Inbox is set to completed, it is possible to also confirm the alert in the Alert Inbox automatically.

Another example of a follow-up action from the Alert Inbox is a notification. It is possible here to automatically generate an email or SMS when an error situation is identified. The recipients or recipient lists used here can be maintained in Notification Management in the *Technical Administration* work center (see Section 10.5). You can centrally assign recipients of one or more alerts and choose how these recipients are automatically notified in the templates for monitoring configuration. As with Service Desk messages, it is also possible to generate notifications manually from existing alerts in the Alert Inbox. For example, a processor of an alert can notify a colleague of the existing problem by email. The email contains all of the details of the problem.

Reset alerts

If you cannot rectify the cause of an alert immediately but you do not want the alert to be displayed in the Alert Inbox, you can put alerts on hold for a specific period of time; for example, there is a performance problem on a server that can only be solved by installing additional hardware. If this hardware is not available until a later date, the performance alert is displayed until this time as a red alert in the Alert Inbox. To avoid this problem, the alert can be put on hold in the list until a specified time. The alert is then hidden in the Alert Inbox until the specified time, although it continues to be updated in the background. At any time, you can display all the alerts on hold or return them to the Alert Inbox.

To display additional information about a monitored object in the landscape, the Alert Inbox provides various options for navigating to other SAP Solution Manager components. These include displaying the current state of the monitored landscape object in the System Monitoring application. For ABAP or Java systems, it is possible to log directly on to the system; additional information about all of the landscape objects can then be displayed in the landscape browser itself.

Methods for analyzing the problem can be started from the Alert Inbox. For example, you can schedule regular snapshots of the ongoing work processes in an ABAP system or of the users logged on to the ABAP system. The recorded snapshots can then be displayed from the Alert Inbox to analyze the cause of a problem. It is also possible to schedule regular thread dumps for Java systems.

To minimize the number of displayed alerts, individual alerts concerning the same problem are brought together in what are known as *alert groups*. This means that metrics that are recorded at five-minute intervals do not lead to a new alert for each notification. Instead, the system checks whether an alert already exists for the problem identified. If so, the existing alert is expanded into an alert group containing a start time and an end time. This ensures that the user is not informed of the same problem multiple times.

Alert groups

To reduce the workload of multiple users in the Alert Inbox, alert groups can be assigned to a person. That way, a processor can either assign an alert group to himself or to another person, as well as adding a comment. This is useful if there is a small team processing the alerts, and there is to be no tracking by means of a full Service Desk message.

To display the cause of a generated alert or an alert group, you can examine the alert detail view (see Figure 10.5). This displays all of the information for an alert group, such as the start and end times of the alert, the current status and processor, and also the number and status of any Service Desk message that has been generated. You can also display additional documentation for an alert, which can contain context-sensitive links to various analysis tools in the SAP Solution Manager, or to transactions of the monitored systems. Customers can configure this to store their own documentation containing customer-specific instructions, as well as the alert documentation

Alert detail view

provided by SAP. In addition, the alert details can display all of the monitored metrics that contributed to the alert group. Because the alert group can cover a large period of time, the minimum, maximum, and last reported values are displayed for each metric to make it easier to localize the problem. A description and the applicable threshold value can be displayed for each metric. In the configuration, customer-defined documentation can be saved for each individual metric. To find out more information about the progress of a metric, the user can switch from each of an alert's metrics to metric monitoring. Here, the progress of an individual metric is displayed together with the applicable threshold values, either in a graph or a table. This way, the Alert Inbox enables a complete representation of the problems identified in a monitored system landscape.

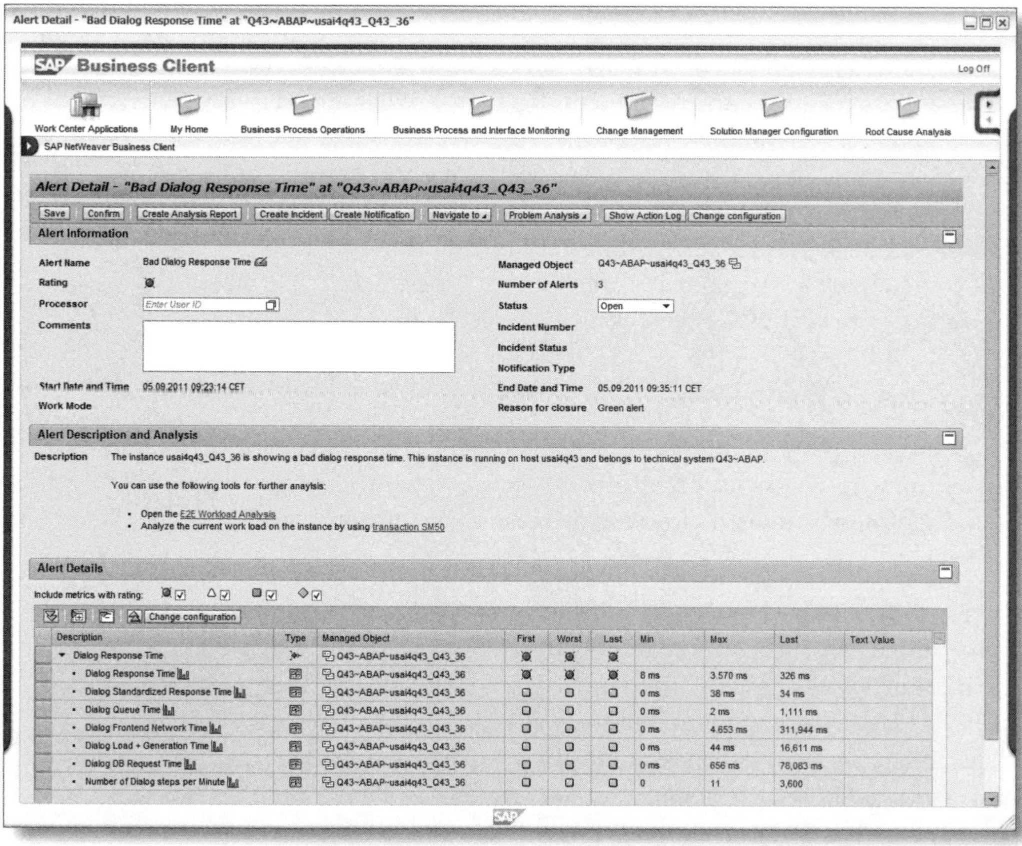

Figure 10.5 Alert Details

10.1.2 System Monitoring

The System Monitoring application provides an overview of the current status of the monitored technical systems, together with their instances, databases, and hosts.

On the entry screen, the user selects one or more systems from a list and displays the current status of those systems. As with the other monitoring applications in the work center, the selection list can be personalized, and multiple personalized queries can be saved.

After the systems have been selected and the System Monitoring application has started, an overview page is displayed showing the current status of the systems (see Figure 10.6). This overview page shows the status of the individual monitoring categories, such as the current availability or performance of the systems. A system administrator can use this overview to gain a quick look at whether a system is currently in a bad state and whether unconfirmed alerts exist for a system. From here, you can switch selectively to the Alert Inbox by clicking on the ALERT icon to display in detail and process the unconfirmed alerts for a system. The system list also displays the current work mode of the individual systems that were set in Work Mode Management in the *Technical Administration* work center (see Section 10.5).

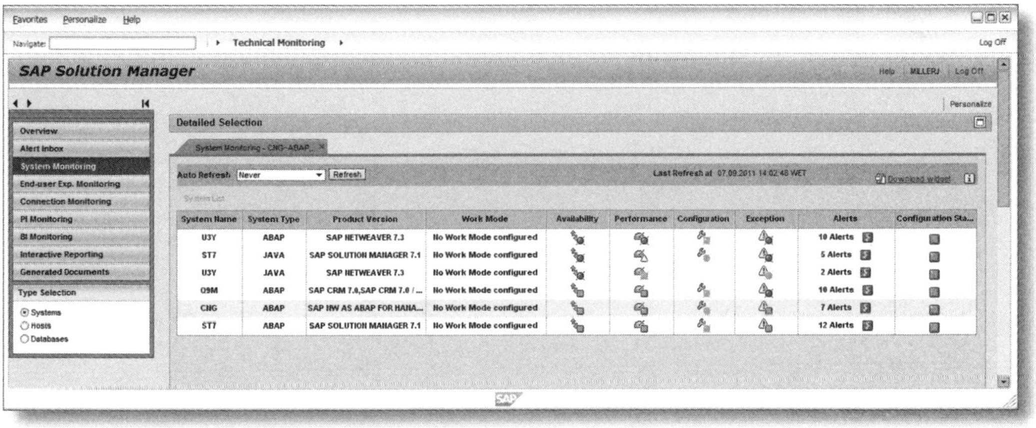

Overview page

Figure 10.6 System Overview in SAP Solution Manager

The System Monitoring application can automatically update the screen. This means that the application can remain open all the time, and new problems are displayed without any additional user interaction. The period until the next automatic update can be set on the top screen border.

System hierarchy   From the system list, you can switch to the system hierarchy display by clicking on the name of a system (see Figure 10.7). The system hierarchy displays all of the monitored landscape objects in the selected system, such as instances, databases, and hosts, in a graphical ranking order, and maps the logical connection between these landscape objects. This hierarchy does not have to be configured manually; instead, the SAP Solution Manager landscape configuration is identified during configuration. The hierarchy display shows the individual categories for each landscape object, as well as the number of unconfirmed alerts. Context-sensitive navigation to the Alert Inbox is also possible from here to display the alerts for the monitored object. You can return to the system list via the navigation links on the top screen border.

Figure 10.7 System Monitoring with System Hierarchy Display

Events and metrics   In addition to the graphical representation of the system hierarchy, System Monitoring displays a tree with all of the events and metrics collected from the monitored objects. This makes it possible to navigate from the general status of each landscape object, through the individual categories, to the individual metrics. The last measured value is displayed for each metric. Additionally, the tooltips for each metric specify additional information, such as the set threshold value or the time of the last measurement. Additionally, you can view the history of all measured values for each metric from the reporting to assess the time at which a metric began to worsen. The value history is initially displayed as a graph that enables further navigation via time selection (see Figure 10.8).

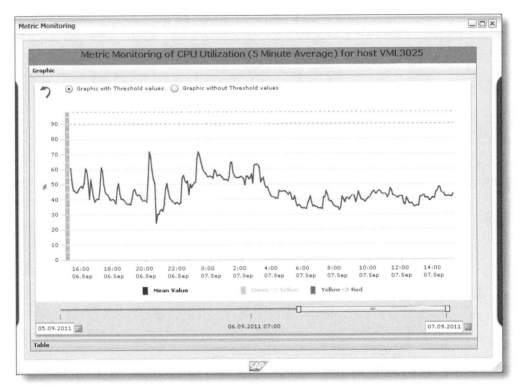

Figure 10.8 Metric Monitoring

The System Monitoring application therefore enables end-to-end navigation, from the rough overview, through the current state of a list of systems, to the individual metrics and their value history.

10.1.3 Connection Monitoring

The System Monitoring application is restricted to monitoring metrics that are measured within the technical systems. However, to achieve overarching landscape monitoring, it is often also necessary to monitor the technical connections between systems. This is made possible by the *Connection Monitoring* application (see Figure 10.9).

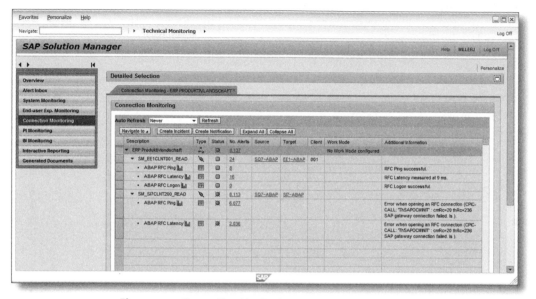

Figure 10.9 Connection Monitoring

Various technical systems are grouped together here in what is known as a *Technical Scenario*. Within the systems in this technical scenario, selected RFC and HTTP connections can then be monitored in terms of availability and performance.

Connection tests When configuring monitoring, you first define which of the existing system connections are used live and should therefore be monitored. These connections are then tested at regular intervals. The general availability of the connection, the latency time of the connection, and a logon test can be carried out.

The result of the connection test is displayed in a list that contains the names of the connections, the last result of the connection test, and the source and target systems. Additionally, if problems are identified, alerts are generated. These alerts can be processed in the Alert Inbox. The number of generated alerts is displayed in Connection Monitoring. From here, you can switch directly to the Alert Inbox.

For further processing, Service Desk messages or notifications by email or SMS can be generated from the alerts that are generated. Depending on the configuration, this either occurs automatically, as soon as an alert is generated, or manually from the Connection Monitoring application or the Alert Inbox.

10.2 Central Monitoring of SAP NetWeaver Process Integration

Today's system landscapes and business processes are often decentralized and have to be connected using various different interface technologies. SAP NetWeaver Process Integration (SAP NetWeaver PI) makes it possible to integrate business processes across multiple departments, organizations, or enterprises. The key issue here is choreographing the data exchange between the process components and, from a technical perspective, transferring business data in the form of XML messages between applications and systems. Figure 10.10 shows an integration scenario with participating process components that exchange messages with each other.

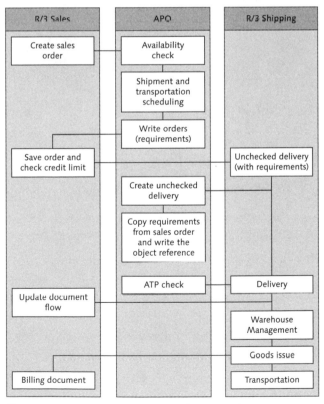

Figure 10.10 Integration Scenario with Process Components

Distributed
landscape

SAP NetWeaver PI translates and processes these messages and acts as the hub of a system landscape, thereby playing a central role. On the other hand, to prevent a *Single Point of Failure,* the runtime components of an SAP NetWeaver PI domain are mostly distributed in a decentralized way. This makes regular and automated monitoring of SAP NetWeaver PI essential to the smooth operation of your business processes. Figure 10.11 shows the technical view of a typical scenario with a distributed SAP NetWeaver PI domain and SAP Solution Manager.

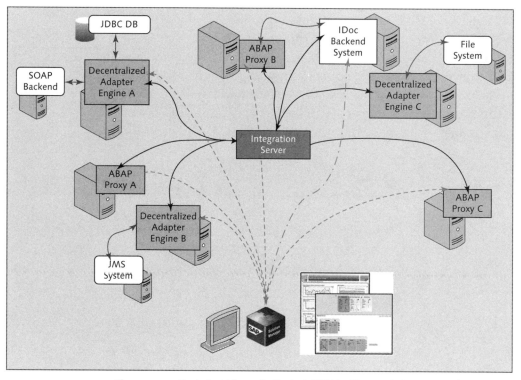

Figure 10.11 Technical View of a Typical SAP NetWeaver PI Domain and SAP Solution Manager

Monitoring
application

As a component of the *Technical Monitoring* work center, SAP Solution Manager 7.1 SP1 offers a monitoring application for SAP NetWeaver PI 7.11 SP6 and higher. This bundles and prepares important information about availability, message throughput, and message backlog. This enables centralized and automated monitoring of all the runtime components in all the connected SAP NetWeaver PI domains, which reduces the manual activities and the overall costs associated with these activities. The following aspects are in focus:

- With growing system landscapes, the SAP NetWeaver PI domains are also growing, leading to an increased need for centralized monitoring solutions. The primary objective is to bundle the variety of monitoring points in a centralized dashboard.

- The total cost of administration can be reduced by saving time and simplifying the monitoring processes for the following:

  - Regular system status checks

  - Shift handovers

  - Problem identification through to problem analysis

  - Context-sensitive navigation to the expert tools

- The following other functions of SAP Solution Manager can be closely integrated:

  - System Monitoring and End-to-End Root Cause Analysis

  - Alerting Infrastructure

  - Notification/Incident Management

- Manual monitoring activities for production systems can be reduced by means of central data collection.

- In some situations, it is necessary to find a specific message again to confirm its processing status to the specialist department, for example. Because message processing is seldom limited to one runtime component only, it is very useful to have a central content-based message search across all runtime components, including the message archives of an SAP NetWeaver PI domain.

This application gives you answers to the following questions: Detail view

1. What's the overall status of all SAP NetWeaver PI components in the live domain? Are there problems in the underlying technical systems?

2. How is the error trend developing for message processing of the business-critical interfaces?

3. What have the typical causes of errors been in the current calendar year? Have these also occurred in the past seven days? At what time of day do these errors usually occur?

4. Is there a backlog in message processing today? Is this backlog related to the total volume of processed messages?

5. Colleagues from the application departments are asking if messages for a business-critical interface are failing and how long this has been happening. On which runtime components did these errors occur, and what were the root causes?

6. Which channels of communication currently have errors, and which detail monitors are relevant to error handling?

7. On which runtime components are there currently the most failed messages, and which interfaces are affected?

8. How many messages arrived in the system this month via communication channel "XYZ"?

10.2.1 Starting and Navigation

SAP NetWeaver PI Monitoring is a component of the *Technical Monitoring* work center and includes all of the connected SAP NetWeaver PI domains, together with their technical systems and components (see Figure 10.12).

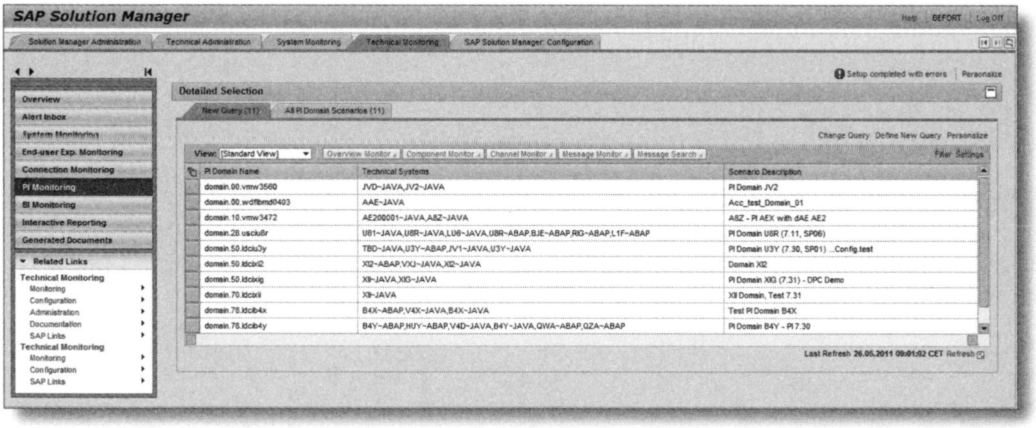

Figure 10.12 Selecting the Connected SAP NetWeaver PI Domain

10.2.2 Overview Monitor

The OVERVIEW MONITOR provides a view of the overall status of the selected SAP NetWeaver PI domain (see Figure 10.13).

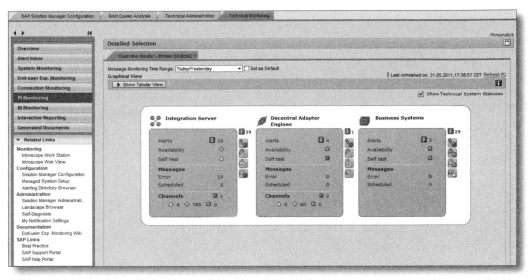

Figure 10.13 Aggregated Status Overview

Depending on the component type (integration server, non-central adapter engines, and business systems), you see details about the following:

▶ Number of accumulated alerts

▶ Availability

▶ Self-test of applications

▶ Communication channels per status group

▶ Number of messages with error status, currently in processing, total volume in selected time interval

If you select one of these component types, you can see further details. From Figure 10.14, you can see that the integration server consists of one ABAP and one JAVA stack. You can also see the SAP NetWeaver PI components developed in these. The individual SAP NetWeaver PI components run on technical systems. Their status, which is represented by the four icons on the right side of the gray box, comes from the System Monitoring application.

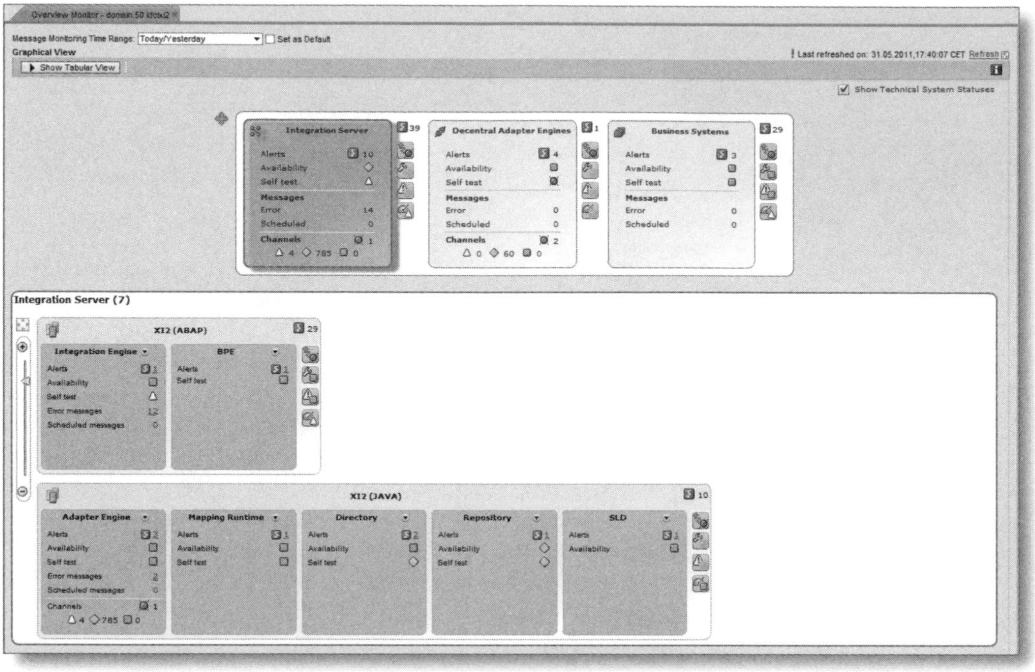

Figure 10.14 Overview of the Integration Server

Metrics In addition to the metrics for SAP NetWeaver PI, this information also makes it possible to monitor the metrics for the underlying technical systems (see Figure 10.15). This is important because even if the SAP NetWeaver PI system is stable, there could be problems in the underlying layers (technical system, application server, host, or database). The following metrics are available:

- Availability status
- Exception status
- Configuration status
- Performance status

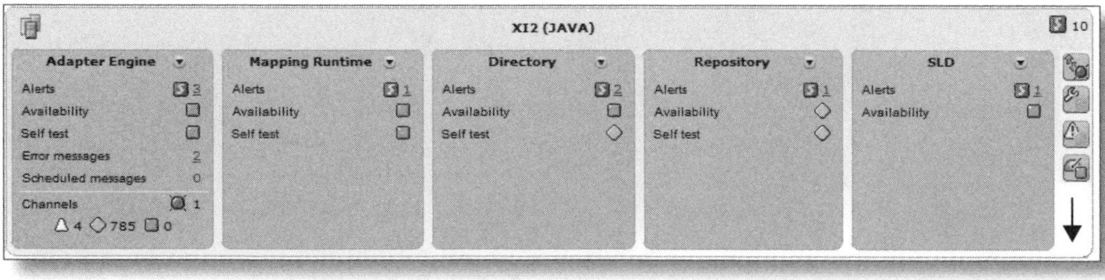

Figure 10.15 Aggregated Status from System Monitoring

Clicking on an icon (see the red arrow in Figure 10.15) takes you directly to the System Monitoring application (see Figure 10.16), where you can view further details (find out more in Section 10.1.2).

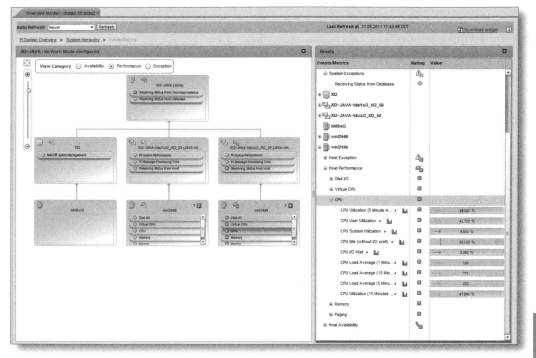

Figure 10.16 System Monitoring

10.2.3 Component Monitor

The COMPONENT3 MONITOR (see Figure 10.17) provides detailed information about the availability and status of individual application components. In addition to this, these tests can also be triggered manually, or specific notifications can be created in the selected context via email, SMS, or support tickets. The system selectively displays only the navigation options to expert tools for follow-up activities that are useful for the selected component and its release.

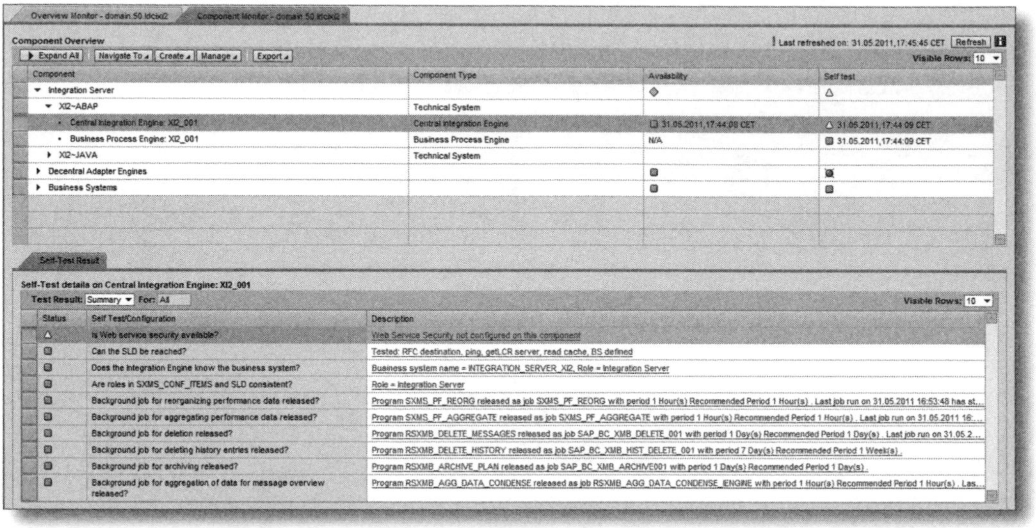

Figure 10.17 Component Monitor

10.2.4 Channel Monitor

Communication channels

Communication channels are adapter-specific, technical connections for exchanging data or business objects via defined protocols between different sources of data. If a communication channel has an error status, it cannot be used to receive or generate messages. In the SAP Solution Manager, you have the option of monitoring the communication channels for all adapter engines at a glance. In addition to the activation and processing status, the Channel Monitor (see Figure 10.18) also shows the relevant Channel Short Log and gives you the option of testing (ping), stopping, or starting communication channels. To carry out these activities, the dialog user must, of course, have the necessary authorizations on the target system.

10.2.5 Message Monitor

The *Message Monitor* is also a central monitor of all the runtime components in an SAP NetWeaver PI domain. The Message Monitor displays aggregated information about message processing and is divided into three submonitors.

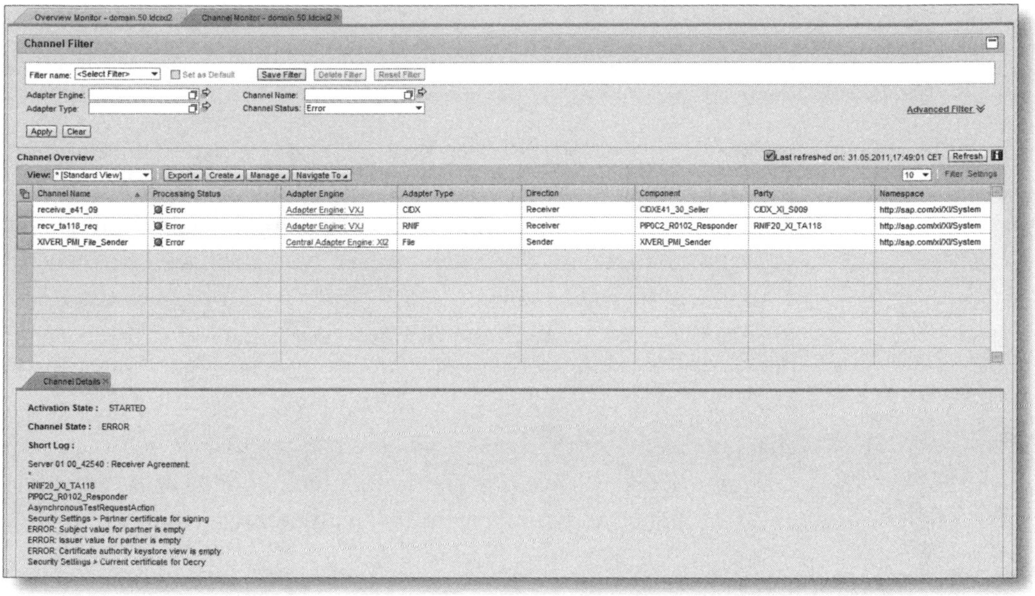

Figure 10.18 Channel Monitor

Selection Filter

The selection filter is the same in all three submonitors and it gives you the option of further restricting the output. You can restrict the time window and message status, as well as the sender and receiver attributes, and save these in *filters* to repeat the selection at any time (see Figure 10.19).

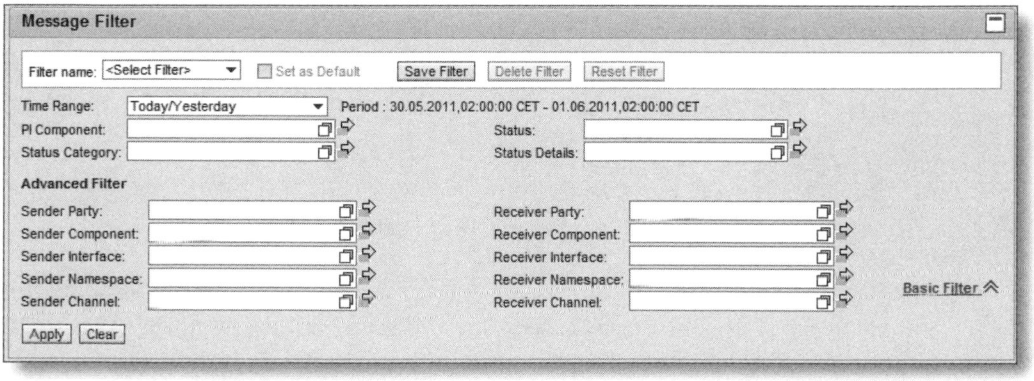

Figure 10.19 Filter in Message Monitor

Error Monitor

The Error Monitor only considers messages with any of the error statuses, and it consists of two layers.

View By Components Components displays the number of messages on each runtime component that have an error status. These messages are broken down in the drill-down section according to the top-10 sender or receiver components or sender or receiver interfaces (see Figure 10.20). On the right side, you can see the trend for either the Daily values for last 7 days or the Hourly values for last 24 hours. In the example below those options, you can see that of the 39,780 messages with an error status, 25,428 messages failed on the central adapter engine. At the same time, you can see that no message processing has taken place on this runtime component in recent days, and that therefore there have not been any error messages, either.

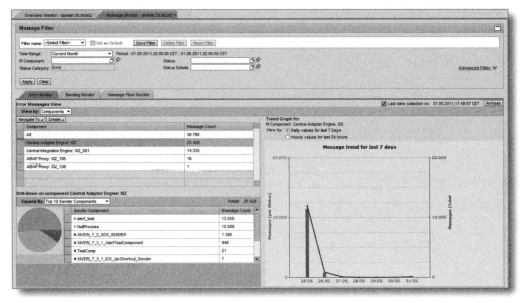

Figure 10.20 Message Error Monitor—Component View

View by Status View by Status shows how the failed messages are divided among the various error statuses for the selected time window. This view also offers a drill-down by sender or receiver component or sender or receiver interface. In Figure 10.21, you can see that most of the messages in the current month failed due to problems in the file adapter and that this error has also occurred in the previous seven days.

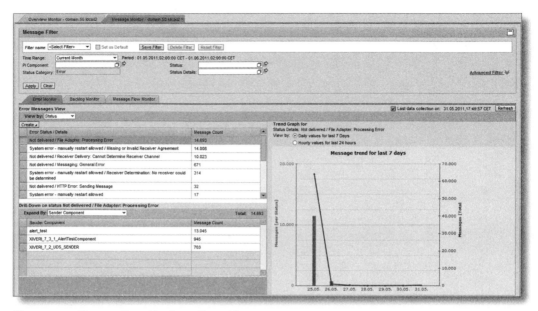

Figure 10.21 Message Error Monitor—Status View

Backlog Monitor

The Backlog Monitor is identical to the Error Monitor. The only difference is that the Backlog Monitor only considers messages that do not yet have a final status. These are messages that are still being processed and could therefore be in one of the queues.

Message Flow Monitor

The MESSAGE FLOW MONITOR (see Figure 10.22) considers all message statuses and can also be used across runtime components; in other words, you can select messages by means of their attributes, without having to know exactly which of the many runtime components the messages were processed on. You also have the option here, in the context of the selected messages, of switching to a local detail monitor for the current runtime component, at any time, or restarting or canceling the selected messages.

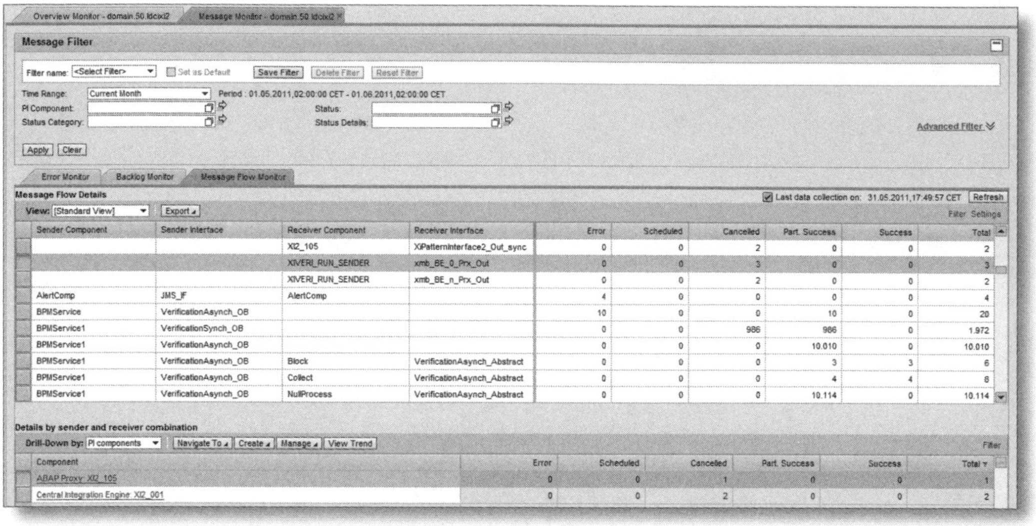

Figure 10.22 Message Flow Monitor

Example   In Figure 10.23, messages of sender component XI2_105 were selected. You can see that although 15 messages were successfully processed on the ABAP PROXY: XI2_105, they were then forwarded to the CENTRAL INTEGRATION ENGINE: XI2_001. There, all 15 messages encountered an error. In the next step, you could display the cause of the error.

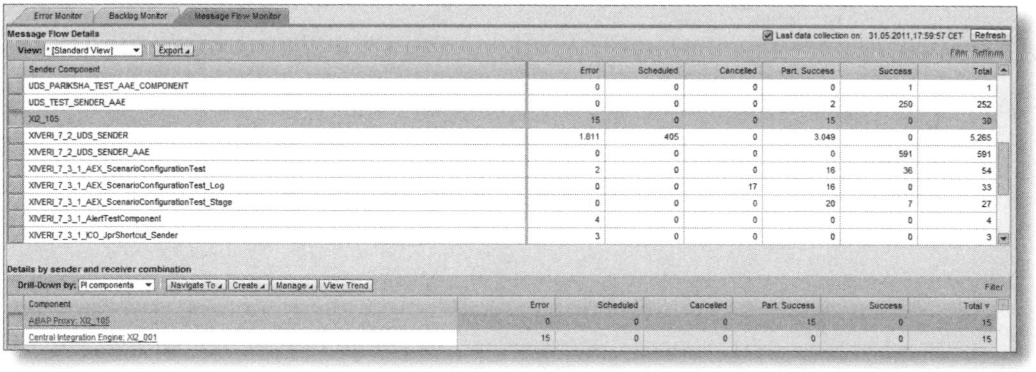

Figure 10.23 Message Flow Monitor—View by Sender Component

For reporting purposes, you can export the information for all the available time periods to Microsoft Excel.

Like the Error Monitor, the *View Trend* function (see Figure 10.24) also offers the option of displaying the message trend for the selected message scenario as a graph.

View Trend Function

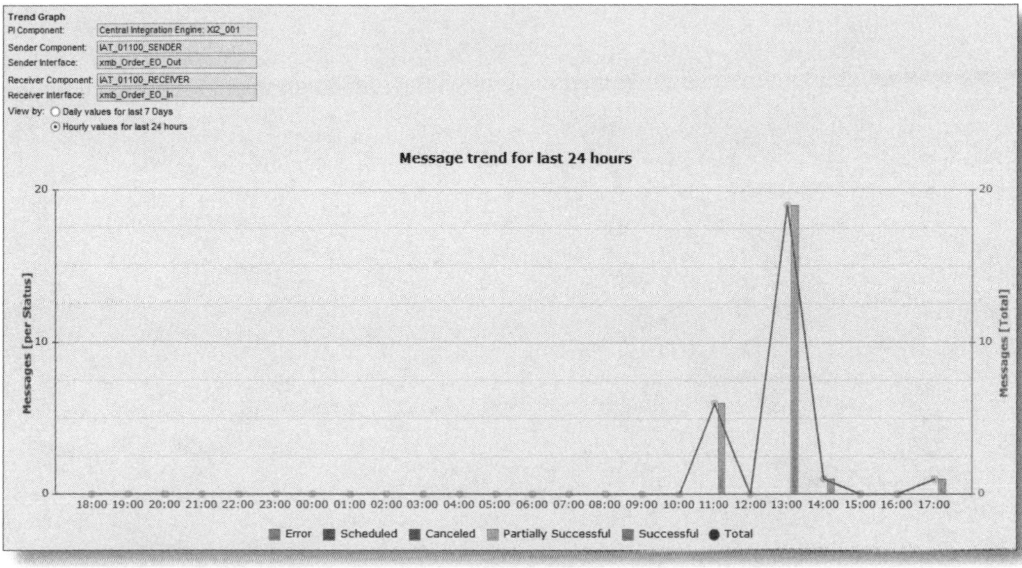

Figure 10.24 Message Flow Monitor—Message Trend View

10.2.6 Central Content-Based Message Search

If you had to find a very specific message, for example, one for customer name Smith and order number 1234567, this type of search was often very time-consuming in the past. Not only did you have to search separately on each runtime component but also the message might already have been archived, meaning you had to include both the runtime persistency and the archives in the search.

Central Message Search

There is a new function available, in cooperation with the SAP Solution Manager 7.1 SP2 and SAP NetWeaver PI 7.3 EHP1: *Central Message Search*. This new function makes it possible to search for messages on the basis of their content, across multiple runtime components, their runtime persistency, and archives. It is based on the *user-defined search* (UDS) of the local runtime components, which indexes selected message attributes during the runtime of message processing, in accordance with a previous configuration.

In Figure 10.25, the search is for messages with "Firstname = Hans" and any "Lastname = *". At the same time, the search is restricted to a time window and four out of the six runtime components on the selected domain.

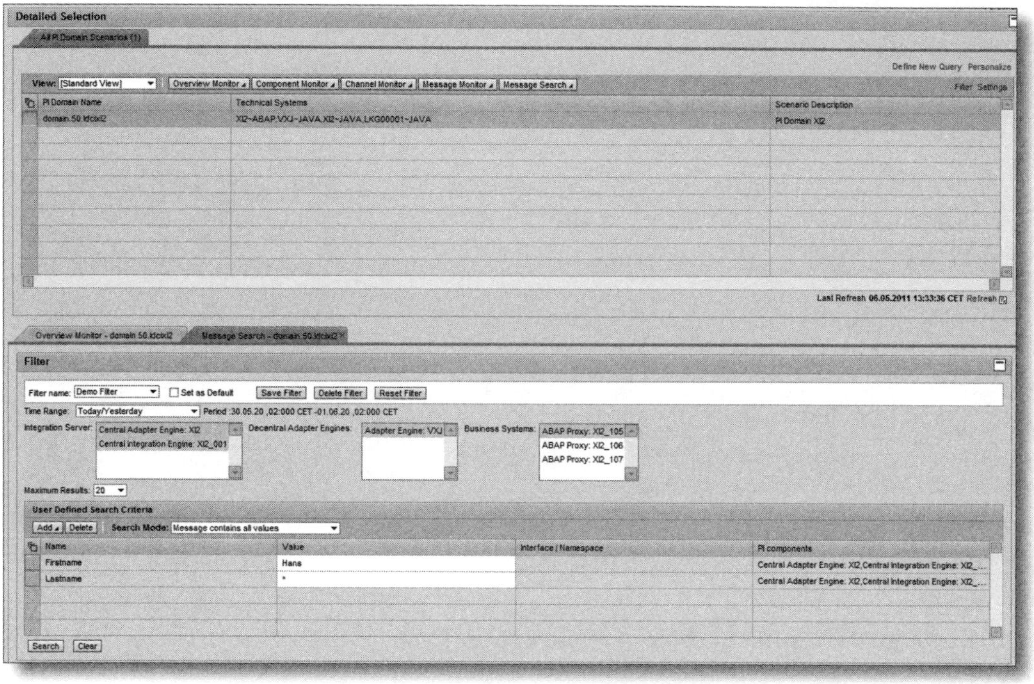

Figure 10.25 Central Message Search—Selection Criteria

The initial result of the search (see Figure 10.26) is information regarding the number of hits per runtime component. Below this, you will find a list of the messages found matching the search together with their attributes.

Follow-up activity

You can also create a support message (incident) at this point (see Figure 10.26), send a notification via email or SMS, or navigate directly to this message for the relevant runtime component to edit, for example.

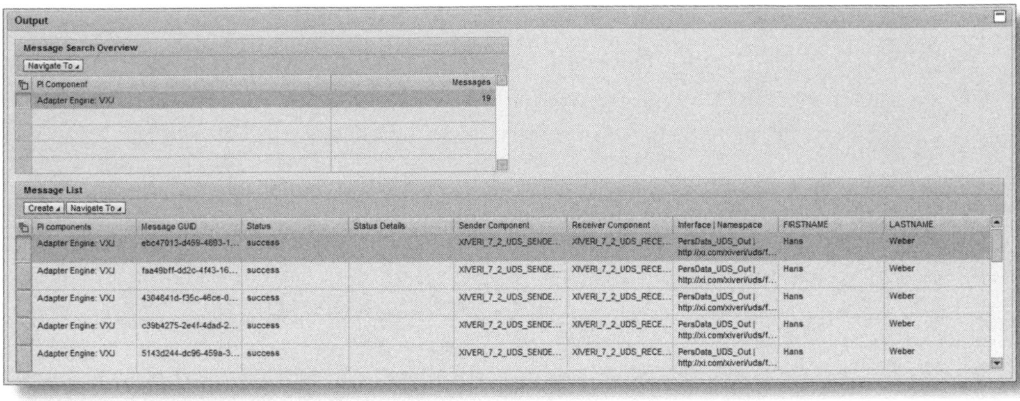

Figure 10.26 Central Message Search—Results List

10.2.7 Connecting to the Alert Infrastructure

Many companies do not simply rely on manual monitoring of their systems but instead expect these processes to be automated. This means automated notification of the responsible persons by means of alerts that can be sent by email or SMS.

SAP NetWeaver PI Monitoring was fully integrated in the alert infrastructure and offers configuration options for generating alerts for all the metrics specific to SAP NetWeaver PI. Figure 10.27 shows an example of the SAP NetWeaver PI alerts in the ALERT INBOX.

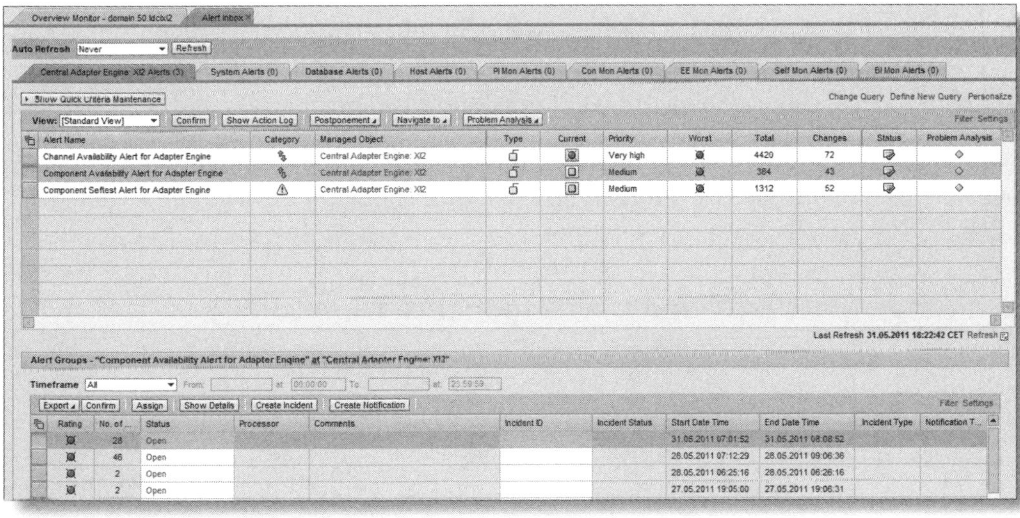

Figure 10.27 Alert Inbox

10.2.8 Connection to the Service Desk

The Service Desk function (see Figure 10.28) creates a central working platform, transparency, and traceability for the incidents that occur and the underlying support processes.

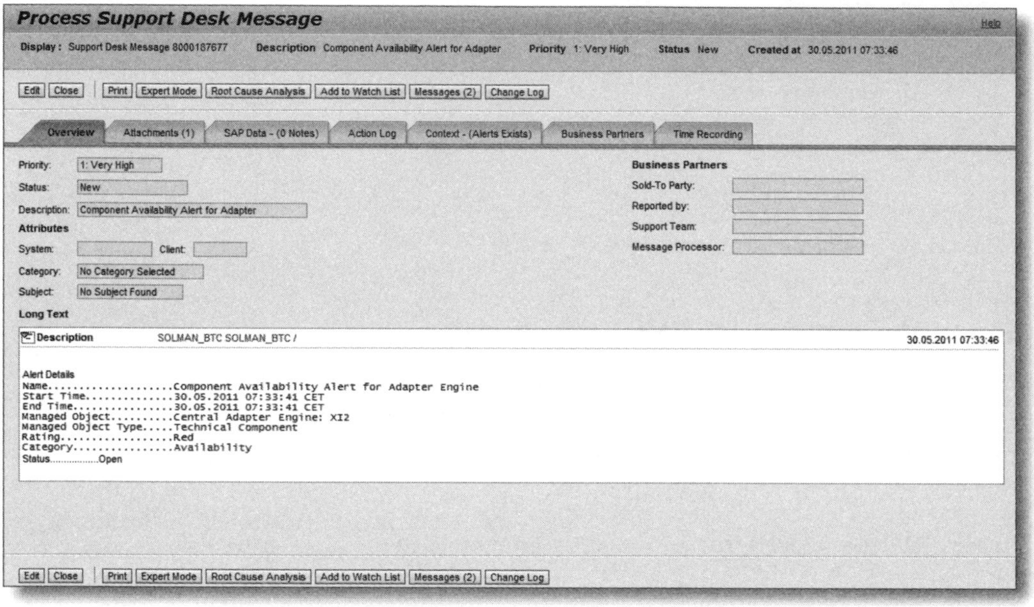

Figure 10.28 Service Desk

Support tickets

SAP NetWeaver PI Monitoring was fully integrated in the Service Desk and makes it possible, in the event of incidents, to create support tickets either fully automatically or manually. All of the relevant and known context information is automatically added to the support ticket.

For more information about the Service Desk function, see Chapter 9.

10.3 End User Experience Monitoring

In IT, the term *End User Experience Monitoring* (EEM) stands for procedures that provide feedback about the actual availability and performance of data processing systems from the point of view of the user. In other words, the results of the EEM provide you with information about whether users can complete a set task correctly and on time. The aim of reflecting the actual availability and performance of your systems is achieved by these procedures by collecting data as far away from the server spaces as possible, and therefore closer to the system users.

This method seems unusual at first, and it quickly takes you away from your familiar terrain as an IT specialist. After all, in the past, the aim was always to document the proper functioning of a system by collecting a variety of technical measured values without any gaps. The goal was to gather more and more data in ever shorter measurement intervals to describe the system more completely. However, this method is not feasible in practice. After all, regardless of the variety of available measured values, end users evaluate your system according to statements such as "It doesn't work" and "It's slow." These are exactly the kind of statements that you can confirm with the aspects considered in EEM, namely availability and performance. EEM measures, monitors, and substantiates what users and customers ask about and understand. That way, you can analyze (on a factual basis) faults that users have experienced subjectively and, possibly, rectify the faults effectively and efficiently.

What is measured?

There are essentially two starting points for technical implementation: The obvious method attempts to look over the user's shoulder, so to speak, and to send the measured data about the observed transactions to the central evaluation server. Depending on the configuration and manufacturer, this can either occur permanently (monitoring) or only lead to analysis in the event of an error. To counteract the suspicion that they are intended for the purpose of monitoring employees, these solutions offer various sophisticated anonymization and safety settings.

Measurement types

If, despite this, the method is not accepted in your enterprise, the new SAP Solution Manager provides an alternative approach that offers decisive technical benefits.

EEM is available via the *Technical Monitoring* work center and does not rely on human users as a source of data. Instead, EEM relies on a network of automatic helpers (known as *robots*) that execute transactions locally in the various geographical regions and report the availability and performance of the systems they use to the SAP Solution Manager. These robots are script-based and act like real employees or customers in the system landscape. For example, they access portal pages, check shopping carts, search through databases, and fill out SAP GUI forms. The executed scripts were recorded in advance by

Robots

recording these activities, which are actually reserved for human users. On the system side, the activities of the EEM robots are therefore completely inconspicuous and can hardly be differentiated from the activities of normal users. They are executed on an equal footing and are therefore a representative measure.

Benefits of automatic load generation

The benefits of automatic load generation more than make up for the initial effort of recording the scripts. Like an industrial robot, the EEM robots carry out their activities unswervingly without ever getting tired, without any careless mistakes, and without time off. Instead of waiting for a problem, you can observe transactions seamlessly and proactively, even if no real users are currently using the function in the region in question—either because of the local time or because the transaction is needed only rarely, when it becomes urgent. That way, you save valuable time in an emergency and, depending on the type of error, the application can be productive again before it is needed in day-to-day activities.

Major benefits of the robot strategy include the reproducibility of script executions, which makes it possible to compare individual executions locally or across regions, using the different robots as a source of data. This makes it comparatively easy to assess whether a problem is locally restricted (i.e., it can be observed from one position only), or if the business operation is faulty globally for all robots, and there is therefore probably a problem with the central backend system. You therefore observe the behavior of a specific script for a variety of robots. The opposite approach, observing a specific robot and the various different scripts executed by it, makes it easy to differentiate a generic network problem from more specific root causes. If multiple scripts with different contents are affected simultaneously by failures, the common technical root cause is probably located in the branch.

As you can see, the EEM provides important information about the causes of the error simply because of its distributed measurement arrangement and easy status comparison, and you do not require more detailed knowledge of the script processes.

Realtime Monitoring UI EEM

The *Realtime Monitoring UI* EEM also displays the individual steps of scripts and detailed error messages for each step. This makes it possible to evaluate and analyze the executed business process as a whole (and also its substeps) according to the criteria: availability

448

and performance. Put simply, the script therefore represents a business transaction, and the script step represents a user interaction, such as pressing a button or filling out a query screen by the robot. Knowing which step in a script was executed with which error status significantly restricts the variety of possible causes. If the system acknowledges the first step with WRONG PASSWORD OR USERNAME, there is probably a more obvious method for finding the error than an intensive check of lock tables or heap dumps.

Unfortunately, human users in production and the EEM have diametrically opposed ideas of what makes an ideal business transaction. To enable the best evaluation, it is desirable from the EEM's perspective to proceed in a linear direction in steps that are as small as possible. The more that subtasks can be divided into separate steps, the easier it is to identify a particular component that could be responsible for a malfunction. On the other hand, a more user-friendly application is designed to keep complexity out of the user's sight while executing as many activities as possible in the background. A single press of a button triggers a cascade of activities in the background, dozens of RFC connections to various databases and systems are used, data is consolidated, transactions wait for work processes, and lock entries are written and deleted. The user (and, therefore, the EEM robot, as well) waits until the result or an error message is displayed. In this case, the measured values that the EEM robot can send to the SAP Solution Manager are not very helpful for narrowing down a problem. However, the measurement makes it possible to quantify the bottleneck in a localized, objective manner and provides this information proactively before a real user has to report the problem. Nevertheless, a properly satisfying solution would have to go one step further and illuminate the hidden transactions behind the scenes.

The EEM uses SAP Passport technology that is also used by the end-to-end trace analysis. An *SAP Passport* is attached to each message that is sent by the EEM robot to the data processing system. The SAP Passport contains a unique identification number and details about which information should be retained for analysis purposes when the actual request is processed. If the processing has to be continued on another component in the background, the SAP Passport is forwarded together with the request, and the target systems are instructed to also retain information about the processing.

SAP Passport

In the Realtime Monitoring UI, the execution of a script is first reported together with all its assigned steps by an EEM robot and evaluated, as before, in terms of availability and performance. In a downstream step, SAP Solution Manager addresses the participating background components in the system, and the information stored in these components is retrieved in line with the SAP Passport identification number in question. The Realtime Monitoring UI then shows more details about the individual steps and lists the participating SAP systems, RFC times, client times, and HTTP times, for example. When you jump to the end-to-end trace analysis, at the latest, a bottleneck can be analyzed very precisely, depending on the configured detail level, by ABAP, Wily, or SQL trace, for example. In order not to have to decide between minimal effect on the system by tracing and more in-depth analysis possibilities, the EEM offers you three options for raising the detail level when needed:

▸ You can execute a script again at any time with a freely configurable detail level, without making any permanent changes to the regular execution configuration.

▸ You can increase the detail level for a specified time, after which the script automatically returns to the normal settings.

▸ The third variant automatically repeats the measurement with a freely configurable detail level when a runtime overrun is measured.

The last two methods mentioned are particularly well suited to examining phenomena that occur sporadically and can rarely be reproduced deliberately. In practice, because errors often fail to recur immediately, users often have to put in a lot of work before convincing others that a problem really exists. The responsible support agent repeats the transaction again and again successfully while more and more examples of the same complaint continue to accumulate. With EEM, the EEM robot takes on the time-consuming detective work and reports its results in the Realtime Monitoring UI.

Realtime Monitoring UI

The Realtime Monitoring UI is the central analysis platform for data from EEM. The Adobe Flash-based application can be accessed via the *Technical Monitoring* work center and essentially consists of tab pages that retrieve from the SAP Solution Manager a select group of script executions in specific locations over a certain period of time. Here, you specify which scripts you are interested in, which robots to focus on, and how far you want to consider the history. In the next step, you decide how to display the requested data by selecting one or more views (apps) for the tab page. There is a choice of several variants, including tree structures, pie charts, curves, and tile views. Depending on the task, these are variously suited to gaining an overview or comparing the different versions in detail. However, they all share the fact that they always operate on the data requested in the tab page and therefore enable different views of the same source data. If the requested dataset is no longer in a local data buffer, the Realtime Monitoring UI retrieves compressed data from the SAP NetWeaver Business Warehouse (BW). This can involve the BW integrated in the SAP Solution Manager or a separate BW system. You can therefore take a quick look at the data for the previous year without having to switch to an unfamiliar BW Web templates environment.

The possibilities and processes in the Realtime Monitoring UI are wide-ranging but can be learned intuitively. For an initial impression, see the executable demo version at *http://wiki.sdn.sap.com/wiki/display/EEM/Home.*

Being able to observe the usability of business transactions in real time, globally, and carrying out a far-reaching technical analysis when needed are fascinating opportunities. However, even if Realtime Monitoring UI is attractive and functional, it will not be the center of focus around the clock and it will only be the initial point of entry to EEM. Normally, the EEM robots will carry out their tasks in the background while you concentrate on more important things. In the event of exceptions or malfunctions, you will be reliably notified by the alerting infrastructure of SAP Solution Manager 7.1.

Alert Inbox

If a script measures unexpectedly long response times or uncovers functional deficits, an alert event is stored in the *Alert Inbox*, and it informs the responsible person by SMS or email; depending on the configuration, an incident can be optionally created. A direct jump to Realtime Monitoring UI makes it easier to investigate without delay. Additionally, an algorithm prevents the inbox from being filled with a constant stream of alert events for a problem that has already been reported but whose solution requires a little more time, which would make it harder to note other events. For the details of the Alert Inbox, see Section 10.1.1.

SAP NetWeaver
Business
Warehouse

EEM data from the local data buffer is compressed at regular intervals and stored in the BW. You can access this overview via the Realtime Monitoring UI and various BW Web templates in Interactive Reporting. The criteria for evaluating whether the measured response times are expected values or critical threshold infringements are adopted strictly from the alerting configuration. That way, the reporting exactly matches the data displayed in the monitoring application.

Service level
agreement (SLA)

If, however, BW is used for providing proof in the context of a service level agreement (SLA), this approach soon leads to a conflict of interests. On one hand, the threshold values and the related alerts are important indicators for early identification of inconsistencies and, if possible, eliminating the inconsistency before a really critical point is reached. On the other hand, the SLA defines the thresholds precisely and reduces the advance warning time to close to zero. The way out of this problem is to create an independent set of threshold values for SLAs in EEM and additional reporting that is independent of interactive reporting. This enables a suitable advance warning time with a useful alert and, simultaneously, precise reporting for the SLA. In this context, precise also means that an agreement is either complied with or infringed, and you therefore only have to define one threshold to clearly define this limit.

Dashboard display

An SAP BusinessObjects dashboard-based application is used to display the data collected for the SLA; the application is restricted to relevant core data. You can therefore see at a glance what percentage compliance there is with the defined thresholds in the categories of availability and performance. The figures are colored green or red, showing you whether the percentages comply with the specifications in the SLA. In addition, the data from previous months is also displayed.

It is no longer necessary to have detailed knowledge of the underlying threshold value approaches and mechanisms to interpret the data. Researching root causes and searching for administrative countermeasures remain the sole preserve of the Realtime Monitoring UI and end-to-end trace. Reporting in the area of the SLA is therefore aimed primarily at external or internal customers of an IT solution who have only limited interest in the technical background details, as long as usability can be guaranteed and shown.

10.4   End-to-End Root Cause Analysis

Heterogeneous systems and increasingly complex customer solutions require you to take a systematic approach to identify the precise cause of a fault. This standardized process must first broadly identify the components concerned and then analyze them more closely to arrive at the cause of the fault by process of elimination (top-down approach).

If, for example, a user notices a performance problem in a browser-based application, the problem might have to do with the user's PC, the server landscape made up of components based on different technologies, or the network. If the problem concerns the server, it may originate from a Java-based SAP NetWeaver Portal, an ABAP-based SAP ECC backend system connected by remote function call (RFC), or a database that retrieves data from a storage subsystem. A performance problem or functional fault can occur at any time in any of the components, from the browser to the storage subsystem.

The aim of end-to-end Root Cause Analysis (referred to in the following as Root Cause Analysis) with SAP Solution Manager is to provide the support organization with tools and methods that reliably identify the affected component while minimizing the time needed to solve the problem.

The Root Cause Analysis is an integral part of SAP Solution Manager and constitutes a basis on which standardized support can be provided by SAP, customers, and SAP partners. The Root Cause Analysis covers the following elements:

Elements of the Root Cause Analysis

▶ A central, comprehensive console for all tools required to perform cross-component and component-specific problem analyses. All of the tools it contains offer a secure way of providing support because it is not possible to make changes unless they are explicitly requested by the customer. In addition, you can open all tools in the Web browser via an HTTP connection, eliminating the need for operating system access.

▶ Standardized, proven procedures for systematically analyzing problems in a top-down process.

▸ An open diagnostics infrastructure with interfaces for different types of data relevant for diagnosing problems (workload, exceptions, technical configuration, traces, changes, client diagnosis).

No changes to production landscapes

SAP is not only enhancing the SAP technologies supported in the past, but is continuously integrating components from independent software vendors (ISVs) for which SAP has a maintenance contract with customers (OEM).

The end-to-end Root Cause Analysis tools in SAP Solution Manager do not rely on the SAP system administration tools that were developed to manage and make changes to production landscapes. Changes to the production landscape are managed by the customer and made either centrally in the *System Administration* work center or locally with the SAP NetWeaver Administrator tool. In other words, you use the Root Cause Analysis tools to analyze problems and plan measures, and then the system administration tools to implement these measures.

With the Root Cause Analysis tools, SAP maps the different roles required to provide second-level support for an IT solution. The SAP NetWeaver Administrator is a tool used to manage daily system operations. Therefore, the Root Cause Analysis tools are used by customers in Customer Centers of Expertise (CCoEs), partners, or SAP, while the SAP NetWeaver Administrator is used in outsourcing or customer operations.

10.4.1 Procedure for Root Cause Analysis

Cross-component

If the Service Desk is unable to solve a problem that has occurred in the business units, the customer's application management team first performs a cross-component root cause analysis to isolate the component responsible for the performance problem or functional fault: client, network, different SAP systems (e.g., SAP NetWeaver Portal, SAP CRM, SAP ERP, etc.), database, or storage subsystems.

The Root Cause Analysis in SAP Solution Manager helps you identify the component responsible for the fault. This approach helps you systematically determine the cause of the fault without involving countless experts, therefore allowing you to avoid an unfocused approach based purely on intuition.

After the application management team has performed the cross-component root cause analysis and identified the component responsible for the fault, you can use incident management to call on the required experts from development, business process operations, SAP operations, or the IT infrastructure to solve the problem. This component-specific root cause analysis is supported by SAP Solution Manager with a range of tools, which can be found in the different systems in the system landscape. The Root Cause Analysis represents a central console that enables all experts involved central access to the tools.

Even after performing a root cause analysis on a fault, customers are not always in a position to solve the problem straight away due to a lack of knowledge of the component concerned. In this case, they need to include SAP or the respective SAP partner in the analysis. The experts must be able to access the customer's IT landscape to perform the analysis efficiently. The Root Cause Analysis grants SAP and SAP partners access to the required tools, while ensuring that no changes can be made to the customer's production environment. In addition, it also guarantees that the customer, SAP, and the SAP partner use the same tools and therefore also the same data basis to analyze the problem.

The Root Cause Analysis offers the following advantages:

- **Safeguard availability of critical business processes**
  The greatest benefits of the Root Cause Analysis tools are that they speed up the process of solving the problem and therefore ensure higher availability of the critical elements of the customer solution.

- **Costs for support experts kept to a minimum**
  By taking this standardized, focused approach to analyzing problems, you can identify the experts you need to solve the problem in just one analysis step. This not only cuts the time required to come up with a solution but also minimizes the number of resources involved.

  In addition, the method used to gather data across components and technological boundaries greatly reduces the knowledge required to isolate the problem.

- **Reduced license costs**
  The license to use all tools provided in the Root Cause Analysis

and the required third-party tools is included in SAP Solution Manager; no further license costs are incurred.

▶ **Necessary Root Cause Analysis tools are shipped as part of the solution**
Because the tools required to perform the Root Cause Analysis are included in the shipment, the customer does not need to invest time in bringing together the right tools. In addition, SAP ensures that all tools are preconfigured before being shipped, and the necessary data extractors are provided. This means customers are not required to develop their own tools and infrastructures to analyze problems.

▶ **Data basis for monitoring and IT reporting**
After the Root Cause Analysis has been implemented, you have the required data basis for the SAP technology and monitoring applications at your fingertips. The integrated SAP NetWeaver BW system provides data for IT reporting supported by this data basis.

Work in Technical Operations is simplified for you in the long term as you benefit from the newly developed tools. When SAP Active Global Support (SAP AGS) offers you assistance for problems relating to the Java environment, you do not have to give SAP support employees access to the operating system for them to perform a Root Cause Analysis. In this way, you can maintain the security of your solution, retain full control, and ensure that any changes made are traceable.

10.4.2 Architecture

Diagnosis database and agents

The Root Cause Analysis in SAP Solution Manager is based on the central diagnosis database, which is filled by diagnosis agents installed on every managed system that have direct access to the managed systems. These agents are preconfigured and shipped by SAP. It is their task to gather the data from the connected components that is required to analyze the problem. Data gather continuously by these agents includes exceptions, for example, critical log entries, dumps, queue errors, configuration snapshots, and workload data relating to the operating system, host, and database of each managed system.

This data is gathered in the SAP Solution Manager from all technologies and made available to the different tools. The data gathered is compressed, correlated with landscape data, and presented in aggregated form for extensive IT reporting.

The third-party products used to gather data demonstrate the openness of the Root Cause Analysis as a transparent diagnosis platform for customers. The Root Cause Analysis includes a license for *CA Wily Introscope* (subsequently referred to as Introscope), which enables you to obtain special performance statistics for Java and .NET components without the need to access the application source code. To achieve this, Introscope uses its own byte code instrumentation technology (BCI), which can set and evaluate measuring points during the runtime of applications. The Introscope license included in SAP Solution Manager covers measuring techniques and dashboards, which are preconfigured by SAP before being shipped. On the basis of this technology, it is possible to integrate performance statistics for both ABAP and non-ABAP components in the Root Cause Analysis tools.

CA Wily Introscope

In addition to CA Wily Introscope, SAP Solution Manager contains a license for *BMC Appsight for SAP Client Diagnostics* (subsequently referred to as Appsight). Appsight is a tool for analyzing problems on users' PCs. It records not only all interactions between the user and the SAP application but also all calls and actions executed in the background at the level of the application code and operating system. To do so, it uses a patented blackbox technology that records the data on a profile basis in the background. The recorded data can be used to analyze client-specific problems and performance bottlenecks or make cross-client comparisons to identify differences between two users' PCs. For example, by comparing registry entries or driver versions, you can investigate why the performance of one user's PC is adequate while another's is not.

BMC Appsight

After you have logged on to SAP Solution Manager, you have access to all Root Cause Analysis functions and tools in the *Root Cause Analysis* work center (see Figure 10.29).

Work center

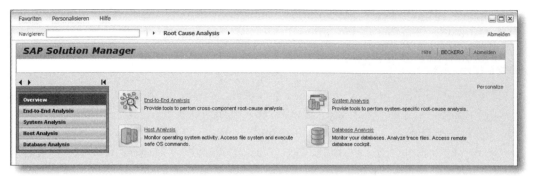

Figure 10.29 "Root Cause Analysis" Work Center

10.4.3 Tools in the "Root Cause Analysis" Work Center

Views of the work center

The navigation area in the *Root Cause Analysis* work center consists of four tool groups (views) that correspond to the top-down approach:

▸ END-TO-END ANALYSIS

▸ SYSTEM ANALYSIS

▸ HOST ANALYSIS

▸ DATABASE ANALYSIS

Each of these four views offers the tools you need to perform further reaching analyses. When you choose the END-TO-END ANALYSIS view, you have access to freely definable queries that allow you to group the systems according to your needs. In doing so, you can use different filter criteria such as system identification (system ID, SID), system type, solution, and so on.

After you have selected the required systems, you can start the tools contained in the view on your selection.

End-to-end analysis

The end-to-end analysis tools are designed to perform the following tasks:

▸ **Exception analysis**
The exception analysis allows you to centrally analyze all exceptions from connected systems, such as serious error messages in logs or dumps. From here, you can start component-specific tools.

▸ **Workload analysis**
The workload analysis comprises server-related workload statistics for the connected systems.

► **Change analysis**

The change analysis creates transparency for all changes (technical configuration, code, content) that have been made in the connected system landscape. This is particularly useful in the event of faults that occur after changes have been made to the production landscape.

► **Trace analysis**

The trace analysis records performance-related and functional faults in a specific user activity from the user's browser to the storage subsystem. The measurement is triggered by the user interface and automatically activates recording of the relevant traces on every component processed by the user query.

The following tools are among the most important instruments for system analysis:

System analysis

► **CA Wily Introscope**

CA Wily Introscope provides historical and real-time data for analyzing system responses and resource consumption. The dashboards give you a quick status overview. A hierarchical search query in the component-specific dashboards and the detailed analysis in investigator mode provide detailed system-specific and component-specific data for expert analyses.

► **Change reporting tool**

The change reporting tool allows you to compare configurations from different points in time and thereby identify changes that may cause a fault to occur. It also gives you the option of comparing configurations from different landscapes if, for example, problems appear in the production landscape that you are unable to reproduce in the quality assurance (QA) landscape.

► **Thread dump analysis**

The thread dump analysis is a tool that enables you to centrally trigger and schedule thread dumps for one particular or all J2EE nodes. You can also analyze thread dumps and the memory-clearing characteristics of your monitored system. The thread dump represents a snapshot of the current status of all Java threads and provides important information enabling you to spot problems such as performance bottlenecks.

Host analysis

There are also dashboards available in Wily Introscope in the host analysis. Here you can display, for example, the current CPU utilization, paging, free main memory, and free swap memory per host in the OS CPU AND MEMORY dashboard:

▶ **OS analysis**
In the OS analysis, you can also display host-related metrics directly in the Root Cause Analysis work center. The CPU view shows historical values of the CPU utilization and the CPU load average in an hourly resolution, for example.

▶ **File system browser**
The file system browser gives you secure, central access to files for performing Root Cause Analysis. The restriction to preconfigured paths that lead to files relevant for the Root Cause Analysis ensures that access to business-relevant data is not granted.

▶ **OS command console**
The OS command console provides you with central access to the managed system's operating system. This means you can use analysis tools that are specific to the network and operating system. For the sake of security, only read-only commands are permitted.

Database analysis

Finally, there is one other important tool for analyzing the database: database analysis. In the new *database analysis*, it is possible to identify database-related problems (mainly performance problems). Depending on the system database used, historical performance indicators are displayed in various categories. The following databases are currently supported: DB2 for LUW, MaxDB, MS SQL Server, and Oracle. The displayed reports are a subset of the reports from the DBA Cockpit. For this reason, the DBA Cockpit configuration must, of course, have been carried out during configuration of the managed systems.

Further tools for component-specific root cause analysis are referred to in the corresponding sections.

10.4.4 Root Cause Analysis in Detail

The following section introduces the most important tools for the Root Cause Analysis.

End-to-End Exception Analysis

In a landscape with different components based on different technologies, for instance, the ABAP stack and J2EE stack of an SAP NetWeaver Application Server (SAP NetWeaver AS Java), the task of analyzing exceptions is becoming increasingly complex. Each of the components writes different log files. A range of tools is needed to access and evaluate the log files. To analyze the actual fault in a business process that makes use of several components, you need to use all of the tools. The end-to-end exception analysis (subsequently referred to as exception analysis) offers a central access point to facilitate this task.

The exception analysis supports two approaches: Procedure

- An exception trend analysis in which the system is monitored over an extended period can be used to clarify, for example, which component in a system is responsible for an unusually high number of errors. You might also use the exception trend analysis to tell whether the number of errors has increased or a particular error has been eradicated after you make a change to a component, perhaps with a patch, a support package (SP) update, or a configuration change.
- If you know the exact time at which an error occurred, you can use the exception analysis to identify the component responsible. In this case, it helps to analyze not only the exact time of the error but also the periods immediately preceding and following the error.

When you start the exception analysis, an overview of all the systems   Overview involved is shown. To the right of the OVERVIEW, the most important KPIs for all components are displayed (see Figure 10.30), such as the number of dumps that occurred in the selected SAP ERP system or the number of serious application messages in the Java system.

Each of the other views contains a table of the most important information on the selected error category. You can show additional table fields with a hierarchical search query. When you click on the marker shown, a new window opens with further analysis options. For ABAP system log errors, you are taken directly to Transaction SM21 in the managed system, and the selected exception is shown for analysis (see Figure 10.31). Here you can see which user caused the dump on which component and at what time.

461

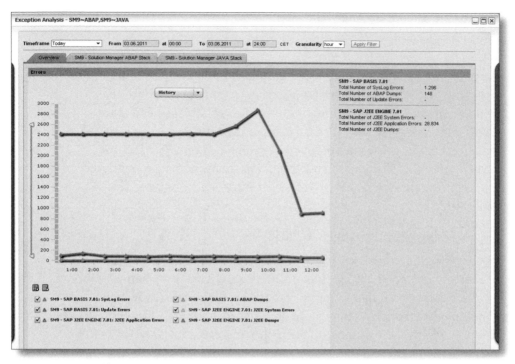

Figure 10.30 Exception Analysis Overview

Figure 10.31 Exception Analysis—ABAP Dumps

Ideally, the exception analysis leads you to the point where you can trace an error in the system back to one component and one exception. If you want to analyze the exception in detail, component-specific tools are essential.

End-to-End Workload Analysis

The end-to-end workload analysis (subsequently referred to as workload analysis) provides all workload information independently of components, enabling you to analyze general performance bottlenecks in complex landscapes. Different monitors and tools deliver all important KPIs for the different components. Initially, in most cases, the response times of all systems are verified. For this purpose, the workload analysis offers an overview of all selected systems.

Component-independent workload information

The graphical view shown in Figure 10.32 maps the time profile of a given period. On the Y-axis, the average response times are related to the respective hour on the X-axis. This type of display enables you to identify peak workload times that usually occur during users' typical working times. To analyze a performance problem in greater depth, you have to take into account not only the average but also the accumulated response time. This example shows a relatively uniform distribution of system load with a peak in the time between 1 and 3 a.m., although with a value of under 2000 ms, it is still negligible.

Time profile

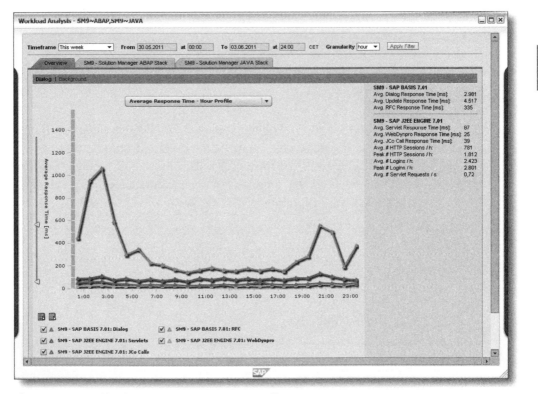

Figure 10.32 Workload Analysis Overview—Hour Profile

463

To do so, you switch the view to AVERAGE / TOTAL RESPONSE TIME – BUBBLE CHART in the diagram selection. The overview then shows the average response time on the Y-axis. The size of the circle reflects the accumulated response time. Critical situations are represented by large, ascending circles (see Figure 10.33).

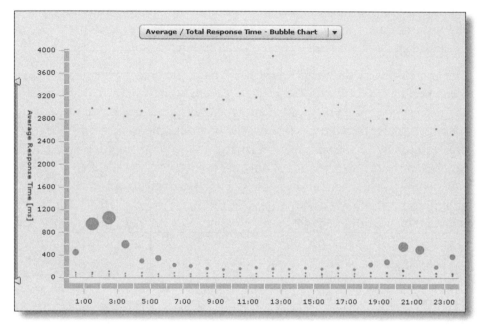

Figure 10.33 Workload Analysis—Bubble Chart

In addition to the overview displayed, analysis tab pages are provided for all connected systems showing application-specific workload data. Figure 10.34 shows the accumulated and average response time itemized by task type, as well as the itemization by CPU, database, wait, and roll times for an ECC system based on ABAP.

Analysis of system changes

The parameters you can analyze with the end-to-end change analysis (subsequently referred to as change analysis) include the following:

- OS parameters
- DB parameters
- ABAP parameters
- Java parameters
- Transport requests
- Support packages

464

ABAP Basis	RFC	BI Reporting	Host

Workload Summary | Top Dialog | Top Update | Top Batch | Top HTTP | User Load | ICM Load | Work Process Load | GW RegisteredTP

▷ Conditions

▷ Navigation

▽ Metric Data Display

Task Type	Tot. Resp. Time (s)	Avg. Resp. Time (ms)	Avg. CPU Time (ms)	Avg. DB Time (ms)	Avg. Wait Time (ms)	Avg. Roll Wait Time (ms)	# Dialog Steps
Overall Result	646.807	534	124	146	1	150	1.211.042
AutoABAP	6.288	4.495	1.578	1.601	0	0	1.399
AutoTH	77	18	2	1	3	0	4.318
Batch	195.675	4.508	1.583	1.163	2	0	43.408
DELAY	49	7	0	0	5	0	6.850
Dialog	68.412	2.981	98	106	2	2.736	22.949
HTTP	409	84	22	39	7	0	4.893
RFC	375.576	335	68	108	1	106	1.120.638
RPC	84	3.121	1.047	2.245	0	0	27
Spool	138	21	2	9	5	0	6.539
Update	90	4.517	148	3.499	6	0	20
Update2	8	8.061	109	801	125	0	1

Figure 10.34 Workload Analysis—ABAP DetailsEnd-to-End Change Analysis

▸ Changes to RFC connections

▸ Safety-critical changes

The change analysis is the central access point to start a root cause analysis. Arranged by system, category, and change date, it gives you access to all changes in a system landscape. You can establish whether a given error has occurred due to changes to a connected system and which changes have been made. The change analysis provides an overview of the total number of changes to the managed systems in the landscape. The changes are grouped according to main instances. Figure 10.35 shows an example of an SAP Solution Manager system with the main instances SOLUTION MANAGER ABAP STACK and SOLUTION MANAGER JAVA STACK.

By selecting the system details, you can analyze changes per category in a selected period.

Figure 10.36 shows changes to the ABAP server grouped by days. The legend below the graphic reveals the types of changes that have been made. A further hierarchical search query in the respective category then displays the actual details of the change.

Navigating further forward, you can analyze the details of each change and a change history. This makes it possible for you to identify individual transport requests or SAP Notes that were imported on a specific day to the system being analyzed, for example (see Figure 10.36).

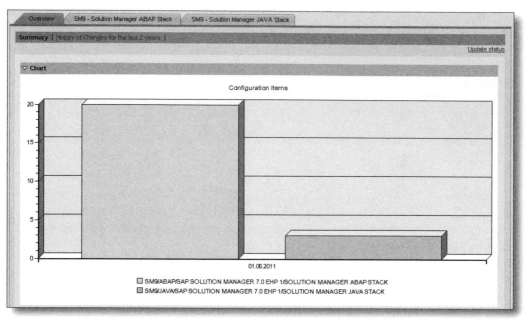

Figure 10.35 Change Analysis Overview

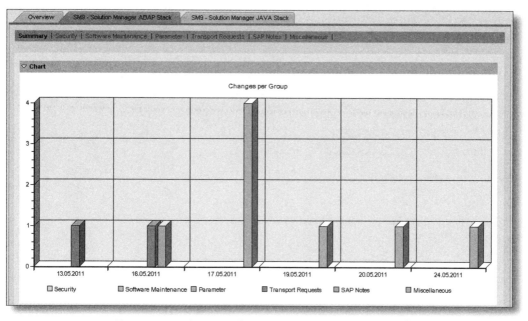

Figure 10.36 Change Analysis—ABAP Details

End-to-End Trace Analysis

The end-to-end trace analysis is used mainly to identify why certain user requests take so long in complex landscapes. You can use it to isolate a single user action and identify the component causing the problem. It records the response times of the components involved in the request and the path the request takes and makes this data available for detailed analysis.

The trace analysis is split into two phases. In the first phase, the trace is performed and recorded. In the second phase, the recorded traces are then evaluated. Before you start recording, you must ensure that you are able to reproduce the problem.

Trace analysis phases

To record a new trace on web applications (or applications that use Microsoft Office products as their frontend), the user's browser must have a plug-in added to it. Its purpose is to instrumentalize the browser's queries so that the components used to execute them can activate particular trace functions. To record a trace for applications that are executed in the SAP GUI, you have to start Report /SDF/ E2E_TRACE before you start the actual program. You then trigger the actual transaction using this report (see Figure 10.37).

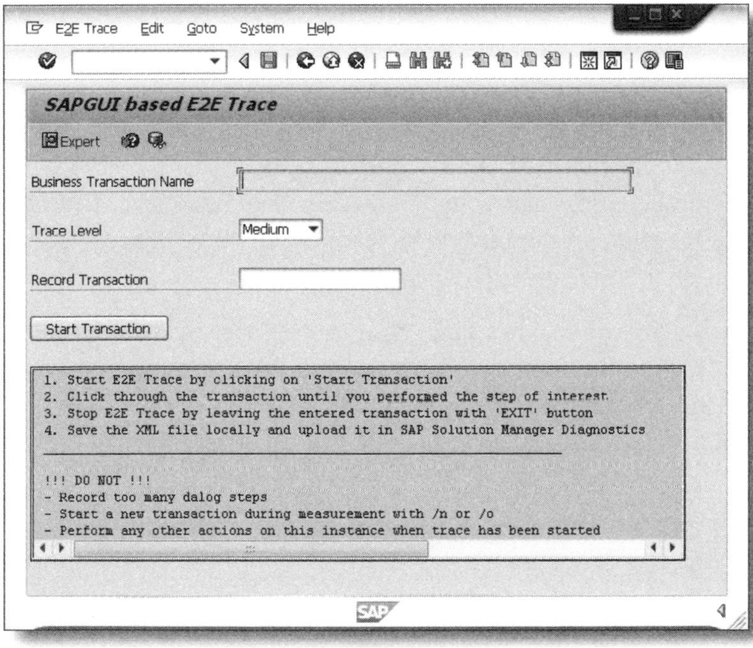

Browser plug-in

Figure 10.37 SAP GUI Trace Recording

After you have successfully performed the trace and uploaded it to SAP Solution Manager, you can use it for further analysis. Figure 10.38 shows an overview of the detailed information about the recorded trace. The scenario shown here involves a trace that was recorded in a scenario from SAP BusinessObjects. You can easily see that the majority of the response time was taken up on the server side, and the response times on the client and in the network are negligible.

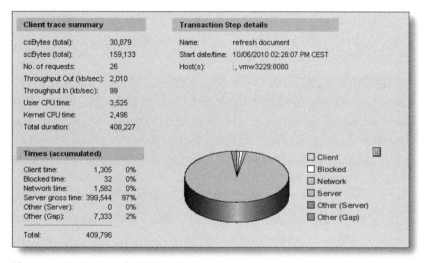

Figure 10.38 Trace Analysis Overview

The data shown under TIMES (ACCUMULATED) lets you quickly identify the component that has taken the most time (client, network, or server). In the example provided in Figure 10.39, the server takes up most of the time. In the SERVER ANALYSIS view, you can break down the time spent into server components.

Figure 10.39 clearly shows that about 90% of the time is consumed in the ABAP application servers for the scenarios, whereas the front-end business objects and the server layer only take up about 10% of the time.

In the REQUESTS TREE view (see Figure 10.40), you can trace the request through all components involved and, after identifying the problematic components, navigate to the respective analysis tools. In the selected example, the RSR_MDX_BXML_GET_INFO function module is the cause of the lengthy response time.

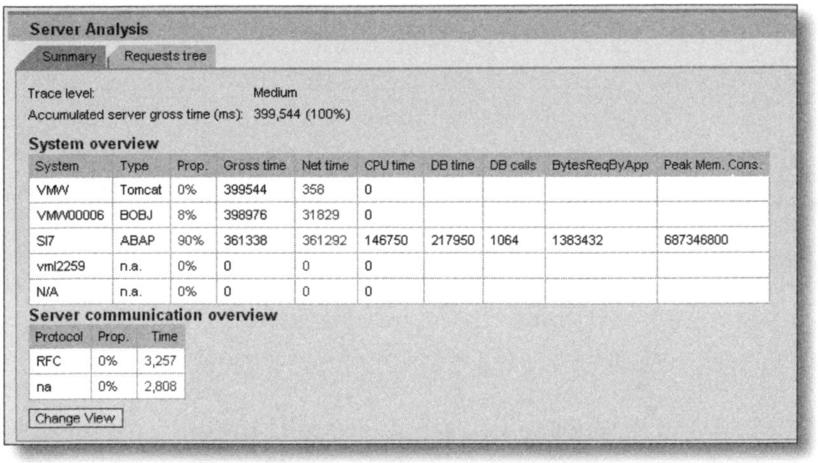

Server Analysis

Summary | Requests tree

Trace level: Medium
Accumulated server gross time (ms): 399,544 (100%)

System overview

System	Type	Prop.	Gross time	Net time	CPU time	DB time	DB calls	BytesReqByApp	Peak Mem. Cons.
VMW	Tomcat	0%	399544	358	0				
VMW00006	BOBJ	8%	398976	31829	0				
SI7	ABAP	90%	361338	361292	146750	217950	1064	1383432	687346800
vml2259	n.a.	0%	0	0	0				
N/A	n.a.	0%	0	0	0				

Server communication overview

Protocol	Prop.	Time
RFC	0%	3,257
na	0%	2,808

Change View

Figure 10.39 Server Analysis in the Trace Analysis

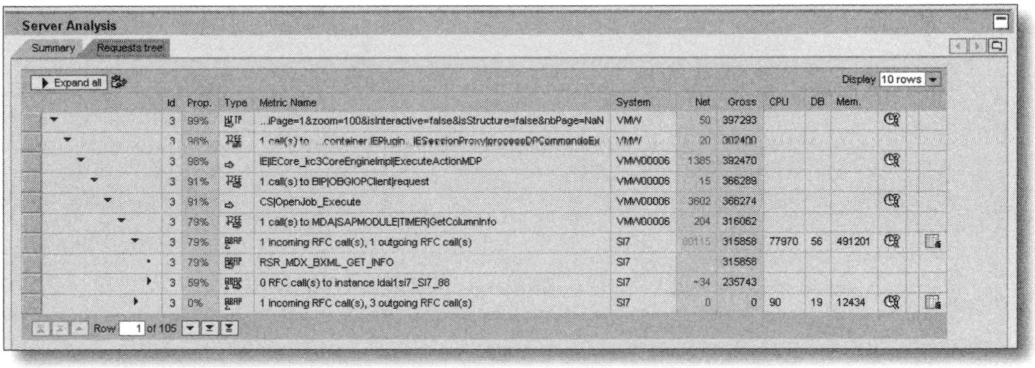

Server Analysis

Summary | Requests tree

Expand all Display 10 rows

	Id	Prop.	Type	Metric Name	System	Net	Gross	CPU	DB	Mem.
▼	3	99%		...iPage=1&zoom=100&isInteractive=false&isStructure=false&nbPage=NaN	VMW	50	397293			
▼	3	98%		1 call(s) to ...container.IEPlugin_.IESessionProxy|processDPCommandoEx	VMW	20	392400			
▼	3	98%		IE|ECore_kc3CoreEngineImpl|ExecuteActionMDP	VMW00006	1385	392470			
▼	3	91%		1 call(s) to BIP|OBG|OPClient|request	VMW00006	15	366289			
▼	3	91%		CS|OpenJob_Execute	VMW00006	3602	366274			
▼	3	79%		1 call(s) to MDA|SAPMODULE|TIMER|GetColumnInfo	VMW00006	204	316062			
▼	3	79%		1 incoming RFC call(s), 1 outgoing RFC call(s)	SI7	00115	315858	77970	56	491201
•	3	79%		RSR_MDX_BXML_GET_INFO	SI7		315858			
▶	3	59%		0 RFC call(s) to instance Idai1sI7_SI7_88	SI7	~34	235743			
▶	3	0%		1 incoming RFC call(s), 3 outgoing RFC call(s)	SI7	0	0	90	19	12434

Row 1 of 105

Figure 10.40 Requests Tree

In this example, jumps to the BW statistics and the ABAP trace provide further analysis options.

10.4.5 Quality Assurance with the Root Cause Analysis Tools

The methods and tools for the Root Cause Analysis can be used not only reactively in the problem and incident management process but also in the quality management process. The aim of a quality process supported by analysis is to implement changes discreetly in production for the business unit; in other words, it should be possible to implement changes without affecting ongoing business. This goal should be achievable with a reasonable level of testing effort.

Code freeze

As part of the stabilization activities undertaken in the test phase of a project, the quality manager needs ways to monitor development activities in the customer's system, particularly a development stop or code freeze. In this phase, no changes may be imported to the QA system unless they have been agreed with the quality manager. The change analysis enables the quality manager to check the entire customer solution for uncontrolled imports to establish if the code freeze has been flouted.

After you have performed functional QA, SAP recommends that you trace the critical core business process steps, such as creating a sales order, in single user mode. This helps you detect problems with performance, data consistency, and technical correctness before they occur in the load test or production operations. By analyzing the end-to-end trace effectively, you can anticipate performance problems that will occur during multi-user operations. You can also identify data consistency problems by analyzing the commit behavior in the trace (SQL behavior) as well as technical exceptions that are not visible on the interface but nevertheless have the potential to cause significant problems in production operations.

Reducing the effort of load tests

By precisely tracing the program flow with the trace analysis, you can reduce the need for effort involved in performing load tests, as well as significantly improve the continuity of business processes after changes. Simulating parallelism in load tests requires considerable effort with regard to script management and providing test data. Each time you reduce the effort needed to perform load tests, you make a major contribution to lowering total cost of ownership (TCO).

The load test itself can be efficiently monitored and statistically analyzed with the workload and exception analyses. Rather than logging on to the individual systems manually, you can monitor and analyze the load test centrally in SAP Solution Manager.

Integration validation

The process associated with the functional integration test for systematically analyzing performance, data consistency, and technical correctness is referred to by SAP as *integration validation*. In this process, SAP is enhancing traditional quality management with Best Practices and the validation of integrated, cross-technology, cross-component solutions—something that must be given special attention in distributed, heterogeneous landscapes.

10.5   Technical Administration

The Technical Administration covers all initial and ongoing administrative tasks and activities you need to manage SAP solutions and therefore constitutes the starting point for production operations. This area contains the tools and activities that you require to guarantee your SAP systems operate smoothly from a technical viewpoint.

SAP Solution Manager allows you to manage recurring administrative tasks centrally and ensure that they can always be executed by saving them as recurring tasks to be completed. This simplifies the system administrator's tasks and lowers costs in production operations.

The *Technical Administration* work center provides all of the essential functions for managing the SAP landscape:

Functions

▶ Periodic and non-periodic administration tasks can be controlled. System administrators and end users can be informed centrally about events that affect them.

▶ Business hours and maintenance windows can be planned centrally for multiple systems, and the plans are displayed instantly in the IT Calendar.

▶ The work center provides a central access point to tools for the administrators of ABAP, Java, and Master Data Management (MDM) systems. Tools for other SAP system types will be added successively.

With central access to the systems to be managed and the option to manage periodic and ad hoc administrative tasks, you can realize major savings in terms of both time and costs.

The *Technical Administration* work center gives you access to a range of functions in the following views (see Figure 10.41):

Views

▶ Task Inbox

▶ IT Calendar

▶ Work Mode Management

▶ Notification Management

▶ MDM Administration

▶ Central Tool Access

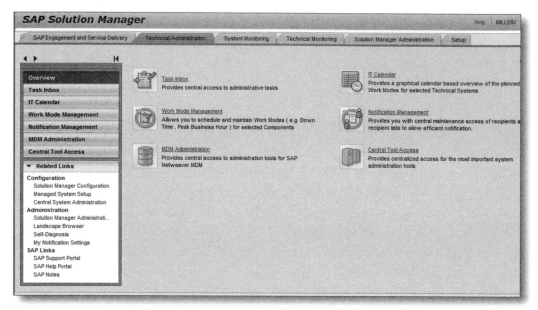

Figure 10.41 "Technical Administration" Work Center—Overview

The individual areas are presented in the following subsections.

10.5.1 Work Mode Management

Work modes

Planning the times in which system functions are not available to carry out maintenance work, and planning the times in which operations have to be guaranteed, is one of the most important tasks of the system administration team. Planned downtime and business hours are grouped together under the umbrella term *work modes*. The SAP Solution Manager enables you to handle work modes systematically in the WORK MODE MANAGEMENT view in the *Technical Administration* work center.

The following key functions are supported:

▸ Planning work modes for technical scenarios, technical systems, instances, databases, and logon groups

▸ Controlling how Technical Monitoring functions in SAP Solution Manager respond during planned downtime

▸ Carrying out downtime; that is, stopping or starting systems and instances

▶ Announcing downtimes by SMS, email, or SAP system message

▶ Reporting functions concerning downtime and main load times.

The work modes can be divided into the following types:

▶ **Planned downtime**
Planned downtime is needed to carry out tasks that require technical components to be shut down. Examples of this include database upgrades, hardware maintenance, and much more. During planned downtime, the system is not available to end users.

▶ **Modified planned downtime**
Creating modified planned downtime is only useful in association with a planned downtime with IN PROCESS status when it is apparent that its end time will have to be brought forward or put back. Because a modified planned downtime can only exist together with a planned downtime and after this planned downtime has been created, it is described as a *phase* of downtime.

▶ **Maintenance**
These work modes are scheduled if there is a pending maintenance activity that requires the system to be shut down but that does not impair operations, such as importing ABAP SPs. During maintenance, end users cannot access the system.

▶ **Peak business hours**
Peak business hours are the times during which the most users work in the system and when peak loads are expected. One example would be the month-end closing, or the days before Christmas when the most turnover is generated. System availability, throughput, and performance are especially critical in these phases.

▶ **Normal business hours**
Normal business hours are the times during which an average number of users work in the system and when no peak loads are expected. System availability must be guaranteed during normal business hours.

▶ **Outside business hours**
Outside business hours covers the times that are outside normal working times, during which no or only few users work in the system, but the system is still available.

All phases and types have certain core attributes in common (as shown a bit later in Figure.10.42): START TIME and END TIME are self-explanatory. The TITLE of the work mode helps you recognize it again more readily. The CATEGORY makes it possible to separate work modes according to their reasons, such as hardware maintenance of the database server. The textual descriptions refer to the detailed reason for downtime (REASON FOR WORK MODE), for example, or how it affects business processes (BUSINESS IMPACT OF WORK MODE). You can also link a downtime to documents.

The remaining attributes depend on the type or phase of the downtime.

Long-Term Planning for Work Modes

Sequences
Over the course of your planning period (for example, six months), you can schedule planned downtimes and business hours as either single events or a recurring sequence of events.

The SAP NetWeaver appointment calendar is used for the time pattern of recurring work modes. This allows you to make use of complex weekly and monthly patterns that you can refine with exceptions, for example, by using holiday and workday calendars.

After you have selected and saved a recurrence pattern once, a verbal expression of the pattern appears on the input screen, for example EVERY TWO SATURDAYS IN THE PERIOD FROM 01/03/2009 TO 05/30/2009 FROM 10 P.M. TO 11 P.M., together with a complete list of the individual elements in the sequence, that is, all the days on which work modes are planned.

Homogeneity
The principle of homogeneity applies to every individual component in a sequence of work modes; that is, all attributes of the components in the sequence match each other—with the obvious exception of timing. The same applies for the status. In practical application, this means that when you select a downtime of this type, you are first asked whether you want to work with the entire sequence behind it or just that individual downtime. If you select the individual downtime and change it, before you save, you are advised of the fact that the downtime you have just edited will no longer belong to the superordinate sequence but will become independent.

You cannot alter the basic recurrence pattern of a sequence of work modes after it has been defined. This means that you cannot change a sequence from weekly to monthly, for example. However, it is possible to define exceptions for a sequence of work modes after the sequence has been created; that is, you can delete individual components of a sequence or convert them to real, individual work modes.

The status of work modes is changed automatically by the system (an example is shown in Figure.10.42). If a planned downtime still has INACTIVE status at the time it is due to start, it is changed to AUTOMATICALLY CANCELLED when the downtime commences. If the planned downtime originally had ACTIVE status, it changes to IN PROCESS and then COMPLETED at the start and end of the downtime. For the first planned downtime in a sequence of work modes, automatic and manual status changes result in the downtime being removed from the sequence.

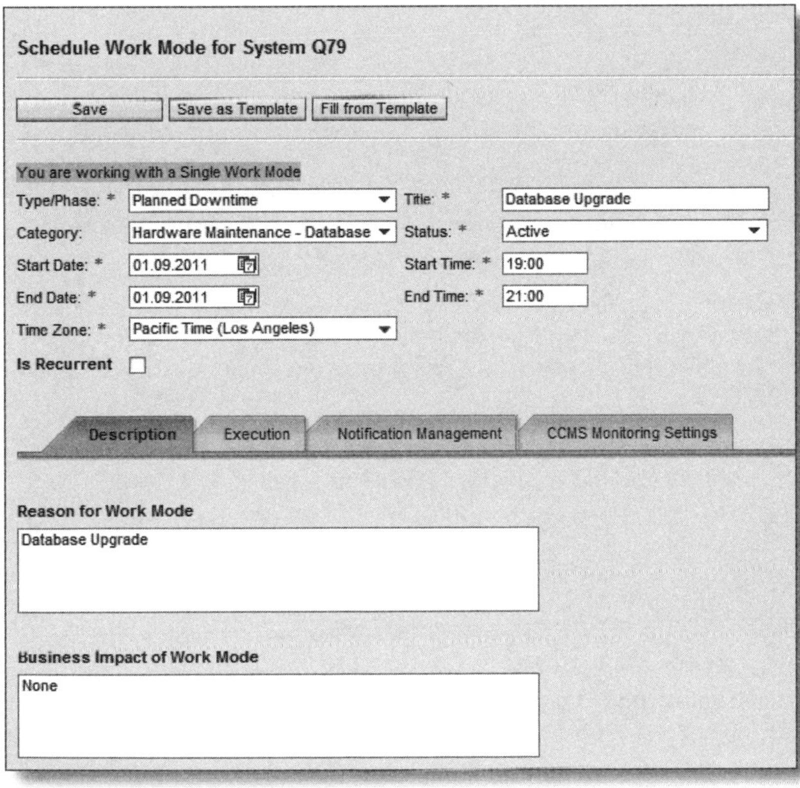

Status

Figure 10.42 Scheduling Work Modes

475

> **Example**
>
> A typical scenario is as follows:
>
> A system administrator wants to schedule downtime every second Saturday for the next six months to carry out maintenance on the hardware of his production system.
>
> First, the administrator contacts the people in charge of the business units that might be affected by the planned production system downtime and asks them to provide information about their business-critical uptimes.
>
> The system administrator records these critical uptimes and the downtimes he would like to schedule in the WORK MODE MANAGEMENT view in the *Technical Administration* work center, categorizes the downtime, for example, as HARDWARE MAINTENANCE: DATABASE SERVER, and enters a detailed account of the reasons for these measures and the impact they will have.
>
> The administrator can export this information to Excel and forward it to colleagues in the business units. The planned downtime retains the INACTIVE status for the time being.
>
> After checks have been completed, for example, with some requests for changes around times at which end-of-quarter closing is due to take place, and alterations have been included in downtime planning, the administrator sets the status of the planned downtime to ACTIVE. At the same time, the administrator makes certain settings, such as who should be informed in advance about downtime. These options are discussed in detail in the upcoming section.
>
> Because the databases of the corresponding development, test, and demo systems must also be maintained, the system administrator can copy the downtimes initially planned for the production system to DEV, TST, and DMO.
>
> Finally, the administrator configures the details of the processes for executing the individual downtimes, for example, configuring tasks that then appear in the task inbox and instruct him to take action as soon as a downtime is due. On the day of the first planned downtime, a task appears in the administrator's task inbox telling him to stop the production system at 10 p.m. and start it again at 11 p.m. The administrator performs this task by opening the upcoming downtime in the WORK MODE MANAGEMENT view in the *Technical Administration* work center in SAP Solution Manager. He then performs either a *hard* or a *soft* shutdown by choosing STOP SYSTEM NOW on the EXECUTION tab page.

Example (Cont.)

If the production system is running on an SAP NetWeaver release that contains the Adaptive Computing Controller (ACC) (and this has also been installed), you may opt to use this tool to shut down the system or otherwise use SAPControl.

At 10:45 p.m., the administrator becomes aware that the downtime is not going to be sufficient. Therefore, he goes to the DOWNTIME MANAGEMENT view in the *Technical Administration* work center and schedules a modified planned downtime that starts at 10 p.m. and ends at 11.30 p.m.

If necessary, he can then inform all relevant parties of the delay using the notification function, for example, by email or SMS. Rather than simply extending the planning downtime, the administrator must add a new phase to the original downtime to ensure that the subsequent history reflects events accurately. After all, by performing a statistical analysis, this history enables you to compare planned downtimes with modified planned downtimes. If planned downtimes are systematically too short or too long, you can identify and remedy this problem in future planning periods.

The administrator completes this maintenance work at 11.20 p.m. and uses the start function on the EXECUTION tab page for the opened modified planned downtime to restart the production system (or, again, using the ACC or SAPControl).

Notification of Downtimes

First, you can choose SET UP NOTIFICATIONS to define notification recipients for each system who may be interested in downtimes in that system.

Internal and external recipients

After you have defined the notification recipients at the system level, you can edit the text templates for each notification mode (email, SMS, system message) that these recipients will receive in a genuine situation. The editor provided allows you to put together texts on the basis of a number of keywords that are set dynamically at runtime. For example, the keyword SURNAME is filled with the last name of the recipient when the notification is sent.

The editor also features a preview function that fills keywords with sample contents to help you create suitable texts. Finally, you can define when you want notifications to be sent in relation to the core event—in this case, at the start of the planned downtime. You are free to change the basic setting shipped by SAP (two SMS messages and three emails, the first of which are sent five days before the downtime, and the last is sent one hour beforehand) or just change the sending schedule for selected recipients.

Notification Management

After you have defined the settings for possible notifications for every relevant system, you can elaborate on them further in the planned downtimes for these systems as required. When you open the respective downtime, you can—in the simplest scenario—go to the NOTIFICATION MANAGEMENT tab page and choose RELEASE SCHEDULED NOTIFICATIONS to copy the notification settings made at the system level exactly as they are for this downtime. When you choose the pushbutton, the contents of the NOTIFICATIONS RELEASED column changes from NO to YES, and the SAPconnect communication service (Transaction SOST) is triggered so that the respective emails and SMS are placed in the SAPconnect processing queue. If a recipient is deleted at a later point in time, or an entire downtime is canceled or removed, the content of the SAPconnect queue is adjusted to suit the new circumstances.

If you want to change the notifications pertaining to a specific downtime relative to the predefined notification settings, you can modify the recipient list as required on the NOTIFICATION MANAGEMENT tab page. In addition, notifications must not necessarily be sent according to the schedule in the notification settings; if the circumstances demand it, you can send notifications immediately by choosing SEND INSTANT NOTIFICATION. Before messages are sent immediately, you can adapt the text for each communication channel (email, SMS, system message). With system messages, you can also bypass the defined recipient list and instead contact all system users.

Integration with Technical Monitoring

Unwanted alerts

With regard to monitoring in SAP Solution Manager, system administrators often complain that monitoring produces unwanted alerts during planned downtimes. The administrators then face the tedious task of removing them. These "phantom alerts" do not occur in Technical Monitoring because alerts are suppressed during scheduled downtime.

Work mode-specific monitoring settings

Furthermore, there is the option in Technical Monitoring of reacting to metrics depending on the current work mode. So, for example, notifications can be sent automatically during peak business hours if the average response time increases to more than 1.2 seconds so that administrators can react immediately. During normal business times, however, this notification is not sent.

The Technical Monitoring configuration offers many possibilities for reacting work-mode-specifically to metrics, but we cannot go into these in detail here.

In addition to this, there is also integration with Computing Center Management System (CCMS) monitoring. The following selection options exist for CCMS monitoring:

CCMS monitoring

▶ FULL MONITORING: The CCMS continues to operate unchanged during downtime.

▶ MONITORING PAUSE: The CCMS stops all activities concerning the managed system, including the gathering of monitoring data.

▶ SUPPRESS ALERTS: CCMS continues to gather data but does not analyze it, which means no alerts can be triggered.

Supported Applications

Downtime processes are logged by the application log in SAP NetWeaver (Transaction SLG1, object SOLAR, subobject DTM or object DTS, subobject API). Log entries are kept for seven days. You can also deactivate logging if required.

Logging

Alternatively, or in addition to executing downtimes directly using SAPControl or ACC, you can create tasks for stopping and starting systems at the start or end of a planned downtime and assign these tasks to the responsible persons.

Task management

Reports

The WORK MODE MANAGEMENT tab page offers many SAP NetWeaver BW reports for checking the success of previous work mode planning and making future planning easier.

Reporting

The *downtime evaluations* (see Figure 10.43) display, for selectable time intervals, the PLANNED DOWNTIME, the USED PLANNED DOWNTIME, and the UNPLANNED DOWNTIME. This lets you quickly establish whether there were problems with unscheduled downtime.

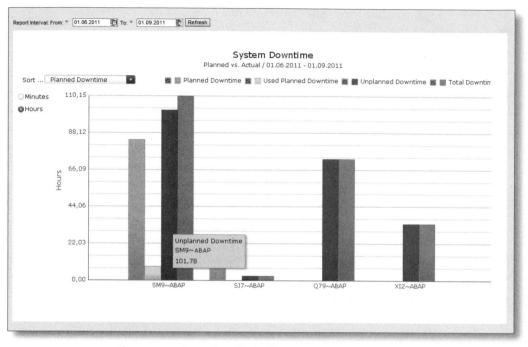

Figure 10.43 Downtime Evaluations

Furthermore, WORK MODE MANAGEMENT provides reports that display the measured downtime and measured performance KPIs in time series, overlaid with the scheduled work modes. Here, you can quickly determine when peak loads or downtime occurred and whether these matched the scheduled downtime or peak business hours.

10.5.2 IT Calendar

Previously, the planning process for downtime and business hours often involved an Excel spreadsheet of varying complexity that had to be made available to every interested party. Changes to the schedule were added manually to the planning sheet. This is now obsolete.

The IT Calendar from SAP (see Figure 10.44) is a convenient tool that shows you the scheduled work modes in a calendar view. You can switch among daily, weekly, and monthly views. You can filter work modes so that only scheduled downtime is displayed, for example.

The display lets you show the work modes in various time zones to check whether a scheduled downtime clashes with business hours in another time zone, for example.

Time zones

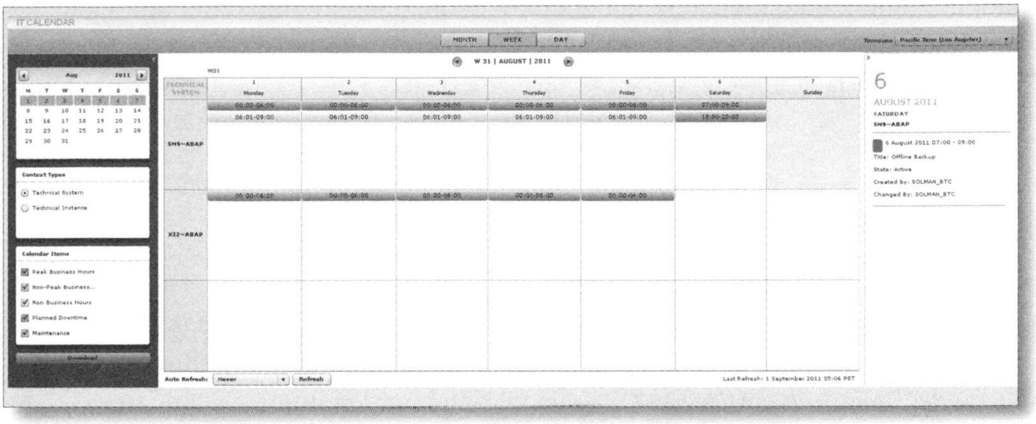

Figure 10.44 IT Calendar

The IT Calendar therefore helps you share current planning information concerning system availability and downtime with all interested persons and departments and keep this information constantly up-to-date.

10.5.3 Managing Notifications

You can use Notification Management to centrally manage recipients or recipient lists for various SAP Solution Manager applications, such as Work Mode Management, Alert Inbox, System Monitoring, PI Monitoring, and BI Monitoring. You can create different recipient lists for different application cases.

Global recipient pool

Notification Management lets you load the communication data for users and business partners of both the SAP Solution Manager system and managed systems to the *global recipient pool*. From there, you can assign the users to recipient lists, as needed.

You can also import notification recipients from LDAP server distribution lists or directly enter communication data for external recipients, if they are not available in the sources mentioned previously.

Notification Management is used by Technical Monitoring and Work Mode Management.

Technical
Monitoring

In technical monitoring, you can save recipients or recipient lists for each system; these recipients are automatically notified by email or SMS in the event of an alert. It is also easy to use manual notifications for alerts in the Alert Inbox and in most monitoring applications.

Work Mode
Management

In Work Mode Management, you can use recipient lists from Notification Management to efficiently notify end users about scheduled system downtime.

The MY NOTIFICATION SETTINGS link lets SAP Solution Manager users set the times during which they want to receive SMS or email notifications, or specify that they do not want to be notified. If, for example, you are in the office from 9:00 a.m. to 1:00 p.m. and are then on call until 6:00 p.m., you can set that you want to be notified by email from 9:00 a.m. to 1:00 p.m. and by SMS from 1:00 p.m. to 6:00 p.m. If you go on vacation or a business trip, you can also enter absences and specify who the notification should be sent to while you are away.

10.5.4 Central System Administration (CSA)

System administration is a key IT instrument for ensuring that your IT landscape is set up in the best possible way and is fully functioning. Proactive monitoring and regular administration make it possible to detect problem situations and remedy them early. The underlying operational events can be addressed to the expert network to be solved even before live operation is impaired.

An integrated documentation and reporting function is an important part and basis for administration-related communication within an IT organization. Unusual application and system events can be documented in detail and reported to the organizational groups involved.

It is equally important to show that the administration tasks are carried out regularly and properly. The administration reporting function has another benefit that should not be underestimated: It offers a platform with clear proof of provision of services for the ordering party, providing confirmation that the SLA has been fulfilled.

Know-how
and tools for
administration

The Central System Administration (CSA) integrated in the *Technical Administration* work center contains the current know-how for administration, as well as tools for documenting administration tasks and procedures. Daily system administration within SAP solutions is supported by a logically structured collection of typical administration tasks. The task structure is dynamically structured and offered by SAP system type and application component. SAP Solution Manager allows you to manage administration tasks centrally and ensure that they are always executed regularly by saving them as recurring tasks to be completed. The tasks of a system administrator are simplified and easier to understand. This makes it possible to significantly increase the safety and quality of system administration in production operations.

SAP Solution Manager provides all of the necessary functions for managing the SAP landscape centrally. It contains all of the tools for both ABAP-based SAP systems and for non-ABAP systems, such as SAP NetWeaver Portal, SAP NetWeaver AS JAVA, Sybase, and SAP BusinessObjects. The Web connection that is also integrated completes the scope of functions, making it possible to monitor and administer the entire IT landscape. This includes functions such as monitoring and managing applications, SAP instances, databases, and output devices; starting and stopping systems; archiving; and much more. With central access to all systems to be managed and the option to manage periodic and ad hoc administrative tasks automatically, you can realize major savings in terms of both time and costs.

With central task management, SAP facilitates initial knowledge transfer and offers a tool for standardizing SAP solution maintenance. This knowledge transfer is especially practical with new solutions, for which minimal knowledge has been established in your company. Furthermore, CSA provides the option of creating your own tasks in addition to the standard tasks predefined by SAP. You can store detailed task and process descriptions and documentation for the tasks that you create and for those provided by SAP. Documentation can either take place inside the administration session or outside, anywhere in your IT landscape, and it can be displayed directly when the task is executed via a URL or a link to your central document server. This documents and captures internal knowledge and therefore ensures that standard administration can also be carried out while you are on vacation or sick leave or in the event of organizational changes within your company. Task completion is logged automatically (along with the comments and notes created as

Standardized administration and knowledge transfer

needed) and can also be summarized and accessed in report form at regular intervals.

If you create a solution in SAP Solution Manager and assign systems to this solution, the CSA session automatically offers you the most important administration tasks for those systems. SAP supplies the administration tasks via SAP Solution Manager in the form of general and component-specific templates that you can either copy in full or make individual selections. These templates are arranged according to SAP's own experience of the base and applications and should be seen as administration templates recommended by SAP.

The CSA functions allow you to centrally access local administration tools in the managed systems from SAP Solution Manager. The major advantage of this concept is that you can incorporate tools that are provided in the latest SAP releases but are not available in SAP Solution Manager, and you can access these tools centrally. In addition to providing central access to daily tasks, therefore, the work center also guarantees that you can integrate and use tools from newer SAP system components in SAP Solution Manager in the future.

The OVERVIEW view in the *Technical Administration* work center (see Figure 10.45) offers all of the tasks and activities you perform regularly when managing the SAP system and solution landscapes. Selecting TASK INBOX takes you to SAP Solution Manager's task management. Various views are available here as a working environment, such as RECURRING, PRECONFIGURED TASKS (CSA), or CSA TASKS IN FAVORITE SYSTEMS.

Alternatively, you can define your own queries to preconfigure an individual, personalized administration area. By using the work center's filter and sorting function, you can also select and sort the task display according to SAP Solution Manager solutions, systems, or task names.

This gives you a quick overview of the system landscape and the pending, open tasks within an SAP Solution Manager solution or for a specific system.

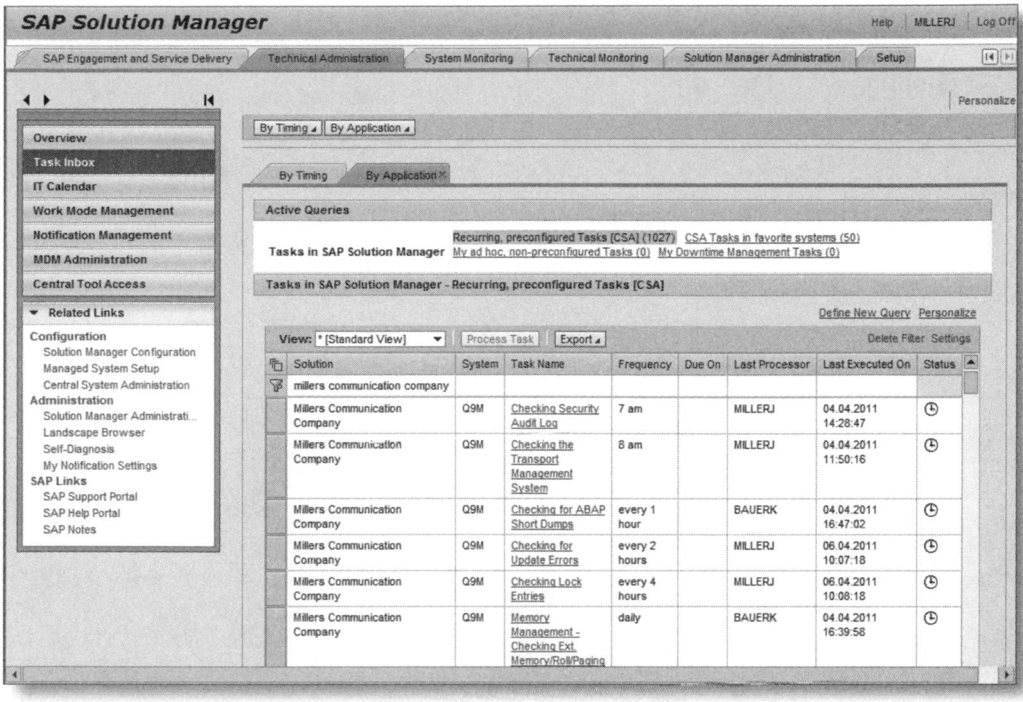

Figure 10.45 "Technical Administration" Work Center—Task Management

Open Tasks List

After you select the application area Task Inbox in the Task Management area, the list of open tasks from all SAP solutions and systems is displayed (refer to Figure 10.45).

List of open tasks

The open task list shows all planned but not yet completed tasks, according to the selection you chose beforehand (in full, per SAP Solution Manager solution, or per system), organized by urgency and due date. The display includes rapid information in the form of the planning execution frequency of the task, as well as the user, date, and time of the last execution. You can also see from the status display whether the task is not currently open and awaiting processing but is already overdue because it was not completed within the specified time frame. You can process the open tasks directly from this list.

Task Structure of the Administration Session

CSA session If you select an open task from the list of open tasks, you go straight to the CSA session for the assigned system (see Figure 10.46). From here, you can execute the administration tool (SAP transaction, program, URL, operating system command, etc.) that is assigned to the task, in the selected system.

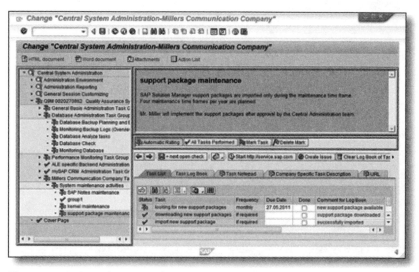

Figure 10.46 Central System Administration Session

The infrastructure of the session provides standardized information and tasks for analyzing the system and for administration. The tasks and information are entered hierarchically in what are known as check groups, checks, and the underlying tasks. You can systematically process all of the open tasks in the administration session according to their due date, or you can process them individually from the work center's list of open tasks.

Functions of the CSA The CSA makes it easier for the administrator team to complete daily tasks, thanks to the following main functions:

▸ Direct jumps to the transactions, programs, URLs, operating system commands and expert monitors in the managed system that are assigned to processing.

▸ Direct access to the managed system without having to log on.[1]

---

1 This requires use of the trusting-trusted RFC connection recommended by SAP.

▶ Optional display of SAP standard documentation in the task description or your own internal task description (COMPANY-SPECIFIC TASK DESCRIPTION).

▶ Compiling brief comments for documenting the completed tasks in the task log book (COMMENT FOR LOG BOOK).

▶ Compiling detailed problem descriptions in the TASK NOTEPAD for the task, if a more comprehensive description or documentation of the completed task is needed, in addition to the brief comments. You can also store URLs or document links.

▶ Creating issues in the SAP Solution Manager's standard issue management, directly from the task, if problems need to be processed further.

▶ Marking uncompleted tasks with a "red flag" to make it easier to find tasks that have not been fully processed later.

▶ Automating recording of the user ID, date, and time in the task log book after the task has been completed.

▶ Creating your own company-specific task structures with your own tasks and task documentation.

▶ Detailed reporting function as a proof and documentation of administration activities.

The CSA session consists of the following five areas:

Structure of the administration session

▶ ADMINISTRATION ENVIRONMENT (personal administration environment)

▶ ADMINISTRATION REPORTING

▶ GENERAL SESSION CUSTOMIZING (session configuration)

▶ SAP TASK STRUCTURE (SAP standard task area)

▶ USER TASK AREA

In the ADMINISTRATION ENVIRONMENT, you can set your personal view of the task structure. You can select the standard views provided by SAP, or you can define your own views using the Task View Master. For example, you can display open tasks only or completed tasks only. Or you can select only open tasks with the planning frequency EVERY HOUR. You can select and combine any number of selection options.

Personal task structure

Administration session configuration

You carry out configuration of the CSA (GENERAL SESSION CUSTOMIZING) for each system within the CSA session. This function is protected by an SAP authorization object and should only be carried out by the central administration team with overall authority. The session is structured so that you first make the settings independently of the task. The work that is independent of the tasks includes specifying the number and time frame for the TASK LOG entries to be saved and the size of the TASK LOG BOOK HISTORY, as well as defining the report layout and the report content. These defined parameters form the basis for automatic self-reorganization of the saved logging data.

The task-specific Customizing settings include assigning the execution frequencies (TASK FREQUENCIES), creating the internal task description (COMPANY-SPECIFIC TASK DESCRIPTION), and, if desired, defining your own company-specific tasks (USER TASKS).

Processing frequencies

In SAP Solution Manager, you can use the processing frequencies recommended by SAP for your tasks, developed in line with Best Practice, by choosing LOAD DEFAULT FREQUENCIES. If you do not want to select individual tasks or their processing frequencies, deactivate the task, or select your own processing frequency. You can choose from a large selection of processing frequencies, ranging from hours and days, specific days of the week, the start of the month, the end of the month, through to weekly, monthly, or yearly intervals, and much more. You can specify a due date to temporarily overwrite the regular processing frequency for the task and schedule the task for a specific date.

Company-specific task description

Your own company-specific description of the task in the COMPANY-SPECIFIC TASK DESCRIPTION part of the document provides the administrator with all of the important information about the type and scope of the activity to be carried out. External documents can also be attached to the description by web links: The documentation therefore does not have to be carried out in SAP Solution Manager itself. The documents can be located anywhere in your system landscape, on document servers or portals.

At this point, you can also save a predefined problem management system with information routes, follow-up activities, and escalation paths for the relevant, task-specific error situations. The problem management description fulfills the process required by ITIL-compliant IT service management (ITSM).

The COPY Customizing function makes it possible to distribute the Customizing settings and the user-defined tasks of a system anywhere in the system landscape. You have the option of copying all or some of the settings data from another system. Alternatively, you can copy a system's settings to individual or multiple systems across landscapes. Copying system settings makes it possible to use predefined administration templates. This can be used to create a highly standardized administration environment.

Configuration templates

General Task Area (SAP Task Structure)

The actual system-specific and component-specific administration tasks connect to the Customizing part. The CSA session contains the three standard areas GENERAL BASIS ADMINISTRATION, DATABASE ADMINISTRATION, and PERFORMANCE MONITORING, which are always present in each ABAP-based system and are processed generally.

SAP task structure

After the general administration areas, the dynamically structured task structure contains, depending on the system type of the system to be administered, the specific tasks of the SAP standard components, such as SAP Customer Relationship Management (SAP CRM), SAP Supply Chain Management (SAP SCM), SAP Supplier Relationship Management (SAP SRM), SAP NetWeaver Business Warehouse (SAP NetWeaver BW), and Internet middleware administration. The standard SAP task structure contains a large number of tasks, but these are only the most important tasks to be carried out for a system or a system component.

User-Specific Task Area (Customer Task Area)

In the user-specific task area, you can put together and define your own task structure, according to your company-specific IT administration needs. You can use task areas and task groups to organize the structure. This structure makes it possible to arrange and organize the individual task areas for an application or system hierarchically. In general, the user-defined task area for administration and reporting functions has exactly the same administration and reporting functions available as the SAP standard task area. There is no functional difference here.

Central documentation tool
The architecture of the user-specific tasks can also be used to create special operations handbooks, business process documentation, or process manuals with detailed task sequences and task descriptions for your IT operations. These tasks do not necessarily need to be backed by technically executable transactions or actions. Equally, the environment described does not necessarily have to be an SAP system landscape. In this case, the CSA session would be used as a program-controlled, central documentation and description tool.

Problem Management and Message Processing

Issue list and action list
The administration session gives you the opportunity to trigger follow-on processing if certain system states, events, or specified problem situations occur, and they require further processing by other employees or organizational units.

You can select from two options. One is to include the SAP Solution Manager standard ISSUE MANAGEMENT function in the administration session and use it to implement message processing. Within the session, you create the *issues* at the system level or the task level. These system-relevant issues can be monitored and processed further either directly from the administration session or centrally in the ISSUE MANAGEMENT area.

Alternatively, you can enter the necessary follow-up activities centrally in the administration session's ACTION LIST for the session and the entire system. When you create the activity to be carried out, you enter the priority, type of action, date of completion, person responsible, and detailed description of the activity in the various input fields. You also update and manage the ACTION LIST within the administration session.

The administration reports also issue the ISSUE LIST and ACTION LIST, which provide important additional information and the basis for subsequent activities.

Administration Reporting

Administration Reporting is an important part of system administration. It is necessary and advisable to document the system states and results of System Monitoring and system administration and to save this information in report histories. This provides proof without gaps, as per the requirements of IT compliance, as part of IT governance. When there are audits in the IT area, verification of the monitoring and administration report histories is a fundamental auditing characteristic. To comply with this requirement, various report areas and reports were developed within Technical Administration.

Task log book history

The TASK LOG BOOK HISTORY report (see Figure 10.47) shows, in detail and for specific systems, the administration activities that were carried out and the results of those activities. The report contains data such as the task carried out, the processor carrying out the task, and the date and time that individual tasks were carried out. The comments that can be entered during administration, the detailed descriptions documented in the TASK NOTEPAD, the monitoring results, and the description of the problem situations that occurred are also listed to complete the information.

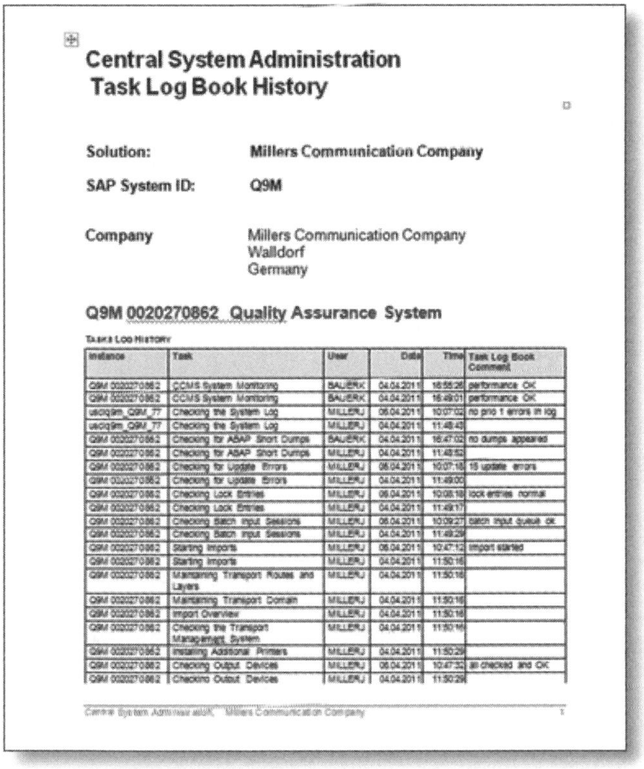

Central System Administration
Task Log Book History

Solution: Millers Communication Company

SAP System ID: Q9M

Company: Millers Communication Company, Walldorf, Germany

Q9M 0020270862 Quality Assurance System

Tasks Log History

Instance	Task	User	Date	Time	Task Log Book Comment
Q9M 0020270862	CCMS System Monitoring	BAUERK	04.04.2011	16:55:26	performance OK
Q9M 0020270862	CCMS System Monitoring	BAUERK	04.04.2011	16:49:01	performance OK
usciq9m_Q9M_77	Checking the System Log	MILLERJ	06.04.2011	10:07:02	no prio 1 errors in log
usciq9m_Q9M_77	Checking the System Log	MILLERJ	04.04.2011	11:48:43	
Q9M 0020270862	Checking for ABAP Short Dumps	BAUERK	04.04.2011	16:47:02	no dumps appeared
Q9M 0020270862	Checking for ABAP Short Dumps	MILLERJ	04.04.2011	11:48:52	
Q9M 0020270862	Checking for Update Errors	MILLERJ	06.04.2011	10:07:18	15 update errors
Q9M 0020270862	Checking for Update Errors	MILLERJ	04.04.2011	11:49:00	
Q9M 0020270862	Checking Lock Entries	MILLERJ	06.04.2011	10:08:18	lock entries normal
Q9M 0020270862	Checking Lock Entries	MILLERJ	04.04.2011	11:49:17	
Q9M 0020270862	Checking Batch Input Sessions	MILLERJ	06.04.2011	10:09:27	batch input queue ok
Q9M 0020270862	Checking Batch Input Sessions	MILLERJ	04.04.2011	11:49:29	
Q9M 0020270862	Starting Imports	MILLERJ	06.04.2011	10:47:12	import started
Q9M 0020270862	Starting Imports	MILLERJ	04.04.2011	11:50:16	
Q9M 0020270862	Maintaining Transport Routes and Layers	MILLERJ	04.04.2011	11:50:16	
Q9M 0020270862	Maintaining Transport Domain	MILLERJ	04.04.2011	11:50:16	
Q9M 0020270862	Import Overview	MILLERJ	04.04.2011	11:50:16	
Q9M 0020270862	Checking the Transport Management System	MILLERJ	04.04.2011	11:50:16	
Q9M 0020270862	Installing Additional Printers	MILLERJ	04.04.2011	11:50:29	
Q9M 0020270862	Checking Output Devices	MILLERJ	06.04.2011	10:47:32	all checked and OK
Q9M 0020270862	Checking Output Devices	MILLERJ	04.04.2011	11:50:29	

Central System Administration, Millers Communication Company 1

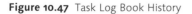

Figure 10.47 Task Log Book History

No report is provided for tasks that have not been completed. Administration reporting as a list output refers only to the tasks that were actively carried out in the CSA. However, you can also use the OVERDUE LIST within the administration session and the status in the list of open tasks in the *Technical Administration* work center to display online the tasks that were not fulfilled within the specified time frame.

Reporting as background job

As with all other reporting functions in SAP Solution Manager, you can also schedule the Task Log Book History report to be created as a recurring background job. This enables the report to be executed automatically at regular intervals without any manual intervention. When reporting is carried out as a background job, the data is also issued as an SAP spool list. Using what is known as an email printer and the SAPconnect environment (Transaction SCOT), you can set the reports to be sent automatically by email. The automated administration reporting is located in the *System Monitoring* work center within the REPORTS area.

Task session report

In addition to the *Task Log Book History*, IT specialists and system administrators can use another report, the *Task Session Report*, to gain a full overview of all the tasks that were actively set within the CSA for one or more of an SAP Solution Manager installation's systems. You can generate the *Task Log Book History* and *Task Session Report* either as HTML or Word reports.

You choose the layout of the cover page and the content of the evaluation. URLs, file links, and document links added to the report also function within the report.

10.6 Technical Analysis

The technical analysis of solutions covers the areas of TECHNICAL EVALUATIONS and MANAGEMENT EVALUATIONS. This subdivision is an attempt to satisfy the various requirements that arise, on one hand, from displaying and evaluating purely technical metrics and, on the other, highly compressed and interpreted data.

10.6.1 Technical Evaluations

Technical measured values

The evaluations in this area are restricted to displaying technical measured values that are of particular relevance to operation of the solution. These evaluations enable early identification of situations that could, under certain circumstances, endanger smooth operation of the solution. The following functions are available in the TECHNICAL EVALUATIONS area in the SAP Solution Manager:

▶ EarlyWatch Alert/EarlyWatch Alert for solutions

▶ Interactive reports

EarlyWatch Alert/EarlyWatch Alert for Solutions

The SAP EarlyWatch Alert is a weekly diagnosis service for monitoring SAP systems in the SAP Solution Manager. After the relevant data has been downloaded from the managed system to SAP Solution Manager, the data is processed, and a report is created. You can display the report as an HTML document or generate a Microsoft Word document. You can use the documents as status reports for a system and use them as the basis for analyzing or avoiding any problems that might occur.

Weekly diagnosis

Before setting this up, the following prerequisites must be fulfilled:

▶ You have set up your systems in a solution landscape in SAP Solution Manager.

▶ You have set up the Service Data Control Center (SDCCN) in the relevant systems of the solution landscape.

You set up the EarlyWatch Alert in the *Solution Manager Administration* work center after selecting the menu item SOLUTIONS (see Figure 10.48).

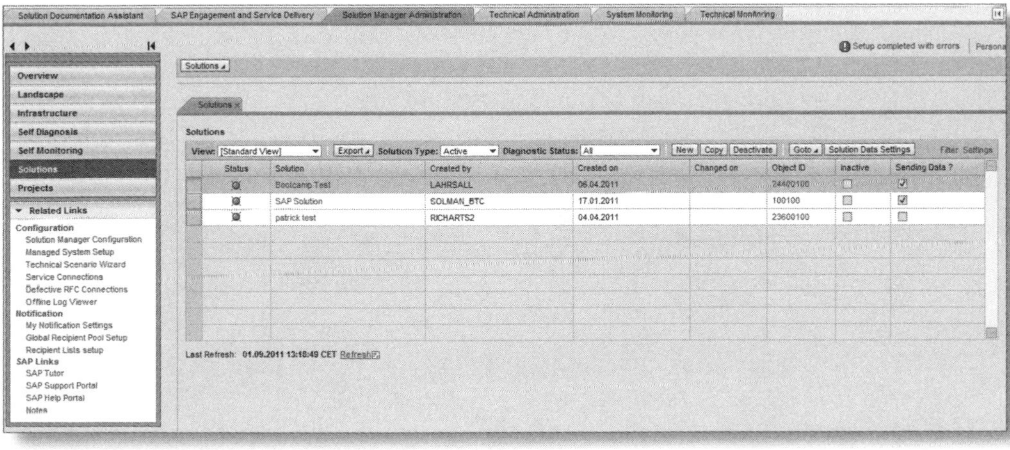

Setup

Figure 10.48 Solutions in the "SAP Solution Manager Administration" Work Center

The details of a selected solution are displayed in the lower part of the screen. Here you will find the components assigned to the solution and a view for setting up operations. You can select the EarlyWatch Alert and start the configuration by clicking on SETUP EARLYWATCH ALERT (see Figure 10.49).

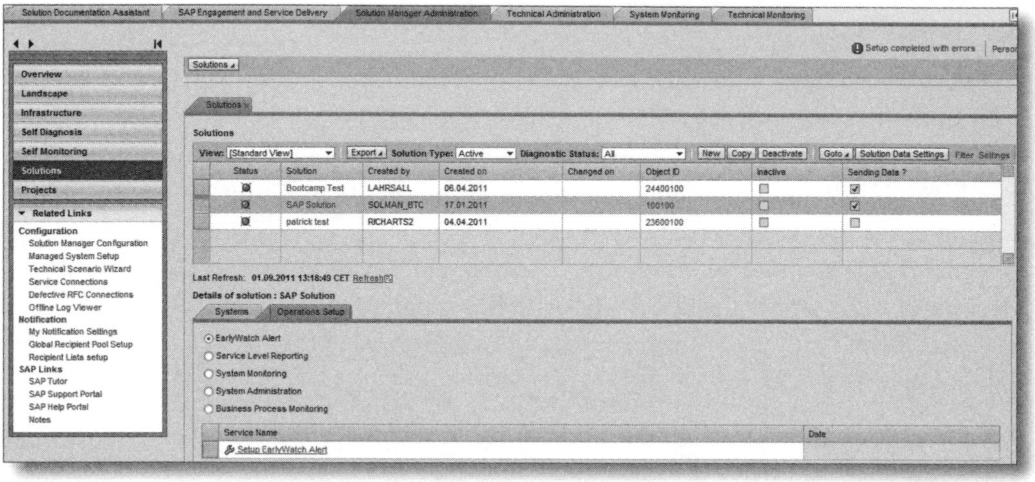

Figure 10.49 Setting Up Operations for a Solution

The settings are displayed in the new window EarlyWatch Alert Administration (see Figure 10.50).

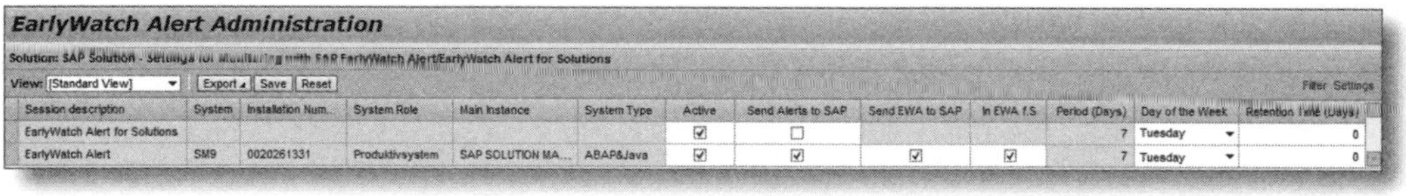

Figure 10.50 EarlyWatch Alert Administration

Here, you can set up the capture of your monitoring data for SAP EarlyWatch Alert per system or per solution. To do this, select the relevant fields according to your requirements (see Table 10.1).

Field	Note
ACTIVE	If you do not set this indicator, the system does not collect any data.
SEND ALERTS TO SAP	Only set this indicator if you set data collection to ACTIVE.

Table 10.1 EarlyWatch Alert Administration

Field	Note
SEND EWA TO SAP	Only set this indicator if you set data collection to ACTIVE.
IN EWA F.S	You can decide which SAP EarlyWatch Alerts per system appear in your SAP EarlyWatch Alert per solution.
DAY OF THE WEEK	The day on which data is collected for SAP EarlyWatch Alert per system and SAP EarlyWatch Alert per solution can vary.
RETENTION TIME (DAYS)	After the retention time, the SAP EarlyWatch Alerts are saved.

Table 10.1 EarlyWatch Alert Administration (Cont.)

To display the generated EarlyWatch Alert reports, select the function GENERATED DOCUMENTS in the *Technical Monitoring* work center. In the upper part of the screen, you can filter the displayed sessions by solution, date, and context. The EarlyWatch Alert sessions are displayed in a table with their evaluation, session ID, solution name, date, and context (see Figure 10.51).

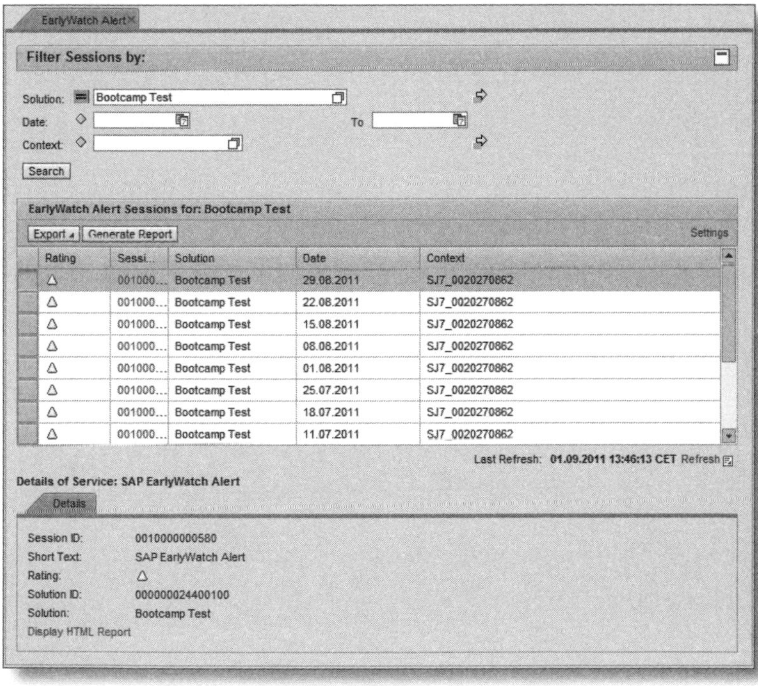

Displaying reports

Figure 10.51 Selection Screen for EarlyWatch Alert Sessions

If you select a session in the table, you can use the GENERATE REPORT function to generate the report in Word format or display it. Furthermore, you can create the report in HTML format. The relevant function call for a selected session is in the detail view in the lower part of the screen (see Figure 10.52).

Analysis from 16.05.2011
Until 22.05.2011
Bericht: Y55, Productive
Installation: 0120003411
Sitzung: 2000000005431

THE BEST-RUN BUSINESSES RUN SAP

EarlyWatch Alert-RKT_Solution

1 Service Summary

During this EarlyWatch Alert Session, we detected issues that could potentially affect your system. We recommend that you take corrective action as soon as possible.

Alert Overview

	Standard users including SAP* or DDIC have default password.
	Secure password policy is not sufficiently enforced.
	There are aborted postings (errors in UPDATE). Reprocess them to ensure consistent data.
	We found more than 30 ABAP dumps in your system.
	Security weaknesses identified in the Gateway or the Message Server configuration.

Figure 10.52 Example of an EarlyWatch Alert Report in HTML Format

Evaluated data   The EarlyWatch Alert report provides a detailed evaluation of the following data for the managed systems:

- General component status
- System configuration
- Hardware
- Performance development
- Average response times
- Current system load
- Critical error messages and interrupted processes
- Database administration

Interactive Reports

You can use *interactive reports* at any time to centrally display the development over time of the most important metrics for your managed systems and solutions. This makes it possible to evaluate various parameters over time, allowing you to identify trends. The measured values are collected via the monitoring and alerting infrastructure and saved in the SAP Solution Manager's BW. The configuration is largely automatic and the result of setting up Technical Monitoring in SAP Solution Manager. This ensures that all of the values that you can display in the interactive reports are stored in the BW in the necessary resolution. Older data is also automatically reorganized into lower resolutions and ultimately deleted, to prevent the storage requirements in BW from increasing unchecked. The interactive reports are a component of the *Technical Monitoring* work center and can be executed there via detailed navigation (see Figure 10.53).

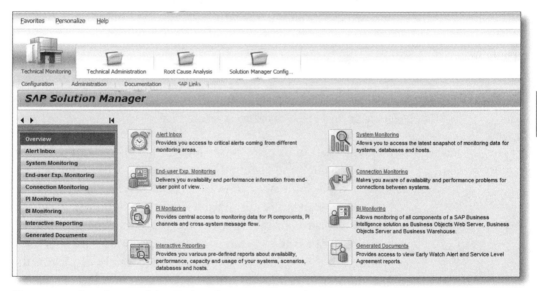

Figure 10.53 Start Screen of the "Technical Monitoring" Work Center

After you call the interactive reports, your first option is to select the type of evaluation you require. You can choose from the following:

Evaluation types

- ▶ Systems
- ▶ Scenarios
- ▶ Hosts
- ▶ Databases

497

The Systems area is selected by default. You can now select the systems you require by means of detailed selection, and you can decide whether to display the reports in the same window or in a new window. To do this, click the System Reports button, and select the relevant option. The reports are now displayed for the selected systems in the content area of the screen (see Figure 10.54).

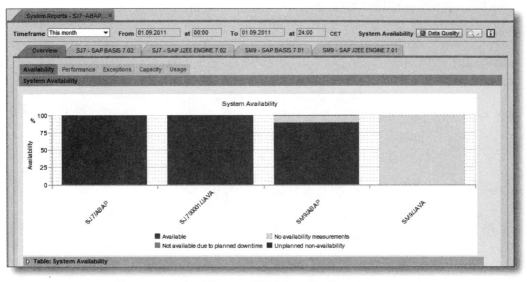

Figure 10.54 Start Screen of the Interactive Reports

Header   In the upper part of the screen (see Figure 10.55), you now have the option of selecting the required reporting period from an expandable list. On the right side, you can see the Data Quality pushbutton. A colored icon in the pushbutton shows the status of the data on which this is based. To the right of this is the Analysis pushbutton. This makes it possible to jump to an appropriate analysis tool, depending on the evaluation shown or to separately display in the metric monitor the values on which the evaluation is based. The last function in this line is the documentation call. This function provides a detailed explanation for each evaluation displayed; the explanation is shown in a new window.

Figure 10.55 Header of the Interactive Reports

For a detailed evaluation of the data, you can use the DATA QUALITY pushbutton to call the BI Diagnostic Center. This is a tool that helps you find errors in the BW-based evaluations. Figure 10.56 shows the start screen of the BI Diagnostic Center.

BI Diagnostic Center

BI Status

BI - Solution Manager Connectivity		BI Database	
BI System ID:	SJ7(001)	Database space used (GB):	181.39
RFC destination from Solution Manager to BI:	NONE	Database usage in %:	77
RFC destination from BI to Solution Manager:	NONE	DB space used by all Scenarios (GB):	5.25
		BI Reporting Data in %:	2.89

Reporting Scenarios

Scenario Setup | Refresh | Expert Mode

Scenario	Last Loading Date	CET	Next Loading Date	CET	Load Interval	Total DB space	Performance (s/call)
System Reporting	01.09.2011	13:55:14	01.09.2011	14:55:14	1 hour	4287 MB	6.42
Test Workbench Reporting		00:00:00		00:00:00		144 MB	-
Incident Management Reporting		00:00:00		00:00:00		144 MB	-
End User Experience Monitoring	01.09.2011	13:51:17	01.09.2011	14:51:17	1 hour	196 MB	-
Alert Management Reporting	01.09.2011	13:51:58	01.09.2011	14:51:58	1 hour	1526 MB	-

Data Loading | Self Checks | Data Quality

Details | Filter

Sources of Reporting Data

Data Load	System ID	Type of Data	Data Load Status Description	Last Load	CET	Next Load	CET	Load Interval	Timeslot	Records loaded	Connection
	SJ7	Monitoring Data	Dataload finished without problems	01.09.2011	14:01:48	01.09.2011	15:01:33	1 hour		209	Edit
	SJ7	System Thresholds	Dataload finished without problems	01.09.2011	02:07:30	02.09.2011	02:06:54	24 hours	02:00-04:00	975	Edit
	SJ7	Scenario Thresholds	Dataload finished without problems	01.09.2011	02:08:12	02.09.2011	02:06:54	24 hours	02:00-04:00	1.553	Edit
	SJ7	Database Data	Dataload finished without problems	01.09.2011	13:44:25	01.09.2011	14:44:24	1 hour		0	Edit
	SJ7	Statistical Data	Dataload finished without problems	01.09.2011	14:01:25	01.09.2011	14:59:01	1 hour		831	Edit
	SJ7	Java Monitoring Data	Loading has not been activated for this type of data		00:00:00		00:00:00			0	
	SM9	Monitoring Data	Dataload finished without problems	01.09.2011	13:55:14	01.09.2011	14:55:04	1 hour		27	Edit
	SM9	System Thresholds	Dataload finished without problems	01.09.2011	02:07:10	02.09.2011	02:06:55	24 hours	02:00-04:00	245	Edit
	SM9	Statistical Data	Dataload finished without problems	01.09.2011	13:50:52	01.09.2011	14:49:57	1 hour		608	Edit
	SM9	Java Monitoring Data	Dataload finished without problems	01.09.2011	13:16:54	01.09.2011	14:16:44	1 hour		0	Edit

Figure 10.56 Start Screen of the BI Diagnostic Center

The upper area contains information about the status of the RFC connections between the SAP Solution Manager and SAP NetWeaver BW. Next to this is displayed information about how much space the BW data occupies in the database. The center part of the screen contains a table showing all of the scenarios that report various values to self-monitoring:

▶ SYSTEM REPORTING

▶ TEST WORKBENCH REPORTING

▶ INCIDENT MANAGEMENT REPORTING

▶ END USER EXPERIENCE MONITORING

▶ ALERT MANAGEMENT REPORTING

For each scenario, the following is displayed: status information, the scenario name, the date and time of the last loading process, the data and time of the next loading process, the loading interval, the memory space that is currently used by the scenario on the database, and the average time for each call of an evaluation from the corresponding scenario. Additionally, the lower part of the screen shows, for each selected scenario, various information about the data loading process and the self-monitoring. The view of the data loading process (see Figure 10.57) issues the relevant status messages for each connected system.

Data Load	System ID	Type of Data	Data Load Status Description	Last Load	CET	Next Load	CET	Load Interval	Timeslot	Records loaded	Connection
◇	Q79	System Thresholds	Loading has not been activated for this type of data		00:00:00		00:00:00			0	
◇	Q79	Java Monitoring Data	Loading has not been activated for this type of data		00:00:00		00:00:00			0	
▣	SJ7	Monitoring Data	Dataload finished without problems	01.09.2011	14:01:48	01.09.2011	15:01:33	1 hour		209	▣ Edit
▣	SJ7	System Thresholds	Dataload finished without problems	01.09.2011	02:07:30	02.09.2011	02:06:54	24 hours	02:00-04:00	975	▣ Edit
▣	SJ7	Scenario Thresholds	Dataload finished without problems	01.09.2011	02:08:12	02.09.2011	02:06:54	24 hours	02:00-04:00	1.553	▣ Edit
▣	SJ7	Database Data	Dataload finished without problems	01.09.2011	13:44:25	01.09.2011	14:44:24	1 hour		0	▣ Edit
▣	SJ7	Statistical Data	Dataload finished without problems	01.09.2011	14:01:25	01.09.2011	14:59:01	1 hour		831	▣ Edit
◇	SJ7	Java Monitoring Data	Loading has not been activated for this type of data		00:00:00		00:00:00			0	
▣	SM9	Monitoring Data	Dataload finished without problems	01.09.2011	13:55:14	01.09.2011	14:55:04	1 hour		27	▣ Edit
▣	SM9	System Thresholds	Dataload finished without problems	01.09.2011	02:07:10	02.09.2011	02:06:55	24 hours	02:00-04:00	245	▣ Edit
▣	SM9	Statistical Data	Dataload finished without problems	01.09.2011	13:50:52	01.09.2011	14:49:57	1 hour		608	▣ Edit
▣	SM9	Java Monitoring Data	Dataload finished without problems	01.09.2011	13:16:54	01.09.2011	14:16:44	1 hour		0	▣ Edit
◇	SM9	Database Data	Loading has not been activated for this type of data		00:00:00		00:00:00			0	
◇	XI2	Monitoring Data	Dataload of this system not yet started		00:00:00	01.09.2011	15:01:33	1 hour		0	
◇	XI2	System Thresholds	Dataload of this system not yet started		00:00:00	01.09.2011	14:55:04	24 hours	02:00-04:00	0	

Figure 10.57 Information about Loading the Data in the BI Diagnostic Center

Automatic tests are carried out for each scenario; these check the prerequisites and that the scenario is functioning without errors. The result of this transaction is grouped by inspection and displayed in a list in the SELF CHECKS view (see Figure 10.58).

Results of BI based Reporting Health Checks

Self Check results

	Status	Description	Check result text	Long ...	Recheck
▼	▣	System Reporting Operating			Check all again
▼	▣	Checks whether all required extracto...			Check again
•	▣		Statistic records extractors for all ma...	ⓘ	
▶	▣	Checks whether all aggregation profil...			Check again
▶	▣	Checks whether internal BI data admi...			Check again
▼	▣	Errors reported by BW background p...			Check again
•	▣		(DATA_LOAD_CUBE_CHECK)		
•	▣		1. Check of Cube 0CCMDAY1 failed ...		
▶	▣	Checks whether the BI client is set u...			Check again
▶	▣	Checks whether needed ICF Service...			Check again
▶	▣	Checks whether MYSELF source sy...			Check again

Figure 10.58 Information about Self Checks

Now we return to the start screen of the interactive reports. Under the header, there is a choice of evaluations that can be displayed in accordance with the selection. This always starts with the overview evaluation, which is also shown first on starting. Next to this are the system-specific evaluations, depending on the choice you made. These evaluations are displayed directly beneath the selection toolbar and contain the following categories:

- ▶ AVAILABILITY
- ▶ PERFORMANCE
- ▶ EXCEPTIONS (ERRORS)
- ▶ CAPACITY
- ▶ USE

In Table 10.2, you can see which reports are displayed in each category for the overview selection.

Reports

Category	Evaluation
AVAILABILITY	System availability
PERFORMANCE	Response times
	Response time distribution
	Java garbage collection (if the list of selected systems also includes Java systems)
EXCEPTIONS (ERRORS)	ABAP exceptions (errors)
CAPACITY	CPU utilization
	Database utilization
USE	Logons
	User activity

Table 10.2 Categories and Evaluations Available in the Overview

Which evaluations are available for a managed system depends on the basic technology used in the system. For an ABAP system, the reports shown in Table 10.3 can be accessed by default via the interactive reports.

Evaluations for ABAP systems

Category	Evaluation
AVAILABILITY	System availability
	Instance availability
	Host availability
	Database availability
PERFORMANCE	Response times
	Response time distribution
	Response time composition
	Database performance
EXCEPTIONS (ERRORS)	ABAP exceptions (errors)
CAPACITIES	CPU utilization
	Database utilization
	Main memory
	File system
	Paging rate
USE	Applications
	Transactions and evaluations
	RFC destinations
	Web service consumer
	RFC and web service providers
	Database
	User activity

Table 10.3 System-Specific Categories and Evaluations (ABAP)

Java evaluations

In a Java-based system, the evaluations shown in Table 10.4 can be called.

Category	Evaluation
AVAILABILITY	System availability
	Instance availability

Table 10.4 System-Specific Categories and Evaluations (Java)

Category	Evaluation
AVAILABILITY (Contd.)	Host availability
	Database availability
PERFORMANCE	Threads
	Garbage collection
	Response times
	Old space usage
	Memory consumption
	Database performance
CAPACITIES	CPU utilization
	Main memory
	File system
	Paging rate
USE	Number of HTTP sessions

Table 10.4 System-Specific Categories and Evaluations (Java) (Cont.)

When you call a report, it contains a graph showing the progress of the measured values over time and a table beneath this listing the values in numerical form (see Figure 10.59).

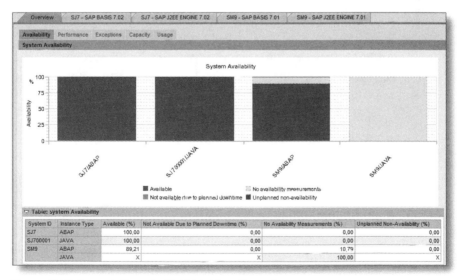

Figure 10.59 Example Report with Table View Opened

Type selection   In addition to the interactive reports for SYSTEMS, you can display other evaluations of SCENARIOS, HOSTS, and DATABASES by selecting the report type. You can select the type on the left screen border, directly underneath the buttons for calling the work center functions (see Figure 10.60).

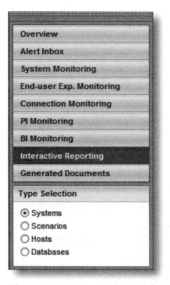

Figure 10.60 Type Selection for the Interactive Reports

"Scenarios" type   If you select the SCENARIOS type, you can display the most important performance and availability values from EEM. The relevant metrics are issued for the following entities:

▸ **Scenario**
An EEM scenario contains one or more technical systems that are relevant to a business scenario. EEM is used to determine the availability and performance of these scenarios.

▸ **Script**
Normally, multiple scripts run within a scenario; each of these scripts maps a sequence of dialog steps within a scenario, such as part of a business process. The scripts are created centrally and distributed to various robots, on which the scripts run.

▸ **Robot**
The scripts are executed on a robot. The robot is a special form of diagnostic agent that, unlike normal diagnostic agents, is not installed in the managed systems themselves but instead is installed in an user environment.

▶ **Step**

A script consists of multiple steps, which represent the smallest units that can be assigned to a measurement of the performance or availability. A step can contain the execution of a dialog step, for example.

The available evaluations for scenarios are divided into the following two subject areas:

▶ **Availability**

These evaluations contain information about availability of the entities mentioned previously. At the scenario level, information is also provided about scheduled downtime.

▶ **Performance**

These evaluations contain information about the response times of the entities mentioned previously.

Figure 10.61 shows an example of the SCRIPT AVAILABILITY scenario.

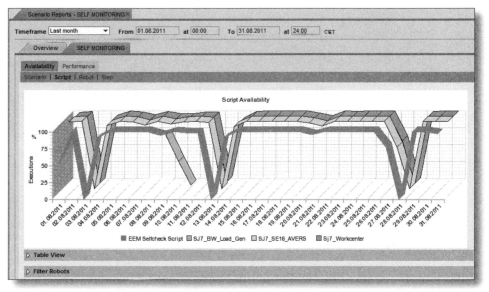

Figure 10.61 Example Report for Script Availability

If you choose the HOSTS type and select the desired objects, evaluations are displayed for the following subject areas: "Hosts" type

▶ **Availability**

These evaluations contain information about the availability of the selected host.

► **Capacity**

These evaluations contain information about the utilization of available capacities in the selected host. You can evaluate how much free capacity is still available in the utilization of various memories or the existing CPU, for example.

"Databases" type The final option is to select the DATABASES type. The evaluations for this type are divided into the following subject areas:

► **Availability**

These evaluations contain information about the availability of the selected database.

► **Performance**

These evaluations contain information about the performance of write and read access to the selected database.

► **Exceptions (errors)**

These evaluations contain information about the number of deadlocks that occurred in the selected database.

► **Capacity**

These evaluations contain information about the utilization and growth of the selected database. Furthermore, you can evaluate how much free capacity is still available in the utilization of various memories or the existing CPU, for example.

► **Use**

These evaluations contain information about the number of read accesses and changed data records.

10.6.2 Management Evaluations

For the management evaluations, data collected previously for display is associated and prepared to provide the basis for strategic decisions and for checking the agreed service level. The management evaluations can be divided into the following two reports:

► Document-based service level report

► Dashboard-based evaluations

Document-Based Service Level Reports

Checking KPIs With document-based service level reporting, you can regularly check the technical KPIs you specified, such as system availability and performance thresholds. Depending on your requirements, you can set up different variants of service level reports and schedule automatic generation. Like the EarlyWatch Alert reports, you can display the service level reports as detailed HTML reports or send them as Microsoft Word reports. Before setting this up, the following prerequisites must be fulfilled:

▶ A solution landscape has been set up in SAP Solution Manager.

▶ SAP EarlyWatch Alert has been set up for all managed systems in SAP Solution Manager.

To set up document-based service level reporting on your SAP Solution Manager, proceed as follows:

Setup

1. Start the SAP *Solution Manager Administration* work center.

2. In the SOLUTIONS area, select a solution, and then switch to the OPERATIONS SETUP tab page.

3. Choose SERVICE LEVEL REPORTING and SET-UP SERVICE LEVEL REPORTING. The session for setting up the service level reporting is opened in a new window.

4. Perform the following checks in change mode:

   ▷ Specify variants of service level report

   ▷ Edit general settings

   ▷ Determine and enter systems and contents for service level report types

   ▷ Specify business processes based on Business Process Monitoring

To display the generated reports, select the function GENERATED DOCUMENTS in the *Technical Monitoring* work center, and switch to the service evaluations view. In the upper part of the screen, you can filter the displayed sessions by solution, date, and context. The sessions for the service level reports are displayed in a table with their evaluation, session ID, solution name, date, and context. If you select a session in the table, you can use the GENERATE EVALUATION function to generate the report in Word format or display it. Furthermore, there is the option of creating the report in HTML format. The relevant function call for a selected session is in the detail view in the lower part of the screen (see Figure 10.62).

Displaying reports

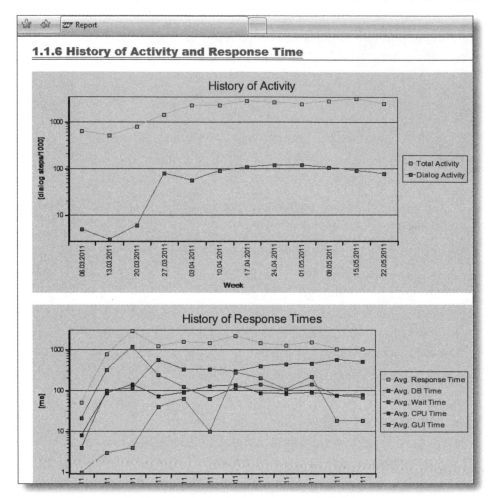

Figure 10.62 Example of a Service Level Report in HTML Format

Dashboard-Based Evaluations

Starting with SAP Solution Manager 7.1, dashboard-based evaluations provide another option for management evaluations. During their development, great care was taken to ensure that users have the opportunity to examine multiple evaluations at the same time, and that users can determine which evaluations to display and can configure which issues are relevant to them. Dashboard-based evaluations essentially consist of two elements during runtime: the dashboard framework and the dashboard applications (see Figure 10.63).

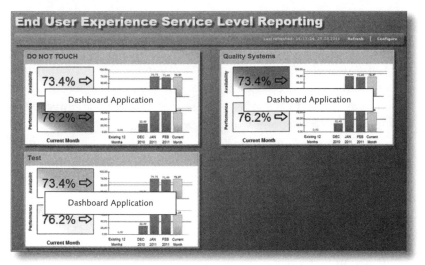

Figure 10.63 Dashboard Framework with Three Dashboard Applications

Double-clicking on an application focuses on it and enlarges it in the center of the dashboard. The time stamp with data is displayed on the top-right edge of the dashboard. By clicking the REFRESH button, you can have the system read the data again. Next to this is the CONFIGURE button for calling configuration mode. In this mode, you have the option of changing the sequence of applications by dragging and dropping them. You can also edit, copy, or delete an individual application.

Applications

At time of going to press, the dashboard can be accessed via the *Technical Monitoring* work center from the EEM application. The applications that can be displayed there are used to evaluate SLAs and were described in detail in Section 10.3. In the future, it will be possible from the dashboard configuration mode to call an area containing a rich selection of further applications for the various aspects of Technical Operations. In addition to this, you will have the option of creating your own dashboard applications here and integrating them in the dashboard infrastructure via a registration tool.

10.7 Data Volume Management (DVM)

Now, for the first time, the new SAP Solution Manager offers you all-round support in every area of defining and executing an efficient and sustainable data management concept.

The latest technological innovations in the field of applications for analyzing business processes and the continuing growth of data in enterprises provoked new debates about efficient, enterprise-wide data or Data Volume Management (DVM). In preparing strategically and technically for the new world, the subject of DVM is coming up again in the project plans of enterprise architects who are investigating the future compatibility and efficiency of existing concepts.

Growing system landscapes, upcoming release upgrades, and subjects such as cloud computing and virtualization have also played a part in the comprehensive expansion of this subject. These continuing trends play a major role in making the very complex issue of data management transparent because, for the first time, DVM project costs and the benefits of DVM projects can be quantified and expressed in real terms.

Governance model To manage the constantly growing demand for data, it has become indispensable to establish what is known as a *governance model*, or a corporate guideline. This defines which data is needed for how long in which format and on what medium—cost-intensive data storage in the online database (level 1), including high availability and multiple data mirroring, versus cost-efficient storage of the data in level 3 archive memories. In today's landscapes, it is no longer rare to find the various SAP and non-SAP products in different product versions. This has led to an enormous increase in the complexity of data distribution within system landscapes that have grown and become heterogeneous.

10.7.1 Position Determination

The biggest hurdle you have to face when creating the necessary transparency and taking the first step toward a global data management concept is what is known as *position determination*. Where am I in my landscape? How is my data distributed? Does the growth in data match the growth of my operations? Is all of the data really used? Am I addressing the right objects? Are there any quick results? Can I use synergies?

Examining the system landscape as a whole First you have to answer these and many other questions. Unfortunately, this type of project is rather inefficient, even today. Whereas it was possible, years ago, in small system landscapes with few SAP systems, to consider the systems as isolated entities and evaluate them separately, this is no longer feasible in today's world of global systems with global interfaces and distributed processes. In certain areas, this approach would even be misleading because data can only be examined in relation to the upstream and downstream systems to avoid far-reaching technical and even legal consequences. It is therefore crucial to consider the system landscape as a whole.

To make the first step in any DVM project easier for you, SAP Solution Manager includes the *Data Volume Management* work center. The idea of the work center is to provide the right tools and appropriate analysis environment for all of the demands of a DVM project. This lets you speed up the various work processes in the project phases. The main focus is on supporting decision making, particularly by setting the right priorities.

"Data Volume Management" work center

10.7.2 Analyzing the Data Distribution

To quickly answer the most important question—data distribution in a landscape—the *Data Volume Management* work center includes a tool-supported analysis. As mentioned earlier, it is important to first gain a complete picture of your landscape. The STATISTICS & TRENDS area includes the function DATA ASSIGNMENT STATISTICS (see Figure 10.64).

When you create the general overview of your system landscape, it is important to examine the data distribution according to various criteria. To do this, you can use the following display levels, which can be found in all reports in the DVM area:

▶ Product

▶ System

▶ Application area

▶ Document type

▶ Archiving object

▶ Table

Display Levels in the DVM area

In the second navigation level, you will find preconfigured reports for the specific selected view, such as the SUMMARY view, which always shows you the latest information for the category in question (see Figure 10.65).

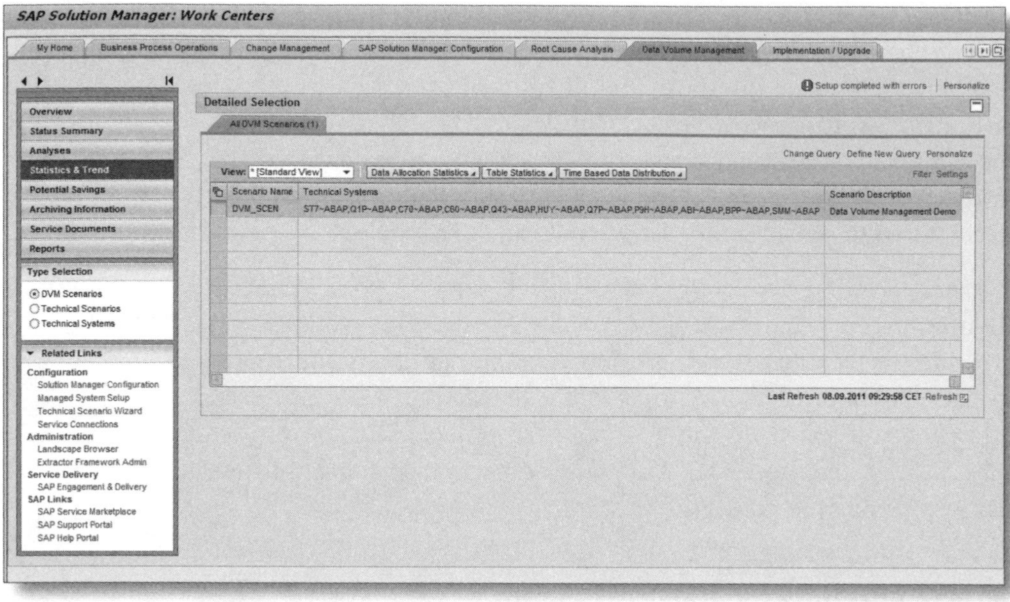

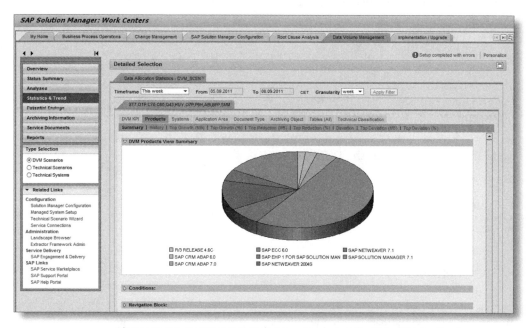

Figure 10.64 Statistics & Trends Area in the "Data Volume Management" Work Center

Figure 10.65 Statistics & Trends Area, Displaying the Data Distribution by SAP Products in a Sample Landscape (Data in MB)

Displaying the data distribution is especially interesting in land-scapes with a large number of legacy systems. The analysis helps you in your evaluations and makes it easier to reach decisions concerning shutting down or virtualizing systems. After the system view, which gives you an insight into how the data is distributed across all the connected systems, the most important evaluation is the data distribution across application areas (see Figure 10.66).

Application areas

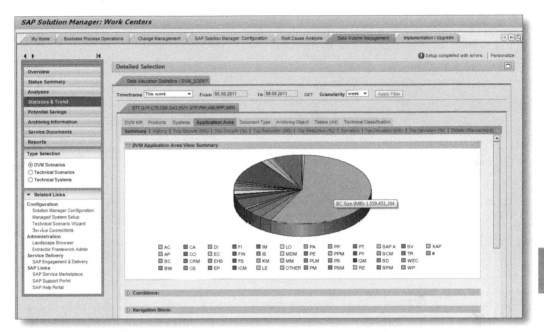

Figure 10.66 Displaying the Data Distribution by SAP Application Areas per the Application Hierarchy in a Sample Landscape (Data in MB)

The example from Figure 10.66 clearly shows the added value of a landscape view across application areas. In most system landscapes, a large proportion of the data consists of data records that belong to the Basis component (BC) application layer—experience suggests an average proportion of 40 to 50%. This includes all types of data that can be found in the lower software layers. These layers primarily control technical communication between system units and therefore mostly write purely technical information about monitoring or system logging of business process execution.

Data from Basis

As you can see from the percentage of the total data, there is an enormous potential here to significantly reduce data before you even deal with application-specific and business process-relevant data. Experience has shown that it is relatively easy to reach decisions in a small group of people about the maximum lifetime of this data.

Data from CA objects

Another application area that you can approach in the same way is the area of *cross-application data objects* (CA). These include data records and tables that are used in a similar way by multiple applications. Examples of this are change documents, change pointers, integration technology or intermediate documents (IDocs), and workflow work items.

Handling these objects is made easier because a DVM concept that considers these data objects is mostly generic in character, and all of the connected systems can be implemented in the same way. Even if the data consumption of Basis and cross-application objects may at first seem minor when you examine your individual systems, examining the landscape as a whole has very different results. When you define the priorities and order for analyzing your objects in your global DVM concept, this information is invaluable.

Detailed analysis

To understand which specific objects and data are involved, SAP Solution Manager offers various detailing levels for each evaluation. For example, you can display the associated document types that have led to this large proportion of BC or CA data. This type of drill-down generally displays a detail view like the one in Figure 10.67.

Figure 10.68 shows the data distribution within the Basis application component. Of course, this also includes the fundamental system units in any SAP system, such as the ABAP runtime environment or the ABAP Dictionary, which are necessary for basic operation. In the top document types, you find the application log mentioned previously, as well as the IDocs.

Naturally, you have the option at any time of also going down to the lowest technical layer to display details via tables or indices for a selected document type (see Figure 10.68).

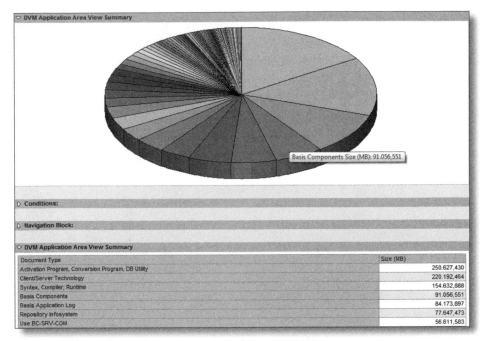

Figure 10.67 Drilldown of the BC Application Area by Associated Document Type per the Application Hierarchy in a Sample Landscape (Data in MB)

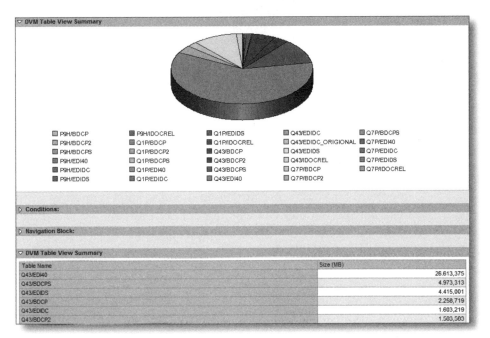

Figure 10.68 Drilldown of Document Type ALE Integration Technology (IDocs) by Associated Tables (Data in MB)

10.7.3 Prioritizing Objects

After you have gained an initial overview of your system landscape, you can determine the project scope for your objects. Due to the variety of objects and document types, you have to prioritize your data according to various classification options. You have already become familiar with the necessary evaluations in the initial appraisal. You will also find these in the *Data Volume Management* work center. The different ways of looking at the data in your landscape also make it possible to establish different procedures for prioritizing the objects accordingly. Experience has shown that the available resources and the time to carry out this type of DVM project are very limited.

Complexity of archiving

To give you an idea of how complex the data in today's system landscapes can be, Table 10.5 shows some sample figures from selected SAP applications. The values are average specifications across various release and EHP states (without industrial solutions).

Archiving complexity

SAP Application	Tables[2]	Archiving Objects[3]
SAP ERP	100.000	800
SAP NetWeaver BW	75.000	80
SAP CRM	30.000	150
SAP NetWeaver PI	25.000	80

Table 10.5 Number of Transparent Tables and Available Archiving Objects in Selected SAP Products[4]

The numbers speak for themselves. Setting up a project that addresses all the tables in all systems and considers all associated archiving objects is practically inconceivable. It is therefore very important for you to concentrate on the most important objects. In the following sections, you will find out more about tried-and-tested prioritization models and how to implement them.

---

2 Only transparent tables were considered.
3 This does not include generated or customer-specific archiving objects; objects that only provide options for deleting data were not considered, either.
4 All the specifications are based on rounded average values, identified across various SAP-internal systems with different release, SP, and EHP levels, as well as different business processes.

10.7.4 Prioritizing by Memory Consumption

One proven method for classifying objects is to prioritize them according to their current memory consumption. The various views of the total landscape are also useful here for first identifying the application area that consumes the most memory, for example.

Using the various drilldown options, you can easily find the associated document types, archiving objects, and tables that you want to investigate in detail.

Another favorite method is to analyze the landscape growth. Which application areas are contributing the most to growth? Which document types and tables are behind this? The variety of available evaluations will give you answers to all these questions (see Figure 10.69).

Landscape growth

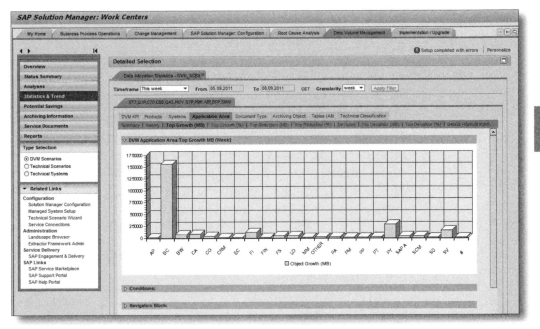

Figure 10.69 Growth of a Landscape Aggregated Across Application Areas (Data in MB and Growth per Week)

You can choose between different time frames. For example, you can display monthly or weekly growth. In addition, you can use the HIS-TORY view to analyze the growth trend for selected objects, as shown in Figure 10.70.

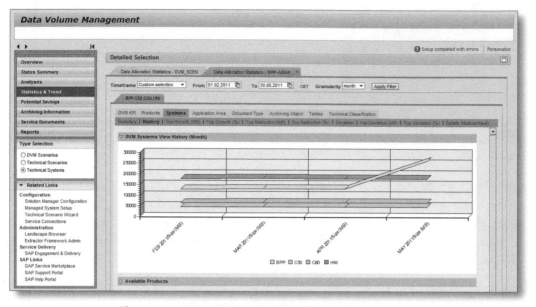

Figure 10.70 Historical Examination of System Parameters in a Selected Period (Data per Month in MB)

10.7.5 Prioritizing by Age Structure of the Data

In DVM, the most important statistic in the decision-making process is the age of your data. The core issue in every discussion with departments and the SAP Basis team concerning deletion activities or retention periods for archiving objects is the issue of how long the data should stay in the system. How long is data needed online for operations?

When defining your priorities, it therefore makes sense to choose objects that have already reached a certain age and therefore have a potential for reduction.

Analyzing the age structure

To make the age structure in your system landscape transparent, the *Data Volume Management* work center offers you the option of scheduling analyses that calculate the temporal distribution of data in the systems you select (see Figure 10.71).

These evaluations have considerable potential and a wide variety of possible uses. Within a few minutes, you can identify the oldest data ranges across application areas, for example. This is the first step in archiving your data. For the first time, it is possible to easily identify technical problems or the weak spots in archiving concepts.

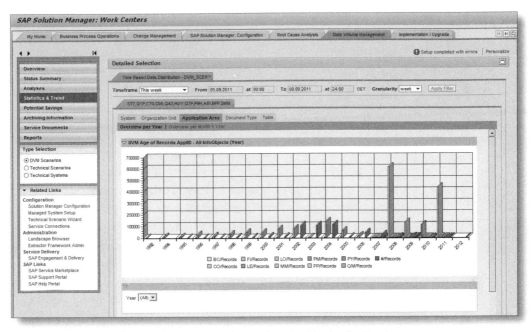

Figure 10.71 Age Distribution of a System Landscape Organized by Application Area (Number of Table Entries per Year)

As mentioned previously, this view provides a very valuable set of information for prioritization. If you apply a few general rules when examining this type of evaluation, it should be easy to identify the most relevant archiving objects. As a rule of thumb, all document types with data that is more than two years old are worth looking at in more detail and considering for archiving, for example. Generally, the older the data is, the greater the potential savings.

Here, you also have the option of displaying details and examining various levels, such as the distribution of data records at the level of a month in a specific year.

10.7.6 Prioritizing by Frequency of Use

In addition to the classic methods of prioritizing objects according to their size and their growth characteristics, evaluating by frequency of use is another very useful classification option. Normally, these objects are only examined after the objects with the largest growth and memory consumption have been examined and deleted or archived.

Analyzing the frequency of use

The evaluations of frequency of use in the *Data Volume Management* work center have two different aims. One is to identify document types and tables that are not among the largest or the fastest growing objects but that have to be examined because of their importance to daily operations. The other aim is to find unused objects that occupy memory space but do not show any read accesses and can therefore be deleted.

In the first case, you can assume that tables that are frequently read by, written to, and changed by processes of all kinds, every day, are relevant to your day-to-day activities. However, these objects are often only considered if they affect the general execution and performance of individual processes. In classic approaches, the measures can only be made *reactively*. One measure that can be taken to optimize performance during operation is processing these objects with the DVM analysis tools in the SAP Solution Manager and then applying data archiving or deletion to keep the affected tables small and slim. This keeps read, write, and change processes as efficient as possible.

Proactive identification

This tried-and-tested approach is taken up by SAP Solution Manager in the *Data Volume Management* work center. In other words, you can use the available evaluations to *proactively* identify the objects with the maximum access frequency. Here, you can also choose between the views SYSTEM, APPLICATION AREA, DOCUMENT TYPE, and TABLE when examining your data.

Figure 10.72 shows an evaluation of access frequency taking DOCUMENT TYPE as the example.

In the second application case, you can use the same statistics to find out which document types or tables show no activity at all on the database interface. The idea is to analyze whether objects that have not been read, written, or changed for a long period of time are still relevant to your day-to-day activities. In principle, you can work out relatively easily which data you can reduce quickly.

Unused data

A typical example of data of this type is data that was migrated to the SAP system from feeder systems via customer-defined tables as part of a migration and was then stored in temporary tables in the SAP system. After the migration is complete, these tables are no longer relevant and can be deleted. Another example is legacy data from customer-defined developments that were only used temporarily or were replaced by SAP standard functions.

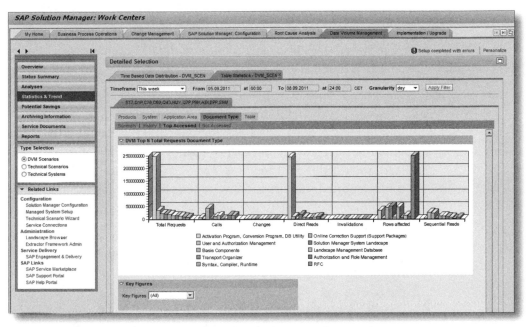

Figure 10.72 Evaluation of Access Frequency Using the Document Type in a System Landscape as an Example (Top 10 Total Accesses)

It should be mentioned here that this type of use analysis poses a risk: Data that seems to be lying around in the system unused could be very important in the context of critical business processes such as month-end or year-end closing. As a result, the longer the period in which you extract this type of data statistic from the connected systems, the more reliable the results of the analysis. However, depending on the origin of the data (e.g., evaluations of the document type), the dataset can often be basically classified to make statements about the relevance of the data to core business processes.

10.7.7 Evaluating the Data

After you have identified the objects on which your analysis should focus, you can start working on the project: What is the data that occupies the most memory used for? Why is the data volume so large in certain application areas? Which business process is this connected to? From experience, how long should this type of data be retained? With which people in my company do I have to discuss these objects?

In preparation for actually discussing the analyses with the business process owners, you first create a technical draft containing a variety of technical and business background details for the objects under consideration.

SAP DVM—Best Practice Session

The *Data Volume Management* work center and its tools also provide help here, simplifying the process. You can fully automate a large number of the steps. The associated function is called SAP Data Volume Management – Best Practice Session and is one of the self-services provided in SAP Solution Manager (see Figure 10.73). This is a tool-supported, standardized procedure for grouping together all of the information that is important when examining a data object (table or document type).

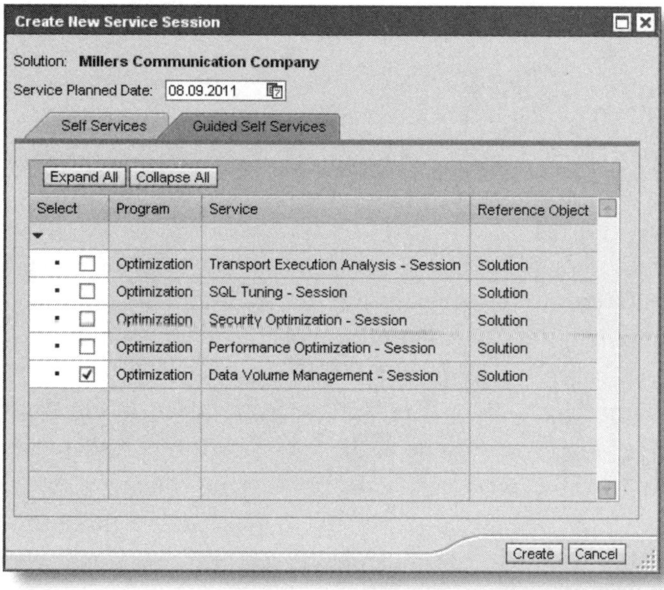

Figure 10.73 Creating a Guided Self-Service for Data Volume Management

To execute this *guided self-service*, you need hardly any technical knowledge of operating SAP Solution Manager or the necessary analysis programs. All of the activities that have to be carried out are stored in a predefined, guided sequence of steps, the *guided procedure* (see Figure 10.74).

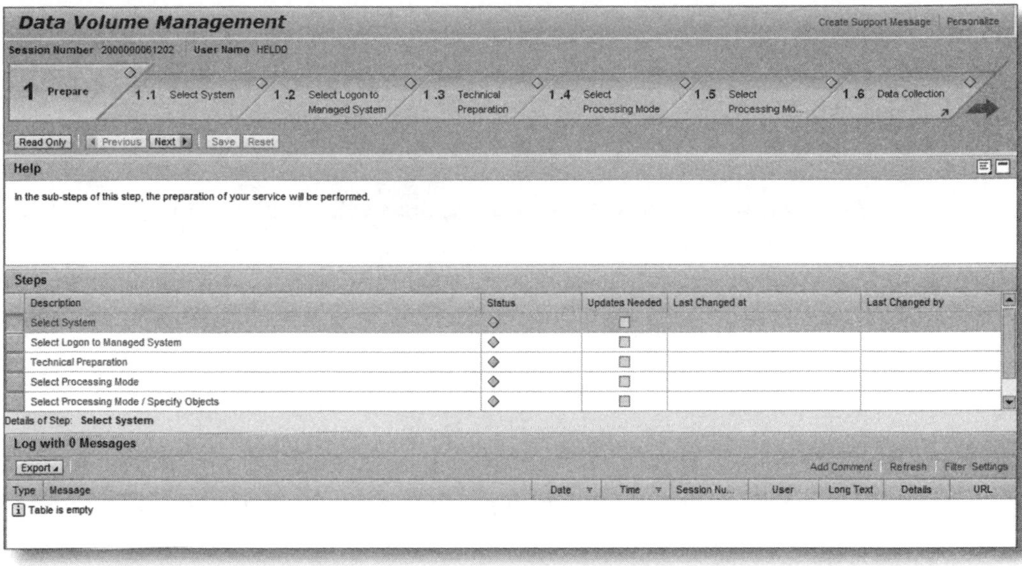

Figure 10.74 Guided Procedure for Scheduling Data Collections for the Guided Self-Service

As a result of these preparatory measures, a complete analysis is started for the freely selectable objects; this analysis is executed in the background of the system in question. In this data analysis, the system checks the data model, for example, to examine as a unit all of the tables that belong together logically and functionally. Additionally, there is a summary of the specialist and technical background of the table group being examined. This makes it possible to draw conclusions about its business process context. Furthermore, special analyses are carried out for data distribution within the associated objects, and the system calculates possible savings based on Best Practice values for retention periods of the objects in question. These data analyses take the particular, customer-specific environment into account. In other words, the SAP application, release, use, and business process configuration are evaluated to make a reliable statement about the possibility of reducing data (prevention, compression, deletion, and archiving) in a specific landscape. You have the option at any time of generating a Word or HTML document with the results of the analysis.

Data analysis

10.7.8 Discussions with the Departments

Different requirements and expectations

Compared to the technical analyses you carry out in advance, the discussions with user departments are far more time-consuming. Simply answering the core question of how long the data should be retained in the online database can lead to long negotiations with the various business areas. During this evaluation, if not before, it often becomes apparent how far apart the different proposals and requirements from the business areas are. Differences of several months or even years are not uncommon. It is therefore very difficult to reach an agreement on reporting periods and the legal and tax requirements. To make this even harder, the specialist departments often lack the basic technical knowledge to understand how far-reaching the consequences of their decisions are in terms of data consumption and growth. It is also important to consider that in multi-national enterprises, various persons working in different geographical locations are often responsible for the same business process. This adds a further dimension to the complications in fulfilling these country-specific requirements.

The overall costs of providing the memory space, including associated costs such as hardware, power, building costs, the costs of data mirroring, personnel, training, and so on, are not transparent for many departments or seem irrelevant to their deliberations. Often, when considering the costs of data storage, people seem to be influenced by advertising from electronics suppliers, who advertise hard disks in the terabyte range for two figure sums. As a result, people quickly assume that storage space entails very few costs.

In this context, it is understandable that negotiations about data retention periods are difficult. Tool-based support, as used in the technical considerations earlier, is hardly possible.

However, experience has shown that creating transparency and, especially, aggregating and displaying information at the right level can make the decision-making phase significantly easier and quicker.

You will also find many helpful functions in the *Data Volume Management* work center that can support you in this phase. We will focus on two of these functions.

Simulating potential savings

To display the positive benefits of data archiving and data deletion and to make the discussions about residence times easier, there is a central scenario for calculating potential savings. This involves analyses that can be scheduled in the background for selected objects that simulate different residence times. You can configure this in a few minutes and display the effects of various residence times in graphs (see Figure 10.75).

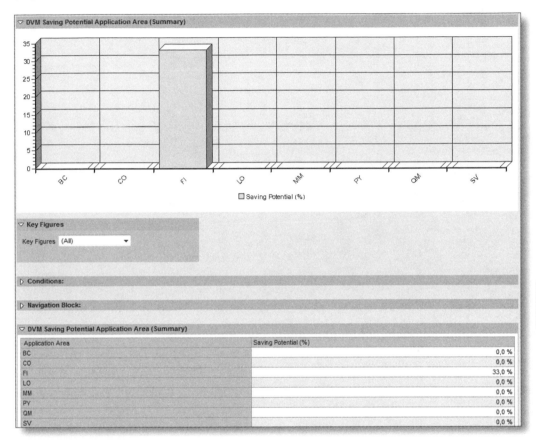

Figure 10.75 Displaying Potential Savings at the Application Area Level

A second approach to communicating the necessary transparency to a department consists of translating the technical subject of data management into universally understood language. By making a few settings, you can take the evaluations that were described earlier in Section 10.7.2 (such as displaying the current memory consumption by document type in gigabytes or megabytes) and display them as costs (such as costs in EUR) by specifying a calculation factor (see Figure 10.76).

Presentation of costs

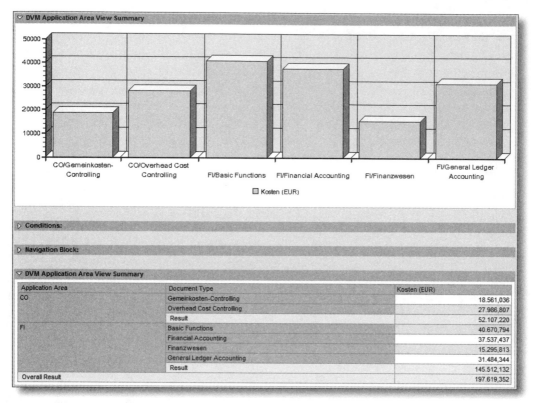

Figure 10.76 Sample Display for Costs of Data Retention at the Document Type Level

If you demonstrate to a business process owner the costs that arise in data retention from data that is directly or indirectly linked to executing that owner's processes, you not only create a new awareness of DVM in all the enterprise groups involved (Basis team and application areas), you also create a more effective working environment.

10.7.9 Project Reporting

Making success transparent

Let's now assume that you have put the first DVM project into live operation and have taken the first measures to reduce your data. SAP Solution Manager also provides special evaluations for making success transparent and displaying the data objects that have benefited most from these measures. For example, you can use the landscape view discussed earlier to gain an excellent overview of what has been achieved, especially for cross-system projects.

However, an overall examination of all the achievements in reducing your data is just as interesting and even more important. As a project leader and a manager, you should be interested in what you have already achieved in your system landscape by means of data archiving and subsequent data deletion. You will also be interested in what your dataset and memory consumption would look like today if you had not taken these data archiving measures.

And even more important than taking a snapshot after the project has begun is a continuous examination of the balance between business growth and technical growth. In the management reporting area, there are various graphical evaluation options for displaying this balance (see Figure 10.77).

Management reporting

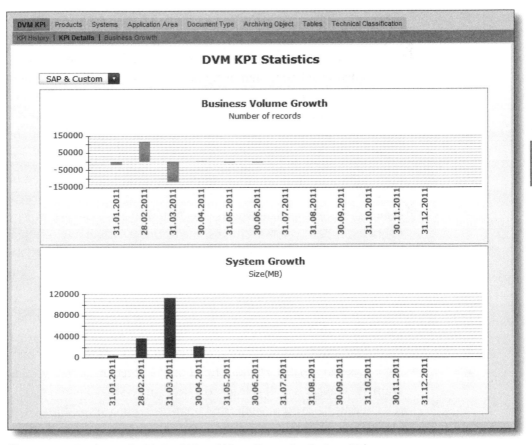

Figure 10.77 Displaying the DVM KPI Detail View; Comparing Business Volumes and Landscape Growth

Technical
foundation

From a technical perspective, this data is calculated on the selection of tables that are directly connected to the core business processes. SAP delivers a template containing a certain number of main tables that you can expand as desired. The concept consists of calculating the growth of business on the basis of these tables. This key figure is compared to the total size or the growth of the overall system landscape. At the highest level, it is very easy to observe the ratio between these values to work out whether further projects are necessary in the area of DVM. If the overall system landscape is growing disproportionately faster than business operations, this is the first important indicator that there is still room for improvement in the global definition of a DVM strategy. On the other hand, if there is an increased volume of business, it is perfectly reasonable to see a greater growth in the landscape.

Daily operations

The tools presented previously clearly show their strengths in the most important phase of all: daily operations. You can now easily use the familiar evaluations and analysis functions available in the *Data Volume Management* work center to identify anomalies in the data distribution or the growth ratio, or to spot potential savings. Various report and analysis options are available to everyone involved in the area of DVM, making it possible to answer any reporting query.

Due to the constant change in today's system landscapes caused by expanding business fields, the introduction of new processes or changes to existing ones, as well as technical changes (such as release upgrades), it is now almost impossible to find a system environment that is stable in terms of data growth. Naturally, this also changes the use characteristics of individual applications, with potentially serious consequences for data distribution and growth.

This means that the analyses that we presented here are generally used regularly, perhaps even daily, because previously unknown data objects will suddenly appear on monitors and in reports, making it necessary to analyze their functional and technical background again. As you can see, this leads to a cycle of actions that you should carry out using the tool-supported options in the SAP Solution Manager's *Data Volume Management* work center so that, little by little, you can come closer to the ideal of a system landscape that is unaffected by data growth.

The Business Process Operations process includes the entirety of the most important application-related activities needed to ensure a stable and problem-free process flow of the core business processes within a company.

11 Business Process Operations

Due to the complexity of today's system landscapes and the associated business processes, it is becoming increasingly difficult to understand the overall picture and provide a correct and efficient response in the event of an error. The early and automatic detection of exceptional situations that affect the normal flow of information are particularly important. Defined processes and responsibilities help ensure that you can respond quickly to such exceptional situations and resolve them promptly.

Proactive and regular checks ensure the required data integrity in all components of an IT solution. Key performance indicators (KPIs) create a certain transparency that indicates the status of business process operation.

Areas of the process

The following areas belong to the area of Business Process Operations described by SAP whose implementation you will find in the Run SAP methodology:

▶ Business Process Monitoring

▶ Job Scheduling Management

▶ Data Consistency Management and Interface Monitoring

▶ Business Process Performance

All areas that belong to the process *Business Process Operations* are interrelated. For example, if the execution of background jobs is taking too long, this could be due to performance problems in the business process or problems with an interface. However, there could also be an error message in Business Process Monitoring due to an inconsistency. You should schedule the program that checks the data consistency using Job Scheduling Management.

For this reason, you should not look at any of these operating areas in isolation but always in relation to other areas.

With SAP Solution Manager, SAP offers a platform that helps you implement Business Process Operations and execute them in all areas.

The following sections provide a more detailed description of the areas Business Process Monitoring, Job Scheduling Management, Data Consistency Management and Interface Monitoring, as well as Performance of Business Processes.

11.1 Business Processes and Interface Monitoring

This section first describes what tools SAP Solution Manager offers to support the operation of business processes. These are mainly *Business Process Monitoring* to stabilize business processes and *Business Process Analytics* to improve business processes.

11.1.1 Tools that Support the Operation of Business Processes

Business process stabilizations as investment protection

If we now look at the lifecycle of business processes of SAP customers, we see that everything starts with the design and implementation. For you as a customer, this means a significant investment first of all; for example, in SAP licenses but also in the actual implementation project. After you start using the processes in operation (go-live), the first task is to (technically) stabilize the business processes to protect this investment in SAP software. This means you have to ensure the following, for example:

▶ All interfaces (e.g., IDoc or qRFC) in the process run without errors as far as possible.

▶ All background processing jobs run without errors, start at the right time, and their data is processed.

▶ The most important (core) transactions have an average response time that users find good or satisfactory.

▶ Functional errors (e.g., in the form of posting terminations or ABAP dumps) do not occur.

This task of business process stabilization (see Figure 11.1) is usually the responsibility of the IT organization and is optimally supported by Business Process Monitoring in SAP Solution Manager. You can use automatic notification functions (e.g., email or SMS) to automatically alert the persons responsible to exceptional situations. This way, you can support the operation of the SAP solution more efficiently than you could, for example, with manual monitoring activities. This means that you can regularly monitor the respective transactions. The IT organization can usually respond quicker and, if necessary, solve problems before they are reported by the user departments.

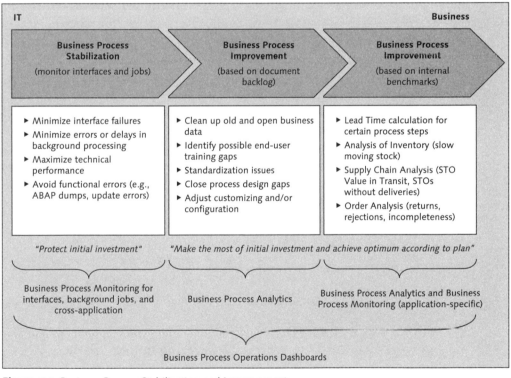

Figure 11.1 Business Process Stabilization and Improvement

Business process improvement for getting the maximum for the SAP investment

As soon as your business processes are running stable, you should check whether your processes are used efficiently or whether there are deviations from the processes defined in the implementation project. You can easily identify these deviations through documents in the system, if they should have been long processed based on the planned date but are still open (processing backlog). These deviations are usually caused by the configuration, master data maintenance or inappropriate use of the SAP system by users. Practice has shown that more than 90% of all SAP customers have deviations in their business processes. Hence, these customers find it difficult to activate the application-specific part of Business Process Monitoring directly with sensible threshold values. If they tried that, all traffic lights would immediately go red, and the persons involved would be unhappy with Business Process Monitoring. Therefore, we used Business Process Monitoring as the basis for Business Process Analytics for user-specific key figures. Section 11.1.4 explains how you can use Business Process Analytics to improve your business processes.

As soon as you have processed or completed backlogged documents, you have the option of including the corresponding user-specific key figure in Business Process Monitoring. If the situation deteriorates again, you are informed.

KPIs

If, in addition to the reduction of backlogged documents, you want to improve your business processes further, you can use selected key figures by comparing your organizational units to each other. An example of this is the measuring of turnaround times for your documents. That is, how long does it take from the creation of a sales order to the goods issue posting?

Dashboards

You can display the data of Business Process Monitoring and Business Process Analytics in self-configured dashboards for operating business processes. You can use these dashboards to display additional target group data as well.

11.1.2 Business Process Monitoring in SAP Solution Manager

SAP Solution Manager is capable of graphically depicting the flow of business processes and their corresponding process steps, interfaces, and different technical components.

You can use the requirements of the IT and user departments to define *monitoring objects* that have to be monitored to ensure the business process flow. When an error occurs, object alerts are triggered that are assigned to the respective process steps or interfaces during the monitoring process. This approach ensures that problems can be assigned immediately to a specific business process step and that their relevance for the entire business process can be analyzed without delay, allowing the appropriate escalation measures to be implemented as required. A three-stage alert system (green, yellow, and red), for which individual threshold values can be defined, also allows the significance of a problem to be weighted accordingly.

A basic distinction can be made between two types of monitoring objects: application-specific monitors and cross-application, more technical, monitors.

Since 2006, Business Process Monitoring has been continuously equipped with more application-specific monitors. As a result, you can now easily find out how well the most common business processes supported by the SAP Business Suite run. Are sales orders delivered as quickly as set out in service level agreements (SLA), for example? Are planned orders converted into production orders on time, and are these production orders released on time and then technically completed? To answer these types of questions, Business Process Monitoring offers more than 500 preconfigured key figures for SAP ERP, SAP CRM, SAP SRM, and SAP SCM (including SAP Extended Warehouse Management [SAP EWM]). You can rapidly adapt these key figures to your needs by making restrictions according to document types and organizational units (e.g., sales organization or plant). Use in practice has revealed that precisely these application-specific monitors are capable of uncovering a broad range of problems, for instance:

▶ Lack of user training, which results in the system being used incorrectly

▶ Customizing errors causing unnecessary follow-on documents to be created

▶ Errors in process design with the result that processes are never completed conventionally

▶ Incomplete or non-existent archiving strategies resulting in old documents remaining in the system

If measurements show large numbers of backlogged documents, we recommend starting with a business process analysis (as described in Section 11.1.4) and using Business Process Monitoring for the respective key figure at a later date. In addition to the monitors for SAP Business Suite, industry-specific monitors exist that cater, among other things, to the monitoring requirements of industries that rely on mass processing (such as energy providers or banks). Other industry-specific monitors are available for the automotive, retails, and apparel and footwear solutions (AFS) sectors.

Technical monitors

In SAP Solution Manager, you've had access to technical monitors in the context of Business Process Monitoring for many years. You can use these monitors, among other things, to manage background jobs (individual jobs as well as SAP NetWeaver BW process chains). For example, you can monitor a background job to see if it started on time or ended late from a business perspective (see also Section 11.2). You can also analyze the average response times of dialog transactions and check for critical messages in the general application log. Interfaces can also be checked to detect any IDocs with a particular error status for a previously defined IDoc message type. Similar monitors also exist for other types of interfaces such as queued remote function calls (qRFCs), business documents (BDocs), business workflows, SAP NetWeaver Process Integration (PI) messages, batch input sessions, and flat files.

Dedicated objects

Dedicated monitoring objects can be defined using customer exits and can be integrated into Business Process Monitoring to configure the functions to meet your specific needs. For more information, see the SAP Developer Network (SDN) at *www.sdn.sap.com/irj/scn/weblogs?blog=/pub/wlg/17437*. Because SAP Solution Manager is based on the standard monitoring infrastructure (Computing Center Management System, CCMS), you can also integrate CCMS monitoring objects into Business Process Monitoring.

11.1.3 Handling Business Process Monitoring in SAP Solution Manager

The central point of contact for Business Process Monitoring is the graphical monitoring interface in SAP Solution Manager as part of the *Business Process Operations* work center. On a single screen, it offers a complete overview of the status of the systems used and the business processes to be monitored (see Figure 11.2).

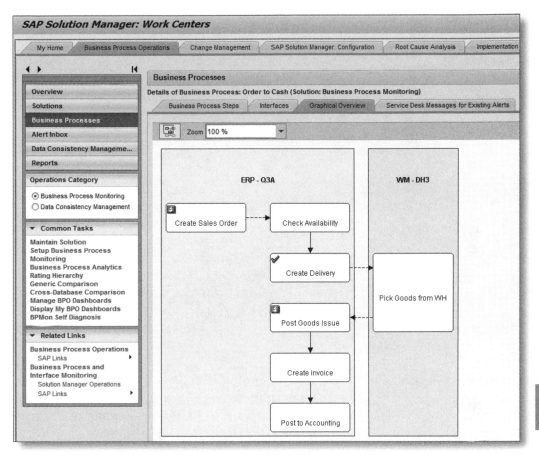

Figure 11.2 Business Process Monitoring

The business processes are assigned an overall alert that corresponds to the highest single alert that occurred for the respective business process. Similarly, the highest single alert is displayed as the overall status for each process step. This allows the technical problem to be assigned to the business process step affected, making it clear which functional areas of the business process require attention and how the problem affects the overall process.

Alerts

From the business process overview, you can navigate via the process flow graphic to the ALERT INBOX (see Figure 11.3) and thus to the individual problem. You can also call this Alert Inbox separately, directly in the web browser. Every user can thus decide which of the

Alert Inbox

alerts that have appeared are interesting to him and for which he feels responsible.

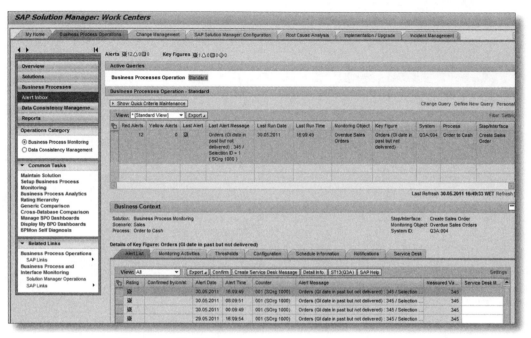

Figure 11.3 Alert Inbox

Monitoring tasks

Monitoring tasks in the form of to-do lists, problem-solving procedures, and escalation paths can be defined in SAP Solution Manager for end users. The employee responsible for monitoring can then access all of the information required in one central tool. For example, from SAP Solution Manager, the employee can access the job log showing canceled background jobs or the list of open application documents and obtain information to resolve the alert situation. The employee also knows who to contact if the problem seriously threatens the overall business process flow. Furthermore, notifications can be sent to the employee via email or SMS.

After an alert has been successfully processed in SAP Solution Manager, it can be marked as completed. If the problem cannot be solved immediately, a message can be created in the Service Desk to allow the problem to be tracked and the message sent to SAP if necessary.

Reporting

In addition, it is possible to extract the collected values to a SAP NetWeaver Business Warehouse system (SAP NetWeaver BW) (we recommend BW 7.0, which runs on SAP Solution Manager 7.1). In the BW, trends that have emerged in recent weeks and months can then be analyzed so that problem situations can be tackled earlier. For more information, see *www.sdn.sap.com/irj/scn/weblogs?blog=/pub/wlg/11931*. For example, it may be possible to identify a worsening in the runtimes of important background jobs before the respective critical threshold values are reached. You can also compare how may sales orders were not delivered on time in your Germany, United States, and Japan sales organizations. Finally, you can configure service level reporting to automatically create a Word document containing these business process trends over predefined periods (one week, one month, or six months) as graphics and tables.

11.1.4 Using Business Process Analytics to Improve Business Processes

Section 11.1.1 explained why Business Process Analytics was developed as an enhancement to Business Process Monitoring. Business Process Analytics basically collect the same (application-specific) key figures as Business Process Monitoring. However, Business Process Analytics does not assess the results in the same way and does not send automatic notifications either.

Instead, it saves the measuring results in an InfoCube of SAP Solution Manager where they can be systematically analyzed for deviations using Business Process Monitoring. You can use (internal) benchmarking to get an initial impression of whether the document processing backlog is a problem in your entire company or whether it affects certain organizational units (e.g., plants or sales organizations) or document types (i.e., process variants) (see Figure 11.4).

Benchmarking

In a second step, you can check the age structure of the affected documents. You can find out whether you are dealing with an already solved problem from the past for which the document was not closed or whether the problem still occurs. Older documents (e.g., older than 6 or 12 months) generally no longer influence operations and are treated differently from more recent documents. However, old documents can influence your business indirectly, as described in the article "Protect Your SAP ERP Investment & Improve Your Core Business Processes" (see *www.sdn.sap.com/irj/scn/weblogs?blog=/pub/wlg/19668*) on SDN.

Age analysis

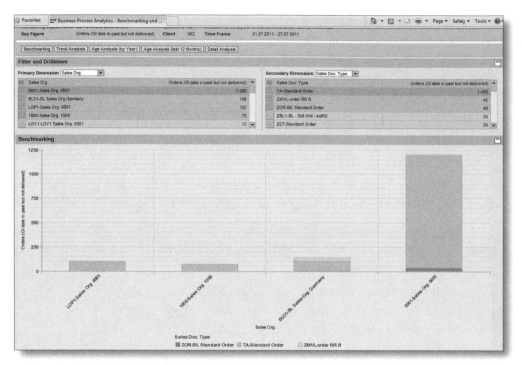

Figure 11.4 Business Process Analytics

Trend analysis

Just like Business Process Monitoring, Business Process Analytics let you branch to the corresponding document list in the respective backend system. From there, you can also branch into the individual document for a more in depth root cause analysis. For each key figure and cause, you should then define a catalog of measures for improving your business process. You can then use Business Process Analytics to monitor whether or not the situation improves. Ideally, there will be a declining trend in your document backlog. As soon as you are happy with the results of the respective key figure, it makes sense to activate Business Process Monitoring for this key figure. That way, you are informed immediately should the situation deteriorate again.

Additional Business Process Monitoring offerings

SAP offers the following services to help create and configure a Business Process Monitoring concept using SAP Solution Manager:

▶ For SAP MaxAttention and SAP Safeguarding customers, a business process operations service is available

▶ The SAP CQC service Business Process Analysis & Monitoring is available to SAP Enterprise Support customers

- Course SM300, Business Process Management and Monitoring

- Course E2E300, Business Process Integration & Automation Management

- Expert-guided implementation session for Business Process Monitoring

For a guide to Business Process Monitoring as well as additional information, see the SAP Service Marketplace at *www.service. sap.com/bpm*. In addition to the aforementioned blogs on SDN, there are additional blogs on certain technical topics, such as monitoring IDocs, qRFCs, or BW process chains, and blogs on monitoring the order-to-cash, procure-to-pay, or manufacturing processes. The central blog (see *www.sdn.sap.com/irj/scn/weblogs?blog=/pub/wlg/15153*) contains links to all these blogs. There are also links to frequently asked questions on the SDN at *http://wiki.sdn.sap.com/wiki/display/ SM/FAQ+Business+Process+Monitoring*. For more information on Business Process Monitoring, see the book *Business Process Monitoring mit dem SAP Solution Manager* by Thomas Schröder (SAP PRESS, 2009).[1]

11.2 Job Scheduling Management

The aim of Job Scheduling Management is to automate business processes fully or partially taking into consideration the available hardware and any time restrictions. Many people see Job Scheduling Management as simply choosing the right tool for scheduling background jobs in one or more backend systems. This, however, is only one of many aspects to Job Scheduling Management. Generally speaking, the following three challenges must be overcome:

- Ensure existing background jobs are documented in full and centrally to achieve a complete overview of the entire workload.

  Challenges

- Distribute the background job processing load evenly and reach the required throughput for mass processing.

- Monitor background jobs efficiently and automatically, and identify potential negative effects on existing business processes.

---

1 This book is currently only available in German.

But how can you tackle these challenges and support a well-defined, standardized process? An example of such a process appears in Figure 11.5.

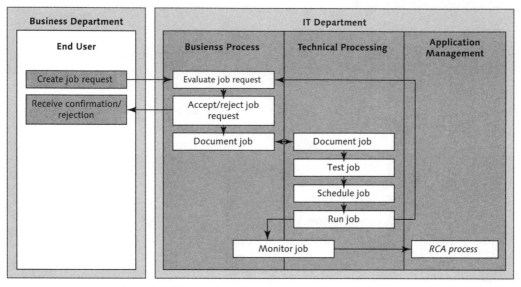

Figure 11.5 Standardized Process for Job Scheduling Management

Section 11.2.2 describes this process on the basis of a concrete example. You discover the extent to which such a process is supported when SAP Solution Manager and the SAP Central Process Scheduling application by Redwood are deployed together. For more information, see the white paper on the subject of Job Scheduling Management and the Job Scheduling Management Best Practice document at *https://service.sap.com/supportstandards* or *https://service. sap.com/solutionmanagerbp*.

Scheduling by users

In addition to the challenges already mentioned, many customers also have to answer two more specific questions in everyday operations. In particular in the SAP ERP environment, users schedule many jobs directly and thus undermine central job scheduling. The question here is whether it is possible to control these user activities. How can you make transparent which load in the current backend system is caused by background processing?

However, this section begins by describing the challenges listed previously in greater detail.

11.2.1 The Challenges of Job Scheduling Management

Extensive job documentation is crucial to achieve transparency across background processing jobs that run daily in your systems and to know exactly which jobs are running unnecessarily. You also need it to see which jobs are no longer needed, perhaps because the respective production plant no longer exists (in the system). Until now, you have been using Microsoft Excel or Lotus Notes for this, for example. However, this type of documentation is rarely particularly transparent and usually only accessible to a limited group of people. Worst of all is that the job documentation usually fails to cover all of the aspects of complete documentation. For instance, documentation often only contains technical data (ABAP report and variant) and states in which system a job runs and when. Information about the business reasons behind a job and the business processes and business units it benefits is normally not provided. Details of contact persons, error-handling methods, and scheduling restrictions are also generally overlooked.

Complete, centralized job documentation

This is where SAP Solution Manager comes in. It provides central job documentation (for individual jobs as well as for job chains). This documentation takes into account all of these aspects and offers standardized job documentation directly as a tool. This job documentation can have different statuses (e.g., in processing, testing, production), and it supports version management. Each job document also has an effective date. In the *Job Management* work center, you can use a simple query to check for which documents the job validity will expire soon or has already expired. This way you can query which job documents should be checked to identify jobs that are no longer required and remove them from the backend system. It is always easy to schedule new jobs in the system, but it is very difficult to unschedule them because they are simply forgotten about.

This job documentation application can also be called up in a web browser and therefore made available centrally to multiple users, at least in display mode.

You can use Transactions SM36 and SM37 to schedule background jobs locally in your SAP backend systems or each individual system (if you have several networked SAP systems). However, along with certain other restrictions, Transaction SM36 notably does not support the scheduling of jobs with dependencies that cross system boundaries.

Improved load distribution and increased document throughput

To map such dependencies and better distribute the background job load, SAP provides *SAP Central Process Scheduling by Redwood*, which is associated with the SAP NetWeaver license. Using the standard XBP interface (*External Batch Processing*), this application also enables you to technically intercept background jobs scheduled by end users and reschedule them in a centralized and controlled fashion. In this way, you can minimize the danger of the SAP backend system being overloaded by jobs scheduled by end users with no control mechanisms in place. This application is not part of SAP Solution Manager but integrated via an interface. For more information about interception, which also includes the earlier question of whether it is possible to control user activities, see the SDN article "Job Interception: Controlling End-User Scheduled Jobs" (at *http://www.sdn.sap.com/irj/scn/weblogs?blog=/ pub/wlg/14715*). However, this function will not enable you to include these background activities in your standard requirements process including job documentation. Section 11.2.3 describes how you do that.

Automated job monitoring in the business process context

Job monitoring is also a multifaceted subject. Some customers monitor nothing at all in practice, while many limit their monitoring activities to manual monitoring in Transaction SM37. This might involve checking sporadically throughout the day if jobs have terminated and need to be restarted. Some customers have at least automated job monitoring to the extent that system monitoring tools are used to automatically check if jobs are canceled or take longer than expected. But here too, many questions are left open and can only be answered by Business Process Monitoring in SAP Solution Manager. In addition to the functions that system monitoring tools present for job monitoring, Business Process Monitoring can also assess whether jobs have failed to start or end on time from a business perspective. Checks on content can also be performed by automatically verifying whether certain messages have been written to the job log. At the same time, jobs are linked to business processes and, in particular, business process steps. This means that if a job is canceled, you know straight away if it supports a sales or production process or belongs to the process for period-end closing.

Monitoring process chains

In addition to monitoring individual jobs, you can also monitor complete process chains in SAP NetWeaver BW. There, you have the same monitoring options as described earlier. In addition you can also check, from a content perspective, whether more or fewer data records were processed than planned. In doing so, you can monitor the process chain as a whole (simple identification using the process chain ID), or you can also monitor individual elements within a chain. For more information on process chain monitoring in SAP Net-Weaver BW, see the article "Best Practice: BW Process Chain Monitoring with SAP Solution Manager – Part 1" (at *www.sdn.sap.com/irj/scn/weblogs?blog=/pub/wlg/20204*).

11.2.2 Case Study: A Job Scheduling Management Process as Conceived in the SAP Standard System

This section takes a fictitious example to illustrate which functions SAP Solution Manager provides for Job Scheduling Management and how they interact with SAP Central Process Scheduling.

Step 1: Job Request Submitted by User Department (or Project Team)

Our model company, Millers Communication Company, is due to open a new plant in the United States. The user department in the company would like to request a new background job to begin performing material requirements planning regularly for this new plant in the near future.

In the past, you had to create your own Word, Excel, or web forms for this purpose. With SAP Solution Manager, you can now use a standardized web form to submit a new job request or a change to an existing job. You can link this web form into SAP NetWeaver Portal or any other intranet. End users can save the form in their web browser favorites. There are two forms with different levels of detail (see Figure 11.6): a basic form that fits on one screen, and a detailed form that has several tab pages. Project team members can use the detailed form during an implementation project. The basic form, in contrast, is intended more for departmental users or key users who submit job requests as part of their daily activities. Our example explains only the basic form. The user department enters details of the JOB DOCUMENTATION NAME (in this case, "S_DE_PP_MRP_1000_6H"), PRODUCT SYSTEM, and CLIENT for which the job is required. The form can also make suggestions regarding the naming convention used. For information on how you can adjust this naming convention to your requirements, see the article "Implementation of a Naming Convention in Job Scheduling Management" (at *www.sdn.*

Web form for job request

543

sap.com/irj/scn/weblogs?blog=/pub/wlg/14716). Scheduling information is also entered here (date, time, or free text descriptions of scheduling requirements, e.g., every six hours).

In addition, you can save organizational information, for example, the Region (EMEA), country Germany (DE), Organization, and the Business Process for which the job is relevant. The user department must specify the business requirements in the mandatory BUSINESS REQUIREMENTS field provided so that the IT department subsequently has a basis on which it can rate how important the job is and how best to fit it into the existing job scheduling arrangements.

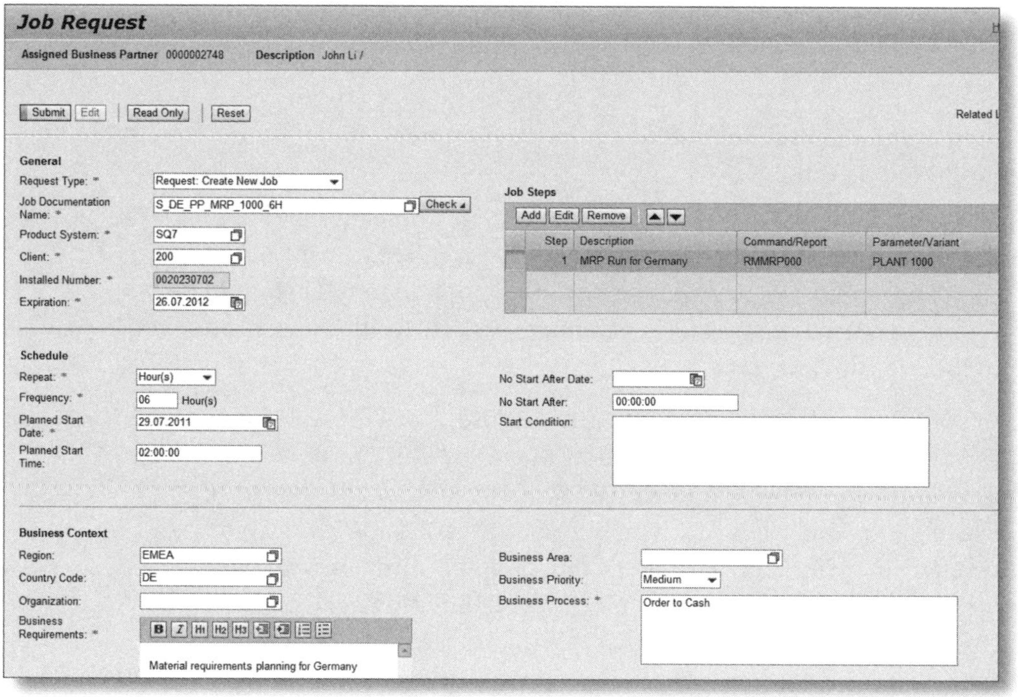

Figure 11.6 Job Request Form

Integration with Incident Management

Following that, data is queried to ensure the integration with Incident Management (Transaction SMIN) or Change Request Management (Transaction SMCR) works. This happens because when you save the form, a SAP CRM document is created in the background in SAP Solution Manager to establish the integrated connection between the request form and job documentation. Accordingly, the reporter must be a business partner in SAP Solution Manager. However, it is not necessary for all users to have a corresponding business partner in SAP Solution Manager. You can also use a generic business partner and enter the contact details of the reporter as free text. In this case, though, the generic business partner must be released for all relevant systems, or a business partner must be created for each system. For information on how you can adjust this request form to your requirements, see the article "How to Configure SAP's Standard Job Request Form – Part 1" (at *www.sdn.sap.com/irj/scn/weblogs?blog =/pub/wlg/20698*).

Step 2: Notifying the IT Department and Evaluating the Request

So far, the user department has simply submitted a request that the IT department is unaware of. Because, however, a document in Incident Management or Change Request Management is created from the job request, the missing connection between the two departments can be established. The IT employee can navigate to the JOB REQUESTS view in the *Job Management* work center to see all new job requests to be processed by him or his team. If the employee chooses the corresponding job request, the job request or corresponding SAP CRM document appears, whereby the job request appears in the Job Scheduling Management assignment block.

The IT employee then switches to change mode (if he is not already in it) and can select from a range of actions in the action profile. The IT employee can now view or process the job request.

Note that the same SAP CRM document for the job requests also appears in the Incident Management or Change Management work center. Hence, your Service Desk employees can also process the job requests from there or use the integration with Change Request Management, which supports an additional formal approval process.

Step 3: Creating a Corresponding Job Document

The colleague from IT has now looked at the job request and confirmed that the newly requested job can be included in existing job scheduling in its present form. The employee has also used the reporting functions in the *Job Management* work center to verify that corresponding job documentation does not yet exist. The job request will now be adopted together with the scheduling information and all other data provided by the user department. To do this, the employee chooses the action to create a corresponding job document in the Service Desk message (Figure 11.7).

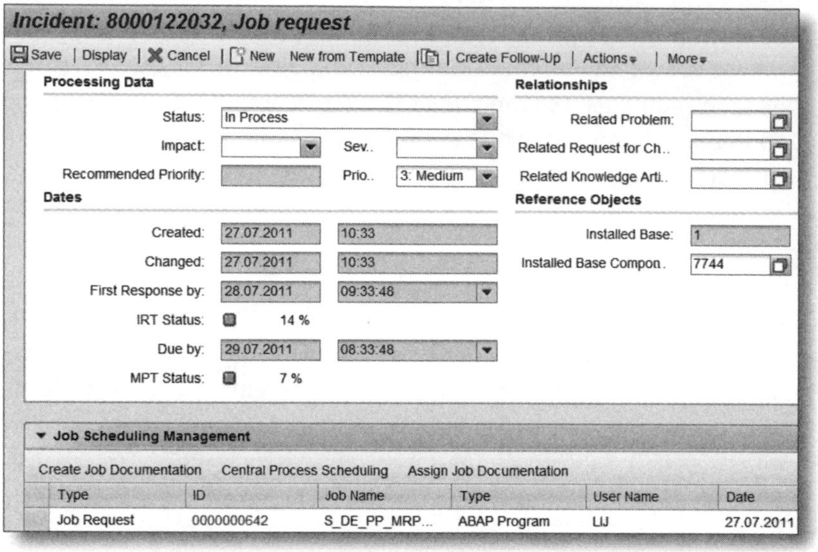

Figure 11.7 Creating Job Documentation from a Service Desk Message

Assignment to business processes

The action is only performed when the Service Desk message is saved. Because no assignment to a logical component or business process has been made in the job request, the IT employee must specify in the popup that appears whether the job is to be assigned to a particular business process step (in which case the respective logical component is selected implicitly) or whether process assignment is not required and the job is only to be assigned to a logical component. The latter case would, for example, apply to an IT Basis job. Job S_DE_PP_MRP_ 1000_6H in this example is assigned to the order-to-cash process (i.e., from creating the sales order to receiving the payment for the invoice) and the run MRP process step.

If the detailed job request form had been used in step 1, assignment to a logical component or a business process could have been made at that stage. Had this been the case, the dialog box would not have appeared when the SAP CRM document was saved.

In our example, the job document has been successfully created and now contains all of the information saved in the job request by the user department employees. In other words, from the point at which the job request was created, all data has been passed on to job documentation automatically without external steps or any need for manual copying and pasting.

Step 4: Completing the Job Document on the IT Side

The fourth step involves taking any necessary steps to complete the job document. First, it must be located. To do so, you either have to open the SAP CRM document again and navigate to the JOB SCHEDULING MANAGEMENT assignment block or open the document flow. From there, you can navigate to the follow-on document (here, job document) by double-clicking it.

Alternatively, you can call up the JOB DOCUMENTATION view in the *Job Management* work center and filter by job name, for example. If you call up the job document from the work center, you see individual tab pages that you can fill. Each of these tab pages represents aspects (Best Practices) of complete job documentation. This allows you to enter general technical data, business data, and organizational data in the same way. You can save different contacts and enter descriptions for error handling. You can also note restrictions in scheduling. If you document a job chain, you can link all job documents that belong to the chain elements. In the corresponding job documentation of the chain element, you can also see to which job chain the element belongs. You can also navigate in both directions, that is, from the documentation of the chain to the documentation of the element and vice versa (see Figure 11.8).

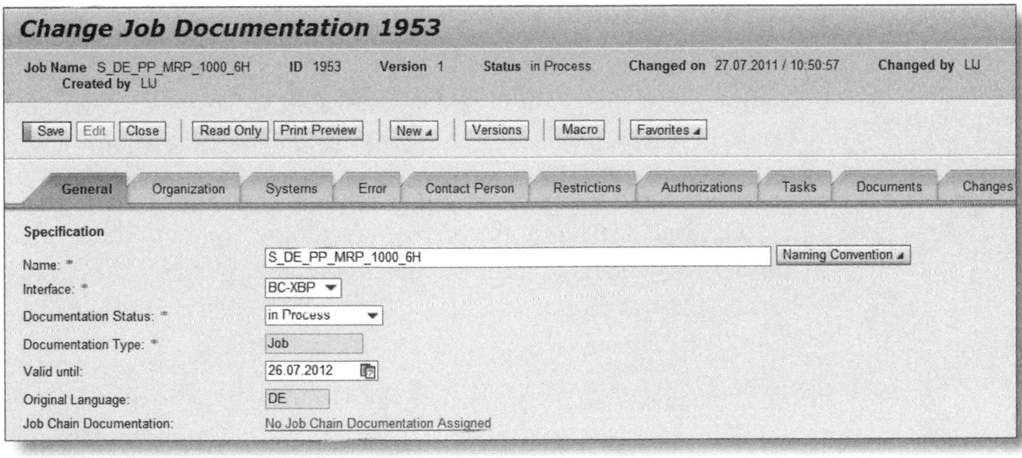

Processing from the work center

Figure 11.8 Job Documentation

547

The SYSTEMS tab page is particularly important in the job documentation because it enables you to configure scheduling as well as monitoring.

Step 5: Configuring Scheduling in SAP Solution Manager and Transferring Data to SAP Central Process Scheduling by Redwood

To configure scheduling, navigate to the JOB DOCUMENTATION view in the *Job Management* work center, and choose the SYSTEMS tab. First, you select a logical component or a solution with a business process and process step. After you have done so, all of the systems belonging to the logical component are displayed in the lower screen area. You then select one of the lines containing a system. In our example, you select the production system. By choosing the SCHEDULE pushbutton, you are then taken to a new window in which you can enter the job scheduling in detail. The user interface appearance changes depending on the chosen scheduling tool. It either looks similar to the standard Transaction SM36 or contains the same fields that you see when you schedule jobs directly in SAP Central Process Scheduling (as in this example).

Creating a job

You enter all of the important scheduling data and choose the CREATE pushbutton. A job is now created in the background in the connected SAP Central Process Scheduling system. Depending on whether the SCHEDULE STOPPED indicator has been set in SAP Solution Manager, the job acquires either STOPPED or SCHEDULED status in SAP Central Process Scheduling. In the former case, the job must still be explicitly released in SAP Central Process Scheduling before it can run in the backend system. In the latter, the job is started as soon as the start conditions are met. Authorizations are used to verify whether SAP Solution Manager is permitted to create and even release jobs in SAP Central Process Scheduling.

If you want SAP Central Process Scheduling to send status data directly to Business Process Monitoring, you have to set the STATUS NOTIFICATION indicator.

Step 6: Configuring Job Monitoring as Part of Business Process Monitoring

If you want to configure and activate monitoring, you must assign the job to a business process step. Assignment to a logical component alone is not sufficient. In our example, the job has been assigned to the run MRP step. On the SYSTEMS tab, you now choose the line that represents the assignment of solution, business scenario, business process, and step. A list of all system and client combinations covered by the assigned logical component is then shown in the lower screen area. You choose the line containing the system with the leading role (in most cases, this will be the production system, just as in our example).

Assignment to business process step

When you choose the MONITORING pushbutton, a new dialog box opens in which you can save information describing when you want the job to be monitored. You can enter whether you consider the job to be particularly critical. Accordingly, a check is run every 5 minutes or once an hour to establish if there is a new status. Next, you enter the data source. You either receive the data directly from SAP Central Process Scheduling, or (if you are not using that application) SAP Solution Manager receives the data from the connected SAP backend system. The former case offers the advantage that SAP Central Process Scheduling can enable monitoring to be extended to non-SAP systems. Next, you enter the days on which you want to receive monitoring data because the job does not necessarily need to be monitored on every day that it is scheduled to run. For example, the job may only be time-critical on workdays and not on the weekend. On the ALERT CONFIGURATION tab, you can enter the respective threshold values for the different key figures. After you have saved all of the data, you activate monitoring directly from this application.

To ensure this is successful, you must first activate Business Process Monitoring for the respective process (in this case, order to cash) and set the CONSIDER JOB DEF. indicator for the process in the general setup area of Business Process Monitoring. You can close the dialog box now that monitoring is active. SAP Solution Manager begins monitoring.

You can also use the SAP Solution Manager Job Request, Job Documentation, and Business Process Monitoring functions together with other scheduling tools. However, to do so you are required to transfer

Summary

the scheduling data from SAP Solution Manager to the planning tool manually. This also results in Business Process Monitoring being restricted to background jobs in the SAP environment. For the future, we are planning a new certifiable interface (Solution Manager Scheduling Enabler). This interface will also give other scheduling tools the chance to establish comparable integration with SAP Solution Manager as has been the case with SAP Central Process Scheduling by Redwood for years (see Figure 11.9).

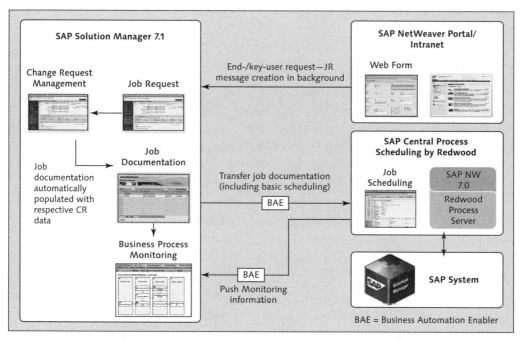

Figure 11.9 Integration of SAP Central Process Scheduling in SAP Solution Manager via the Business Automation Enabler Interface

11.2.3 Automatically Redirecting a User from the Backend System to the SAP Solution Manager Application Form

At the start of the chapter, we already pointed out that many customers find it difficult to control the background activities that end users schedule directly, thus avoiding the central scheduling team. Section 11.2.1 already introduced the function that can be used to intercept such user activities. That solves the problem at least technically. It also prevents the corresponding backend system from being overloaded, which is important in particular during period-end closing times. However, many customers do not find this technical solution satisfactory because it leaves some problems unsolved. The intercepted jobs generally do not follow any naming convention, and there is no documentation for the respective job. This means that nobody knows what to do in case of an error and who to contact in case of questions. Problems can occur in particular if job scheduling is operated by an outsourcing partner.

That is why SAP Solution Manager offers a more comprehensive solution. In Section 11.2.2, we introduced how SAP Solution Manager provides a job request form and a job document in integrated form. However, access into the process was merely optional until now. That is, a user has to actively call one of the job request forms. Alternatively, you can also use SAP Solution Manager to force respective users to be taken automatically into the request process if they want to call Transactions SM36, SM37, or SA38 to schedule jobs in the connected backend system.

In the first step, you determine for each backend system whether this redirection should be activated and, if so, which users are supposed to be redirected and which users should be excluded (e.g., administration or regular scheduling users). Before you activate the redirection, you should have set up and configured the integration scenario for the job request form and job documentation in SAP Solution Manager so that the process can actually be used in production. For more information on the redirection of Transactions SM36, SM37, and others, see the article "Re-directing Transactions SM36, SM37, SA38: Controlling End-User Scheduled Jobs – Part 1" on the SDN site (at *www.sdn.sap.com/irj/scn/weblogs?blog=/pub/wlg/17544*).

Process flow

11.2.4 Job Scheduling Management Health Check

During their everyday work, IT organizations keep having the problem that the influence background processing has on their backend system is not clear. That is, they cannot see what load background processing causes in the respective system. One problem that makes it harder to achieve this transparency was described earlier: Many users independently schedule jobs in the system without the IT department knowing about it.

To create this type of transparency, the new SAP Solution Manager offers the *Job Scheduling Management Health Check* (see Figure 11.10).

SAP Solution Manager uses this function to collect the relevant background processing runtime data from the respective backend systems. (By default, only the header data is extracted from Table TBTCO, but you can also extract the item data of Table TBTCP.) It then saves this data in selected InfoCubes and displays it in a standardized form. You can call the corresponding web templates (the data is aggregated every day, week, or month) directly in the web browser. However, you can also call them from the *Job Management* work center.

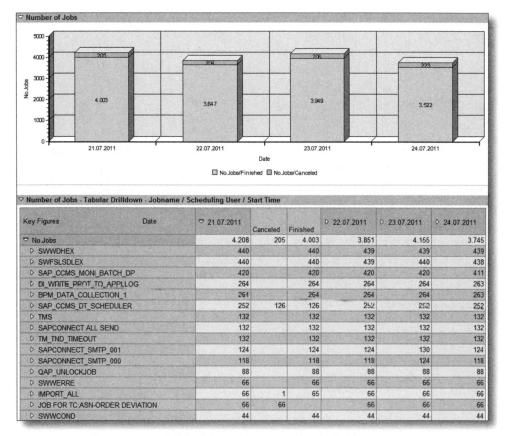

Figure 11.10 Job Scheduling Management Health Check

Possible reports | You can use the web templates to answer the following questions:

- How many jobs have been processed successfully, and how many jobs have been terminated?

- What is the cumulated runtime of all successful jobs or all terminated jobs?

▶ How many jobs had a runtime of < 1 minute, 1-5 minutes, 5-15 minutes, 15-60 minutes, and > 1 hour?

▶ How many jobs had a delay of < 1 minute, 1-5 minutes, 5-15 minutes, 15-60 minutes, and > 1 hour?

▶ Which user name created the most jobs? And which users accumulated the longest runtimes with their jobs?

▶ On which application instances were the most jobs executed? And which application instances had the longest accumulated runtime?

11.3 Data Consistency Management

Data Consistency Management is an important aspect in Business Process Operations. In the following sections, we first show you why it plays such an important role and the tasks that Data Consistency Management should include (see Section 11.3.1). In Section 11.3.2, we then give you an overview of the tools provided with SAP Solution Manager.

11.3.1 Introducing Data Consistency Management

Current standard business processes store central master data such as material masters or customer master data as well as transactional documents such as sales orders in several systems and redundantly with different data models. However, this data should contain the same information at all times on one hand so that processes can run correctly and, on the other hand, so that business decisions are based on identical data records. To check this consistency, SAP provides different application-specific consistency reports in the individual SAP systems.

The consistency of the data used in the business process is essential for the successful operation of an SAP system landscape because the decisions of each user and management, and therefore the company's success, depend on correct and up-to-date data being available at the right time. Many people think that standard systems like those that occur in an SAP landscape should provide transaction security and data consistency without particular effort. In fact, however, ensuring this data consistency is one of the biggest challenges faced in today's landscapes. In the past, ensuring and restoring data

Motivation

consistency were made easier by the fact that the application ran on only one database in one system. These days, application processes tend to span across several systems and use several databases in parallel without sufficient synchronization.

It is therefore absolutely necessary to create a comprehensive operation concept that explicitly takes into account data consistency because data inconsistencies can arise in a number of ways. Typical causes are, on one hand, customer programs that violate the LUW (logical unit of work) concept; user errors, in particular in the interface environment; and technical errors, such as errors in network controllers. This can lead to errors between systems but also between different functionalities such as Sales and Distribution (SD) and Materials Management (MM). Hence, you must regularly check the consistency of the most important application and master data to be able to detect and correct errors at an early stage.

For application support, this gives rise to the question of how to find the most important inspection reports and how to use them as efficiently as possible. In addition, the solution landscape often has integrated non-SAP systems, which cannot be intended for use in the SAP standard as such but are subject to the same data consistency requirements. Central data management must also make available tools for handling at least the most important data, if this data can be exchanged between the systems.

Consistency cycle   In addition to the early detection of potential inconsistencies, Data Consistency Management should naturally try to avoid inconsistencies right from the start as well. If you discover potential inconsistencies, you must, of course, correct them but also analyze what caused them. Data Consistency Management should therefore cover the following four phases:

1. Avoiding inconsistencies
2. Discovering inconsistencies
3. Analyzing inconsistencies
4. Correcting inconsistencies

11.3.2 Overview of the Tools for Data Consistency Management

Ideal Data Consistency Management should cover these phases and include the non-SAP systems involved in the business process. It should also provide central access to all required functions. For this purpose, SAP Solution Manager provides central and efficient Data Consistency Management in the *Business Process Operations* work center (see Figure 11.11).

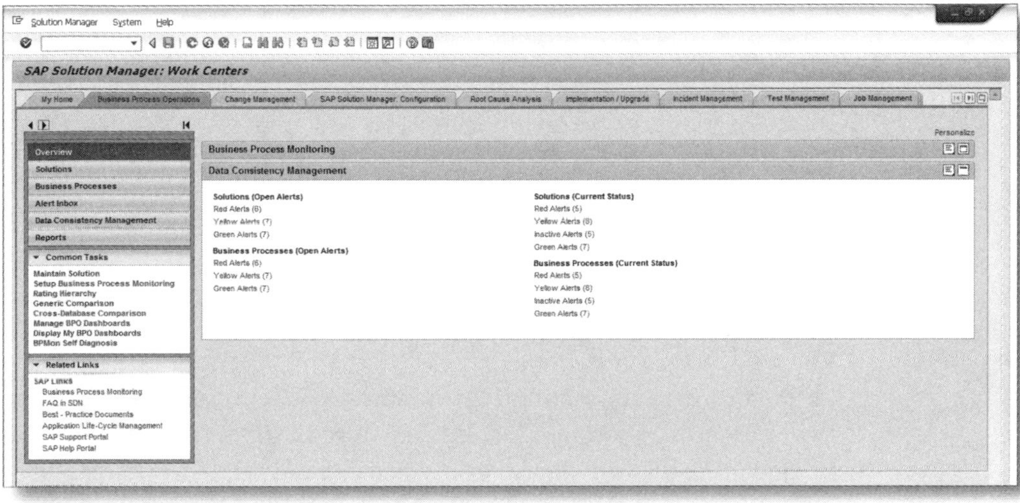

"Business Process Operations" work center

Figure 11.11 Data Consistency Management in the "Business Process Operations" Work Center

Various functions of the *Business Process Operations* work center cover the individual areas of the data consistency cycle. Table 11.1 provides an overview of which functions in the work center support which phase.

Phase of the Consistency Cycle	Function in the Work Center
Avoiding data inconsistencies	Best Practice documents
Monitoring the data consistency	Data Consistency and Interface Monitoring

Table 11.1 Coverage of the Phases of the Consistency Cycle by the Work Center

Phase of the Consistency Cycle	Function in the Work Center
Analyzing the data consistency	Data consistency toolbox in the Data Consistency Management area Cross-database Comparison
Correcting inconsistencies	Data Consistency toolbox in the Data Consistency Management area

Table 11.1 Coverage of the Phases of the Consistency Cycle by the Work Center (Cont.)

Data Consistency Management and Business Process Monitoring

To monitor the data consistency, SAP Solution Manager provides an efficient tool as part of Business Process Monitoring with data consistency and interface monitoring. This tool enables you to check all your data automatically. The most important key figures available to you are the following:

▶ The results of central consistency reports

▶ The age of the last correct execution of these consistency reports

▶ Errors during data exchange between the two systems

Data consistency monitoring and interface monitoring perform two different monitoring tasks. Interface monitoring provides high-frequency checks for current errors that could put the data consistency at risk so that they can be corrected quickly. The data consistency check based on the respective consistency report, in contrast, should be set up as an additional safety net to discover inconsistencies that have occurred due to other causes. Hence, you should set up this check in addition to interface monitoring.

Alerts

To get an overview of whether there are Data Consistency Management alerts, you can set a filter for these alerts in the ALERT INBOX and in the business process view (see Figure 11.12).

To make it easier to set up interface monitoring, you can copy the technical data entered in the interface documentation, for example, the queue name(s) or IDoc types used, into the monitoring object settings. Aside from the purely technical monitoring of interfaces, you can also display the errors in the process context. That way, you see at a first glance how different processes are affected by an interface error that occurs.

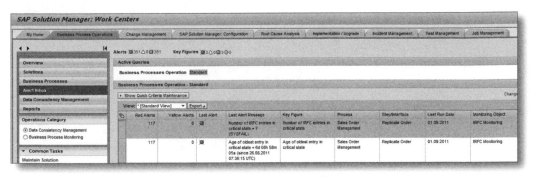

Figure 11.12 Data Consistency-Relevant Alerts Using a tRFC Interface as the Example

As an integral part of Business Process Monitoring, you have access to all functions described in Section 11.1.3; for example, to-do lists, procedural documentation for problem solving, escalation paths, and trend reporting.

When operating a solution, you not only need to take care of the regular monitoring of the data consistency, but you're also faced with user questions regarding suspected inconsistencies. You also want to check the data consistency after a data transfer or hardware error. In this case, you have to specifically check the consistency of certain application tables or application areas and analyze typical causes if inconsistencies are detected.

DCToolbox

Here, the *Business Process Operations* work center supports you by providing the *DCToolbox*. It first queries important information using a guided procedure and then uses this information to derive an approach based on Customizing data. This procedure is made available as a session from which you can directly start all necessary actions such as the execution of consistency reports or checking the affected interfaces and documents for potential errors in the connected satellites.

Figure 11.13 shows, for example, which data the guided procedure queried to analyze sales documents. Figure 11.14 shows the approach generated from this data, including possible actions, background information, and the option to document the results.

Of course you can expand the Customizing data underlying the session generation to take into account customer data, reports, or transactions.

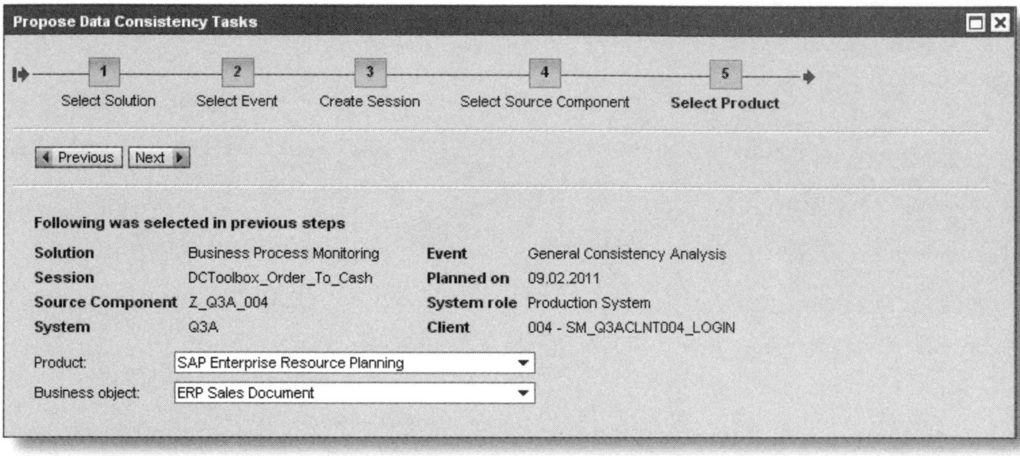

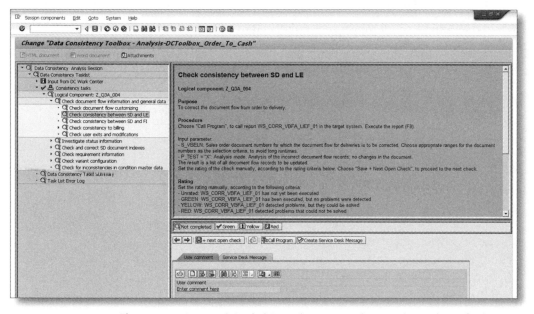

Figure 11.13 Guided Procedure Using the Analysis of Sales Documents as an Example

Figure 11.14 Proposed Guided Procedure Approach Using the Analysis of Sales Documents as an Example

Cross Database Comparison

In the preceding sections, you learned how SAP Solution Manager helps you with Data Consistency Management in situations that usually occur in standard systems. But what is the situation with regard to the usual application reports for common tasks that are not supported, for example, a consistency comparison arising due to the use of third-party systems? To cover fundamental data consistency also in these cases, SAP Solution Manager offers the *Cross Database Comparison* (CDC). CDC is an easy-to-use tool for modeling and setting up comparisons between different source systems and displaying the results.

To do so, you first define a *comparison object*; that is, a model, of which data is to be compared in which system and how this data is supposed to be mapped. CDC helps you with this modeling with F4 helps for ABAP systems integrated via RFC, but also for non-SAP systems that are connected to SAP Solution Manager using ADBC.

Comparison object

After you have defined the data model, you use it to generate a *comparison instance* that defines which systems are supposed to be compared using the underlying comparison object. In addition, you can also enter filter values in a comparison instance, if this is permitted in the comparison object. This allows you, for example, to define comparison instances for different organizational units on the same data model.

Comparison instance

After you have completed the comparison instance, you can execute the comparison, that is, a *comparison run*. For each comparison run, you can display the following results in CDC-UI:

Comparison run

- Statistical values
- Number of data records compared
- Absolute number and percentage of each:
  - The correct (identical) data records
  - Data records that exist only in system 1
  - Data records that exist only in system 2
  - Data records whose key values are available in both systems but have different data values

For the last three cases, you can display additional details; for example, key and field values that differ between the systems (see Figure 11.15 and Figure 11.16).

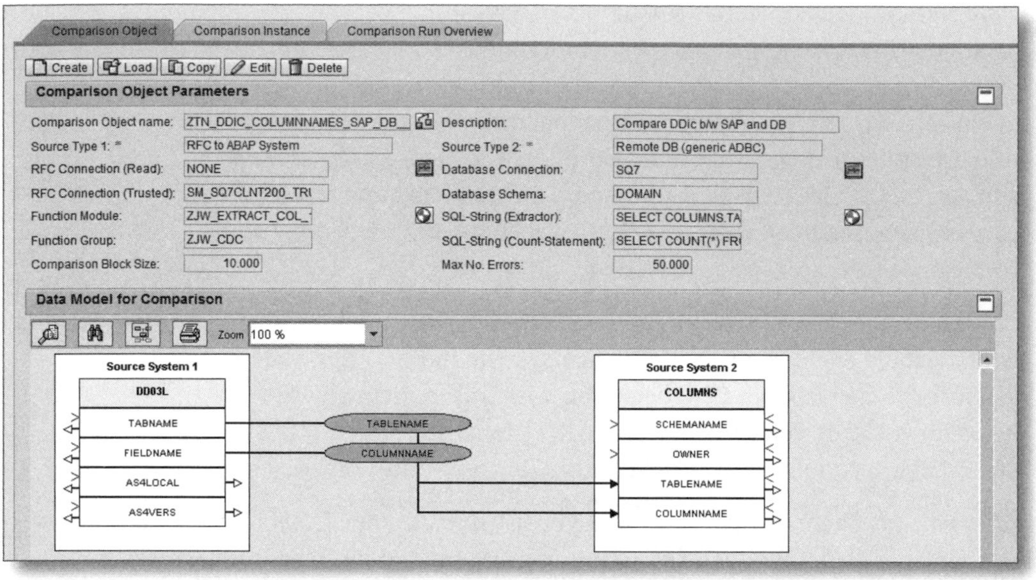

Figure 11.15 Display of a Comparison Object in the Cross Database Comparison

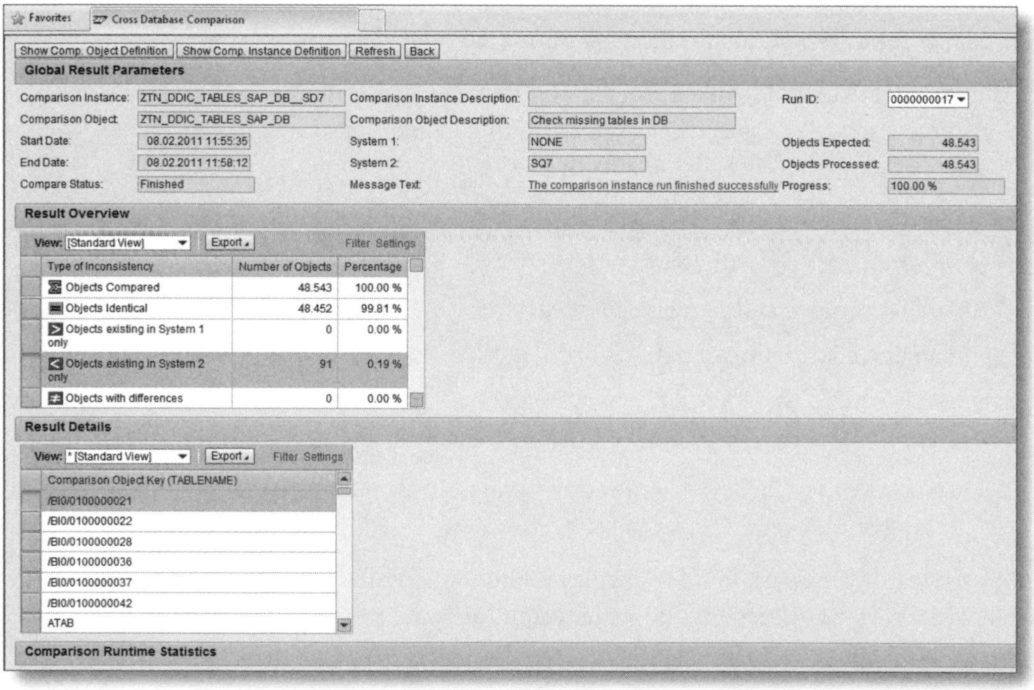

Figure 11.16 Display of Inconsistencies Found in Cross Database Comparison

11.4   Business Process Performance

To successfully operate an SAP solution, it must be smoothly integrated into the user's work. In addition to aspects such as functional correctness, ease of use, security, and data protection, the performance of the business processes plays a crucial role. Here, performance refers to the system response time per user action and the runtime of critical background jobs.

Business process performance plays a special role because users can feel it directly, it frequently deteriorates only over time, and it is not visible directly in system monitoring (e.g., the average response time of the overall system). Hence, it is important to monitor the performance of the most important business processes and take the necessary countermeasures if response times deteriorate.

Motivation

For performance bottlenecks, you should first analyze the cause of the bad response times. The SAP Solution Manager functions and dashboards offer guidance here (see Chapter 10, Section 10.4). However, if you are using mainly ABAP applications (without Web Dynpro ABAP) you can execute the analyses as usual directly in the backend using the corresponding analysis functions in the SAP GUI.

It is often not possible to solve complex performance problems with simple system and program optimization tools. In addition, this can have the effect that not all performance optimization options are utilized. Even with additional hardware, performance problems can still occur. In those cases, you should proceed as described in Section 11.4.1.

11.4.1   Business Process Performance Optimization

The procedure for optimizing the performance of business processes should be used in particular for complex performance problems and for validating new business process implementations. The method includes the steps described in the following sections.

Step 1: Description of the System Landscape and the Technical Components Used

This also includes the descriptions of all server and network components; for example, including those that ensure high availability:

System landscape

- ▶ Hardware (number of servers, memory size, number of CPUs, CPU types, database type and version, and database size)
- ▶ Additional important information, for example, use of logical partitions or database clusters
- ▶ Network layout
- ▶ Technical sequence of the business process (see Figure 11.17)

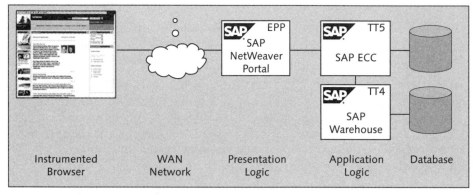

Figure 11.17 Example of a Technical Process Flow of a Business Process

Business process graphic

Step 2: Description of the Business Process to Be Analyzed and Highlighting of Individual Critical Steps in a Suitable Graphical Display

Figure 11.18 shows an example of a sales process.

Step 3: Description of the Requirements (KPIs) for Each Individual Critical Business Process in a Table

KPIs

Here, it is important to document the data volume and the number of users. It makes sense to set the required response time in relation to the data volume. For example, in many areas of logistics, it makes sense to define the requirement for the response time per item. In addition, you have to document information about components, interfaces, and changes that the business process step uses. Table 11.2 shows an example of the description of requirements for an individual critical business process step.

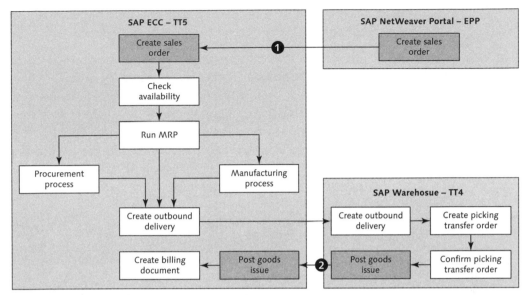

Figure 11.18 Example of a Business Process Graphic

Description	Information	Execution	Interface	Notes
Create sales order	► Document volume, for example, 6,000 per day with an average of 15 items per document ► Possible time restrictions or dependencies with other processes ► Time window with highest data volume	► Portal: Online ► SAP ECC: Transaction VA01	Interface: SAP ERP → SAP ECC	Is the call center used?

Table 11.2 Example of KPI Documentation

Step 4: Monitoring and Analysis of the Business Process Step

You should execute the analysis in an environment with a representative data volume and realistic examples. If you want to execute the analysis in a test environment, you should make sure that it contains representative data.

Analysis

In the context of the analysis of critical business processes before production startup, this means that you first have to find out whether there actually is a performance problem. For example, we recommend copying the production data and distributing it to the test system for further performance analyses.

Before you analyze the performance of your business processes, you should make sure that there are no general system performance bottlenecks within your SAP architecture (database, application server, frontend, and network). An important gauge for that is SAP EarlyWatch Alert (EWA), which your system administrator should schedule once a week in every production system. You should use the EWA report to answer the questions in the checklist shown in Table 11.3 to search for the cause of bad performance.

Question	Examples
How good is the general system performance?	Average dialog response time
How high is the load on hardware resources?	CPU load, memory consumption, buffer quality
Are there database bottlenecks?	Locks, expensive statements
How good are the systems I/O response times and network performance?	Long I/O wait times, long NiPing times
Are the database and system parameters configured correctly?	SAP EarlyWatch Check

Table 11.3 Checklist for the Analysis

Note
Note that inefficient ABAP programming or inefficient database access can also lead to a hardware bottleneck (e.g., unnecessary locks, incorrect use of database indexes, incorrect buffering of tables, too much memory consumption).

When you have made sure that there is no system performance problem, you should first execute the runtime measurements of the critical action (e.g., a single click in a transaction or a step of a job) without a trace. The purpose of this execution is to fill the buffers in the database and SAP application server. You should document the second measurement using the corresponding statistical records (Transaction STAD).

If you want to analyze a web transaction, you can use the end-to-end Trace Analysis (described in Chapter 10, Section 10.4) or another suitable tool, for example, the HTTP trace. This often shows that performance problems are located on the server, if the client does not process any logic. You should then start an HTTP/RFC-ST12 trace on the server. You can also, for example, check the interface for errors to find out which data is transferred to the server through the interface. In case of long network times, you can use the niping tool to measure individual legs.

End-to-end Trace Analysis

In the GUI or HTTP/ABAP case, only the third execution should use the ABAP and SQL trace. You usually use the ABAP trace (with internal tables) and the SQL trace of the *Single Transaction Analysis* (Transaction ST12). This transaction is available with the ST-A/PI plug-in. In some cases, you are directed to special traces such as the GUI trace for the analysis of statistical records.

With the new SAP Solution Manager, you can also use the Guided Self-Service *Performance Optimization* (GSS PERF), which supports E2E Trace Analysis and Single Transaction Analysis.

Guided self-service performance optimization

In some use cases, for example, material requirements planning (MRP) run or SD pricing, you have to analyze the SAP Customizing. For that, the GSS PERF service offers a small selection of application checks. They provide an initial indication as to whether there is potential for optimizing the performance in the setup of the individual applications (e.g., unnecessary SD pricing rules, use of expensive MRP parameters).

Step 5: Creation of the Optimization Recommendation (System or Application)

Depending on the scope of changes (e.g., additional index versus restructure of the program), you can use your change management to trace the changes in the system, or you have to execute a new project. Test Management and Change Management are described in more detail in Chapters 7 and 8, respectively. For more information on ABAP performance optimization, see the two books *ABAP Performance Tuning* by Hermann Gahm (SAP PRESS, 2009) and *Performance-Optimierung von ABAP-Programmen [Performance Optimization of ABAP Programs]* by Siegfried Boes (dpunkt-Verlag, 2009).

Creation of the optimization recommendation (system or application)

Step 6: Implementing the Optimization in the Test/Production System

Implementing the optimization in the test/production system

Before you transport changes into your production system, you should check the improvements in a test environment and compare the results before and after the change. A repeated trace or debugging analysis can be helpful for verifying the program changes. You should also make sure that the optimization has no negative effect on any other business process steps, as when you implement additional indexes, for example.

Step 7: Checking the Improvement and, If Necessary, Repeating the Analysis/Optimization/Validation

Verification

You should perform the final acceptance of the performance improvement in the product system and document it accordingly. It is possible that the runtime response changes if the document volume changes. If your changes do not suffice for reaching your KPIs, you should execute another performance analysis.

11.4.2 Performance Optimization with SAP Self-Services

SAP Active Global Support (SAP AGS) offers different services for optimizing the performance of your business processes. Depending on the complexity of your SAP solution, there are different options for ensuring operation and implementation with regard to performance.

SAP BPPO and SAP CQC BPPO

In the context of SAP MaxAttention and SAP Safeguarding, SAP offers the *SAP Business Process Performance Optimization* service (SAP BPPO). For SAP Enterprise Support customers, a similar service, *SAP Continuous Quality Check BPPO* (SAP CQC BPPO), is available but it has a reduced service scope.

Both services have the same objective, to optimize the performance of your core business processes and ensure that the necessary data throughput is achieved in the available time window. First, they try to find technical optimization options that do not require the business process to be modified.

In these services, SAP Solution Manager reuses already documented information about the core business processes as well as problems that have been identified in the processes. This enables the efficient analysis of individual process steps (see Section 11.4.1 for the method).

These two services start with those points that, as experience has shown, most frequently lead to performance problems:

- Expensive SQL statements
- Customer developments and modifications
- Ineffective use of SAP standard transactions

Long running SQL statements not only cause long runtimes in the programs in which they are called, but also indirectly cause performance problems in other transactions. For a few expensive SQL statements to cause more than 50% of the total load on the database server is not an exception.

Expensive SQL statements

Despite optimal database access, it is possible to have unsatisfactory performance. This is often due to customer developments and changes in the SAP standard, user exits, BAdIs, or enhancements options. You can also identify, analyze, and optimize these in the context of the described SAP CQC. Throughput is increased, the response times of long running transactions are improved, and the smooth operation of the core business processes is thus ensured. Practical experience has shown that significantly more than 50% of all performance problems in ABAP programs are due to inefficient database accesses in combination with inefficient program algorithms.

Customer developments

Aside from expensive SQL statements and customer developments, the ineffective use of SAP standard transactions can also affect performance and thus the throughput of core business processes. When SAP experts carry out SAP CQCs, they analyze (locally or remotely) the individual steps and actions of the core business processes with regard to performance, technical correctness, and transactional security. They identify the optimization potential with focus on the following subject areas:

Ineffective use of SAP standard transactions

- Optimization of task functions
- Parallel processing and use of mass data capable programs
- Database locks
- Queues
- Sizing

▶ Load distribution by time

▶ Load distribution to database and application server

▶ Shared resources

The results of this analysis are documented directly in a service session in your SAP Solution Manager. The identified problems and the steps required to solve them are recorded in a central issue list in issue management in SAP Solution Manager, from where they can be processed further and addressed. A service report with the results of the analyses is also generated for you. This report contains the technical process description, a concrete action plan, and service recommendations. For on-site deliveries, your local staff members acquire comprehensive knowledge, enabling them to independently analyze and optimize other business processes in your SAP solution in the future. From SAP Solution Manager 7.1 onward, you can use the SAP GSS PERF. You can also participate in an Expert-Guided Implementation (EGI) for this service. An SAP expert explains in detail how you can best execute this guided self-service.

Guided Self-Service Performance Optimization (GSS PERF)

This guided self-service is an enhancement to the SAP Services that is available as of Solution Manager 7.1 You also need the *Support Tools Application Plug-In* ST/A-PI 01N to be able to fully use all self-service features. You can create the service as a guide self-service in the *SAP Engagement and Service Delivery* work center. The service consists of four steps:

1. **Preparation**

   This preparatory step serves to check whether all important prerequisites for the guided self-service delivery are met. In the preparation, you have to decide which type of analysis (refer to Figure 11.19 for the scope selection) you want to execute. You can choose from the following analysis methods:

   ▶ **End-to-end Trace Analysis**
   You can use the end-to-end Trace Analysis with a connected Solution Manager Diagnostics or by uploading the E2E trace downloaded from diagnostics as an XML file into the analysis section.

   ▶ **Single Transaction Analysis (ST12)**
   To analyze a performance trace in the analysis session, certain prerequisites must be met. You must have installed at least the

service and support plug-in ST-A/PI 01N in your SAP Solution Manager and the connected system that contains the performance trace. You also need a read and a trusted RFC connection with the corresponding authorizations. These are required for loading trace information or reading source code, among other things. For more information, see the SDN at *http://wiki.sdn.sap.com/ wiki/display/ABAP/Single+Transaction+Analysis.*

▶ **Application analysis**

Within the application analysis (Transaction ST14), you can choose additional options for the individual application components (SAP CRM, SAP SCM, SAP ERP). Make sure that you have maintained a trusted RFC connection in the corresponding system to schedule the application analysis from SAP Solution Manager as a job. After the job has been executed, the results are available in the next step, the analysis.

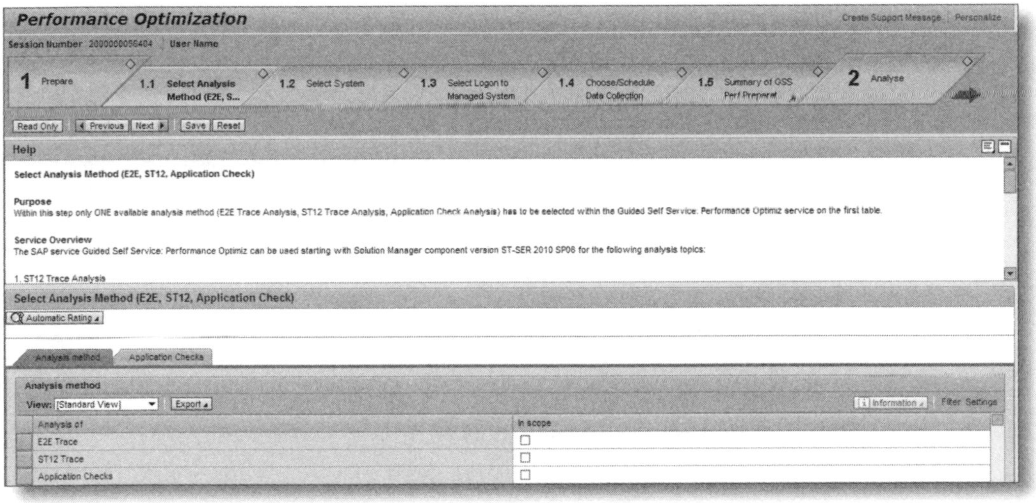

Figure 11.19 Sample GSS PERF Preparation Step—Scope Selection

2. **Analysis**

After successfully completing the preparations and selecting the analysis method, you can execute the analysis step. Depending on the method, you can choose and analyze a trace. You have several options for that, for example, identify expensive SQL statements or long running table calls. In addition, you can also execute, for example, an SAP Note search in the connected OSS system during Single Transaction Analysis if SAP program parts are causing the performance problems. You can document the resulting actions and recommendations in issue management of SAP Solution Manager directly from the session.

3. **Report**
If you have completed the analysis, you should generate the final report. This also starts the follow-up step.

4. **Follow-up**
In the follow-up step, you can choose which actions and issues you want to pursue and process further.

11.5 SAP Solution Manager at Bayer Material-Science

Business Process Monitoring and Business Process Analytics—a key tool within SAP Solution Manager—provides automatic, standard KPI functionality, and helps our teams achieve low-cost leadership, flexibility, and efficiency. Business Process Monitoring and Business Process Analytics is ultimately making us a more efficient and effective business.

Laurie Miller, O&I, Head of Global Support Services,
Bayer MaterialScience

Bayer Material-Science AG

Bayer MaterialScience (BMS) is one of the largest companies in the global chemical industry, with sales of over 10 billion Euros In 2010. BMS develops, manufactures, and markets high-performance products in the areas of polyurethanes, polycarbonates, coating and adhesives raw materials, and specialties such as functional films. The company also manufactures and markets selected inorganic basic chemicals. BMS is divided into the Polyurethanes, Polycarbonates and Coatings, Adhesives, Specialties business units, and the Industrial Operations area. BMS employs approximately 14,700 people and operates 30 major production sites worldwide.

Project overview

BMS is currently implementing a companywide business-process and IT transformation project called ProgramOne (P1), with the objective of defining a standardized set of global processes and merging the company's different SAP ERP systems into a single global platform which to support the global processes. Running from now until January 2012, the project will provide a single global template for approximately 12,000 end users worldwide. SAP MaxAttention knowledge, applications, and tools are playing a critical role in P1P's success. SAP Solution Manager's Business Process Analytics has given team members a highly transparent overview of the company's business processes, providing them with the full benefits of what the SAP environment can offer. In the words of CIO Kurt De Ruwe: "We are convinced that Business Process Analytics is SAP's best-kept secret."

The business process improvement project based on Business Process Analytics was kicked-off in September 2010, after an initial analysis of the business processes on the P1P system (BMS' ERP system) via SAP Active Global Support. Based on the analysis results, BMS decided to pilot two business process workstreams *Demand to Supply* and *Maintain to Settle*. With the preliminary analysis, BMS saw already not only the potential for improvement, but also a new approach for an issue-orientated procedure to measure process performance. The BMS process owner community will ensure that business processes are sustainable and stable after the transition from the P1 project phase into the global operative ERP system.

Simplification, automation, and standardization are the key goals to be achieved by:

Key goals

1. Systematically analyzing the business processes and defining critical milestones within the processes

2. Setting up different BP Analytics data collectors to map critical milestones to use different functionalities of BP Analytics, e.g., internal benchmarking of organizational units and age-structure analysis of backlog documents over the last years

3. Detecting process issues at an early stage using Business Process Monitoring (BP Mon) and Alerting

The identified exceptions can be classified into the following five main areas:

Exceptions

▶ Standardization issues

▶ Systematic end-user failures and end-user training gaps

▶ Process design gaps

▶ Master data issues

▶ Configuration and customizing needs

DMAIC cycle   In the following, I will explain how our project team used the DMAIC cycle (see Figure 11.20) within the project, and what we experienced throughout the project.

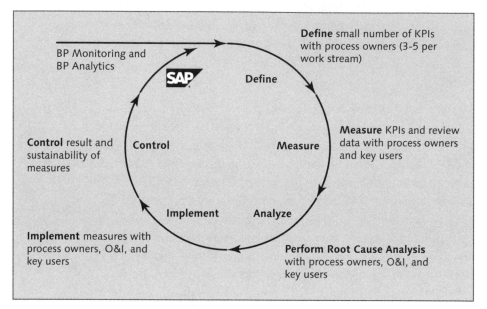

Figure 11.20 DMAIC Cycle

Define   During the first phase of the cycle, the business processes are chosen for which the project is carried out. During this phase the project team focused on the workstreams *Maintain to Settle* and *Demand to Supply*. The tasks in this phase also included those that addressed the question: Who should be the first business department or unit to work with? We then gathered requirements and defined target values. Key performance indicators were also chosen during this phase, with the selection of the key figures dependent on business impact, probable benefit, estimated savings, and sub-process lead time. We started with four key figures for both workstreams.

Measure   Measuring and evaluating the respective key figure is done with Business Process Analytics based on Business Process Monitoring in SAP Solution Manager. During this phase, we incorporated the feedback of the business process owners and community as well as colleagues from Organization & Information (O&I – those members responsible for the technical realization of business defined processes) in order to adjust the set-up regarding our needs, and including only those process variants that are relevant to the chosen pilot workstreams.

Within the third phase, we started to dig into the different root causes for deviations and exceptions from expected business process performance, i.e., what led to the high backlog? Business Process Analytics' *Detailed Analysis* function provides a detailed list of all documents in backlog, including the possibility to jump directly into the affected business document. Here, primarily the business departments and units checked the documents with support from O&I. Usually, the same root causes could be determined, e.g. process work-arounds to address business exceptions. For instance, further automation potential within the last process steps for *Maintain to Settle* was identified.

Analyze

During implementation, the actual change and adaption of the business process through countermeasures for the root causes took place. The project team defined and executed actions to re-install or adjust business process designs. For each root cause identified, one or more action items had been created, including the assignment of deadlines and responsibilities.

Implement

Within the last cycle, the team set up monitoring and alerting functionality on the respective business process, in order to stabilize process performance and improve the process efficiency and effectiveness. This was managed by defining thresholds and alerting the appropriately identified business person(s) in case of critical deviations. The *Trend Analysis* functionality within Business Process Analytics was used to monitor the reduction of document backlog.

Control

Initially we had it in mind to rollout Business Process Monitoring and Business Process Analytics in a phased approach. Due to the strong interest within the BMS organization, the team is now working with each workstream in parallel, allowing for more balance and earlier realization of first impacts and results. The project rollout therefore now includes *Order to Cash*, *Procure to Pay with Accounts Payable*, as well as *Finance to Manage*.

Rollout

In addition to the continued rollout of Business Process Monitoring and Business Process Analytics, the team is focused on an increased awareness of the tool and the approach taken at BMS. Within BMS, up to now we have had discussions and involvement across all work streams, regions and business departments and units. We will also continue to expand the knowledge and further reach out to our key users in all areas.

The true power of a strong process owner community along with Business Process Monitoring and Business Process Analytics lies for us in the transparency, visibility, flexibility, and collaboration it enables. The business and O&I team members are working together, and when preliminary results are seen between the team members the issue and the measure to be taken is typically readily apparent.

Business Process Monitoring and Business Process Analytics—a key tool within SAP Solution Manager—provides automatic, standard KPI functionality, and helps our teams achieve low-cost leadership, flexibility, and efficiency. Business Process Monitoring and Business Process Analytics is ultimately making us a more efficient and effective business.

The Author

Laurie Miller, Head of BMS O&I Global Support Services at Bayer MaterialScience holds responsibility for several areas spanning the BMS O&I organization, one of which is a governance role ensuring that the global O&I teams work according to quality standards and procedures, as well as ensuring the relevant security practices are in place and that all teams adhere to them. In 1988 Laurie Miller graduated Magna Cum Laude in Accounting from Robert Morris University, Pittsburgh, PA. She completed her MBA program in 1994, focusing on marketing and international business at the University of Pittsburgh – Joseph M. Katz Graduate School of Business. Throughout her career, Laurie has held positions and responsibility in several areas, including controlling, marketing, strategic marketing, acquisitions, and divestitures before she became a member of the global ProgramOne Design Team and subsequently Head of ProgramOne Finance to Manage NAFTA Deployment at BMS.

SAP Solution Manager provides comprehensive support for the maintenance of your system landscape. This chapter provides an overview of the Maintenance Optimizer as a central maintenance tool and the System Recommendations function for tailored recommendations for SAP Notes.

12 Maintaining an SAP Solution Landscape

As SAP software is continuously enhanced, you are constantly presented with new functions and flexible ways to integrate services on the basis of open architecture. The new possibilities offered by the introduction of new SAP technologies have been accompanied by an increase in the number of software components in your system landscape. SAP has introduced the *Maintenance Optimizer* so that you can perform maintenance transactions efficiently and utilize innovations as easily as possible. It provides you with support for planning, downloading, and implementing enhancements and new functions.

A typical customer landscape consists of a development, consolidation, and production environment (three-system landscape). All changes from the development environment are transferred to the consolidation environment. As soon as the system is error-free, all changes are transferred to the production environment and can be used in the company.

Three-system landscape

Changes in an SAP landscape include the following:

▶ Patches for the operating system, databases, and SAP kernel

▶ Support packages (SPs)

▶ Enhancement packages (EHPs)

▶ Legal changes

▶ Customer developments and changes to customer-specific settings

▶ Corrections included in SAP Notes

All of these changes must be distributed and imported in the system landscapes in different ways. In the ABAP environment, you can use the SAP transport system to do this, and in this way distribute the changes (customer developments, customer-specific settings, or changes to the code from SAP Notes). Changes outside of the ABAP stack, SPs, and kernel updates previously had to be distributed in the landscape manually and imported into the individual systems. These activities were executed independently of each other without centralized control. The completeness and correct order of the import into the system could not be ensured in this way. With the Maintenance Optimizer, SAP offers a function that provides central access to the maintenance activities in SAP Solution Manager.

Maintenance certificate

To import the SPs into the individual systems, you need a valid maintenance certificate (see Section 12.1.6). These maintenance certificates can be distributed manually or automatically by SAP Solution Manager.

Landscape Verification Tool

To ensure that your maintenance processes flow smoothly, you must have correct and complete documentation for your system landscape. In particular, in preparation for an upgrade or installing EHPs, SAP recommends using the Landscape Verification Tool. This tool checks your system landscape and corrects any possible inconsistencies. For more information about the Landscape Verification Tool, see Chapter 4, Section 4.1.2.

12.1 The Maintenance Optimizer

With the Maintenance Optimizer, SAP addresses the challenges associated with maintaining a solution landscape as just described:

Functions

▶ For the selected product system, it determines which SPs and/or EHPs are relevant and available for each software component in your solution and guides you through the necessary implementation steps using a guided procedure.

▶ The Maintenance Optimizer enables you to centrally manage all maintenance activities in your customer landscape.

▶ The Software Lifecycle Manager (SLM) is available in the Maintenance Optimizer to automate the downloading of the selected SPs. This service is used to automatically save the SPs you require in a central directory. At the same time, existing SPs are recognized and not requested again for download from the SAP global support backbone. The latest enhancements in SAP Solution Manager mean that it is now possible to control the distribution and import of SPs on the particular servers centrally using the Maintenance Optimizer. To import the SPs, the Maintenance Optimizer centrally calls up the existing import programs, such as Support Package Manager (SPAM), Java Support Package Manager (JSPM), SAP Add-On Installation Tool (SAINT), and SAP Enhancement Package Installer.

▶ The SAP transport system enables you to distribute changes such as SAP Note corrections, modifications, and configuration changes within the system environments. In the past, this function was only available for the ABAP stack. The functions needed to support it were not available in the non-ABAP environment, for example, the ability to distribute an iView (application in SAP NetWeaver Portal). SAP NetWeaver 7.0 SP14 has enhanced the transport system. These enhancements allow you to use the transport system for any enhancements outside of the ABAP stack. You can now use the Maintenance Optimizer to control the transport system thanks to the latest enhancements.

Figure 12.1 provides an overview of the maintenance processes of the system landscape.

To summarize, the Maintenance Optimizer facilitates the following improvements in the maintenance process:

Aims and advantages of the Maintenance Optimizer

▶ **Transparency**
The Maintenance Optimizer provides an overview of all maintenance activities in your system landscape.

▶ **Control**
You control the entire maintenance process using the Maintenance Optimizer.

▶ **Efficiency through standardization**
The Maintenance Optimizer is the central entry point for planning and implementing your maintenance activities. It guides you through the necessary steps, simplifies maintenance, and helps you lower your operating costs.

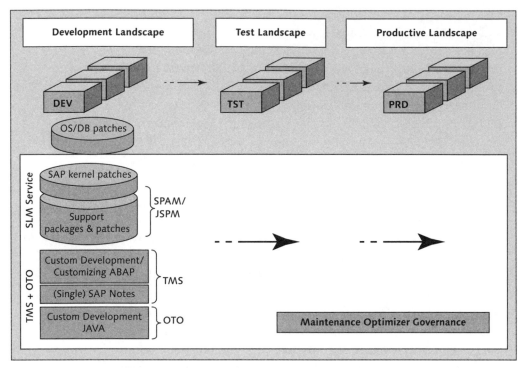

Figure 12.1 Overview of Maintenance Processes in the System Landscape

12.1.1 The Maintenance Optimizer in Detail

The basic concept

The Maintenance Optimizer supports you in managing and implementing maintenance activities in your system landscape.

The system and solution information in SAP Solution Manager accessible in the Solution Manager System Landscape transaction (SMSY) serves as a basis and reference for maintenance transactions. You can assign a solution or one or more systems to your maintenance transaction for the greatest possible flexibility. The Maintenance Optimizer interacts with the SAP global support backbone to download the SP you have selected from there. To make this possible, S-users for SAP Service Marketplace must be created and assigned to the SAP Solution Manager users. Figure 12.2 provides an example of how the Maintenance Optimizer and the SAP global support backbone interact.

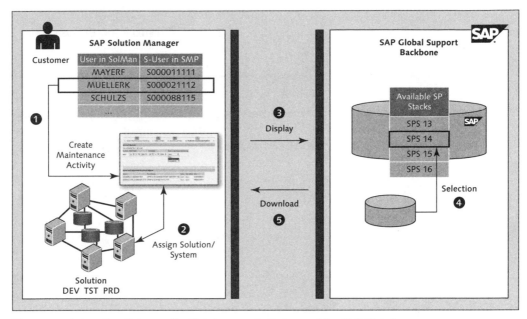

Figure 12.2 Interaction Between the Maintenance Optimizer and the SAP Global Support Backbone

The end user creates a maintenance transaction ❶ and assigns a solution/system to it ❷. SAP Solution Manager establishes a connection to the SAP global support backbone and calculates all currently available SPs ❸ for the selected solution. The SPs selected by the user are added to the download basket ❹ and can be downloaded for further processing from there ❺.

Process

The Maintenance Optimizer leads you through the following steps intended for the maintenance transaction:

1. Planning maintenance

2. Selecting the required SPs

3. Downloading the selected SPs

4. Implementation (*optional when using SLM*):

   ▸ Distributing and importing the SPs in the system landscape

   ▸ Controlling transports and distribution in the system landscape

5. Closing the maintenance transaction

In SAP Solution Manager, you can call the Maintenance Optimizer in the *Change Management* work center (see Figure 12.3) There, you first see an overview of all the maintenance activities you have created. You now create a new maintenance transaction in the CHANGE MANAGEMENT work center.

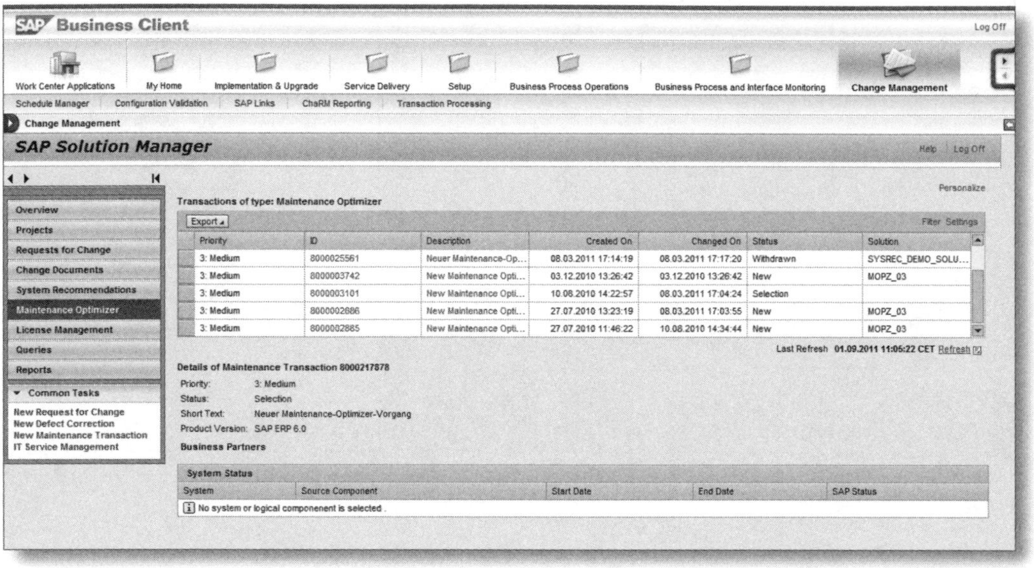

Figure 12.3 Maintenance Optimizer in the "Change Management" Work Center

Planning maintenance

You enter a priority and a short text for your maintenance transaction in the PLAN MAINTENANCE function step. You also assign it a solution or the systems that you want to maintain. You have the option of assigning documents containing project information to your maintenance transaction, as well as persons, to whom you can assign release authorization. When you implement a corresponding authorization concept, you can ensure that only selected persons can perform a release for your maintenance transaction.

Selecting the support packages

SAP Solution Manager now establishes a connection to the SAP global support backbone and offers you the options described here. First, you receive an overview of all the SP stacks available for your product. After selecting the target stack you want, the Maintenance Optimizer calculates all SPs required. The calculation is based on the software status of the systems you have referenced in the maintenance transaction.

After you have selected the SPs you want, you go to step 3, downloading the relevant SPs. The SPs you have selected are now in the

SAP Service Marketplace download basket and can be downloaded from there.

To download the selected SPs, you have the following options: You can continue to use the SAP Download Manager preinstalled on your PC, which connects to SAP Service Marketplace and downloads all SPs in the download basket to your local PC. A significantly easier option is to use the Maintenance Optimizer. It now controls the SLM service, which saves the selected SPs automatically in a central download directory. Existing SPs are thus not downloaded again. The SLM service is optional and requires prior configuration.

Downloading the selected support packages

All selected SPs are referenced in the maintenance transaction so that you can always see which SPs are assigned to the transaction. You can also request a report on the side effects of SAP Notes. It contains a list of SAP Notes that correct errors that can occur when SPs are imported. In addition, you see security-related SAP Notes that you should also implement after the implementation to ensure the security of your SAP systems.

After the SPs have been successfully downloaded, they have to be distributed to the particular systems and imported there. Previously, the Maintenance Optimizer offered the option of managing the status of implementation in each system. This provided a quick overview of the status of maintenance activities but meant that the statuses had to be saved reliably. Activities, such as distributing and importing SPs into the systems and distributing transport requests, previously had to be performed independently of the Maintenance Optimizer with the existing tools.

Implementation

The latest enhancements mean that precisely these functions have now been integrated into the Maintenance Optimizer. The Maintenance Optimizer controls the distribution and implementation of SPs. It also calls up the appropriate implementation tools, ensures that the individual steps are called up in the correct order, and takes you through the maintenance transaction step by step. If you use this preconfigured function, you benefit from enhanced navigation for the implementation step, which provides the functions and tools you require.

The current version of the Maintenance Optimizer also provides a single system update function. The single system update assumes that you want to install a new system on a system release defined by

Single system update

you, for example, when creating a development system for a new system landscape. In this case, the initially installed system is provided with the latest SPs.

The Maintenance Optimizer finds the SPs required for the system and, with confirmation from the end user, downloads them into the download directory. The Maintenance Optimizer helps to ensure that the import tools are available and started in the current version. The SPs are imported into the target system, and the Maintenance Optimizer displays the current status for each step in the procedure.

Enhanced implementation process

The enhanced implementation process includes the following steps:

1. **Planning**
   The Maintenance Optimizer checks the import tools and, if necessary, updates them to the current status. It also checks if all required SPs are available.

2. **Development**
   The required SPs are first imported into the development system. The development system is now at the required status.

   ▶ You can now create a transport request and release it. It contains all changes that need to be transported into the production system. With the enhanced SAP transport system, you can use the transport system for enhancements outside of the ABAP stack.

   ▶ After the final release of the transport request, it is ready to be imported into the test system along with all further changes.

3. **Test**
   The required SPs are now imported into the test system, followed by the transport request. The test system now has the required status, and you can begin the tests.

   ▶ If errors are detected during the tests, you correct them in the development system and transport the corrections into the test system to repeat the tests. As soon as the test system is working free of errors, you can skip to the next phase: Go-Live.

4. **Go-Live**
   In this phase, the SPs and transports are imported into the production system. Your production system now has the required status, and the maintenance transaction can be closed.

This takes you to the last maintenance step, and you can close the maintenance transaction so that it can no longer be changed.

The Maintenance Optimizer in SAP Solution Manager offers you all the support you need to plan and maintain your systems and solutions. It guides you through the individual steps using tried and tested SAP tools to import SPs and transports. You start the tools directly from the Maintenance Optimizer. The Maintenance Optimizer is therefore the central application for carrying out comprehensive maintenance activities in your system landscape.

12.1.2　Maintenance Optimizer for SAP ERP

SAP's release strategy is to make all new functions of the SAP ERP standard software available as a series of optional enhancements (SAP EHPs). This allows you to enhance your business applications with new technology and processes using a flexible, modular approach without having to upgrade your current SAP ERP system. As an SAP ERP customer, you therefore avoid the effort associated with complex upgrades and can implement new product-specific or industry-specific functions and enterprise services with greater speed and ease.

You can find details of the SAP EHPs for SAP ERP on SAP Service Marketplace at *http://service.sap.com/erp-ehp*.

The Maintenance Optimizer provides you with support for using SAP EHPs. When performing maintenance for SAP ERP, the Maintenance Optimizer offers you two options:

▶ Maintenance
▶ Installation of SAP EHPs

In the case of maintenance, you import the new SPs for your SAP ERP system without using a new function. This involves importing SPs for SAP products that do not support any SAP EHPs. You therefore benefit from technical improvements or changes in the law/taxes but do not use any new business functions.

An important advantage of using SAP EHPs is that no release update is required. SPs are imported instead. The Maintenance Optimizer offers the following options for this:

▶ Employ an additional *technical usage* of the SAP EHP already installed.

▶ Install a more recent version of SAP EHPs and an additional technical usage.

You currently have the option of installing SAP EHPs for SAP ERP 6.0. On the basis of the referenced systems in the maintenance transaction, the Maintenance Optimizer recognizes that you want to maintain a product that supports SAP EHPs. In the SELECT FILES step, select the ENHANCEMENT PACKAGE INSTALLATION option. The Maintenance Optimizer provides the following selection options:

▶ Install additional technical usages.

▶ Install a new SAP EHP with the option of selecting another technical usage.

Configuration file   It also determines the files you require. During the guided selection, the Maintenance Optimizer creates a configuration file (XML format) that contains details of the files to be selected. When this configuration file is being imported, it is used by the SAP Add-On Installation Tool (SAINT) or the SAP Enhancement Package Installer. This ensures that all files are imported into the systems in the correct order, thereby preventing possible errors and simplifying the import process. You can find out which SAP products are used by SAP EHPs in the current SAP release strategy at *http://service.sap.com/release-strategy*.

Upgrade to
SAP ERP 6.0   To benefit from the simplified use of additional business functions in SAP EHPs, you first have to upgrade to SAP ERP 6.0. The Maintenance Optimizer also assists you with this. All SAP releases (from Release 4.0B) can upgrade to SAP ERP 6.0.

If an upgrade to SAP ERP 6.0 is possible for the product version selected in the maintenance transaction, the UPGRADE option is automatically available.

As well as a simple upgrade to SAP ERP 6.0, it is also possible to combine the upgrade to SAP ERP 6.0 with the installation of an SAP EHP.

Support from the
Maintenance
Optimizer   The Maintenance Optimizer provides you with support for determining and implementing the corresponding SAP EHP and calculates

all files that you have to download in addition to the files on the upgrade DVD provided by the SAP global support backbone. It also guides you through the implementation of these files. The files you select are saved in a configuration file that the installation tools then use to import all necessary files in the correct order.

12.1.3 Supporting Complex Landscapes

The Maintenance Optimizer supports the maintenance of complex SAP landscape configurations, for example, landscapes with systems that have been assigned the *hub* or *sidecar* landscape pattern.

Landscape pattern: Sidecar

Technical systems that have the sidecar landscape pattern assigned are used by exactly one production system. The target status of these technical systems defined as sidecar is determined only by the active product version of the production system. For different release levels of the software components used, a current and synchronized combination is always determined as the target status.

Technical systems assigned the landscape pattern hub are used by several production systems and therefore by several SAP applications. You can execute a separate maintenance transaction for each of these individual production systems. The technical system classified as the hub is part of each of these maintenance transactions.

Landscape pattern: Hub

To calculate a consistent target status for each of these technical systems classified as a hub, you ideally change as few software components as possible. This should ensure that no additional dependencies arise between the technical system and the production systems that use it.

In such a configuration, the Maintenance Optimizer takes into account possible dependencies and accordingly calculates the files required for a maintenance transaction. It ensures that the system environment always remains functional after a maintenance transaction, even if there are existing dependencies. And it keeps the effects of a maintenance transaction to the system environment to a minimum.

12.1.4 Country Legal Changes Packages for SAP ERP HCM—Integrating Solutions and HR Support Packages in the Maintenance Transaction

Automatic calculation of legal change packages and HR SPs

To keep your HR solutions up-to-date, in particular in regard to legal changes, *Country Legal Changes packages* (CLCs) and HR support packages (SPs) have to be installed in these systems. The Maintenance Optimizer provides the option to also calculate the relevant CLC packages and HR SP in the context of a maintenance transaction for an HR system and include them in the download.

To use this function, the system selected for the maintenance transaction must be an HR system. In the Maintenance Optimizer, you can display a list of all CLC packages and HR SPs available for the selected HR system. You can also add the desired files to the list of files to be downloaded. This can happen either in the context of the regular maintenance transaction or directly through the manual selection of files for maintenance.

The Maintenance Optimizer checks which country versions are installed on the selected HR system, which is a particularly helpful feature. It then displays only the files that are relevant for these country versions in the overview list.

You can also directly call the function for displaying the relevant recommended CLC packages and HR SPs, if you want to use them independently of the installation of an SP. In the guided procedure of the Maintenance Optimizer, you select the respective HR system. In the next step, you then select the manual maintenance activity. In the next step, you can branch directly to the selection of the CLC packages and HR SPs for the selected system and add the desired files to your download basket for further processing.

12.1.5 Authorizations and Reports in the Maintenance Optimizer

Authorizations

The Maintenance Optimizer specifies the individual process steps for planning and implementing your maintenance transaction. The process steps adapt themselves to the particular scenario but cannot be changed.

Authorizations can be flexibly and easily granted to individuals so that you can implement your company-specific requirements.

Predefined roles are already available to you on delivery, which allow you to create, change, or just display maintenance transactions. You can use these roles as the basis for your maintenance transaction.

You can assign the authorizations you require for each individual step in the maintenance transaction and distribute them to the relevant people. This means that it is easy to separate substeps such as planning, requesting, or implementation, and distribute them to different people.

You use the QUERIES view in the *Change Management* work center to get a list of all activities and their statuses. You can limit the search according to various criteria, for example, status, referenced solution/system, or priority, to obtain a quick overview of the maintenance transactions.

Evaluation

12.1.6 Maintenance Certificate and License Management

A *maintenance certificate* is required to import SPs. This also applies to all SAP products. The maintenance certificate makes it possible for the software logistics tools to recognize the exact scope of the maintenance contract and render tailor-made services. It also helps you to improve the quality of your SAP solution. The maintenance certificate prevents SPs from being downloaded accidentally and distributed to the wrong systems.

Maintenance certificates

You can view your maintenance certificates in the SAP Support Portal using a self-service. However, to make it easier for you, you can also call it up automatically from SAP Solution Manager. After it has been set up, SAP Solution Manager regularly receives maintenance certificates for managed systems and ensures the certificates are distributed to them. You can find further information about maintenance certificates at *http://service.sap.com/maintenancecertificate*.

Figure 12.4 shows how maintenance certificates are automatically distributed with SAP Solution Manager. SAP Solution Manager requests a maintenance certificate for the managed systems once a day in the SAP global support backbone ❶. The maintenance certificates are then generated in the SAP global support backbone ❷. The next

License management

587

time a connection to the SAP global support backbone is established, maintenance certificates are received and are available in SAP Solution Manager ❸. As soon as the managed system communicates with SAP Solution Manager, the available certificate is received ❹. SAP Solution Manager always requests a maintenance certificate from the SAP global support backbone if none is available for a managed system or one that is valid for less than 30 days. This ensures that the whole process runs smoothly.

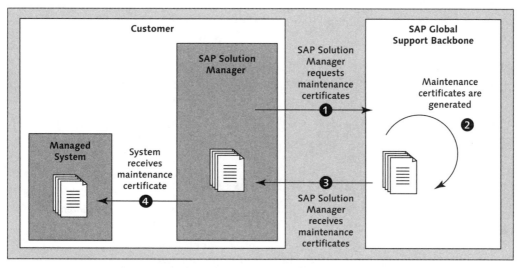

Figure 12.4 Automatically Distributing Maintenance Certificates

From the LICENSE MANAGEMENT view in the *Change Management* work center (see Figure 12.5), you can see the status of the maintenance certificates for all systems managed by SAP Solution Manager. This means that you can see whether a valid maintenance certificate has been received by SAP Solution Manager for each system and whether it is on the managed system. You can activate automatic maintenance certificate distribution in license management. You also have the option of downloading all maintenance certificates received together and distributing them to systems not connected to SAP Solution Manager. License management also provides information about the license keys for your systems; for example, whether valid license keys are available for your systems or whether a license key might expire.

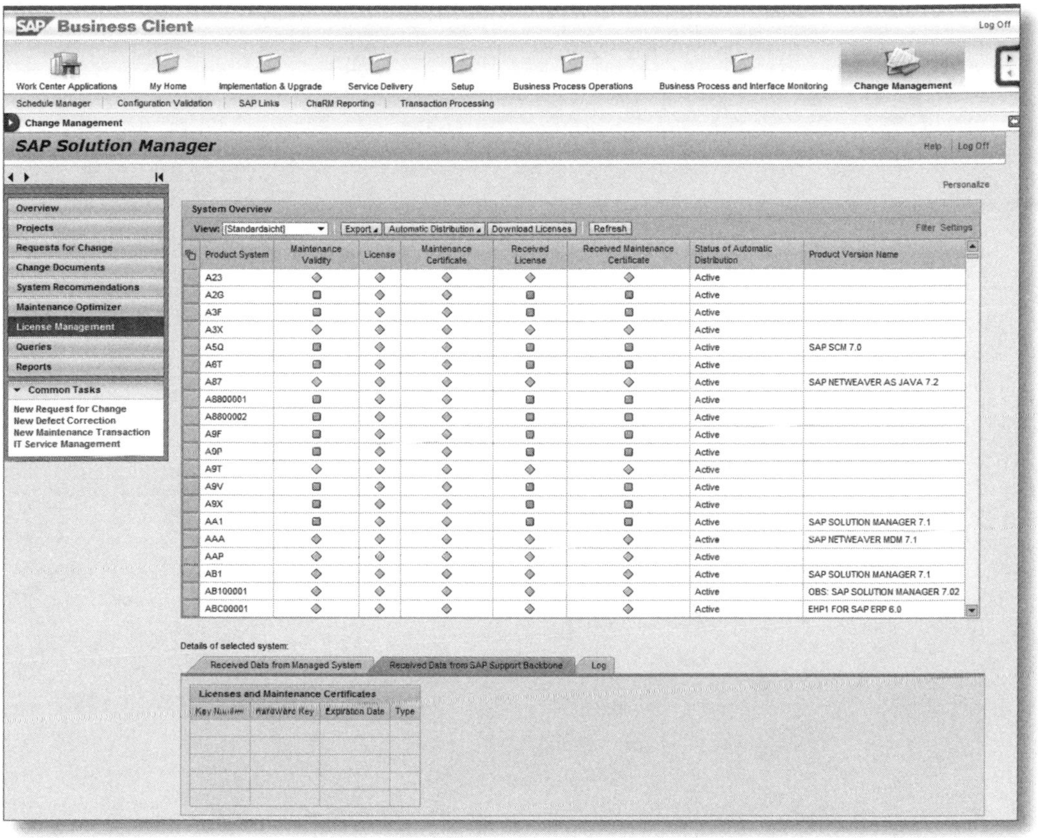

Figure 12.5 License Management in the "Change Management" Work Center

12.2 System Recommendations

To ensure that your SAP landscape is always up to date with regard to security, performance, and error corrections, you have to install not only the aforementioned SPs but also SAP Notes, Java patches, and other corrections. The new SYSTEM RECOMMENDATIONS function simplifies this task significantly. It recommends available SAP Notes or patches for implementation in the respective system.

To give you a tailored recommendation for the selected system, system recommendations take into account the SP level as well as already implemented SAP Notes and other versions. Hence, you also get recommendations to implement new versions of SAP Notes, for example.

System recommendations for SAP Notes

You use SYSTEM RECOMMENDATIONS (see Figure 12.6) to get recommendations for the following categories:

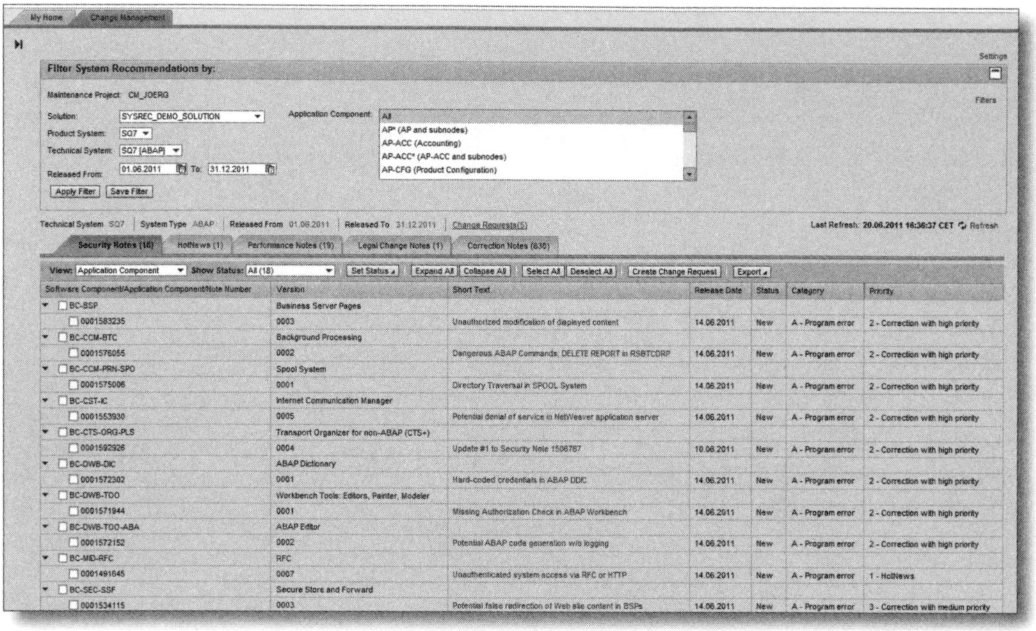

Figure 12.6 System Recommendations

► SECURITY NOTES

► HOTNEWS (SAP Notes whose implementation SAP rates as particularly important)

► PERFORMANCE NOTES

► LEGAL CHANGE NOTES

► CORRECTION NOTES

► JAVA PATCH NOTES

12.2.1 Receiving Recommendations for your Systems

To receive recommendations for your systems, open the SYSTEM RECOMMENDATIONS function in the *Change Management* work center. To start with, you can now set corresponding filters for a solution, production system, or technical system. Additional filter options are available by setting a restriction to a time span for the publication date of the corresponding SAP Notes and by filtering by application component.

After you have made these filter settings, you see the relevant SAP Notes and/or Java patches for the selected product system or technical system, structured according to the categories described previously. You can have the additional filter option filter by application components to set further restrictions.

To make it easier to manage the recommended SAP Notes, status management has been integrated into the SYSTEM RECOMMENDATIONS function. You can assign each SAP Note a status such as TO BE IMPLEMENTED, POSTPONED, IRRELEVANT, and TO BE IMPLEMENTED (NEW VERSION AVAILABLE) and filter the display of SAP Notes according to this status.

Status management

You can now export by category the list of recommended SAP Notes filtered by status into an Excel table. With this worklist, you can then implement the SAP Notes with the SAP Note Assistant (or Transaction JSPM for JAVA patches) in the system.

12.2.2 Integration with Other Tools in SAP Solution Manager

The SYSTEM RECOMMENDATIONS function offers you the option to put recommended Java patches directly in the download basket on SAP Service Marketplace. You can then download the patches directly for further processing. To approve this download basket quickly and easily, you can generate a maintenance transaction in the Maintenance Optimizer directly from the system recommendations. If you are using SAP Solution Manager Change Request Management, you can use the direct integration to create a change request for the recommended SAP Notes.

You can use the *configuration validation* described in Chapter 8, Section 8.4.4, for optionally validating certain configuration statuses across the system landscape. In the context of system recommendations, you can, for example, validate whether recommended SAP Notes have been implemented on all systems for which these notes are relevant to ensure the security of these systems.

Configuration validation

12.2.3 Setting Up the System Recommendations Function

You call the SYSTEM RECOMMENDATIONS function in the SAP Solution Manager *Change Management* work center.

To use system recommendations, we recommend scheduling background job BG_JB_SR in your SAP Solution Manager system. It collects the required information of all managed systems and thus enables you to quickly calculate which SAP Notes and corrections are required.

You can control the display of the individual tab pages using authorization object SM_FUNCS. This enables you, for example, to make only certain categories of system recommendations available to certain users.

12.2.4 Summary

The SYSTEM RECOMMENDATIONS function gives you the option to quickly and easily get a list of SAP Notes for a technical system, which should be implemented in the system. This recommendation is calculated automatically and takes into account the current patch level of the selected system. You thus get a recommendation for SAP Notes to be implemented that is tailored to the system and organized in clear categories, which offers you the following benefits:

Advantages
- Time is saved thanks to the automatic calculation of an exactly tailored recommendation and the display of the recommendation at a central point in SAP Solution Manager.

- The clear organization of recommendations in different categories increases clarity and facilitates the implementation of certain categories of SAP Notes.

- The calculation of the recommendation happens at SAP and can thus always access current information about SAP Notes.

SAP Solution Manager supports upgrade projects with numerous tools for the upgrade management process. This chapter explains the individual tools and how integrating them can help you complete upgrade projects effectively and cost efficiently.

13   Support for Upgrade Projects

Upgrading to SAP ERP or within another SAP product line poses many challenges for customers and their current SAP landscapes.

In particular, if you are already using SAP Solution Manager for project support, using it for an upgrade project or regular maintenance projects can offer benefits such as cost savings and increased efficiency in the planning and execution of these tasks. Integrated and supplementary parts of SAP Solution Manager, such as *Upgrade Dependency Analyzer* (UDA), *Upgrade Roadmap* or upgrade service offerings, also contribute. They play a critical role in minimizing the costs and risks associated with upgrading to a newer release, while at the same time maximizing the value added.

Cost savings and increased efficiency

In addition to support for classic upgrades, you can use the tools and offers introduced here also for maintenance projects using *SAP enhancement packages*. Even though the scope of activities is not comparable to an upgrade project, individual tasks such as the synchronization of modifications and testing the new solution are very similar.

Identifying cost drivers

SAP Solution Manager addresses a number of upgrade-specific cost drivers such as project management, test administration, implementation of new functions, and end user training.

Organizations can draw on SAP's upgrade offerings available via SAP Solution Manager to tackle other known cost drivers, such as modification adjustments and the technical upgrade itself. The classic cost drivers of an upgrade project also appear in maintenance projects with enhancement packages. Identify the cost drivers for your upcoming upgrade project, and use this analysis to decide which tool offers the best cost/benefit ratio. In this analysis, also look at the long-term cost benefit of the tools used; for example, by reusing regular maintenance activities.

Identifying potential savings SAP Solution Manager is designed to save time and costs in upgrade projects. Methodological upgrade knowledge and predefined scenario contents at SAP help reduce operating costs and increase efficiency in many project tasks.

Customers that already deploy SAP Solution Manager extensively reap extra benefits when they upgrade: Information stored in implementation projects can form the basis for an upgrade project; reporting functions supply important information concerning the solutions, systems, and products in use.

When used consistently, SAP Solution Manager also sets the prerequisite for responding to future requirements from application management. For example, you can use upgrade projects for new implementation projects. All of the information can be copied in full or in part to new implementation projects. Business Process Monitoring lets you monitor live business processes during production operations. SAP Solution Manager features a Change Request Management scenario for tackling changes that may become necessary over the course of an upgrade project (see Chapter 8).

In this chapter, we introduce a selection of integrated tools for the new SAP Solution Manager, which can be used in the context of an upgrade project (see Sections 13.1 to 13.6). This chapter is supplemented with the introduction of additional upgrade service offerings by SAP (see Sections 13.7 to 13.9). For a detailed list with additional offers related to upgrades, see UPGRADE SERVICES on SAP Service Marketplace at *http://service.sap.com/upgrade*.

13.1 Upgrade Dependency Analyzer

SAP applications such as SAP ERP, SAP CRM, and SAP SCM are normally part of an SAP system landscape and connected to several other systems therein. In this system landscape, business processes can be operated via various systems.

To successfully complete an upgrade project, you need a strategy that is thought-through, comprehensive, and adapted to the company.

The procedure you choose, for example, directly influences the duration and/or effort of your project.

If you are planning to upgrade one or more SAP systems in your system landscape, it helps to know whether the upgrade affects the other systems and maybe also the processes running on this system in your landscape. Knowing this at an early stage saves costs and provides transparency as well as planning security. This is where the *Upgrade Dependency Analyzer* (UDA) can support your upgrade project.

Identifying dependencies

The UDA is a planning tool that identifies dependencies that can arise due to upgrades to individual application systems within your existing system landscape. For a planned upgrade of individual systems in your system landscape, it can point out potential problems at an early stage and thus guarantee planning security. This tells you, for example, whether an independent upgrade of individual production systems is possible. If there are restrictions or dependencies, you can clarify which additional steps are required before you start the upgrade project. As a consequence—depending on the complexity of the dependencies—you might have to implement individual support packages (SPs), use a single SAP Note, or upgrade several production systems.

The UDA assumes that the system landscape is intact and working and ensures that this is also the case after an upgrade.

You can determine potential dependency statements directly online on the SAP Service Marketplace at *http://service.sap.com/uda*.

How can you use the UDA?

Alternatively, you can query dependencies that might appear in your system landscape under consideration of the system landscape data that you have maintained in SAP Solution Manager (as of SAP Solution Manager 7.1, *Implementation/Upgrade* work center under the UPGRADE DEPENDENCY ANALYZER entry). The query of dependencies that can occur within an existing system landscape due to the upgrade is created as a project. You can thus reproduce it at any time. You can individually assess the determined dependency statements and add your own information. (A dependency declared to be critical by SAP does not have to be critical for you.) You can save the entire UDA project in SAP Solution Manager, print it, and export it as a PDF file.

The following prerequisites and conditions apply to using the UDA:

- No statements are made regarding possible dependencies between SPs.
- Dependency statements refer to the purely technical level between the product systems.
- The dependency statements assume that the system landscape is intact and functional before the upgrade starts.
- Possible dependencies to new functions that are available in a newer release are not taken into account.
- The dependencies between the product systems always refer to two separately installed product systems.
- In general, the dependency statements do not contain any information about SAP NetWeaver, PI/XI, or portal content.
- No statements are made regarding possible dependencies of SAP Solution Manager releases.

13.1.1   Possible Dependency Statements

The following dependency statements can occur in the context of an upgrade:

- No known upgrade dependencies exist; independent upgrade is possible.
- An independent upgrade is possible but with known restrictions.
- An independent upgrade is not possible.
- Cross-system functions are lost.
- No interaction occurs.
- No interaction occurs in the combination of existing releases.

The following sections provide a brief description of these statements and illustrate the use cases.

No Known Upgrade Dependencies; Independent Upgrade Is Possible

If you execute an upgrade to the target release, all default, cross-system functions that could be executed before the upgrade remain available. For new cross-system functions, you might have to upgrade the specified existing components. For more information, see the scenario component list (SCL) and process component list (PCL) on the SAP Service Marketplace at *https://service.sap.com/scl*.

SAP uses this dependency statement when it knows that all previously available cross-system functions are retained when the product system is upgraded. This upgrade as such includes all possible activities from the SAP upgrade guide. It is possible that additional information is appended to the dependency statement in the form of an SAP Note.

To use this dependency analysis, there must be at least one cross-system function between the product systems.

An Independent Upgrade Is Possible But with Known Restrictions

If you execute an upgrade to the target release, all default, cross-system functions that could be executed before the upgrade remain available. If there are any restrictions, an attached SAP Note explains these.

The following restrictions are possible:

Possible restrictions

▶ You have to make adjustments to some cross-system functions after the upgrade.

▶ Additional support packages might be necessary after the upgrade.

▶ It is possible that you have to perform additional manual steps after the upgrade.

SAP uses this dependency statement when it is ensured that all cross-system functions can be restored with the aforementioned options.

There is no need to upgrade the other product system.

An SAP Note is attached, which describes in detail the cross-system functions that might be temporarily unavailable and how these functions can be restored.

To use this dependency analysis, there must be at least one cross-system function between the product systems.

An Independent Upgrade Is Not Possible

After executing the upgrade to the target system, selected or all default cross-system functions no longer work. You either have to upgrade the specified existing component, or you have to manually implement the affected cross-system functions some other way.

SAP uses this dependency statement if you also need to upgrade the other product system to retain one or more cross-system functions.

To use this dependency analysis, there must be at least one cross-system function between the product systems.

Cross-System Functions Are Lost

After executing the upgrade to the target system, selected or all default cross-system functions no longer work. You have to manually re-implement the affected cross-system functions some other way. An upgrade of the existing component is either impossible or insufficient.

SAP uses this dependency statement if the upgrade of the product system means that a cross-system function is lost, and this function cannot be restored by upgrading the other product system either. This dependency statement can also be temporary.

To use this dependency analysis, there must be at least one cross-system function between the product systems.

No Interaction Occurs

By default, the specified components do not share any cross-system functions, or the specified releases define a combination of existing releases without standard cross-system functions. There is no direct interaction. You can upgrade the components independently.

SAP uses this dependency statement if the two affected product systems do not share any cross-system function in any of the existing releases.

If appropriate, check whether the two product systems you have selected do interact.

No Interaction Occurs in the Combination of Existing Releases

The specified releases define a combination of existing releases that does not share any standard cross-system functions. There is no direct interaction before the upgrade. You can upgrade the components independently.

SAP uses this dependency statement if the two affected product systems can have a cross-system function in general, but a cross-system function is not possible in the underlying defined combination of start releases. If appropriate, please check whether the cross-system function you selected exists between the two product systems.

13.1.2 Distinctions Among the UDA, the Maintenance Optimizer, and the Scenario and Component Lists (PCL/SCL)

As already mentioned, the UDA is a planning tool that identifies dependencies that can arise due to upgrades to individual application systems within your existing system landscape. The UDA does not make any direct statements about the possible effects of an upgrade of one of your product systems on the function of your business processes.

To get detailed statements at the scenario level of your existing business processes, include the SCL and PCL on the SAP Service Marketplace in planning. For more information, see *http://service.sap.com/scl*.

Statements at the scenario level

The Maintenance Optimizer helps you with your system update under consideration of the system landscape stored in SAP Solution Manager. The Maintenance Optimizer automates activities that used to be manual and error-prone.

System update

The Maintenance Optimizer can assist you with the following maintenance activities:

► Installation of SPs and SP stacks

► Installation of SAP enhancement packages

► Upgrade of SAP applications

► Installation of SAP ERP HCM legal change packages

▶ Support of add-ons

▶ Support of Java patches

The Maintenance Optimizer also calculates any updates that might be required for connected product systems. In doing so, it starts with a final status to be reached by the product systems in your SAP system landscape. A maintenance transaction might require an incremental change though. For these interim steps, the UDA can make the required dependency statements.

13.1.3 Data Quality and Legal Disclaimer

The dependency statements centrally maintained at SAP reflect the current state of knowledge at SAP. Any changes are made available to all UDA users as quickly as possible. You have to query the possible dependencies several times during the course of an upgrade project. SAP tries to make the UDA's dependency statements available immediately after new software releases become generally available.

Note that the UDA is a planning tool that can support you with your upgrade project. However, it is not possible to map all dependencies that are relevant to your upgrade project. For more information, especially on scenario and process component lists, see the SAP Service Marketplace at *https://service.sap.com/scl*.

Also note all other required documentation; for example, master guides, upgrade master guides, SP stack guides, and SAP Notes. Do not rely solely on the UDA statements.

SAP does not accept any responsibility for errors in or misunderstandings of the statements of the UDA or damage that arises due to the use and interpretation of the UDA statements. SAP can change the contents of the UDA statements at any time and without notice.

13.1.4 Examples of Using the UDA

This section provides examples of using the UDA on the SAP Service Marketplace (*http://service.sap.com/uda*) and a description for using the UDA in the new SAP Solution Manager.

The objective of the dependency analysis with the UDA is to plan all combinations of product systems in your system landscape so that all statements are non-critical. Several iterations might be required.

Example 1: UDA Use on SAP Service Marketplace

Let's assume that you have an SAP system landscape with three product systems X, Y, and Z as depicted in Figure 13.1. You are planning to upgrade product system X to X' (whereby X' and Z' refer to the respective system after the upgrade).

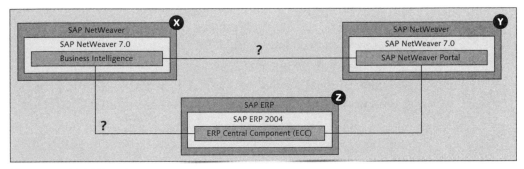

Figure 13.1 Initial Situation

At the start of the planned maintenance transaction (release upgrade), product system X corresponds to an SAP NetWeaver 7.0 with the Business Intelligence (BI) instance, product system Y is an SAP NetWeaver 7.0 with the SAP NetWeaver Portal instance, and product system Z is an SAP ECC SERVER product instance of SAP ERP 2004.

Initial situation and assumptions

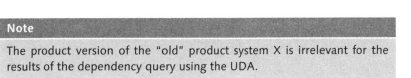

Note

The product version of the "old" product system X is irrelevant for the results of the dependency query using the UDA.

You are planning to upgrade product system X to the SAP NetWeaver 7.3 product version and the BI product instance.

Task

You would like to know whether, after upgrading product system X to X', all cross-system functions between the connected product systems Y and Z still work in the same way as before the upgrade.

The dependency analysis only takes into account the existing functions of the existing system landscape.

Approach   Follow these steps:

1. On the SAP Service Marketplace at *http://service.sap.com/uda*, enter the details of product system X' as the TARGET COMPONENT and the details of product system Y as the EXISTING COMPONENT.

   The result of the query is the following:

   ▶ *No known dependencies; independent upgrade is possible.*

   ▶ *If you execute an upgrade to the target component, all default, cross-system functions that could be executed before the upgrade remain available. For new cross-system functions, you might have to upgrade the specified existing components. For more information, see the scenario and process component list (SCL, PCL) on SAP Service Marketplace at https://service.sap.com/scl.*

2. On the SAP Service Marketplace at *http://service.sap.com/uda*, enter the details of product system Y' as the TARGET COMPONENT and the details of product system Z as the EXISTING COMPONENT.

   The result of the query is the following:

   ▶ *An independent upgrade is not possible.*

   ▶ *After executing the upgrade to the target component, selected or all default cross-system functions no longer work. An upgrade of the specified existing component is necessary. Alternatively, you have to manually implement the affected cross-system functions some other way.*

> **Note**
>
> The decision for or against an upgrade depends on your company's individual assessment of the dependency statement. If the loss of cross-system functions between product systems X' and Z is not critical for you, you can upgrade to X' without carrying out other activities.

Based on the results of the first two dependency queries as depicted in Figure 13.2, there is a dependency between product systems X' and Z. Upgrading product system Z is recommended to ensure that all cross-system functions can still be used after the upgrade to product system X'. To do so, you should check all possible dependencies between product systems Z' and Y. For your query, choose the latest successor for product system Z if possible.

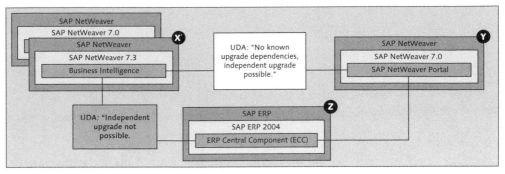

Figure 13.2 Result of the Dependency Analysis for a Simple Upgrade to Release X'

Product system Z' thus corresponds to an SAP ECC Server product instance of SAP ERP 6.0 EHP5.

For the dependency query, follow these steps: Approach

1. On the SAP Service Marketplace at *http://service.sap.com/uda*, enter the details of product system Z' as the TARGET COMPONENT and the details of product system Y as the EXISTING COMPONENT.

   The result of the query is the following:

   ▶ *No known dependencies; independent upgrade is possible.*

   ▶ *If you execute an upgrade to the target component, all default, cross-system functions that could be executed before the upgrade remain available. For new cross-system functions, you might have to upgrade the specified existing components. For more information, see the scenario and process component list (SCL, PCL) on SAP Service Marketplace at https://service.sap.com/scl.*

Figure 13.3 illustrates the result.

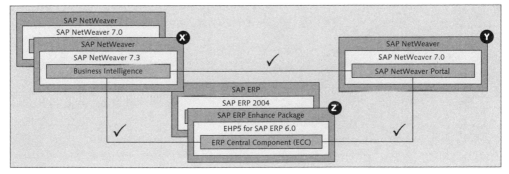

Figure 13.3 Result of the Dependency Analysis for a Double Upgrade to Releases X' and Z'

603

As depicted in Figure 13.3, you need to upgrade product system Z to Z' in addition to the upgrade to product system X' to restore all cross-system functions completely.

Example 2: UDA Use in SAP Solution Manager 7.1

For a dependency analysis of your system landscape, you need to have at least SAP Solution Manager 7.1.

To create a new analysis project, use Transaction SOLMAN_ WORKCENTER. and then go to the *Implementation/Upgrade* work center.

There, switch to the upgrade analysis, and create a corresponding upgrade project on the basis of your existing system landscape.

"Implementation/ Upgrade" work center
Figure 13.4 shows how the *Implementation/Upgrade* work center could look with your various planned upgrade projects. There are different filter options for designing your work center individually. In an already created upgrade project, you can, for example, change the status of the planning phase, add your own assessment of the dependency statements made by SAP, or add your own documents to the respective assessed dependency statements.

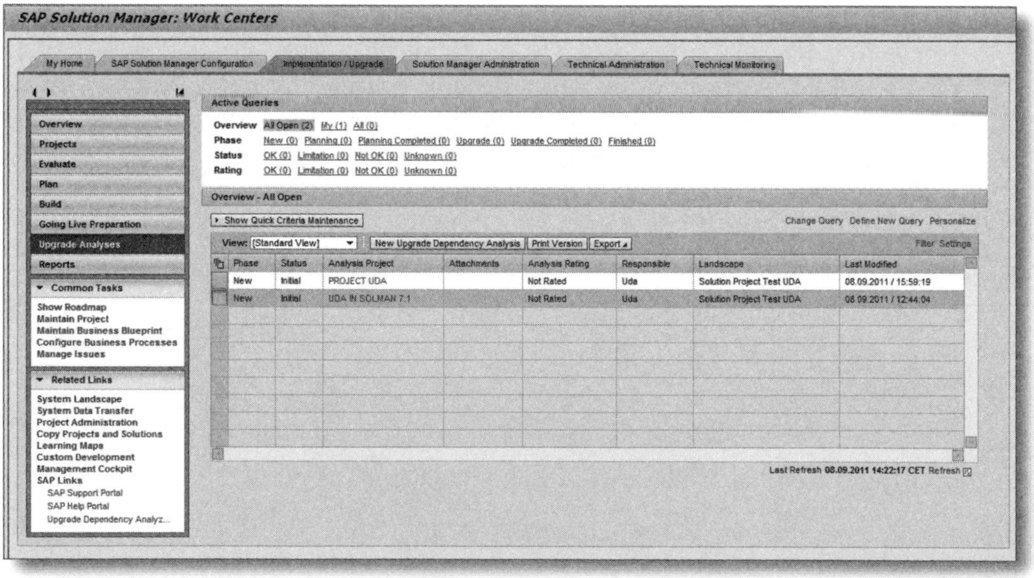

Figure 13.4 Upgrade Projects in the "Implementation/Upgrade" Work Center

An upgrade project could look like that in Figure 13.5. The depicted project corresponds to the system landscape described in example 1.

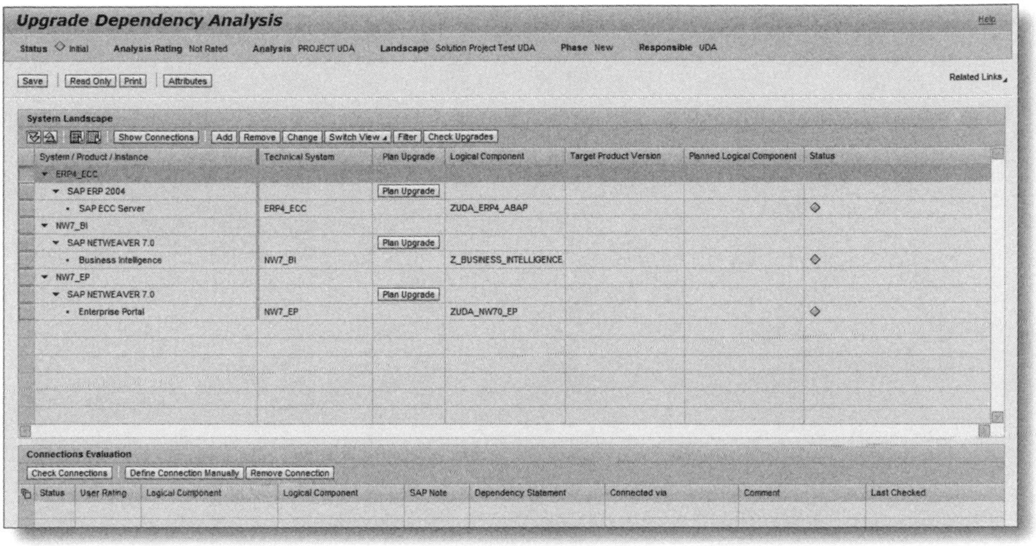

Figure 13.5 Upgrade Project for a System Landscape as in Example 1

By default, the SYSTEM/PRODUCT/INSTANCE column shows your product systems with the assignment to product versions and product instances.

As in example 1, you plan an upgrade of the BI product instance. Here, SAP Solution Manager 7.1 offers a selection of possible target releases as well as a recommendation for the target release.

As in example 1, Figure 13.6 also shows you the respective dependencies to other product instances here.

Due to the depicted dependency between the SAP NetWeaver BI and the SAP ECC server, you also have to plan another upgrade of the SAP ECC product instance.

Because product version EHP5 for SAP ERP 6.0 is an add-on, you have to add it manually as a planned product instance for technical system ERP4_ECC to get correct dependency statements (see Figure 13.7).

Taking EHP5 into account

If you want to plan additional possible upgrade dependencies on the basis of a previously non-existing product instance in your system landscape, you can also insert these manually in your landscape.

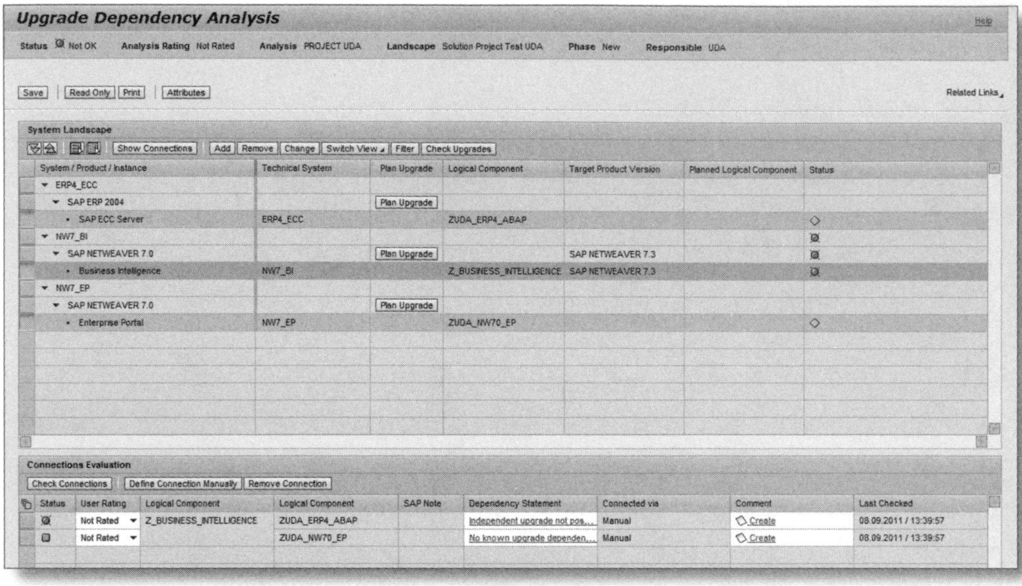

Figure 13.6 Dependencies between Product Instances

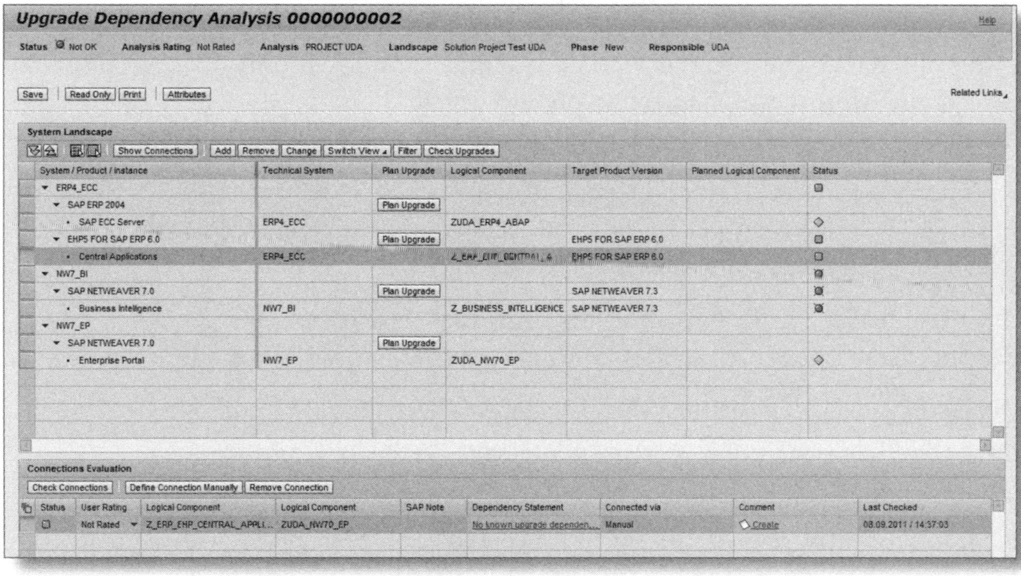

Figure 13.7 Details for SAP ERP 6.0 EHP5

Individual upgrade plans based on an existing system landscape are not automatically transferred into your system landscape in SAP Solution Manager. These adjustments exist only in connection with your upgrade project.

If necessary, you can enter additional technical connections between the product systems in SAP Solution Manger and individually assess the results as well as the other upgrade dependencies.

As a result, you get a complete analysis of the possible dependencies that could arise due to the upgrade of one or more product systems in your system landscape in SAP Solution Manager, as you can see in Figure 13.8. If any other upgrades are necessary, a corresponding note is displayed. If only minor manual activities are necessary to restore the functions, SAP Notes will inform you of these.

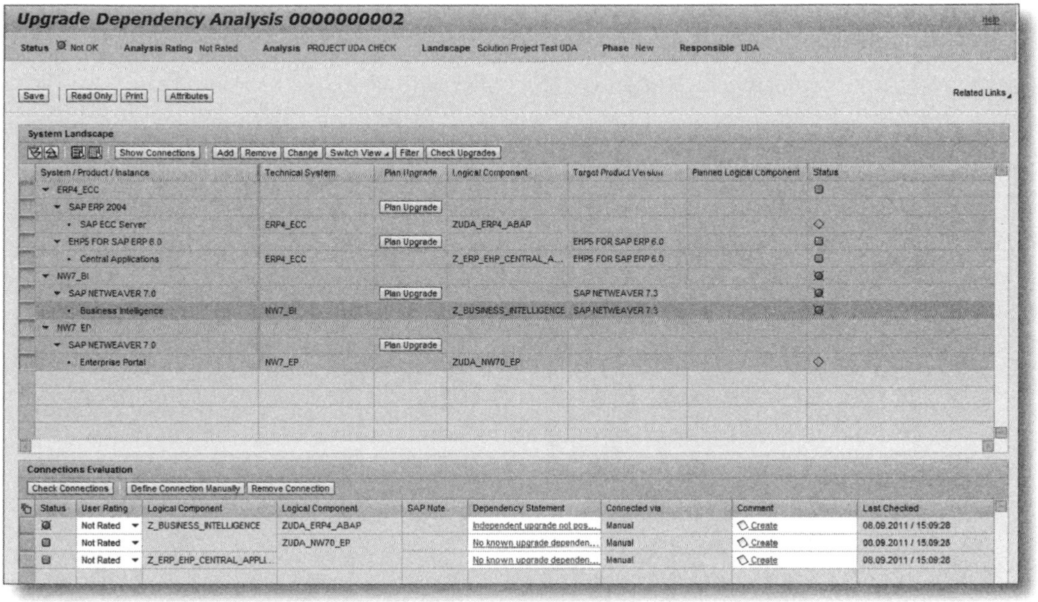

Figure 13.8 Complete Depiction of Dependencies

13.2 Project Planning and Project Management Using the Upgrade Roadmap

In the context of project planning and project management, SAP Solution Manager supports you with a standard SAP project methodology, the *Upgrade Roadmap*. The Upgrade Roadmap provides methodical, phase-based guidelines to take you through your upgrade. It thus facilitates more transparency and high quality for all important project tasks. The Upgrade Roadmap also addresses aspects such as analyzing and defining objectives for existing business processes, the underlying

Upgrade Roadmap

IT infrastructure before and after the upgrade, the upgrade configuration, and testing for processes in the new release.

Accelerators

In a separate area, you can access additional information and tools, called *accelerators*. These accelerators link you to transactions in SAP Solution Manager, SAP upgrade offers, and other sources of SAP information, such as Best Practices documents and project templates to accelerate your upgrade. In addition, *Expert Guided Implementation* (EGI) documents are generated. These provide targeted instructions for the SAP Solution Manager tools.

Personalization of the Upgrade Roadmap

During an upgrade, you can choose to display only Upgrade Roadmap content that is relevant to your specific upgrade path, such as from SAP R/3 4.6C to SAP ERP 6.0 with SAP EHP5 or from SAP CRM 2007 to SAP CRM 7.0 with SAP EHP1. You can then use this selection to restrict the upgrade-specific contents offered for support.

The Upgrade Roadmap guides you directly to the upgrade functions in SAP Solution Manager; for example, central system administration, (CSA) documentation, and business process testing. You can monitor your project activities using the overview of documentation, statuses, and problem messages. In short, with the Upgrade Roadmap, you can always access all the sources of documentation required for adapting the system's functions and technical settings. When you plan the details of the project, you can use SAP Best Practices for orientation.

Like all the other roadmaps, the Upgrade Roadmap is available as a project-specific working version in SAP Solution Manager or as a self-contained HTML version. SAP is constantly adding to the list of available content.

You access the Upgrade Roadmap in your SAP Solution Manager through the *Implementation/Upgrade* work center.

For more information on the Upgrade Roadmap and the user guide *Upgrade Projects with the SAP Solution Manager*, see the SAP Service Marketplace at *http://service.sap.com/upgraderoadmap*.

13.3 Custom Development Management Cockpit

When it comes to determining how to handle custom developments such as modifications and interfaces, the *Custom Development Management Cockpit* (CDMC) can provide a valuable contribution. CDMC has two main parts: *clearing analysis* and *change impact analysis*. The clearing analysis analyzes your custom developments in your SAP system and identifies, for example, custom developments that are no longer in use. They might be superfluous in the new target release. The objective is to exclude these in all further steps in an upgrade project. Typically, this significantly reduces the amount of adjustment work for custom developments for the new release.

Analysis of custom developments

The upgrade/change impact analysis in contrast determines the influence of the SAP target release on existing custom developments. You can also use it for EHPs, SPs, and SAP Notes. This enables you to determine the amount of work required for custom developments for an upgrade even before you begin testing. In addition, you can also plan major adjustments and changes at an early state, which reduces the planning risk.

You can start CDMC in SAP Solution Manager via the *Implementation/Upgrade* work center under the CUSTOM DEVELOPMENT MANAGEMENT COCKPIT menu item. For more information on Custom Code Management, see Chapter 15, Section 15.3.

13.4 Maintenance Optimizer

The *Maintenance Optimizer* guides you through the process of planning and downloading SAP software stacks and the aforementioned EHPs.

Planning maintenance activities

With this tool, you can compile EHPs and SPs, and it is a prerequisite for upgrading to SAP ERP 6.0. The Maintenance Optimizer also generates a *package configuration file* that the upgrade tool subsequently requires in the actual technical upgrade. The Maintenance Optimizer also resolves issues such as the handling of add-on products in an upgrade and offers the required update packages for direct downloading.

For more information on and prerequisites for using the Maintenance Optimizer, see the SAP Service Marketplace at *http://service.sap.com/mopz* as well as Chapter 12, Section 12.1.

13.5 Test Management

With the integrated Test Management in SAP Solution Manager, you can cover the following activities:

▶ **Test cases**
Generate process-oriented test plans. You can upload test cases, irrespective of the format, and store them centrally.

▶ **Test case management**
Assists you with the creation and editing of test plans and test case packages according to the respective test phase. You can assign individual test packages to a tester.

▶ **Test execution**
The TEST EXECUTION menu option enables you to directly access the test execution for test processing.

▶ **Central Test Workbench**
You can use the central Test Workbench function to maintain test settings, for example, status, messages, profiles, and others.

Holistic test concept — SAP Solution Manager thus offers holistic support for managing all the test planning and execution processes. The use of test tools guarantees the coverage of holistic test management and leads to increased efficiency and thus reduces test effort and costs. For example, you can divide test plans into smaller work packages and assign them to testers, who use them to perform acceptance tests. The test coordinator uses the test evaluation function to monitor all important activities and status information in a single, central overview. For more information on test management, see Chapter 7.

13.6 User Training

Training materials — The process and role-oriented generation of *training materials* makes it easier to create training documents and user training. Training experts can use the *Learning Map Builder* integrated into SAP Solution Manager to create HTML-based Learning Maps such as SAP

Tutor learning units, PowerPoint presentations, or other documentation. Learning Maps compiled in this way can be sent centrally to the relevant end-users by email.

For more information on the subject of E-Learning Management, see Chapter 5, Section 5.7.

13.7 SAP Upgrade Assessment

SAP Upgrade Assessment is a service offering for customers who are planning to upgrade a product of the SAP Business Suite (e.g., upgrade to SAP ERP 6.0 with an EHP installation). The offering focuses on a comprehensive technical system analysis.

Different factors influencing an upgrade are analyzed and evaluated, for example, the number of customer developments and modifications as well as installed add-on products. The analysis result is rounded off with an individual action plan of important preparations. An SAP Upgrade Assessment should be executed before the actual start of the project and helps you with the preparation phase of your upgrade project.

Comprehensive system analysis

13.8 SAP GoingLive Functional Upgrade Check

The *SAP GoingLive Functional Upgrade Check* is a service offering by SAP that analyzes your SAP production system with regard to the impending upgrade. This makes it possible to identify and address weaknesses and problems at an early stage. For example, one of the focal points is whether the planned hardware is sufficient for handling the expected load in the new SAP release. The report specifically includes the settings of the hardware, operating system, and database. An analysis of the system load and performance after the upgrade rounds off the analysis. The SAP GoingLive Functional Upgrade Check thus supports you during the current upgrade project.

For more information and order details, see the SAP Service Marketplace at *www.service.sap.com/goinglive-fu*.

13.9   Near Zero Downtime Method

Significant
reduction of
downtime

The *Near Zero Downtime method* (NZDT) was developed to reduce the
planned downtime that is caused by the SAP software update. This
method can be used for classic upgrade projects as well for the installation of EHPs and SPs. In addition, the NZDT method can be used
for Unicode conversions and maintenance activities without contributing to the originally planned downtime.

In the NZDT method, several maintenance activities are usually executed in bundled form to fit them into one maintenance window
during which production availability is ensured. In doing so, core
business processes are always available. However, customizing settings are significantly limited for a duration of up to approximately
14 days.

For background information about the NZDT method, see the SAP
Architecture Bluebook *Near Zero Downtime—Reduction of Business
Downtime* in the SAP Community Network (*http://www.sdn.sap.com*)
using the search phrase "Near Zero Downtime—Reduction of Business Downtime."

SAP Landscape Transformation software helps you speed up your business and IT transformations and plan, analyze, structure, and execute complex business requirements using transformation solutions.

14   SAP Landscape Transformation

To keep up with constantly changing market conditions and business requirements, SAP Landscape Transformation (SAP LT) software helps you speed up your business and IT transformations and implement complex business requirements using highly standardized transformation solutions. The software enables you to plan, analyze, structure, and execute transformation projects in the context of business scenarios, for example, mergers and acquisitions (M&A), sales, internal reorganization projects, and projects for harmonizing existing business processes.

Harmonizing IT and corporate goals

Companies are regularly confronted with transformation requirements. This is often the result of numerous external influences. Organizations can face changed market requirements, which are supposed to be reflected in the company structure or product portfolio. In addition, many companies try to achieve more transparency and effectiveness. However, the need for adjustments can also be due to internal conditions. For example, companies not only have to deal with regional differences and system complexity but also with internal restructuring. Hence, it is important for companies to always be able to adjust their operational processes and structures in the affected SAP system landscape(s) to new situations as quickly and effectively as possible.

Companies have a constant need for transformation

SAP offers the SAP Landscape Transformation (SAP LT) software to help companies keep up with constant market changes, stay flexible, and reach their own goals. SAP has developed this software to enable customers to adjust their organizational structures, unify and optimize their business processes, and to consolidate them using a structured process.

Based on the knowledge and expertise acquired in more than 10,000 transformation projects over the past two decades, the software can help you achieve your goals (for example, to reduce total costs of ownership (TCO) and ensure data quality and consistency). Proven methods and standardized technologies form the basis for realizing the desired transformation scenario (see Figure 14.1).

In addition, the software helps with the consolidation and optimization of existing processes. Structured roadmaps, preconfigured templates, and analyses support the versatility of SAP LT for planned consolidation and optimization processes.

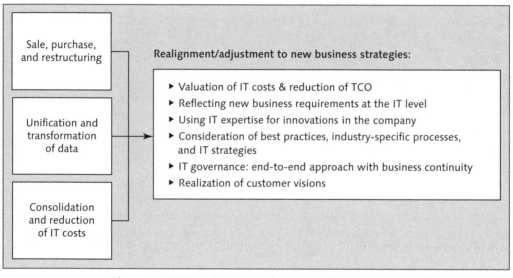

Figure 14.1 SAP Landscape Transformation Helps You Align Your IT Landscape with New Business Strategies

Market requirements make transformation necessary

Many SAP customers manage a number of different system landscapes that include different SAP systems and solutions of the SAP Business Suite; for example, SAP ERP, SAP Customer Relationship Management (SAP CRM), and applications for SAP Supplier Relationship Management (SAP SRM), as well as SAP Business Intelligence (BI) and industry solutions. The requirement to take into account regional and statutory requirements frequently increases the variety and complexity of such system landscapes. Over time, established processes become increasingly complex, costly, and non-transparent. The following influencing factors increase complexity:

▶ Multiple instances, different release levels, and platforms

▶ Redundant and inconsistent master and transaction data

▶ Different process structures and incomplete business processes

▶ Numerous user interfaces in SAP and non-SAP systems

Companies respond to these recurring transformation requirements with IT-based initiatives of significantly varying scope. Options for restructuring initiatives include, for example, reorganization of the internal company structure at the system level, simplification of processes or harmonization of master and transaction data. Irrespective of the scenario, reliable software and expertise are prerequisites for implementing the desired transformation project in an effective and cost saving manner.

If you are faced with the challenge of transforming your IT landscape, SAP LT can help you implement your desired company structures. The software is integrated into SAP Solution Manager as an add-on, which creates synergies with other processes, for example, solution documentation and test documentation. The software meets all technical and business transformation requirements, ensures data consistency, and takes system integrity aspects into account.

Harmonizing the IT infrastructure and corporate goals

SAP LT covers the following business scenarios:

▶ Management of *mergers and acquisitions* (M&A) and spin-off projects

▶ Execution of reorganization projects

▶ Optimization and/or simplification of business processes

▶ Harmonization of master data and preparation of the introduction of global templates

▶ Reduction of the TCO thanks to system consolidation and data centralization

One of the main benefits of SAP LT is that it includes predefined and scenario-based roadmaps. These roadmaps offer support and include best practices as well as detailed documentation. The software also includes tutorials, which show users how to create and execute projects step by step. The work center-based structure of the software helps you master your project efficiently and reliably. Proven transformation functions enable customers and partners to correctly schedule and execute the different project phases.

The analysis functions of the software are the first step to a successful transformation. They provide a comprehensive overview of general system and database characteristics. It is important to evaluate and assess the expense, duration, technical feasibility, and application-specific requirements of the project at an early stage. Hence, an intensive analysis of data to be converted is very important.

SAP LT constantly evolves. With SAP LT software version 2.0, users have access to additional transformation solutions (see Figure 14.2).

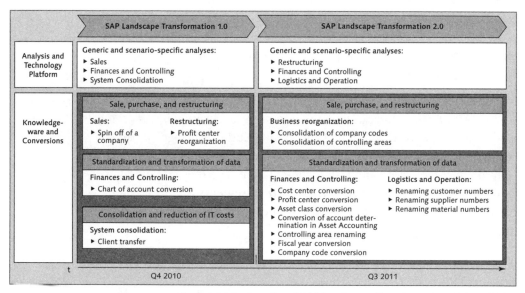

Figure 14.2 Scope of Functionality of SAP Landscape-Transformation: 1.0 and 2.0

14.1   The Greenfield Approach

Selecting the most effective and cost-efficient transformation approach

The *Greenfield* approach (the complete reconstruction of a system) is the most widespread method for implementing IT transformation requirements. At the same time, however, this approach is also deemed the most costly because it means that all existing SAP ERP solutions, structures, and interfaces have to be rebuilt in the new target system. The process is complex and can include the following tasks:

- Developing a new process design
- Creating a new authorization concept

- Generating new master data and setting up new organizational structures
- Setting up new interfaces

In addition, the Greenfield structure bears its own risks. The combination of different transformation approaches and manual tasks can result in errors in the data selection and transfer. It can also result in incomplete data structures, missing data history, and gaps in the integration of applications.

In addition, this approach requires a lot of work by the company's internal IT department as well as the individual user departments. All these factors limit the company's ability to continuously adapt the system landscape to recurring transformation requirements.

14.2   SAP's Approach to SAP Transformations

With the SAP LT software and supplementary services, SAP now offers its customers a holistic approach to SAP ERP system transformation. Some of the benefits of this approach are the following:

- Enables customers to build up their own transformation skills and realize transformation requirements with internal resources
- Smooth and consistent data transfer through test cycles taking into account the entire data history
- Reduction of the overall project duration and downtime of the production system
- Guaranteed maintenance and ongoing support while the software is used

For more complex and customer-specific transformation requirements as well as projects that require other SAP applications to be adapted, for example, SAP CRM, SAP SRM, SAP Business Warehouse (BW), or industry-specific solutions, the System Landscape Optimization area offers a comprehensive service portfolio.

Figure 14.3 shows a comparison of the Greenfield approach and the SAP LT approach.

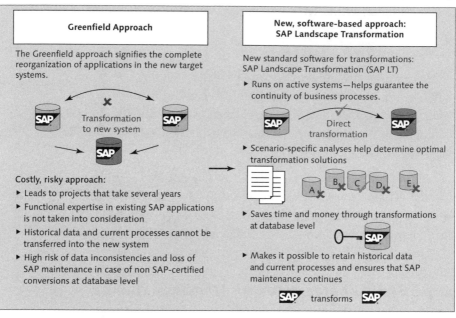

Figure 14.3 Comparison of Transformation Approaches

14.3 Phases of Executing a Transformation Project

Based on modern project-management techniques and many years of experience with transformation projects, SAP LT provides ideal customer and partner support in all project phases (see Figure 14.4).

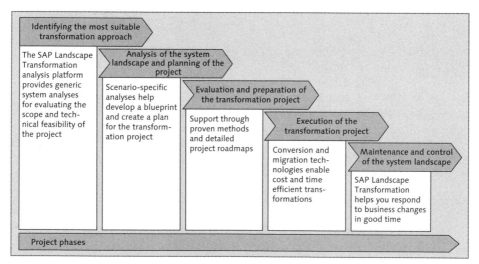

Figure 14.4 Typical Phases of a Transformation Project

14.3.1 Identification of the Transformation Approach

The software's analysis platform enables you to execute generic system analyses that help companies assess the scope and technical feasibility of a transformation project. Software-based analyses have the advantage that they use existing system information for cost and risk estimates as well as for feasibility studies.

14.3.2 Analysis of the System Landscape and Planning of the Project

After a company has selected a suitable approach for executing a transformation project, customers can compile projects according to their individual requirements and include the desired transformation components. This process results in a project template, which contains all relevant project steps and transformation requirements. Scenario-specific analyses provide customers and partners with valuable insights, such as the following:

▶ A detailed overview of the respective system landscapes

▶ Database characteristics and scenario-specific information

▶ Estimates of time, costs, and project resources at an early point in time

▶ Comparison of fundamental system settings and data structures such as repository objects and different Customizing settings

▶ Identification of conflicts, missing information, and duplicate entries

Based on these analysis results, you can then create a blueprint and set up a detailed project plan.

14.3.3 Evaluating and Preparing a Transformation Project

With Best Practices, SAP LT offers scenario-specific roadmaps, which provide a detailed overview of all phases of the project.

14.3.4 Realizing a Transformation Project

The SAP LT software enables you to implement your transformation scenarios using proven conversion and migration technologies. Dedicated test runs facilitate minimal system downtimes and maximum data security during the conversion of the production system. Depending on the complexity of the project, the test phase includes one or more test cycles in a dedicated test system. After each test conversion, you should check the following:

- Data consistency of the data structures
- Data access after the conversion
- Verification of test results
- Verification of prerequisites for the conversion

As soon as you get satisfactory test results, you can make the conversion in the production environment. All project steps are executed using a process structure. This is similar to this IMG that is usually used for system configuration in an SAP system landscape.

You can start using your production system for daily operation again directly after the successful conversion. You are guaranteed that all system data, including open items, complete data history, and archives, are consistent.

14.3.5 Typical Approach for Executing a Client Transfer

SAP LT is suitable for implementing different business scenarios and can help you identify potential for improvement. The software also enables companies to respond early to pending business changes and adapt their organizational structures accordingly. Companies benefit from higher efficiency, data quality, and improved transparency.

Proven and standardized project management

Based on the extensive experience in transformation projects that has contributed to SAP LT, projects are introduced along standardized phases. A project that uses SAP LT software to execute a transfer of clients includes the following phases:

- Organizational preparations:
  - Comparison analysis of differences between the affected systems, including SAP Repository und user exits, and client-independent Customizing
  - Creation of a transformation concept
  - Identification of differences between the systems and their harmonization
  - Definition of test scenarios

- Technical preparations:
  - Test system setup
  - Setting up the SAP transformation project in SAP Solution Manager
- Test cycles:
  - Test conversions in the test system
  - Performance monitoring
  - Analysis of the results of the test conversions for business processes
- Production conversion (usually on a weekend)
  - Conversion of the production system
  - Final test

14.4 Transformation Scenarios

The standard SAP transformation software is suitable for a number of transformation requirements that can be grouped in specific business scenarios. This categorization helps convert your business requirements into a suitable transformation scenario.

Focus on specific business-scenarios

14.4.1 Transformation Solutions for Sales, Purchasing, and Restructuring Initiatives

These scenarios include M&A as well as restructuring projects. SAP LT offers a holistic approach for realizing your transformation projects in these areas and helps you be prepared for future business situations.

Efficient IT support

If you are planning to sell or spin off part of your company, you must reflect company-wide organizational structures in your system landscape. This requires an approach that guarantees transaction integrity and meets legal requirements. Data security, compliance with statutory requirements, and profitability are success factors for adapting to constantly changing business requirements.

Sale of a company or a company unit

Scenario: Spin Off of a Company or Business Unit Using "Clone and Delete"

Carve-out   If your company plans to spin off a subsidiary company, the *carve-out* transformation scenario (see Figure 14.5), helps you remove the selected company code from your existing SAP system. In a copy of the original system, only the company code of the carved out part of the company is transferred to the system landscape. This part now represents a legally independent company.

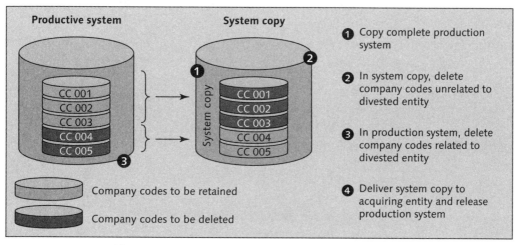

Figure 14.5 A Typical Company Carve-Out Scenario

The *carve-out* scenario allows you to execute transformations without affecting your day-to-day activities. By providing project roadmaps, which include detailed instructions, predefined templates as well as links to the individual project steps, you can independently master all of the phases of the project.

In the context of sale or spin-off projects, SAP LT offers the following benefits:

▸ Review/analysis of the IT landscape before the carve-out
▸ Evaluation of the different carve-out options
▸ Best practices and assistance with project evaluation and methodology and project execution
▸ Retention of historic data in case of a *share deal*
▸ Minimal system downtime

Scenario: Consolidation of Company Codes

A consolidation of company codes (see Figure 14.6 for an example) can become necessary if integration requirements have to be met in the context of M&A and/or organizational structures have to be mapped adequately at system level. The consolidation of company codes can support a realignment of your company structure and improve company-wide reporting functions and the transparency of your company data.

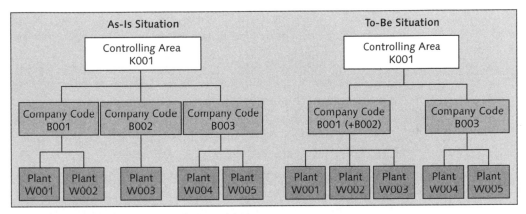

Figure 14.6 A Typical Company Code Consolidation

Other triggers for company code consolidations are listed here:

► Tax or commercial law reasons

► Objectives that increase cost efficiency

► Expansion of the company portfolio or adjusting it to changed market requirements

SAP LT helps customers identify and transfer all of the relevant data of the respective company codes.

It also includes structured procedures and integrated analysis functions that help make decisions about which business objects and organizational units are relevant for consolidation (e.g., Financial Accounting [FI] and Controlling [CO] master data, accounting documents, plants or sales organizations, etc.).

Analysis of affected business objects

A prerequisite for executing a transformation project is to check the following points first:

- All company codes to be consolidated must belong to the same controlling area.

- All company codes must use the same local currency, chart of accounts, and fiscal year variant.

Scenario: Reorganizing Profit Centers

Different external and internal reasons can give rise to the need to reorganize profit centers. For example, a changed corporate structure, which also means changed areas of responsibility, can make it necessary to adjust controlling processes and existing profit centers.

Other internal objectives (for example, simplifying the existing profit center structure, simplifying the company-wide report structure, or changing from a structure based on a cost center to a structure based on a profit center) can give rise to reorganization. Irrespective of the scope, changing the profit center also means reassigning all objects related to the profit center (e.g., materials, purchase orders, and sales orders). This often means changing thousands of objects and making the corresponding correction postings. In addition, the restructuring of profit centers can affect not only the use of a profit center in the general ledger (GL) but also all GL-specific data.

Companies planning such a reorganization project are often faced with numerous problems, for example, the required manual calculations and transfers, manual reconciliations, and unstructured audit logs.

SAP LT offers customers a proven solution for reorganizing profit centers (separate, consolidate, and change), assigning master and transaction data, and changing the assignment of profit centers on a key date basis.

Predefined standards

You can profit from the following predefined standards of SAP LT:

- Provision of a defined point of access for all parties involved in the reorganization process

- Automated calculations and logs

- Complete audit log

Scenario: Consolidation of Controlling Areas

In the context of transformation projects, a number of complex business requirements have to be mapped at the system level. This also includes adjusting the controlling data, for example, the consolidation of controlling areas (see Figure 14.7).

Preparation for company code consolidation

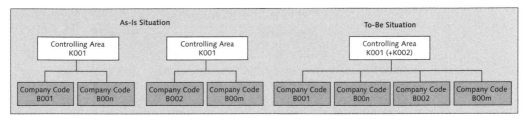

Figure 14.7 A Typical Controlling Area Consolidation

Controlling area consolidation is an important preparatory step for consolidating company codes that belong to different controlling areas. This is also relevant if the company has decided to move from decentralized to central, uniform controlling.

To achieve the objectives, the changes must be mapped adequately at system level. This can mean consolidating two or more controlling areas in one new controlling area or an already existing controlling area.

From the system perspective, you must take into account several other objects in controlling area consolidation, for example, cost centers, activity types, service types, cost types, charts of accounts, and so on.

The SAP LT analysis functions enable you to determine in advance whether your system meets all of the prerequisites for controlling area consolidation, such as uniform charts of accounts, identical fiscal year variants, operating concerns, profit centers, and so on.

The standardized function for consolidating controlling areas provides you with the option to cover all these requirements and implement them in the project.

Possible Combinations of Transformation Scenarios

In the *Sales, Purchasing, and Restructuring* scenario, you can combine the following scenarios and execute them in one downtime:

▶ Consolidate company codes

▶ Consolidate controlling areas (including profit center and cost center consolidation)

14.4.2 Standardization and Transformation of Data

Consistent and high-quality data forms the basis for reliable and efficient business processes. Hence, companies want to increase the transparency of their financial processes and take measures to unify and align data structures and processes across the company.

Regional and local differences also have a decisive effect on the overall business processes of a company and are therefore frequently a reason for the decision to introduce widespread accounting standards, such as the *Generally Accepted Accounting Principles (GAAP)* and the *International Financial Reporting Standards (IFRS)*.

Standardization in FI
Regionally organized structures can increase administrative complexity and make adjustments necessary. Standardizing your FI and CO structures enables you to redefine your existing company structure. Establishing a company-wide, centralized SAP ERP application can help make your business processes more effective and increase profitability. The following objectives, in particular, drive transformation projects:

▶ More precise reporting and increase of corporate transparency

▶ Changing and enhancing account or organizational structures

▶ Meeting statutory requirements and introducing defined reporting standards

▶ Adjustment of processes and structures to meet statutory requirements

Chart of Accounts Conversion

SAP LT helps you introduce standardized financial guidelines and harmonize your charts of accounts.

If you are planning to replace your local and regional charts of accounts with a new corporate chart of accounts, SAP LT also supports this.

Integrated scenario-specific analyses of your FI and CO data help your company create a project plan and determine the feasibility and scope of your planned chart of accounts conversion project.

In the conversion phases, you can choose to rename or consolidate your account and cost types. SAP LT uses detailed, predefined methods to guide you safely through the transformation process. It is important to include all organizational and operational requirements and to provide optimal support for future business processes.

Renaming or merging

In particular, the retention of existing processes and data specific to your company code, and the enabling of efficient accounting and period-end closing procedures are taken into account.

Renaming Company Codes and Controlling Areas

For a client or *controlling area* consolidation, you might have to rename controlling areas. You have to make sure that all controlling areas only occur once per client after the consolidation. This can result in renaming and adjusting the company code keys. Another example could be that your company or corporate family plans to introduce uniform naming conventions for all controlling areas.

Controlling areas

Company codes can be renamed due to a company acquisition or restructuring with a group to standardize company data. To cover the business requirements at the SAP system level, data consistency must be ensured across all existing SAP components.

Company codes

A *fiscal year conversion* allows you to adjust the fiscal year that exists in your system to the current calendar year. This can be necessary if you have introduced a shortened fiscal year, for example, due to a merger or acquisition. As a consequence, it's possible that the fiscal year defined in the SAP system precedes the actual calendar year. This difference often affects company-wide workflows and cross-company code processes. Other adjustment requests for your current fiscal year can arise due to task, statutory, or harmonization reasons.

Fiscal year conversion

SAP LT guarantees to eliminate this difference consistently across all components and thus match the fiscal year in your SAP system to the current calendar year. The conversion is made for all company codes belonging to a fiscal year variant. Figure 14.8 shows an exemplary fiscal year conversion.

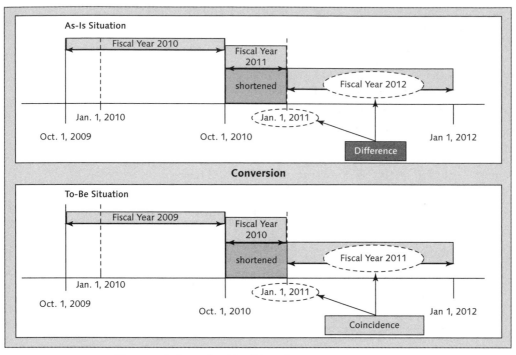

Figure 14.8 Exemplary Fiscal Year Conversion

Conversion of asset classes

The conversion of asset classes can be necessary for many different reasons:

▶ Introduction of uniform conventions and IDs

▶ Consolidation of asset classes with the same values and different IDs

▶ Changes to asset classes due to chart of accounts conversions

SAP LT supports the function to change numbers of asset classes (1:1 conversion) and to consolidate asset classes (renaming several asset classes to the same number). In addition, the software makes it possible to change the text descriptions of the asset classes during the conversion. In the context of the project preparations, the prerequisites would have to be checked in detail.

Because asset classes are defined at the client level, changes to asset classes can only be made for all company codes that belong to the same client at the same time.

The conversion of the account determination (FI-AA) can be neces- sary, for example, if the following occurs:

▶ The assignment of GL accounts to asset accounts is changed.

▶ New requirements must be implemented in the context of a chart of accounts conversion with regard to the account determination.

SAP LT makes it possible to rename the account determination in a 1:1 relationship, consolidate the account determination in an *n*:1 relationship, and change the descriptions (texts) of the account deter- mination.

To maintain the *flexibility of your FI and CO structures*, SAP LT offers the following scenarios:

▶ Simplification and systemization of the existing profit center and cost center structure.

▶ Restructuring or company acquisitions make it necessary to change your controlling structures. For example, you might have to change the names of profit centers and cost centers or introduce company-wide naming conventions for profit centers and cost centers.

In these scenarios, SAP LT helps you ensure data consistency across all applications. The adjustment includes all transaction, master, and Customizing data. In addition, the software helps you change profit centers and cost centers differently in every controlling area while redefining the descriptions (texts) at the same time.

Simplification in the Logistics and Sales Area

A solid and reliable data foundation is an important factor for han- dling your business processes. Hence, it is crucial for companies to have transparent and valid customer, supplier, and inventory data as well as sales figures to map complex and cross-application processes such as requirements planning, order processing, sales activities, and production planning.

However, different activities, such as migrations from different source systems, for example, can create redundant entries, for exam- ple, for customers and suppliers in your SAP system. Here, deleting duplicate entries can increase the transparency of your data and sim- plify company-wide access to the relevant data.

To simplify global processes with suppliers and customers as well as reporting structures, you might also want to introduce new criteria or categorizations (e.g., by country, hierarchies). As a preparation for introducing additional applications from SAP CRM or SAP NetWeaver Master Data Management (SAP MDM), a cleaned up database can generate enormous added value and simplify the implementation significantly. With SAP LT, you can adjust customer and supplier numbers by specific customer and eliminate duplicate entries.

Preparation for SAP MDM introduction

The expansion of business activities and the related adjustment of the product portfolio is often a reason for companies to redesign the structures in their Materials Management (MM). For example, the current structure of your material numbers might no longer be sufficient for servicing your company's product portfolio. One possible solution is to add additional digits to your material number structure (e.g., eight instead of six digits). In addition, reorganization measures and acquisitions can lead to an unstructured and complex material number structure over time. Here, you can use SAP LT to establish a uniform structure or adjust the current structure to new naming conventions. A unification of the structure can also be helpful to prepare for the introduction of (SAP MDM).

For all of these objectives, SAP LT provides predefined scenarios that help realize the most varied transformation requirements with regard to the adjustment of customer, supplier, and material numbers at the system level. From a technical perspective, SAP LT enables the following possible solutions:

▸ Conversion of numbers in master and transaction data as well as Customizing

▸ Renaming of customer, supplier, and material numbers (1:1 relationship) or consolidation of customer and supplier numbers (n:1 relationship)

▸ Moving a series of numbers from one number range to another (according to a specified rule)

▸ Combination of predefined rules and individual assignment requirements

▸ Individual execution or combination of customer, supplier, and material number conversions

Possible Combination of Transformation Scenarios

In the *Unification and Transformation of Data* area, you can combine the following transformation scenarios with each other:

▶ Chart of accounts conversion, conversion of cost centers, asset classes, and asset account determination

▶ Renaming of company codes and controlling areas together with the conversion of cost centers and/or profit centers

14.4.3 Consolidation of Systems and Reduction of IT Costs

Many international companies operate a globally distributed system landscape with different data centers. This often leads to strongly diverging systems with different datasets, which can result in higher operating costs and expenses. Hence, it is a priority for many companies to unite strategic data centers. That is why a clearly structured data system is crucial for transparent data management and a prerequisite for fast and sustainable company decisions in the future.

A system consolidation can be a first step in the context of designing a more rational, efficient, and robust IT infrastructure that is suitable for the target business model. For example, setting up a one-system landscape with standardized processes, add-ons, programs, and business data can significantly reduce system complexity. In addition, the centralization can reduce the total cost and effort for maintenance and administration.

A centralized IT environment with independent clients can significantly facilitate data management and global reporting. It also has the effect that your FI and sales data is always available across the company and supports the establishment of standardized and uniform business processes.

SAP LT helps you set up a centralized SAP ERP application that significantly reduces the effort required for system maintenance and upgrades. You can reduce not only the number of systems and interfaces but also delete redundant data and thus improve the quality of your company data.

Client transfer

With the client transfer approach (see Figure 14.9), you can plan and set up an IT infrastructure that provides targeted support for your long-term company requirements.

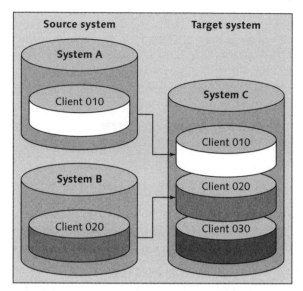

Figure 14.9 A Typical Client Transfer Scenario

No need for process harmonization

In an SAP system environment, a client transfer supports the centralization of data from different source systems in a single target system. This approach makes it possible to quickly achieve results because every client retains its structure, and no process harmonization is necessary. By consolidating your data centers, you can improve your operational performance while lowering operating costs and the communication effort of your IT department at the same time. System administration is simplified significantly because only one system landscape has to be managed. The new system environment also facilitates future implementations and upgrades.

Using SAP LT offers the following advantages:

▶ Software-based, detailed checks of the system and comparisons

▶ Identification of a suitable consolidation approach

▶ Use of Best Practices and instructions for the project evaluation as well as methodologies for preparing and executing the project

▶ Transfer of all data, including the entire data history, into the existing target system

▶ Minimal system downtimes and minimal disruptions to operations

14.5   Using SAP Landscape Transformation

SAP LT is an SAP product that requires a license and is installed on an SAP Solution Manager system. You download the software from the Software Download Center at *http://service.sap.com/swdc* on the SAP Service Marketplace. There you have the option to download add-ons for the installation as well as corrections in the form of support packages (SPs). SAP recommends using the software with the latest SPs and taking into account SAP Note 1527123 during installation because of possible consequences.

Buying and down-loading the software

SAP LT consists of two add-ons (DMIS and SHC_CONT), which are installed using the standard add-on installation process.

In SAP Solution Manager, which is the control system that enables central access to all important SAP LT functions and the administration of SAP LT projects, both add-ons (DMIS; SHC_CONT) must be installed. The most important configuration measures in SAP Solution Manager are the activation of certain Web Dynpro services and the preparation for use with the SAP NetWeaver Business Client. In other SAP systems (execution systems) that are affected by the SAP LT project, only the DMIS add-on needs to be installed.

Installation and configuration

An authorization concept with predefined roles—which correspond to the typical user roles of the SAP LT—gives you the option to restrict the use of SAP LT functions. This enables you also to easily and efficiently implement the required security standards for the remote execution of SAP LT functions in the execution system.

Authorization concept

Additional Information Regarding Installation and Configuration

All details regarding the installation and configuration of the SAP LT are available in the following documents:

▶ SAP Landscape Transformation 2.0 Master Guide
▶ SAP Landscape Transformation 2.0 Security Guide
▶ Central SAP LT Note: 1465272

Please note the specific requirements for the installation of the transformation solutions for profit center reorganization (SAP Note 1534197).

14.5.1 Working with SAP Landscape Transformation

Using
transformation
solutions in
projects

The supplied transformation solutions are an elementary part of the SAP LT software. Depending on the type and scope of the transformation requirement(s), they include several analyses and transformation applications. Transformation applications are standardized and control the technical conversion of the affected system data. The modular structure enables you to use a combination of several transformation applications in one project and configure them according to your customer situation and your project requirements. This efficient approach provides maximum flexibility and ensures the quick and consistent conversion of the affected system data. Corresponding project roadmaps provide extensive methodological support also to ensure quick and smooth progress for all other aspects of the project.

"SAP LT" Work
Center

In the *SAP LT* Work Center, you can flexibly combine transformation solutions in project templates or use a project template already predefined by SAP. You can use project templates in different projects.

Typical user roles

Depending on the complexity of the transformation project, it can make sense to first execute analysis applications to analyze the affected systems in an early phase of the project. To ensure that the project flow is as smooth as possible, we recommend assigning team members different roles. By default, three role profiles are designed for executing a transformation project.

One of the role profiles offered is that of project manager, as you already know from other SAP projects. The other SAP LT role profiles are described here:

▶ **Business expert**
The business expert should provide the business know-how for the affected SAP application and ideally have already worked on implementation and transformation projects. Basic knowledge of and experience with using SAP Solution Manager are also advantageous. His requirements in the context of a transformation project are basically to define the scope of the required transformation solutions, assess analysis results, and provide user-specific information for the technical conversion.

▶ **Technical execution expert**
The technical execution expert should have basic knowledge of the SAP applications and their architecture. In-depth knowledge of SAP NetWeaver and the use of SAP Solution Manager are also

required. The main tasks include the execution of analyses and preparation of the results as well as the technical execution of the transformation applications.

14.5.2 Structure of the Work Center of SAP LT Software

As soon as you have successfully installed the software, you can call the work center *SAP LT* (Transaction LTS) in SAP Solution Manager (see Figure 14.10). The work center is the central user interface for calling all important functions of SAP LT and for the central administration of the projects.

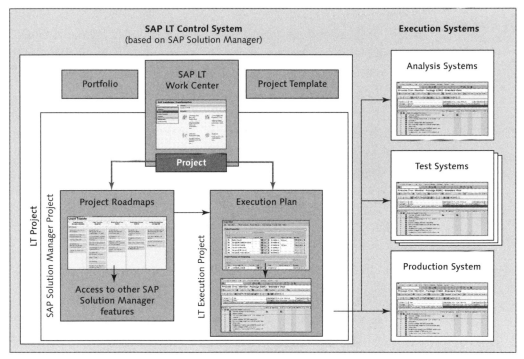

Figure 14.10 Structure of the "SAP LT" Work Center

The navigation area of the *SAP LT* work center is structured as follows:

▶ OVERVIEW

    The *SAP LT* work center offers quick access to your transformation projects, including team members, analysis results, test results, documentation, and roadmaps.

Navigation area

▶ PORTFOLIO

Portfolios contain all transformation solutions structured according to the typical transformation requirements of SAP customers. The portfolios enable you to flexibly combine all relevant transformation solutions for an SAP transformation project. The project roadmaps provide methodological explanations.

▶ PROJECT TEMPLATES

A project template provides a concrete project scope of a transformation project. These templates contain the required transformation solutions from the portfolio. You can use a project template for several projects.

▶ PROJECTS

A project centrally manages all project activities for the technical implementation of the transformation solutions in a project execution plan.

▶ PROJECT STATUS

The project status enables the user to get a quick and targeted overview of current projects and makes it possible to navigate directly into the project execution plan of an SAP LT project.

▶ SYSTEM LANDSCAPES

System landscapes enable the central definition of system landscapes that can be used for one or more transformation projects. For relevant information, use the integrated access from the system landscape maintenance of SAP Solution Manager.

Application help

In addition to useful help documents in the OVERVIEW navigation panel, the *Application Help* is a comprehensive and easy to understand source of information. The RELATED LINKS area gives you central access to the application help. The HELP CENTER area provides detailed explanations of the available functions for every subarea of the work center.

Transformation offer and project templates

The SAP LT portfolio structure consists of four parts (see Figure 14.11):

▶ LEVERAGE SELL, BUY, AND RESTRUCTURE

▶ UNIFY AND TRANSFORM DATA

▶ CONSOLIDATE AND REDUCE IT COST

▶ ANALYSES

For more information on the available transformation components, see Section 14.4.

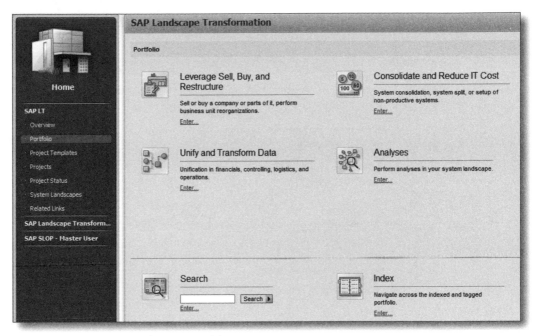

Figure 14.11 Initial Screen of SAP LT Portfolio

As an alternative to menu navigation, a search function enables you to locate specific transformation solutions.

Searching in the portfolio

Descriptions explain the supported transformation requirements as well as typical areas of use and the function scope of the corresponding transformation solutions.

PROJECT TEMPLATES contain the corresponding transformation solutions and analyses for executing one (or more) transformation project(s). You can create your own project templates on the basis of SAP project templates and your own selection of transformation requirements and solutions.

Project templates

Subsequent adjustments to a project template can be saved as a new version. In addition, you can use the note function to document changes to the contents of project templates.

14.5.3 Creating Projects

The project manager creates a project in three steps (see Figure 14.12):

1. Define the PROJECT NAME.

2. Assign the PROJECT TEMPLATE.

3. Adjust the suggested SOLUTIONS in the project execution plan.

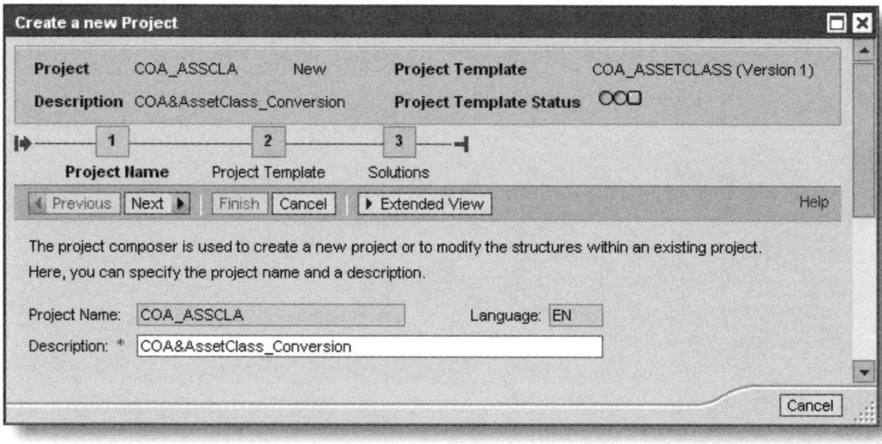

Figure 14.12 Creating Projects

Starting with the transformation solutions included in the assigned project template, step 3 (SOLUTIONS) includes a suggested project execution plan. With the project execution plan, the technical execution expert receives a comprehensive overview of all recommended steps for the technical implementation of the SAP LT project. This overview is structured according to the project phases.

You can customize the proposed project execution plan. This also enables you to remove transformation solutions marked as optional from the project execution plan and specify the number of analyses yourself.

Assigning system landscapes and editing the project execution plan

After the initial creation of the project execution plan, you can edit this plan further. Important steps here are the assignment of project members and the assignment of system landscapes. Prior to this, you can centrally create System landscapes in the system landscape navigation area and also define the remote connections to the execution systems (see Figure 14.13).

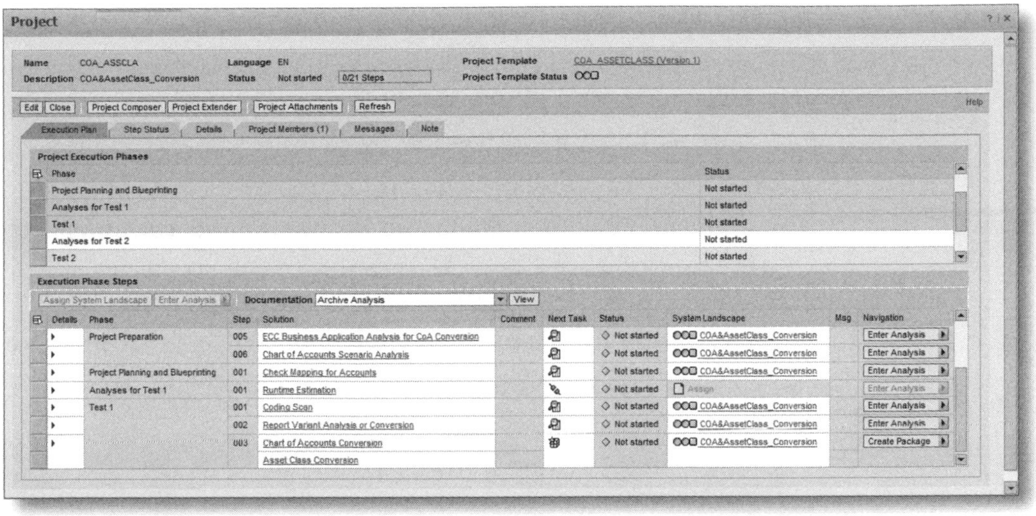

Figure 14.13 Project Execution Plan, Including System Landscape Assignment for Example Chart of Accounts and Asset Class Conversion

14.5.4 Combining Transformation Solutions

If your company is implementing several transformation projects at the same time, one project template can contain several transformation applications, for example, chart of accounts conversion and conversion of asset classes. You can use the ENHANCED VIEW button to specify to which extent the technical execution is supposed to be combined to keep the system downtime to a minimum.

You can combine the following transformation solutions: *(margin note: Possible combinations)*

- Sales, purchasing, and restructuring scenario:
  - Consolidate company codes
  - Consolidate controlling areas (including profit center and cost center consolidation)
- Standardization and transformation of data scenario:
  - Chart of accounts conversion, conversion of cost centers, asset classes, and asset account determination
  - Renaming of company codes and controlling areas together with the conversion of cost centers and/or profit centers

14.5.5 Executing Projects

Using project road-maps and critical success factors

The project execution plan is the central navigation environment for executing analyses and transformation applications and contains information about the current project status and degree of processing.

The PROJECT ROADMAPS button takes you to the corresponding project roadmap (see Figure 14.14), which contains detailed information and useful notes for general planning, preparation, and successful execution of the transformation project.

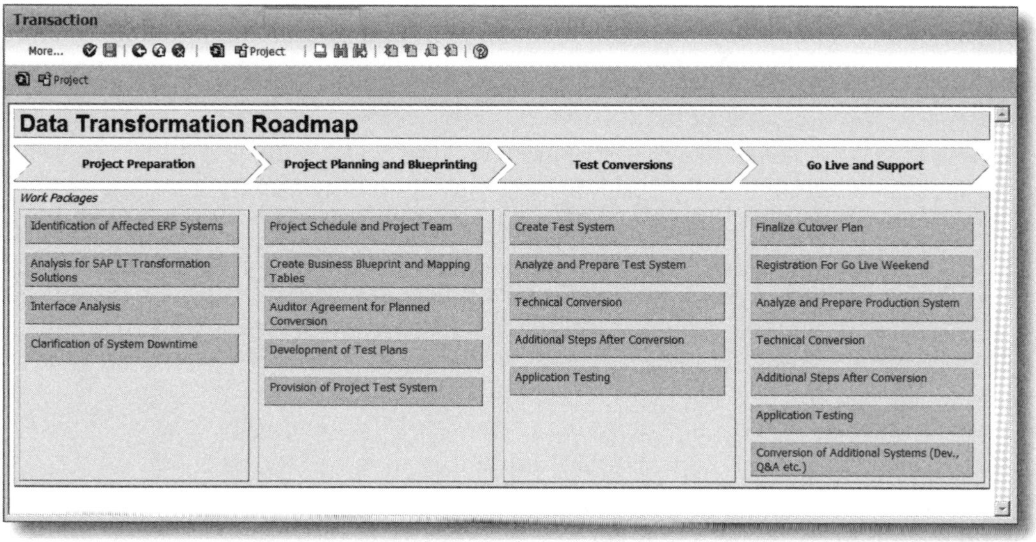

Figure 14.14 Project Roadmap

The following aspects must be taken into account throughout the entire project:

- Consult your auditor and provide mapping information in good time.
- Adjust and clean up data and data structures on the basis of the analysis results.
- Schedule several test runs (integration test, application test, performance test, etc.).

Test system
- Validate the test results.
- To get meaningful test results, we recommend setting up the test system on the basis of a copy of the production system and with a

comparable hardware configuration. This enables you to make reliable statements regarding the duration of the conversion and the required system downtime.

▶ Back up your data before you start the technical conversion of the production system.

▶ Register your go-live date (see SAP Note 1463386) to make sure that a competent SAP Support employee is available if you experience any unexpected problems.

14.5.6 Executing Analyses

The analyses suggested in the project execution plan have different objectives depending on the project phase. In the project preparation phase, they help you determine the amount of work required for the conversion more precisely or check the technical feasibility for the respective affected system constellation. Examples of such upstream analyses are the *ECC Business Application Analysis*, the *Archive Analysis*, and the *Runtime Estimation* (runtime and downtime). These analyses are usually executed in the affected production systems or a current copy. Analyses like the *Coding Scan* also help you determine to which extent customer programs will still work after a technical conversion and whether they have to be modified.

After you have assigned a system landscape, you can execute the analyses centrally using the project execution plan. Depending on the type and scope of the analysis, several execution steps are executed. After the successful execution, you can access the analysis results. You can display these in different output formats (e.g., as an HTML file that can be downloaded to Excel; see Figure 14.15).

In preparation for a chart of accounts conversion combined with an asset class conversion, the ECC Business Application Analysis, for example, provides valuable insights about whether special conversion steps are necessary for using the new GL or whether the workflow should be adjusted manually at a later point in time.

SAP Landscape Transformation – ECC Business Application Analysis

Home Contact ©Copyright

Home
▼ Analysis Information
▶ Organizational Structure (Graphic)
▼ Active SAP Modules
  GTS - Global trade services
  Switch Framework
▶ Financial Accounting
▶ FI - Asset Accounting
▶ Controlling
▶ Material Management
▶ Sales and Distribution
▶ Human Resources
▶ Plant Maintenance
▶ Project System
▶ Production Planning
▶ Quality Management
▶ Archiving
▶ Workflow
▶ Inconsistencies

Active SAP Modules

In this section, you can view which SAP modules are actively used in the system.
A SAP module is considered actively used when at least one of its transactional data tables has more than 20 entries.

The table below also includes the largest tables (max. 3) for each of the actively used SAP modules.

SAP Module	SAP Module Description	Largest tables (Transaction Data)
AC	Accounting - General	SMCOPC (505)
AP-CFG	Product Configurator	COMM_CFGVALTX (3656),COMM_CFGCLACOM (3373),COMM_CFGVALSYM (2694)
AP-CFG-CBA	dBASE / Configuration Store	IBINVALST_SYM (3319),IBINST_OBJ (950)
AP-LIM	AP-LIM Logistics Inventory Management Engine	/LIME/GEN_IDXCOL (1248),/LIME/GEN_IDXTAB (114)
AP-MD-BF	Basic Functions	MDSM_SYNC_HIST (1504),MDSM_SYNC_RUNT (1080),MDSM_SYNC_HIST_F (1024)
AP-MD-BP	SAP Business Partner	BUT100 (6651),BUT000 (5832),BUT020 (4838)
AP-MD-IBA	Installed Base	IBEXTINST (19461),IBINVALUES (12459),IBIN (10551)
AP-MD-PCA	Payment Cards	CCSEC_LOG (128)
AP-MD-PRO	Central Part of Product Master	COMM_CATEGORYT (3083),COMM_PRCAT (1391),COMM_CATEGORY (1391)
AP-PPE	Integrated Product and Process Engineering	POSVID (14497),PNODID (8384),PVSDEX (6946)
AP-PRC-CON	Condition Technique	/SAPCND/CONDINDX (116)
AP-PRC-PR	Pricing	PRCD_ITEM (4364),PRCD_HEAD (4240),PRCD_COND (2608)
BC-ABA-LA	Syntax, Compiler, Runtime	INDX (149124),ABAPHTML (6946),TSKBA (256)
BC-ABA-TO	Logical DB, Selection Screens, Selection Variants	VARINUM (22465)
BC-BMT-OM	Organizational Management	SWWUSERWI (109339),PLOG (28992),HRMDORIGIN (3797)

Figure 14.15 Example of an Analysis Result

14.5.7 Executing Transformation Applications

Creating a package   Depending on the degree of complexity of the transformation project, numerous test conversions are necessary. To centrally start a transformation application using SAP Solution Manager in the respective application systems, you first need to assign a system landscape. You use the CREATE PACKAGE step to initialize the transformation application in the assigned system.

The technical application expert then gets a process structure as the central work environment for the technical execution. Depending on the transformation application, this structure contains different numbers of steps that have to be processed in sequence.

In case of a chart of accounts conversion in combination with an asset class conversion, for example, important configuration steps are the restriction of the technical conversion to certain organizational units (e.g., only one company code) as well as the definition of *mapping tables*.

Central status management logs every step of the conversion and stores it centrally in SAP Solution Manager. For each step in the process tree (see Figure 14.16), the detailed view provides a wealth of useful information (e.g., documentation or runtime of the conversion program). If errors occur (marked with STATUS red), additional functions such as *troubleshooting* can help you correct the error automatically by providing useful hints. For each execution step, you can store notes and product documentation or optimize the runtime of the technical conversion programs.

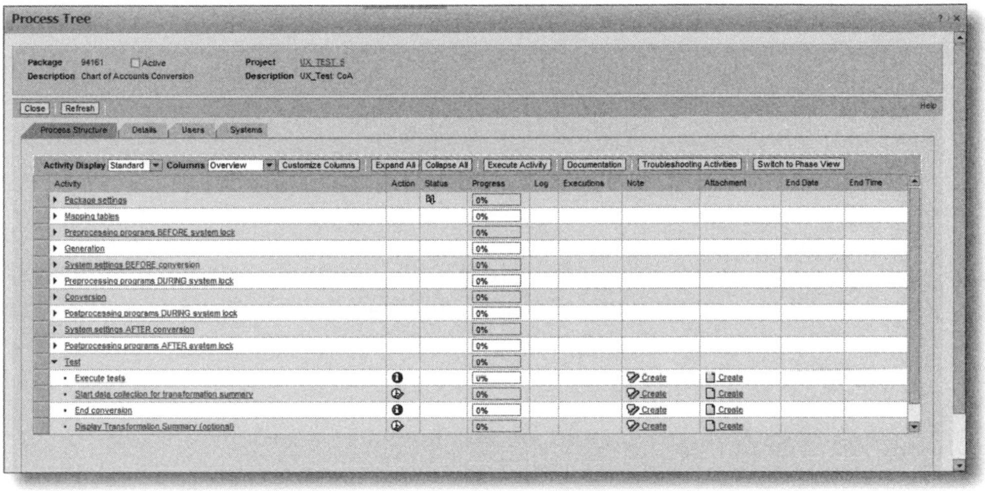

Figure 14.16 Process Tree in SAP LT

14.5.8 Important Notes and Recommendations Regarding the Technical Execution

SAP recommends using the number of test conversions suggested in the project execution plan. You must check the results of the technical test conversions in extensive application tests. Executing the technical execution steps incompletely or incorrectly can lead to data inconsistencies. Hence, it is important to follow the instructions and notes in the documentation for each execution step.

After the complete execution of a transformation application, the result of the technical conversion is formatted in a *transformation summary*, which can be used as the documentation basis for auditors.

Transformation summary

14.5.9 Troubleshooting and Support

If you experience problems using SAP LT, proceed as follows:

▸ Check the current SP status of the software.

▸ If appropriate, implement SAP Notes made available in the meantime.

Searching for SAP Notes

Use the following keywords to search for SAP Notes:

▶ Transformation solutions for SAP LT, for example, chart of accounts conversion

▶ Technical name of the affected activity

▶ Message number

▶ Program name

If necessary, enter an error message.

To search for notes and create error messages, use SAP component CA-LT*.

SAP recommends registering the conversion of production systems with SAP to ensure that quick and competent support is available on the respective production startup weekend. For more details, see SAP Note 1463386.

For more useful notes on problem solving and available support for SAP LT, see SAP Note 1465272.

14.6 Additional Services for SAP Landscape Transformation

In addition to SAP LT, SAP offers a range of different services for support and consulting during the entire project cycle: from strategic consulting to help with analyses to optimization services during the implementation phase and support during production startup (see Figure 14.17). If you want to learn more about transformation, additional course offerings are available on request.

Individual service packages

This flexible approach enables companies to compile a service package that is tailored to their individual requirements for implementing the planned transformation project. The services assist companies with the following requirements, for example:

▶ Identifying the most suitable transformation scenario for the business strategy

▶ Speeding up projects with regard to the preparation, project scope, and technical feasibility

▶ Integrating enterprise-specific requirements

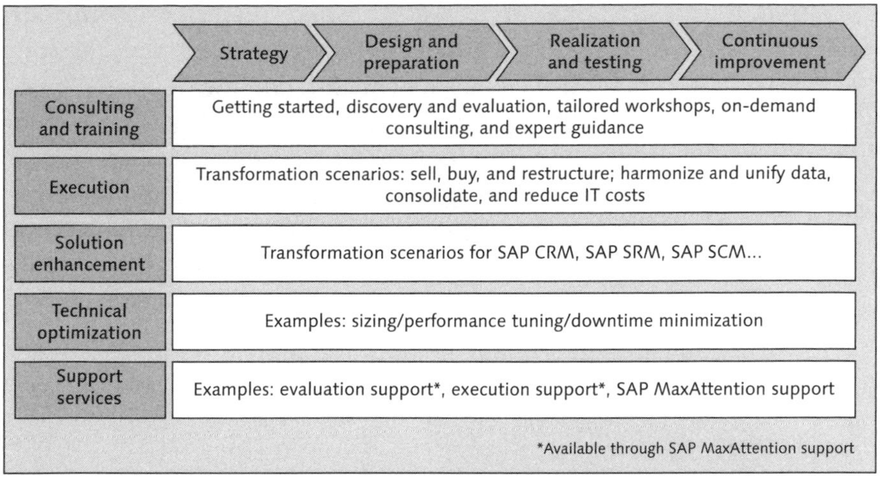

	Strategy	Design and preparation	Realization and testing	Continuous improvement
Consulting and training	Getting started, discovery and evaluation, tailored workshops, on-demand consulting, and expert guidance			
Execution	Transformation scenarios: sell, buy, and restructure; harmonize and unify data, consolidate, and reduce IT costs			
Solution enhancement	Transformation scenarios for SAP CRM, SAP SRM, SAP SCM...			
Technical optimization	Examples: sizing/performance tuning/downtime minimization			
Support services	Examples: evaluation support*, execution support*, SAP MaxAttention support			

*Available through SAP MaxAttention support

Figure 14.17 Overview of Supplementary SAP Service

▶ Implementing transformation requirements that are not yet covered by SAP LT

▶ Acquiring extensive knowledge of the transformation scenarios covered by SAP LT with training provided by the System Landscape Optimization group

▶ Complete control over all phases of a transformation project (technical implementation, project management, test management, performance tuning)

Many companies have difficulties implementing the transformation requirements necessary for business reasons in a suitable IT program. This is often due to missing information about existing solutions, methodologies, project plans, and so on. In this phase, SAP transformation experts can help you create transformation plans that offer the best and fastest solutions based on your individual requirements. During the startup phase of the project, the extensive knowledge of the SAP experts helps your company master specific challenges such as combining already-existing solution components; estimating the cost, duration, and risk of the project; and coordinating projects running in parallel.

Support with IT transformation strategies and project preparations

SAP offers training and consulting, which can be combined flexibly to meet customer-specific and project-specific requirements. Companies faced with a transformation project sometimes have difficulties setting it up appropriately or look for an option to learn more about

Project-specific requirements

specific project tasks. Here, SAP LT offers extensive information about scenario-based transformation projects. In addition, the software also includes detailed documentation on how to use the product. Furthermore, the software includes an Online Knowledge Product (OKP), which consists of numerous presentations and audio recordings. Additional training and consulting can support the activities of the project team and thus make it possible to get started with the transformation project as soon as possible. These services include the following:

- Support with the planning of transformation projects
- Participation in planning workshops, proof of concept, and design phases
- Provision of documentation for evaluating the analysis results of the SAP LT analysis functions
- Planning and optimization of project test cycles

Customer-specific consulting projects

The System Landscape Optimization Group of SAP Consulting offers numerous services for all SAP Business Suite applications to cover the whole range of transformation scenarios. These services are suitable in particular for companies who are not planning to implement several transformation projects in a certain period and are therefore not interested in building up in-house SAP LT expertise. The services of the System Landscape Optimization Group are tailored specifically to your individual requirements during analysis, planning, execution, and production startup. By providing you with the option to have experts accompany the entire process, SAP enables you and your departments to focus on your core business.

SAP LT was developed with the aim to address specific business scenarios. For example, if your company is planning on implementing a scenario related to the *International Financial Reporting Standards* (IFRS), you might have to expand the transformation requirements with regard to additional controlling aspects and asset values. You can implement most of your transformation project with SAP LT (e.g., by using the functionality for converting charts of accounts). To implement additional project requirements, such as the consolidation of controlling areas, the introduction of controlling templates, and changes to cost structures as well as adjusting your BW solution, you might have to use customer-specific consulting projects. Such a consulting project usually includes the following requirements:

▶ Additional transformation requirements such as a system or client consolidation, changes to the product hierarchy, and adjustments to depreciation runs

▶ Adjusting different SAP solutions such as SAP NetWeaver BW, components of SAP NetWeaver Information Lifecycle Management, and applications for SAP CRM and SAP SCM

In the planning phase, companies are often faced with technical challenges regarding, for example, performance and downtimes. If your company would like to receive support in these areas, SAP's Service for Hardware Sizing and Performance Tuning can be a suitable solution. The Minimized Downtime service enables you to significantly reduce your system downtime by means of online data processing.

Technical services

In addition to the standardized SAP consulting offers, there are two SAP Support services exclusively for SAP MaxAttention customers.

Special MaxAttention services

▶ **SAP SLO Evaluation Service**
This service helps you evaluate the feasibility of a project by analyzing the current situation. Experienced consultants discuss your transformation and harmonization requirements with you, and you develop the best approach for the planned transformation — including schedule, cost estimate, and details for the technical implementation.

▶ **SAP SLO Execution Support Service**
This service provides comprehensive support with the execution and use of transformation solutions using SAP LT software. You receive guidance while building up in-house knowledge that enables you to complete technical conversions in subsequent projects as well. This approach is particularly interesting for SAP MaxAttention customers for whom the IT side conversion of their *Customer Competence Center* or *Customer Center of Expertise* (CCoE) is performed.

For more information on SAP LT and related services, see *www.service.sap.com/saplt* or contact *slo.consulting@sap.com*.

14.7 SAP Solution Manager at SKW Stahl-Metallurgie Holding AG

Thanks to SAP Landscape Transformation, installed as an add-on on SAP Solution Manager, SKW Stahl-Metallurgie Holding AG can now access its newly adjusted company structure in their SAP ECC 6.4 application that meets the requirements of the company, which have grown over time.

Hartmut Koch, Project Manager at SAP Partner Consinto

SKW Stahl-Metallurgie Holding AG

Dynamic company development, as described by the history of SKW Stahl-Metallurgie Holding AG, is often the trigger for internal restructuring within a company. The current SKW Stahl-Metallurgie Holding AG developed from a global group whose colorful company history extends back to the start of the 20th century, a fact that is also reflected in the IT landscape. The SKW Metallurgie group is a global market leader for numerous chemical substances for iron desulphurization and secondary metallurgy. The primary focus is on the efficient production of high-quality steel products, which is based on more than 50 years of metallurgy expertise. In addition, the group produces and sells special Quab chemicals that are mainly used to produce starch and paper. The main customers of the SKW Metallurgie Group are manufacturers of high-grade steel, as is required, for example, in the automotive industry, for building ships and mechanical engineering, and plant engineering for the chemical and petrochemical industry, and well as the manufacture of white goods.

With its headquarters in Unterneukirchen (Germany), the SKW Metallurgie Group is active in more than 40 countries. It has a clear growth strategy: to build on its market leadership by opening additional production sites in developing countries to profit from the high demand in these regions. It currently has production sites in France, the United States, South Korea, Canada, Mexico, Brazil, Bhutan, Russian, Sweden, the PR of China, and India (joint ventures).

From SAP R/2 to SAP ECC 6.0

The consistent growth of today's SKW Metallurgie Group is based on numerous—national and international—start-ups and acquisitions, which let the company's IT environment grow increasingly complex over time. In addition to this, the SKW Metallurgie Group did not have an independent IT or SAP ERP system, despite the changes in the company's history.

Coming from the SAP R/2 world, different companies and subsidiaries of the SKW Metallurgie Group were mapped as company codes in a client of an SAP ECC 5.0 system. This goes back to former group affiliations which significantly restricted day-to-day business.

SKW entrusted the SAP partner Consinto with the project to split up the previous system environment with the objective to set up an independent SAP ECC 6.4 system for the SKW Stahl-Metallurgie Holding AG. Central steps of the project were these:

Project description

▶ Separation of the previous system landscape

▶ Setting up an independent SAP system for SKW Metallurgie

▶ Creating an archive system for all old SKW data

▶ The subsequent deletion of the SKW company code and data from the old system environment

The project was broken down into several parts. First of all, the relevant client that contained the SKW company code had to be copied from the source system (SAP Basis ECC 5.0), followed by an adjustment of the authorization concept.

In parallel, a blank SAP ECC 6.0 system was installed, which was to become the SKW system. To do so, the Customizing accounting for the *New General Ledger* (NGL) including a revised chart of accounts had to be set up. The Customizing logistics could be applied directly. Required repository objects were either adjusted or copied. Master data was transferred with the LSMW (Legacy System Migration Workbench). Finally, key date (balance sheet, P&L) had to be converted to a date after the conversion.

In the next step, an archive system (copy of the source system) had to be created, which was to contain only SKW-related company codes and data. This is where we used the new standard SAP Landscape Transformation software (SAP LT v.1) for the first time. This software was responsible for deleting all non-SKW company codes and data in this system. At the same time, we deleted all SKW-related company codes and data from the source system—also with SAP LT. Hence, there were two systems at the end: one system for SKW contents and one for all non-SKW-related contents.

SAP Landscape Transformation

The software, which is a fully integrated add-on for SAP Solution Manager 7.0, makes it possible to implement technical and business requirements while retaining data consistency under consideration of system integration aspects. The SAP standard tool is based on proven SAP business procedures—generated through various projects of the System Landscape Optimization Group—and has its own work center for controlling the entire process flow. The main thing is to adapt new processes, reporting structures, and controlling functions to the target structures of the company and adjust the technical infrastructure to the new business processes. This is mainly a task for the company's IT department.

The SAP *LT* work center of SAP Solution Manager provides an optimal way to delete company codes within a client and monitor the deletion. By merely specifying the company code, it was possible to derive all relevant SAP organizational elements, such as plants, controlling areas, and statistical data, and thus consider them for deletion. It was also easy to determine and take into account customer objects provided they were defined rule-compliant by means of SAP tools beforehand.

The SKW project was the first project in relation to deleting company codes with the new standard software SAP Landscape Transformation. It shows that the *Landscape Transformation* work center is very well integrated into SAP Solution Manager and thus enables consistent project management using only the work center. Thanks to SAP Landscape Transformation, installed as an add-on on SAP Solution Manager, SKW Stahl-Metallurgie Holding AG can now access its newly adjusted company structure in their SAP ECC 6.4 application that meets the requirements of the company, which have grown over time.

Mr. Ertl, Chief Financial Officer (CFO) at SKW is also happy with the project flow and confirmed that "the use of the SAP LT tool supports leaving the old, integrated SAP installation in an orderly and contract-compliant manner."

The Author

Hartmut Koch, Manager of SAP Solutions & Architecture at Consinto, completed a Master of Mathematics and Business at RWTH Aachen and then taught at the University Seminar of Economic Schloss Gracht, Erftstadt (today ESMT Campus Schloss Gracht). He has more than 20 years' experience as an SAP systems analyst and worked as an organizer and departmental manager for application development (with focus on SAP) for various manufacturing companies and service providers. He managed SAP migration projects (R/2-R/3), SAP installation projects, and currently manages projects related to spin-off and restructuring of companies and SAP landscapes.

Optimizing your custom code and enhancements for your SAP standard solutions sustainably reduces the costs of running SAP.

15 Custom Code Management: Efficient Management of Custom Code

The new SAP Solution Manager supports you in the management and optimization of your custom code and individual enhancements to the SAP standard solutions run by your company. It provides numerous tools that you can use effectively as part of the Application Lifecycle Management (ALM) process, Custom Code Management. Using these tools, you can analyze your specific custom code and enhancements with regard to their use in your systems, and thus get an overview of the totality of customer developments. Based on the results of the analysis, you can identify the customer developments that actually get used, and structure and control them better using the functions provided by SAP Solution Manager. The objective is to improve the quality and technical implementation while reducing the quantity and impact of enhancements on other objects. This helps you achieve sustainable cost reductions for the operation and maintenance of your SAP system landscape.

15.1 Introduction to Custom Code Management

Today's IT system landscapes are seldom comprised of homogeneous solutions. Beyond established software modules, gaps in the landscape are closed ad hoc, or standard business processes are enhanced in line with requirements. Your custom developments are an important element in your system landscape. Such developments become necessary when your standard software cannot map certain business processes as desired, and there is no specialized, ideally certified,

The current situation

solution on the market. A complex amalgamation of standard software, enhancements, and custom code quickly develops, driven by the need to respond to changing business requirements in a timely manner. The result is fast implementation of program code with a less pronounced focus on sustainability and transparency. Important factors such as complete documentation, the impact of changes on core business processes, and maintainability are not taken into account until planned or unplanned events change the overall system landscape and leave a multitude of questions regarding custom enhancements unanswered.

Testing requirements for custom code

Planned, recurring events such as minor and major software updates, or the introduction of new standard functions, can lead to increased testing requirements and significantly higher implementation costs for your custom developments. Unplanned events such as the need to implement new legal requirements, the use of new technology, or the need to adapt interfaces for external reasons also frequently present unexpected challenges with regard to custom enhancements. SAP proactively supports you in the targeted handling of all of these aspects.

15.1.1 The City Model

In light of the known characteristics (number, quality, type of implementation, degree of documentation, etc.) of custom enhancements and custom code, four primary dimensions were defined that can be measured and evaluated. The four dimensions are *quantity*, *quality*, *rating of the impact on core business processes,* and *classification of the technical implementation* in relation to the SAP standard. The model also considers the aspects of management and software lifecycle.

The visualization of custom enhancements and custom code with these metrics corresponds to the abstract representation of a city with buildings of various heights, colors, and locations within the city. Every city reflects an individual system within your system landscape.

Dimensions of the city model

Staying with this metaphor, as the forward-looking mayor of your own city comprised of multiple custom enhancements and custom code, you have a number of ways of beautifying or redeveloping the city. To keep this "beautification of the city" from devolving into a costly and arbitrary process, in the following, we will present the individual dimensions, tools, and services with which SAP supports you in your pursuit of a well-run, cost-effective, and forward-looking system landscape (see Figure 15.1).

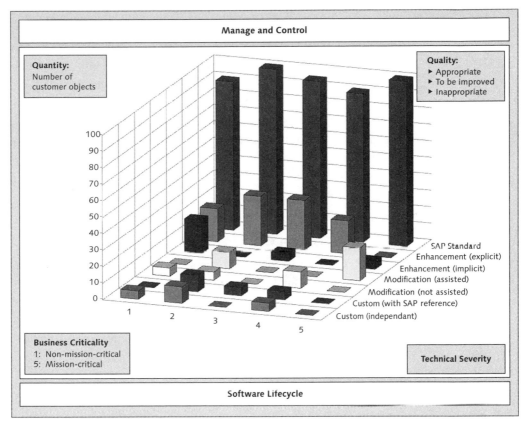

Figure 15.1 The City Model for Custom Code

In the QUANTITY dimension, customer-specific objects are recorded according to their object characteristics and categorized according to their technical implementation.

Quantity

The quality of program code is an often neglected but highly important factor in the development of custom adjustments. In the QUALITY dimension, SAP has made it possible to measure quality in a comparable way and thereby maintain quality standards.

Quality

Criticality and impact on core business processes

Your core business processes must be stable, ensure maximum availability, and correctly map your functional requirements at all times. SAP supports you in the analysis of the most frequently used system processes and shows you which of your frequently used core business processes are impacted by modifications or enhancements. You receive important information that is helpful for planning software updates or optimization.

Technical implementation

SAP NetWeaver provides a multitude of enhancements that in some cases go far beyond classical Customizing, enabling you to enhance and adapt standard processes to meet your requirements. Beyond the ability to implement and define implicit and explicit extension points (BAdIs, user exits, enhancement spots), you have the freedom to change SAP standard code at will through logged and unlogged modifications. Each of these system modifications has specific strengths and weaknesses, which should be evaluated based on maintainability, risk, and complexity.

15.1.2 The Custom Code Management Process

After you have assessed the current situation and transferred to the city model with your key indicators, you can start optimizing individual dimensions or improving your system landscape as a whole. *Custom Code Management* addresses precisely the aspects of the city model that deal with current business and IT requirements and the sustainable use of custom code, which will help you lay the groundwork for making the right decisions.

Three phases of the ALM process

This process, with its three phases TRANSPARENCY, OPTIMIZATION, and CONTROL (see Figure 15.2), is a fixed element of the Optimize phase of application management. It reflects the results of the other phases, in particular the early phases Design and Build & Test.

Transparency

The TRANSPARENCY phase allows you to use the application *Custom Code Lifecycle Management* (CCML) to get off to a structured start in the new SAP Solution Manager. The corresponding subpoints ensure that the definition is compatible with your requirements for a sustainable, generic, and always up-to-date custom code library. For more information about CCML, see Section 15.2.

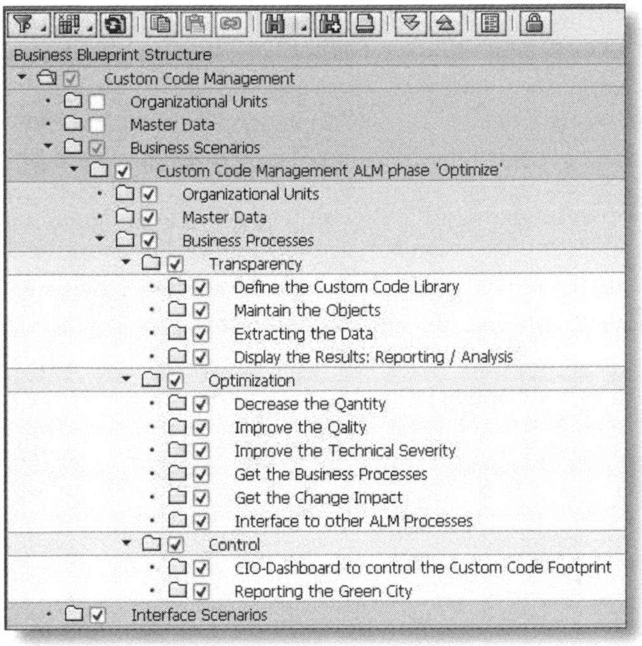

Figure 15.2 Custom Code Management in the Business Blueprint

The next phase utilizes the transparency and starts optimization. Here we look at the dimension *Technical Implementation*. This involves analyzing the nature and manner in which customer-specific business applications and enhancements are implemented. The objective is to move the individual implementations back toward the SAP standard. For example, a modification may be replaced by the use of a BAdI implementation. SAP supports this with the *Clonefinder* tool.

Site optimization— back to the standard

Product standards with key indicators such as the performance or maintainability of custom code and enhancements should be analyzed within their life phases and ideally improved as early as possible. SAP supports this with the *SAP Code Inspector* tool.

Quality optimization

Experience shows that within a few years, a third of custom developments are no longer in use or need to be adjusted. Before a software update such as an upgrade to a higher SAP release or the import of a support package (SP), all custom code and enhancements first have to be checked and adjusted manually. Then all objects have to be checked one by one to ensure that they do not cause problems in the new context. The *Custom Development Management Cockpit* (CDMC)

Custom Development Management Cockpit (CDMC)

has a project-based approach and supports you in the first step of analyzing the custom code and enhancements in your system. At the same time, it helps you identify obsolete objects and, in the second step, helps you determine the effects of an upgrade or SP installation. CCML supports you with a long-term approach with current usage key figures (see Section 15.2).

Any insights from the optimization area can be used to identify the optimization potential of other ALM phases and scenarios. Of particular interest here, for example, is raising the bar in the actual decision-making process for or against custom code or adding an additional check step to ensure quality in the software development process.

The final decisive area always reflects the success of the management or optimization. The data from CCML is extracted to the BW of SAP Solution Manager and can be used to assess success. Control and checking can thus be performed at any time.

15.2 Custom Code Lifecycle Management — Managing Custom Code

The management of custom code (CCLM) supplements tools already available in SAP Solution Manager such as the CDMC. CCLM was developed especially for the purpose of accompanying your ABAP enhancements and new developments throughout their lifecycles. This cycle begins when you create an object (program, transaction, table, class, etc.), followed by its use in production systems, and extends through the deletion of the object in case of non-use or a reorientation of the development.

This newly developed application is a part of the new SAP Solution Manager. The heart of the application is a generic library with which you can classify and manage objects developed by you. Information about the use of these objects, their quality (Code Inspector, Transaction SCI), and versions in the connected systems can also be collected if desired. You get an application that provides total transparency for your custom code and records its use in a complex landscape.

Generic library The generic library is used by SAP as the central data source for all information on customer objects. You benefit particularly from the possibilities of individual assignment of responsibilities and contracts, consolidation of developments within an organization, and total control over new developments. It is possible to assign any object or list of objects to a contract or other predefined attributes.

The objective in introducing this application is to ensure that you can achieve the best possible adaptation of custom code to SAP code and therefore receive the best possible support. You can also benefit from cost savings in possible upgrades to higher SAP releases.

> **Note**
>
> The version in the SAP Solution Manager currently only takes ABAP developments into account because extractors have only been provided for them. Expansion to include Java objects is technically possible and is already supported by the design.

15.2.1 Process and Architecture

The process steps and work with CCLM (Transaction CCLM) are shown in Figure 15.3. To begin, you must initialize the process and the application (steps 2–4). During ramp-up, SAP offers a service to execute the setup of the application. The following steps are described in detail in SAP Note 1547234.

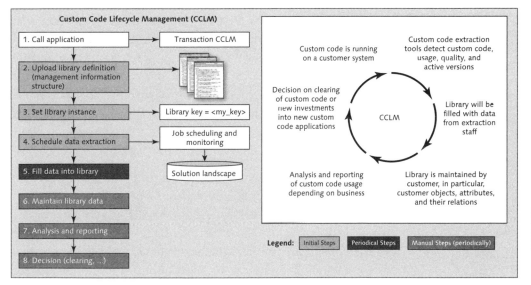

Figure 15.3 CCLM Process Overview

Defining the library

After the first call of Transaction CCLM, you first upload the library definition (step 2). You can change this definition to add your own input helps for predefined attributes or additional new attributes. You define a name for the library (step 3) and can then schedule the data collectors defined as part of the configuration (step 4). More information about the definition of the library and data collectors follows in the coming sections.

Periodic step 5 in Figure 15.3 illustrates the process of filling the library. The uploaded definition of the library contains a schema indicating which attributes exist for which objects with a particular cardinality and can be filled manually or automatically. The periodically scheduled programs ensure that information is collected and written or overwritten in accordance with this active definition. The information entered by you manually is not overwritten and is retained long-term.

The attributes for your individually developed objects that are not collected automatically, such as a lifecycle status or distribution rule, and particularly references to contracts and responsible persons, must be maintained manually. This is in step 6 in Figure 15.3. For more details about maintaining customer objects, see Section 15.2.5.

Analysis and reporting

Additional manual steps are possible in the analysis and reporting area (see step 7 in Figure 15.3). Depending on your installation of an SAP NetWeaver BW with the respective content, web templates are provided. You can also make your own reports. Reporting and the retention of historical data for use in the BW simplifies the decision regarding the deletion or consolidation of custom code. The BW is optional and is not active in the default setting in Transaction CCLM. The same applies to ad hoc reporting, which at the time of delivery is considerably more powerful than BW reporting.

Architecture

Figure 15.4 shows the general architecture of CCLM. The central rectangle stands for the generic library for managing custom code. In addition to the library definition, it contains the master data for customer objects and their transaction data such as use, quality, or version. The flexible structure of the library allows multiple instances of a library, though only one can be active. Control on the frontend is performed using a Web Dynpro interface. This interface is also used for additional elements such as settings, library definition, and object maintenance as well as analyses and reporting. The stored master and transaction data is collected by collectors. The collectors are controlled through the settings. The horizontal box in the lower part of Figure 15.4 represents the collector framework, which controls the data collection for customer objects, their use, and other data.

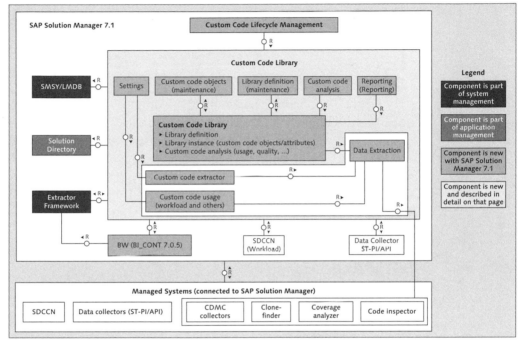

Figure 15.4 CCLM Architecture

The SOLUTION DIRECTORY in Figure 15.4 is used to get information about the individual solutions and the systems maintained within them. The SMSY/LMDB component (system landscape maintenance) is used to determine the product and product versions of the individual systems. The Extractor Framework is used to extract data to the BW system (generally SAP Solution Manager itself). In the managed systems, there is a series of data collectors (long box at the bottom end of Figure 15.4), of which the CDMC collector for the collection of customer objects, a collector for quality, and a collector for versions of the individual objects are connected. The use of objects—in particular in programs and transactions—is secured with the workload data from the analysis of the *Workload Monitor* (Transaction ST03N) collected by the SAP EarlyWatch Alert, whose collection modules are scheduled with the SAP EarlyWatch Alert using the administration tool Service Data Control Center (SDCCN). The data is formatted and transaction usage passed on to a corresponding report. There is also the *ABAP Coverage Analyzer* (Transaction SCOV), which documents the use of objects in the kernel. This application, also known as *Usage Procedure Logging* (UPL), as of basis version SAP NetWeaver 7.01 collects considerably more information about usage and in greater detail and documents dynamic calls not listed in the workload.

15.2.2 The CCLM Application in Detail

The application for managing custom code was completely developed in the Web Dynpro and is structured like a work center. The following sections provide detailed descriptions of all elements and their functions with which you can manage the lifecycle of your custom code. These include the following areas and views in Transaction CCLM:

▶ OVERVIEW

▶ SETTINGS

▶ LIBRARY DEFINITION

▶ OBJECTS

▶ REPORTS

Integrated applications
There are also three integrated applications you can use: the CDMC, the Extractor Framework, and an extensive ad-hoc reporting function. The CDMC application is primarily used as a project-based application and is therefore linked with Transaction CCLM. The Extractor Framework is a prerequisite for BW integration, and ad hoc reporting is used to evaluate data in the library. For more information about CDMC, see Section 15.3.

Overview
Figure 15.5 shows the initial screen of Transaction CCLM, which can be called with the SAP NetWeaver Business Client, among others. This screen gives you a quick overview of your custom code and allows you to navigate to the various views.

Every view contains different groups, and the number next to a group indicates the number of objects in the group. You can access the selected view and group directly using a link. The first area in the

OVERVIEW is the SETTINGS. Here the following groups are displayed for all systems and active systems:

- MY SYSTEMS – <MY SOLUTION>
- ALL SYSTEMS – ALL SOLUTIONS
- MY ACTIVE SYSTEMS – <MY SOLUTION>
- ALL ACTIVE SYSTEMS

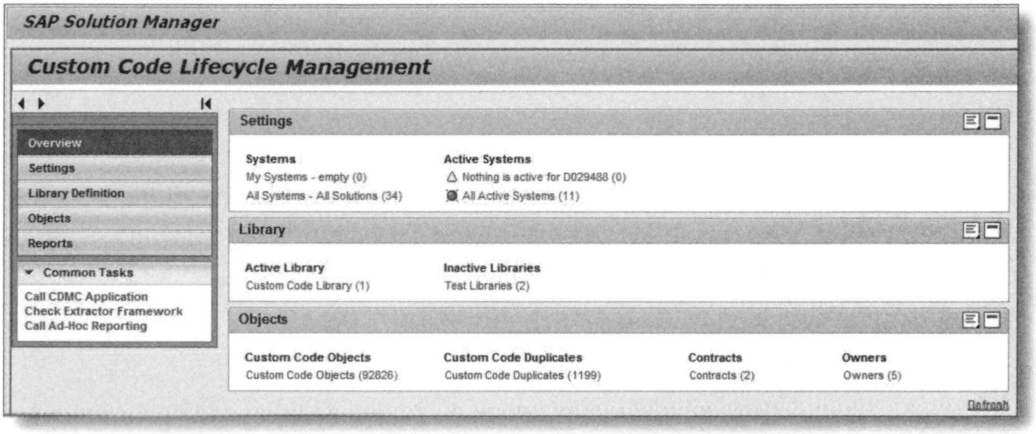

Figure 15.5 Transaction CCLM Overview

The personalized displays depend on which solution you selected the last time you called Transaction CCLM. Nothing is displayed here the first time you call it.

For the active systems, a status is displayed as well. The following statuses have a fixed definition: **Status**

- **Green**
  All collectors are scheduled and are running without errors.
- **Yellow**
  At least one collector has not been scheduled.
- **Red**
  At least one collector has terminated or encountered an error.

The second area in the OVERVIEW is the LIBRARY. Generally, only one active library is displayed here, that is, the one that was uploaded during the technical configuration:

▶ ACTIVE LIBRARY

One or no active library is loaded in the application.

▶ INACTIVE LIBRARIES

Inactive libraries have been uploaded for testing purposes.

Objects   The third area—OBJECTS—shows the objects that have been created in the library. The focus is on the objects developed by you, their duplicates, and the objects that you can create, such as the CONTRACTS and OWNERS. The value in parentheses stands for the respective number of objects in the library. From a technical standpoint, duplicates are objects that have identical entries in the TADIR table, which is only possible if there is more than one development system in which the same object can be created again. The system does not distinguish whether the duplicate has the same function or not. Distinguishing such objects is done through the source system, which is also stored in the TADIR table.

15.2.3 Settings

Figure 15.6 contains a view of the settings that can be made for the selected systems. The list of systems contains additional information about the product and version for each system. The first column displays an overall status for the collectors of the system with the status defined above.

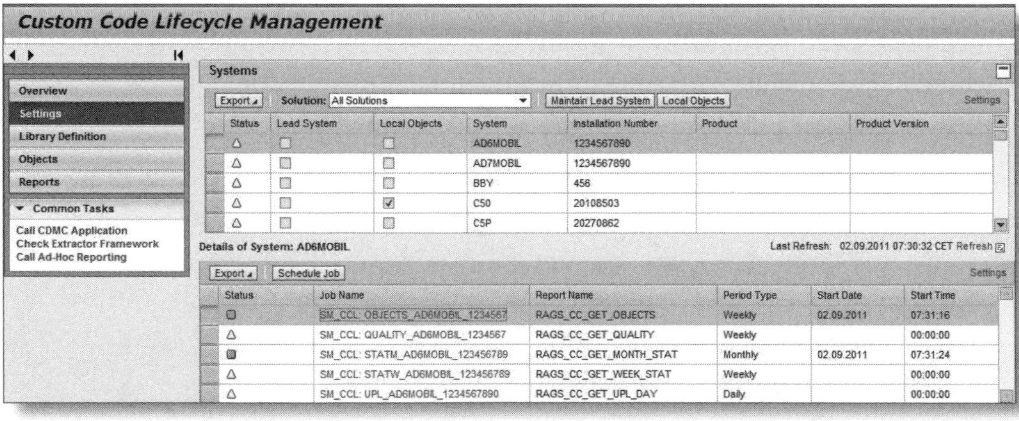

Figure 15.6 Custom Code Lifecycle Management Settings

The status displayed is always the worst status; that is, if all jobs are running or scheduled successfully but one, the red or yellow status of the terminated or unscheduled job is displayed as the overall status. A configurable propagation does not exist.

The system list also contains columns for setting a leading system and settings for local objects. Development systems should be set as the leading systems because collectors are set so that only the attributes of the leading system are overwritten. This prevents the characteristics of objects being overwritten by collectors in an uncontrolled manner. If, for example, the development class of an object in the development system has been changed, and the object is released and transferred to the test system, the production system has an old development class. Depending on the order in which the collectors are currently running, only the attribute DevClass may be updated, which is not the objective. Local objects are another story. It is not a good idea to collect these objects in a development system; developers want to test or try things, and such objects do not belong in the library. Moreover, such local objects will never be transported to a production system. But there are local objects in production systems, and here it makes sense to collect this information and write it to the library to establish transparency with regard to such objects.

Leading system

The setting for the leading system has another important meaning for the management of custom code. The attribute ObjectFound is automatically updated when the object is found in a leading system by the collector. If an object is deleted, this attribute is no longer updated, and the attribute Deleted_Flag can be set by a periodically scheduled job. This makes the deletion of objects transparent without the connection to a transport repository.

For each selected system, there is a list with detailed information about scheduled collectors (refer to Figure 15.6). The first column displays the rating with the status. The following columns display the name of the collector, the name of the report, the type of periodic scheduling, and, for a scheduled job, the last successful execution or next scheduling as well.

Information about collectors

The most important collector that collects data from the managed systems is the collector for customer objects. This collector also collects the version of the object in the respective system, if a version exists. Transactions, for instance, have no version because generally a report (program) is stored that has a version and is executed separately. There are also collectors that determine statistics regarding the use of programs and transactions (workload data). To do so, the SAP EarlyWatch Alert Service scheduled in SAP Solution Manager and its download are used. Therefore, it is not necessary to collect additional data from the collected systems. Depending on the SAP Basis version of the connected system, there is also a kernel-based data collector that collects data on the use of other objects such as classes, methods, or tables (usage procedure logging). You also have the option of importing quality information about custom code from the Code Inspector. However, we recommend using the latter collectors only in production and test systems.

15.2.4 Library Definition

The library definition is delivered with an XML file and is part of the general SAP Note 1547234. This definition contains objects, attributes, and the relationships between objects and attributes. Changes and modifications can be executed during the technical implementation. Figure 15.7 shows an active library definition and additional inactive test versions.

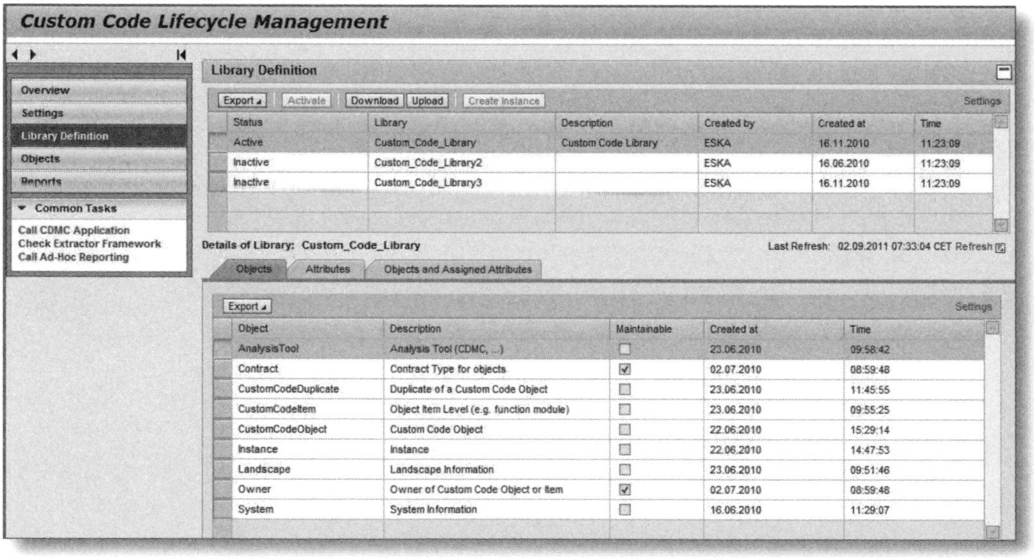

Figure 15.7 Custom Code Lifecycle Management Library Definition

It is possible to add any attribute. A distinction is made between maintainable and automatic or standard attributes. Only maintainable attributes can be created, changed, or deleted using Transaction

CCLM. Value helps (search helps) can be stored for any attribute. An automatic check of the values is then executed. This is particularly useful for references to objects or special attributes with default values.

The data model is designed so that it can be extended at will. At first, however, there is only a library definition. Only one instance of the library can be active at a time. In the current version, you can freeze at least one instance and continue working in another.

15.2.5 Objects in the Library

The objects collected by the collector are displayed in Figure 15.8 as a list. In addition to the object ID, the object class, and the technical name, the creation date in the library as well as the change date and the last changer are displayed. There is a filter area above the list that can be expanded. There are also filtering options for every column in the list. An additional search function enables the search for special attributes that can be assigned to the objects. This search function may be rather time-consuming depending on the number of objects and the hit list. We recommend setting a filter to 200 or 500 hits to ensure that the result can be displayed quickly.

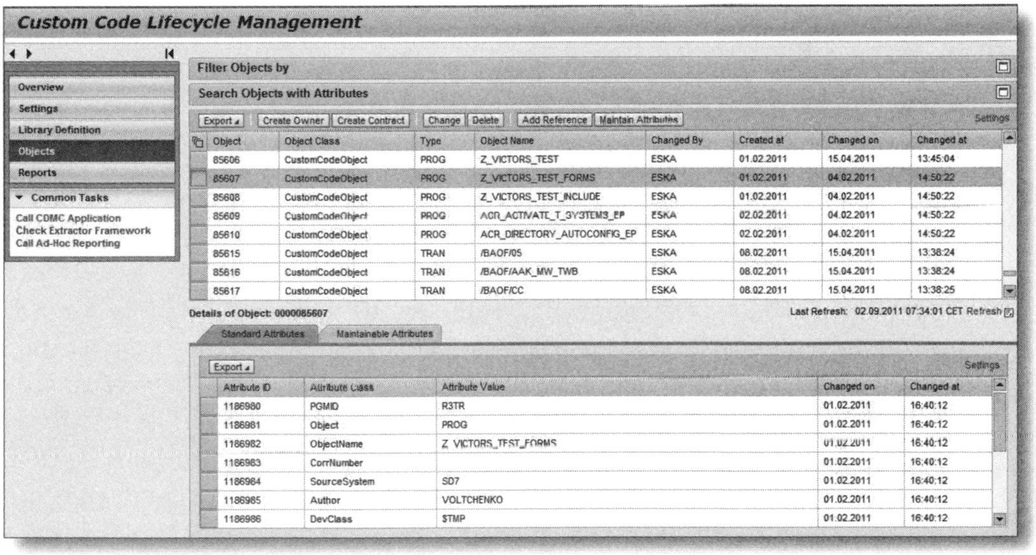

Information about objects

Figure 15.8 Objects in the Library

Functions for objects

There are numerous functions for the displayed objects, such as the assignment of references and maintenance of attributes. You can also create, change, and delete the objects OWNER and CONTRACT. The list is designed so that you can select multiple objects and thus perform a sort of mass maintenance. One example would be the assignment of a maintenance contract to all objects of a particular development class. To do so, you must set a filter for the respective development class in the list. In this way, you can select all objects in the first column before the object ID at once. Then you can click the ADD REFERENCE button, select the desired contract in a popup, and confirm your selection.

Which attributes have been set or maintained by you are displayed in the object details for each object in the list below the object list in Figure 15.8. The standard attributes for a customer object either come from the TADIR table or are defined and non-maintainable attributes from the definition that are automatically filled; for example the attribute Ref_2_System, where the system in which the object with the respective object ID was found is listed. Optionally, there is a tab that stores changeable attributes. Here you have the option of creating, changing, or deleting changeable attributes. The attributes of an object that can be changed or created are defined in the library definition.

15.2.6 Reporting

Ad-Hoc Reporting

A comprehensive reporting function known as *Ad-Hoc Reporting* is available. You can find this application as a link under COMMON TASKS. Figure 15.9 shows the initial screen for reporting with various areas.

The library information with key, ID and version must always be filled to get results. Then you can make a preselection as to whether you want to evaluate ALL OBJECTS, NEW OBJECTS, USED OBJECTS, or UNUSED OBJECTS. There is then a system selection for the transaction data, which is the only data for which system information is saved. The most common scenario is the use of objects, but evaluation can also be done on the basis of quality or version. The latter option is especially interesting if you want to ensure for particular objects that the same version exists in all connected systems. The time selection option enables you to restrict reporting to a particular time period.

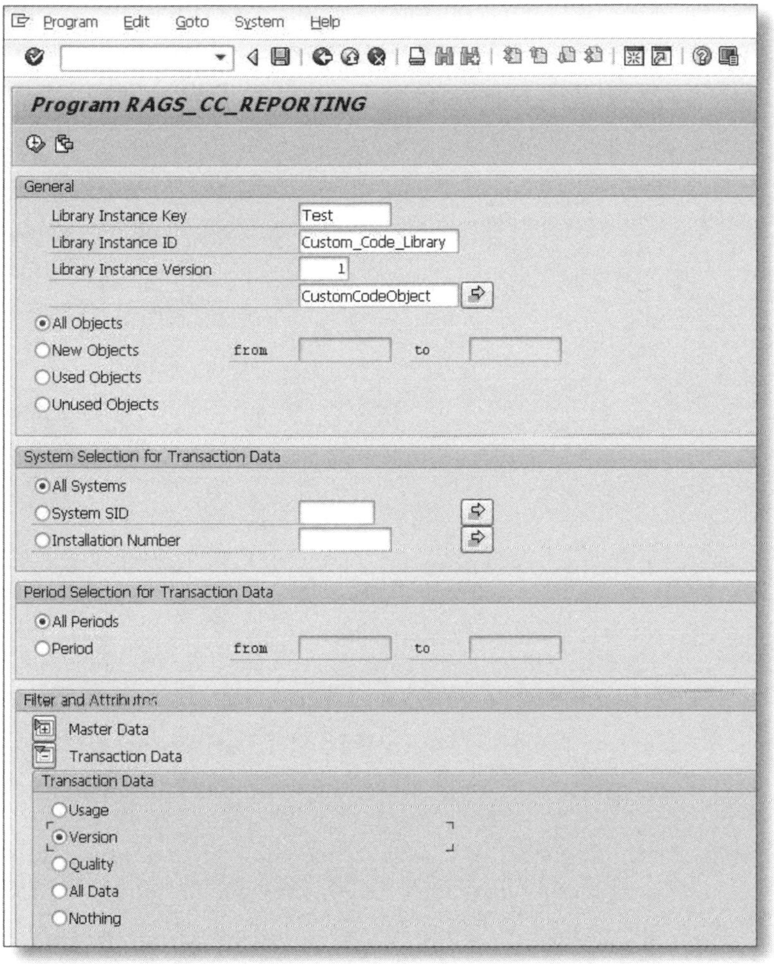

Figure 15.9 Ad-Hoc Reporting

Filters and attributes allow you to control the search for particular data as well as the output with the number of columns. You can filter by any particular attribute or combination of attributes. This also applies to references to the objects OWNER and CONTRACT. Here, the columns that appear depending on the entries in the output list are also predefined. Subsequently, you can select the attributes that you want to appear as columns in the output list.

Filter and attributes

For transaction data, you can select by use, version, quality, or none of these. We recommend that you save your frequently used settings as variants of the report. This allows you to start reporting faster and get results faster.

BW reporting There is also a BW-based reporting function, and you can load your own or SAP Web templates in the report view. Figure 15.10 shows the view with a report; this is the same view that is used in two other applications (business process operations and job management).

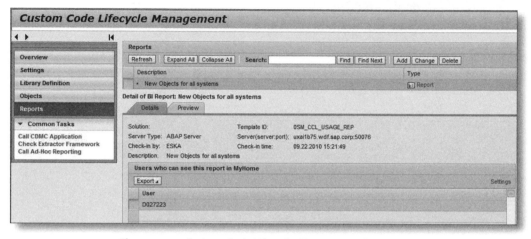

Figure 15.10 Custom Code Lifecycle Management Reports

15.3 Custom Code Development Management Cockpit

Many SAP customers modify or enhance their SAP standard software. For example, they may create company-specific reports or custom (externally or internally developed) add-ons. Using custom code and modifications enables companies to adapt business processes to market requirements. The result of this natural development is a multitude of customer objects and modified SAP standard objects in circulation.

Obsolescence of customer objects However, requirements change so quickly that many customer objects and changes to SAP standard objects quickly become obsolete. Experience shows that after just a few years, a third of custom code is either no longer in use or has been modified, not only due to fast-changing requirements but also because new versions of the SAP standard software contain objects that render custom code useless. This can lead to unnecessarily high maintenance costs, which in turn cause high operating costs.

For customers, it can be difficult to keep up with the pace of modifications to the standard system and produce custom code. Numerous changes and customer objects also raise the cost of upgrades and importing SPs. Before a system can be upgraded to a newer SAP version or a SP can be imported, all custom code must be checked and manually adjusted. Then all objects have to be checked one by one to ensure that they do not cause problems in the new context.

Using the Custom Development Management Cockpit (CDMC), you can determine how custom code is used (based on the call statistics provided by the system) and which customer-specific developments are obsolete. The CDMC then evaluates the effects of an upgrade or a SP installation on custom code. The business process documentation for custom code is also determined (maintenance using Transaction SOLAR02). CDMC supports the project or release manager in evaluating risk by analyzing objects from transport orders before importing them into the production system.

You must ensure that planned changes are implemented in line with business requirements. CDMC simplifies upgrade projects by reducing the amount of obsolete custom code. Upgrades can be performed more quickly because you only have to modify your custom code if it is absolutely necessary. CDMC supports project planning by enabling early estimation of the costs of adjusting object types that are required for a more current version. You profit from better and more reliable planning, shorter project runtimes, and thus reduced costs. Another advantage is that the objects in transport orders are analyzed before being imported into the target system.

Speeding up upgrades

Using key figures and collected data, you can optimize the performance of a solution and reduce costs. CDMC simplifies the deletion of obsolete custom code based on the usage analysis executed as part of the requirements analysis and the Build & Test phase.

Deleting objects

The CDMC determines the scope of customer developments. CDMC has three phases:

CDMC phases

1. **Clearing Analysis**
   This phase analyzes the use of customer objects. Obsolete objects and the corresponding business process documentation of the customer objects are determined (in Transaction SOLAR02). The result of the Clearing Analysis is the starting point for cleaning up

the developments. Detailed instructions guide you through the *clearing process*.

2. **Upgrade/Change Impact Analysis**
   This phase identifies the technical effects of an SAP upgrade or the installation of a SP on customer-developed objects and makes it possible to produce an estimate of the time and effort required to adjust these objects. The function determines the custom code to be used after the upgrade and the scope of the respective business process documentation.

3. **CTS Analysis (change and transport system)**
   In this phase, the use of objects in a transport order, the test scope, and the test coverage are analyzed. It is determined whether the state of the objects in the transport order is identical throughout the transport system landscape.

The CDMC can be called in the *Implementation/Upgrade* work center of SAP Solution Manager or in the Custom Code Management application (see Figure 15.11).

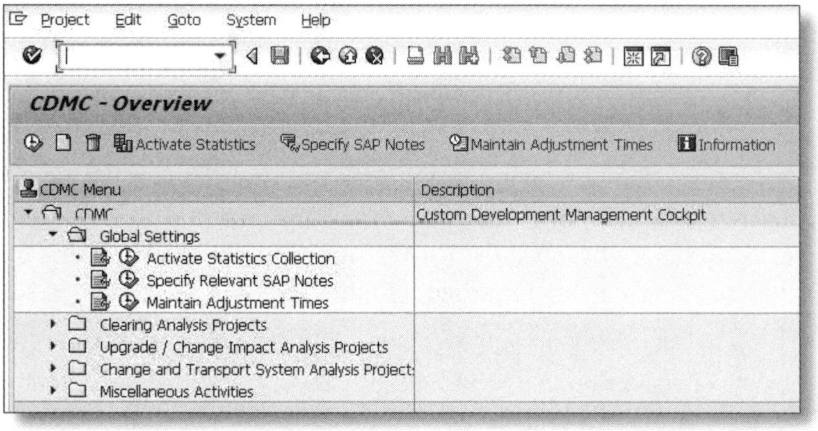

Figure 15.11 CDMC Overview Screen

Clearing Analysis project — Figure 15.12 shows the system landscape of a Clearing Analysis project.

In the statistics system, statistical data, such as data about executed transactions, is gathered and saved in CDMC database tables. All project-relevant analyses are executed in the analysis system. The control system includes the control center where all activities are triggered and monitored. The systems are connected by remote function call (RFC). Several pairs of statistics and analysis systems can be assigned to a control system.

Custom Development Management Cockpit - Clearing Analysis

Project ID : 00001
User : TEGI_GENERAL

The landscape for this project is as follows

System Type	RFC Destination
Control Center	NONE
Analysis Systems	CDMC_ANALYSIS
Statistics Systems	CDMC_STAT

Figure 15.12 Clearing Analysis System Landscape

In a typical system landscape (as represented in Figure 15.13), the statistics system represents the production system, and the analysis system corresponds to the consolidation system. The platform for the control system is SAP Solution Manager.

CDMC Customer Project	Status	Activity Log	Start Date	Start Time	End Date	End Time
00004						
Project Settings						
Define Project Landscape	OOO		21.11.2010	22:37:10		
Display SAP Notes						
Collect						
Determine Customer Objects	OOO		21.11.2010	22:37:25	21.11.2010	22:37:32
Determine SAP Modifications	OOO		21.11.2010	22:37:30	21.11.2010	22:43:32
Import Statistics	OOO		21.11.2010	22:55:38	21.11.2010	22:55:39
Analysis						
Duplicate Domains	OOO		21.11.2010	22:56:04	21.11.2010	23:00:50
Determine Empty Databases	OOO		21.11.2010	22:56:03	21.11.2010	22:59:22
Syntax Check	OOO		21.11.2010	22:56:34	21.11.2010	22:59:11
Transport Frequency	OOO		21.11.2010	23:12:59	21.11.2010	23:13:14
Inactive Customer Objects	OOO		21.11.2010	23:13:01	21.11.2010	23:13:01
Perform Usage Analysis	OOO		21.11.2010	23:13:09	21.11.2010	23:13:34
Objects with no Reference	OOO		21.11.2010	23:13:45	21.11.2010	23:20:22
Enhancements	OOO		21.11.2010	23:13:49	21.11.2010	23:19:30
Confirm Analysis	OOO		21.11.2010	23:24:18	21.11.2010	23:24:36
Display						
Display Results						
Clearing						
How to guide for Clearing						

Figure 15.13 Clearing Analysis Phases

The Clearing Analysis has five phases (see Figure 15.13):

Clearing Analysis phases

1. PROJECT SETTINGS

   In this phase, the system landscape is defined, and the relevant SAP Notes are called. You can select the systems for the project landscape from the SAP Solution Manager system landscape.

2. COLLECT

   The activities in this phase include collecting statistical data in the statistics system and identifying the custom code and modified SAP objects in the analysis system. The collected statistical data is then imported from the statistics system into the central system. The scope of the customer-developed objects for the analysis can be selected from the list of development classes, SAP Solution Manager projects, and SAP Solution Manager solutions.

3. ANALYSIS

   In this phase, duplicate domains in the customer namespace and empty database tables are determined; syntax is checked; the transport frequency, inactive objects, and objects without references are determined; and top-down analysis is performed. These are the most important functions for determining the usage of customer-developed objects. The syntax check and all activities associated with empty databases are executed in the statistics system. You can control the execution by entering date and time information.

4. DISPLAY

   In this phase, you can view the results. There are numerous options for displaying and filtering the data.

5. CLEARING

   This phase completes the Clearing Analysis project with the *clearing process*, in which objects from the customer namespace (Z*, Y*, and namespaces with customer-specific prefixes) are deleted or changes to standard objects in the SAP namespace are undone. The clearing process is different for these two cases. Obsolete modifications to SAP objects are removed using SAP standard tools, while obsolete objects that are assigned to the customer namespace are physically deleted according to SAP clearing guidelines. To optimize the clearing process, the clearing tools you use should correspond to the SAP standard procedure for deleting objects (ABAP Workbench) so that when you delete a master object (e.g., an object of type PROG) all other dependent objects (e.g., text elements) are automatically deleted. This ensures that all relevant objects are really deleted. Otherwise, dependent objects would remain in the system even if they are no longer used, and then be found by later clearing projects. This process of deleting and restoring (accidentally deleted) obsolete objects is described in the clearing instructions.

The system landscape in an Upgrade/Change Impact Analysis project is displayed in Figure 15.14.

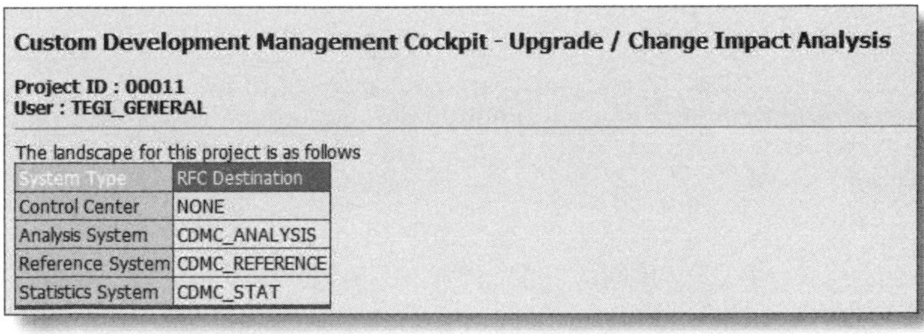

Upgrade/change impact analysis project

Custom Development Management Cockpit - Upgrade / Change Impact Analysis

Project ID : 00011
User : TEGI_GENERAL

The landscape for this project is as follows

System Type	RFC Destination
Control Center	NONE
Analysis System	CDMC_ANALYSIS
Reference System	CDMC_REFERENCE
Statistics System	CDMC_STAT

Figure 15.14 System Landscape in a CDMC Upgrade/Change Impact Analysis Project

The Change Impact Analysis project is managed in the control system. Analysis systems and reference systems are part of the same project but have different product versions. In the analysis systems, objects developed by the customers are analyzed to determine how the modifications of SAP objects affect them. The reference system shows the system in which the upgrade or other planned change has already been made so that the SAP objects appear in this system in the changed version. When analyzing the effects, this version is compared to the unchanged version in the analysis system. In the statistics system, statistical data, for example about executed transactions, is gathered and saved in CDMC database tables.

In a typical system landscape, SAP Solution Manager is the platform of the control system. The analysis system can be a quality assurance system. The reference system is a non-production system, for example, a test system or the reference information basis. The statistics system is optional and can be added to obtain usage information for customer-developed objects or to execute a Change Impact Analysis. This is generally the production system.

When defining a project landscape for an Upgrade/Change Impact Analysis, you can choose between a reference system and a reference information basis. The reference information basis represents an alternative to the reference system. You use the reference information basis to collect the SAP objects that are modified by an upgrade. The reference information basis determines the upgrade project budget to decide whether a test upgrade is required. You can select the

Defining a project landscape

systems for the project landscape from the SAP Solution Manager system landscape.

UCIA phases   The Upgrade/Change Impact Analysis is divided into three phases (see Figure 15.15 Upgrade/Change Impact Analysis Phases):

CDMC Customer Project	Status	Activity Log	Start Date	Start Time	End Date	End Time
▾ 🗂 00011						
▾ 🗂 Project Settings						
• 📄 ⊕ Define Project Landscape	⚬⚬⚬	🖳	24.11.2010	21:02:58		
• 📄 ⊕ Get Copied Program List	⚬⚬⚬	🖳	24.11.2010	21:00:08	24.11.2010	21:20:25
• 📄 ⊕ Maintain Copied Program List						
• 📄 ⊕ Display SAP Notes						
• 📄 ⊕ Maintain Adjustment Times	⚬⚬⚬	🖳	24.11.2010	21:03:06		
▾ 🗂 Analysis						
• 📄 ⊕ Find Referred SAP Objects	⚬⚬⚬	🖳	24.11.2010	22:10:05	24.11.2010	22:17:40
• 📄 ⊕ Import Statistics	⚬⚬⚬	🖳	24.11.2010	22:35:31	24.11.2010	22:35:31
• 📄 ⊕ Perform Usage Analysis	⚬⚬⚬	🖳	24.11.2010	22:35:34	24.11.2010	22:37:12
• 📄 ⊕ Find Changed SAP Objects	⚬⚬⚬	🖳	24.11.2010	22:38:14	24.11.2010	22:38:14
• 📄 ⊕ Perform Remote Comparison	⚬⚬⚬	🖳	24.11.2010	22:38:18	24.11.2010	22:39:32
• 📄 ⊕ Calculate Adjustment Times						
• 📄 ⊕ Customer Batch Input Analysis						
• 📄 ⊕ Analyse Ext. Subroutine Calls						
▾ 🗂 Display Results						
• 📄 ⊕ Display Results						

Figure 15.15 Upgrade/Change Impact Analysis Phases

1. PROJECT SETTINGS

    In this phase, among other things, the system landscape is defined, the list of cloned/copied programs is called, the SAP Notes relevant to the upgrade are displayed, and the time and effort required for adjusting the individual object types is estimated.

2. ANALYSIS

    In the second phase, various analyses are executed. For example, a list is created of all SAP objects referenced in custom code, which will be changed in an upgrade. Finally, the SAP objects in the currently active version in the analysis system are compared to their new counterparts in the reference system. CDMC evaluates the effects of each change to an SAP object and classifies the affected customer objects according to these effects. In the second phase, you can also call usage information for the customer objects and a Change Impact Analysis. An estimate of the effort required to adjust the customer objects is also made at this point. In this phase, CDMC determines the effects on all customer objects referenced in batch data communication programs and in calls of external subroutines.

3. DISPLAY RESULTS

    After the comparison has been executed, the results of the analysis can be displayed in the last phase. The CDMC environment provides various options for displaying and filtering the data. You can also assign a processor. In this procedure, you grant someone the authorization to analyze the object in greater detail and make a decision regarding the further use of the object.

In the results list, all customer objects are listed according to the probability of a required change:

Probability of changes

▶ A green traffic light means that the object does not have to be changed due to the planned upgrade or change.

▶ A yellow traffic light means that the object probably has to be changed.

▶ A red traffic light means that the object very probably has to be adjusted to ensure that it functions correctly after the upgrade or change.

Classifying the affected customer developments enables a more precise estimation of the time and effort required to adjust the objects. CDMC ensures a high degree of transparency for customer developments and modifications and thus plays a significant role in reducing maintenance and project costs.

The system landscape of a CTS analysis project is displayed in Figure 15.16.

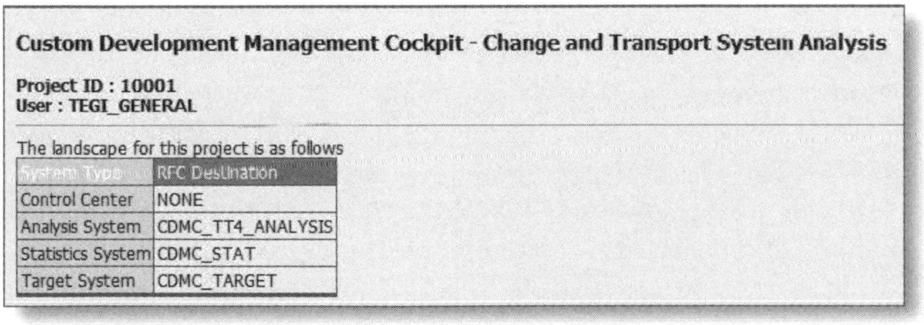

Clearing Analysis project

Custom Development Management Cockpit - Change and Transport System Analysis

Project ID : 10001
User : TEGI_GENERAL

The landscape for this project is as follows

System Type	RFC Destination
Control Center	NONE
Analysis System	CDMC_TT4_ANALYSIS
Statistics System	CDMC_STAT
Target System	CDMC_TARGET

Figure 15.16 System Landscape of a CDMC-CTS Analysis

The CTS analysis project is also managed in the control system. The analysis system is the consolidation system that contains a list of the objects in the transport order that are to be released in the target system. The statistics system is the production system that is used to call the actively used reports and transactions. The target system is the system into which the transport order is imported.

In a typical system landscape, the statistics system represents the production system, and the analysis system corresponds to the consolidation system. The platform for the control system is SAP Solution Manager.

CTS analysis phases

The CTS analysis is divided into four phases (see Figure 15.17):

1. PROJECT SETTINGS

   This phase includes tasks such as defining the system landscape and determining the object list for the transport order in the analysis system. The object list defines the scope of the analysis.

2. COLLECT

   In this phase, modified SAP objects, enhancements (customer exits, BAdIs, business transaction events, etc.), and the customer objects are identified using the object list in the transport order. This enables you to identify custom code in the transport order.

CDMC Customer Project	Status	Activity Log	Start Date	Start Time	End Date	End Time
10001						
Project Settings						
Define Project Landscape	OOO		22.07.2011	16:43:15		
Determine Object Set	OOO		22.07.2011	16:43:31	22.07.2011	16:43:31
Collect						
Determine Modified Objects	OOO		22.07.2011	16:43:39	22.07.2011	16:43:39
Determine Enhancements	OOO		22.07.2011	16:43:40	22.07.2011	16:43:45
Customer and Ref SAP Objects	OOO		22.07.2011	16:43:48	22.07.2011	16:43:49
Analysis						
Test Scope Identification	OOO		22.07.2011	16:44:03	22.07.2011	16:44:04
Perform Environment Analysis	OOO		22.07.2011	16:44:08	22.07.2011	16:44:11
Test Coverage Analysis	OOO		22.07.2011	16:44:15	22.07.2011	16:44:26
Perform Remote Comparison						
Display						
Display Results						

Figure 15.17 System Landscape of a CTS Analysis

3. ANALYSIS

   In this phase, you can display the modifications to reports and transactions that are already in use in the production system and define the test scope of the objects before releasing them in the production system. Changed reports or transactions that are not executed in the analysis system are also determined to ascertain the test scope of the objects in the test phase. You must specify the time period for the collection of data from the statistics/analysis system. In this phase, you can also call up the result of the version comparison in the transport orders as well as the comparison result for the dependent objects. In this way, you can avoid errors due to missing dependent objects, for example, before the import of transport orders, and ensure that all objects in all systems have the same version.

4. DISPLAY

In this phase, you can view the results. You have numerous options for displaying and filtering the data.

In the results list, each originally selected object in the transport order is classified according to the status that resulted from the comparison of the analysis and target systems:

Status

▶ A green traffic light means that the object has the same version in both systems.

▶ A red traffic light means that the object occurs in different versions or that the object does not exist in one of the systems.

This evaluation applies also to dependent objects that were called up in the environment analysis of the objects in the transport orders. The usage analysis of the objects in the statistics and analysis systems is displayed in the results list.

The CDMC-CTS project analyzes the objects as a record of transport orders. This enables the project or release manager to estimate the risk before the transport orders are imported into the production or target system.

15.4 Analyses for Custom Code

In the world of custom code, there are two defining questions. How is the quality of custom code, and how did the customer programs come about?

There is no general answer to these two questions, and any attempt to find a generally valid answer always leads to discussions. We therefore want to approach the problem pragmatically and, with the aid of tools, outline a comprehensive analysis of the problem.

To this purpose, SAP offers the new *Custom Code Analysis* tool, which can help you resolve the fundamental issues regarding custom code. We divide the tool into different use cases. Let's begin with the simplest use scenario: identifying clones.

Custom Code
Analysis

679

15.4.1 Distinguishing SAP Original Objects from Clones

Clowns

An amusing play on words describes the problem with clones quite simply, combining the words *clone* and *own* to create "clowns." While the creation of a clown is a simple matter and appears to avoid the need to pursue an unwanted customer-specific modification, shortly thereafter it is creating havoc in the system. Perhaps unknown or seldom executed, the clown always carries the risk of not containing a required standard correction. Perhaps the clown is based on an obsolete software status or release and is maintained in the customer namespace with each new upgrade. Only in rare cases is it possible to derive the SAP original object from its clone. That would require comprehensive project documentation. While this problem may sound trivial, the potential effects of undocumented clones are difficult to foresee.

Clonefinder

SAP now offers you an effective tool, the Clonefinder (see Figure 15.18), which provides an easy way for you to find the SAP original program for a clone.

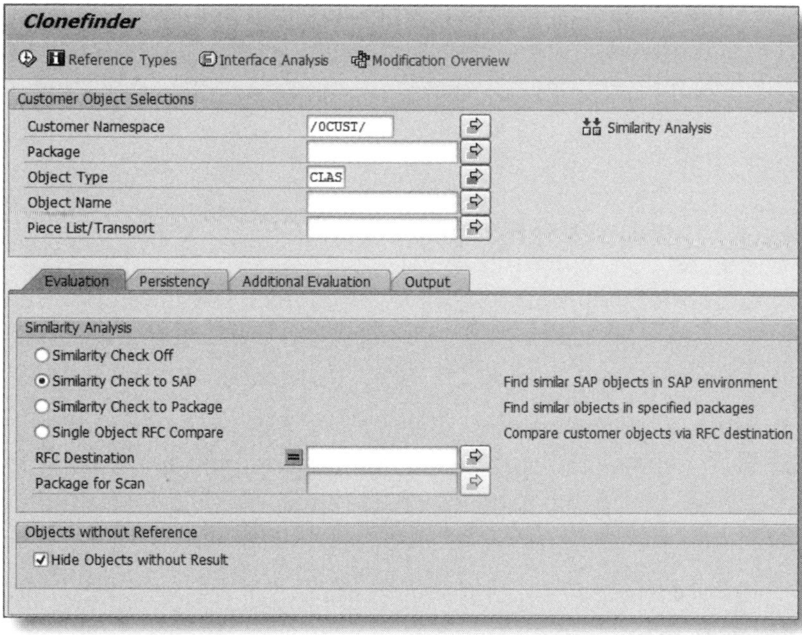

Figure 15.18 Clonefinder

Potential similarities are not determined on the basis of names alone. Rather, notable places in the coding, such as typos in comment lines or patterns in contiguous program sections are used to determine unique system-wide fingerprints for each customer program to be analyzed. In a subsequent step, the logical SAP environment of the customer program is determined and the potential SAP program candidates output by a complex similarity algorithm. The advantage of this approach is the incredible speed and reduced number of theoretically necessary comparison operations. The main distinguishing characteristic compared to other tools is the possibility of real similarity analysis. This tool even recognizes sections of code that have been copied and pasted from the SAP program library to the customer namespace.

Using the Clonefinder, in just a few steps you can determine the name of the SAP original object and how it has been further developed through notes and corrections (see Figure 15.19). It also enables you to identify your custom code, which, through inheritance, has followed an evolutionary path of its own, and distinguish the different versions. Even without a similarity analysis with SAP objects, the tool provides you with the ability to analyze completely unknown user-developed code. You find out which logical application areas and how many lines of code the program being analyzed has, as well as how many versions of it are in circulation.

Customer Object Name	Size	Creation Date	G	S	Refer.	Reference Type	Object Type	SAP Interface Object Name
Z_PROJ_DOCUMENTATION	55	11.03.2010			📄	Very Similar Source Code	Program	AGS_SOLAR_EVAL_TRAN_TBOM
ZDTABREORG	88	27.05.2010			📄		Program	/SSF/DTABREORG
LZSMD_FUNCTOP	125	04.06.2008			📄	Similar Source Code	Report Source Code	LSMD_FUNCTOP
SAPLZSMD_FUNC	4	04.06.2008			📄		Report Source Code	SAPLSMD_FUNC
Z_SGEN_SPEEDUP	100	05.02.2010			📄		Program	RSPARAGENLOD
Z>DCAU39	66	18.12.2010			📄		Program	/SSF/SYSINFOS
Z>EXSF01	98	22.10.2008			📄		Program	/SSF/DLBROWSER
Z>XDYU01	17	11.09.2008			📄		Program	/SSF/ULIB
ZRSCVR_COLLECT	244	25.01.2010			📄		Program	RSCVR_COLLECT
Z_GET_ST14_DOWNLOADS	71	01.12.2008			📄	Partly Similar Source Code	Program	/SSF/DLTRANSFER
Z_SCOV_ON	79	25.01.2010			📄		Program	RSCVR_TRIGGER_COLLECT
Z_TRANSFER_BENCHMARK_GUIDS	160	13.04.2010			📄		Program	/SSF/DLBROWSER
Z_TRANSFER_GUIDS	161	05.12.2008			📄		Program	/SSF/DLBROWSER

Figure 15.19 Finding Clowns Results List

The Clonefinder offers you a fast and simple introduction to the area of Custom Code Management and helps you actively reduce clones. SAP focuses on the identification and evaluation of clones and intentionally stays away from a method of comparing deltas between the clone and the original. Our goal is to reduce "clowns" and not simply make them more manageable.

15.4.2 Identifying the Usage Area of Clones

Static where-used list

To answer the question of where custom code is used, many developers use the familiar where-used list in the ABAP Workbench. This works rather well, as long as the search index is current, and a static programming model was used. Unfortunately, in new SAP applications in particular, dynamic use of program elements pushes the limits of the static where-used list. This becomes clear very quickly when you talk about engines, frameworks, or enhancement concepts. Customer developments and customer-specific implementations for such frameworks are generally dynamically integrated, but even customer developments themselves follow modern programming models such as ABAP-OO with increasing frequency, rendering the classical where-used list obsolete.

Dynamic Interface Analysis

With its *Dynamic Interface Analysis* tool, SAP has developed a means of closing this gap. From re-implemented classes and interfaces from the ABAP-OO world to BAdI implementations or framework enhancements and the identification of classical customer exits, to classical user-exits, the tool covers all the bases. For a list of the enhancements, see Figure 15.20.

Custom Code Interface Analysis

Obj.Type	Customer Object Name	Size	A..	Creation	Refere	Reference Type	Object Type	Interface Object Name	Func	Link	Componen
Class (ABAP Objects)	Z CL CI COLLECTOR STAT	218	5	10.06.2010		SAP Class Redefinition	Class (ABAP Objects)	CL CI COLLECTOR ROOT			SAP_BASIS
Function Module	Z CODE INSPECTOR RESULTS	99	4	07.02.2011		SAP Table Link	Table	SWD FUNCS-FUNCTION			SAP_BASIS
Class (ABAP Objects)	Z JUERGEN	218	2	14.06.2010		SAP Class Redefinition	Class (ABAP Objects)	CL CI COLLECTOR ROOT			SAP_BASIS
Enhancement Implem	Z VENKATAM ENHO1	0	1	16.02.2011		SAP BAdI Enhancemer	Enhancement Spot	SEEF BADI TEST DEFS			SAP_BASIS
Class (ABAP Objects)	ZCL ABSTRACT ENH SPOT T(	200	1	21.02.2011		SAP ABAP Interface	Interface (ABAP Obje	IF ENH CWB SPOT			SAP_BASIS
Class (ABAP Objects)		383	4	24.02.2011		SAP ABAP Interface	Interface (ABAP Obje	IF ENH OBJECT			SAP_BASIS
Class (ABAP Objects)		383	4	24.02.2011		SAP ABAP Interface	Interface (ABAP Obje	IF ENH OBJECT DOCU			SAP_BASIS
Class (ABAP Objects)		383	4	24.02.2011		SAP ABAP Interface	Interface (ABAP Obje	IF ENH SPOT TOOL			SAP_BASIS
Class (ABAP Objects)	ZCL IM DOMINIK BADI	11	2	09.02.2010		SAP BAdI Interface (cl	Business Add-Ins - De	TAANA VIRTUAL FIELDS			SAP_BASIS
Class (ABAP Objects)	ZCL IM TEST	18	1	30.06.2009		SAP BAdI Interface (cl	Business Add-Ins - De	CRM DNO MONITOR			BBPCRM
Class (ABAP Objects)	ZCX SAPLINK	36	2	15.06.2008		SAP Class Redefinition	Class (ABAP Objects)	CX STATIC CHECK			SAP_BASIS
Program	ZXRSRU01	586	0	29.05.2008		SAP SMOD Exit	Function Module	EXIT SAPLRRS0 001			SAP_BW
Enhancement Implem	Z UBB TEST	0	0	07.04.2005		Broken Enhancement					
Class (ABAP Objects)	Z CL NET310 MES1	7	1	16.12.2010		SAP Class Redefinition	Class (ABAP Objects)	CL WD COMPONENT ASS			SAP_BASIS
Class (ABAP Objects)	ZCL IM COEF DNO MONITOR	74	4	09.02.2009		SAP BAdI Interface (cl	Business Add-Ins - De	CRM DNO MONITOR			BBPCRM
Class (ABAP Objects)	ZCL DOMI	11	2	16.04.2009		SAP BAdI Interface (ke	Enhancement Spot	/POSDW/CONV EXIT			BI_CONT
Enhancement Implem	ZDOMINIK IMPL	0	1	16.04.2009		SAP BAdI Enhancemer	Enhancement Spot	/POSDW/CONV EXIT			BI_CONT

Figure 15.20 Enhancements Results List

Smart forms and SAPscript programs can now also be checked with regard to usage. The most effective function, however, is the identification of custom code, the control of which is hidden somewhere in Customizing. This is where the tool begins, and it uses all the possibilities of SAP NetWeaver. No other tool is able to utilize this integration aspect so completely. Now you have the possibility of deleting custom code without running the risk that it is still used dynamically somewhere else. This enables complete transparency and a basis for long-term code reduction.

15.4.3 Monitoring and Evaluating Modifications

The actual technical number of modifications in their SAP systems surprises many customers, and the attempt to explain the difference between the technical number of objects and the perceived number is often fruitless. With its *Modification Browser* (Transaction SE95), SAP does offer a tool for developers, but it does not support targeted analysis or continuous monitoring of modifications.

For this reason, there is the new *Modification Overview*, which enables table-based filtering, sorting and classification of modifications (see Figure 15.21).

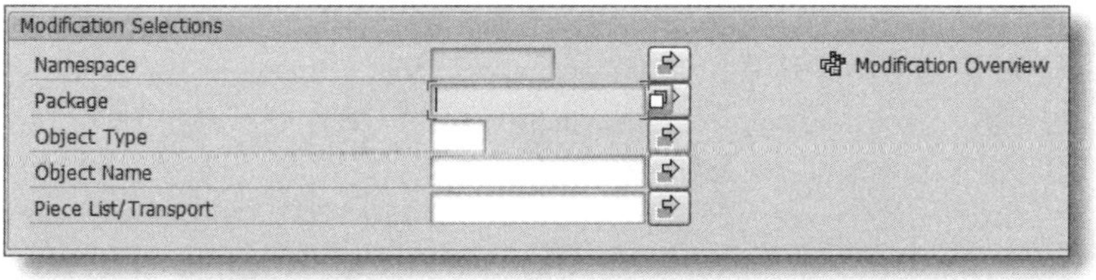

Modification Overview

Figure 15.21 Modification Overview Initial Screen

The Modification Overview tool enables you to achieve comprehensive transparency with regard to your modifications and maintain an overview at all times. It also enables you to find out when a particular developer created what type of modification and what area of application it affects. You can also focus your testing activities on the modified application areas and know beforehand where side-effects may arise. You can also use the tool to distinguish between manual activities from SAP Notes or incorrect operation of the modification adjustment (SPAU) from true modifications. Only with full transparency with regard to modifications can you improve the bad reputation of modifications and cost-intensive clones through targeted modifications or, ideally, enhancements. Modification is a highly flexible means of adapting your SAP system. But it should always be used judiciously, with an eye to necessity and control. Figure 15.22 shows a results list of modifications in the Modification Overview.

SAP Object Text	SAP Object Name	Size	V	G	Refe	Reference Type	Status	Func	Link	Date	Modif.Req.	Author
Role	SAP BWC SOLUTION MANAGER CLIENT(	0	0			Modification (assisted)				18.01.2010		ZHOUDE
	SAP CDMC ST14 CLIENT001	0	0			Modification (assisted)				12.01.2010		KETTNERB
	SAP DVM SERVICE CLIENT001	0	0			Modification (assisted)				19.04.2010		HEFFNERS
Table Definition	CRMT DNO SERVICE MONITOR	0	0			Modification (assisted)				09.02.2009	SMMK900076	SAP
Function Group	SMD COMPL	0	0			Modification (unassisted)				23.06.2010	SMMK900169	RUBINSHTEYN
Function Module	SMD MD LOADER100	365	2			Modification (assisted)				25.01.2009	SMMK900070	SAP
Report Source Code	LSMD FUNCTOP	104	2			Modification (assisted)				27.01.2009	SMMK900070	SAP
Transformation	EP CFG 2004S	0	1	X		Modification (unassisted)				05.11.2008		FALKNER
Method (ABAP Objects)	CL EMMA ANALYZE JOB LOG GET LOG	0	1			Modification (assisted)				30.06.2008	SMMK900018	
	CL EMMA ANALYZE JOB LOG GET MESS	0	1			Modification (assisted)				30.06.2008	SMMK900018	
	CL EMMA ANALYZE JOB LOG VALIDATE	0	1			Modification (assisted)				30.06.2008	SMMK900018	
Private Header (ABAP Obj	CL EMMA ANALYZE JOB LOG	0	3			Modification (assisted)				30.06.2008	SMMK900018	SCHABRAM
Protected Header (ABAP		0	3			Modification (assisted)				30.06.2008	SMMK900018	JAFFERY
Public Header (ABAP Obje		0	3			Modification (assisted)				30.06.2008	SMMK900018	SCHABRAM
Private Header (ABAP Obj	CL EMMA CASE	0	1			Modification (assisted)				06.08.2008	SMMK900035	SCHABRAM
Protected Header (ABAP	CL EMMA PREP PAROBJ RUNID	0	1			Modification (assisted)				19.06.2008	SMMK900018	JAFFERY
Public Header (ABAP Obje		0	1			Modification (assisted)				19.06.2008	SMMK900018	JAFFERY
Report Source Code	REMMALOADAPPLLOG	277	3			Modification (assisted)				07.08.2008	SMMK900034	SCHEUSS
	REMMALOADJOBLOG	175	3			Modification (assisted)				07.08.2008	SMMK900034	SCHEUSS
Domain Definition	ATTYP	0	1			Modification (assisted)				14.07.2009		KETTNERB
		0	1			Modification (unassisted)				14.07.2009		KETTNERB
Table	SCICHKV ALTER	0	0			Modification (unassisted)				27.09.2010	SMMK900221	MAHLER
Technical Attributes of a		0	1			Modification (unassisted)				27.09.2010	SMMK900221	MAHLER
Private Header (ABAP Obj	CL COVERAGE EVAL	0	3			Modification (assisted)				07.04.2010	SMMK900147	CHRIS

Figure 15.22 Enhancements Results List

Customers who have already used the analysis function intensively have been impressed by the advantages. Not only were they able to reduce the number of modifications; they were also able to proactively limit the creation of new modifications because they were able to find enhancement options instead. They were also able to prevent modifications from their old release from being transferred to their system during an upgrade.

15.4.4 Distinguishing Versions of Your Program

Problems distinguishing the different versions of your programs usually only arise in a multi-system landscape in which the systems are distributed around the world and are subject to different business requirements. The same business processes in different countries often require customer-specific adjustment. Often, the same objects are used for this because the differences are frequently marginal. A central development system precludes the uncontrolled growth of customer developments but can lead to a proliferation of program versions.

Cross-System Comparison

Strict control of the transports and development policies help keep a lid on the problem. The *Cross-System Comparison* tool analyzes customer developments across system boundaries and indicates which version of the program in the development system matches the actively used product version (see Figure 15.23).

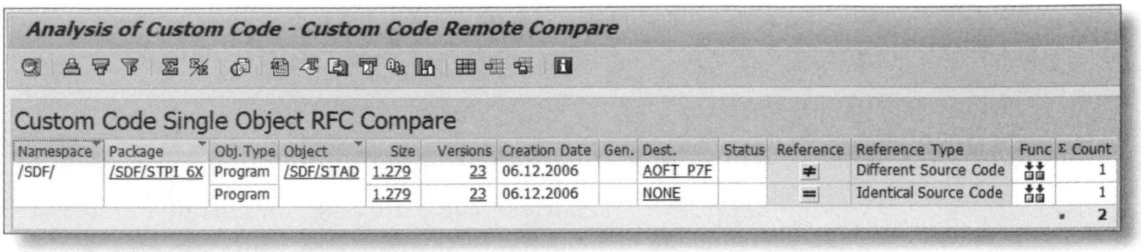

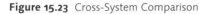

Figure 15.23 Cross-System Comparison

This function enables you to identify where real differences exist and where transports are missing (if any) or have yet to be imported. It is also possible to identify any code differences in the objects of one or more transports. You also receive information about the size and complexity of the objects. One very special scenario focuses on the implementation of user exits. Multiple projects change the same user exit and transport it to the project landscapes for testing purposes. Changes due to SAP corrections are usually not taken into account. So use Cross-System Comparison to monitor code adjustments and thereby support a central code strategy in your company.

The *top-20 analysis* scenario maps out some ideas (see Figure 15.24). **Top-20 analysis** Concentrate on your company's business processes that are used every day. Using the workload statistics and freely definable parameters with regard to the number of objects or the number of periods to be analyzed, the systems are either checked to ascertain which customer developments were cloned or display a marked similarity, or the used SAP programs are checked for the characteristic *modified*.

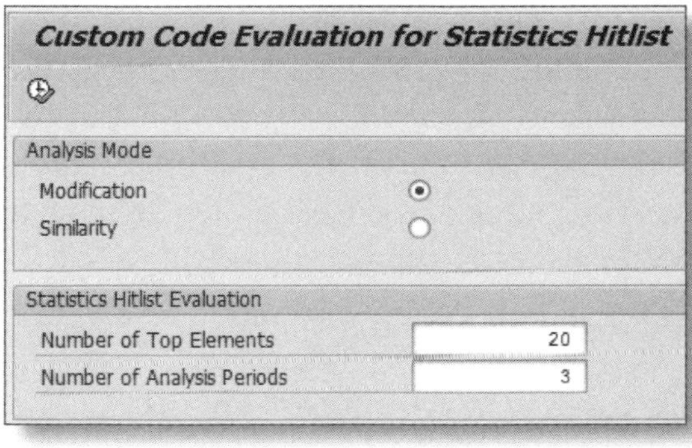

Figure 15.24 Top-20 Analysis Selection

This gives you the capability to analyze your most frequently used programs in detail and thus provides a starting point for other supporting

SAP Active Global Support (SAP AGS) services such as the *modification justification check*.

15.4.5 Time for Improvement

Various application scenarios have been described from a theoretical standpoint. There are certainly many more uses that can emerge from using the Custom Code Analysis tool on a daily basis. The tool is started with Transaction /SDF/CD_CCA or by executing the Program /SDF/CD_CUSTOM_CODE_CONN_GUI in the managed system (see Figure 15.25).

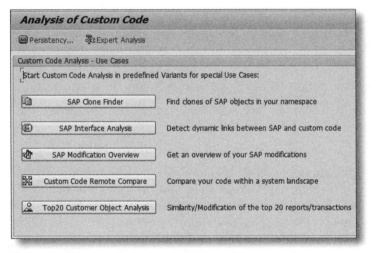

Figure 15.25 Custom Code Analysis Tool Initial Screen

In addition to the predefined application scenarios, you can execute standard runs as background processes and adapt the results lists to your personal requirements using user-defined layouts. You can also use object lists to further restrict or enrich the results. For more information and messages from other users, see our blog on the SAP Developer Network (SDN).

15.5 Custom Code Lifecycle Management at Procter & Gamble

Custom Code Lifecycle Management (CCLM) is a critical step on the way to continuous management of custom developments and the life-

cycle status of each program and transaction. The introduction of CCLM has given us a clear view of our own developments, across the entire SAP system landscape, and gives us central Reporting functionality—a true "single source of truth."

Cristopher Herzfeld, Procter & Gamble

Procter & Gamble is well known for its brands such as Ariel, Lenor, Duracell (household), Oral-B, Wick (health), Pampers (family and baby care), Pantene, Head & Shoulders, Gillette, and Braun (beauty), and is one of the largest companies in the consumer goods industry.

Procter & Gamble

Sustainability is very important to us not only in the environmental sustainability of our products, but it is also deeply embedded in our company culture. It means for us that we are always aware of our social and economic responsibility so can we assure the long term success of our company. This objective is also reflected in an ambitious ecological sustainability vision, which was announced in 2010.

IT at Procter & Gamble belongs to an organization called Global Business Services (GBS). Within GBS, the application management team is responsible for the processes, methodologies, and tools used in the application management lifecycle—specifically during design, build, and deploy.

The motivation for a single source of truth for CCML was the fact that Procter & Gamble has a significant and growing number of custom developments in our SAP system landscapes, without significant cleanup of obsolete or unused developments. This causes the following problems:

Motivation

1. The increasing number of transactions and programs make it gradually more difficult to clean up obsolete developments.

2. Because no information is available about the actual usage of the transactions and programs, we do not know which transactions and programs are no longer relevant in the productive systems. This leads to wasted effort in upgrade or SP projects because a lot of unused programs are reviewed, updated, and tested (including regression testing).

3. These problems are costly and resource-intensive, without adding any value. Through CCLM's single source of truth, we tackle the problems by first making them visible. We wanted to use the

reporting data for targeted and measurable cleanup activities because you cannot improve what you do not measure.

Development of a prototype

A collaboration project between SAP and Procter & Gamble was defined, and a solution was implemented that covers the following use-cases:

1. Create a database to automatically gather and store information on custom code transactions, programs, and tables. The database is located in SAP Solution Manager, and it stores the information retrieved from the managed systems.

2. Maintain additional information per object, for example, the owning person/organization or the lifecycle status in addition to the automatically collected object information.

3. Refresh the automatically gathered information at any time, without overwriting the manual information maintained per object.

4. Embed the implementation in SAP Solution Manager, allowing seamless integration of CCLM with other accelerators and tools, both now and in the future.

5. In the current version of CCLM, numerous attributes are collected automatically per transaction, table, or program object (the prototype is currently restricted to these three most important types of custom development) and stored in the central database. We also collect the following information from the managed systems:

   ▸ Is the object still available in the development system?

   ▸ In which productive system does the object exist?

   ▸ In which version and with which transport were the objects applied to the productive system (version information is available for programs and tables)?

   ▸ The usage of the programs and transactions (also for programs called via transactions). This information is currently retrieved monthly from the SAP EarlyWatch Alert (EWA), which is already in our SAP Solution Manager system.

Rollout dimensions

After the stabilization of the solution in our system landscape, we are currently planning the rollout of CCLM in several dimensions into our landscapes. One rollout dimension is the functional enhancement of the solution to cover additional use cases. There is now a close relationship between SAP and Procter & Gamble. One of the next steps for us is the implementation of an improved mechanism to detect the usage of the objects in the SAP systems. The solution has already been developed by SAP and is ready for prototyping and testing.

A parallel rollout dimension for Procter & Gamble is to connect more landscapes and systems to the central database to complete the picture.

The final rollout dimension is a cooperation with the business and subject matter experts from the development teams to drive cleanup activities in the system landscape. One of the next steps in this regard is to define the ownership of the objects, based on their functional or application area, and store them in the database. This will make it easier to find out who is responsible quickly and define clear measurable actions with them.

Conclusion

The power of the CCLM solution in SAP Solution Manager lies in its ability to provide one single source of truth for information about custom-developed objects, which can be kept up to date automatically. Central reporting makes the situation transparent, and can be made available to the relevant application managers. Cleanup targets can be defined, executed, and measured, by translating data into insight.

CCLM is a critical step on the way to continuous management of custom developments and the lifecycle status of each program and transaction. The introduction of CCLM has given us a clear view of our own developments, across the entire SAP system landscape, and gives us central reporting functionality—a true single source of truth.

The Author

Cristopher Herzfeld is manager of the area Build Solution in the Procter & Gamble Application Management horizontal team, in which he is responsible for the global IT processes, tools, and methodologies for implementing SAP software.

He has a total of 17 years of experience in SAP SD/MM and program development (for Tetra Pak and Gillette, among others).

He has been involved with SAP Solution Manager for the past two years, especially with the processes, methods, and tools for managing the lifecycle of customer developments.

A   The Authors

Marc Oliver Schäfer,
Director Product Management
SAP Solution Manager

Marc Oliver Schäfer studied English and German literature and linguistics at the University of Tübingen, Germany. Prior to joining SAP in 2000 as product manager for the Customizing tools development group, he worked at DaimlerChrysler AG as a trainer in language courses and intercultural courses. Since 2008, Mr. Schäfer has been head of the Communication and Marketing Team for SAP Solution Manager. You can reach Marc Oliver Schäfer at *marc.oliver.schaefer@sap.com*.

Dr. Matthias Melich,
Vice President of Product Management
SAP Solution Manager

Dr. Matthias Melich studied English literature at the University of Rochester, New York, and mathematics and English philology at the University of Cologne, Germany, where he wrote his doctoral thesis on computer-based language acquisition in 1993. He began working for SAP in 1995, and after working in various positions, he assumed responsibility of product management for Customizing tools in 1998. Since becoming vice president in January 2005, he has been responsible for the SAP Solution Manager product management worldwide. You can contact Matthias Melich at *matthias.melich@sap.com*.

Susan Großer, Product Manager

Susan Großer studied English and American studies, romance studies, and adult education/business training at the Chemnitz University of Technology, Germany, and the Università degli Studi di Modena e Reggio Emilia, Italy. She joined SAP in 2008 as a student employee, and supported the SAP Solution Manager project management in creating the second edition of the *SAP Solution Manager* book. Since 2010, Susan Großer has been a permanent employee at SAP and coordinates the SAP Solution Manager user documentation in product management. For the third edition of the *SAP Solution Manager* book, she shared responsibility with Marc Oliver Schäfer for the overall project management. Susan Großer can be reached at *susan.grosser@sap.com*.

Melanie Klingenfuß-Marquart, Team Assistant

Melanie Klingenfuß-Marquardt studied language, culture, and translation (English and Spanish) at the Johannes Gutenberg University in Mainz, Germany, and at the Universidad de Granada in Spain. After completing her studies, she joined SAP in 2011 as a team and management assistant, and she supported the SAP Solution Manager project management in creating the third edition of the *SAP Solution Manager* book. You can contact Melanie Klingenfuß-Marquardt at *melanie.klingenfuss@sap.com*.

Werner Arlt, Service Architect

Werner Arlt joined SAP in 1990 as a systems analyst. In the first nine years, he worked at SAP Consulting as a technical consultant focusing on SAP R/2 Basis for IBM and Siemens mainframe systems and SAP R/3 Basis with Unix and database systems. After this, he spent four years as a service architect in SAP Active Global Support in the Technical Competence Center of Expertise group. Since 2004, Werner Arlt has been a quality manager responsible for SAP Solution Manager and the Support Service Development area. Alongside his tasks in quality management, he is responsible for the design, development, and content of the Central System Administration tool within SAP Solution Manager. You can contact Werner Arlt at *werner.arlt@sap.com*.

Waldemar Befort, Product Manager

Waldemar Befort studied information management at the Baden-Württemberg Cooperative State University, Germany, and came to SAP in 2003. There he supplied services in the system and process optimization field. Later he worked on the development of the Business Process Monitoring in SAP Solution Manager and was responsible for the Service SAP Interface Management. Since 2010, he has been in SAP NetWeaver Product Management and is responsible for the operation of SAP NetWeaver Process Integration. You can reach Waldemar Befort at *waldemar.befort@sap.com*.

David Birkenbach, Senior Solution Manager

David Birkenbach studied industrial engineering at the Saarland University for Technology and Economics, Germany. He started his professional career in 1998 as an SAP consultant in the SAP CRM area at SAP Retail Solution in St. Ingbert. In 2001, he moved to T-Systems, a subsidiary of Deutsche Telekom, where he worked intensively with SAP Solution Manager in international projects. He moved on to taking over the project management for SAP Solution Manager projects while also working as application service manager for customers of T-Systems. In 2007, he returned to SAP AG, where he has been product manager for SAP Solution Manager. His responsibilities include the technical roll-in and roll-out of the application incident management scenario within SAP Solution Manager. David Birkenbach can be contacted at *david.birkenbach@sap.com*.

Mathias Bley, Service Architect

Mathias Bley completed his studies in electrical engineering at the University of Karlsruhe, Germany. From 1995 to 1998, he worked at Kiefer & Veittinger in Mannheim in IT services. In 1998, he moved to SAP Deutschland, where he worked as a technology consultant specializing in SAP CRM systems. In 2005, he started working at SAP AG in the CoE CRM Technology area of SAP Active Global Support. Today he works as a service architect in the Application Lifecycle Management area, where he is responsible for the topic of technical monitoring and alerting with SAP Solution Manager. You can contact Mathias Bley at *mathias.bley@sap.com*.

Dr. Veit Eska, Service Architect

Dr. Veit Eska studied physics from 1989 to 1994 at Rostock University and at the Institute of Atmospheric Physics in Kühlungsborn, Germany. He then worked for six months at the institute as a scientific assistant, completing his doctorate in applied physics three years later. In 1998, he joined SAP, where he is now working as a service architect in SAP Active Global Support. With regard to SAP Solution Manager, he is responsible for managing development projects in the custom code, monitoring, reporting, and business intelligence areas. In SAP Solution Manager 7.1, he is responsible for the Custom Code Lifecycle Management. You can contact Veit Eska at *veit.eska@sap.com*.

Volker von Gloeden, Service Architect

Volker von Gloeden studied mathematics at the University of Düsseldorf, Germany, from 1997 to 2002. After obtaining a master's degree in mathematics, he began working at SAP in 2003. He initially worked in the area of Business Process Monitoring, before focusing on performance optimization in the business process context. Since 2006, he has held overall responsibility for Business Process Monitoring in SAP Solution Manager, and he also manages the project for job scheduling management, in which the corresponding functions in SAP Solution Manager are integrated with the SAP Central Process Scheduling by Redwood. He also developed the idea of services for the business process analysis and is centrally involved in the development of a systematic method for business process improvement using the business process analysis. Volker von Gloeden can be reached at *volker.von.gloeden@sap.com*.

Rajeev Gollapudi, Senior Product Manager

Rajeev Gollapudi studied computer engineering, business administration, and marketing, and worked for Oracle in India and IBM in the United States before joining SAP. Rajeev Gollapudi now has more than 12 years of experience in the areas of software development, strategy, product management, and consulting. The main emphasis of his work at SAP now is in end-to-end test management, where he is mainly responsible for the Business Process Change Analyzer and the integration of the new SAP Solution Manager with IBM Rational tools. He is Head of the Application Lifecycle Management team in India and is the customer consultant for the business development strategy in the Application Lifecycle Management area. Rajeev Gollapudi can be reached at *rajeev.gollapudi@sap.com.*

Esther Hardt, Senior Product Manager

Esther Hardt studied business administration at the Universität des Saarlandes in Saarbrücken, Germany, and at the University of Southern Colorado (now CSU-Pueblo), USA.

She began her career in management consulting at PriceWaterhoseCoopers and joined SAP as a consultant in 2004. Since 2006, Ms. Hardt has been working as a senior product manager in the SAP Solution Manager area. Her responsibilities include the application lifecycle process solution implementation, the SAP contact role for the SAP Solution Manager, and the Support Infrastructure user group of the German-speaking SAP User Group e.V. (DSAG). Esther Hardt can be reached at *esther.hardt@sap.com.*

Martin Harnacke,
SAP Internal Strategic Consultant

Martin Harnacke has been at SAP Deutschland since October 2000, in Walldorf, Germany. After completing his master's degree in computer science and economics, he initially worked as a technical consultant and technical project manager in numerous customer projects in SAP Supply Chain Management (SAP SCM/SAP APO), SAP Business Warehouse (SAP BW), and the SAP Strategic Enterprise Management (SAP SEM) environment. In 2005, he moved to SAP AG to work on the technical product modeling of the SAP ERP enhancement packages in the areas of solution management for SAP ERP and Development ERP Technical Coordination, among other projects. Since 2007, he has been in the Global Upgrade Office, where he provides dedicated support on upgrade tools. His tasks and responsibilities include the Upgrade Dependency Analyzer (*www.service.sap.com/uda*), the Solution Browser (*www.sapsolutionbrowser.com*), and the central overview of the upgrade-relevant tools at SAP (*www.service.sap.com/upgradetools*). You can contact Martin Harnacke at *martin.harnacke@sap.com*.

Tobias Hauk, Product Manager

Tobias Hauk studied applied informatics at the Baden-Württemberg Cooperative State University in Karlsruhe, Germany. While studying, he worked at SAP, gathering experience in various areas of the company, such as CRM development, widget development, user interface design, and product management. He joined SAP on a full-time basis in 2009 and works as a product manager for SAP Solution Manager. Tobias Hauk works in the IT service management (ITSM) area and is responsible for technical developments and the rollout of Change Request Management. You can reach Tobias Hauk at *tobias.hauk@sap.com*.

Dominik Held, Service Architect

Dominik Held studied information management at the Berufsakademie Mannheim, Germany. Within the framework of the dual system, he worked in many areas of SAP AG while still studying, but in 2002 decided on the service and support area, where he has worked since. In the beginning, he focused on the development of services and tools for complex SAP products. He was introduced to the topic of Data Volume Management at an early stage, and this is still one of his main areas of expertise. In his role as a service architect in a global Service and Support development department, he now defines and develops IT concepts, services, and tools for strategic and complex IT environments. You can contact Dominik Held at *dominik.held@sap.com.*

Wolf Hengevoss, Senior Product Manager

Wolf Hengevoss studied natural science at the University of Kaiserslautern, Germany. In 1999, he took on a position in product management at SAP, as a member of the Basis Group. Since the beginning of the development of the Exchange Infrastructure—one of the main consumers of landscape data—he has been in contact with the topic of the landscape. Today, the main emphasis of his work is on product management for the tools for managing landscape data in SAP systems, the System Landscape Directory, and the landscape description in SAP Solution Manager. Wolf Hengevoss can be contacted at *wolf.hengevoss@sap.com.*

**Oliver Kapaun,
Expert Technical Support Consultant**

Oliver Kapaun studied information management at the Technical University in Darmstadt, Germany, and has been working at SAP since 2002 in the organizational area of SAP Active Global Support. He develops services for SAP MaxAttention customers and has experience in the Java and ABAP Basis areas and in upgrade and Near Zero Downtime (NZDT). His expertise also encompasses applications such as ESS, MSS, MDM, and other areas of SAP technology. Oliver Kapaun can be contacted at *oliver.kapaun@sap.com*.

Martina Kaplan, Senior Support Consultant

Martina Kaplan has been working as a senior consultant in the technical consulting of SAP Deutschland AG & Co. KG since 2006. Previously, she spent five years in technology consulting at CSC Ploenzke AG in Wiesbaden, Germany, gaining knowledge of SAP technology topics such as upgrade. The main emphasis of her work as a senior consultant was in the enhancement packages, upgrade, and upgrade project management areas. From 2008 on, she was leader of the Upgrade focus group, and in this function she worked on many national and international customer projects, from planning to execution. Alongside her project work, Ms. Kaplan was responsible for the service development and positioning of the EHP portfolio. Since 2011, as senior support consultant in the SAP Active Global Support of SAP AG, she has shared responsibility for the development of the global service portfolio for SAP MaxAttention customers for the upgrade and enhancement packages topics. She is also the author of the book *Implementing SAP Enhancement Packages*. You can reach Martina Kaplan at *martina.kaplan@sap.com*.

Michael Klöffer, Service Architect

Michael Klöffer joined SAP in 2004, initially working in Strategic Research and Development on the topics IT services and application management, and in the Global Technology Center of Expertise within SAP Active Global Support. As the service architect in Application Lifecycle Management, his responsibilities include the roll-out of the technical operation in SAP Solution Manager and the new functions in IT service management (ITSM). Michael Klöffer can be reached at *michael.kloeffer@sap.com.*

Sonal Kumar, Senior Product Manager

Sonal Kumar studied computer engineering, marketing, and finance, and worked as a software developer for Hewlett-Packard before coming to SAP in 2004 to work as a developer in the SAP Portals area. He took over the responsibility of product owner in the SAP NetWeaver area, and now works as senior product manager in Application Lifecycle Management, where he is responsible for SAP Test Acceleration and Optimization and the SAP Solution Manager adapter for SAP Quality Center by HP. Sonal Kumar can be contacted at *sonal.kumar@sap.com.*

Stefan Lahr, Technical Support Consultant

Stefan Lahr studied communication technology at Harz University, Germany. In 2003, he began working in the SAP Active Global Support of SAP AG. Since 2009, Stefan Lahr has been responsible for the technical analysis of interactive reporting and management reporting in SAP Solution Manager. His area of responsibility includes both the rollout of the functions in this area and their continued development. You can contact Stefan Lahr at *stefan.lahr@sap.com*.

Jürgen Mahler, Service Architect

Jürgen Mahler studied industrial engineering (sensor system technology) at the University of Karlsruhe, Germany. As a service architect he is globally responsible for innovation, development, portfolio planning, and the positioning of the topic of Custom Code Management within the SAP Active Global Support of SAP. Since 1996, he has worked at SAP in various areas of software development, support, project management, and the worldwide implementation of SAP products. This is rounded off by his experience in customer support, application know-how, and technical application and risk management. Jürgen Mahler can be reached at *juergen.mahler@sap.com*.

Michael Merzbach, Senior Product Manager

Michael Merzbach studied business administration at Cologne University of Applied Sciences, Germany, specializing in IT and general management. In 2008, he joined SAP, where he began as a developer, later becoming scrum master in end-to-end alerting and monitoring. Since 2010, Michael Merzbach has worked as a product manager in the Application Lifecycle Management area. His area of responsibility in the SAP Solution Manager environment is template management. Michael Merzbach can be contacted at *m.merzbach@sap.com*.

Robert Müller, Service Architect

Before joining SAP AG in 2001, Robert Müller studied physical technology at the University of Applied Sciences in Zwickau, Germany. At SAP AG, he began in support in the Customer Center of Expertise–Logistics department. In 2006, as an expert in performance optimization, he took over global responsibility as the service owner for the Business Process Performance Optimization (BPPO) service. From 2007 to 2009, Robert Müller supported major customers in Philadelphia, Pennsylvania, mainly within the framework of SAP MaxAttention and SAP Safeguarding projects, in the implementation and stable operation of complex SAP solutions. Since 2010, as service architect, Robert Müller has been head of the Global Service development for SAP Active Global Support services, focusing on application performance optimization. Robert Müller can be reached at *robert.mueller@sap.com*.

Jan Musil, Director,
Global Project Management Office

Jan has more than 15 years of consulting, general management, and operations experience in the informational technology industry. He is currently leading the global Project Management Practice in the SAP field services where he advises customers implementing SAP solutions. Since starting in 1996 at SAP, Jan has held various roles in product development, quality management, customer support, consulting organization, and operations in the United States, Germany, and the Czech Republic. You can contact Jan Musil at *jan.musil@sap.com*.

René Muth, Service Architect

René Muth studied computer science at the University of Applied Sciences in Würzburg, Germany, and then worked as a consultant. In 1997, Renè Muth joined SAP and worked in the service development area on various topics such as the database management system IBM DB2, SAP NetWeaver Business Warehouse, and SAP NetWeaver Business Warehouse Accelerator. Since 2007, he has been responsible for the development of options for change diagnostics in SAP Solution Manager. René Muth can be contacted at *rene.muth@sap.com*.

Dr. Christoph Nake, Service Architect

Dr. Christoph Nake completed his PhD in experimental physics at the University of Bonn, Germany, before starting at SAP in 1996 in the training area for SAP Basis administrators. In 2001, he moved to the product management of SAP NetWeaver. There, as product manager, he was responsible for the topics of system management, background processing, printing, and adaptive computing. In 2008, he started as a service architect in the IT Planning Team, where he works in the United States in particular on the optimization of the IT support processes for SAP MaxAttention customers. You can reach Dr. Christoph Nake at *christoph.nake@sap.com.*

Rainer Nerding, Service Architect

After studying physics, Rainer Nerding began working in application support in the client-server environment, and later in the SAP environment of a midsize company in the car delivery industry. Since January 2000, he has worked in the customer support of SAP AG, in the software change management area. He was initially responsible for processing problem messages. The focus of his current work is on the development and delivery of services and consulting packages, in particular in the areas of software change management and support packages. He is responsible for the development of various services for analyzing and optimizing the transport processes in the customer systems. He has project experience from many customer assignments and service deliveries. Rainer Nerding can be reached at *rainer.nerding@sap.com.*

Björn Panter, Service Architect

Björn Panter studied computer science and design and production technology at the Saarland University, Germany. Since 1998, SAP has benefited from his experience with algorithms and data structures in areas such as product development, global support, and product management. As the service architect responsible for Custom Code Management and reverse business process documentation, he is currently responsible for innovations, new developments, and the holistic positioning of services and tools, as well as the integration into the overall SAP product portfolio. You can contact Björn Panter at *bjoern.panter@sap.com*.

Patrick Richarts, Service Architect

Patrick Richarts studied medical technology at Hamburg University, Germany. In 1998, he joined SAP, where he worked in the customer support and service development areas. Since 2006, Richarts has worked in the SAP Solution Manager technical operation area. He is responsible for product integration and technical administration. Patrick Richarts can be reached at *patrick.richarts@sap.com*.

Marcus Ronellenfitsch, Service Architect

Marcus Ronellenfitsch studied business administration at Ludwigshafen Technical College, Germany, specializing in tax, auditing, and finance. Afterwards, he worked for two years as a financial analyst. The main focus of this work was carrying out company valuations, especially for market-listed companies in the IT area. In 2001, Marcus Ronellenfitsch started at SAP in CoE Financials Support, specializing in finance (Asset Accounting). Since 2003, he has worked in support for banks and is currently a service architect in global banking support. The main focus of his work is on the creation and delivery of SAP support services for operating the SAP Banking solution, and the creation of various Best Practices in this area, in particular day-end processing and exception management. Marcus Ronellenfitsch can be contacted at *marcus.ronellenfitsch@sap.com*.

Mirco Rotzlawski, Senior Product Manager

Mirco Rotzlawski studied translation and interpreting (English and French) at Heidelberg University, Germany, and Stendhal University, Grenoble 3, France. He began his career in the marketing communication area at Ricoh Deutschland GmbH. In 2006, he joined SAP, where he initially worked as an information developer and knowledge project leader for various industry solutions. Since 2010, Mirco Rotzlawski has worked as a product manager in the solution management of SAP Solution Manager. The main focus of his work is on the test management area within the Application Lifecycle Management. Mirco Rotzlawski can be reached at *mirco.rotzlawski@sap.com*.

Patrick Schmidt, Service Architect

Patrick Schmidt studied information management at the Berufsakademie Karlsruhe, Germany. From 2000 to 2006, he worked as a consulting manager at REALTECH AG, where he was responsible for setting up software solutions in the SAP environment. In 2006, he joined SAP in the SAP Active Global Support organization at the Center of Expertise for Software Logistics. You can contact Patrick Schmidt at *pat.schmidt@sap.com*.

Benjamin Schneider, Senior Product Manager

Benjamin Schneider studied German language and literature and political sciences for teaching at the University of Mannhcim, Germany. During his study, he spent three years in SAP product management of SAP Solution Manager as a student employee. After completing his studies, he spent one year working in technical support for SAP add-on products at REALTECH AG before returning to SAP in 2007 to work as a product manager in solution management for SAP Solution Manager. His responsibilities include the solution documentation and maintenance management areas within the Application Lifecycle Management. Benjamin Schneider can be reached at *benjamin.chneider@sap.com*.

Dr. Thomas Schröder, Service Architect

Dr. Thomas Schröder studied physics and chemistry, completing his PhD in physics at the Max Planck Institute for Energy Research at the University of Göttingen, Germany. After doing research work at international institutions, he joined SAP in 1999. There he worked in SAP Active Global Support, initially at the Regional Support Center Europe and the Customer Center of Expertise (CoE) of SAP Active Global Support for the areas of Sales and Distribution (SD) and Customer Relationship Management (CRM). Since 2006, as a service architect he has led the team for the business process integration area at the Global CoE. His responsibilities in the SAP Solution Manager environment are interface and data consistency management, as well as the integration of non-SAP systems into the Business Process Monitoring. Dr. Thomas Schröder can be reached at *thomas.schroeder@sap.com*

Kirankumar Vangaru, Senior Consultant

Kiran Kumar Vangaru studied information technology, systems, and computer science at the Symbiosis University in Pune and the Kakatiya University in Warangal, India. Before coming to SAP more than four years ago, he worked as a technical consultant in SAP for Capgemini Consulting in India. Today, Kiran Kumar Vangaru is senior consultant for SAP Labs India in Bangalore in the System Landscape Optimization (SLO) team, and he is the product owner of the Custom Development Management Cockpit (CDMC). In the CDMC team, he oversees the areas of design, development, implementation on the customer side, and customer support. He is also responsible for the product and solution management of the Landscape Optimization, and he is working on the ramp-up of the Test Data Migration Server 4.0 (TDMS). Kiran Kumar Vangaru can be contacted at *kirankumar.vangaru@sap.com.*

Stefan Voll, Support Architect

Stefan Voll studied chemical engineering at Karlsruhe Technical College and industrial engineering at Pforzheim Technical College, Germany. From 1996 to 2006, he worked in the ERP Logistics area at SAP AG, and for six years, he was responsible for the material management team in SAP Active Global Support (SAP AGS). Since 2006, as a support architect, Stefan Voll has led the SAP Solution Manager development team in Business Process Monitoring and automation in SAP AGS. You can contact Stefan Voll at *stefan.voll@sap.com*.

Sabine Wachter, Product Manager

Sabine Wachter, product manager for system landscape optimization/STS, studied economic policy at the University of Waterloo, Canada, completing an MBA in business administration at the University of Toulon, France, and a master's in politics and English at the University of Mannheim, Germany. She worked for the Economic Supervisory Committee of the European Commission before joining SAP in 1995 in the R/2 Services area. She held positions in the areas of quality management, SCM product development for System by Design, in consulting, and as global support manager for SAP key accounts. Since 2005, she has been globally responsible for the product management and marketing of system landscape optimization STS/ITTS, overseeing the market launch of the new standard software SAP Landscape Transformation (SAP LT). She is currently working on the introduction of a partner model for SAP LT. Sabine Wachter can be contacted at *sabine.wachter@sap.com*.

Marcus Wefers, Chief Support Architect

As chief support architect in the Active Global Support department of SAP AG, Marcus Wefers is responsible for the strategy, products, and positioning of test management as part of SAP Solution Manager. He has worked at SAP for 21 years, focusing on software development, consulting, project management, quality management, and product management. In the past years, he has been responsible for the areas of financial consolidation, Profit Center Accounting, analytics, performance and strategy management, business planning, corporate governance, modeling of business processes, and Application Lifecycle Management. Marcus Wefers has extensive experience from global customer projects in Europe, America, and Asia, and is a regular speaker at international conferences. You can reach Marcus Wefers at *marcus.wefers@sap.com*.

Heinrich Wegener, Senior Product Manager

Heinrich Wegener studied German language and literature, general linguistics, and ethnology at Heidelberg University, Germany. Before joining SAP, he gathered three years of experience in various IT projects at IBM, and then managed his own IT consulting company for seven years. Heinrich Wegener joined SAP in 1998 and was involved in multiple migration projects in R/2 and SAP Service & Support Infrastructure. Since 2004, he has been responsible for various SAP Solution Manager projects in the product management area. His particular focus is on SAP Solution Manager for SAP partners. Heinrich Wegener can be reached at *heinrich.wegener@sap.com*.

B The Authors of Customer Experiences

Ralf Punga, Sanofi-Aventis

Ralf Punga studied computer science at Darmstadt University from 1983 to 1987. In 1987, he joined Hoechst AG in IT Pharma Controlling, where he was responsible for the introduction of a new global reporting system. In the course of a number of major fusions, he switched responsibilities to the areas of *Financial Reporting/Management IS* and later *Global Finance Integration IS*. Since 2006, he has been at the SAP Customer Competence Center Network Management (CCC) and is responsible for SAP Solution Manager in the Sanofi Group.

Dr. Björn Gelhausen and Johannes Hurst, SNP AG

Dr. Björn Gelhausen is the head of the Training and Quality Management departments at SNP AG. Since 1999, he has directed numerous SAP Solution Manager implementation projects as a consultant and project manager. His special area of expertise is the efficient linking of Solution Documentation, Test Management, and Change Request Management.

Johannes Hurst is the head of consulting at SNP AG. He has more than 20 years' experience in consulting, and he and his team have been working with SAP Solution Manager since 2002. His particular area of expertise is Change Request Management and the integration of third-party products. Since 2007, he has been the spokesperson of the DSAG SAP Solution Manager work stream.

Gerd Siemering, Procter & Gamble

Gerd Siemering is an Application Manager for SAP Solution Manager and other Application Lifecycle Management tools at Procter & Gamble. He has a total of 13 years of experience with SAP, as an in-house consultant in industrial enterprises and an application manager, also for mega solutions (such as SAP SD/MM at Wella). He has been working with SAP Solution Manager for 7 years. He currently works in the Application Management Horizontal Team at P&G, where he shares responsibility for global IT processes in the development, implementation, and delivery stages.

Warren Kaufmann, Colgate-Palmolive

Warren Kaufman is Director of the Governance IT organization at Colgate-Palmolive. The key responsibility of the Governance organization is to ensure the effective and efficient use of IT resources in order for Colgate to achieve its corporate goals. To that end, Warren's primary focus for the past several years has been to standardize the Application Lifecycle Management processes by maximizing Colgate's investment in SAP tools. Warren and his team have implemented global processes and applications consisting of portfolio management and resource planning, project management frameworks and methodologies, project turnover procedures, change management, and business process monitoring. Most recently, Warren and his team have been working on the implementation of an end-to-end test automation framework, as well as implementing centralized governance, and risk and compliance processes and tools.

Martin Flegenheimer, Ferrero Deutschland GmbH

Since 2003, Martin Flegenheimer has worked at Ferrero, where as IT Director, he is responsible for the Central and East European regions (Germany, Austria, Switzerland, Scandinavia, Poland, and other East European countries). In the Ferrero Group, he shares responsibility for the strategy and design of the entire SAP system architecture. He is also responsible for the complete lifecycles of all IT applications and for all the technologies used in the company.

Klaus Wehrle, Ferrero Deutschland GmbH

Klaus Wehrle has worked in IT at Ferrero Deutschland GmbH since 1991. In this time, he has completed a variety of tasks in the development and IT administration areas. He has been head of the SAP Solution Manager IT area for two years. There he is responsible for all SAP Solution Manager processes, for the coordination with all other IT areas, and for training SAP Solution Manager users.

Thomas Volkmann, itelligence AG

Thomas Volkmann studied sports science at Bielefeld University and economics at Bielefeld Technical College. Since 2002, he has been one of the SAP Solution Manager experts at itelligence AG in Bielefeld. Along with overseeing numerous consulting projects in the various areas of SAP Solution Manager, he shares the responsibility for supporting and developing the global SAP Solution Manager used by itelligence AG for the processes designed for customers.

Laurie Miller, Bayer Material Science AG

Laurie Miller, Head of BMS O&I Global Support Services at Bayer Material Science AG, holds responsibility for several areas spanning the BMS O&I organization, one of which is a governance role ensuring that the global O&I teams work according to quality standards and procedures, as well as ensuring the relevant security practices are in place and that all teams adhere to them. In 1988, Laurie Miller graduated Magna Cum Laude in Accounting from Robert Morris University, Pittsburgh, PA. She completed her MBA program in 1994, focusing on marketing and international business at the University of Pittsburgh, Joseph M. Katz Graduate School of Business. Throughout her career, Laurie has held positions and responsibility in several areas, including controlling, marketing, strategic marketing, acquisitions, and divestitures before she became a member of the global ProgramOne Design Team and subsequently Head of ProgramOne Finance to Manage NAFTA Deployment at BMS.

Hartmut Koch, Consinto

Hartmut Koch, Manager of SAP Solutions & Architecture at Consinto, completed a Master of Mathematics and Business at RWTH Aachen and then taught at the University Seminar of Economic Schloss Gracht, Erftstadt (today ESMT Campus Schloss Gracht). He has more than 20 years' experience as an SAP systems analyst and worked as an organizer and departmental manager for application development (with focus on SAP) for various manufacturing companies and service providers. He managed SAP migration projects (R/2–R/3), SAP installation projects, and currently manages projects related to carve out, and restructuring of companies and SAP landscapes.

Cristopher Herzfeld, Procter & Gamble

Cristopher Herzfeld is manager of the area Build Solution in the Procter & Gamble Application Management horizontal team, in which he is responsible for the global IT processes, tools, and methodologies for implementing SAP software. He has a total of 17 years of SAP experience in SAP SD/MM and in program development (for Tetra Pak and Gillette, among others). He has been involved with SAP Solution Manager for the past two years, especially with the processes, methods, and tools for managing the lifecycle of customer developments.

Index

T

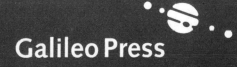

Galileo Press

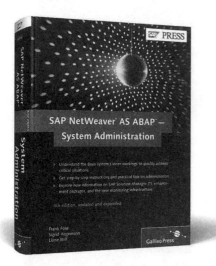

■ Understand the Basis system's inner workings to quickly address critical situations

■ Get step-by-step instructions and practical tips on administration

■ Explore new information on SAP Solution Manager 7.1, enhancement packages, and the new monitoring infrastructure

Frank Föse, Sigrid Hagemann, Liane Will

SAP NetWeaver AS ABAP— System Administration

As a system administrator, you know that SAP NetWeaver AS ABAP is the core of an SAP system. This book provides essential information on the main concepts and tools of SAP NetWeaver AS ABAP, as well as new information about SAP Solution Manager 7.1 and the new monitoring infrastructure. This all-inclusive resource teaches you a holistic approach to administration, and can also be used to prepare for the Certified Technical Consultant exam.

747 pp., 4. edition 2012, 79,95 Euro / US$ 79.95
ISBN 978-1-59229-411-4

>> www.sap-press.com

■ Provides 100 little-known
time-saving tips and tricks

■ Features detailed instructions
and guiding screenshots

■ Presents practical, expert
advice for system administrators

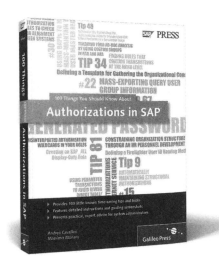

Andrea Cavalleri, Massimo Manara

100 Things You Should Know About Authorizations in SAP

Unlock the secrets of working with authorizations in the SAP Basis system!
In this book, you'll find 100 tips and workarounds you can use to improve
the security of your SAP system. The tips are grouped together based on the
area of authorizations they cover, such as development security, Profile
Generator, upgrades, and more. They have been carefully selected to provide
a collection of the best, most useful, and rarest information.

346 pp., 2012, 59,95 Euro / US$ 59.95
ISBN 978-1-59229-406-0

>> www.sap-press.com

Galileo Press

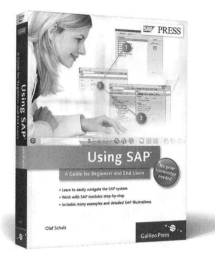

■ Learn to easily navigate
the SAP system

■ Work with SAP modules
step-by-step

■ Includes many examples
and detailed SAP illustrations

Olaf Schulz

Using SAP: A Guide for Beginners and End Users

This book helps end users and beginners get started in SAP ERP and provides readers with the basic knowledge they need for their daily work. Readers will get to know the essentials of working with the SAP system, learn about the SAP systems' structures and functions, and discover how SAP connects to critical business processes. Whether this book is used as an exercise book or as a reference book, readers will find what they need to help them become more comfortable with SAP ERP.

388 pp., 2012, 39,95 Euro / US$ 39.95
ISBN 978-1-59229-408-4

>> www.sap-press.com